In recent years historians of China have focused increased attention on the critical decades of Nationalist rule on the mainland. This recent scholarship has substantially modified our understanding of the political events of this momentous period, shedding light on the character of Nationalist rule and on the sources of the Communist victory in 1949. Yet no existing textbook on modern China presents the events of the period according to these new findings.

The five essays in this volume were written by leading authorities on the period, and they synthesize the new research. Drawn from Volume 13 of *The Cambridge History of China,* they represent the most complete and stimulating political history of the period available in the literature. The essays selected deal with Nationalist rule during the Nanking decade, the Communist movement from 1927 to 1937, Nationalist rule during the Sino-Japanese War, the Communist movement during the Sino-Japanese war, and the Kuomintang-Communist struggle from 1945 to 1949.

THE NATIONALIST ERA IN CHINA

1927–1949

THE NATIONALIST ERA IN CHINA

1927 – 1949

LLOYD E. EASTMAN
JEROME CH'EN
SUZANNE PEPPER
LYMAN P. VAN SLYKE

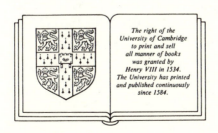

The right of the
University of Cambridge
to print and sell
all manner of books
was granted by
Henry VIII in 1534.
The University has printed
and published continuously
since 1584.

CAMBRIDGE UNIVERSITY PRESS

CAMBRIDGE

NEW YORK   PORT CHESTER   MELBOURNE   SYDNEY

Published by the Press Syndicate of the University of Cambridge
The Pitt Building, Trumpington Street, Cambridge CB2 1RP
40 West 20th Street, New York, NY 10011, USA
10 Stamford Road, Oakleigh, Melbourne 3166, Australia

© Cambridge University Press 1991
The contents of this book were previously published as part of Volume 13
of *The Cambridge History of China,* copyright © Cambridge University Press 1986.

First published 1991

Printed in the United States of America

Library of Congress Cataloging-in-Publication Data
The Nationalist era in China, 1927–1949 / Lloyd Eastman . . . [et al.].
p. cm.
"Contents of this book were previously published as part of volume
13 of The Cambridge history of China, copyright, Cambridge
University Press, 1986" – Verso t.p.
ISBN 0-521-39273-X. – ISBN 0-521-38591-1 (pbk.)
1. China – History – Republic, 1912–1949.   I. Eastman, Lloyd E.
DS774.N38   1990
951.04 – dc20   90-30310
                                                              CIP

British Library Cataloguing in Publication Data
The Nationalist era in China, 1927–1949.
1. China. Political events, 1927–1949
I. Eastman, Lloyd E.   II. The Cambridge history of China
951.042

ISBN 0-521-39273-X hardback
ISBN 0-521-38591-1 paperback

CONTENTS

MAPS

TABLES

PREFACE

This book fills a special need. The two decades of Nationalist rule on the mainland (1927–1949) were among the most critical in recent Chinese history. During those years, the Nationalist Party, led by Chiang Kai-shek, endeavored to consolidate its revolutionary victory of 1927–1928 and to build a nation based on Sun Yat-sen's Three Principles of the People. At the same time, the revolutionary party led by Mao Tse-tung, drawing inspiration from the principles of Marx and Lenin, grew from a seemingly insignificant guerrilla band in the rural hinterland of Kiangsi Province into a military and political force that shook not only China but the world.

Yet none of the existing college textbooks on modern China presents the events of this momentous period comprehensively or on the basis of the most recent scholarly literature. Until the 1970s, most of what Westerners knew about the Nationalist period was gleaned from such journalistic accounts as Edgar Snow's *Red star over China,* Theodore White and Annalee Jacoby's *Thunder out of China,* and Jack Belden's *China shakes the world* – wonderful books that can still be read with excitement and benefit. In recent years, however, academic historians have been turning their attention to these critical decades. As a result, a spate of books, articles, and doctoral dissertations have substantially modified our understanding of the Nationalist period, shedding new light on the character of Nationalist rule and on the sources of the Communists' revolutionary victory.

The five essays that make up this volume synthesize this new research. Students will find here, I believe, a more complete, accurate, and interpretatively stimulating discussion of the history of the years preceding the Communist 'liberation' in 1949 than in any of the standard texts on modern China.

These essays were first published in 1986 in *The Cambridge History of China.* This monumental work, to comprise fifteen volumes when completed, is designed to provide a summary, but comprehensive, account of the whole of Chinese history. *The Cambridge History,* however, was intended not as a textbook but as a reference. The five essays here, which pertain specifically to the political history of the Nationalist period, were therefore selected from Volume 13 of *The Cambridge History* in order to make them more readily available for classroom use. Students interested in other aspects of the Nationalist period, such as the economy, literature, education, local government, peasant movements, or international relations, should consult the original edition of *The Cambridge History*. Anyone wishing to probe the literature on the period more fully will find the bibliographical essays at the end of that volume especially useful.

The editors of *The Cambridge History of China*, Volume 13, were Professors John K. Fairbank and Albert Feuerwerker. But for their original inspiration and organizational talents, these essays would never have been written. And but for their support now, this separate volume would not have been published. The volume is gratefully dedicated to them.

LLOYD E. EASTMAN
University of Illinois, Urbana

PUBLISHER'S NOTE

References to other volumes or to chapters not in this book are to *The Cambridge History of China*.

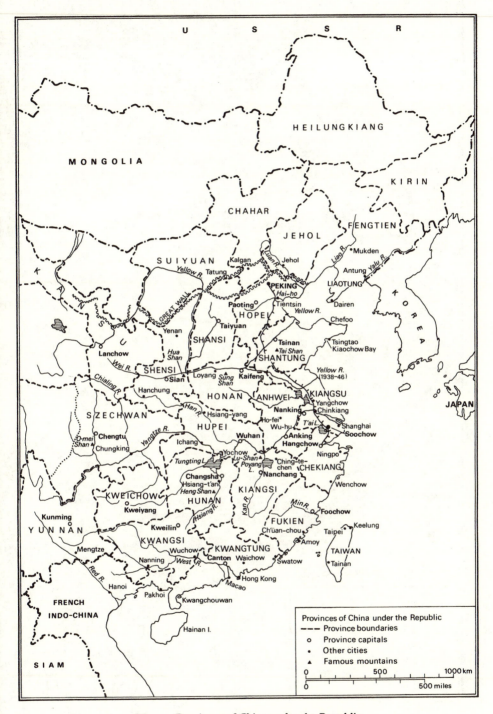

MAP 1. Provinces of China under the Republic

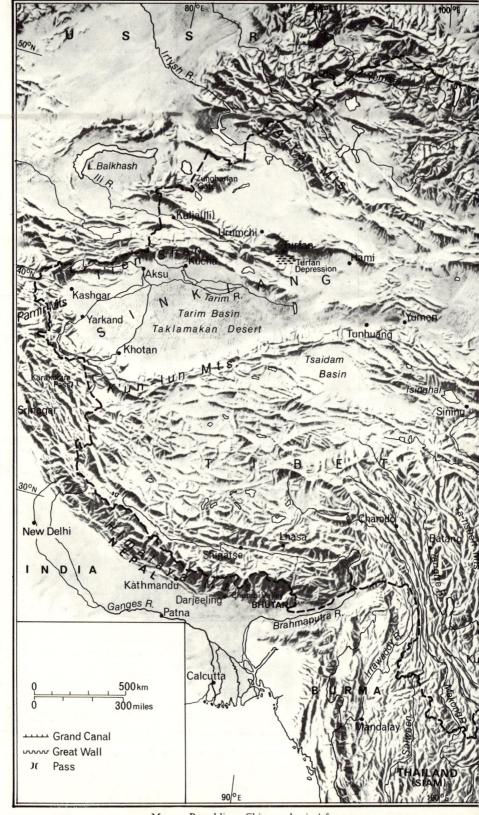

MAP 2. Republican China – physical features

CHAPTER 1

NATIONALIST CHINA DURING
THE NANKING DECADE 1927–1937

The Nanking regime was born of factional strife and bloodshed. In the early morning of 12 April 1927, gangs of thugs belonging to the Mafia-like Green Gang plunged through the streets of Shanghai, seized Communists and suspected Communists, and executed them on the spot with pistols or broadswords. Several thousand were massacred then and during the ensuing month. Chiang Kai-shek had split with the Communists; the first united front was ended. Six days later, on 18 April, the Nationalist government was inaugurated at Nanking.

The challenge confronting the new government was awesome – nothing less than to turn back the tide of national disintegration that, for a century and more, had been washing over the Chinese nation. A central, national government had virtually ceased to exist. Political power had devolved into the hands of regional militarists, 'warlords', who too often were unconcerned for the popular welfare and sought only to enhance their wealth and power by reliance on military force. The sense of moral community – the broad and pervasive consensus regarding the values and proper relationships of cultural and social life, which had so richly contributed to the stability of traditional China – had disintegrated, and in its place were confusion and contention. Even the economic foundations of the traditional political system had eroded.

THE INITIAL CONSOLIDATION OF POWER

Because the Chinese were profoundly sensitive to the abject condition of their nation, to the ravages of warlord struggles, and to the humiliations of imperialist aggression, the Nationalist revolutionary armies had been greeted exultantly as their Northern Expedition moved from Canton in the south (beginning in July 1926) to Peking in the north (occupied in June 1928) (see volume 12). To many Chinese, Nationalist rule marked the beginning of a new era, when China would again be unified and strong, when there would be economic plenty for all, and when they would no longer feel shame at being Chinese. As early as 1929, however, these extravagant expectations turned ashen. For the Nationalists, before turning their attention to the constructive tasks of the new era, had first to resolve who among them was to wield the power of the new government.

Since the death of Sun Yat-sen in March 1925, there had been a bitter, even bloody, struggle for leadership of the Nationalist movement. These power rivalries had been papered over during the Northern Expedition. Early in 1927, however, with the prize of national power within reach, the intraparty struggles resumed with a new and unprecedented ferocity. When the Nanking decade dawned, therefore, the Nationalist movement was in utter disarray. Indeed, in the spring of 1927, there existed two Nationalist governments (that of Chiang Kai-shek and the 'Centrists' in Nanking, and that of the Left-Kuomintang, still allied with the Communists, in Hankow) and three headquarters claiming leadership of the Kuomintang (besides those in Hankow and Nanking, the extreme right-wing Western Hills faction claimed sole legitimacy for its Central Executive Committee in Shanghai). Complicating the situation was that each of these power centres was backed by the armed forces of one or more provincial militarists. These had only recently declared allegiance to the revolution; they had little or no commitment to the ideological goals of the movement; and they were now simply indulging in political manoeuvres which, they hoped, would result in the preservation, if not the enhancement, of their personal and regional power.

Early in these struggles, Chiang Kai-shek was nearly eliminated from the competition. Only three months after establishing the government in Nanking, his troops were defeated by the warlord army of Sun Ch'uan-fang while he was attempting to push the Northern Expedition toward Peking. The result was a rout, during which Sun Ch'uan-fang's army threatened even to occupy Nanking. Chiang Kai-shek's prestige was badly tarnished as a consequence, and a new coalition within the Nanking government, headed by the Kwangsi faction of Li Tsung-jen and Pai Ch'ung-hsi, forced him from power in August 1927.

The Left-Kuomintang at Hankow, headed by Wang Ching-wei, had meanwhile followed Chiang's example and purged the Communists from their own ranks. With Chiang Kai-shek in retirement and with the Communists eliminated, the two chief causes of intraparty altercations had been removed, and the way lay open to a reconciliation of the warring factions. In September 1927, representatives of the Nanking and Hankow governments and of the Western Hills faction formed a 'Central Special Committee' which established a new, supposedly unified, Nationalist government at Nanking.

This new government was no more stable than its predecessors. The two most powerful leaders in the Nationalist movement, Chiang Kai-shek and Wang Ching-wei, had been excluded from it. And it never became financially viable. By January 1928, therefore, the government of the Special Committee had crumbled. Chiang Kai-shek, after five months in retirement (during which time he married the comely Soong Mei-ling), returned to office more powerful than before. In February he was named chairman of the Central Executive Committee of the Kuomintang and commander-in-chief of the army. In October, he also assumed the office of chairman of the State Council (and thus was the formal head of state). He now controlled all three legs of the Nationalists' triad of power – the party, government and military.

Under Chiang's aegis, the Nationalist government in Nanking was transformed into a military dictatorship. Prior to his rise to leadership, the Nationalist movement (whether in the form of the Kuomintang or one of its organizational antecedents) had never been a cohesive, ideologically unified, or tightly disciplined political party. Since Sun Yat-sen first formed the Hsing-Chung-hui (Revive China Society) in 1894, his following had comprised persons of widely diverse orientations and motivations. Indeed, he seems never to have refused membership in his party to anyone who applied. In at least one instance he even enrolled the entire army of the warlord Ch'en Chiung-ming into the Kuomintang. As a consequence, wrote T'ang Leang-Li, who was a member of the party, the Kuomintang before the 1924 reorganization was not a political party but simply 'an agglomeration of different individual politicians, the majority of whom, caring little for the principles Sun Yat-sen stood for, were merely out to exploit his great reputation and prestige among the population for their own ends'.[1] The agglutinative tendencies of the Kuomintang had worsened as the movement approached the threshold of national power. For then careerists and opportunists of every political stripe leapt onto the victorious bandwagon; membership in the party grew from only 150,000 in 1926 to 630,000 in 1929. The party organization, never tightly controlled, admitted the new applicants with utter disregard for their backgrounds, character, or commitment to the goals of the revolution. 'Party headquarters at all levels,' complained Ho Ying-ch'in, chief-of-staff of Chiang Kai-shek's army, in January 1928, 'are concerned only about the quantity, and pay no attention to the quality [of the new members]. The spirit of the party therefore becomes more rotten by the day'.[2] The Kuomintang membership by 1927 had therefore become

[1] T'ang Leang-Li, *The inner history of the Chinese Revolution*, 330.
[2] *Ch'en-pao* (Morning post), 11 Jan. 1928, in Hatano Ken'ichi, comp., *Gendai Shina no kiroku* (Records of contemporary China), Jan. 1928, 110.

intolerably disparate, and Chiang Kai-shek accordingly began to screen out many of the members that to him appeared to be undesirables. In the process, he fundamentally altered the character of the Nationalist movement.

The first to be purged from the movement were the Communists. Never, in all probability, could the Nationalists have gained national power had it not been for the united front that Sun Yat-sen formed with the Chinese Communists and the Soviet Union in 1923–4. With the advice, material aid and organizational skills of the Communists, the Kuomintang had been reorganized on the model of the Russian Communist Party; a party-led and politically indoctrinated army had been created; and young revolutionary cadres had gone among the peasants and workers in the warlord-held areas, stirring up and organizing support for the revolution. Significantly, those who had engaged in the difficult and dangerous work of organizing the masses were more closely identified with the Communists than with the Kuomintang. 'Kuomintang members were unwilling to do the real and lower-level work,' Ho Ying-ch'in admitted, and consequently 'the Communists naturally took on this work to split our party from the peasants and workers'.[3] Those less committed to the revolution avoided working among the masses and thus avoided the taint of communism. The purge of the Communists therefore had a filtering effect, leaving the self-servers untouched, but removing from the revolutionary movement many of those who had infused a degree of vigour, discipline and commitment into the Kuomintang during the period of revolutionary success.

Even after the purge of the Communists, however, there remained a broad stratum of Kuomintang members who advocated more radical solutions to the nation's problems than those favoured by Chiang Kai-shek. This was the left wing of the party, which during 1928 and 1929 was Chiang's most formidable political rival and which he successfully suppressed only after nearly two years of bitter struggle. These leftists loudly denounced the 'one-man military dictatorship' that Chiang was creating, and they demanded that the Kuomintang revive the policies and spirit that had energized the movement during the period of Sun Yat-sen's revolutionary leadership in 1924. The party, they contended, and not the army, should control and provide direction to the regime. The leftists, in contrast to the Communists, rejected the concept and policies of class struggle, but they believed that the party must maintain and strengthen its relations with the masses by means of peasant, worker, and other mass organizations. Only with such a mass base, they insisted, could they

[3] Ho Ying-ch'in, 'Chin-hou chih Chung-kuo Kuo-min-tang' (The Chinese Kuomintang from now on), *Chung-yang pan yueh-k'an* (Central semi-monthly), 2 (Oct. 1927) 102.

prevent the revolution from becoming a plaything of bureaucrats and militarists.[4]

Many Kuomintang members, perhaps a majority, supported these radical views. But the estimate of T'ang Leang-Li, himself a member of the left, that 80 per cent of the party members in this period belonged to the left wing was surely an exaggeration.[5] Still, it is clear that many of the low-ranking and young members of the party (one-third of the Kuomintang members in 1929 were under twenty-five years of age) were sympathetic with the views of the left wing.

Wang Ching-wei was the recognized leader of the left, but he was sojourning in Europe during 1928 and 1929, and formally at least dissociated himself from the movement opposing Chiang Kai-shek. Moving spirit behind the left-wing organization, therefore, was Wang's loyal associate, Ch'en Kung-po, a one-time Communist, who in May 1928 began publishing the weekly *Ko-ming p'ing-lun* (Revolutionary critic) as a mouthpiece for the left wing. Although this journal never exceeded a circulation of 15,000 copies, it enjoyed such popularity and influence that the Nanking government suppressed it in September after an existence of only 4½ months.

Facing the prospect of government suppression, Ch'en Kung-po decided that the left wing, hitherto an amorphous body of Wang Ching-wei supporters, should organize. Although Wang himself was ambivalent about the plan, viewing himself as a leader of the entire Kuomintang rather than merely a factional leader, Ch'en in late 1928 organized the Chinese Kuomintang Reorganizationist Comrades Association (Chung-kuo kuo-min-tang kai-tsu t'ung-chih hui) – the name symbolizing the group's advocacy of the revolutionary principles that the Kuomintang had adopted at the time of the 1924 reorganization. The Reorganization clique, as it was called, was a formal organization with a written constitution, a party headquarters in Shanghai, and branches throughout much of the country. During 1928, too, Ch'en organized the Ta-lu University in Shanghai, the purpose of which was to indoctrinate youth with the political views of the left and to train cadres for the faction.

The leftists, although they all recognized Wang Ching-wei as their leader, were not unified. Ku Meng-yü led a faction within the Reorganization clique that was notably less radical than the faction led by Ch'en

[4] Ssu-ma Hsien-tao, *Pei-fa hou chih ko-p'ai ssu-ch'ao* (The doctrines of the various cliques after the Northern Expedition), 133–99; T'ang Leang-Li, *Inner history*, 331–3; Arif Dirlik, 'Mass movements and the left Kuomintang', *Modern China*, 1.1 (Jan. 1975) 57–9.

[5] T'ang Leang-Li, *Inner history*, 334. Actual membership in the leading left-wing organization (the Reorganization clique) at this time was perhaps 10,000. See Chiang Shang-ch'ing, *Cheng-hai mi-wen* (Secrets of the political world), 72.

Kung-po. Ku, whose views were publicized in his own journal, *Ch'ien-chin* (Forward), disapproved of Ch'en's emphasis upon peasants, workers and petty bourgeoisie as the core of the Nationalist Revolution. Ku also expressed greater mistrust of the mass movement. Other leftists, like Ho Ping-hsien, disliked Ch'en Kung-po and held aloof from the Reorganization clique, although they remained loyal to Wang Ching-wei. Thus, the left wing of the Kuomintang suffered much the same kind of internal fragmentation that plagued the right wing led by Chiang Kai-shek.[6]

Left-wing opposition to Chiang and the authorities in Nanking was not limited to ideological theorizing and propaganda, for the radicals, often dominant in the local and provincial party branches, worked strenuously to bring the revolution to fruition. In Chekiang, for example, leftists organized boycotts of foreign goods and led popular demonstrations against foreign churches and hospitals. They organized special tribunals to judge and punish counter-revolutionaries. They also began a programme of rent-reduction, which stirred the enmity of the landlord class and consequently damaged Nanking's efforts to raise money from that group. In Kiangsu, similarly, the radicals provoked Nanking's displeasure by organizing the masses and by confiscating temples which were then converted into welfare centres for the local people.[7]

The activities of the radicals, and the implicit political challenge of Wang Ching-wei, deeply disturbed the right wing of the party. Immediately following Chiang's return to power in January 1928, therefore, there began an intensive, albeit generally bloodless, suppression of the left wing. At the fourth plenum of the Kuomintang's Central Executive Committee in February, for example, all provincial party organizations 'not creditable to the party' were ordered dissolved. A re-registration of the party membership was ordered; and all party members were ordered to conduct themselves in the 'spirit' of the party leadership. The move to re-register the members was patently designed to weed out those who had displayed radical tendencies, and to guarantee a membership that would complaisantly accept the dictates of leaders then ensconced in power. Mass movements were also, for all intents and purposes, suspended. Henceforth, the mass organizations would serve as Nanking's instruments of control, not as organs for the expression of popular opinions or initiatives. In Chekiang, where landlord opposition to the land redistribution policy was

---

[6] Chiang Shang-ch'ing, 68–73; Ssu-ma Hsien-tao, 140–52; Ch'en Kung-po, *The communist movement in China*, 178–90.

[7] Noel Ray Miner, 'Chekiang: the Nationalists' effort in agrarian reform and construction, 1927–1937', 64–79; Patrick Cavendish, 'The "New China" of the Kuomintang', in Jack Gray, ed. *Modern China's Search for a political form*, 158–9; Bradley Kent Geisert, 'Power and society: the Kuomintang and local elites in Kiangsu province, China, 1924–1937', 96–131.

fierce, at least one leftist leader was assassinated, and others were beaten and stabbed. Landlords may have been responsible for this violence. But the Chekiang provincial government, under Chiang Kai-shek's intimate supporter Chang Jen-chieh (Chang Ching-chiang), sided with the landlords by arresting recalcitrant leftists and suspending the provincial party newspaper *Min-kuo jih-pao* (Republic daily), which had been dominated by the leftists.[8]

Youth, who were most susceptible to the idealism and radicalism of the left, were unequivocally instructed to get out of politics. 'The most deplorable fact,' read the manifesto of the fourth plenum (February 1928) 'is the participation by immature students today in our political and social strifes. To permit these young boys and girls, not yet [having] attained maturity, and without sufficient knowledge and experience, to participate freely in the affairs of the nation is not only to sacrifice the life of our race in the future, but also to allow them to treat the entire nation and human society as playthings'.[9]

The paramountcy of the right wing was finally and formally established at the Third Party Congress in March 1929. Recognizing that the lower ranks of the party were permeated by adherents of the left, Chiang Kai-shek's faction took special measures to guarantee its control of the congress. On the grounds that re-registration of party members had not been completed and that the organization of the party at the local level was still in disarray, only one-fourth of the delegates to the congress were elected by the party members. The remaining delegates were appointed by the central-party headquarters.[10] The leftists vehemently denounced this violation of democratic principles within the party, and declared that the Third Party Congress was illegal. The denunciations were in vain, however, for Chiang Kai-shek had now placed his own supporters in control of the Kuomintang, and imposed his own conception of the revolution upon the party and the government. Leaders of the left wing were disciplined: Ch'en Kung-po and Kan Nai-kuang were 'expelled forever' from the party; Ku Meng-yü's party membership was suspended for three years; and Wang Ching-wei was reprimanded for his error of 'straddling parties'.[11] Thereafter, the leftists' contention that the govern-

[8] Hsiao Cheng, *T'u-ti kai-ko wu-shih-nien: Hsiao Cheng hui-i-lu* (Fifty years of land reform: the memoirs of Hsiao Cheng), 27–9; *China year book* (hereafter *CYB*), *1929–30*, ed. H. G. W. Woodhead, 1163–73; Miner, 'Chekiang', 64–79; Cavendish, 158–9; Geisert, 'Power and society', 144–66.

[9] *CYB, 1929–30,* 1170.

[10] Jürgen Domes, *Vertagte Revolution: die Politik der Kuomintang in China, 1923–1937,* 325. Most of the elected delegates were Overseas Chinese. In actual fact, therefore, only a tenth of the elected delegates represented party branches within China. See *CYB, 1929–30,* 1202.

[11] *I-shih-pao* (Social welfare post), 21 Mar. 1929, in Hatano Ken'ichi, *Gendai Shina no kiroku* (Records of contemporary China), Mar. 1929, 276–8; *Fan-Chiang yun-tung shih* (History of the anti-Chiang movement), 46–7.

ment ought to be simply the administrative arm of the party and that the party should be the superior organ during the period of revolutionary construction was conclusively rejected. Instead, during 1929–31, the party was stripped of most of its power, and it ceased to play a significant role either in policy formation or as a supervisory organ. Somewhat earlier, Chiang had also dismantled the system of party commissars in the army.[12] Ineluctably, the left wing was repressed, and the status of the party was correspondingly reduced.

Even as he purged Communists and Kuomintang leftists from the movement, Chiang Kai-shek relied increasingly upon old-style bureaucrats and the army. As soon as the revolution gave evidence of success, large numbers of former bureaucrats in the various warlord regimes had descended on Nanking seeking new and remunerative employment. And Chiang, confronted with the challenge of administering a national government, welcomed them into his camp. By 1929, at least four of the ten ministries were headed by these new converts to the revolutionary cause. They filled so many other bureaucratic posts that Quo Tai-chi (Kuo T'ai-ch'i), a long-time member of the Kuomintang, angrily resigned his vice-ministership of foreign affairs, charging that 'the Party is nearly usurped by the old mandarin influence even as it was usurped last year by the Communists'.[13] The effects of this mandarin influence on the new regime were far-reaching. These groups brought with them the same outlooks, the same lust for power cum disregard for the public weal, that they had displayed in their former jobs. The bureaucracy became routinized; bureaucrats wrote innumerable documents and shuffled papers, but paid minimal heed to the actual implementation of policy; and corruption quickly seeped through the administration. Thus, the values, attitudes and practices of the old warlord regimes had been injected into the new government. Even eighteen years later, in 1946, would-be Kuomintang reformers surveyed the corruption of their government and attributed it to the political opportunists and bureaucrats who in this period had swarmed into the Nationalist ranks.[14]

Perhaps even more decisive in determining the future course of the Nationalist movement was the pervasive influence of the military. During Sun Yat-sen's lifetime, the military had been a relatively disparaged

---

[12] The system of political commissars was reinstituted beginning in 1932. See Joseph H. Heinlein, Jr. 'Political warfare: the Chinese Nationalist model', 268–330.

[13] *North China Herald*, 14 Apr. 1928, 48.

[14] See e.g. Ch'eng Yuan-chen, 'Ko-hsin yun-tung chih-hsu ch'eng-kung pu-hsu shih-pai' (The renovation movement can only succeed and must not fail), in *Ko-hsin chou-k'an* (Renovation weekly), 1.5 (24 Aug. 1946) 3–5; and Li Ta, 'Ko-hsin yun-tung ti ta ching-shen' (The great spirit of the renovation movement), in *Ko-hsin chou-k'an*, 1.6 (31 Aug. 1946) 5.

element in the movement. Under Chiang, however, Sun's relative ranking of these groups – first the party, then the government, and lastly the army – was turned upside-down, and the army now became the preponderant element. Some indication of this is found in the fact that, in 1929, more than half the members of the Kuomintang in China were soldiers, not civilians. Of the party leaders – members of the Central Executive Committee – 43 per cent in 1935 were military officers. Twenty-five of the thirty-three chairmen of provinces controlled by the Nationalists between 1927 and 1937 were generals.[15] And about two-thirds of the government's expenditure during the decade was allocated for the military and payments on debts (most of which had been contracted to pay military outlays).[16] The true measure of the dominance of the military is provided less by these statistics, however, than by the overshadowing presence of a single soldier, Chiang Kai-shek – a presence that would grow in importance as the Nanking decade advanced.

THE STRUGGLE IN THE PROVINCES

With his victory over the left wing, Chiang Kai-shek's power within the councils of the Nanking government was secured. Then, however, the main arena of internecine struggle shifted to the provinces.

By 1929, the flag of the National government flew over the whole of China proper and Manchuria. Peking had been occupied by Nationalist forces in June 1928, at which time the city's name was changed from Peking (Northern capital) to Peiping (Northern peace). And on 29 December 1928, Chang Hsueh-liang, warlord of the four provinces of Manchuria, proclaimed his loyalty to the Nationalist government. With the nation now nominally unified for the first time since 1916, the authorities in Nanking could look ahead to the tasks of peaceful national reconstruction.

A major obstacle, however, remained. The military phase of the revolution had been successful in large part because many of the provincial militarists had not been defeated on the field of battle but instead had been coopted into the revolutionary movement. Although these warlords had gained membership in the Kuomintang and accepted prestigious posts in the Nanking hierarchy, they distrusted Chiang Kai-shek, were jealous of his growing power, and were largely indifferent to the ideology of the Nationalist movement. During the Northern Expedition, Chiang and the

---

[15] Robert C. North, *Kuomintang and Chinese Communist elites*, 53; Domes, 572; Hung-mao Tien, *Government and politics in Kuomintang China, 1927–1937*, 140.

[16] Arthur N. Young, *China's nation-building effort, 1927–1937: the financial and economic record*, 75, 147.

authorities in Nanking, who were committed to the unification of the nation and to the centralization of authority, had necessarily tolerated the independent power of the provincial militarists. They had, in fact, even institutionalized the position of the provincial militarists by creating a number of branch political councils. These councils, established in 1928, were nominally subordinate to the Central Political Council in Nanking. In fact, however, they were autonomous administrative organs that, momentarily at least, legitimized the regional dominance of the major warlord groupings. Thus, Feng Yü-hsiang, who controlled Kansu, Shensi and Honan, headed the branch political council at Kaifeng; Yen Hsi-shan's administration of Shansi was legitimized by the branch political council at Taiyuan; and the so-called Kwangsi clique dominated the councils at Hankow, Peiping and Canton, which were headed respectively by Li Tsung-jen, Pai Ch'ung-hsi and Li Chi-shen. A sixth branch political council was established at Mukden after Chang Hsüeh-liang's capitulation in Manchuria.[17]

Chiang Kai-shek regarded the branch political councils as temporary expedients, for he aspired to centralize all power, administrative and military, under the Nanking government. Soon, therefore, he challenged the autonomous power of the provincial militarists. First, in late 1928, Nanking announced that the branch political councils would be abolished in March 1929. Then, in January 1929, a National Reorganization and Demobilization Conference convened in Nanking, at which the central government authorities presented a plan for the reduction of China's armed forces.

The desirability of military demobilization was generally recognized. Armies in China had swollen prodigiously since the fall of the Ch'ing dynasty, and in 1929 probably numbered about two million men (as compared with about 400,000 under the dynasty, and about 1,200,000 in 1922). Now that the military phase of the revolution was concluded, these huge forces were no longer needed and were, moreover, an insupportable burden on the nation's financial resources. In 1928, for example, Nanking's own army, which totalled roughly 240,000 men, cost approximately Y360 million a year (Y = *yuan*, Chinese dollars), although Nanking's revenue (after payments on debts) amounted to only Y300 million a year.[18] Furthermore, while the armies of the provincial militarists did not constitute a direct financial burden upon Nanking, they did absorb revenue that might otherwise have been channelled to the central government. It was therefore argued that, unless the armies were reduced,

[17] Diana Lary, *Region and nation: the Kwangsi clique in Chinese politics, 1925–1937*, 117.
[18] Young, *Nation-building*, 15.

the government would have no means with which to undertake the social and economic reconstruction of the nation.

At the demobilization conference, the nation's leading militarists – Chiang Kai-shek, Feng Yü-hsiang, Yen Hsi-shan, Li Tsung-jen and others – agreed to trim the nation's armies to 800,000 men, to limit military expenditures to 41 per cent of the government's revenues, and to establish a unified command structure. The conference was a failure, however, because the militarists' suspicions of Chiang Kai-shek were exacerbated during the meetings. Using the principle that the less efficient armies should be demobilized first, and because his own Whampoa-led troops tended in fact to be the best-trained and best-led units in China, Chiang Kai-shek was asking greater sacrifices of the provincial militarists than of himself. Because their armies were their principal source of political power, the provincial militarists felt that Chiang was merely using the issue of military disbandment to establish a political advantage over them. However dedicated they might have been to the national interests – and that was debatable – the provincial militarists were disinclined to abandon their own ambitions so that Chiang might enhance his power. For they did not perceive that he had any greater claim to national power and leadership than did they. They therefore left the conference in late January 1929 applauding the principle of military disbandment, but determined to maintain their military and political positions against Chiang. Chiang, on his part, was equally determined to establish the dominance of the central government over the provinces. The result was a long and costly series of civil wars.

The first of the civil wars erupted in March 1929, only two months after the demobilization conference, when the Kwangsi clique – as a result of a crisis seemingly provoked by Chiang Kai-shek – revolted against Nanking. This was a formidable challenge, for the Kwangsi leaders were skilled tacticians and commanded about 230,000 troops. There was also the possibility that Feng Yü-hsiang, commanding 220,000 men and perhaps Chiang Kai-shek's most ardent military rival, would join forces with the rebels. This challenge might have doomed a lesser man, but it was tailored to Chiang Kai-shek's talents. For Chiang bought off Feng Yü-hsiang, reportedly with Y2 million and a promise of control over Shantung province. Then, with his superior troops, he defeated the Kwangsi armies in less than two months. The empire of Li Tsung-jen and Pai Ch'ung-hsi in Hopei and Hunan-Hupei thereupon collapsed. They hastily retreated to their home province of Kwangsi to nurse their humiliation and to plan for another day.

Only one month later, in May 1929, Chiang provoked Feng Yü-hsiang into rebellion by reneging on his pledge to hand Shantung over to Feng's control. In this confrontation, half of Feng's army – fully 100,000 of his best troops – suddenly defected to the central government, a shift of loyalties precipitated again by massive bribes. During this struggle, Yen Hsi-shan in nearby Shansi watched passively as Feng's remaining forces were pushed out of Shantung and Honan.

With Feng Yü-hsiang's army now badly mauled by the central government forces, the balance of power in North China had clearly shifted in Nanking's favour. Yen Hsi-shan therefore felt threatened, and in February and March 1930 he, together with the now much weakened Feng Yü-hsiang, formed a new anti-Chiang movement. This Northern Coalition, as it was called, posed the most serious challenge yet to Chiang's power. For Yen and Feng had now formed a broad alliance of anti-Chiang forces. Li Tsung-jen and Pai Ch'ung-hsi of the Kwangsi clique promised to coordinate their attack from South China. Many of Chiang's civilian opponents – including such diverse groups as Wang Ching-wei and his Reorganizationist clique, and the extreme right wing Western Hills faction – provided administrative and ideological muscle to the movement. Soon these disparate elements began creating the institutional structures of a separate and permanent regime. An 'Enlarged Conference of the Kuomintang', functionally equivalent to a Central Executive Committee of the party, convened in Peiping in July. And in September a new National government was instituted, with Yen Hsi-shan as chairman of the State Council. By promulgating a provisional constitution (yueh-fa), which contained articles guaranteeing personal freedoms, the new regime also attracted much popular support, especially from the nation's intellectuals, who had begun to feel the sting of Nanking's political repression.

As early as July, however, Chiang ordered his troops against the Northern Coalition. The fighting in this civil war fitted none of the stereotypes of warlord battles. Nanking and the northerners fought furiously. Physical devastation was enormous; in four months of fighting, the two sides incurred some 250,000 casualties. By September, just when the Northern Coalition announced the formation of a new government, Nanking was gaining the upper hand in the war, and the rebel government fled from Peiping to Yen's provincial capital of Taiyuan. To the very end, however, the leaders of the Northern Coalition and of Nanking realized that Chang Hsueh-liang, warlord of Manchuria, could tip the scales of battle either way. Both sides therefore wooed him. Finally, apparently won over by Nanking's bribe of 10 million yuan and by the promise that he might administer all of China north of the Yellow River, Chang in mid-September issued a public declaration in support of the central government. The Northern Coalition was thereby doomed. Still, Nanking gained little from its victory. For Chang Hsueh-liang quickly led 100,000 of his own troops into the Peiping-Tientsin area, and took control of the major railroads and of the rich revenues from the Tientsin customs. North China, therefore, still lay outside the administrative sway of Nanking.

The concatenation of revolts was still not ended. The next one actually succeeded – for six weeks – in forcing Chiang Kai-shek from power. The basic causes of the revolt were identical to those of the preceding ones: jealousy of Chiang Kai-shek's growing power and fear of Nanking's centralizing pretensions. As always, however, there were secondary issues that provided the rebels with a facade of moral justification. In this case, the catalysing event was Chiang Kai-shek's arrest of Hu Han-min. Stung by the Northern Coalition's popularity as a result of proclaiming a provisional constitution, Chiang Kai-shek in February 1931 declared his determination to promulgate a similar document. 'Without a Provisional Constitution,' he insisted, 'there could be no security for the lives and property of the people...without guarantees to person and property there could be no real unification of the country and an end of civil wars.'[19]

Hu Han-min, however, heatedly rejected this proposal. He publicly avowed that the proclamation of a provisional constitution would be contrary to the intention of Sun Yat-sen – although the actual cause of his objection may well have been the fear that Chiang meant to enhance his power by having himself named president under a new constitution. In protest against Chiang's unilateral decision to promulgate the provisional constitution, Hu resigned his position as head of the Legislative Yuan. Chiang Kai-shek thereupon arrested Hu, because – as Chiang explained – 'It is only in this way that his glorious past may be preserved intact.'[20]

Ostensibly in protest against Hu Han-min's arrest, the provincial militarists of Kwangtung and Kwangsi, and a mixed assortment of Chiang Kai-shek's civilian rivals (such as Wang Ching-wei, the Western Hills partisans, and Sun Yat-sen's son, Sun Fo) established a new separatist regime in Canton in May 1931. An 'Extraordinary Conference' of the Kuomintang's Central Executive Committee was formed, and this in turn created a new National government on 1 June.[21] Real power rested with the provincial militarists, most notably Ch'en Chi-t'ang, chairman of Kwangtung province.

Mutual denunciations and impeachments emanated from the new Canton regime and from the Nanking government. Canton asserted that

[19] CYB, 1931–32, 529.
[20] Ibid. 530; Lei Hsiao-ts'en, San-shih-nien tung-luan Chung-kuo (Thirty years of China in turmoil), 205.
[21] Domes, 439–44.

it would abandon its opposition only if the dictator Chiang Kai-shek relinquished his positions in Nanking.

Had not the Japanese invaded Manchuria on 18 September 1931, this conflict, like its predecessors, would presumably have been fought on the battlefield. As a result of an impassioned anti-Japanese reaction from the Chinese people, especially the students, pressures to terminate the intraparty squabbling and to form a united government to oppose the foreign aggressor became irresistible. After extraordinarily arcane negotiations and complex conferences, including two Fourth Party Congresses held separately in Nanking and Canton and a joint peace conference in Shanghai, an agreement between the rival regimes was worked out. On 15 December, Chiang Kai-shek resigned his posts of chairman of the National government, president of the Executive Yuan, and commander-in-chief of the army. Retaining only his membership on the standing committee of the Kuomintang's Central Executive Committee, Chiang 'retired' to his native village of Hsi-k'ou in Chekiang.

A new government was thereupon formed in Nanking. Lin Sen, a venerable but ineffectual old revolutionary, was named chairman of the National government. Sun Fo assumed the presidency of the Executive Yuan and became effective head of the new administration.

The Sun Fo government, which took office on 1 January 1932, survived only twenty-five days. All three of the Kuomintang's leading personalities – Wang Ching-wei, Hu Han-min and Chiang Kai-shek – were excluded from or refused to associate with the new government. The regime failed to win the support of the Shanghai financial classes, and consequently could not meet its financial responsibilities. The central army remained loyal to Chiang. And the leaders of the new government were overwhelmed by the problems of the crisis confronting them – even as early as 2 January entreating (unsuccessfully) Chiang Kai-shek and Wang Ching-wei to return to Nanking so that the government might benefit from their advice.

The plight of the Sun Fo government worsened with each passing day, and Chiang Kai-shek discerned in that plight an opportunity to regain power. So virulent had the opposition to his 'dictatorship' been, however, that he knew he could not simply reassume the offices that he had held prior to his retirement. The solution to this predicament was thrashed out at Hangchow in three days of intense negotiations between Chiang, Wang Ching-wei, and Sun Fo. On 21 January 1932, the three men together returned to Nanking. Soon the outlines of those negotiations became clear. On 25 January, Sun Fo and his cabinet resigned. Three days later Wang Ching-wei was sworn in as president of the Executive Yuan, and on 29 January Chiang Kai-shek became head of the newly created Military Affairs Commission. Wang, as 'prime minister', was formally the chief administrative officer of the civilian branch of the regime. Progressively it became apparent, however, that real power rested in the hands of Chiang Kai-shek, and from 1932 until 1949 he was the overwhelmingly dominant leader of the Nationalist regime.

FACTORS CONTRIBUTING TO CHIANG KAI-SHEK'S POLITICAL DOMINANCE

Assessments of Chiang Kai-shek have varied greatly over the course of his long career. Some Chinese revered him as a flawless national leader; others reviled him as a feudalistic militarist. Some foreigners lauded him as a Christian and defender of democracy; others denounced him as an outmoded Confucian and ruthless dictator. Whether friend or foe, however, all recognized that Chiang was no ordinary man.

Chiang Kai-shek's succession to the mantle of Sun Yat-sen could not have been predicted in, say, 1925 at the time of Sun's death. At that time, leadership of the Kuomintang seemed destined for Wang Ching-wei, Hu Han-min, or perhaps Liao Chung-k'ai, each of whom had a much richer revolutionary background and more intimate ties with Sun than did Chiang. Yet Chiang held three advantages over his rivals, and to these his rise to power was largely attributable. First, he was a soldier, and military force had become the primary political coinage of the time. The most important step in his rise to power was his appointment by Sun Yat-sen in 1923 to command the party's military academy at Whampoa. As commandant of the academy, Chiang oversaw the training of thousands of cadets (during 1924–6, 5,000 graduated in just the first four classes), and with many of these he formed what in China was the powerful bond between teacher and student. After graduation, these young officers assumed commands in the party army, which was generally better trained and equipped than were the armies of the warlords. This army became a loyal and powerful instrument that Chiang effectively employed in his subsequent political career. After he was forced into retirement in August 1927, for example, he retained the loyalty of, and hence effective control over, the party army. Without Chiang's cooperation, therefore, the Central Special Committee was virtually impotent to resume the Northern Expedition against North China. On 20 December 1927, moreover, eighteen of the army's leading commanders, including Ho Ying-ch'in, sent a wire to the Special Committee demanding that Chiang be renamed supreme military commander.[22] Using this military backing – together with the support of various political and financial elements – Chiang

---

[22] *Ko-ming wen-hsien* (Documents of the revolution), comp. Lo Chia-lun, 18.10–11; Domes, 295; Ch'ien Tuan-sheng, *The government and politics of China*, 96.

forced the resignation of the Special Committee, and in January 1928 resumed the dominant positions in the army, party and government.

Chiang also in 1928 began employing Germans, such as Colonel Max Bauer, as military advisers and instructors. The military training and knowledge that Bauer and others imparted to Chiang's army (although still generally rudimentary by Western standards), together with that army's bonds of loyalty to Chiang, made it far-and-away more effective militarily and dependable politically than were those of any of his rivals. Wang Ching-wei in the summer of 1927, for example, headed the rival Nationalist government at Wuhan, and his most powerful military supporter was the warlord of Hunan, T'ang Sheng-chih. T'ang, however, had political aspirations of his own. As a result, Wang in September 1927 was suddenly stripped of power and forced to seek a coalition with his archrival, Chiang Kai-shek. Similarly, Hu Han-min after 1932 cast his fortunes with the militarist of Kwangtung, Ch'en Chi-t'ang. Ch'en found Hu useful, because Hu, the leading Kuomintang ideologue, lent an aura of legitimacy to Ch'en's otherwise purely warlord administration. Never, however, was Hu able to impose his will upon Ch'en Chi-t'ang or significantly influence Cantonese policies.

A second advantage that Chiang enjoyed in his political struggles was a superior financial base. During the Northern Expedition, some revolutionary leaders had counselled Chiang to by-pass Shanghai, which was then heavily defended, in order to occupy North China. Shanghai would then drop, it was argued, into the hands of the revolutionaries without a fight. Chiang, however, like Sun Yat-sen after 1913, regarded the great city on the Yangtze as his primary military target.

More than most other Nationalist leaders, Chiang recognized the financial importance of Shanghai, and knew that control of its revenues would be worth more than the command of many army divisions. Between 1912 and 1922, he had spent much time in the city. He had close ties there with leaders of the financial community and, allegedly, with bosses of the Green Gang (Ch'ing-pang), a secret society that controlled the city's underworld. The financial resources of Shanghai, of course, had to be tapped. This initially would not be difficult, for the city's capitalists were panic-stricken now in the spring of 1927 by the approaching spectre of communism, and they appealed to Chiang to prevent the outbreak of revolutionary excesses in the city. This precisely suited Chiang's wishes. Although he had in the past sometimes voiced the radical rhetoric of the left, he too was disturbed by the growing radicalism of the Communists. He was disturbed even more, perhaps, by the political threat to his leadership being mounted in Wuhan by Borodin and the Chinese leftists.

Chiang and the capitalists therefore needed each other. The capitalists of Shanghai agreed in late March to provide him with an initial advance of Y3 million. In return, he promised to put an end to the labour disturbances in the city and to eliminate Communist influences from the revolutionary movement. In the predawn hours of 12 April 1927, Chiang faithfully fulfilled his part of the bargain by launching a massacre of the Communist-led labour unions in the city. Hundreds, perhaps several thousands of Communists and workers were murdered in this bloody purge. But the capitalists had attained their wish; the Communists no longer posed a threat to Shanghai.

The Shanghai businessmen and bankers, however, still had to pay Chiang for his service. On 25 April, they gave him an additional Y7 million. But this merely whetted Chiang's financial appetite, for his military expenses were running at about Y20 million every month. His agents went from shop to shop and factory to factory demanding contributions. The Nanyang Tobacco Company, for instance, was ordered to give Y500,000; the Nantao Electric and Gas Works, Y300,000; and the Sincere Company Department Store Y250,000. When the capitalists balked, Chiang's agents threatened, blackmailed, and even kidnapped. 'Wealthy Chinese would be arrested in their homes or mysteriously disappear from the streets... Millionaires were arrested as "Communists"', reported Owen Chapman. 'Under no previous regime in modern times had Shanghai known such a reign of terror'.[23] Chiang's minister of finance, T. V. Soong, even admitted publicly after the Northern Expedition that 'in time of war, we have perhaps been forced to resort to extraordinary means to raise funds'.[24]

Although the Nationalists ceased to employ such tactics after mid-1928, Shanghai and its environs continued to serve as the government's primary source of revenue. During the Nanking decade, it derived approximately 85 per cent of its tax revenue from the trade and manufacturing sectors of the economy – much of which was centred in the Shanghai area. The government was also heavily dependent for its fiscal survival on loans. Here again, it was the Shanghai capitalists who subscribed to most of the government loans. Able to tap the wealth of China's largest and most modern city, Chiang enjoyed an enviable advantage over his rivals. Feng Yü-hsiang, for example, complained bitterly that he could not compete with Chiang, because the Nationalist armies were invariably better paid, fed, and armed than his own. Chiang also, he claimed, was sufficiently wealthy that he could cripple his opponents by purchasing defections from the rival armies.[25]

[23] H. Owen Chapman, *The Chinese revolution, 1926–1927*, 232.   [24] *CYB, 1929–30*, 629.
[25] Feng Yü-hsiang, *Wo so-jen-shih-ti Chiang Chieh-shih* (The Chiang Kai-shek I know), 17–18.

The third ingredient that contributed to Chiang's ascendancy in the Nationalist movement was his mastery of the techniques of factional and warlord politics. He seldom committed himself irreversibly to an ideological position or factional policy. He easily accommodated himself to – without becoming a part of – any faction if it was politically advantageous to do so. In late 1927 and early 1928, for instance, he associated himself with the Left Kuomintang and the *yüan-lao* (genrō in Japanese; a group of former anarchists and elder statesmen represented by Chang Jen-chieh, Wu Chih-hui, Ts'ai Yuan-p'ei, and Li Shih-tseng); by August 1928, he was allied with the *yüan-lao* and the right against the left; and by March 1929, he had allied with the right against both the *yüan-lao* and the left. Within a year and a half, therefore, he had associated himself with groups at most points of the Kuomintang's political spectrum. He also had a talent for holding the loyalties of factions that were bitterly antagonistic to each other. In the mid-1930s, for example, the CC clique and the Blue Shirts were ready to fight each other – yet each revered him as their leader. And both the CC clique and the Blue Shirts despised the Political Study clique – yet many of Chiang's most intimate advisers and trusted officials were members of the Political Study clique.

This skill in political manipulation was discernible also in Chiang's relations with the provincial militarists. These quondam warlords were jealous and distrustful of Chiang, and, at one time or another, nearly all of them raised the flag of revolt against him. Invariably, the rebelling militarists expected other provincial militarists to join forces with them, and it is certain that, if Chiang's enemies had acted in concert, he could have been crushed. Yet he isolated his opponents and eliminated them one by one. He, more than any of the other militarists, was a master of the use of 'silver bullets', bribes used to induce defections from opposing armies. And, when not employing silver bullets, he cajoled, promised, and threatened in order to gain the support, or at least the neutrality, of his provincial rivals – until he was ready to turn on them.

Although Chiang's ideology was flexible, his drive for power was unswerving. But his ambition for power was fuelled not solely by the desire for personal gratification, for he was deeply committed to the welfare of the Chinese nation. He was, however, so deeply convinced of his selflessness and moral rectitude that he perceived his power interests as being identical to those of the nation. What was beneficial to Chiang, therefore, was beneficial to the nation. And – in Chiang's view – one who opposed him was thereby acting against the best interests of the nation. Such persons, he claimed, were 'perverse', 'opportunistic', and lacked 'innate goodness'.[26] There was no room in Chiang's world for a loyal opposition; if they opposed him they were, ipso facto, disloyal to the nation. This self-righteousness was one of Chiang's great strengths; it gave him determination in the face of criticism and adversity. It was also, however, the tragic element in his character, for it pushed him ineluctably to his defeat in 1949.

IDEOLOGY, STRUCTURE AND FUNCTIONING OF THE NANKING REGIME

The regime that took shape in Chiang Kai-shek's hands after 1927 was neither totalitarian nor democratic, but lay uncertainly between those points on the political spectrum. Its structure, which was preserved in its essential features even after 1949 on Taiwan, had been erected in a governmental reorganization of October 1928. The blueprint for the new government had been drafted by Sun Yat-sen in his lectures on the Three People's Principles and in his *Fundamentals of national reconstruction.* Underlying the whole structure of government was Sun's concept of political tutelage. Sun Yat-sen was committed to the goal of popular sovereignty but he was also convinced that the Chinese people were unprepared for the responsibilities of self-rule. He had therefore predicated three stages of the Nationalist Revolution. First was the stage of military rule, during which the revolutionaries would rely on military force to consolidate their power. Following the capture of Peiping in June 1928, the Nationalist government declared that this initial stage of the revolution was completed, and that it had now progressed to the second stage, that of political tutelage. During this phase, the revolutionary party, the Kuomintang, was to exercise the sovereignty of the nation on behalf of the people. At the same time, the party was to train the people at the local level in the exercise of self-government. Through elections of *hsien* (county) magistrates, the convening of hsien representative assemblies, and the making of laws so that the hsien could become fully self-governing, the people would be educated in preparation for the third stage of the revolution, that of democratic, constitutional rule.

Political tutelage ostensibly meant that the Kuomintang was to exercise 'party rule' (*tang-chih*) on behalf of the people. Party rule was expressed institutionally in the authority invested in the party organs, the Central Executive Committee and the Central Political Council. The former was

---

[26] 'Tzu-shu yen-chiu ko-ming che-hsueh ching-kuo te chieh-tuan' (Stages traversed in studying revolutionary philosophy), *Chiang tsung-t'ung yen-lun hui-pien,* 10.50.

the supreme organ of party power (except during the brief sessions of the National Party Congress, only three of which were convened during the Nanking decade). It and especially its Standing Committee were charged with the formulation of the guiding principles of party rule and with the overall direction of party administration.

The Central Political Council was a bridge between the party and the governmental structure. Although it was merely a subcommittee of the Central Executive Committee, it was, formally at least, the supreme authority over the National government, combining both legislative and executive functions. As a legislative body, it could initiate legislation or transmit decisions of the Central Executive Committee to the government. As an executive body, it was empowered to provide general direction to and supervision of the government. Theoretically, then, the Political Council wielded virtually unlimited powers over the civilian branch of the government. In practice, too, the Political Council was the locus of authority in the government, for the head of the council was Chiang Kai-shek.[27]

Under the Political Council, in accordance with Sun Yat-sen's specific prescription, was established the five-*yuan* (or five-branch) system of government. This was similar to Montesquieu's threefold division between the executive, legislative and judicial branches of government. In addition to these three branches of government, however, Sun had added two branches that were derived explicitly from traditional institutions. These were the Examination Yuan (for determining the qualifications of government employees by means of civil-service examinations) and the Control Yuan (an ombudsman of government, similar to the imperial system of censors who supervised the policies and morals of officials). Of these five branches, the Executive Yuan was preponderant. The president of the Executive Yuan served as prime minister, directing the work of the subordinate ministries of foreign affairs, finance, education, commerce and so on.

It would be a mistake, however, to devote exclusive attention to the structure of the Nationalist government or to the formal relationship between, say, the Executive Yuan and the Legislative Yuan. For, regardless of the formal positions that Chiang Kai-shek held in the party, government or army, he wielded ultimate authority over the regime as

[27] Ch'ien Tuan-sheng, *Government and politics of China*, 139–145. Because the government was formally subordinate to the Kuomintang, and because the actual locus of authority frequently lay in an indeterminate relationship between the party, government and military, it is frequently appropriate in this chapter to employ the term Nationalist regime rather than Nationalist government. No pejorative connotation is intended by use of the term regime.

a whole. He exercised that authority with minimal concern for formal chains of command. 'The real authority of the government,' recalled Franklin Ho, one-time adviser to Chiang, 'went wherever the Generalissimo went. In terms of authority, he was the head of everything.'[28] Or, as an American foreign service officer observed in 1934, 'The shadow of Chiang Kai-shek extends over this whole scene. [Before coming to Nanking,] I would have been unwilling to believe that he dominated the Government set-up here to the extent that is now so apparent. Where his interest touches, there you will find a certain governmental activity; elsewhere, if not paralysis, at least a policy of drift.'[29]

As a result of Chiang's overriding dominance of the regime and of his predilection for ignoring formal chains of command, the government, as a policy-formulating and administrative organization, languished. The bureaucracy did formulate numerous plans for social and economic reconstruction, and the Legislative Yuan assiduously drafted new laws and a draft constitution. Much of this governmental activity, however, had little relation to political realities. For the civilian apparatus had neither the money to finance its various projects nor the power to enforce its decisions. Only 8 to 13 per cent of the total budget during the 1930s, for example, was allocated for the operations and maintenance of the civil bureaucracy – as contrasted with the much larger expenditures of the army.[30] T. V. Soong, minister of finance until 1933, endeavoured strenuously to restrain Chiang's military spending so that the government could proceed with the tasks of peacetime reconstruction, but Chiang ignored him. The civil government thus always remained subordinate to the interests of Chiang and the military, and it never generated a momentum of its own.

The party, the Kuomintang, atrophied even more than did the governmental administration as a result of Chiang Kai-shek's transformation of the revolutionary movement into a military-authoritarian regime. Where Sun Yat-sen had regarded the party as the ultimate locus of authority and as the trustee of the people's sovereignty during the pre-constitutional phases of the revolution, Chiang Kai-shek emasculated the party. After 1929, with the suppression of the left wing of the party, the Kuomintang performed no independent role. It became merely the propagandist, journalist and historian for the regime.

This emasculation of the party, together with the rise to prominence in the regime of old-style bureaucrats and warlords, had a deadening effect

[28] Franklin L. Ho, 'The reminiscences of Ho Lien (Franklin L. Ho)', 160.
[29] United States, State Dept. doc. 893.00/12842, Gauss to Johnson, 16 Sept. 1934, p. 1.
[30] Lloyd E. Eastman, *The abortive revolution: China under Nationalist rule, 1927–1937*, 221.

on the morale of formerly idealistic party members. A former Kuomintang member recalled that he 'like many...schoolmates, originally joined the Kuomintang in the belief that it was the only agency in China capable of destroying the powers so long held by provincial warlords'. As a result of Chiang Kai-shek's deradicalization of the movement, however, he and many like him 'were understandably disillusioned with the Kuomintang and many of us virtually withdrew'.[31] Party membership continued to be a prerequisite for government employment, but during the 1930s the party became a hollow shell, its role – as Arthur N. Young remarked – becoming 'almost nominal'.[32]

The Kuomintang continued in existence, however, because its committees and congresses provided a stamp of legitimacy for decisions already made by Chiang Kai-shek. The party therefore provided some substance, however transparent, to the regime's claim that it was not a military and personal dictatorship but rather – in accordance with Sun Yat-sen's instructions – a one-party dictatorship on behalf of the people until they were prepared to undertake the responsibility of ruling themselves.

The Nationalist regime was ambivalent in nature: at times it was despotic and arbitrary; at other times it was compliant and feeble. In its authoritarian guise, its power was derived largely from control of a superior military force. Consequently, individuals or groups that challenged its power or criticized its policies were, if within the reach of the Nationalists' army or police, often forcibly suppressed. Labour unions, for example, had become powerful, well organized, and highly politicized during the mid-1920s. After 1927, the leadership of these unions was removed and replaced by agents of the regime. The guiding principle of the unions now was not class conflict but cooperation with the employers and with the government. Independent union activities were proscribed, and the unions became weak, complaisant instruments of the regime.

The student movement, which since the May Fourth Movement (1919) had been a potent factor in national politics, was also suppressed – albeit less effectively and permanently than were the unions.[33] In 1930, for example, the Kuomintang's Ministry of Training proscribed all non-academic student organizations except those that were stringently regulated by the party. Students were simultaneously directed to concen-

---

[31] Wang Cheng, 'The Kuomintang: a sociological study of demoralization' (Stanford University, Ph.D. dissertation, 1953), 150.

[32] Young, *Nation-building*, 424.

[33] John Israel, *Student nationalism in China, 1927-1937*.

trate upon their studies and to avoid political activities. The students were, however, among the most passionately nationalistic groups in the country. And in 1931–2, and again in 1935–6, when Japanese imperialist pressures mounted and the Nanking authorities seemingly took refuge behind a policy of appeasement, the students' patriotism erupted into demonstrations, boycotts, and even physical attacks on government officials. To these student protests the regime invariably responded, ultimately, with force. Distrustful of any political movement that it had not initiated and did not control, and immoderately sensitive to the fact that a few Communists were among the student agitators, Nanking threw at least one thousand, and perhaps several thousand, students into prison. Students were terrorized by the presence of government informers in their classes, surprise searches of their rooms, and sudden disappearance of fellow students. The regime was thus largely successful in controlling the student movement as a political force. In accomplishing this, however, it alienated the students and pushed them politically leftward, many of them eventually becoming members of the Communist Party.

Political repression became a primary instrument of Nationalist rule. As early as 1929 and 1930, by which time the corruption, factionalism, and maladministration could no longer be varnished over, the regime was no longer sustained by popular support. 'Contrasted with the enthusiasm of less than eighteen months ago,' wrote the *North China Herald* in May 1930, 'the sense of hopelessness...among all Chinese today is perhaps the worst feature of all.'[34] Three years later, the much respected *Kuo-wen chou-pao* (National news weekly) observed that 'the masses unconcealedly dislike and detest the Kuomintang'.[35]

Determined to quash this rising tide of discontent, the regime tightened controls over its critics. Political opponents were assassinated; captious newsmen were arrested; newspapers and journals were censored. Because the territorial control of the government was still limited, its critics could find refuge and relative safety in the foreign-administered treaty-port concessions or in the provinces controlled by Chiang Kai-shek's opponents, such as in Hupei province under Chang Hsueh-liang or in Kwangtung under Ch'en Chi-t'ang. During the Nanking decade, therefore, China enjoyed a considerable intellectual and political vitality. In the areas of Central China controlled by Nanking, however, opposition to Chiang Kai-shek's policies was muted. Organizations and groups that might have imposed restrictions on the regime's power or policies were either

[34] *North China Herald*, 20 May 1930, 297.
[35] Liu Chen-tung, 'Chung-kuo ch'u-lu wen-t'i' (The question of China's way out), *Kuo-wen chou-pao* (National news weekly), 10.24 (19 June 1933), 2.

dissolved or rendered harmless through the imposition of controls by the regime.

Like the relationship between *yin* and *yang*, however, the authoritarian character of the regime was balanced by its essential weakness. Factionalism and corruption eroded the movement's early revolutionary commitment, and rampant bureaucratism stifled its policy initiatives. Even within itself, therefore, the regime lacked the drive, dedication and efficiency that might have enabled it to realize the programmatic goals of Sun Yat-sen. But the regime was also weak, because it lacked a firm footing in society. A characteristic of strong, modern nation-states is that significant segments of the population are mobilized in support of those governments' political goals. But the Nationalists, placing a premium on political control and social order, distrusted mass movements and private initiative; they therefore failed to create the kinds of broadly based popular support that, in the twentieth century, generate true political power.

As a result of these inherent weaknesses, the regime had to accommodate itself, at times grudgingly, to the leaders of the existing social order, most notably the landlords and capitalists. Indeed, this accommodation has caused many – perhaps most – non-Kuomintang writers to infer that the Nationalist regime was a class instrument of those classes.[36] And, in fact, the interests of the capitalists and landlords did sometimes correspond closely to the interests of the ruling regime. Nanking avoided, for example, implementing even a moderate rent-reduction law as a result of landlord opposition, and the Nanking leaders sometimes went to extraordinary lengths to maintain the landlord system. It was customary, for example, for the Nationalists, after recovering areas where the Communists had carried out their policy of land redistribution, to dispossess the tillers and restore the lands to the original landlords. This policy was sometimes exceedingly difficult to implement, because the Communists had in some areas held these lands for over six years and the boundary-markers and deeds of ownership had in many cases been destroyed.

The regime also formed an intimate relationship with the nation's more powerful bankers. Having surrendered collection of the important land tax to the provinces, the central government never contrived a means of supporting itself financially from taxes or state-operated enterprises. It consequently borrowed, approximately one-fifth of the government's revenues being derived through the sale of government bonds or through

---

[36] See, e.g. Ho Kan-chih, *Chung-kuo hsien-tai ko-ming shih* (History of the modern Chinese revolution), vol. 1, 119–23; Barrington Moore, Jr. *Social origins of dictatorship and democracy: land and peasant in the making of the modern world*, 187–201.

bank loans and overdrafts. For a time, therefore, the regime was heavily dependent on the banks and bankers. The banks, for their part, profited hugely from the relationship, especially because the government customarily sold its bonds to them at less than – often only 60–75 per cent of – face value. The banks in this way could often realize an effective annual return on their loans to the government of 12–25 per cent.[37] Many contemporaries, as a result, concluded that the regime represented capitalist class interests.

Assuredly, the interests of the capitalist and landlord classes did overlap with those of the regime. Each was opposed to social revolution; each feared the Communists; each was distrustful of the mobilization of the peasants and workers. But sometimes their interests conflicted. The capitalists had first been apprised of this truth in 1927–8 when the regime resorted to threats, blackmail and kidnapping to finance the last phase of the Northern Expedition. In 1935, too, the government broke whatever political power the bankers had wielded. By simply issuing new government bonds, and forcing the privately owned Bank of China and the Bank of Communications to accept these bonds as capital, H. H. Kung with a single blow made the government the banks' major stockholder. Using similar tactics, Kung quickly gained control of several lesser private banking corporations, and by 1937 the Nanking government controlled about 70 per cent of the nation's total banking assets.[38] These banking coups effectively ended the bankers' role as a political pressure group, and demonstrated beyond doubt that it was the regime that controlled the capitalists rather than vice versa.

The long-term interests of landlords were also frequently in conflict with those of the regime. These landlords generally wished to maintain, or even increase, their dominance of their local areas. They organized militia, operated schools, managed construction and other local programmes. They also collected taxes, ostensibly to support these projects, although indeterminately large portions of these revenues were siphoned into the pockets of the local elite. The regime, by contrast, endeavoured to maximize its control, constantly pushing its administrative, fiscal and military authority downward into the villages. Proposed reforms of the tax system, for instance, threatened to restore to the tax rolls landlord-held lands that for years and decades had escaped the tax-collectors' grasp. The government's attempts to install its own cadres in local government posts

---

[37] Young, *Nation-building*, 98, 507–8.
[38] Parks M. Coble, Jr. *The Shanghai capitalists and the Nationalist government, 1927–1937*, 161–207. A recent study shows in detail that cotton-mill-owners in the Shanghai area were by no means powerless vis-à-vis the National government, but neither did they control the government. See Richard Bush III, 'Industry and politics in Kuomintang China: the Nationalist regime and Lower Yangtze Chinese cotton mill owners, 1927–1937'.

likewise threatened to oust members of the local elite from positions that assured them power, preferment, and wealth.[39] There were, as a result, fundamental contradictions between the interests and goals of the regime and of these landlords.

During the Nanking decade, however, the conflicts generated by those contradictions were usually muted and localized, because the regime's attention was then focused much more on the Communist and Japanese problems than on questions of local administration. The relationship between the government and the local elites during this decade might therefore be described as mutual toleration and limited cooperation. But to baldly ascribe a class character to the Nationalist regime, without noting its important differences with the landlords and capitalists, conceals its fundamental nature. For the regime was dependent, first of all, on the support of the military. From that fact, all else followed. It was not in any basic way accountable to this or that social-economic class or indeed to any forces outside itself. It was, in many respects, its own constituency. This is a basic reason why the regime's modernizing and developmental impulses were so weak; why the Nationalist bureaucracy could be sustained so long despite its corruption and administrative lethargy; and why the regime could perpetuate itself with so few new faces or new ideas for over two decades. Some members of the regime were, of course, enlightened, dedicated, and competent. Too many, however, took advantage of the institutional character of the regime to maximize their own power, prestige and wealth rather than to strive for the national good.

KUOMINTANG FACTIONS

In this kind of regime, which was customarily free of the constraints of public opinion and which tolerated no meaningful political activity that it did not control, the competition for political power was conducted not in society at large but within the councils of the regime itself. And, because the distribution of political authority was determined less by formal chains-of-command than by the personal decisions of Chiang Kai-shek or one of his favoured aides, allocation of power was determined inordinately by personal influence. It was a common practice, for example, for a new minister or bureau chief to dismiss the previous employees in that office and to replace them with his cronies and supporters. The key to political success, therefore, lay less in the possession of technical

---

[39] Geisert, 'Power and society', 167-242; Philip A. Kuhn, 'Local self-government under the Republic: problems of control, autonomy, and mobilization', in Frederic Wakeman, Jr. and Carolyn Grant, eds. *Conflict and control in late imperial China*, 284-98.

expertise than in the maintenance of personal relationships with leaders of the regime. Factionalism, in other words, was the principal medium for political struggle.

Factions proliferated. There were, for example, the factions of Wang Ching-wei, T. V. Soong, H. H. Kung, Ho Ying-ch'in, Chu Chia-hua, Sun Fo – the list goes on and on. The largest factions, however, and those which were generally the most influential in the policy-making process, were the CC clique, the Political Study clique, and the Whampoa clique.

The CC clique coalesced around the brothers Ch'en Kuo-fu and Ch'en Li-fu. Bound to Chiang Kai-shek by extraordinarily close personal and emotional ties – they were nephews of Ch'en Ch'i-mei, who, until his assassination by Yuan Shih-k'ai in 1916, had been Chiang's mentor and father-figure – the two Ch'en brothers after 1926 directed the organizational operations of the Chiang-dominated Kuomintang. In June 1927, they first created the secret organization that became known as the CC clique (CC-hsi) – a term that was thought to represent either 'Central Club' or the 'two Ch'ens'. The actual name of the organization may, instead, have been the Ch'ing-pai-she (lit. Blue-white society) or the Kuo-min-tang chung-shih t'ung-chih-hui (Kuomintang loyal-and-faithful comrades' association), although details of the clique's names, structure, and operations remain obscure.[40]

Using the Organization Department of the Kuomintang as their institutional base, the Ch'en brothers placed adherents throughout the party and governmental apparatus, particularly in the middle and lower strata of those organizations. In this way, the CC clique became a dominating influence in the civilian branches of the regime, controlling much of the bureaucratic administration, educational agencies, youth organizations and labour unions. The clique also controlled various publications, such as the *Shih-shih yueh-pao* (Times monthly) and *Wen-hua chien-she* (Cultural reconstruction), and operated the Kuomintang's Central Bureau of Investigation and Statistics (Chung-yang tiao-ch'a t'ung-chi chü) which was one of Chiang Kai-shek's two principal secret police organizations.

By contrast with the civilian oriented CC clique, the Whampoa clique (Huang-p'u hsi) was formed preponderantly of military officers, but it too had broad political concerns that potentially at least touched all aspects of national life. Loosely defined, the Whampoa clique denoted the former

[40] Ch'en Tun-cheng, *Tung-luan ti hui-i* (Memoirs of upheaval), 29; Ch'en Shao-hsiao, *Hei-wang-lu* (Records of the black net), 290–1. Ch'en Li-fu, however, denied the existence of such an organization. See Shu-wen, 'Ch'en Li-fu t'an CC' (Ch'en Li-fu chats about the CC), *Hsin-wen t'ien-ti* (News world), 20 (1 Feb. 1937) 13.

faculty and students of the Whampoa Military Academy, who maintained strong bonds of loyalty to Chiang Kai-shek. The faction thus defined had, however, no organization, and some of the members – such as Ho Ying-ch'in, Ch'en Ch'eng and the younger officers – were bitterly antagonistic one to the other. The operative nucleus of the Whampoa clique, therefore, at least during the period 1932–8, was a tightly disciplined, clandestine organization known popularly as the Blue Shirts (Lan-i she).

The Blue Shirts were organized in early 1932 by a small group of young military officers, former students of Chiang Kai-shek in the Whampoa Military Academy, who were alarmed by the condition of the nation and of the Kuomintang movement. The Japanese were invading Chinese territory; the Communists survived in the interior despite repeated annihilation campaigns against them; and, perhaps most alarming, members of the Nationalist movement had become corrupt and were more concerned about enhancing their power than they were about attaining the goals of the revolution. That is, in the Blue Shirts' view, the revolution had failed and the nation lay in peril.

With Chiang Kai-shek's consent, financial support, and at least formal leadership, these young officers – represented, for example, by Ho Chung-han, Tai Li, Teng Wen-i and K'ang Tse – created a pyramidal organization comprising three basic levels. At the top, the dominant leadership constituted the Li-hsing she (Vigorously-carry-out society); the middle echelon was named the Ko-ming ch'ing-nien t'ung-chih hui (Revolutionary youth comrades association); and the foot-soldiers of the movement, drawn from lower levels of the army, from students and from governmental agencies, were organized into the Chung-hua Fu-hsing she (Chinese revival society). In reaction against the disarray and poor discipline of the Kuomintang, the Blue Shirts stressed the need for absolute, unquestioning obedience to the leaders of the organization. Frugality, incorruptibility and secrecy were also emphasized.

Progressively, as a result of the growing power of Mussolini's Italy and Hitler's Germany, fascist doctrines became attractive to the Blue Shirt leaders. Chiang Kai-shek, too, made extensive efforts to learn about Nazi methods of organization and operation and in about 1935 he reportedly declared to a gathering of Blue Shirts, 'Fascism...is a stimulant for a declining society.' 'Can Fascism save China? We answer: yes. Fascism is what China now most needs.'[41] As a result of this fascination with the apparent successes of fascism in Europe, the Blue Shirts likewise

[41] 'Ranisha no soshiki to hanman kōnichi katsudō no jitsurei' (The organization of the Blue Shirts and examples of anti-Manchukuo, anti-Japanese activities), in Ranisha ni kansuru Shiryō (Materials on the Blue Shirts), 11.

propounded ultra-nationalism, the cult of the Leader, elimination of liberalism and individualism, and the 'militarization' of society.

The Blue Shirts became highly influential during the 1930s. They dominated political training within the army, thus helping to assure Chiang Kai-shek of the continuing support of that ultimate source of political power. The Blue Shirts also became involved in various civilian activities, such as the schools, the Boy Scouts and the police. They provided many, perhaps most, of the cadres of the New Life movement. And they also operated the much feared Military Bureau of Investigation and Statistics (Chün-shih tiao-ch'a t'ung-chi chü) under Chiang Kai-shek's Military Affairs Commission. This secret police organization, headed by Tai Li, conducted intelligence operations against Chiang Kai-shek's putative enemies (who ranged from the Japanese and the Communists to corrupt officials and even political rivals within the Kuomintang). It was involved in press censorship. It was also responsible for many of the most notorious assassinations during the decade, such as that in 1934 of Shih Liang-ts'ai, editor of Shanghai's leading newspaper, *Shen-pao*.

In contrast to the CC and Whampoa cliques, the Political Study clique (Cheng-hsueh-hsi) was all head and no tail; its members were each men of prominence, but it had no following among the rank-and-file of the regime. It had no organization or clear-cut leadership, but consisted informally of a group of friends, or friends-of-friends, who shared generally similar political views. Two of the clique's foremost representatives, Huang Fu and Chang Ch'ün, were sworn-brothers of Chiang Kai-shek, a relationship which in China signified the closest possible tie of loyalty outside the family. Probably in large part through this relationship, the Political Study clique became enormously influential in Chiang Kai-shek's coterie of advisers and leading administrators. On the recommendation of Huang Fu and Chang Ch'ün, for example, Chiang Kai-shek in 1932 appointed Yang Yung-t'ai as his secretary-general in the headquarters of the Military Affairs Commission. From that position, Yang – until he was assassinated in 1936 – was one of the two or three most powerful political figures in the nation. Other members of the clique included Wang Ch'ung-hui, Hsiung Shih-hui, Wu Ting-ch'ang, Chang Kia-ngau, Weng Wen-hao and Huang Shao-hung. To name these and other members is to list many of the leading figures in the nation and in the regime. Significantly, however, the relationship of these clique members to the Kuomintang was, at best, tenuous. Huang Fu, for example, steadfastly refused even to become a member of the party. They were less politicians than they were specialists – economists, industrialists, bankers, publishers, intellectuals – who adhered to no ideological doctrine but stood instead for technical expertise and bureaucratic professionalism.

The relations among these several factions were complex. Each of them publicly expounded the doctrines of Sun Yat-sen; each supported Chiang Kai-shek as the leader of the regime. At the same time, their dealings with each other were sometimes exceedingly strained, because they were the principal vehicles in the intra-party struggle for power. Ch'en Kuo-fu and Ch'en Li-fu, for example, were extremely jealous of the Political Study clique's position in the civilian apparatus and competed with them for bureaucratic office. The Blue Shirts viewed the others as corrupt civilian politicians, and were particularly hostile to the CC clique, because the political, educational and intelligence operations of the two factions overlapped, thereby generating intense frictions.

Ideological and policy differences, significantly, were not the main cause of these frictions. Although the differences between the factions would frequently be expressed in terms of policy orientations, the fundamental issue was power and position. The Blue Shirts and the CC clique expressed differences, for example, on how to implement Sun Yat-sen's Principle of Economic Livelihood. A former Blue Shirt leader admitted, however, that 'any [factional] struggle is not a struggle resulting from differences of policy, but is a struggle for the rice bowl'.[42]

Chiang Kai-shek knew of these intra-party conflicts, but unless they threatened to erupt into violence – as one did in 1934 between the Blue Shirts and the CC clique – he did not intervene. Indeed, he appears actually to have fostered the competition among the factions. For the struggle among factions prevented any one of them from becoming overly powerful. Chiang thus assured his supremacy over all of them.

Nationalist rule has customarily been labelled 'conservative'. This is misleading, however, for leaders of the regime were in fact intensely dissatisfied with the status quo, and they envisioned drastic, even 'radical', departures from China's existing condition of national decrepitude. They admired, for example, the scientific and industrial progress of the West, and they aspired to employ Western technology to improve the economic well-being of the Chinese people. They wished also to restructure the Chinese socio-political order. The model for Chiang Kai-shek's ideal society lay not in the Chinese past, but in the specifically militaristic aspects of Japan, Italy and Germany. He recalled his student days in a Japanese military academy, and declared that the rigorous barracks discipline there represented precisely his ideal for Chinese society as a whole.[43] He thought that fascist Italy and Germany fulfilled that ideal. 'In fascism,' he declared

---

[42] Interview with Liu Chien-ch'un, Taipei, 27 May 1969.
[43] Chiang Kai-shek, 'Hsin-sheng-huo yun-tung chih yao-i' (Essentials of the New Life movement), *Chiang tsung-t'ung ssu-hsiang yen-lun chi* (Collection of President Chiang's thoughts and speeches), 12.110.

admiringly, 'the organization, the spirit, and the activities must all be militarized...In the home, the factory, and the government office, everyone's activities must be the same as in the army... In other words, there must be obedience, sacrifice, strictness, cleanliness, accuracy, diligence, secrecy... And everyone together must firmly and bravely sacrifice for the group and for the nation.'[44]

It was precisely this image of a militarized society, strictly disciplined and unconditionally obedient to the Leader's will, that Chiang aspired to re-create in China. These were the goals of his vaunted New Life movement, inaugurated in 1934, which he regarded as providing the basic cure for China's ills. 'What is the New Life Movement that I now propose?' Chiang asked. 'Stated simply, it is to militarize thoroughly the lives of the citizens of the entire nation so that they can cultivate courage and swiftness, the endurance of suffering and a tolerance for hard work, and especially the habit and ability of unified action, so that they will at any time sacrifice for the nation.'[45] Patently, his image of fascism had been translated virtually intact into the New Life movement.

Chiang Kai-shek and the Nationalist leaders also, however, paid obeisance to the ethics of Confucianism, and it was this that convinced many observers that the Nationalist regime was actually a conservative, even reactionary, force. Customarily, for example, Chiang declared that the goals of the New Life movement were the Confucian virtues of *li*, *i*, *lien* and *ch'ih*, loosely translated as social propriety, justice, integrity, and sense of self-respect. He greatly admired the great conservative, Confucian officials of the late Ch'ing dynasty, Tseng Kuo-fan and Hu Lin-i. And, under his aegis, the official worship of Confucius was restored; Confucius's birthday was proclaimed a national holiday; and study of the Confucian classics by students and military officers was encouraged.

This traditionalism of the Nationalist regime was comparable to the classicism promoted in fascist Italy and Nazi Germany. Confucianism, that is, was not propounded as a goal in itself, but as a moral ingredient that would contribute to the cohesiveness of the Chinese people as they moved forward to a new society. It provided, as a member of the CC clique asserted, a 'central belief', without which the Chinese people became politically anarchic and morally confused.[46] Thus, Chiang Kai-shek frequently spoke in the idiom of Chinese tradition. Indeed many of his

---

[44] [Iwai Eiichi], *Ranisha ni kansuru chōsa* (An investigation of the Blue Shirts), 37–8.

[45] Chiang Kai-shek, *Chiang tsung-t'ung ssu-hsiang yen-lun chi*, 12.111. On the New Life movement, see Arif Dirlik, 'The ideological foundations of the New Life movement: a study in counterrevolution', *JAS* 34.4 (Aug. 1975) 945–80; Eastman, *Abortive revolution*, 66–70.

[46] Fang Chih, 'Min-tsu wen-hua yü min-tsu ssu-hsiang' (National culture and national thought), *Wen-hua chien-she* (Cultural reconstruction), 1.2 (10 Nov. 1934) 20.

methods and outlooks – such as his stress on traditional morality, his conception of the political utility of education, and his elitism – did reveal that his vision of the modern world was limited. But his political goal, that of a thoroughly regimented society, bore no resemblance to China's Confucian past. He was a would-be totalitarian, aspiring to extend the controls of his regime down to the local level, and to subordinate the individual and all of society to the regime to a degree that emperors of the Ch'ing dynasty had not even dreamed of. This was not a conservative ideal, for it differed fundamentally from either the ideals or realities of the past.

ACHIEVEMENTS OF THE NATIONALIST REGIME

There exists no consensus regarding Nationalist achievements during the Nanking decade. Some historians have concluded that the Nationalists established a fundamentally sound system of rule and laid the foundations upon which a strong, democratic and prosperous nation could be constructed – although this promising beginning was aborted by the onslaught of the war with Japan in 1937. Others contend that the government established by the Nationalists was corrupt and inefficient, that the Nationalist leaders did not comprehend the problems confronting them, and that they were ignorant of alternative political and economic strategies available to them. Accordingly, in this view, the regime was doomed to failure even if the Japanese had not launched their war of aggression.[47]

These issues are passionately debated. They are perhaps irresolvable, because what would have occurred had the Japanese not attacked is, by its very nature, unprovable. Two facts, however, are clear. First, the task confronting the Nationalists – namely, reversing the tide of national disintegration – was gargantuan. Second, the circumstances under which they attempted the task were extraordinarily uncongenial to successful or rapid solutions. Economic depression, foreign invasion and civil strife – conditions that were largely beyond the control of the Nationalists – militated against the implementation of meaningful reforms. They were, moreover, allotted only about six years in which to accomplish those reforms, because the first four years of the Nanking decade had been devoted chiefly to securing the regime in power.

The outstanding achievement of the Nationalists was to reverse the trend toward territorial disintegration. When they seized power in 1927,

[47] Studies that are generally favourable to the Nationalists are Domes and Young; less favourable are Hung-mao Tien and Eastman, all cited above.

they controlled only Kiangsu, Chekiang, and part of Anhwei. As a result of the civil wars in 1929–31, the central government forces cowed the provincial militarists, thus guaranteeing the existence of the Nanking government, but the writ of the central government in 1931 was still restricted to a constellation of provinces, or parts of provinces, in central China (most notably in varying degree in Chekiang, Kiangsu, Anhwei, Honan, Kiangsi, Hupei and Fukien).[48]

Nanking's effective authority expanded rapidly, however, after Chiang Kai-shek's fifth annihilation campaign against the Communists. A central premise in Chiang Kai-shek's strategic thinking was that, before China could repulse the Japanese aggressors, it must be unified internally. 'The Japanese,' he liked to say, 'are like a disease of the skin, but the Communists are like a disease of the heart.' To cure this disease of the heart, Chiang, in October 1930, immediately after his victory over the Yen Hsi-shan Feng Yü-hsiang rebellion, had launched his first annihilation campaign against the Communists in Kiangsi. The Communists, however, employing the mobile tactics of guerrilla warfare, repulsed the Nationalist attackers by 1 January 1931. Other annihilation campaigns followed. But not until the fifth annihilation campaign of 1933–4 – in which Chiang employed about 800,000 troops, was advised by German and Japanese advisers, and augmented his military offensive with a stringent economic blockade of the Communist areas – did he gain a nearly decisive victory over the Communists. The Communists, defeated militarily and suffering incredibly from shortages of food and especially salt, summoned their last reserves of strength and courage, broke out of the Nationalist encirclement, and in October 1934 commenced what was to become the Long March.

The Long March, which has become a legend in the history of the Communist Revolution, provided Chiang Kai-shek with an unprecedented opportunity to inject his military forces and political power into the provinces of South and West China. Pursuing the retreating Communists, Chiang's well-equipped armies entered Hunan, Kweichow, Yunnan and Szechwan. The provincial militarists, feeling endangered by the presence of the Communists, welcomed the Nationalist armies – not whole-heartedly, because these too threatened their provincial autonomy, but as the lesser of two evils. Chiang Kai-shek fully exploited the opportunity. For, once Chiang's bandit-suppression army had entered a province, his agents began imposing 'reforms' designed to break down that province's isolation. In Szechwan, for example, the garrison areas (*fang-ch'ü*), which had been the military and economic bases of operations of the several Szechwanese warlords, were abolished, and a more centralized system of

<hr />

[48] Domes, 486.

provincial administration was instituted. A massive road-construction programme, designed to integrate the province politically and militarily with the rest of the nation, was launched. Szechwan was also drawn into Nanking's economic orbit as a result of the widespread use of Nationalist currency (*fa-pi*) in place of the several currencies that had been issued by various banks in the province.[49] Prior to the war with Japan, such reforms as these had attenuated, without breaking, the south-west provinces' accustomed independence, and the local authorities continued to strain against the tightening tentacles of the central government. In the spring of 1937, for example, relations between Chiang and Liu Hsiang, the dominant warlord in Szechwan, became so tense that a renewed outbreak of civil war was narrowly avoided. As a result of Chiang's anti-Communist campaigns of 1934–5, however, the autonomy and political manoeuvrability of the provincial militarists in Hunan, Yunnan, Kweichow and Szechwan had been sharply reduced. And the power and prestige of the Nanking government had been commensurately enhanced.

The ultimate fruit of the anti-Communist campaign did not ripen until 1936 when Kwangtung was finally and completely brought under the control of the central government. Although Kwangtung had been the revolutionary base of the Kuomintang prior to the Northern Expedition, it had never been effectively incorporated into the political and financial system of the Nanking government. Especially since 1931, when the militarist Ch'en Chi-t'ang became provincial chairman, Kwangtung had conducted its affairs virtually without reference to the central government. Ch'en, together with Li Tsung-jen and Pai Ch'ung-hsi, leaders of the Kwangsi faction, in late 1931 had established the South-west Political Council and the South-west Headquarters of the Kuomintang Central Executive Committee. These governmental and party organs formed the basis of a formidable regional coalition against Nanking, uniting the rich economic resources of Kwangtung with the military expertise and fighting qualities of Kwangsi. The political challenge of this coalition against Nanking was enormously enhanced by the participation of Hu Han-min, the party's leading theoretician and venerated elder (albeit only fifty-two years old in 1932), who imparted to the so-called South-west separatist movement a legitimacy that other anti-Chiang movements had lacked. For some five years, Chiang Kai-shek had endured the taunts and criticisms of Kwangtung and Kwangsi, because they were a formidable political and military power and more especially because they lay protected behind a buffer formed by the semi-autonomous provinces of Fukien, Hunan and

[49] Robert A. Kapp, *Szechwan and the Chinese Republic: provincial militarism and central power, 1911–1938*, 99–120.

Kweichow. As a result of his pursuit of the Long March, however, Chiang by late 1935 had eliminated that buffer. Chiang was also assembling troops near the Kwangtung-Kwangsi borders, constructing airfields in neighbouring Hunan, and rushing the Hankow-Canton railway to completion.

In May 1936, Hu Han-min suddenly died, and Chiang seized the occasion of Hu's funeral to throw down the gauntlet to the Kwangtung-Kwangsi leaders, demanding that they now submit to the central government. The ultimatum was rejected, and the South-west authorities in early June began moving their troops northward into Hunan province. Their purpose was avowedly to fight the Japanese aggressors in North China. Chiang inferred, however, probably correctly, that Ch'en Chi-t'ang and the Kwangsi leaders were planning to attack, in an attempt to overthrow the Nanking government.

Chiang Kai-shek's genius for political manipulation shone at its brightest in this kind of situation. On the one hand, he bribed the Cantonese air force, causing it in July to defect *en masse* to the central government. Then, with a combination of military threats and offers of alternative official posts to the rebel leaders, Chiang brought about the collapse of the rebellion in September. As a consequence, Kwangtung, for the first time in the Nanking period, was brought under the effective administration of the central government. Kwangsi, which retained some vestiges of its former autonomy, was subdued, no longer in a position to challenge Nanking.

By late 1936, therefore, Chiang Kai-shek had consolidated political control over the greater part of the nation – only seven of the eighteen provinces in China proper continued to be essentially autonomous – and he had thus laid the foundation for a viable political system. Yet he had attained his control at enormous cost. Not only had his strong reliance upon armed force cost the nation heavily in terms of the destruction of life and property, but it had diverted the regime's attention from the exigent demands of social, economic and political reform. Chiang's advisers sometimes warned him against relying excessively on force to attain political ends. In introspective moments he even admitted this failing. He was, however, a soldier, and alternative strategies of attaining national unity seem never to have engaged his interest. He might, for example, have contented himself with merely the nominal allegiance of the various provincial militarists, and then have endeavoured to create a model of political, economic and social reform in the areas that he did control. Doing this he might have avoided the bloody and costly civil wars, established economic and fiscal stability, and developed the administrative and technical expertise that would serve him when other provinces were gradually drawn into the economic and political orbit of the Nanking government. Perhaps this scheme of creating a model area in the Lower Yangtze provinces – which was in fact envisioned at the time by Nanking's economic adviser, Arthur N. Young[50] – betrays the naïvety of the intellectual rather than the realism of the man of action. The history of the decade suggests, however, that it could not have been less successful than were the policies pursued by Chiang. For Chiang attempted to control too much, with the result that nothing was controlled well. Nowhere was this more evident than in the economy.

The Chinese economy was overwhelmingly agrarian and traditional. In 1933, for example, the modern sector of manufacturing, mining, and utilities accounted for only about 3·4 per cent of the net domestic product. Four out of every five Chinese, on the other hand, were employed in agriculture, and produced about 65 per cent of the net domestic product. The farmers lived in appalling poverty, a year of sickness or poor weather plunging them over the edge of subsistence. Destitution is not easily measured, but some rough indication of the misery of the Chinese masses is the fact that in 1930 China's death rate was about the highest in the world, two and a half times higher than that of the United States and markedly higher even than that of India.[51]

Many contemporary observers, both Chinese and Westerners, believed that the basic cause of this rural poverty was the unequal distribution of land. They contended that a small number of landlords owned a disproportionate number of the farms, and rented these to tenants at extortionate rates. As the League of Nations' leading agricultural specialist in China, Ludwig Rajchman, remarked in 1934, 'Of the economic and social factors [contributing to the rural crisis], perhaps the system of tenancy is the most disquieting'.[52]

The Legislative Yuan, under the leadership of Hu Han-min, had attacked this problem by drawing up a Land Law. This law, promulgated in 1930, imposed a maximum on rents (37·5 per cent of the harvest). It also held out the prospect of eliminating landlordism by authorizing tenants of an absentee owner to purchase their farms if they had farmed the land for more than ten years. The 1930 Land Law remained nothing more than an admirable expression of intent, for it was never implemented by the Nanking authorities. Rents, 50-70 per cent of the main crop,

[50] Young, Nation-building, 425.

[51] T. C. Liu and K. C. Yeh, The economy of the Chinese mainland: national income and economic development, 1933-1959, 66 and 89; John Lossing Buck, Land utilization in China, 387.

[52] League of Nations, Council Committee on Technical Cooperation between the League of Nations and China, Report of the technical agent of the Council on his mission in China from the date of his appointment until April 1st 1934, 18.

continued to be exacted, and approximately half the Chinese farmers continued to rent all or part of their land. The Nationalists feared to tamper with the social-economic relations in the villages. They may have had, as Arthur Young suggests, an empathy for the landlord class, and they therefore wished not to dispossess or alienate the landlords by redistributing the land.[53] Or, as has been suggested alternatively, they feared that an attack on the system of tenancy would provoke a social revolution, the outcome of which they could neither control nor predict.[54] Whatever the reasons, tenancy rates remained virtually unchanged during the Nanking decade.

The system of tenancy was, however, only a proximate cause of the social and political inequities in China's villages. The fundamental cause of rural impoverishment was the unfavourable ratio between population and food production, and this was the problem that the Nationalists primarily attacked.

Largely through the National Economic Council, which was assisted by prominent League of Nations' specialists such as Rajchman and Sir Arthur Salter, and the agriculture-related bureaus of the Ministry of Industries, the Nanking government undertook a broad programme to increase the farmers' productivity. It sponsored research on new seed varieties, pesticides and fertilizers. To prevent floods, the Yangtze, Yellow, and Hwai Rivers were dredged and the dikes were strengthened. Irrigation systems were constructed, and efforts were made to revitalize the production of silk, cotton and tea through the introduction of disease-resistant plants, and improved marketing techniques.

These reform projects had slight impact on the rural areas. Less than 4 per cent of the government's total expenditures for the years 1934–6, for example, was devoted to economic development.[55] And much of even this minuscule amount was dissipated in bureaucratic boondoggling that resulted in little positive achievement. As a Nationalist partisan wrote in 1937, 'The year before last, the work was to survey such-and-such an area; last year the work was also to survey such-and-such an area; this year the work is still simply to survey, gather statistics, draw maps, and hold conferences. Because the appropriations have been expended, however, the actual engineering work cannot be carried out.'[56]

There is some indication that Nanking's agricultural specialists did

[53] Young, Nation-building, 389.
[54] Eastman, Abortive revolution, 217.
[55] Computed from figures in Young, Nation-building, 437 and 439. ('Reconstruction' was the term used for economic development. See Young, 77.)
[56] Kao T'ing-tzu, Chung-kuo ching-chi chien-she (Chinese economic reconstruction), 122–3.

achieve some progress in the realm of research, but results of that research were not brought effectively to the farmers. 'In agricultural extension,' wrote Franklin Ho, 'nothing went beyond the planning stage at the national level during the period from 1927 to 1937.'[57] The irrigation projects were also utterly insignificant relative to China's needs, bringing water to an area that totalled only about 6,000 square miles. A government apologist in 1936 summed up the ineffectuality of the Nationalists' rural reconstruction policies and the regime's fear of provoking social revolution, when he admitted that 'The direct benefits to the people [from the government's reconstruction measures] were very small,' because 'the Government was not seeking to give immediate and direct help to the people by drastic changes, but preferred to follow a slow and gradual policy that would avoid too great a disturbance in the country.'[58]

The Nationalists thus did little to ameliorate rural impoverishment during the Nanking decade. The problems were, however, so great, and the time allotted to the regime so short, that it would be absurd to expect that prior to 1937 the agricultural sector could have been transformed. A combination of economic and climatic factors, moreover, plunged China's farmers into even more straitened circumstances during the years 1932-5. A major reason for the crisis was a deflationary trend that hit China in the wake of the world economic depression. Farm prices consequently fell precipitously, and in 1934 struck a low that was 58 per cent below the 1931 level. This deflation caused especial hardship for peasants, who had to pay cash for debts, taxes or rents. During this same period, also, large parts of the country suffered the worst weather within memory. Particularly during 1934-5, when the monetary depression was at its depth, drought, floods, winds and hail wreaked widespread devastation. According to a highly respected agricultural specialist at the Academia Sinica, the rice harvest in 1934 was 34 per cent below that of 1931; soy-beans were down nearly 36 per cent, and wheat was down 7 per cent. Cotton was the only major crop that year to exceed the 1931 level.[59] The value added by agriculture to the gross national product dropped from Y24·43 billion in 1931 to Y13·07 billion (in current prices) in 1934.[60] Such data are not wholly reliable in detail, but eyewitness

57 Franklin L. Ho, 'First attempts to transform Chinese agriculture, 1927–1937: comments', in Paul Sih, ed. The strenuous decade: China's nation-building efforts, 1927–1937, 235.

58 W. L. Holland and Kate L. Mitchell, eds. Problems of the Pacific, 1936: aims and results of social and economic policies in Pacific countries, 166.

59 Chang P'ei-kang, 'Min-kuo erh-shih-san nien ti Chung-kuo nung-yeh ching-chi' (China's agricultural economy in 1934), Tung-fang tsa-chih, 32.13 (1 July 1935): 134.

60 Liu Ta-chung, China's national income, 1931–36: an exploratory study, 10, 35–40.

accounts at the time confirm that the villages suffered severe destitution, especially during 1934 and 1935.[61]

Governmental policies and actions, whether by the central or various local governments, had not been the cause of this agricultural crisis. They had, however, in many cases exacerbated the peasants' plight by imposing new burdens. Because the Nationalists endeavoured to extend their control down to the villages, the size of the bureaucracy at the hsien, or district, level grew. More administrators and tax-collectors were appointed, and the size of the police and militia expanded. These new local authorities provided few palpable services that benefited the peasants, but they had to be paid. The rural tax burden thus increased at the very time that the countryside was in a depression. Surtaxes were added to the main land tax. *T'an-p'ai*, or special assessments, were levied in increasing amounts. There were also indirect taxes – on salt, tobacco, wine and matches; on sales of pig bristles and animal hides; on slaughtering of pigs and chickens; on stamps for receipts and legal agreements – that assailed the villagers in bewildering variety. Some of these taxes were not new. And it is impossible to generalize how much the farmers' tax burden increased during the 1930s, because the variations between localities were often great. Chiang Kai-shek's assessment in 1935 did, however, reflect the general situation:

Government expenditures grow steadily higher. Whenever a programme is begun, new taxes arise. Surtax charges are often attached to the regular taxes as needed, and miscellaneous taxes are also created. Occasionally, [the local authorities] collect unspecified taxes from house to house according to their own wishes. As a result tax items are numerous. The people have suffered immensely under this heavy tax burden.[62]

Peasants were subjected not only to the increased demands of the tax collectors; they were also faced with onerous and unpredictable demands of the government and army for labour, supplies and land. Nanking's armies, for example, especially while on the march or engaged in a campaign, frequently suffered from supply shortages, and they therefore requisitioned food from local sources. These troops were often like a plague upon the landscape, seizing homes, food, carts and manpower. Such requisitions, declared one writer (perhaps with forgivable hyperbole), cost the peasant 'forty times more than the regular taxes'.[63]

---

[61] Eastman, *Abortive revolution*, 190–4.
[62] Hung-mao Tien, 168.
[63] Ch'en Chen-han, 'Cheng-fu yin-hang hsueh-shu chi-kuan fu-hsing nung-ts'un' (Government, banks, academic institutions, and revival of the villages), *Kuo-wen chou-pao*, 10.46 (20 Nov. 1933) articles, 4.

Any attempt to draw up a balance-sheet of the Nationalist record in the rural sector is fraught with difficulties. The nation was so large, local conditions so varied, and the available data so skimpy and imprecise that definitive conclusions are elusive. During 1936 and 1937, moreover, the agrarian crisis ended. Clement weather in those years resulted in the best crops (except in Kwangtung and Szechwan) that China had known in almost twenty years. Farm prices were simultaneously high, largely as a result of an inflationary trend that began in late 1935. As a result of this adventitious set of circumstances, China's farmers generally enjoyed a prosperity they had not known for a decade. The basic character of the political, economic and social system that ensnared the peasants had not changed, however, and the relative prosperity of 1936–7 proved, therefore, to be a transient phenomenon.

Leaders in Nanking were largely uninterested in the problems of the peasants. To the extent that they concerned themselves with economic problems, they were oriented primarily to the modern sectors of the economy. They aspired to create a significant industrial base, and they produced numerous plans and issued innumerable directives to realize that aspiration. It is a signal fact that industry grew at an impressive rate during the Nanking decade. According to one reliable estimate, industry in China (exclusive of Manchuria) grew at an annual rate of 6·7 per cent from 1931 to 1936. Other indicators of economic development generally support this estimate. The output of electric power, for example, doubled during the decade, increasing at an annual average of 9·4 per cent; cotton cloth, 16·5 per cent; bank deposits (at 1928 prices), 15·9 per cent; and so on. These indicators compared favourably with those of most other countries in the world. In Germany, for example, production in 1936 was only 6 per cent above the 1929 level, while in the United States and France production in 1936 was still, respectively, 12 per cent, and 21 per cent *below* the 1929 levels.[64]

To assess the significance of these figures, however, it is necessary to note that the base upon which production increases were calculated was exceedingly small. China's electric-power output in 1928, for instance, was a mere 0.88 million megawatt-hours – compared to 5 million in Russia the same year and 88 million in the United States.[65] Relative increases therefore appeared large, whereas absolute increases remained minuscule by comparison with the more advanced industrial nations and with China's real needs. Still, in view of the adversities afflicting the Chinese

[64] Young, *Nation-building*, 310 and 396–9.
[65] John K. Chang, *Industrial development in pre-Communist China: a quantitative analysis*, 119; Abram Bergson, *The economics of Soviet planning*, 84; *Statistical abstract of the United States, 1929*, 367.

economy during the 1930s – the effects of the world depression, civil war and Japanese aggression – it is remarkable that the Nanking decade witnessed any industrial growth at all.

The impact of the National government upon China's industrial development during the 1930s has been the topic of intense debate. The economist John K. Chang has contended, for example, that the increases were the result of the 'growth-inducing measures' of the government.[66] Douglas Paauw, by contrast, remarked that the Chinese economy remained stagnant during the Nanking decade and that 'the government had less capacity to promote economic development in 1937 than a decade earlier'.[67]

Paauw's contention that the industrial sector of the economy remained stagnant is no longer sustainable, but Chang's conclusion that the growth of industry resulted from government policies is also suspect. The government, it is true, did undertake a number of reforms that helped lay a groundwork for a unified and modern economic system. In 1929, for example, it threw off the restraints on tariffs that the foreign powers had imposed under the unequal treaties. In 1931, it abolished the likin (transit tax) that since the mid-nineteenth century had impeded the development of inter-regional trade. It began to impose some order on the monetary system – described by the Kemmerer Commission in 1928 as 'unquestionably the worst currency to be found in any important country'[68] – by banning use of the tael and in 1935 proclaiming *fa-pi* to be the sole legal currency. The government proscribed taxes on inter-port trade and proclaimed a uniform system of weights and measures. It also markedly improved the nation's communications network, expanding the postal and telegraphic services, instituting regular airline routes, and constructing some 2,300 miles of railway track – an increase of 47 per cent over the 1927 trackage.[69]

Unfortunately, some of these reforms were only partially effective, because – as in other areas of Nationalist administration – there frequently existed a broad gap between the formulation and the implementation of policy. The likin, for instance, was abolished, but provincial governments often replaced it with a 'special consumption tax' or some other euphemistic substitute. Uniform weights and measures were enforced only in the official bureaus. And the banks of the various provinces, such as

---

[66] John K. Chang, 'Industrial development of Mainland China, 1912–1949', *Journal of Economic History*, 27.1 (Mar. 1967) 73-81.

[67] Douglas S. Paauw, 'The Kuomintang and economic stagnation, 1928–1937', *JAS* 16.2 (Feb. 1957) 220.

[68] Young, *Nation-building*, 163.

[69] *Ibid.* 317.

those in Yunnan, Kwangtung and Shansi, continued to issue their own paper notes.

Some measures of the government, moreover, appear to have run counter to the requirements of industrial growth. The government was heavily dependent upon borrowing, for example, and, by providing high returns on bonds and loans to the government, fully 70 per cent of the country's investment capital was channelled to the government and, therefore, away from industrial and commercial enterprises. To obtain loans in competition with the government, private industries had to pay interest rates of 18–20 per cent annually. These were rates, Frank M. Tamagna observed, that 'most Chinese industries were unable to pay; as a result, industrial activity was turned into speculative ventures'.[70]

Taxation also inflicted hardships upon the industries. Because the central government had surrendered the revenues of the land tax to the provincial governments in 1928, it became almost wholly dependent upon the manufacturing and trade sectors for its tax revenues. The full impact of Nanking's tax policies remains to be studied, but it is clear that such exactions as the consolidated taxes (excise taxes levied on rolled tobacco, cotton yarn, flour, matches, etc.) and the business tax (a levy on the assets of commercial enterprises, instituted as a partial replacement for likin) created grave difficulties for entrepreneurs in the Nationalist-controlled area. Fully two-thirds of the 182 Chinese-owned cigarette companies in Shanghai in 1927, for example, closed down by 1930 – and the owners generally agreed that the chief reason was Nanking's taxation. Cotton-textile manufacturers, too, felt heavily burdened by the consolidated tax on cotton yarn, and in 1934 they repeatedly appealed for a reduction in the tax rate. The tax burden on these cotton-texile manufacturers is not known, but in 1936 taxes took fully 38·7 per cent of the Nanyang Brothers Tobacco Company's total income – a burden that the family owners could not sustain. Besides the legal exactions, companies were also subject to occasional demands for payoffs or 'gifts' to the government or to individual officials.[71]

All these facts raise substantial doubts regarding the reputed efficacy of Nanking's 'growth-inducing measures'. That Nanking's policies may not have significantly contributed to the growth of industry is also suggested by the fact that industrial production grew at a generally constant rate throughout the period from 1912 to 1936.[72] This demon-

[70] Frank M. Tamagna, *Banking and finance in China*, 211–12.
[71] Sherman Cochran, *Big business in China: Sino-foreign rivalry in the cigarette industry, 1890–1930*, 188–190; Bush, 'Industry and politics', 250; Coble, 155.
[72] John K. Chang, 'Industrial development', 66–7.

strates that fundamental social and economic forces were working toward industrial development regardless of political regimes or governmental policies.

During the Nanking decade, the Nationalist government assumed an increasingly direct role in the management of economic enterprises. The economic consequences of this trend are unclear, but the political implications are patent. Initially, after 1927, government participation in economic enterprises had been slight. After the banking coup of 1935, however, the government quickly became involved in other areas of the economy, acquiring ownership of at least 12 per cent of the Chinese-owned industries in the country by the end of 1936. It was even more extensively involved in commercial enterprises, and its share of the modern sector of the economy was growing rapidly in the months before the war with Japan.

A prime instrument of government participation in the industrial economy was the China Development Finance Corporation. This was a private-stock corporation, organized in 1933 by T. V. Soong for the purpose of mobilizing Chinese and foreign investments in support of economic development in China. The corporation initially floundered, because it was unable to attract sizeable amounts of capital. After the banking coup, however, the government-controlled banks invested heavily in the corporation. Its assets leaped from Y12·6 million in late 1934 to Y115 million in June 1936, the government-controlled banks providing nearly Y90 million of the added assets.[73] With this capital, the corporation extended loans to and undertook joint management of various electrical, mining, water-control, and other enterprises. Because the bulk of the corporation's capital was obtained from the government, and because most of the leading stockholders of the corporation were either government officials (like H. H. Kung) or officers in government-controlled banks (like T. V. Soong), the government had thereby become directly and actively involved in the economy.

Other prominent instruments of government participation in industry and commerce were the Bank of China and the Ministry of Industries. The Bank of China was now headed by T. V. Soong, and after the 1935 banking coup was a leading component of the government-controlled banking group. When the war broke out in 1937, the Bank of China was operating fifteen spinning mills, which comprised 13 per cent of all the spindles in Chinese-owned mills. It also held investments in, inter alia, flour, meat-packing, telephone, paper, and vegetable-oil companies.

[73] Coble, 220.

Sun Yat-sen, in his lectures on economic development, had instructed that only heavy industry, transportation and communications should be nationalized. But Sun's prescription was honoured more in the breach than in the practice, for most of this direct and indirect governmental involvement in the economy was either in light industry or in marketing and speculation. The China Cotton Company, for example, which was headed by T. V. Soong and indirectly controlled by the government, was in 1936 and 1937 one of the largest commodity trading firms in China. The Ministry of Industries, too, established the Central Fish Market in Shanghai. This joint government-private undertaking instituted a virtual monopoly on the fish trade in Central China, reaping big profits for both the ministry and the selected private individuals who were permitted to invest in the venture. The ministry also traded in vegetable oils, paper, tea, and miscellaneous 'national products'.[74]

The Nanking government's quest for revenues – combined with individual officials' efforts to enrich themselves – was clearly the primary reason for these ventures into the fields of light industry and commerce. Among the government's many economic undertakings, only Chiang Kai-shek's National Resources Commission appears both to have accorded with Sun Yat-sen's economic model in its emphasis on heavy industry, and to have been motivated strictly by concerns for the nation's economic development. This commission, created in 1935, was an agency of Chiang's Military Affairs Commission, and its purpose was to create an industrial base that would support the nation's armed forces. To accomplish this goal, the National Resources Commission in 1936 drafted a five-year plan of industrialization, with a planned capitalization of Y270 million. Central to the commission's work was the creation of an industrial zone in the interior, safely removed, supposedly, from the coastal centres which were vulnerable to enemy attack. During the two years prior to the war, the National Resources Commission's most ambitious projects were located in Hunan, where work was begun on factories to produce steel, heavy machinery, and radio and electrical equipment. Coal, iron, zinc, tin and copper mines were also planned in Hunan, Hupei, Kiangsi and Szechwan.

From the beginning, however, the commission suffered from financial shortages; it received only Y30 million of the projected Y270 million. As a result of the paucity of funds, the commission succeeded in completing only three new factories; fifteen of its projects remained in the planning stages. Significantly, the commission's most measurable growth was

[74] *Ibid.* 245–6.

attributable to the several previously existing private enterprises – coal mines, a copper mine, an oil field, and an electrical company – that had simply been taken over, in part through confiscation, and then operated by the commission. Otherwise, the work of the commission was still largely on paper when the war broke out.[75]

Participation by the National government in these economic enterprises was by no means unprecedented in Chinese history. Throughout much of the dynastic period, merchants had been relegated to secondary status, often subject to the domination and intimidation of the emperor's officials. During the self-strengthening movement of the late nineteenth century, officials had become deeply involved in the operations of the several Western-inspired economic ventures, even those that were ostensibly privately owned and managed. In these enterprises, the interests and money of the government were inextricably mixed up with the private interests and money of leading officials. During the warlord period, however, this intimate bond between the government and the economy had loosened; as the governments weakened, the private entrepreneurs achieved an unaccustomed freedom from official intervention and control. But when the Nationalists at least partially restored the power of government, the government again began participating in the economy. Officials such as T. V. Soong and H. H. Kung became involved in economic ventures, both officially and privately, much as had Li Hung-chang in the 1890s. The growing entrepreneurial role of the National government was actually, therefore, a reassertion of a traditional mode of political behaviour.[76]

CHINA'S NEW MOOD, 1936–7

Beginning in the autumn of 1936, a new sense of optimism and national unity suffused the nation. The turning-point was marked by Nanking's suppression of the revolt of Kwangtung and Kwangsi in June-September of that year. These were the last provinces that had blatantly proclaimed their opposition to Nanking rule, and with their defeat China for the first time since 1916 appeared to be unified. The suppression of the revolt, moreover, had been largely peaceful, convincing many Chinese – now profoundly weary of civil strife – that the Nanking authorities were not mere militarists and that Chiang Kai-shek was a wise and able statesman.

[75] *Ibid.* 235–40. On the secret origin of the National Resources Commission (under the geologist Weng Wen-hao) and the Nationalist programme to use German military and industrial support, see the thorough study by William C. Kirby, *Germany and Republican China*.

[76] Coble, 259–60.

A second reason for the new mood of the nation was that Chiang Kai-shek now appeared to have aligned himself with the prevailing anti-Japanese sentiment. Hitherto, he had consistently stressed that China was too weak and divided to resist imperialist aggression, and he had used all the resources at his command, including secret police and censors, to repress the critics of his policy of appeasement. The anti-Japanese stance of the Kwangtung-Kwangsi rebels had, however, forced Chiang on 13 July 1936 to declare that China, rather than agree to further territorial concessions to the Japanese, was prepared to make 'the ultimate sacrifice' of an all-out war of resistance. Although Chiang had doubtless timed this declaration so that it would defuse potential popular support for the rebels, the declaration may in fact have resulted from a hardening of his determination to resist further Japanese encroachments. When in November 1936 the Japanese attempted to establish a satellite state in Suiyuan province, for example, a Nationalist army under General Fu Tso-i strongly and successfully resisted. In November and December, too, the Chinese foreign minister, Chang Ch'ün, unflinchingly rejected a set of Japanese demands, displaying thereby a defiance of the Japanese that the Nationalists had not shown throughout their entire tenure in Nanking. No doubt Chiang Kai-shek still hoped to postpone what was felt to be the inevitable war with Japan. Strong nationalistic sentiment, both among the people and perhaps especially within his army, however, persuaded him now to assume an unprecedentedly firm stance against the Japanese.

A third factor contributing to China's new national mood was its emergence from the economic depression that had gripped the country since the winter of 1931-2. In November 1935, with silver flooding out of the country to foreign buyers – thereby badly eroding public confidence in *fa-pi* – Nanking abandoned the silver standard and switched to a managed currency. This enabled Nanking to meet its financial needs by increasing the volume of note issues, and in just a year and a half the volume of *fa-pi* in circulation more than tripled. The effect was to stimulate an inflationary trend that by mid-1937 had restored agricultural prices to their 1931 level. Farm credit now also became more readily available and interest rates fell. Thus, although the inflationary effects of the currency reform had been unanticipated and actually unwanted by Nanking's fiscal experts, that reform started the entire economy on the road to recovery.

Coinciding in 1936 and 1937 with the rising agricultural prices were bumper harvests, the best in nearly twenty years. As a consequence of this happy juxtaposition of excellent crops and high prices, the value of China's harvest in 1936 was 45 per cent higher than the average for the years 1933-5. With relative prosperity in the villages, peasants began buying the industrial commodities that they had denied themselves since 1931. The result was a fresh stimulus also to the urban economy.

The upturn of the economy in the autumn of 1936, together with the enhanced unity of the nation and the government's new-found determination to resist the Japanese, had an extraordinary effect on the national spirit. 'At the moment,' reported Columbia University professor Nathaniel Peffer in October 1936, 'Chinese are inclined to a mood of confidence and impassioned patriotism.'[77] Likewise an editorial in China's leading independent newspaper, the *Ta-kung-pao* ('L'Impartial'), declared in December, 'In the period of the last few months, the people's confidence seems as though it were revived from the dead.'[78]

Chiang Kai-shek was the principal political beneficiary of this new national mood. Earlier in the decade, he had been widely viewed as an ill-educated militarist striving only for personal power. Now, however, he was praised as a far-seeing leader who, so long as the nation had been torn by internal struggles, had wisely avoided a confrontation with the Japanese. Chiang for the first time had become a popular and seemingly inexpendable leader.

At the crest of this new popularity, however, the Nanking regime was suddenly plunged into a brief but unprecedented crisis when Chiang Kai-shek was kidnapped at Sian. Despite his expressed determination to resist further Japanese encroachments, Chiang's *bête noire* was still the Communists. And he was convinced that, with just one further campaign, the Communists – located since the completion of the Long March in northern Shensi, and reduced to about 30,000 armed men – could be finally annihilated. But the North-west Bandit-Suppression Force that Chiang assigned to this operation had not responded to his marching orders. This army, commanded by Chang Hsueh-liang and composed largely of natives of Manchuria, felt little zeal for the anti-Communist campaign. They were convinced that the real enemy was not the Communists, whom they had learned to respect as true patriots, but the Japanese, who had invaded their homes.

Unable to enforce his orders from Nanking, Chiang Kai-shek flew to the army headquarters in Sian on 4 December, where he exhorted Chang to commence the attack. The Manchurians were adamant, however, that they should, in concert with the Communists, fight the Japanese. And, when their entreaties failed, they overpowered Chiang Kai-shek's body-

---

[77] *New York Times*, 4 Oct. 1936, 25.
[78] *Ta-kung-pao* (L'Impartial) (13 Dec. 1936), sec. 1, p. 2.

guard in the pre-dawn hours of 12 December and placed their commander-in-chief under arrest.

For two weeks, Chiang Kai-shek was held prisoner in Sian. Radical young Manchurian officers demanded that he be put to death. But the calmer voice of Chang Hsueh-liang, who sought not to kill Chiang but only to change his policy, prevailed. That Chang Hsueh-liang succeeded in this purpose has never been officially admitted, although it is now clear that Chiang Kai-shek did make a verbal promise to cease attacking the Communists and to resist the Japanese. Finally, on 25 December, with the concurrence of Communist representatives who were in constant consultation with the mutineers, Chiang was released and flew back to Nanking.[79]

The Sian incident had been a traumatic episode for the Chinese. Public response – marked by profound agony and concern during his captivity, and by unrestrained relief and joy upon his release – confirmed Chiang's widespread popularity and buttressed his increasingly autocratic powers within the regime. Despite his asseverations that he had made no concessions to his captors, there were no further attacks against the Communists. Indeed, negotiations between Nanking and the Communists, leading to the formation of a united front, were soon under way. For the first time in a decade, the Chinese seemed to be putting aside their domestic quarrels in order to resist the foreign aggressor.

AN ASSESSMENT OF NATIONALIST RULE DURING THE NANKING DECADE

The Nationalists were granted only ten years from the establishment of their government in Nanking until the nation was engulfed in a long and devastating war. Ten years was too brief a time to establish a completely new national administration and to turn back the tide of political disintegration and national humiliation that for a century and a half had assailed the nation. Even if conditions had been ideal, the new government could have done little more than initiate political, social and economic reforms.

Despite the adverse conditions afflicting the nation, there had been progress during the decade. By mid-1937, the central government was seemingly ensconced in power, so that there was greater political stability than at any time since 1915. The economy was on the upturn; the

---

[79] Tien-wei Wu, *The Sian Incident: a pivotal point in modern Chinese history*, 142–8 and *passim*.

government was pushing ahead with various transportation and industrial schemes; the currency was more unified than ever before. Many observers, both Chinese and foreign, believed that the Nationalists had in just ten years reversed the tide of disintegration. The American ambassador, Nelson T. Johnson, for example, wrote in April 1937 that 'An observer... cannot but be impressed by the energy with which the Chinese government is pushing its program of economic reconstruction on all fronts, agricultural, industrial and communications.'[80] The British commercial counsellor at about the same time noted 'the increasing, justified confidence which the Chinese themselves as well as the world at large have in the future of this country, a confidence based on the remarkable growth of stability achieved in recent years and the improved political, financial and economic conduct of affairs – government and private'.[81]

The conditions that had generated this swelling optimism, however, were of such recent vintage – appearing less than a year before the war began – that it would be folly for a historian to insist dogmatically that those conditions necessarily portended long-term success and stability for the regime. The improved economic situation, for example, was directly related to the vagaries of China's weather and to the uncertainties inherent in the inflationary trend set off by the creation of a managed currency. The political and military unity of the nation was also extremely fragile, as would become grievously apparent later in the war years. And the popularity of Chiang Kai-shek was attributable to his avowed determination to resist the Japanese rather than to any fundamental reforms in the regime itself.

The new mood of the nation, in other words, had been generated largely by superficial and possibly transient phenomena. Peering beneath those surface features, one discerns that the regime continued to be, even at the end of the Nanking decade, a clumsy and uncertain instrument of national renewal. The civil bureaucracy remained inefficient and corrupt. Government offices were filled with nepotistic appointees who had few if any qualifications for office, but filled the government bureaus with superfluous and self-serving personnel. Wages of these employees were low, and corruption was consequently rife in the administration. As late as September 1936, Chiang Kai-shek bemoaned the ineptitude of the bureaucracy, asserting that 'If we do not weed the present body of corruption, bribery, perfunctoriness, and ignorance, and establish instead a clean and efficient administration, the day will soon come when the revolution will be started against us as we did against the Manchus.'[82]

---

[80] Quoted in Young, *Nation-building*, 419. [81] Quoted in *ibid.* 420.
[82] *North China Herald*, 16 Sept. 1936, 482.

Some of the civilian leaders in the bureaucracy were educated, modern-minded men. Since 1935, in particular, Chiang Kai-shek had brought into government service a number of respected bankers, journalists and intellectuals, such as Chang Kai-ngau, Weng Wen-hao, Wu Ting-ch'ang and Tsiang T'ing-fu, who were generally highly capable and relatively progressive. These new men, however, exerted minimal influence on basic government policy. The men who in fact controlled the regime seldom comprehended how to cope with the tasks of social and economic regeneration. Franklin Ho, who became a close political and economic adviser to Chiang Kai-shek in 1936, recalled that 'One can only be surprised to know just how unaware people at the top were of what was going on, how little they knew of actual conditions in the country, and how they were even less aware of the theoretical basis of those conditions.'[83] Some of these people at the top were skilled technicians, but they tended to be almost exclusively oriented to the urban, modernized sectors of society. They therefore had little understanding of the problems or of the potentialities of the rural areas, which constituted the soul of the nation. T. V. Soong and H. H. Kung, for example, were skilled financiers and budget managers, but they never confronted the problem of how to mobilize the resources of the agricultural sector – which provided two-thirds of the national product – if China were to develop any momentum in its programmes of transport and industrial development.

The military continued to hold ultimate power in the Nationalist regime and to establish the regime's priorities. However enlightened the civilian administrators might have been, therefore, they were little more than tools of the military. And the military men tended to be considerably less worldly than the civilians, and were much less oriented to the problems of social and economic reconstruction. They found solutions to the national problems chiefly in authoritarianism and political repression. 'All too often,' remarked Arthur Young, these militarists 'were incompetent, reactionary, and/or corrupt.'[84] With this kind of men dominant in the upper reaches of the regime, the prospects of the government responding creatively to the nation's exigent problems were exceedingly unpromising.

One of the problems for which the Nationalist leadership provided no solutions, for example, was that, as Arthur Young put it, 'The government failed to identify with the people, but rather stood above them.'[85] The regime was a dictatorship built on and maintained by military power. Its leaders were jealous of their power, disinclined to share that power and

---

[83] Franklin L. Ho, 'The reminiscences of Ho Lien', 144.
[84] Young, *Nation-building*, 423.   [85] *Ibid.* 423.

its perquisites with others, and repressive of political rivals and critics. In a modernizing and increasingly nationalistic polity, where the citizens are inevitably becoming more politically alert, this kind of exclusivist wielding of power is generally self-destructive. Certainly this is not to suggest that China needed to adopt Anglo-American institutions of democracy, for assuredly those were not suitable to China at the time. The Nationalists should, however, have allowed and even encouraged the politically mobilized elements to become involved in the processes of government. It might, for example, have permitted trade unions, student and professional associations, and local self-government assemblies to become vehicles of political mobilization. Or it might have injected life into the Kuomintang by making it an instrument for the supervision of government rather than being an atrophied limb of the regime.

During periods of extreme political crisis, the regime did go through the motions of expanding political participation. In 1932, for instance, when public opinion had turned strongly against the regime for its unmilitant response to the Japanese attacks on Manchuria and Shanghai, the government convoked a National Emergency Conference designed to allow prominent persons outside the regime to advise the authorities. Whenever such crises passed, however, the regime returned to its accustomedly authoritarian and exclusivist methods of rule. In some regimes, such as Franco's Spain or Salazar's Portugal, such authoritarian solutions have been remarkably stable. China, however, was many times larger and therefore incomparably more difficult to control than were those European states.

Exacerbating the inherent instability of the Nationalist regime were the unresolved problems in China's villages. Scholars are currently debating whether the peasants' standard of living was declining during the Republican period or remaining at about the same level. There is little dispute, however, that the life of the peasants generally was impoverished and occasionally even brutish. As a consequence, peasant rebellions, banditry, and other forms of social pathology had become endemic in the rural areas. These dissident activities had, however, lacked the political awareness and the organization needed to transform them into politically revolutionary movements. By the 1930s, however, both the aspirations and the organization were being brought to the peasants. As a result of the increasingly rapid process of modernization in China, the peasants were learning of ways of life different from their own mundane existence. Largely through the flow of commerce, they learned of worlds beyond their villages, and commerce had expanded dramatically by the 1930s. In 1935, for instance, about 54 per cent of China's families bought kerosene;

cigarettes and cigarette advertising penetrated even to the farthest provinces. Rural youths, moreover, who were being recruited to work in urban factories, vastly broadened their intellectual horizons by exposure to the cities and to workers from other provinces – and, returning home periodically, they communicated what they had learned to their fellow villagers.[86] Radio and newspapers were also making inroads into the hinterlands, conveying information about alternative modes of existence. 'Nothing,' Samuel Huntington has observed, 'is more revolutionary than this awareness.'[87] Although little research has yet been attempted on this question of changing peasant attitudes and outlooks in modern China, the probability that peasants were becoming aware not only that they were suffering, but that those sufferings were not inevitable, suggests the presence of a potentially powerful destabilizing factor in the countryside.

The Communists, moreover, had begun providing the organization that could transmute peasant discontents into political power. The Nationalists might, in the absence of a Japanese invasion, have continued employing repressive measures against the Communists. But the facts that the Nationalists assigned such a low priority to the elimination of the socio-economic causes of peasant discontent, and that the Communists had already demonstrated their tenacious capacity to survive, also suggest that the rural areas of Nationalist China were destined to remain a tinder-box even if there had been no war with Japan.

These several factors – the ineffectual administration of the Nationalists, their incomprehension of the tasks of national reconstruction, their failure to accommodate into the political process the broadening strata of the population that were becoming politically alert, and the persistence of the rural problem – did not mean that the Nationalist regime was fated to be overthrown. They did, however, portend continuing instability.

---

[86] Dwight H. Perkins, *Agricultural development in China, 1368–1968*, 111–12, 126–7; Jean Chesneaux, *The Chinese labor movement, 1919–1927*, 48–9, 66–70; Cochran, 18–22; Albert Feuerwerker, 'The foreign presence in China', *CHOC* 12.196; Martin M. C. Yang, *Chinese social structure: a historical study*, 339.

[87] Samuel P. Huntington, *Political order in changing societies*, 298.

CHAPTER 2

THE COMMUNIST
MOVEMENT 1927–1937

The decade between the first and second united fronts, from the KMT-CCP break-up in mid-1927 to mid-1937, was a time of disaster, trial and tribulation for the Communist movement that brought it close to extinction. Yet from this period emerged an experienced and tested leadership with a capacity not only to survive but to win power. The severity of the problems met and surmounted by the CCP in these years can be best understood by looking first at its crisis of membership and organization.

RECONSTITUTION AND LEADERSHIP OF THE PARTY

In brief, the CCP from its Second Congress in 1922 had been a branch of the Communist International (CI) which, in spite of differing views occasionally expressed by Chinese leaders, had its way throughout the period of the first united front of 1923–7. After 1927, however, the prestige of the CI plummeted and vigorous efforts were needed to restore it. This meant the deposition and criticism of Ch'en Tu-hsiu, the recall and rebuke of Ch'ü Ch'iu-pai, the trial of Li Li-san; more significantly, this also meant the convocation of the Sixth Congress in Moscow and the reconstruction of the party presided over by Pavel Mif. From the autumn of 1927 to January 1931 the CI's interference in the affairs of the CCP virtually reduced the Chinese party to the status of a 'colony'. After the fourth plenum of January 1931, however, the CI's influence over the CCP declined, due to complex factors, including Stalin's increasing preoccupation with Russian and European affairs, the destruction of the liaison organization in Shanghai by the KMT police in the summer of 1934, and Stalin's bloody purges that by 1937 had rendered the CI an unreliable vehicle for transmitting his policies.

Meanwhile, Ch'en Tu-hsiu's leadership of the CCP had ended in mid-1927. His successors were younger men – Ch'ü Ch'iu-pai in the second half of 1927, Li Li-san from summer 1928 to summer 1930, and the International Faction (or the 28 Bolsheviks, *erh-shih-pa shu*) from

January 1931 to January 1935. Under the guidance of the CI they undertook to rebuild the shattered party and develop a new, feasible revolutionary strategy. The membership of the party dropped from its peak of nearly 60,000 in April 1927 to probably less than 10,000 by the end of the year. It was perhaps to Ch'en's credit that the CCP had not been entirely destroyed in the debacle of 1927. Some attribute this resilience to the inculcation of 'a common state of mind', or, in other words, the strength of the ideology that had been disseminated through the party organs, chiefly *The Guide Weekly* and the theoretical journal, *New Youth*.[1] As the intellectuals were the people in whose minds the ideology had taken firmest root, it was they who remained firm in the face of the anti-Communist upsurge, to carry on the torch of revolution. In the words of one such survivor of the persecution of 1927, 'to lose contact with the party or the [Communist Youth] Corps was like losing one's loving mother'.[2] It was this sentiment that turned the politically alienated to brotherly comradeship with each other and gave them a ruthless determination against their foes within and without the party.

When the storm broke in 1927, the attention of the party had shifted to a young man, only twenty-eight years of age, perhaps not nearly as resolute in action as Ch'en, but certainly more Leninist and adventurist and with considerable theoretical sophistication. Ch'ü Ch'iu-pai had been opposing Ch'en's leadership on several issues for some time before Ch'en's retirement from his commanding position. A prolific polemicist in the party organs he edited, he was fluent in Russian and thus gained access to Lenin's writings on party organization and strategy, such as *What is to be done?* and *Two tactics*. Upon taking over the secretaryship in July–August 1927, Ch'ü proceeded to bolshevize the CCP. Then, as later in 1928, he regarded the party as an elite organization clearly different from any mass organization under its leadership. Its vanguard status came from its capability of exposing and learning from its own mistakes through intra-party struggles.[3] Here he echoed not only Lenin but also Stalin's 1925 definition of bolshevization.[4] Putsches attempted at Swatow in

[1] This chapter is a continuation of the same author's 'The Chinese Communist movement to 1927' in *CHOC* 12.505–26. See also *ibid.* 430–3, 'Introduction of Marxism-Leninism' (B. Schwartz); and 566–73, 'The Russian role by early 1926' (C. M. Wilbur). For a survey narrative, see James P. Harrison, *The long march to power: a history of the Chinese Communist Party, 1921–72*. The other major account is Jacques Guillermaz, *A history of the Chinese Communist Party 1921–1949*.

[2] *Hung-ch'i p'iao-p'iao* (Red flags flying), hereafter *HCPP*, 6.15.

[3] Previously no intra-party differences had reached this dimension. See 'Letter to all the members', *Hung-se wen-hsien* (Red documents), 96. On Ch'ü Ch'iu-pai's background and literary interests see Jonathan Spence, *The Gate of Heavenly Peace: the Chinese and their revolution 1895–1980*, 145–8 and *passim*; Tsi-an Hsia, *The gate of darkness: Studies on the leftist literary movement in China*, 3–54; and ch. 9 below.

[4] Published in *Pravda*, 3 February 1925 and included in Boyd Compton, *Mao's China: party reform documents, 1942–44*, 269–71.

September and at Canton (the 'Canton commune') in December 1927 both failed. The CCP leadership was decimated. At a time when the existing structure of the party was fractured by blows from without and rent by factionalism within, Ch'ü could do only as much as the circumstances allowed. His attempt to introduce the democratic process of consultation at least at the top level, when often a quorum of the Politburo was scarcely possible, only aggravated the sectarian wrangles.[5] However, through Ch'ü's emphasis on the land revolution, the party branched out from the urban underground to the embryonic rural base areas, some fifteen of which were now taking shape.

Class composition

After a series of disastrous adventures known as the Autumn Harvest uprisings, in April 1928 Ch'ü vacated the party secretaryship in favour of Hsiang Chung-fa, a colourless proletarian. Under persecution and in war conditions, along with the omnipresent concern with safety and defections, the party centre faced a host of organizational problems. First, the class composition of the membership had changed from urban workers and intellectuals to a rural predominance.[6] The change threatened to transform the class base, the style of work and the policies of the party. Therefore both the resolutions of the Sixth Congress of July 1928 and the letter to the CCP from the ECCI (Executive Committee of the Communist International) on 8 February 1929 urged an increase in urban membership. Second, in order to consolidate the proletarian base of the party, the centre had to re-establish contact with those members who had lost touch with their party cell. It had to find jobs for and to plant back among the non-party masses those activists who had exposed themselves during the period of open work before June 1927 but were now living on the slender resources of the party. Above all it had to unify its control over radical labour unions which were in the hands of the 'real work' group under such union leaders as Ho Meng-hsiung and Lo Chang-lung. Third, the rural branches were for a long period of time completely cut off from any connection with their provincial committees and the centre. The Ching-kang-shan Front Committee in the mountain fastness far

---

[5] Mao Tse-tung, *Hsuan-chi* (Selected works), hereafter Mao, *HC* 3.980 and Harrison, *Long march*, 124.

[6] None of the sets of figures of the CCP membership can be taken without question. I am using the official statistics as a rough guide. See for example, Mao Tse-tung, *Selected works*, hereafter Mao, *SW* 4.270. It is generally held that the size of urban membership in all these reports is exaggerated. But, on the other hand, the exodus of members of the CCP to the countryside may have also inflated the size of the rural membership. Many of the people working in the rural soviets were obviously of urban origins.

south-east of Changsha between Kiangsi and Hunan, for instance, took five months to re-establish its communication with the Hunan provincial committee. A letter from the centre to Mao, then the secretary of the Front Committee, sent on 4 June 1928, reached him six months later. Ho Lung in west Hunan and Hupei knew the resolutions of the Sixth Congress only in the spring of 1929! Fourth, within the central leadership factionalism, especially Ch'en Tu-hsiu's 'rightist' influence, persisted. As the situation worsened after the repeated failures in the second half of 1927, it appeared to dim the hopes for consolidating the party organization.[7]

The Sixth CCP Congress held outside Moscow in June and July 1928 charged the new leadership (principally Li Li-san from Hunan, who had been in France and Russia) with rehabilitating the party along the following lines. The party had to be proletarianized by bringing more workers into its organization and leadership. This should not be done at the expense of ideological and organizational unity, which would happen if localism and factionalism were allowed to continue. To curb localism and factionalism it would be necessary to intensify the education and training of members of the party and at the same time to practise true democratic centralism without, however, endangering the safety of the party and its members. In the widely scattered rural base areas all efforts should be made to arouse the broad masses in the land revolution and soviet movement led by the party. The response of the masses was to be a major criterion of correctness of policy and style; putschism and commandism, which were likely to lose mass support, were deemed erroneous. In the base areas, the Communists should act only as ideological leaders, not as administrators of the soviets themselves, so as to give the masses the power to supervise their own governments, although not to supervise the party itself.[8]

Following these resolutions, Li Li-san took immediate steps to strengthen the central leadership. Although the Sixth Congress showed a distrust of the intellectuals and Li himself noticed a barrier between the workers and intellectuals in the party, he does not seem to have developed an anti-intellectual stand. One can hardly describe Li Wei-han, Teng Chung-hsia, and the cultural workers in Honan, all staunch supporters of Li, as anything but intellectuals.[9] Initially the main threat to the security

---

[7] ECCI to CCP, 8 February 1929; Mao's report, 25 November 1928, *Mao Tse-tung chi* (Collected writings of Mao Tse-tung), ed. Takeuchi Minoru, hereafter *MTTC*, 2.25, 28; *Hsing-huo liao-yuan* (A single spark can start a prairie fire), hereafter *HHLY*, 1, pt. 2, 603–14. After vol. 1 citations are by volume and page.

[8] Resolutions of the Sixth Congress in *Hung-se wen-hsien*, 169–91.

[9] Wang Ming, Postscript to 'Liang-t'iao lu-hsien' (The two lines), in his *Hsuan-chi* (Selected works), 3.140–1.

of Li's leadership came from the labour union leaders and it would have been unwise for him to alienate his intellectual colleagues.[10]

In the first few months of Li Li-san's leadership, when the small rural soviets were still struggling for their existence, the major problems of party unity and consolidation did not lie in the rural bases. It was the remnants of party-led labour unions and their leaders whom Li condemned for excessive democratization, egalitarianism, bureaucratism and un-principled factionalism.[11] His endeavour to curb intra-party democracy in order to safeguard the party under the 'white terror' may have ended in too much centralization of power. The complaint was that he, like Ch'en Tu-hsiu, became a patriarch.[12] Essentially a man of action rather than of intellectual power, Li relied chiefly on the reinforcement of discipline to achieve unity. Now that the CCP's status as a branch of the CI had been reaffirmed at the Sixth Congress, Li had the backing of the CI's authority to help him pursue this line of action. Often he resorted to dismissal to eliminate the opposition. Occasionally he even dissolved an entire provincial committee for the same purpose.[13] Not until September 1930, after the collapse of the Li Li-san line, did he try to lay down some rules on the rampant intra-party struggles.[14] Even then the emphasis was evidently on discipline in a crude and authoritarian manner. Li's attempt to unify the party included the use of party organs. The *Bolshevik* (*Pu-erh-sai-wei-k'e*), created by Ch'ü Ch'iu-pai in October 1927, was continued and Li launched the weekly *Red Flag* (*Hung-ch'i*) in November 1928, which was published twice weekly from October 1929 to July 1930. And finally he formed the General Action Committee, combining the heads of the party, youth corps, and labour unions into one body.[15]

The much discussed differences between Li and Mao related more to their assessment of the revolutionary situation and their corresponding strategies than to party organization. The widely shared anxiety over the increase in peasant membership, hence the possible permeation of peasant mentality in the party, appeared to Mao to be an unwarranted fear. Operating in remote rural areas, Mao and other soviet leaders could

---

[10] Richard C. Thornton, *The Comintern and the Chinese Communists, 1928–1931*, 34.

[11] Conrad Brandt *et al. A documentary history of Chinese communism*, 172–3.

[12] Ilpyong J. Kim, *The politics of Chinese Communism: Kiangsi under Soviet rule*, 183–4.

[13] 'Resolutions of the second plenum' (June 1929), in Kuo Hua-lun (Warren Kuo), *Chung-kung shih-lun* (An analytical history of the CCP); hereafter Warren Kuo, *History*, 2.43–4. This trend culminated in the dismissals of Ch'en Tu-hsiu, P'eng Shu-chih and many others in November 1929. See Wang Fan-hsi, *Chinese revolutionary: memoirs 1919–1949*, translated and with an introduction by Gregor Benton.

[14] Hsiao Tso-liang, *Power relations within the Chinese communist movement, 1930–1934*, 55–6.

[15] All things considered, the tribute paid to Li's organizational achievement by the ECCI expressed a general optimism rather than a description of reality. The ECCI resolution, often dated 23 July 1930 (see *Hung-se wen-hsien*, 354), was drafted in April-May and adopted in June.

depend only to a limited degree on developing small-scale industries in order to increase the proletarian component of the soviet party. Mao in particular had to resort to political education for the proletarianization of the peasants, who were the only masses under the party's influence and the only important source of party recruitment. The anxiety remained unrelieved – all that Li could do was to develop the party's work among the workers. In the context of 1928-30, Li's effort in that respect did not get very far.

Unity of a party so widely scattered and so badly mauled as the CCP under Li was more a matter of ideology than of organization. Yet he was anything but a mighty ideologue. With Moscow divided first between Stalin and Trotsky and then between Stalin and Bukharin, Li had either to evolve his own line or to vacillate as the CI did. Whatever direction he followed, he had to persuade his followers. When persuasion failed, the unconvinced left for Moscow or left the party altogether. But Hsiang Chung-fa, Li Wei-han, Ho Ch'ang, Teng Chung-hsia, and several others supported him to form a caucus powerful enough to control the centre effectively.[16]

In spite of Wang Ming's acrimony against Li's organization line,[17] Li was removed by the CI not on that ground, but because of his strategic blunders to be noted below. After a short interval of confusion, the centre passed into the hands of the '28 Bolsheviks', of whom Wang Ming was the leader, through the authority of the CI. A situation thus arose in the centre where the CI's authority was pitched against the 'real work' group of union leaders who, persistently opposed to Li Li-san, found their power base much eroded by Chiang Kai-shek's persecution.[18] In the countryside it was pitched against the soviet leaders whose power in terms of territory and men had grown enormously since the Sixth Congress.

Of all the crucial intra-party struggles, the issues that triggered the dispute between the 28 Bolsheviks and the 'real work' group led by Ho Meng-hsiung and Lo Chang-lung are perhaps most obscure; so obscure that they defy intelligent speculation. By the time the dispute broke out, the old contention between Ho and Li Li-san had been settled. The only link between the two disputes seems to have been the ways by which the party should be reconstructed and who should be the people to do it. The single intelligible point to emerge from examining the existing docu-

16 Wang Ming, 'The two lines', in his *Hsuan-chi*, 3.70, 100, 108, 140-1, and 143-4; Warren Kuo, *History*, 2.334. I give these names to correct an impression that Li had almost no supporters at all in 1929-30.
17 Wang Ming, *ibid*. 3.68-71.
18 *HHLY* 1, pt. 1, 16; Pei-p'ing she-hui tiao-ch'a so (Peiping Social Survey Institute), *Ti-erh-tz'u Chung-kuo lao-tung nien-chien* (Second yearbook of Chinese labour), preface, 2.

ments, mostly biased against the 'real work' group, was the emergency conference proposed by Ho, Lo, and their supporters with a wider representation than the fourth plenum of the Central Committee proposed by the 28 Bolsheviks and their mentor, Pavel Mif. The emergency conference proposal envisaged a reconstruction of the party from below, whereas the fourth plenum of the Sixth Central Executive Committee – as actually convened in January 1931 – consisted of a narrow representation which preferred to do so from above. As far as the 'real work' group could see, the latter course would have most dire consequences for the party as well as for the revolutionary movement as a whole.[19] Personal factors, for example rivalry for leadership positions and distrust of the inexperienced and young 'Bolsheviks', certainly entered into the dispute; nonetheless they may not have been the deciding factors. When the issues were joined, it turned out that both Ho and Lo had grossly overestimated the strength and unity of the labour union opposition – a miscalculation that ended in their total defeat at the fourth plenum in January 1931. Ho and 22 others, including five young leftist writers, were evidently betrayed to the police and were then shot on 7 February 1931.

Having seized the central leadership, the 28 Bolsheviks might have attempted to 'bolshevize' the party organization – on the one hand by insisting on absolute fidelity to the political line of the CI; on the other by practising 'democratic centralism'.[20] As they were sharp debaters,[21] it is reasonable to assume that they would have preferred committee discussions rather than patriarchal commandism or a system of penalties they seem to have disliked. In fact, however, when the cloak-and-dagger struggles between the secret service men of the KMT and CCP were exacerbated in 1931 immediately after the fourth plenum, and the work of the party in the 'white area' suffered disastrous reverses, it is highly doubtful that committee meetings and democratic centralism could have been attained.[22]

---

[19] 'Centre's resolution concerning the question of Comrade Ho Meng-hsiung' (16 December 1930) in Tang ti kai-tsao (Reconstruction of the party), no. 1 (25 January 1931). See Hsiao Tso-liang, Power relations, 95. Also 'Resolution concerning the removal of Lo Chang-lung as a member of the central committee and the party' (20 January 1931) in Tang ti kai-tsao, 3 (15 February 1931). Full text reproduced in Warren Kuo, History, 2.218–21. See also Hsiao Tso-liang, Power relations, 135.

[20] Wang Ming, 'Chung-kuo hsien-chuang yü Chung-kung jen-wu' (The present situation of China and the tasks of the CCP), speeches at the 13th plenum of the ECCI, Moscow, 1934, 78. On centralism, see the end of his famous pamphlet, 'The two lines', in Hsuan-chi, 3.111.

[21] In 1939 I had a chance to listen to Wang Ming's public speech given in the tennis court of the YMCA, Chengtu, when Wang Yü-chang and Lin Tsu-han were on their way back to Yenan after a session of the People's Political Council. I have not heard any Chinese speaker, before or since, more eloquent than Wang.

[22] Warren Kuo, History, 2.250–9.

The 28 Bolsheviks, however, achieved a greater measure of centralized control over the fifteen or so rural soviets than had Li Li-san. Soon after the fourth plenum, the 'front committees' which had governed the soviets, were replaced by a central bureau of the soviet areas directly under the Politburo, with six soviet areas under its jurisdiction. At least four of these six soviets each had a branch bureau – the central soviet in eastern Kiangsi on the border of Fukien (to which Mao and Chu Teh had removed from Ching-kang-shan at the end of 1928), the O-Yü-Wan (Hupei-Honan-Anhwei) soviet, Hsiang-o-hsi (West Hupei and Hunan), and Hsiang-kan (Hunan-Kiangsi).[23] The other two may have been directed by a special committee.[24] The new institution may have weakened the growing power of Mao Tse-tung in the central soviet; it was certainly possible for the 28 Bolsheviks to use it to eradicate Li Li-san's residual influence in the O-Yü-Wan soviet when Ch'en Chang-hao, Shen Tse-min, and Chang Kuo-t'ao superseded Hsü Chi-shen and Tseng Chung-sheng, while in the Hsiang-o-hsi soviet Hsia Hsi replaced Teng Chung-hsia.[25]

As the 'white area' activities became almost unfeasible, the party centre took steps to remove itself to the central soviet, accompanied by a migration of party members. The transfer of the centre was completed early in 1933, leaving only a skeletal liaison staff in Shanghai, who were soon arrested by the KMT police. The transfer not only exacerbated the struggle over issues and for power, but introduced many urban party members to day-to-day administration in the open countryside that was vastly different from clandestine work in cities. Their old styles of life, work and writing had to undergo appropriate modifications as they were now in close touch with a massive peasantry. Though facing similar difficulties, they differed from the old imperial officials, who under the principle of avoidance had to come in as outsiders, because they did not want to cultivate bureaucratism purposely. Yet they also differed from the old cadre in the soviet areas in the sense that the newcomers had neither participated in the creation of the base areas nor acquired the styles of peasant life and some understanding of local dialects, including Hakka. And they did not eliminate their disdain of the peasants, or prevent the growth of bureaucratism once they had gripped the helm of governmental power.[26]

[23] Hsiao Tso-liang, *Power relations*, 151; *She-hui hsin-wen*, 6.19–20 (27 February 1934), 264; Warren Kuo, *History*, 2.183–4.
[24] Wang Chien-min, *Chung-kuo kung-ch'an-tang shih-kao* (A draft history of the CCP), hereafter Wang Chien-min, *Draft history*, 2.503.
[25] *Hung-ch'i* (Red flag), no. 29 (25 January 1932); Warren Kuo, *History*, 2.335 and 367–8.
[26] Ts'ao Po-i, *Chiang-hsi su-wei-ai chih chien-li chi ch'i peng-k'uei* (The establishment and collapse of the Kiangsi soviet), hereafter Ts'ao Po-i, *Soviet*, 464.

The mass line

Guerrilla fighters everywhere from Algeria to Cuba have depended upon the support of the masses for whom they fight. But the practice of winning popular support through propaganda and action does not necessarily imply a conceptualized 'mass line'. To be sure, both the party centre and the soviet leaders since the Sixth Congress of the CCP accorded high priority to the mobilization of the masses. In fact the political resolution of the Sixth Congress went as far as to say that in the soviet areas the party should expand itself into a mass organization,[27] while Mao in his *Hunan report* of 1927 commented, 'To talk about "arousing the masses of the people" day in and day out and then be scared to death when the masses do rise...'[28] Mass mobilization had become an urgent matter when the CCP in its first wave of migration to the countryside in 1927 encountered the people of rural China. At that time the members of the party had to define: Who were the peasants? How active were they in giving support to the revolution? Or how timid if they lost the protection of the Red Army, thus exposing themselves to reprisal by the reactionaries? How could they be more efficiently mobilized – through organization and technique or through policy and propaganda?

The views of the 28 Bolsheviks also began to change once they came in close touch with the peasant masses. They in no sense formed a monolithic bloc within the party now; nor did they all migrate into the central soviet. But none of them had fully accepted the mass line with all its connotations, as Mao advocated. Although the centre's directive of 1 September 1931 urged the central soviet to do its utmost in mass mobilization so as to consolidate the base area,[29] its tenor was clearly on mobilizing the masses through intensified class struggle. Its criticism of the vaguely phrased army slogan against 'rascals' instead of specifically against landlords, rich peasants and merchants, its insistence that rich peasants be given only poor land, and its dissatisfaction with the neglected anti-imperialist work, all illustrated this point. In the view of the centre, only by sharpening class distinctions and class struggle could the soviet arouse a broader mass of the oppressed. Its criticisms and suggestions were reflected in the resolutions of the first party representatives' conference, the First All-China Soviet Congress, which proclaimed the Chinese Soviet Republic at Juichin, Kiangsi, in November 1931, with Mao Tse-tung as president.[30] There were no indications in these early directives

[27] *Hung-se wen-hsien*, 194.
[28] Mao, *SW* 1.56.
[29] Warren Kuo, *History*, 2.312.
[30] Hsiao Tso-liang, *Power relations*, 165; Warren Kuo, *History*, 2.306.

that the campaigns could be a way of mobilization, no reference to caring for and cherishing the people, and no allowance for the people to supervise and criticize the work of the government and party.

Even in the fifth plenum, held in January 1934 at the height of the line of the 28 Bolsheviks, and before the decisive battles in 1934, the resolution on the present situation and the tasks of the party stated: 'the victory of the revolution depends upon the party, its Bolshevik political line and work, its unity of thought and action, its discipline and ability to lead the masses, and its opposition to any deviation from or distortion of the line of the International and the Chinese party.'[31] Only after the first serious military reverses in that year did dissensions and uncertainties appear in the statements and acts of even the leading 28 Bolsheviks. For example, Chang Wen-t'ien, generally regarded as one of the 28 who drew closest to Mao just before the Long March, said on the one hand

we must always follow the line of mobilizing the masses, working through them and relying on them, regardless whether we arrest and kill counter-revolutionary landlords and rich peasants, organize them into forced-labour corps, or confiscate and requisition their food-stuff. For the problem here is not simply to arrest and kill a few people or to confiscate and requisition some belongings of the landlords and rich peasants. *The problem is how to promote the activism of the masses, raise the degree of their consciousness, and rally and organize them round the soviet regime, when we carry out our clear and definite class line.*[32]

On the other hand, he tightened the 'red terror'. 'Red terror ought to be our reply to these counter-revolutionaries. We must, especially in the war zones and the border areas, deal immediately, swiftly with every kind of counter-revolutionary activity.'[33]

Mao's views on the same set of problems and his solutions to them, which admittedly were still in the process of development, showed a breadth of difference. As a founder of his base area, he had worked, fought and lived with the masses longer than any of the 28 Bolsheviks. Although he may not yet have conceptualized his experiences into a line of policy, the Ku-t'ien resolutions of December 1929 emphasized two essential points – the masses had the right to criticize the mistakes of the Red Army, helping it rectify its mistakes, and the party's resolutions were to be implemented through the masses.[34] To be sure, the Red Army was then dominated by the party commissars.[35] To criticize the army's errors was synonymous with criticizing the party. Mao defined the sources of the

---

[31] *Tou-cheng* (Struggle), 47 (16 February 1930).
[32] *Hung-se Chung-hua*, hereafter Red China, 28 June 1934. My italics.
[33] *Ibid.* 25 May 1934.
[34] MTTC 2.82.
[35] Party centre's directive to the soviet areas, 1 September 1931, in Warren Kuo, *History*, 2.302–4.

party's wisdom and ability to lead correctly in an unambiguous fashion: 'The upper-level organizations must clearly understand the conditions in the lower-level organizations and the living conditions of the masses. This will become the social origins of a correct leadership.'[36] This train of thought led in 1932 to the following conclusion: 'All the methods [of political and economic work] which are detached from the masses are bureaucratic.'[37]

To combat bureaucratism (that is, peremptoriness and pretentious infallibility) was, and still is, the most important single component of Mao's mass line. The required attitude was to be the willing pupils of the masses, not just their leaders, and not to regard the masses as clumsy and stupid country bumpkins but as people who deserved trust and must be involved in administration and political campaigns. Only in this way could the masses be aroused without doing damage to their voluntarism. In Mao's fairly developed conceptualization of the mass line (*ch'un-chung lu-hsien*) of 1933, no one – neither the vanguard nor the class – was presupposed to be perfect, hence the need of education for everyone. Through education for everyone, both the cadre and masses, bad habits and styles could be eliminated so that correct and reliable information might be transmitted from the grass roots to become the basis of correct policy decisions and so that the decisions might be carried out as intended.

In practical terms, this meant every possible care for livelihood and social justice among the people under soviet rule, once that rule was established by the army. The army itself undertook to propagandize and organize the people in preparation for setting up a regime, while land and other property were redistributed, counter-revolutionaries and reactionaries were punished, and relief was provided.[38] When the regime became firm, its economic and financial measures should be aimed at increasing production, facilitating trade, and sharing the tax burden fairly. In some cases, this might entail changes in the economic structure, for instance, cooperativization and mutual aid teams.[39] It might also entail the use of production drives and 'model workers'. Sometimes even the red soldiers took part in farming.[40] To mobilize women, the Soviet Republic introduced and adopted the Marriage Law of December 1931, while women's activities branched out from the hearth to the fields and battlefields.[41] The evacuation of the Red Army from Central China in 1934

[36] *MTTC* 2.82.   [37] *Ibid.* 3.168.
[38] 'The Ku-t'ien resolutions', *MTTC* 2.123.
[39] Information given by Wang Kuan-lan to Edgar Snow, *Random notes on Red China*, 38; *Red China*, 26 July 1934; Ts'ao Po-i, *Soviet*, 345–50; Edgar Snow, *Red star over China*, 183 and 253.
[40] *Red China*, 30 June 1934; Ts'ao Po-i, *Soviet*, 152–4; *HHLY* 2.100; *HCPP* 13.65.
[41] Mao, *SW* 1.142; Ch'ien T'ang, *Ko-ming ti nü-hsing* (Revolutionary women), 13–5; *HCPP* 11.166, 171 and 210.

enhanced the role of women in the remaining guerrilla areas. Less feared by the KMT soldiers and militia, the female activists gathered information, transported food and other necessities to the guerrillas, nursed the wounded, and fought.[42]

In the administration of the law, the masses must be clearly differentiated from their enemy and the laws made understandable to them. The Marriage Law and Labour Laws were obviously designed to protect them, while the laws and acts controlling the activities of counter-revolutionaries were to safeguard the soviet regime.[43] In the application of the mass line the regime became less concerned that justice be done than that justice be seen to be done. The hearings were therefore public under mass supervision, educating and warning the public at the same time.[44] However defective it may have been, the soviet judicial system impressed none other than the leading opponent of the CCP, General Ch'en Ch'eng: 'Its strength lies in its judicial consideration to the exclusion of personal feelings. Its beneficial consequence is shown in the scarcity of cases of embezzlement and corruption.'[45]

If one assumes that the mass line as defined by Mao had won the approval of the party leaders, it follows that the other soviets would have accepted it together with all its organizations and apparatus. It is true that the basic pattern of mass mobilization in the Hupei-Honan-Anhwei (O-Yü-Wan) soviet was similar, with perhaps less attention to economic work but more to the liberation of women than in the central soviet.[46] But the leader there, Chang Kuo-t'ao, had less confidence in the efficacy of land redistribution as a means to arouse people than in the strength of the Red Army to protect the mass work. Therefore he probably relied more on coercion than careful persuasion; and so military reverses often ended in the collapse of his mass work.[47] Conceptualized in this way, Chang's mass line differed from Mao's. Judging from extremely scanty information, the West Hupei and Hunan (Hsiang-o-hsi) soviet under the rough and tough Ho Lung seems to have developed a more elaborate network of mass organization in 1930-1. His soviet tackled problems of production and social welfare by launching production and land reclamation drives and campaigns against superstition, opium addiction and gambling. But Hsia Hsi, one of the 28 Bolsheviks, seems to have

[42] HCPP 1.74; 7.79–108; 9.176–8; 11.151, 200–8; HHLY 4.266–8.
[43] The soviet code was promulgated on 15 October 1933. See Ch'en Ch'eng Documents, roll. 16; Trygve Lötveit, Chinese communism, 1931–1934: experience in civil government, ch. 5, section B; Ts'ao Po-i, Soviet, 404–6.
[44] Ts'ao Po-i, Soviet, 413–14.
[45] Wang Chien-min, Draft history, 2.353.
[46] HHLY 2.462 and 6.379–80; Wang Chien-min, Draft history, 2.192.
[47] Chiao-fei chan-shih (History of the war to suppress the bandits), 4.685.

reversed this approach.[48] As to the other, smaller soviets, information is even scarcer. What is known is no more than that the Japanese discrimination against Chinese women in the factories in the north-east of China drove them to the arms of the guerrillas. And on Hainan island in the early 1930s there was a red detachment of 120 women commanded by Feng Tseng-min[49] – a heroic episode later adapted as the plot of one of the revolutionary operas.

Factionalism and defection

The history of the CCP has witnessed many factional fights, struggles for power in an attempt to control the course of the revolution.[50] Right at the beginning, the party was formed on clientelist ties mainly of the master-disciple type, with Li Ta-chao and Ch'en Tu-hsiu as the two revered figures. The lack of cooperation between them, though not yet carefully documented and analysed, was obvious and may have been attributable to doctrinal differences and personal disagreements. Both Li and Ch'en, being firmly committed Marxists, worked under conditions of intensifying persecution, but did not simply drop out like some of the other early party members. From 1927 onward, the whole revolutionary situation took a sharp turn. Outlawed, the dissidents could defect from the party only by going through a humiliating and agonizing process of confession to the KMT police or secret police, often entailing the betrayal of one's erstwhile comrades with no assurance of one's own safety. Refusal to do so could jeopardize one's life. Under such conditions, members of the party who held opposing views tended to indulge in factional struggles short of separatism or defection.

But to say that it was fear of reprisal that bound the party together in spite of factionalism is to underestimate the strength of the ideology. Whatever divergent opinions these factionalists possessed, they were still Communists fighting for a common goal. Ruptures among them were concerned essentially with organization and political lines; personal traits and power-seeking were secondary factors. In addition to ideology, there was also the 'iron discipline' of the party. It is true that a Communist throve on class hatred and was combative in character. This was, however, only one aspect of his personality; the other was a comradely love

---

[48] *HHLY* 2.100–2; Ho Lung's article in *HHLY* 1, pt. 2, 617.

[49] Ch'en Hsueh-chao, *Man-tsou chieh-fang-ch'ü* (Wanderings in the liberated areas), 94–5; *HHLY* 2.510–22.

[50] For a theoretical treatment, see Andrew J. Nathan, 'A factionalism model for CCP politics', *China Quarterly*, hereafter *CQ*, 53 (Jan.–Mar. 1973) 59; also Harrison, *Long March*, 149–51.

transcending the clientelist ties. The view that brutalization caused factionalism within the CCP must be taken with a large pinch of salt.[51]

Extreme factionalism was usually the precursor of either separatism or defection, both of which implied an ideological reorientation. A separatist might transfer from the predominant ideology of the party to another – Trotskyism in the case of Ch'en Tu-hsiu and P'eng Shu-chih – while a defector perceived a discord between belief and reality – for example, Li Ang, Kung Ch'u and Chang Kuo-t'ao. Dismissed from the party, Ch'en organized the Trotskyist opposition because in the later 1920s and early 1930s he felt that the 1927 debacle was chiefly the responsibility of the CI and he accepted Trotsky's criticism of it.[52] In the spring of 1929, P'eng Shu-chih received two articles by Trotsky – 'The past and future of the Chinese revolution' and 'The Chinese revolution after the Sixth Congress' – which he agreed with implicitly. This, together with his earlier opposition to Ch'ü Ch'iu-pai's putschism, led both him and Ch'en to Trotskyism and opposition to the CCP.[53] Their transfer of faith required a considerable measure of intellectual integrity.[54] Li Ang was quite different. He justified his defection in incredibly naive terms – he wanted to be on the side of the truth forever and he wanted to expose the dark aspects and the conspiracy of the Communist movement. He vehemently opposed the 'dictatorship of Mao Tse-tung', appraising it as 'more despotic than Hitler',[55] Kung Ch'u, an early leader in Kwangsi, left the party when its fortunes were at a nadir. His personal dissatisfaction apart, the main reasons for his action were that the CCP for eleven years had not worked for the independence, democracy and glory of the nation. On the contrary, the party had caused untold suffering to the people and deviated far from the goals of the revolution. It was no more than 'the claws and fangs' of the Soviet Union, 'a big lie'. In 1971, in another series of articles in the Hong Kong monthly Ming-pao, Kung repeated the same reasons for his defection.[56]

[51] Harrison, Long march, 149; Ezra Vogel, 'From friendship to comradeship', CQ 21 (Jan.–Mar. 1965) 46–59.

[52] Ch'en Tu-hsiu, 'Kao ch'uan-tang t'ung-chih-shu' (Letter to all the comrades of the party), 10 December 1929, 7b–8a. For the other reasons for Ch'en's separatism, see Lin Chin's article in She-hui hsin-wen, 9.8 (11 December 1934) 296–300; and Thomas C. Kuo, Ch'en Tu-hsiu (1879–1942) and the Chinese Communist movement, ch. 8.

[53] P'eng Shu-chih, 'Jang li-shih ti wen-chien tso-cheng' (Let historical documents be my witness), Ming-pao yueh-k'an (Ming Pao monthly), hereafter Ming-pao, 30.18–19.

[54] It is because of this that Chinese separatist literature should be treated differently from Chinese defector literature. In this respect, students of the CCP do not share the fortune of their colleagues in the Russian field, where a large body of good and reliable defector literature is available.

[55] Li Ang, Hung-se wu-t'ai (The red stage), 189 and 192. Li even claims to have been a participant of the First Congress of the CCP: ibid.75–6. Li's book is probably one of the least reliable of its genre.

[56] Kung Ch'u, Wo yü hung-chün (The Red Army and I), 2–10, 445.

The process of separatism and defection, not necessarily a protracted one, usually started from differences over issues. When these differences grew in intensity, the actor's belief system itself disintegrated, resulting in his increasing estrangement from the formerly accepted ideology, while he himself went through a period of negativeness and alienation from his comrades. At this stage, a separatist needed an alternative ideology to believe in, whereas a defector had to find an opportunity to survive. If the transfer was from a logically more coherent to a less rigorous ideology (as from communism to Sun Yat-sen's Three Principles of the People), the rationale for the transfer might strike a false note, suggesting opportunism and sheer perfidy. Kung Ch'u's case illustrates this process well. He seems to have had some difficulty in convincing the KMT of his good faith and so he was ordered by the KMT to destroy some red guerrilla bands on the Kiangsi-Kwangtung border and even to attempt to seek out Hsiang Ying and Ch'en I in south Kiangsi.[57] Other defectors, such as Ku Shun-chang, K'ung Ho-ch'ung *et al.*, were either captured by or surrendered to the KMT with almost no ideological concern.

Chang Ku-t'ao was both a separatist and a defector (as to his separatism, see below, p. 96). Arriving at Yenan on 2 December 1936, ten days before the detention of Chiang Kai-shek in Sian, when the policy line he had presented at the Mao-erh-kai Conference in 1935 had completely failed, Chang felt alienated and sank into a negative mood. Then there came the public humiliation of the struggles against him (the 'trials of Chang Kuo-t'ao') in February and November 1937, at which he was accused of all kinds of hideous crimes against the party. Before the return of Wang Ming from Moscow, he had a faint hope of a possible alliance with Wang in opposition to Mao Tse-tung. When Wang came and accused him of 'being a tool of the Trotskyists', his disappointment in the Communist cause in China was complete. It was not the party he had helped found; nor was it the party he wanted.

Earlier he had doubted the viability of the rural soviet movement. Without a proletarian base, only petty bourgeois in nature, he thought the soviets were merely a disguise for power and territorial occupation which had nothing to do with the welfare of the nation.[58] Leaping from one ideology to another, Chang found nationalism and Chiang Kai-shek. He agreed with Mao's Ten Point Programme for the anti-Japanese united front, but blamed Mao for betraying his own principles for the seizure of power and territory. He regarded Mao as no more than 'a traitor in

[57] *HHLY* 4.117–18; *HCPP* 3.229–33.
[58] *Ming-pao*, 57.95; 60.88–90; 61.83–4. See Chang's message to the nation (20 May 1938) in *Ming-pao*, 62; an earlier version appeared in Chang Kuo-t'ao, Liu Ning *et al.*, *I-ko kung-jen ti kung-chuang chi ch'i-t'a* (A working man's confession and other essays), 4.

communist skin', whereas Chiang's effort in the anti-Japanese war should be supported unreservedly since it was anti-imperialist, and Chiang's work in unifying China should be supported also, since it was anti-feudal. As his 'leftist day-dreams' were rudely awakened and Chiang fitted perfectly into the formula of an anti-feudal and anti-imperialist bourgeois national revolution, Chang felt no qualms in his reorientation. Legally speaking one could leave the party voluntarily; therefore Chang thought that there was no question of either betrayal or treachery. Beneath his personal alienation and ideological considerations, his rivalry with Mao cannot be denied. A full generation after his departure from the CCP, he still described his old rival with blazing emotion – 'dictatorial', 'unreasonable to the extent of being barbaric', 'narrow-minded', 'selfish', 'short-sighted', 'ruthless', 'scheming', 'hypocritical', and even 'aspiring to become an emperor of China'.[59]

CREATION OF RURAL SOVIETS

Since the collapse of the first united front in July 1927, the major preoccupation of the CCP had been to create sanctuaries in rural China wherein lay a possibility to continue the revolution and a hope to bring it to final victory. There seemed to be no other feasible choice for that outlawed and persecuted party. These sanctuaries were in fact *imperia in imperio*. Their creation required an army and that was why the Fifth Congress of the CCP at Hankow in April 1927 toyed with three ideas – to push eastward from Central China to defeat Chiang Kai-shek; to march southward to take Canton; or to strengthen the revolutionary forces in Hupei and Hunan. In the absence of any armed force none of these aims could be accomplished.[60] Belatedly, by the end of May 1927, the ECCI advised the CCP to agitate for army mutiny and organize workers' and peasants' troops in order to give teeth to the revolution.[61] This train of thought developed into the CI's call for revolt in July.

The insurrections of 1927

For the rest of the year, in response to this call, the CCP staged a series of insurrections – in Nanchang, Kiangsi on 1 August, the Autumn

[59] *Ming-pao*, 56.86 and 93; 58.89; 59.85–6, 60.85; 61.93–4; 62.85–8. See also Chang's preface to Kung Ch'u, *Wo yü hung-chün*, iii–iv.
[60] Harrison, *Long march*, 105.
[61] Jane Degras, *The Communist International 1919–1943: documents*, 2.390. For the description of the Nanchang uprising, I rely chiefly on C. Martin Wilbur, 'The ashes of defeat', *CQ* 18 (April–June 1964) 3–54.

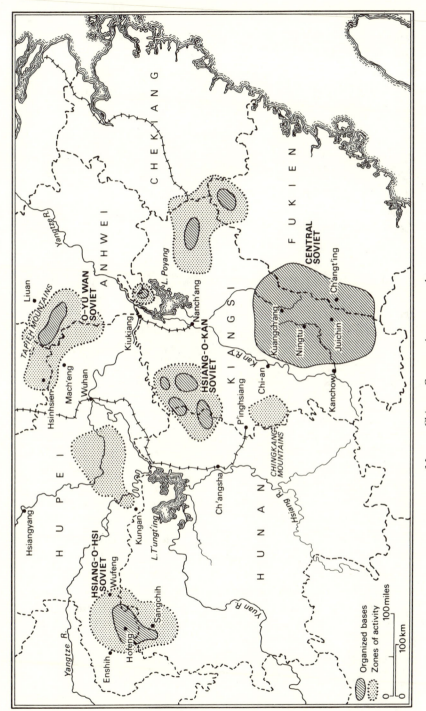

MAP 3. Chinese Communist areas, early 1930s

Harvest uprisings, chiefly in Hupei and Hunan from August to October, and the Canton commune in December. In a sense they were the continuation of the three ideas broached at the Fifth Congress under the assumptions that the city must lead the countryside, that the decisive struggle must be waged in the cities, and that the tide of revolution was rising.

Why Nanchang of all places? The superiority of the Communist and pro-Communist military strength (especially that of the leftist Chang Fa-k'uei) explains the choice of the location of the first armed uprising organized by the CCP. It may have been hoped that by taking this important city, which lay between the quarrelling Nanking and Wuhan, the Communists would be able to turn the whole situation to their favour.[62] Not an industrial city of great importance, Nanchang provided no proletarian base. There was no peasant participation either. Under the command of Chou En-lai, most of the people who took part in the uprising were KMT troops under Communist influence and the revolutionary youth of Hupei and Hunan.[63]

In spite of accusations that poor training and organization of the army units and a lack of coordination and mass support had caused the uprising to fail, the retreating armies from Nanchang under Yeh T'ing, Ho Lung and Chu Teh showed, however, the first of the signs that were to characterize the Red Army later. Chu's 25th Army, which had a large number of revolutionary youths as its low-ranking officers, dispersed into companies and platoons for political propaganda and land confiscation.[64] Yeh and Ho launched their land programme of confiscating landlords' and communal land for redistribution among poor peasants and reducing rent to a maximum of 30 per cent in Ch'ao-chow and Swatow in Kwangtung.[65] Even at this early stage, these units were already different from other troops in China.

After the defeat at Nanchang, the CCP called its historic emergency conference on 7 August 1927 – the type of conference that the 'real work' group demanded later in January 1931. It is not certain whether the party was doctrinally under the persuasion of the CI representatives B. Lominadze and his successor, H. Neumann, who held that Chinese society was less feudal than it was Asiatic with small, fragmented units

[62] Jerome Ch'en, *Mao and the Chinese revolution*, 129; cf. Guillermaz, *A history*, ch. 12.
[63] Su Yü in *HHLY* 1, pt. 1, 19; Chin Fan, *Tsai Hung-chün ch'ang-cheng ti tao-lu shang* (On the route of the Red Army's Long March), 10–11; 'Nan-ch'ang ta-shih chi' (Important events at Nanchang), in *Chin-tai-shih tzu-liao* (Materials of modern history), 4 (1957) 130. Most of these young people were members of either the CCP or the Youth Corps.
[64] Yang Ch'eng-wu in *HHLY* 1, pt. 1, 101.
[65] *Hua-tzu jih-pao* (The Chinese mail), 28 and 30 September 1927.

of production as its chief characteristic. Its bourgeoisie (represented by the KMT) therefore was also weak and disunited, quite unable to lead the bourgeois democratic revolution to completion, which thus stood a good chance of being propelled straight into a socialist stage without interruption, if it was assisted by a foreign proletariat.[66] The 'letter to the comrades' issued after the emergency conference[67] refused, on the one hand, to recognize the land revolution as an anti-feudal revolt but on the other asserted the bourgeois democratic nature of the Chinese revolution. The transition from its present stage to the next was conceived as possibly an uninterrupted one. The conference also stressed the interrelation between the national and social revolutions; the anti-imperialist and anti-feudal struggles were interlocked to make the peasants' participation in them absolutely necessary. Seen from this perspective, the Autumn Harvest uprisings of 1927, that unleashed an attack from the countryside on the cities without planned urban insurrections to give it support, were vastly different from the endeavour a week earlier at Nanchang and provided the only feasible counteraction to the KMT repression.[68]

The Autumn Harvest uprisings, 'tak[ing] advantage of the harvesting period of this year to intensify the class struggle', were directed at the overthrow of the Wuhan government of the left KMT, to create a state within a state so that the CCP could survive to carry on the revolution. It was planned to cover the Hunan-Kiangsi border, south Hupei, the Hupei-Hunan border, south Kiangsi, north-west Kiangsi, and other places from Hainan to Shantung.[69] The three components of the strategy were: to use assorted armed forces as a shield to protect and arm the peasants, to seize local power either to transfer it into peasant committees or restructure it into soviets, and to redistribute land. The key to the success of the strategy was the expectation that the peasants could become an effective combat force so that the gains of the uprisings could be preserved and enlarged to win victory in one or more provinces. As this assumption was proved invalid, the uprisings were doomed.

However, this is not to say that the peasants, especially those in the hills, were unready for insurrection. If they were unready, the rest of the land revolution cannot be explained, except by an unconvincing conspiracy theory. Nor was the failure due to the leaders' conscious neglect of the peasants. Both the party centre and Mao, for example, regarded workers

---

[66] Thornton, *Comintern*, 5 and 15–16.

[67] *Hung-se wen-hsien*, 93–135.

[68] Brandt *et al. Documentary history*, 118. Hsiang Chung-fa did start an abortive strike in Wuhan in support of the uprisings. See *Hua-tzu jih-pao*, 5 August 1927.

[69] Brandt *et al. Documentary history*, 122. For this geographic plan, consult Roy Hofheinz, 'The Autumn Harvest insurrection', *CQ* 32 (Oct.–Dec. 1967) 37–87.

and peasants as the main force of the uprisings.[70] Strategic errors abounded. The party conceived the attack on cities from countryside as being a short process; starting from county towns the armies were to capture large cities and then to overthrow the Wuhan government in a matter of months or weeks. When the party found that even the county towns were either too well defended or too hotly disputed to be taken by the motley troops under Mao and the other leaders of the uprisings, it then scaled down its ambitions to a more cautious and protracted guerrilla warfare in remote rural areas like Ching-kang-shan.[71] From the ashes of defeat, Mao reorganized his troops in one regiment (enormous compared with what his comrades in the Hupei-Honan border region and West Hunan could muster) and made a new start. Not until the summer of 1928 did he have a relatively stable base area incorporating one or two county towns, but still relying on mountainous terrain for safety. The future O-Yü-Wan base took and held its first county town, Shang-ch'eng, only in the winter of 1929 and the base area was formally created as late as the eve of Li Li-san's adventures.[72] Ho Lung arrived back in his home county towards the end of 1927 with only eight rifles and twenty members of the party, and did not rally enough following to capture two county towns till May 1929. Although the November conference of the Politburo recognized these strategic mistakes, it did not share the feeling of loneliness and ebbing tide of revolution that hit the guerrilla leaders fighting in the mountains and hills. At this stage of the revolution, as Mao put it in one of his reports, 'You [the party centre] desire us not to be concerned with the military but at the same time want a mass armed force.'[73] There seems to have been both a lack of experience in military operations and costly hesitation, to bear out what Mao said in 1938: 'war had not been made the centre of gravity in the party's work'.[74]

In mass work, too, experience was lacking. Discussion of when and how the soviet form of government should be introduced seems to have hung on such criteria as whether China in 1927 was comparable to Russia in 1905 (that is, ready for a bourgeois revolution) or in 1917 (a socialist revolution). Li-ling in Hunan saw its first soviet at the beginning of the

[70] Brandt et al. Documentary history, 122; Chung-yang t'ung-hsin (Central newsletter), 6 (20 September 1927), in MTTC 2.13.
[71] Even a county town like Huang-an in Hupei was under too strong an attack for the Communists to hold it for any length of time. See Hsu Hsiang-ch'ien and Cheng Wei-san in HHLY 2.363–77 and 1, pt. 2, 734–55 respectively. See also Lo Jung-huan, in HHLY 1, pt. 1, 139–40 and Huang Yung-sheng in HCPP 13.7.
[72] Hsu Hsiang-ch'ien, ibid.; Ch'en Po-lu in HHLY 1, pt. 2, 795–9.
[73] Ho Lung in HHLY 1, pt. 2, 603–14; Hsiao Tso-liang, Chinese communism in 1927: city vs. countryside, 110; Chung-yang t'ung-hsin, 5 (30 August 1927), in MTTC 2.13.
[74] Mao, SW 2.236.

Autumn Harvest uprisings.[75] This and later soviets were formed largely by utilizing old social ties centred on the gentry, for example the clan associations, rural schools and militia units. Sometimes even secret societies were useful. The radicalized and educated young people returned to their native villages from the suppressed cities to infiltrate these organizations both for sanctuary and for agitation. From these organizations they obtained men, arms and money for the creation of soviet base areas. They made their mistakes and paid for them dearly. But by the end of 1927 there appeared clearly two streams of communism in China – the rural soviets and the urban leadership; the former had to be led by the latter, else the whole movement might have sunk into the traditional pattern of Chinese peasant rebellions. As the rural soviets were still weak and unstable, the establishment of the central authority was not particularly arduous.

Continuing to regard the tide of revolution as rising, Ch'ü Ch'iu-pai and the urban leadership went on with their insurrections in I-hsing and Wusih in Kiangsu, Wuhan in Hupei, Nan-k'ou and Tientsin in Hopei – all miserable failures.[76] Then occurred the Canton commune of 11 December 1927. In the background was Stalin's desire, expressed through the CI, for a victory of China to justify his policy there in the face of Trotsky's criticisms. As Yeh Chien-ying recalled, 'A revolutionary must find a direction for him to go forward.' After the Nanchang uprising Canton seemed the only hope of proving that the CCP could not be bullied by its enemies and that a victory in one province was still feasible.[77] The decision to stage such an uprising was indeed taken at the November conference of the party centre, but the operation was directed by the people on the spot who, once again, cherished a forlorn hope of Chang Fa-k'uei's cooperation.[78] When it failed, any attempt to capture a major city was shelved till Li Li-san's actions in the summer of 1930. The revolution was decidedly at a low ebb; no major action could be contemplated.

The need for bases

Small actions towards the end of 1927 included the establishment of base areas in almost inaccessible places – Ching-kang-shan, the Tapieh Mountains, the Hung Lake region, north Szechwan, and the Left and

[75] HHLY 1, pt. 1, 164. On the role of the radical, educated people, see J. M. Polachek, 'The moral economy of the Kiangsi soviet (1928–1934)', JAS 42.4 (Aug. 1983) 805–29.

[76] Ch'ü Ch'iu-pai, 'Chung-kuo hsien-chuang yü Kung-ch'an-tang ti jen-wu' (The present situation in China and the tasks of the CCP), report at the November conference, in Hu Hua, 200–22.

[77] Yeh in HHLY 1, pt. 1, 196–7

[78] Hsiao Tso-liang, Power relations, 147–8.

Right Rivers of Kwangsi – where the rebels had security and could carry on the struggle.[79] But the revolutionaries had to ask: was it necessary to have a base area? Could they win peasants' support? What would be the future of the revolution from the purview of the mountain fastness?

At the beginning of the Ching-kang-shan soviet, Mao told his soldiers:

> While working for the revolution, we cannot simply run here and there. We must have a home; otherwise we will get into all sorts of difficulties. The base area is our home from which we carry on revolutionary struggles against the enemy. If he does not come, we train soldiers and mobilize the masses here; if he comes, we fight him from our home. We chew up or drive away our enemies bit by bit and our days will gradually improve.[80]

The truth is that the red soldiers and their party, engaged in building a base area, needed men and money which could be procured only by confiscating the property of the rich and distributing some of it to the poor. Afraid of reprisals, the poor peasants would not take part in land and property confiscation and redistribution, unless the shield of the Red Army was strong enough to protect them and give the new property system a measure of permanency. Once the new system became settled, the red regime could legitimately recruit soldiers and tax the people. In a sense this was similar to a warlord's satrapy, except that the warlord protected the gentry instead of the poor peasants. By having a sufficiently strong army to defend the new property system and the red regime, the party hoped to introduce social and economic changes with the effect of arousing the loyalty of the poor and oppressed. Mao and a few others like Fang Chih-min had faith in this strategy, while Chang Kuo-t'ao believed that the peasants, opportunistic and concerned only with their own survival, gave support to the Red Army only when the army was winning. In Chang's view, peasant mobilization hinged entirely on the CCP's military strength; it had nothing to do with the land policy.[81]

That the peasants were active and responsive enough to give their allegiance to the CCP as a result of land redistribution appears from another source of information and assessment – the missionaries and foreign journalists who had first-hand knowledge of the Communists in

[79] About the 'ecology' of the Chinese Communist success, see Roy Hofheinz's essay under that title in *Chinese Communist politics in action*, ed. A. Doak Barnett. In Hofheinz's essay quoted here and his earlier article on the Autumn Harvest uprisings (*CQ* 32), he overlooks the existence of peasant associations at Ching-kang-shan. In his report dated 25 November 1928 (*MTTC* 2.61), Mao referred to basic work of the party among the masses in Ching-kang-shan more than a year before his arrival there. About the foundation of the Ching-kang-shan base area, see the detailed discussion with the staff of the museum there on 7 and 8 July 1980, reported by Jerome Ch'en under the title 'Ideology and history' (xeroxed for circulation).

[80] Speech recorded by Huang Yung-shen in *HCPP* 13.8. See Mao's report on 25 November 1928 in *MTTC* 2.28 and 47–8.

[81] Chang in *Ming-pao*, 46.99.

Central China. As early as 1931 an article in the *Chinese Recorder* (a leading missionary journal) admitted that 'god-less as they were', the Communists had the 'support of millions of peasants and workers'.[82] Popular periodicals like the *China Weekly Review* (an American journal published in Shanghai) reported peasants' support of the Communists throughout 1933 and 1934.[83] When the Communists left for the Long March, Hallett Abend and A. J. Billingham inspected the areas formerly under Communist occupation, where they discovered that the peasants preferred the CCP to the KMT.[84] It was this support that enabled the red regimes to survive before the Long March and enabled the guerrilla areas to continue after it. It is curious that in discussing this problem scholars generally ignore the reports by foreign missionaries from Hunan, Kiangsi, Fukien and other provinces affected by the soviet movement.

As soon as the groundwork of the base area was laid, the revolutionaries had to choose between two long-range strategies. The first would be to give up the small base area in the mountains, whose economic resources were inadequate for a large-scale operation, and instead roam about the countryside fighting guerrilla warfare. This strategy would spread the political influence of the party through propaganda and economic dislocation until guerrillas were ready and able to seize power in a nation-wide insurrection. The second strategy would be to hold on to and expand the base area, while organizing and arming the masses, wave after wave outwardly. This would aim at enhancing the influence of the red regime in an orderly manner, benefiting the peasants at the same time, and hastening the arrival of a revolutionary upsurge.[85]

Following a pattern similar to that of Ching-kang-shan, the O-Yü-Wan, Hsiang-o-hsi, and a few other soviets emerged along the foothill regions of China between her highlands to the south and west and the plains to the north and east. The existence of soviets in this region and the unusually frequent civil wars, hence the concentration of troops there, suggest a correlation between the establishment of soviets and peasant misery, which deserves careful and systematic research. The civil wars and concentration of troops in this region in the 1910s and 1920s may have created a social and economic dislocation more severe than, say, on the plains of China. To study the plains, rather than this region, and to come to the conclusion that peasant misery had only marginal relevance to rebellion is like tasting chalk and rating it as cheese. By 1930 the thirteen

---

[82] *Chinese Recorder* 13 (June 1931) 468.
[83] See for instance, *China Weekly Review*, 22 July 1933, 18 November 1933 and 13 January 1934.
[84] Hallett Abend *et al. Can China survive?*, 238–9.
[85] Mao's letter to Lin Piao, 5 January 1930, in *MTTC* 2.128–9.

or so soviets probably had 300 counties under various degrees of Communist control or influence. The guerrilla bands that did not create soviets, such as those led by K'uang Chi-hsun in Szechwan between July and October 1929, vanished into oblivion.[86]

The rich peasant problem

The soviets set out to confiscate land and mobilize the poor peasants, a task usually allocated to revolutionary committees or village and district soviets, which were initially dominated by immigrant intellectuals from cities and towns.[87] This fact implied that a passive role was played by the politically inexperienced peasants and that party cells tended to overshadow the administrative organizations.[88] A period of six months was normally needed for the peasants to break through their passivity and scepticism, and thus involve themselves first in economic problems such as grain scarcity and taxation and then political matters such as the class struggle.[89] Once the wall of passivity was pulled down, the land revolution helped release the long pent-up hatred of the poor against the rich and inspired them to participate more actively in military and political work. To reach through to this peasant activism was the very essence of the land revolution. It is nonetheless an irony that the intellectual thinking of the CCP at that time paid scant attention to this process of politicization and activization of the poor peasants. All the while the party's attention and eulogies went to the urban proletariat, which was bogged down in economic struggles for more money and better working conditions, both issues of limited political significance.

The land policy of the CCP fell victim to the wrangling for power between Stalin and Bukharin. Based on Lenin's attitude towards the kulaks and the Russian experience that the kulaks exploited the masses even more cruelly and savagely than had the landlords, the CI instructed the CCP on 20 June 1929 to radicalize its policy toward rich peasants. Consequently, the Kiangsi soviet in February 1930 adopted a land law that stipulated the confiscation of all communal, landlords' and rich peasants' land; and the conference of the soviet areas held in May 1930 (without Mao Tse-tung)

[86] Hu Hua, *Chung-kuo hsin-min-chu chu-i ko-ming-shih ts'an-k'ao tzu-liao* (Historical materials on the Chinese new democratic revolution); hereafter *Materials*, 230. Estimates of the size, population and strength of the red armies vary widely. Indeed, even the concept of 'Communist occupation' requires stringent definition, as Hofheinz has pointed out (n. 79 above). Although K'uang lost his Szechwan soviet, his guerrilla activities continued in the border region between Szechwan, Hupei and Hunan, as frequently reported in the *Shih-pao* (The eastern times) of Shanghai.

[87] About the structure and functions of the soviet governments, see Lötveit, *Communism* and Kim, *Politics*.

[88] Mao's report of 25 November 1929 in *MTTC* 2.51-2.

[89] Po-ku (Ch'in Pang-hsien) related this experience to Snow, *Random notes*, 19.

advocated the confiscation of that part of rich peasants' land which was rented out to others to farm.[90]

Down at the soviet level the rich peasants presented a tough practical problem. When their vital interests were threatened, they obstructed the work of land redistribution. Trade between the base areas and the nearby towns was in their hands and they could stop this with dire consequences to the Communists. This experience was reflected in the Ching-kang-shan land law of December 1928.[91] Later the land law of Hsing-kuo, April 1929, adopted a milder attitude toward rich peasants.[92] Probably due to the same considerations, the rich peasants of the O-Yü-Wan soviet retained their land up to 1931. Neither the Hsiang-o-hsi nor Hsiang-kan soviet pursued a rigorous policy towards rich peasants.[93]

When the 28 Bolsheviks took power at the party centre, the rich peasant issue sharpened. Mao's way of curbing the influence of the rich peasants by taking away their 'surplus land' (*ch'ou-to pu-shao*) in the first land redistribution and by taking away their 'good land' (*ch'ou-fei pu-shou*) in the second redistribution,[94] without violating the principle of equality, came under fire at the fourth plenum in January 1931.[95] He was directed to change his policy by the centre's letter dated 1 September 1931. To be sure, the rich peasant question formed an important link in the centre's class line which was deemed essential to mobilizing the poor masses. What the centre wanted was to give only poor land to the rich peasants while no compensation was to be considered for the landlords. Theoretically, Mao did not regard all rich peasants as exploiters. They could be semi-landlords or semi-capitalists, but they could also be merely potential exploiters.[96] The 28 Bolsheviks, on the other hand, defined rich peasants as those who 'before the revolution, rented a part of their land, loaned money at usurious rates of interest, and usually hired labour'. They were

---

[90] On the CI directive, see *Hung-se wen-hsien*, 324–7 and Thornton, *Comintern*, 87–91. This and other directives of the CI, contrary to Thornton's impression, are couched in vague terms. The kulak problem, this particular instruction says, could be relegated to a secondary position when the war against imperialists and reactionaries became embittered. It was probably on this qualification that Li Li-san reversed his land policy in the summer of 1930. For texts of these laws see Wang Chien-min, *Draft history*, 2.357–61. But it would be wrong to say that Li Li-san's land law of May 1930 represented a sharp turn towards a radical policy against the rich peasants. As it did not insist upon the liquidation of the kulaks, it stood to the right of the CI instructions.

[91] *MTTC* 2.67–9 and also 47 and 56.

[92] *Ibid.* 2.73–5 and 179–84.

[93] Wang Chien-min, *Draft history*, 2.191–2 and 245–8; *HHLY* 2.99–100.

[94] Ho Kan-chih, *Chung-kuo hsien-tai ko-ming shih* (History of the modern Chinese revolution), 1.143. The Chinese edition of this book is far superior to its English translation published in 1960.

[95] *Hung-se wen-hsien*, 236.

[96] Resolution no. 2 adopted by the Joint Meeting of the Front Committee and the Western Fukien Special Committee, June 1930 in Hsiao Tso-liang, *The land revolution in China, 1930–1934: a study of documents*, 153–5.

thus plainly exploiters.[97] To treat them leniently was to blur the class line or to abandon class struggle altogether.[98]

The difference between taking away a part of the 'good land' of a rich peasant and giving him only 'poor land' might seem trivial. Certain facts, however, should be borne in mind. First, the expansion of soviet areas to include cities and towns and the growth of a trading system under the soviet government or in the form of cooperatives drastically reduced the mercantile function of the rich peasants, whose interests could be impaired for the sake of mobilizing the masses. Second, the rich peasants, making use of clan associations to conceal their actual land holdings, prevented the land revolution from being carried out thoroughly. This became evident during the land investigation campaign of 1933. Third, they leased land from the orphaned or the widowed, the aged or the young, because they had more able-bodied men in their families, more farming animals, more tools, and more liquid capital. Fourth, by falsifying their class category, they could infiltrate and take control of the poor peasants' corps, cooperatives and other mass organizations to make the land revolution and mass mobilization in some places a farce.[99] Therefore from 1931 onward, the land laws of the newly established Soviet Republic of China accepted the class line of the 28 Bolsheviks by distributing only poor land to rich peasants while confiscating their surplus tools, livestock and houses.[100] To what extent this new anti-kulak line was implemented cannot be ascertained. In O-Yü-Wan, Chang Kuo-t'ao accepted this line and seems to have pushed the policy of the First Congress of the Soviet Republic (held in November 1931) with vigour.[101] After the transfer of his soviet to north Szechwan in 1933, Chang and his comrades intensified their drive against rich peasants. Elsewhere, the new line was carried out only half-heartedly.[102] It was to accelerate the struggle against rich peasants that the land investigation campaign was launched.

---

[97] Centre's letter, 10 January 1932 in Wang Chien-min, *Draft history*, 2.508.

[98] Hsiao Tso-liang, *Land revolution*, 49.

[99] *MTTC* 2.166–7; Wang Chien-min, *Draft history*, 2.508.

[100] *MTTC* 2.259–62; Ts'ao Po-i, *Soviet*, 192–3 and 495; Hsiao Tso-liang, *Land revolution*, 53. Land transactions, however, were allowed in Wang Ming's 'Two lines' (*Hsuan-chi*, 3.61). According to the land policy of the First Congress of the Soviet Republic, landlords and rich peasants were not permitted to purchase land. Slightly later, notice no. 2 issued by the Central Revolutionary Military Commission gave rich peasants the right to buy or sell land but they were not allowed to do it in a monopolistic fashion. The questions are: who was actually buying and selling land in the soviet areas and who had the money to buy? See *MTTC* 2.262.

[101] *Ming-pao* 40.98; Wang Chien-min, *Draft history*, 2.245.

[102] For experiences in Hsiang-o-hsi and Hsiang-kan, see Wang Chien-min, *Draft history*, 2.245 and 249–51; *HHLY* 2.99.

The land investigation

Precisely who was responsible for launching this campaign is not easy to say. For a work of this magnitude and importance it is inconceivable that the party centre had no part in the decision, and without involving the entire structure of the soviet government it is doubtful that the decision could be implemented. The party centre in 1933 was firmly in the hands of the 28 Bolsheviks, and yet no one is sure to what extent the influence of the centre reached down to the grass roots. On the other hand, before 1934 Mao was still the dominant figure in the government with his prestige riding high among the masses. In all probability, the campaign began as a joint effort using the authority of the party and the prestige of Mao, a combination of the class line and mass line.[103] In the first phase of the campaign, between June and September 1933, it was obvious that Mao was responsible. Then in October the party centre stepped in to announce its new policy, which interrupted, and for a time suspended the movement till the convocation of the Second Congress of the Soviet Republic held in January-February 1934. Thereafter Chang Wen-t'ien, as the chairman of the People's Commissariat, took it over.[104]

The military situation at the end of the fourth KMT encirclement, when the campaign began, was favourable to the CCP, although food had become a serious problem. Since March 1933 a series of measures had been taken to counteract the KMT blockade – such as setting up a Food Board (Liang-shih t'iao-chieh chü), investigating the supply of foodstuff in the counties, and the prohibition of cornering grain by merchants.[105] Because they were otherwise preoccupied, the soviet government also encouraged the masses to help officials and cadres farm their shares of land.[106] Finally, the land investigation campaign was decreed.[107] Its main purpose was not to redistribute land again, unless the masses demanded it; rather it was to investigate the class background of as many people as possible without affecting production.[108] It was hoped that in this way the hidden counter-revolutionaries and feudal elements could be ferreted out and at the same time the enthusiasm of the masses could be heightened in order to consolidate the defence of the soviet area against the forthcoming fifth encirclement. Take the poor peasants' corps, for instance. In some places

---

[103] Warren Kuo, *History*, 2.409–12; Ts'ao Po-i, *Soviet*, 203–5; Lötveit, 154–84.
[104] For instance, all the directives on the land investigation were now issued by Chang Wen-t'ien.
[105] Directive of the Central People's Commissariat, 4 March 1933 in *MTTC* 3.195–6 and 3.195–6.
[106] Directive of the Central Executive Committee, 14 April 1933, *MTTC* 3.207–8.
[107] Directive of the Central People's Commissariat, 1 June 1933, *MTTC* 3.223ff.
[108] *MTTC* 3.254.

they existed in name only and in other places they had not even been organized until after the campaign was in progress.[109]

Class categorization was obviously a vital but complex problem, especially when it came to deciding who were the kulaks and who were the rich middle peasants. According to Mao's definition, given on 29 June 1933,

The rich peasant as a rule owns land. But some rich peasants own only part of their land and rent the remainder. Others have no land of their own at all and rent all their land. The rich peasant generally has rather more and better instruments of production and more liquid capital than the average and is engaged in labour himself, but always relies on exploitation for part or even the major part of his income. His main form of exploitation is the hiring of labour (long-term labourers). In addition, he may lease part of his land and practise exploitation through land rent, or may lend money or engage in industry and commerce. Most rich peasants also engage in the administration of communal land. A person who owns a fair amount of good land, farms some of it himself without hiring labour, but exploits other peasants by means of land rent, loan interest or in other ways, shall also be treated as a rich peasant. Rich peasants regularly practise exploitation and may derive most of their income from this source.[110]

One can imagine that such a complex definition was difficult to apply. Indeed, the second resolution of the party centre on 8 August 1933 noted the confusion caused by this definition.[111] Subsequently the People's Commissariat took it upon itself to discuss some of the problems arising from the land struggle. A rich peasant was redefined as one whose exploitative income amounted to more than 15 per cent of the total. With this new definition there was the need for a reinvestigation and re-categorization. In Sheng-li county alone, 1,512 households out of 3,125 were changed from landlords or rich peasants to middle or poor peasants; the investigation of class background thus dwindled into a calculation of class background. The situation became an unholy chaos.[112]

If Mao's statistics are to be trusted, the campaign up to September 1933 had succeeded in recovering 307,539 piculs of land (land was measured by its yield in some parts of Kiangsi) and confiscated property worth Y606,916. He also reported that in some counties production had increased by 15–20 per cent from 1932 to 1933.[113] To put these figures in their proper perspective, note that the soviet government floated a public loan of Y3 million in July 1933, issued Y10 million of currency in 1933–34,

---

[109] MTTC 3.223 and 257; Tou-cheng, 24 May 1934; Wang Kuan-lan in HHLY 2.211.
[110] Mao, SW 1.138.
[111] Ts'ao Po-i, Soviet, 211–12.
[112] Tou-cheng, 26 May 1934; Chang Wen-t'ien's directive in Red China, 15 March 1934.
[113] Red China, Second Soviet Congress Supplement, 26 January 1934.

and borrowed 600,000 piculs of grain from the people in July 1933.[114] As an economic measure, the land investigation campaign cannot be described as a seminal success.

When it was resumed in January 1934, the aims of the campaign were no longer principally economic, not even for the food supply to the Red Army, but political. It became a campaign against counter-revolutionaries, a red terror against landlords and rich peasants.[115] As such, it was pursued till the collapse of the central soviet.

The Red Army

The struggle in the border area, as Mao put it, 'is exclusively military'.[116] But since the failure of the Autumn Harvest uprisings followed by the reorganization of his troops at San-wan on his way to Ching-kang-shan, Mao, like the other creators of border areas, had under his command former KMT officers and men who had radical intellectuals as their political officers. At Ching-kang-shan these mercenaries were joined with riff-raff (or the lumpen-proletariat, *yu-min fen-tzu*), who were excellent fighters but totally unruly and unaware of the political purposes of the revolution. The poor peasants looked on, reluctant to take part in whatever they were doing.[117]

In April 1928, Chu Teh and his followers came; they too were former KMT troops. In fact, mutinies of KMT armies seem to have been an important source of recruitment for the Red Army in 1928 and 1929. In the first place, the KMT armies were poorly paid and inhumanly treated by their officers and, second, the jealousies and rivalries among KMT officers could often be exploited by the Communists.[118] In July 1928 two KMT officers, P'eng Te-huai and Huang Kung-lueh, brought their troops over to Mao and a year later there were the mutinies of Lo Ping-hui's army in Kian and K'uang Chi-hsun's in Szechwan.[119] By 1930, however, the peasants showed their readiness to join and some of them were even promoted to officers.[120] This was probably why among the middle-ranking officers of the Fourth Front Army very few could read and write.[121] In

[114] Ts'ao Po-i, *Soviet*, 360 and 368; *Red China*, 26 July 1934.
[115] Chang Wen-t'ien's article in *Red China*, 25 June 1934; Hsiao Tso-liang, *Land revolution*, 285.
[116] Mao, *SW* 1.80.
[117] Mao's report, 25 October 1928 in *MTTC* 2.37; Lo Jung-huan in *HHLY* 1, pt. 1, 139–40; *HCPP* 1.57–9.
[118] *HHLY* 1, pt. 2, 465–70.
[119] Fang Ch'iang in *HHLY* 1, pt. 2, 431–6: *HCPP* 10.186; Snow, *Red star*, 273; Agnes Smedley, *The great road: the life and times of Chu Teh*, 270.
[120] *HCPP* 1.57–9.
[121] Ch'en Hsi-lien in *HCPP* 3.90.

the spring of 1934 the class composition of the First Front Army showed 30 per cent workers and 68 per cent peasants, the majority of whom (no less than 77 per cent) came from the central soviet itself, while KMT deserters and mutineers accounted for no more than 4 per cent.[122]

To make the Red Armies different from those of warlords and the KMT, political training had first priority. Many of the erroneous tendencies listed in the Ku-t'ien resolutions of December 1929 drafted by Mao can be summed up as a lack of discipline, an unawareness of the political goals of the revolution, and an ignorance of the tasks of the Red Army – combat, financing itself, and mass mobilization. Political training required that the Red Army set up a dual system of organization to take charge of strategic command and political work. By a curious coincidence, at the very time when the Red Army introduced its soldiers' committees (*shih-ping wei-yuan-hui*), Chiang Kai-shek abolished political commissars in his army. The soldiers' committees ensured a measure of democracy in the Red Army so that the men would not be treated like animals by their superiors.[123] There were also political officers whose duties were not clearly defined; hence their functions were not firmly delineated till the Ku-t'ien conference. Their main job was to help the Red Army mobilize the masses and set up new regimes.[124] In addition to these, the party representatives (*tang tai-piao*) organized a cell in each squad and a branch in each company, for at Mao's insistence the optimum ratio between party and non-party members in the army had to be one to three. In fact, the ratio in 1934 was 28 per cent to 72.[125] The command and political systems were separate, with independent revenues and a similar ranking system; they had well-developed channels of communication between them. Within the political system, the General Political Department, established in February 1931, controlled both the political officers and the party representatives (now called political delegates, *cheng-chih wei-yuan*) of various ranks, but a party representative of a given rank always took precedence over a political officer of the same rank.[126] In neither of the two systems were salary differences instituted. Everyone in the army, regardless of his rank, received the same pay and shared the same style of life.[127] In battle and in keeping law and order, the army was assisted by the Red Guards and peasant self-defence forces.[128] An army so trained naturally differed considerably from the other troops in China of the same

---

[122] *Ti-erh-tz'u kuo-nei ko-ming chan-cheng shih-ch'i shih-shih lun-ts'ung* (Discourses on the history of the second revolutionary war period), 63–4.
[123] Lo Jung-huan in *HHLY* 1, pt. 1, 139–40.
[124] The Ku-t'ien resolutions in *MTTC* 2.123–4.
[125] Lo Jung-huan, *ibid.* 140.   [126] *MTTC* 2.124 and 253–4.
[127] Mao, *SW* 1.81.   [128] *Ibid.* 85–6.

period. Apart from the Fu-t'ien incident of December 1930, when a Red Army unit mutinied and was suppressed with many hundreds of executions, the Red Army had not fought an internecine battle; seldom did it feel the need to quell peasant hostility towards it. With the party wielding all the ideological authority and political officers holding the purse strings, the Red Army was always dominated by the party. It was a politicized army supported by the masses.

The mass line permeated the Red Army, which was repeatedly reminded of the three disciplines and the eight points of attention worked out by Mao and his colleagues, so that soldiers would not alienate the masses for whom they fought. They propagandized and protected the people, and also helped in productive work. Cementing their relations with the people this way, they could be sure of reliable information on enemy movements, and in defeat they could depend on the people to hide them in safety. This mutual dependence became more important after the evacuation of the First Front Army on the Long March in October 1934 when only small guerrilla bands were left behind to harass the KMT armies.[129]

According to various estimates, the Red Army became better organized under Li Li-san's leadership, and had some 50,000 men in 1930. This was to grow to over 100,000 in 1931, 200,000 in 1932, and 500,000 in 1933. The two most significant reorganizations came before and after Li Li-san's adventure in 1930. Before the summer of that year, the army was reorganized into army corps and, after that, the front armies came into existence. In spite of regrouping in July-August 1935, the front armies continued in this way till their reorganization into the Eight Route Army of three divisions of 1937 and the New Fourth Army in 1938.[130]

THE SEARCH FOR A STRATEGY

Created at the low ebb of the revolution in 1927, the Red Army was considered an important instrument for the CCP's seizing power, even for hastening the arrival of the revolutionary 'high tide' expected in the near future. But nowhere in the political resolutions of the Sixth Congress of 1928 was it stated that military struggle had now become the central form of struggle and the army the deciding factor of victory. The next upsurge was believed to depend on a host of external and internal factors, perhaps even more important than the army.

---

[129] *HHLY* 1, pt. 1, 309–10 and 2.145–8; Smedley, *Great road*, 237.
[130] Tang Leang-li, *Suppressing communist bandits in China*, 99–100; Hollington Tong, *Chiang Tsung-t'ung chuan* (A biography of President Chiang), 1.203.

Stalin's coinage of 'the revolutionary tide', vague as it was, had a leftist bias built into it. To admit the ebbing of the tide without in the same breath asserting it would rise again, in the context of a strong prejudice against right opportunism, would be tantamount to 'liquidationism'. In the spirit of the resolutions of the Sixth Congress, the tide would rise next when the labour movement increased its scope and intensity, the imperialists threatened to disturb the peace of the Pacific, the ruling cliques in China engaged themselves in more ferocious fighting, and the guerrilla war conducted by the Red Army spread further.[131] The resolutions repeatedly stressed the unevenness of the revolutionary situation in China, which would condition the tide to rise unevenly in different areas and different sectors of society. As long as it remained uneven, a nationwide revolutionary situation did not exist. As to when the tide would rise and the upsurge inundate a part or the entirety of the country, no one could tell with precision.

The Li Li-san line

In the second half of 1929 frequent civil wars, worsened intra-party feuds in the KMT, and the Wall Street crash gave the CI reasons for describing the Chinese national crisis as 'deepening' and to blame the CCP for 'lagging behind the growth of mass discontent'.[132] It may be a mistake to interpret this as the CI's call to action;[133] nonetheless it did encourage Li Li-san to shake off his earlier pessimism and to assess the situation with over-optimism. He went on to design his military strategy, which formed the kernel of the so-called Li Li-san line. By early summer 1930, the CI adjudged the high tide in China 'an undeniable fact', though still uneven: 'The direction of recent events is such that if the revolutionary situation cannot embrace the entire territory of China, at least it will cover several important provinces in the very near future.' Under such circumstances the CCP should prepare for the imminence of a war of liberation and the most deadly error would be a right-opportunist tendency.[134]

Thus radicalized by the ambiguous directives of the CI, Li began to exploit the deteriorating economic depression abroad and military disorder at home. Heartened, Li Li-san went even as far as to assert that the outcome of a revolution was not decided by the political forces involved in it but by the tasks to be accomplished. Therefore the bourgeois

---

[131] *Hung-se wen-hsien*, 152–3 and 166.
[132] ECCI to CCP, either 26 October 1929 (*Hung-se wen-hsien*, 334 and 340) or alternatively late December 1929.
[133] Brandt *et al. Documentary history*, 180.
[134] ECCI to CCP, 23 July 1930 (or in June 1930), *Hung-se wen-hsien*, 346–55.

revolution in China could be led by the proletariat. As soon as the proletariat took power and introduced its leadership, the transition to the socialist stage of the revolution could begin. 'There is no need to wait for the conquest of the whole country before the transition. To do so is to commit rightist deviation.'[135] In the vitally important resolution on the new revolutionary high tide and preliminary victory in one or more provinces adopted by the CCP Politburo in 11 June 1930, the call for a preliminary victory did not mean a prolonged war to defend the CCP's occupation of one or more provinces. To seize power in one or more 'important provinces', including key administrative or industrial cities, except in the north-east and south-west, would inevitably threaten the security of the central government and trigger a death duel between the government and the rebellion till one of the belligerents was destroyed.[136] Hence a durable local regime was unlikely; hence the unevenness of the situation would be quickly made even. This is then not a question of Li Li-san's denial of the unevenness; to him the question was how soon the unevenness could be transmuted into evenness. After all, the CI's letter of June or July 1930 did refer to a decisive war in the nearest future and a swifter transition from the bourgeois to socialist revolution in China than had occurred in Russia.[137] The vagueness of the CI's assessment of the situation and its policy proposals on the one hand reflected a lack of clear thinking on the part of the CI and on the other allowed Li Li-san ample room for his own interpretation.[138]

To be sure, Li had refrained from giving military instructions to the soviet leaders for several months after his assumption of power in the summer of 1928.[139] This was perhaps because at the beginning of his leadership he was touched by a streak of pessimism about the future of the revolution. He did not begin to develop his military strategy until the second half of 1929.[140] Insisting on urban leadership and dismissing the idea of depending on the Red Army alone for victory as 'a serious error',[141] Li thought that the key to a preliminary victory in one or more provinces (a goal agreed upon at the Sixth Congress) lay in the workers'

135 Li Li-san, *Fan-t'o* (Anti-Trotsky), 9; see also Mao's comment on this in *HC* 3.982.
136 Wang Chien-min, *Draft history*, 2.42–51; Hsiao Tso-liang, *Power relations*, 22ff.
137 *Hung-se wen-hsien*, 355 and 358. The date of this letter is given vaguely as June 1930 (see A. M. Grigoriev's article in L. P. Deliusin, ed. *Komintern i vostok*, 334–5). These different dates do not help to decide whether the letter was a response to the CCP's strategic plan before or after the momentous Politburo meeting on 11 June 1930.
138 See for instance, Kuusinen's report at the 10th plenum of ECCI, and L. Magyar's article in *International Press Correspondence*, 5.40 (20 August 1929) and 10.18 (10 April 1930), respectively.
139 Kiangsu Provincial Committee's comments on the centre's work in *Chung-kung ti cheng-chih kung-tso*, 1.166–7.
140 Mao, *SW* 3.998.
141 *Hung-ch'i* (Red flag), 29 March 1930; *Chung-yang t'ung-hsin*, 15 (8 November 1928).

struggles in the big cities with the support of the Red Army, peasants' uprisings, and mutinies of KMT troops. The ripening of the revolutionary situation would be signalled by an outburst of workers' struggles. In other words, in February 1930 Li visualized that the workers would start their strikes and armed insurrections, while the Red Army marched on the cities to give them support.[142] Once a preliminary victory was won in one or more provinces, the uneven situation would soon become even enough for the CCP to seize national power. At this stage of Li's strategic plan the target city was Wuhan, and the plan was translated into a letter to the secretary of the Front Committee of the Fourth Red Army on 3 April 1930, directing the army to march along the Kan River towards the riverine city, Kiukiang, and take it.[143]

The army's supporting role was to be fulfilled not by waging guerrilla warfare but by attacking large cities and disrupting the transport lines of the KMT armies. According to the Politburo resolution on 11 June 1930, the army was to capture such administrative centres and medium-sized cities as Changsha, Nanchang, Kiukiang, Shashih and Huang-p'i before its final assault on Wuhan.[144]

The CI, on the other hand, had never spelt out a strategic plan of its own, let alone a programme for action, in its directives to the CCP in February, June, and October or December 1929. Even its directive or letter of June or July 1930 to the Chinese party, perhaps prompted by an uneasy feeling over Li's writings and the Politburo's resolutions in the spring, said no more than that 'Attention must be focused on the organization and strengthening of a Red Army so that one or more industrial and administrative *key cities* can be occupied according to the political and military circumstances *in the future*'.[145] Insofar as the capture of the key cities was concerned, the CI and Li did not differ; as to how such cities could be taken, the CI suggested no strategy; as to the ripening of the revolutionary circumstances, the CI was vague; the meaning of 'the future' was anyone's guess. The uncertainties had presumably to be ascertained by the leaders on the spot, the commanders in the field. This was precisely what Li did when he worked out his programme for action once the uncertainties were made certain. This was why CI's official organ, the *International Press Correspondence*, in its issue on 7 August 1930, could rejoice and praise Li's ephemeral success in capturing Changsha.

From the perspective of a leader of the party centre, urban struggles

[142] *Chung-yang t'ung-hsin*, 70 (26 February 1930).
[143] Hsiao Tso-liang, *Power relations*, 15.
[144] *Hung-ch'i* (Red flag), 16 August 1930.
[145] Benjamin I. Schwartz, *Chinese communism and the rise of Mao*, 143. My italics.

and the capture of cities doctrinally and practically looked larger and more decisive than the guerrilla activities in the widely scattered mountain fastnesses. But from the perspective of the guerrilla leaders, the preservation of their base areas was a life-and-death concern. Even before the collapse of the first united front, Mao had already come to the conclusion that the peasant question was the central issue of the Chinese revolution.[146] The progress around the Ching-kang-shan base that he and his comrades had made in 1928 renewed their confidence in the future of the revolution. Mao had no fear of the peasants' struggle outstripping the workers' struggles.[147] Nonetheless he realized that the struggle was arduous and protracted, for the rule of the landlords and warlords, unlike that of a handful of capitalists of a few key cities, permeated the vastness of rural China.[148] The struggle was directed at the heart and brain, not merely the limbs, of that 'feudal' regime. Based on his gains in 1928 and early 1929, Mao could optimistically forecast at the Juichin Conference on 18 May 1929 that within a year it would be possible for the Red Army under his command to occupy the province of Kiangsi.

At the beginning of 1930, when he wrote his famous letter to Lin Piao,[149] Mao not only corrected his earlier hastiness but also defined his strategy of concentrating armed forces to capture counties, expand red areas in order to spread the political influence of the party and army, and speed up the arrival of the high tide. Kiangsi remained his goal, and that was what he understood by a preliminary victory in one or more provinces which would give the CCP a solid local regime as the basis for future expansion. As to urban struggles, it was time for rallying the masses around the party, not time yet for armed insurrection. In his analysis of the situation, Mao paid almost no attention to either the world economic depression or the larger conflicts among China's military cliques. In any case he was against the dispersal of his troops and their dispatch to take distant cities like Changsha.[150]

Reluctantly Mao accepted Li Li-san's orders to be a part of Li's plan. He tried to take Nanchang at the end of July 1930 when P'eng Te-huai's Third Army Corps occupied Changsha, but was repulsed by the garrison of the city. In less than ten days P'eng had to evacuate the capital of Hunan. Then came the second assault on Changsha, with the combined forces of Mao and P'eng, from 1 September to the 13th. Seeing it as a hopeless struggle, Mao persuaded his comrades to retreat and direct their resources

---

[146] MTTC 1.175.
[147] Ibid. 2.133.
[148] Ibid. 2.59 and 128.
[149] Ibid. 2.135 and 139.
[150] Mao, SW 1.54 and 61.

to the rebuilding and expansion of soviet base areas.[151] In Mao's view Li's strategic directives in the summer of 1930 read like fiction.[152]

Wang Ming's 'two lines'

The defeat of the Li Li-san line was to be followed by a series of encirclement campaigns by Chiang Kai-shek against the soviet areas. But CCP thinking was on an entirely different course. The theoretical framework of the CCP's strategy in this period was laid out in Wang Ming's famous pamphlet, *The two lines* (*Liang-t'iao lu-hsien*), of July 1931 which made much of the crisis of postwar capitalism in its third stage of development, when the contradictions among imperialist powers became increasingly acute.[153] As if to give support to this thesis, the Japanese Kwantung army seized Manchuria after 18 September 1931. Suddenly the anti-imperialist struggle took precedence over the anti-feudal struggle. The Japanese invasion of Shanghai in January 1932 inevitably involved the proletariat there, though to an unascertainable extent, giving the 28 Bolsheviks a gleam of hope of taking the revolution back to the cities. The anti-imperialist thesis and the strategy of urban revolution were to remain the consistent policies of the 28 Bolsheviks throughout the first half of the 1930s, up to the formation of the second united front in 1937.

Under their leadership the strategy still aimed at winning a preliminary victory in one or more provinces, with the Red Army of the rural soviets now their sole weapon. The first stage of this strategy was to consolidate and coordinate the existing and new soviet areas. Only when this was accomplished would the CCP fight for national power in the second stage.[154] The anti-Japanese high tide after September 1931 gave the 28 Bolsheviks fresh hopes, and their strategic plan, the 'Resolution on winning a preliminary victory in one or more provinces' of 9 January 1932, once again contemplated the possibility of capturing key cities. 'What used to be the correct strategy of refusing to take big cities does not hold true any more.'[155] South of the Yangtze all the soviet areas should try to link up with the central soviet, while north of the river they should do likewise, with the O-Yü-Wan soviet as the centre. By this consolidation and coordination the Red Army could in the near future march on Nanchang, Foochow and Kian, while the army north of the Yangtze

---

[151] Mao, *SW* 3.1020, no. 4; Smedley, *Great road*, 278–9; Jerome Ch'en, *Mao*, 156–9. The second attack on Changsha was not ordered by the CI. See Harrison's article on Li Li-san, *CQ* 14.187 and Wang Ming, *Hsuan-chi*, 3.75.   [152] Wang Ming, *Hsuan-chi*, 3.56.

[153] *Ibid.* 246–69.   [154] *Ibid.* 50 and 74.

[155] *Shih-hua* (Honest words), 3 (20 April 1932).

would threaten the security of Wuhan, the Peking-Hankow railway, and transport on the Yangtze. To do this the Red Army could not just wait for the enemy to attack, lure him into the soviet area, and then destroy him. Such a tactic was criticized as designed by 'a country scholar', not by a Marxist revolutionary.[156] Chou En-lai himself showed an intense distrust of it in his well-known Shao-shan report of 1931. The party's directive to the soviet leaders dated 1 September 1931 also regarded guerrilla tactics as of only secondary, supplementary importance. The Red Army must be trained differently under a unified political and military leadership and made fit for positional warfare, so that victories in one or more provinces could be won.[157]

A new strategy required a new army leadership. At the Ningtu Conference of the central bureau of the soviet areas in August 1932 Chou En-lai replaced Mao as the political commissar of the First Front Army and later was made the political commissar of the Red Army as a whole.[158]

DESTRUCTION OF THE SOVIETS

Chiang Kai-shek's first three encirclement campaigns (in late 1931 and 1932) were fought while Mao was still firmly in the military saddle. Grossly belittling the strength and skill of the Red Army and unaware of the importance of mass political work, Chiang tried to kill two birds with one stone by pitching a motley of warlord troops against the Communists in a war of attrition. These 'expatriate' armies, unfamiliar with local conditions, were easily enticed into the soviet area and defeated.[159] The Red Army, on the other hand, relied on the speed of their movement and mass support, 'usually moving at night' and 'appearing suddenly and disappearing quickly', in a situation best described by the KMT's official history of the 'suppression of the bandits':

When the National Armies advanced into an area, they found very few people there. The old and sick left behind were controlled by the bandits' underground

[156] Liu Po-ch'eng in *Ko-ming yü chan-cheng* (Revolution and war), 1 (1 August 1932).
[157] Chou En-lai in *Hung-hsing* (Red star), 4 (27 August 1933); Wang Ming, *Hsuan-chi*, 3.74.
[158] Warren Kuo, *History*, 2.345–8. In place of the generally held view that Mao and the 28 Bolsheviks with Chou En-lai's support waged a power struggle between them, I. J. Kim (*Politics*) advances the theory of 'division of labour' with Mao concentrating on the government, Ch'in Pang-hsien on the party, and Chou on the army work, to form a collective leadership. Kim's basic hypothesis is that the 28 Bolsheviks, having no real power base, only theoretical articulation, did not dare to challenge the military leaders, including Mao. With almost no documentary evidence to support it, Kim's thesis seems unacceptable. See the analysis of personnel and their roles in Lötveit, *Communism*, 86–97.
[159] *Chiao-fei chan-shih* admits this point of inadequacy, 1.93–4; T'ang Sheng-chih and Sun Fo also criticized this intention of Chiang's: see Sun Fo *et al. T'ao Chiang yen-lun-chi* (Anti-Chiang messages), 41 and 133. See also Tang Leang-li, *Bandits*, 42.

organization and therefore would not dare to talk with the government troops. Sometimes they even helped the bandits by hindering the advance of the troops... The National Armies had very little knowledge of the conditions of the bandits.[160]

A similar pattern occurred in the second encirclement campaign (May-June 1932) during which the Communists' mass work showed a remarkable progress. The KMT's official history complained that 'the bandits carried away both men and grain with them'; that people destroyed bridges behind the government troops, denied information to them, and even ambushed them; that the people harassed the supply lines of the government troops to such a degree as to require a full regiment to protect government messengers and quartermasters.[161]

Chiang realized now that he was dealing with a tough enemy. He set up his headquarters in Nanchang and deployed his own crack troops, thus relegating the 'miscellaneous' forces to a supporting role in the third campaign (July-October 1932). Under the able command of General Ch'en Ch'eng, whose quality even Mao admitted,[162] to the chagrin of the Communists, the government troops penetrated deeply into the soviet area. At the same time Chiang became aware of the non-existence of a civil government structure below the county level, so that he had no way of collecting reliable intelligence about the Communists. He also made a beginning in his type of mass work by forbidding the press-ganging of porters and orderlies.[163] But the crisis in relations with Japan, intensifying after the 'Mukden incident' on 18 September 1931, eventually forced Chiang to wind up the third campaign quite abruptly. In the respite, the CCP reviewed the war situation and questioned Mao's strategy of luring the enemy deep into the soviet area before destroying him. As a result, in the summer of 1932, after Ho Lung's soviet in the Hung Lake area was overrun by the KMT troops, Chou En-lai replaced Mao.[164]

When the national crisis with Japan subsided, Chiang resumed his efforts to 'achieve internal peace before dealing with the foreign foe' by launching in 1933 the fourth encirclement campaign. But the Red Armies continued to be elusive, with a speed that 'tired the government troops out in chasing them'. Their mass work had now reached a point that government troops 'had no one to use, thus making us both blind and deaf'.[165] This was the war situation around the central soviet. In O-Yü-Wan

---

[160] *Chiao-fei chan-shih*, 1.107–14.
[161] *Ibid.* 1.128–44.
[162] Mao, *SW* 1.222.
[163] *Chiao-fei chan-shih*, 1.154–67.
[164] Ho Lung attributed the loss to Hsia Hsi's 'mountain top-ism'; see Miao Ch'u-huang, *Chung-kuo Kung-ch'an-tang chien-yao li-shih* (A brief history of the CCP), 90.
[165] *Chiao-fei chan-shih*, 2.170 and 239; Ts'ai T'ing-k'ai remarked in his *Tzu-chuan* (Autobiography), 1.375 that having been converted to communism, the people became united and happy.

the mass work, though well done, tended to become inert and disappear whenever the Fourth Front Army had suffered a reverse and retreated.[166] With Chiang in personal command of the campaign since May 1932, the O-Yü-Wan soviet was destroyed in September, forcing Chang Kuo-t'ao and Hsu Hsiang-ch'ien to go on what might be described as their first long march to north Szechwan. There the fighting between the 24th and 29th Armies of the province gave the Fourth Front Army a chance to set up a new soviet.[167]

Chiang's fifth campaign

Thus at the beginning of the fifth campaign in late 1933 the central soviet had lost the support of both O-Yü-Wan and Hsiang-o-hsi, although Ho Lung was creating another soviet in the north-west of Hunan and there were still the smaller and weaker soviets of Fang Chih-min on the Hunan-Kiangsi border and Hsiao K'o at the old Ching-kang-shan base. Chiang, taking a leaf from his enemy's book, now ascribed greater importance to political work and altered his strategy. In the political sphere he prepared the ground by organizing an officers' training course in the summer of 1933; some 7,000 army cadres took the course. Then he militarized the administration, economy, and social and educational work around the central soviet area, so that the KMT government, party and army cooperated in an all-out effort to defeat the Communists. At the grass roots he gave help to the spring sowing of 1934 and revived the collective security system known as *pao-chia*.[168] People living around the soviet were forced to move into what were prototype 'strategic hamlets' and put under the *pao-chia* so as to create a ring of no-man's-land, intended to blockade and starve the Communists.[169] A road-building programme was initiated, employing 20,000 workers to construct 700 miles of motor roads in order to increase the mobility of Chiang's armies, while wireless apparatus, telephones and aeroplanes were extensively used to achieve better coordination among his army units. While all this was being done Chiang's troops advanced steadily and slowly, lining their routes of penetration with blockhouses. In other words, this was a strategic offensive coupled with tactically defensive warfare, which rendered Mao's

[166] On the mass work of the Fourth Front Army, see *Chiao-fei chan-shih*, 3.467 and 4.683–5.
[167] For the creation of a new soviet by the Fourth Front Army, see *ibid.*, 4.519 and Wang Chien-min, *Draft history*, 2.207–11.
[168] Much of the information used here comes from *Chiao-fei chan-shih*, 2 and 3 *passim* and Tang Leang-li, *Bandits, passim*.
[169] Liu Pei-shan in *Chung-kuo Kung-ch'an-tang tsai Chiang-hsi ti-ch'ü ling-tao ko-ming tou-cheng ti li-shih tzu-liao* (Historical material concerning the revolutionary struggles led by the CCP in Kiangsi), 1.188.

old strategy of luring the enemy into the soviet area obsolete. 'There was no need to seek out the main force of the bandits. We only have to occupy strategic places where the bandits must come out and fight.' This was Chiang's directive on 17 October 1933. In this way the Red Army was forced from offensive mobile warfare to defensive positional warfare. Ironically, Chiang described his strategy as that of the foolish old man who removed the mountains. To be sure, the Red Army did not want to fight a purely defensive war, although Mao was to make that charge against the military leadership at the Tsun-yi Conference in January 1935. But, according to Chou En-lai, a defensive positional war became inevitable.

This [blockhouse warfare, positional warfare and night battles] was unavoidable and this is why we are doing it. But of course our main form of war remains mobile warfare. In the present [February 1934] circumstances, we often see a rencontre of mobile war quickly turn into positional war.[170]

The KMT's blockhouse tactic went through two important stages. At the beginning there were only a few blockhouses, each of which was guarded by a company or a platoon of regular soldiers. In November 1933 more were built with a distance of only two-thirds of a mile between them and guarded usually by a squad or at most a platoon. In this way the blockhouses formed a supporting network and a regiment of troops could defend a line thirteen or fourteen miles long. The second change came early in 1934 when militia units were ordered to guard the blockhouses while regular troops were transferred to offensive duties. At this stage the Red Army's fire-power had been so weakened that the KMT armies could afford to build more earthen blockhouses than brick ones.

As the lines of blockhouses tightened, the Red Army changed its positional warfare to what was known as 'short, swift thrusts' (*tuan ts'u t'u-chi*), a tactic whose invention was attributed to Lin Piao.[171] They depended on the building of 'supporting points' (*chin-ch'eng tien*) – the Communist version of blockhouses, which could help the Red Army move within a few miles of the KMT troops. Making use of its speed and good organization, the Red Army hoped to attack while the enemy was building

---

[170] *Hung-hsing* (Red star), 29 (18 February 1934).

[171] The official history of the war (*Chiao-fei chan-shih*) published by the KMT government speaks of 'the steadily tightening rings' (2.266) and Wang Chien-min's draft history of the CCP supports this description. In accordance with the general strategic plan of the fifth campaign, roads protected by blockhouses were constructed to penetrate the soviet area. On Otto Braun's tactic see Chi-hsi Hu's article in CQ 43.34. Snow's attribution of this tactic to Lin Piao was recently vindicated by an article in *Hung-ch'i* (Red flag), 1 (1975). See also Otto Braun, *A Comintern agent in China 1932–1939*, 68. I myself saw a copy of Lin's pamphlet on this subject in the War Museum, Peking, in 1980.

his blockhouses. The coordination of the units fighting around a supporting point needed telephones of which the Red Army had hardly any; the supporting point itself could scarcely withstand the bombardment of the KMT's heavy artillery pieces. In any case, such a tactical move was no answer to the Red Army's strategic needs. After the decisive battle of Kuang-ch'ang in April 1934, guerrilla warfare, the last resort it seemed, was brought back to the centre of the party's and the army's attention.[172] But the revival of guerrilla warfare at this stage of the struggle was chiefly for diversionary purposes. It was intended to gain time for the eventual evacuation of the central soviet and to mobilize the masses again so that guerrilla bases could be re-established after the evacuation. Writing in the army's organ, *Red Star (Hung-hsing)* on 20 August 1934, Chou En-lai pointed out that the weakest link in the Communist strategy lay in the lack of guerrilla warfare deep behind enemy lines; writing two years after the evacuation, Mao remarked:

but where it is evident that the campaign cannot be terminated on our interior lines, we should employ the main Red Army force to break through the enemy's encirclement and switch to our exterior lines (that is, the enemy's interior lines) in order to defeat him there. Now that the enemy has developed his blockhouse warfare to a high degree, this will become our usual method of operation.[173]

Probably because of this consideration, Fang Chih-min's 10th Army Corps was ordered in July 1934 to move from east Kiangsi to west Chekiang and south Anhwei, ostensibly to engage the Japanese in war but in fact to divert Chiang's attention from the central soviet.[174] In August, Hsiao K'e's 6th Army Corps was ordered to break through the encirclement to join forces with Ho Lung in north-west Hunan.[175] Finally, the central soviet, by now much reduced in size, was abandoned in October 1934, leaving behind Hsiang Ying, Ch'en I, Su Yü and others to spend lonely years fighting in scattered guerrilla enclaves till the formation of the New Fourth Army in 1938. In Central China there remained only the small soviet under Ho Lung and Jen Pi-shih. Further north were Chang Kuo-t'ao's soviet in north Szechwan and Liu Chih-tan's and Kao Kang's soviet in north Shensi. The state so arduously created since 1927 was now destroyed under Chiang Kai-shek's overwhelming might as the First Front Army started on its Long March.

---

[172] *Hung-hsing* (Red star), 55 (25 July 1934).
[173] Mao, *SW* 1.247.
[174] Wang Chien-min, *Draft history*, 2.258–9; Miao Ch'u-huang, *Brief history*, 92–3; Sheng Li-yü, *Chung-kuo jen-min chieh-fang-chün san-shih-nien shih-hua* (An informal history of the 30 years of the People's Liberation Army of China), 16–18.
[175] Hsiao K'e in Nym Wales, *Red dust*, 139; Wang Chen in *ibid.* 101; Miao Ch'u-huang, *Brief history*, 93.

The Long March

This epic hegira covered some 6,000 miles on foot, across a dozen or more big mountain ranges and two dozen rivers in about a year. History offers few comparable triumphs of will-power over circumstance, nor a better example of constant improvisation. There is hardly any doubt that the first destination of the Long March was a junction with the Second Front Army commanded by Ho Lung – an intention which did not escape Chiang's calculation.[176] Chiang seems to have been aware of the incomplete ring of encirclement in the south-west corner of the soviet area which might afford a chance for the First Front Army to slip through to north Kwangtung and Kwangsi. As it was too late to close the ring, Chiang hoped to use the new situation of the Communist invasion to solve to his own advantage the thorny problems of the South-west Political Council under the military dissidents there.[177] But the Kwangtung and Kwangsi leaders let the Red Army pass through without much fighting; they only scorched the earth to create difficulties for the oncoming red soldiers. Therefore they had no need for Chiang's military aid to induce their submission to him.[178] Assured now of the intention of the First Front Army, Chiang laid four lines of defence between the First Front Army and Ho Lung,[179] making it absolutely impossible for the two red forces to unite. Having crossed the Hsiang River and lost nearly two-thirds of the 100,000 combatants and non-combatants of the First Front Army, the leaders of the Politburo held their first meeting on the Long March at Li-p'ing near the Kweichow border (now in Kweichow); the plan to join the Second Front Army was abandoned and the decision to invade Kweichow was taken.[180] This was in December 1934. Chang Kuo-t'ao and Hsu Hsiang-ch'ien of the Fourth Front Army in north Szechwan were informed of the decision and of the plan to join forces with them somewhere in north-west Szechwan.[181] The projected route would cross the Yangtze at I-pin (Sui-fu).

On reaching Tsun-yi in January 1935, the Red Armies suddenly appeared to threaten the security of Szechwan from the north, south and

---

[176] Li T'ien-yu in *HHLY*, Hong Kong, 19; Liu Po-ch'eng, *ibid.* 4; Miao Ch'u-huang, 'Chung-kuo kung-nung hung-chün ch'ang-cheng kai-shu' (A brief account of the Long March of the Workers' and Peasants' Red Army of China), *Li-shih yen-chiu*, 2 (1954), 88. Details of the Long March are in Dick Wilson, *The Long March, 1935*.

[177] Ho Kuo-kuang's statement in Wang Chien-min, *Draft history*, 624. Ho was then the director of Chiang's field headquarters.

[178] Chang Kuo-p'ing, *Pai Ch'ung-hsi chiang-chün chuan* (A biography of General Pai Ch'ung-hsi), 62–4; *Ch'un-ch'iu* (Spring and autumn), 99.14.

[179] Chin Fan, *Tsai Hung-chün ch'ang-cheng ti tao-lu shang*, 45.

[180] Liu Po-ch'eng in *HHLY*, Hong Kong, 4.5.

[181] *Ming-pao*, 48.85.

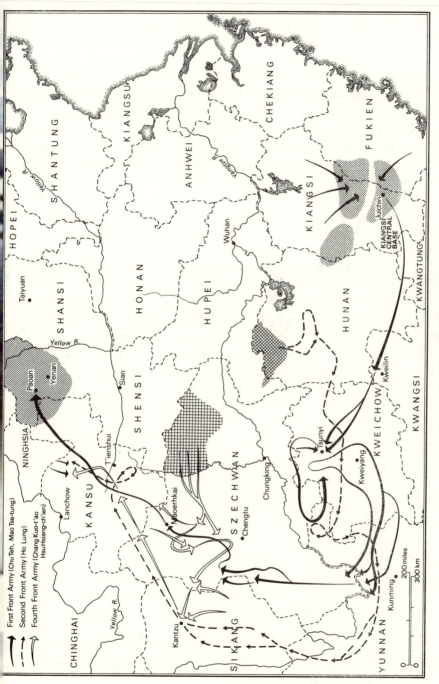

MAP 4. The Long March to Shensi

First Front Army (Chu Teh, Mao Tse-tung)
Second Front Army (Ho Lung)
Fourth Front Army (Chang Kuo-t'ao Hsu Hsiang-ch'ien)

east.[182] This panic situation gave Chiang an opportunity to insert his military and political influence into that province, while the First Front Army gained its first respite since October. It took Tsun-yi on 7 January 1935 and left that small city on the 19th,[183] during which time the army was reorganized while the party leaders sat through the historic conference of the Politburo. The Tsun-yi Conference decided on joining forces with the Fourth Front Army by way of T'ung-tzu, Sung-k'an and Ch'ih-shui, and to enter Szechwan and cross the Yangtze at I-pin as previously planned. When this plan was frustrated by reinforced enemy defences, the First Front Army had to choose another route. According to Teng Fa, the chief of political security, the purpose of going north to join the Fourth Front Army was to be close to the Japanese and engage them in a war of national liberation without Chiang and his allies. Another purpose may have been to find 'the possibility of contact with Russia, the certainty of not being surrounded [again]'.[184]

Strategically the Tsun-yi Conference marked the beginning of a new stage. Before this the First Front Army had had to fight enemies both in front and behind, thus suffering tremendous casualties and desertions.[185] After the eleven days of respite and reorganization, the main anxiety of the army was not the unworthy Kweichow troops ahead but the dogged Nationalist troops behind. The reorganization and abandonment of heavy equipment enabled the army to return to mobile warfare, and use high speed and feints to disengage the pursuing armies under Generals Hsueh Yueh and Chou Hung-yuan.[186]

Chang Kuo-t'ao's separation

At this time Chang Kuo-t'ao gave up his soviet, though not under unusually heavy military pressure from the central and local forces. His own explanation of this move was to enable him to meet the oncoming First Front Army, whereas the Maoist historians have accused him of 'flightism'.[187] The route Chang took led his troops across the Chialing River, through Nan-t'ung, Chien-men, Chien-ko, Tzu-t'ung, then across the Fu River through Chiang-yu, and finally across the Min River to Li-fan and Mou-kung.[188] Chang had an alternative choice of going north to join

[182] *Chiao-fei chan-shih*, 5.883; Hsueh Yueh, *Chiao-fei chi-shih* (A factual account of the campaigns against the bandits), pt. 3, 13–4.
[183] Liu Po-ch'eng in *HHLY*, Hong Kong, 5; Hsueh Yueh, *ibid.*, pt. 3, 7–9.
[184] *HHLY*, Hong Kong, 48 and 50; Hsiao Hua in *HCPP* 13.87; André Malraux, *Anti-memoirs*, 533.
[185] Liu Po-ch'eng in *HHLY*, Hong Kong, 4.4.
[186] *Ibid.* 6; *HCPP* 14.102–3.
[187] *Ming-pao*, 49.78; Liu Po-ch'eng, *HHLY*, Hong Kong, 9.
[188] Hsu Hsiang-ch'ien in Wales, *Red dust*, 161.

forces with Liu Chih-tan and Kao Kang. Had he done so and abandoned Mao and Ho Lung to their fate in the south, the entire Communist movement might have been reduced to political insignificance. What Chang actually did had the effect of enfeebling the First Front Army while preserving it, but it gave him a military edge which might lead to his political supremacy in the party. Later events were to prove that Chang's apparently astute calculations in February 1935 turned out to be the first major mistake he made on the Long March. Either choice, however, implied that he must give up his soviet.

From what is known, the Tsun-yi Conference avoided political polemics, concentrating on criticism of the military line which had led to the losses of the soviets and the disastrous defeats in the initial stages of the Long March. The 'pure defence' tactics, the unwillingness to exploit the disunity among Chiang Kai-shek's ranks during the Fukien rebellion in the winter of 1933–4, the refusal to make a strategic retreat and transfer the main forces behind the enemy's lines of blockhouses in order to crush the encirclement, and the poor preparation for the Long March, all came under Mao's merciless attack in the resolutions he drafted.[189] With Wang Chia-hsiang gravely wounded, Chou En-lai having admitted his mistakes, Chang Wen-t'ien drawing close to Mao, and the German adviser Otto Braun in disgrace, the leadership of the party was in awful disarray. In an atmosphere reminiscent of the 7 August conference of 1927, the enlarged conference at Tsun-yi, including representatives of the military who were unhappy with the leadership, elected Mao to be the first of the three-man commanding team, including Chou En-lai and Wang Chia-hsiang, to act in place of the military commission of the party while the soviet government's military affairs committee was still headed by Chu Teh. In addition Mao regained his seat on the Polituro and probably a secretaryship in the central secretariat headed by Chang Wen-t'ien.[190]

Two major points were to be the bone of contention when the First and Fourth Front Armies met in Mou-kung on 12 June 1935 – the first

---

189 Jerome Ch'en, 'Resolutions of the Tsunyi Conference', CQ 40. In Fukien the 19th Route Army commanded by Ts'ai T'ing-k'ai, which had distinguished itself in the defence of Shanghai in January 1932, having entered into an agreement with the Communists on 26 October 1933 (see Hsiao Tso-liang, Power relations, 49), set up a 'People's Revolutionary Government' in Foochow in November 1933. This seriously weakened Chiang's encirclement in its north-eastern corner. Complicated by many political issues, the situation did not result in any form of cooperation between the 19th Route Army and the CCP, and the Foochow government was soon defeated by Chiang.

190 Dieter Heinzig's article in CQ 46.287. Mao's new position as 'the first' (ti-i-pa-shou) of the three-man commanding team (san-jen chün-shih hsiao-tsu) is now held to be his true position in the party's military hierarchy by the curatorial staff of all the important museums in China and by such authorities as Professor Hu Hua at the People's University, Peking. See Hu's Chung-kuo ko-ming-shih chiang-i (Lectures on the history of the Chinese Revolution), 1.363.

was the legality of the Tsun-yi Conference, as by then several members of the Politburo were not even members of the Central Committee elected at the Sixth Congress in 1928. They included Ch'in Pang-hsien, Chang Wen-t'ien, Wang Chia-hsiang and Chu Teh. The second and more important point which had been avoided at Tsun-yi concerned the future of the soviet movement in China. In Mou-kung the situation was different; Chang Kuo-t'ao wanted to challenge the legality of the new leadership, including Mao, and to change the course of the revolution.

It is generally agreed that at the time the two armies made their junction, the Fourth Front Army was numerically stronger and better equipped, though less well disciplined, than Mao's worn-out First Front Army. Chang Kuo-t'ao knew perfectly well that the CCP lacked a democratic tradition for settling intra-party disputes through committee discussion, and yet he agreed to the convocation of the Liang-ho-k'ou Conference of 24 June 1935. Perhaps he hoped that, with his military preponderance and firm belief that the soviet movement was doomed to fail, he could carry the majority of the party leadership with him, as they and they alone were in a position to legitimize his policy proposals. He was still working with the party; he was not yet a separatist. His close colleague, Ch'en Ch'ang-hao, asked him a crucial question: 'If you come out clear and criticize the mistakes of the centre to hasten the bankruptcy of the leadership, what will be the result?'[191] Chang did not record his reply; nor did he criticize the leadership. Instead, he preferred to argue at the conference over whether the soviet movement had or had not been a success and to discuss what the future would be if all of them marched northward to join forces with Kao Kang and Liu Chih-tan.[192] In other words, what he presented to the conference was not his maximum demand for an overhaul of the central leadership, but his minimum demand, the thin end of the wedge, of replacing the soviet government with a north-west autonomous government based on a coalition of the minority nationalities to be decided at a high cadres' conference. Presumably the high cadres' conference would contain a greater representation of the Fourth Front Army. If his autonomous government proposal was adopted, this would give Chang the supreme leadership of the party which he so coveted.

But Chang's proposal would have obliterated the class base of a government led by the CCP. In spite of its mild social programme, which included land redistribution and the abolition of extortionate taxes, it would not be a socialist government.[193] His policy proposal therefore was tantamount to a transformation of the CCP into a party of minority races.

[191] Ming-pao, 51.82.   [192] Liu Ning, I-ko kung-jen ti kung-chuang, 12.
[193] Ming-pao, 49.80.

It was no surprise that Mao won the day. But as a compromise for the sake of unity, the military commission was reorganized with Mao continuing to serve as its chairman and Chang and Chu Teh as its deputy chairmen. This compromise Chang willingly accepted.[194]

To patch up still other differences, the Mao-erh-kai Conference was convened on 5 August. At this point no one there knew the whereabouts of Hsu Hai-tung's 25th Army Corps or had any inkling of a new united front strategy being formulated in Moscow. The conference did not consider Chang's proposal of a new government again; it concentrated on the question of the march northward. Chang's suggestion to hold a high cadres' conference was rejected on the ground that matters concerning the party should not be treated by the representatives of only two front armies, whose proper jurisdiction was over military affairs such as the command system and the northward march itself.[195] As to the command system, Chu Teh nominated himself as the commander-in-chief with Chang as the general political commissar. All strategic problems were to be determined by the commander-in-chief's headquarters with the final approval of the party's three-man commanding team headed by Mao.[196] Therefore Mao, as the chairman of the commission holding the powers of final decision, was above both Chu and Chang. There was no question of Mao's disobedience of Chang, only Chang's defiance of Mao.

This defiance was exhibited by Chang's different interpretation of the 'northward' march. Mao's destination was the north Shensi soviet, but Chang argued at the conference that the armies should go only as far as to Min-hsien and Kan-nan in Kansu before the next step of the march was decided.[197] Much to Chang's chagrin, Mao began his march with the east column, an act that Chang interpreted as Mao's contempt for his authority. In Mao's view, Chang's demand that he should return to A-pa was sheer disobedience.[198] Behind this disagreement lay the issue of the future of the soviet movement. If the movement was assessed as a success and there was a future in continuing it, there was every reason to go to north Shensi; if it was adjudged a failure, it would be better to heed Chang's advice, to coop up in the remote Sikang-Kansu mountains and wait for another day. At a personal level, to accept Chang's judgment and proposal would result in accepting Chang's leadership and all that that implied. This Mao could not do.

With Mao's refusal to return south, the CCP split. Soon after that, Chang called his cherished high cadres' conference in Cho-k'e-chi to

194 *Ibid.* 50.88.
195 *Ibid.* 51.81–2.
196 *Ibid.* 51–79 and footnote 191.
197 *Ibid.* 52.83.
198 Liu Po-ch'eng, *HHLY*, Hong Kong, 10.

inaugurate a provisional party centre with Chang as its secretary. The army was to be commanded by the provisional centre.[199] Three months later fortune turned against Chang's west column – the cold weather set in and Liu Hsiang, the Szechwan warlord, repeatedly defeated Chang's troops, forcing them to retreat deep into Sikang and Chinghai.[200] Meanwhile Ch'en Ch'ang-hao's attempt to advance to south Kansu was thwarted by Chiang's troops.[201] To add more gloom to his future, Chang made an overture to Yang Hu-ch'eng, a warlord in north-west China, for a non-aggression pact, which was cold-shouldered.[202]

In the meantime the Second Front Army under Ho Lung started its Long March on 12 November 1935. But for the strong KMT defence to the north-west of Hunan, Ho Lung might have gone straight north to join forces with Mao without tramping through half of China.[203] On the other hand, the turmoil in Kwangtung and Kwangsi gave Ho a chance to penetrate south.[204] He followed roughly the footsteps of the First Front Army to reach Chang Kuo-t'ao in Sikang at a time when the frustrated Chang was under pressure to reunite with Mao's centre. Lin Yü-ying, Lin Piao's uncle, had brought back from Moscow a compromise formula for reunification. Exploiting this opportunity, the newly arrived leaders, Jen Pi-shih, Kuan Hsiang-ying and Ho Lung joined with Chu Teh and Liu Po-ch'eng in urging Chang to march north.[205] To explain his long delay in resuming the march, Chang gave the reason that he was training his troops so that they could deal with the cavalry of the Muslim generals in the Kansu corridor.[206] Of course, he had done no such thing. He did not embark upon a programme of training in preparation for crossing the Yellow River to fight the Muslim cavalry until he was persuaded to march again.[207] But now his destination was not north Shensi as his persuaders intended, but somewhere in the Kansu corridor to the north of the Yellow River. This shrewd plan was to regard Mao's north Shensi base as his front line against Japan while using Sinkiang or the USSR as his rear. If the projected united front was formed and the war against Japan broke out, Mao's military strength would be spent in the fighting, while Chang, retaining his own troops behind Mao and with Russian backing, would be the only strong man in the Communist movement of

199 Ming-pao, 52.96.   200 Liu Po-ch'eng, HHLY 10.
201 Ming-pao, 54.88.   202 Ibid. 48.85.
203 HHLY 4.264.   204 Chiao-fei chan-shih, 6.997.
205 Ming-pao, 53.91 and 54.88. As to the formula, according to uncorroborated information, Lin Yü-ying
    suggested that Mao's centre be transformed into a north-west bureau and Chang's into a south-west
    bureau with Lin himself as the mediator between the two to bring about a reunification. See
    Ming-pao, 53.89.
206 Ibid. 50.86.   207 Ming-pao, 54.88.

China. The crossing of the Yellow River was necessary for the western column on another account. It must not remain south of the river if it was to avoid tough fighting against Chiang's troops and run the risk of being driven back to Mao-erh-kai and an impasse. What happened after the crossing was unexpected by Chang. The western column was annihilated by the Muslim cavalry of the KMT. With it went Chang's hope of challenging Mao's leadership. Politically he ceased to be a man of any weight. With his separatism bankrupted, his defection began.[208]

UNDERGROUND WORK IN THE 'WHITE AREA'

Since the creation of the rural soviets, tension as well as cooperation had developed between the 'white area' work and the land revolution. The former was doctrinally blessed to lead the latter, while the latter was all the time outgrowing the former in strength and importance. Still, as summed up in the 'Resolution of some questions in the history of our party' in 1945,[209] the party centre stubbornly refused to subordinate 'white area' work to rural work. It continued to insist on a mechanical interpretation of proletarian hegemony, quite oblivious to the fact that neither the proletarian theory nor the proletarian party was the domain of the proletariat.

It is undeniable that in both the Ch'ü Ch'iu-pai and Li Li-san periods the urban labour movement had become narrowly economic while the peasants, especially the armed peasants, were waging political and social battles to destroy the bastions of what they called 'feudal China'. In the arts and literature, through which many young people were radicalized, the CCP had a greater influence. The creative arts and literature of China began their own radicalization after the May Thirtieth movement of 1925, a tendency clearly shown, for instance, in the writings of Lu Hsun and the transformation of such literary organizations as the Creation Society

---

[208] There are only fragments of information on the provisioning of the Red Army on the Long March. It seems safe to assume that requisitioning from landlords and rich peasants was the usual source (*HHLY* 4.179–80), a pattern similar to the provisioning of the guerrillas after the Autumn Harvest uprisings.

The well-known story of Liu Po-ch'eng swearing brotherhood with a Lolo chieftain (Wales, *Red dust*, 71) is not typical. When the Red Army stayed in the Miao area in Lung-p'ing-chen in Kwangsi for some ten days, fires broke out near the army camps every night (*HCPP* 9.32). On the grassland, Ho Lung and Lo Ping-hui, who had fought the rearguard action almost all the way, were harassed by the Tibetans (Wales, *Red dust*, 130). Whenever there was a tribal feud, the Red Army made skilled use of it in order to obtain supplies (*HHLY* 4.128–30). Naturally they exploited the misgovernment of the KMT to help the poor and the imprisoned, who could not pay taxes and rent, in order to ingratiate themselves with the Yi and other tribes (*HHLY* 4.118–21).

[209] Mao, *HC* 3.978.

(Ch'uang-tsao she). In March 1930 the different strands of the general development of left-wing literature were gathered together in the founding of the Left-wing Writers' League. The magazines under its infuence challenged the academic critics, the proponents of 'art for art's sake', and the Nationalist writers. The league also influenced, to a remarkable degree, the film industry in Shanghai to turn its attention from costumed sword-fighting dramas to contemporary social problems. In both literature and film, this was the most celebrated period before the resistance war. Artists and writers produced praiseworthy works under severe persecution. Many of their writings were proscribed by KMT censorship and many writers were themselves either arrested and executed or driven to the soviet areas.[210]

Curiously enough, the CI's July 1931 instruction on 'white area' work paid almost no attention to art and literature, hardly any to the student movement, but a great deal to labour unions and anti-imperialism. One result of this instruction was the party's effort to organize Shanghai workers during the Japanese invasion of January 1932, to agitate among the soldiers, and to try to carry the war into the foreign settlements. This all came to nothing.[211] The sectarianism of the CCP's urban work led the party to fight against the KMT Reorganizationists led by Wang Ching-wei, the Third Party led by Teng Yen-ta, and the Trotskyists led by Ch'en Tu-hsiu. With the 'yellow' labour unions, the CCP consciously or unconsciously found little in common for cooperation.[212]

The migration of party members to the soviet areas in 1931–3 further weakened 'white area' work. A conscious endeavour was initiated to reverse the flow and to give a semblance of equilibrium between town and country. On record some 150 cadres were sent back to the cities. But on the whole Liu Shao-ch'i's charge of the failure of the 'leftists' (the 28 Bolsheviks) to develop urban work was fully justified.[213]

One obstacle to expanding the CCP's urban work was, of course, the KMT's counter-espionage. To deal with this the CCP set up its own special security branch soon after the Sixth Congress. It was headed by Hsiang Chung-fa, Chou En-lai and Ku Shun-chang. In the underground war between these clandestine agents, the CCP centre in Shanghai was discovered and destroyed no less than fourteen times. The terror that the

[210] See Ch'eng Chi-hua et al., Chung-kuo tien-ying fa-chan-shih (A history of the development of Chinese cinema); Jay Leyda, Dianying, an account of films and the film audience in China; Liu Shou-sung, Chung-kuo hsin wen-hsueh shih ch'u-kao (A preliminary draft history of modern Chinese literature). See also Wang Chien-min, Draft history, 2.137; T. A. Hsia, Gate of darkness.
[211] Hung-se wen-hsien, 386–92; Snow, Random notes, 17; Warren Kuo, History, 2.326.
[212] Wang Ming, Hsuan-chi, 3.51–2.
[213] Ming-pao, 58.87.

KMT's Investigation Department brought against the Communist provincial organizations, Youth Corps, Shanghai General Labour Union, the Workers' Mutual Aid Association (Kung-chi hui), anti-imperialist societies and cultural organizations caused their activities to decline or discontinue. With the arrests of Ku Shun-chang and Hsiang Chung-fa in April and June 1931, the party centre could hardly exist and function in Shanghai, hence its removal to the central soviet. In all, no less than 24,000 members of the CCP were either arrested or killed and 30,000 others had to go through the process of confession to the KMT police.[214] Nonetheless it was not impossible to buy one's way out of difficulty, the KMT special agents being so inefficient and corruptible. Sixty *yuan* was all that was needed for Liu Ning, for example, to have a chest of documents destroyed and himself released from prison.[215]

Around the soviet areas, K'ang Tse organized his Special Activities Corps (Pieh-tung-tui) of five columns, consisting of some 24,000 men to collect red deserters, blockade trade, inspect travellers and mail, and train and organize the masses.[216] The CCP, on its part, tightened the political security system in the soviets. They had anti-counter-revolution committees to ferret out hidden reactionaries and rescue arrested comrades, give aid to the families of the arrested, gather intelligence, set up an intelligence network from Kiangsi to Shanghai and Hong Kong, and take retaliatory action against KMT agents.[217]

Liu Shao-ch'i

Late in 1934 or early in 1935 Liu Shao-ch'i's task of picking up the shattered pieces of 'white area' work was far from easy. Apart from his rich experience in the labour movement, Liu was the man who had tidied up the shambles of urban work after Ch'ü Ch'iu-pai's putschism and replaced Lo Chang-lung as head of the Shanghai General Labour Union before his own exodus to the central soviet. In 1935–6 Liu now focused his attention on students, youth, and writers instead of the inactive labour unions. Because of the weakness of the party branches in the cities and the reluctance of left-wing sympathizers to accept extreme radicalism, Liu was critical of the adventurism manifested in the December Ninth

[214] Warren Kuo, *History*, 2.228–61; Ts'ao Po-i, *Soviet*, 408–14.
[215] Liu Ning, *I-ko kung-jen ti kung-chuang*, 66.
[216] Hollington Tong, *Chiang*, 1.208–9; Lloyd Eastman, 'Fascism in Kuomintang China: the Blue Shirts', *CQ* 49 (Jan.–March 1972), 1–31.
[217] Warren Kuo, *History*, 2.228–38; Ts'ao Po-i, *Soviet*, 408–14. The information given here is uncorroborated and should be accepted only with great care. I have deliberately left out whatever information there is in Kung Ch'u and Li Ang, for it is my view that whenever possible these two authors should be avoided.

movement, an anti-Japanese demonstration organized by Peking students on that date in 1935. The first step Liu Shao-ch'i took was to distinguish clearly between secret and open work and to moderate political slogans in order to improve relations between the party and its front organization and the masses. It was hoped that party members could work in legally recognized organizations and thus be in closer contact with the masses without actually committing the sin of legal Marxism.[218] Liu's style was strictly that of the united front – organizing students' study groups and art circles, establishing students' national salvation associations, and supporting the 29th Army stationed in the Peking area. The village propaganda teams (Nan-hsia hsuan-ch'uan-t'uan) of 400–500 students organized after the December Ninth movement seemed to him too radical, as they only helped expose the hard core of the left-wing youth movement. Instead, Liu encouraged the organization of the semi-open National Salvation Vanguard (Min-hsien) – a small beginning of 300 members in February 1936 which was to grow to 1,300 in July.[219] In the student unions the left-wing played an increasingly important role, with P'eng Chen, Ch'en Po-ta and Huang Ch'eng working behind the scenes. Huang even managed to have himself elected president of the Tsing Hua Union.[220] In this way Liu Shao-ch'i preserved his precious cadres and brought students and the armies stationed in Hopei under their influence. This group – to be known as the December Ninth cadre – who after the outbreak of war migrated to the rural areas of Hopei and Shansi to work among the peasants, helped the 8th Route Army set up base areas. The experience of 1927 was thus re-enacted. In both his urban underground and rural open work, Liu laid a solid foundation for future development. With such attainments, his return to Yenan in 1937 was triumphal, with enough prestige for him to criticize the 28 Bolsheviks and to secure for himself a seat on the Politburo. It was probably then that the alliance between Liu and Mao was forged. However, working in 'white areas' Liu had no administrative routine to deal with, no bureaucratism to tackle. His theoretical aspirations were given vent in his study of a moral philosophy such as was needed for clandestine work. He was the first Communist of any importance to have trodden that forbidden philosophical territory which other Marxist angels feared to tread.

[218] Liu Shao-ch'i, 'Lun kung-k'ai kung-tso yü mi-mi kung-tso' (On open and secret work), in *Kung-ch'an-tang-jen* (The Communist), 1. A handwritten copy of this is in the Hoover Institution.
[219] Li Ch'ang, 'Hui-i min-hsien tui' (Reminiscences of the National Salvation Vanguard), in *I-erh-chiu hui-i-lu* (Memoirs of December 9), 16.
[220] *Ibid.* 187–9.

PREPARATION FOR THE SECOND UNITED FRONT

In September 1935, when Hsu Hai-tung's army eventually reached the north Shensi base area, the reconstructed soviet there was only two years old. Claiming some six counties, with its capital at Wa-yao-pao, this soviet had once been destroyed by Chiang, thanks largely to the motorways built by the China International Famine Relief Commission. This had also prevented it from joining with Chang Kuo-t'ao's soviet in north Szechwan.[221] When Mao and his east column arrived in October, they added to the strength of the soviet and gave it a chance to expand. Its capital was moved to Pao-an in mid-1936 and then to Yenan in January 1937. By the time the second united front came into being it had some 35,000 square miles and 1,500,000 people under its control.[222] Coincidentally, Chang Hsueh-liang's Manchurian army was transferred to Sian to fight the Communists, also in October 1935. The 8,000 strong Red Army was then opposed by seventeen KMT divisions in what was planned to be the final campaign of annihilation.[223]

Largely through their own mistakes and clumsy manoeuvres, the Long March saw the decline of the 28 Bolsheviks and Chang Kuo-t'ao, thus giving the party at long last a measure of unity unknown since the end of Ch'en Tu-hsiu's leadership. The CCP's time in the wilderness was drawing to a close. On the opposing side Chiang, using the suppression of the 'bandits' as his reason, managed to penetrate into the south-west with his army, political apparatus, and economic institutions to give him a measure of national unity unknown since the death of Yuan Shih-k'ai in 1916. In the process of consolidating the situation in the south-west the various local forces had to make a choice in national politics – either to parley with the CCP so as to ward off Chiang's influence, or to succumb to Chiang's pressure in order to keep the Communists out of their territory. This consolidating process was in a sense beneficial to China, and probably helped her to withstand the strains and stresses of eight years of resistance against Japan.

After September 1931, the intensified aggressiveness of Japanese militant nationalism had produced its first reaction from the CCP, a call for a united front, published in October 1932. In this resolution, the party envisioned that Chiang's regime might disintegrate under the pressure of Japan and therefore there was no thought of an alliance with Chiang.

---

[221] K'ang-jih chan-cheng shih-ch'i chieh-fang-ch'ü kai-k'uang (The liberated areas during the anti-Japanese war), 6; HCPP 3.168–80.

[222] Wales, Red dust, 75; US War Department, Military Intelligence Division, 'The Chinese Communist movement', 2355.

[223] HHLY, Hong Kong, 10–11; China year book, 1936, 425–6.

However, this call attracted little attention outside the soviet areas and was interpreted by the country at large mainly as a move to protect the socialist fatherland rather than China. In no sense did the call succeed in gaining the CCP a share in the KMT's leadership of the struggle for national independence. The CCP was still considered by many as a mere instrument of Russia.

The CCP's proposal for a united front acquired a new meaning after the fall of Kuang-ch'ang during Chiang's final encirclement in April 1934; it became an attempt to reverse the worsening civil war situation and to rescue the CCP from its predicament. The central committee's letter to the nation on 10 April 1934 left the role of the KMT in the united front purposely vague. The KMT was not explicitly left out of the alliance; nor was the aim of overthrowing it renounced.[224] The deteriorating war situation moderated the CCP's attitude to the KMT, as shown in Chou En-lai's Six Point Programme of 20 July 1934,[225] which suggested a united front including all anti-Japanese forces, even Chiang Kai-shek's. Pragmatic as the new proposal indeed was, it was not completely opportunistic. In embryonic form it contained a new theoretical formulation to direct the revolution from the withering soviets onto a more hopeful course. Lenin's old theses of a national united front were obviously worth reviving. In Lenin's conception a nation may have no ultimate value; but in a China under the pressure of Japanese aggression, the existence of the Chinese nation was a matter of cardinal importance. In other words, the struggle for national liberation (anti-imperialist) was gradually overshadowing the struggle for social liberation (anti-feudal). In reviving this idea, the CCP had on its mind the bad experiences of the first united front of 1923–7, especially the 'betrayal' by the bourgeoisie and big landlords thought to be represented by Chiang Kai-shek. If the CCP was to mitigate its land revolution for the sake of a united anti-imperialist struggle, the questions that must be answered were (in the language of the day): was it to be a united front on a national-political level with all the anti-Japanese forces who had been at variance with Chiang? Or was it to be a united front of a social revolutionary sort based on the mobilization of the workers, peasants and soldiers with sufficient political consciousness to supervise their leaders so as to ensure its solidarity and success? The contradiction between these two approaches was explicit. Then tactically should the CCP forge a united front before mobilizing and arming the masses or vice versa? The failure of the first united front was to a large measure due to the absence of an independent Communist armed force. In 1935–6, the CCP

[224] Hsiao Tso-liang, *Power relations*, 226.
[225] *Hung-hsing* (Red star) (20 July 1934), 1.

did have an army and an occupied territory. For the sake of unity against Japan, should the party give them up or should the resistance war be left to cement national unity without either of the major parties sacrificing its autonomy? Closely related to this last question was that of the temporary or permanent nature of the united front. If it was merely temporary, it followed that the two opposing parties entered into an alliance for national preservation without at the same time abandoning their long-range goals, whose fulfilment required both to continue their military and territorial expansion. If it was permanent, China must undergo a basic political change in order to permit the parties to contend for their long-term goals by peaceful means. The change would entail the nationalization of all armed forces, the creation of a democratic assembly, the guarantee of the basic freedoms, and so on. Above all, the most difficult question in 1935–6 was: could a united front with Chiang be meaningful and effective in view of Chiang's enmity and fickleness? These questions received serious consideration at the Seventh Congress of the CI in the summer of 1935, when the International called for a general anti-imperialist united front to curb the growth of fascism in the West and Japanese aggression in the East. In the spirit of this call, the August First Declaration was issued in the name of the Central Committee of the CCP by Wang Ming in Moscow.[226]

The scope of the united front envisaged in the declaration was broad enough to embrace all anti-Japanese forces. However, it still attacked Chiang as the enemy of the nation who should be excluded from the alliance. But there was a change in priority – Japan had replaced Chiang as the most feared enemy.[227] The exclusion of Chiang from both the proposed national defence government and the anti-Japanese allied armies provoked further questions: would Chiang stand aside and watch the allied armies fight Japan without taking any action? Would he continue to fight the CCP and other opponents while the anti-Japanese war was in progress? What justification could he have for either his action or inaction? Was he to declare neutrality in the Japanese war or to play the role of an ally of Japan? The illogicality of the declaration was soon realized and remedied by Wang Ming in his speech at the Seventh Congress of the CI on 7 August 1935. 'The path is left open for the Kuomintang if Chiang Kai-shek is to call off his anti-Communist

[226] Hu Hua, *Materials*, 263–9. At the Mao-erh-kai Conference no one even mentioned the possibility of an anti-Japanese united front; no one knew of the publication of the August First Declaration. Chang Kuo-t'ao, *Ming-pao*, 50.85.

[227] For discussions on the various aspects of the second united front, see L. P. Van Slyke, *Enemies and friends*; and Tetsuya Kataoka, *Resistance and revolution in China: the Communists and the second united front*.

campaign and join in the fight against Japan.' Still later, in his essay 'New situation and new strategy', Wang Ming addressed Chiang as 'Mr Chiang', saying, 'If Mr Chiang is willing to change his attitude, the Chinese Communist Party can cooperate with him'. In Wang's view, the national contradiction so outweighed the class contradiction that 'apart from the people's interests the Chinese Communist Party had no other interest in mind'.[228]

The thinking in north Shensi, where the real power of the party resided, if not the real authority, seems to have been different. The Red Army's anti-Japanese manifesto of 13 November 1935 was decidedly against both Japan and Chiang.[229] Two days later Mao drafted his Ten Point Programme, which was discussed and adopted without much revision by the Wa-yao-pao Conference of the Politburo on 25 December. Mao described Chiang as a 'running dog' of Japan, to be opposed by the CCP.[230]

The Wa-yao-pao Conference envisaged a broad alliance of all revolutionary classes against Japanese imperialism and the traitorous group led by Chiang. In order to arouse and mobilize these classes of people, it was necessary to satisfy the peasants' demand for land and workers', soldiers' and intellectuals' demands for improvement in their livelihood. Only in that way could their revolutionary zeal be sustained. It followed that the property of traitors, including Chiang, should be confiscated and redistributed; extortionate taxes should end; wages and salaries should be increased; and relief work should be organized. As to the strategy of this national war, the Red Army and the red territories should under no circumstances be abolished. Instead, in the Japanese and KMT occupied areas, revolutionary bases should be founded, and a two-front struggle against internal oppressors and foreign foes should be carried on from these bases. As conceived at Wa-yao-pao, the war of resistance was to be simultaneously a war of social revolution. Otherwise it could never become the mass war needed to ensure victory. Organizationally the first step was to set up an anti-Japanese government, similar to Wang Ming's national defence government. But organizational development would not stop there. In the base areas, revolutionary committees would serve as a transitional form of government leading to the creation of soviets. A prerequisite for the creation of the base areas was the expansion of all anti-Japanese armed forces and guerrillas. If the situation evolved in this

---

[228] Wang Ming, *Hsuan-chi*, 1.9–10, 11–13, 25 and 53; Van Slyke, *Enemies and friends*, 53–4; Kataoka Tetsuya, 23ff.
[229] Ho Kan-chih, *Modern revolution*, 1.187.
[230] *MTTC* 5.10 and 13–14.

manner, Chiang's China would be subject to external pressure from Japan and internal pressure from his opponents; it would grow weak and disintegrate. The CCP would then make fresh allies with the dissidents from Chiang's clique.[231]

Two points emerged clearly from the Wa-yao-pao resolutions – north Shensi had as yet no appetite for parleying with Chiang; and the peasant war remained the leading form of struggle, with the proletarian struggle in the cities its closest ally. The strategy of encircling the cities from the countryside would continue with little revision. But the application of such a strategy in a national war begged a theoretical and a pragmatic question: how could peasants be aroused to anti-imperialist struggle? Was a united anti-Japanese front without Chiang feasible?

In the nation at large there existed a widespread belief that the Communist movement was at the end of its tether and its grandiose plans did not deserve serious attention. To put teeth in its proposals the CCP launched in February–April 1936 its 'eastern expedition' across the Yellow River into Shansi, ostensibly to engage the Japanese in Hopei and Jehol. As Liu Chih-tan's army pushed towards Taiyuan, Yen Hsi-shan, the perennial governor there, sent a call for help to Chiang Kai-shek. The subsequent death of Liu in action and the withdrawal of the Red Army did not mean that the venture was a total failure. In addition to demonstrating the CCP's determination to fight the Japanese, it recruited 8,000 fresh troops and broke the back of Chiang's encirclement campaign which had been manned by a motley of 'miscellaneous' troops.[232] (See below, chapter 4.)

Another significant result of the 'eastern expedition' was that local military leaders in north-west China, including Chang Hsueh-liang, were now convinced of the CCP's patriotic commitment; consequently they lost their interest in fighting the Red Army. Relations between Chang and the CCP began to improve.[233] It was at this juncture that Lin Yü-ying came back from Moscow with the CI's new policy proposal. On 14 March 1936, Mao could therefore declare to the KMT that if the government troops stopped attacking the soviet area, the Red Army was prepared to conclude a truce with them.[234] The party's policy thus underwent a sharp change from the idea of a two-front struggle against both Japan and Chiang to that of forcing Chiang to join the united front. The way to

---

[231] The text of the Wa-yao-pao resolutions in *MTTC* 5 *passim*.
[232] Mark Selden, *The Yenan way in revolutionary China*, 103; Kataoka Tetsuya, 35–7.
[233] Snow, *Red star*, 370–8.
[234] Van Slyke, *Enemies and friends*, 60.

force him was to provoke a fight with Japan, to struggle first in order to achieve unity later. It was perfectly Maoist.[235]

Now there was at least a basis for bargaining between the two major parties. They could jockey for the most advantageous terms to ensure victory against Japan, and also for hegemony to rule and shape China after the conclusion of the resistance. When Chiang replied by assaulting the soviet area in April 1936, Mao and Chu loosed a tirade of violent language against him; when Chiang's assault was called off, the military commission of the Red Army proposed that the civil war be stopped for the sake of unity.[236] Meanwhile Chou En-lai and other CCP representatives were in Shanghai making contact with KMT leaders, such as Chang Ch'ün and Ch'en Li-fu, over the terms of cooperation.[237]

From the end of 1935, when Japan's East Hopei Anti-Communist Special Regime was established,[238] Chiang's efforts to reach a detente with Japan came to an impasse. The negotiations between Chang Ch'ün and Kawagoe, the Japanese ambassador to China, deadlocked while the Kwantung army instigated Mongolian troops to invade Suiyuan. Students in Peking, leading intellectuals in Shanghai, and military leaders in Kwangtung and Kwangsi criticized Chiang's accommodating attitude to Japan in harsher and more strident tones. Unable to contain Japanese militant nationalism or to destroy the CCP, Chiang's frustration led him to prepare for an eventual showdown with the foreign aggressor. That eventuality required moral and material aid from the USSR, the only major power willing to assist China. According to Chiang himself,[239] he sent an emissary to Vienna to sound out Russia's intention to help and these negotiations for a non-aggression pact and military aid between the two governments went on throughout 1936. It was in the context of popular sentiment against Japanese aggression, of deteriorating Sino-Japanese relations, of improving Sino-Russian feelings, and of a softer attitude of the CCP to Chiang, that the epochal Sian incident took place on 12 December 1936.[240]

[235] Ho Kan-chih, *Modern revolution*, 1.302.
[236] *Ibid.* 1.194; *Red China*, 26 May 1936.
[237] Chiang Kai-shek, *Soviet Russia in China: a summing-up at seventy*, 72–3.
[238] Hollington Tong, *Chiang*, 2.225.
[239] *Ibid.* 245.
[240] Charles McLane, *Soviet policy and the Chinese communists, 1931–1946*, 79–91. Prof. T. F. Tsiang visited Moscow at Chiang's request in late 1934; see Charles Lilley, 'Tsiang T'ing-fu: between two worlds 1895–1935'.

The Sian incident

The plot to arrest Chiang in Sian was hatched in great secrecy. When it occurred it shocked the world, the nation, and the CCP. Understandably, the CCP's initial reaction, based on imperfect information, showed signs of panic. From the point of view of all the anti-Japanese forces concerned – the USSR, the CCP and Chiang's captors – Chiang's death at any stage of the incident would have defeated their purpose of forming a united front. Chiang was narrowly preserved from death during the initial hours of his capture (in the chaos and confusion on the morning of the 12 December), and after that his safety was secured for the duration of his detention in Sian. Since Chang Hsueh-liang, Chiang's captor, gave no orders to kill Chiang, it is safe to assume that he had never entertained the thought of assassinating him. Moscow's directive to the CCP was clearly for Chiang's preservation. Among the rank and file of Chang Hsueh-liang's and Yang Hu-ch'eng's troops and the CCP there may have been a strong enough hatred to demand Chiang's blood, but this hardly reflected the wisdom of the leaders. True, Mao is reported to have gone into a rage when the Moscow directive arrived;[241] even this may have been a way to pacify his followers or an expression of his indignation against Moscow's interference in the CCP's internal affairs. With Chiang captured, the united front was definitely in the offing. The problems to be negotiated concerned the strategies, organizations, and ideologies that in the long term would affect the future of both Chiang's and the Communists' revolutions. (See pp. 47–8 above.)

In Nanking the pro-Japanese wing, represented by General Ho Ying-ch'in, advocated a tough reaction to the Sian incident by starting a punitive expedition against the rebels and the reds, while Wang Ching-wei was to be invited back to strengthen the possibility of a rapprochement with Japan.[242] But the influential press like the *Ta-kung-pao* demanded the release of Chiang and a settlement of the differences between Nanking and the rebels by peaceful means.[243] At the scene of the incident, Chou En-lai, Yeh Chien-ying and others held talks with Chiang, insistently arguing for a united front.[244] On both sides, the toughest problems lay in the reconciliation between erstwhile enmity and future friendship, unity and struggle, revolution and counter-revolution.

---

[241] Snow, *Random notes*, 1ff.

[242] Shigemitsu Mamoru, *Japan and her destiny*, 222–3.

[243] Editorial of *Ta-kung-pao*, 14 December 1936 in Chang Ch'ih-chang, *Chi-luan wen-ts'un* (Taipei ed., 1962), 222–3.

[244] J. M. Bertram, *Crisis in China: the story of the Sian mutiny* (also titled *First act in China*), 170; Kataoka Tetsuya, 46.

Up to this time Chiang's method of resolving these contradictions had been to eliminate the class struggle as represented by the CCP before facing up to the tension between China and Japan – a solution in line with Prince Kung's and Tseng Kuo-fan's policy of the 1860s toward the Taiping rebels. Wang Ming's method was to subordinate class struggle to national struggle so as to achieve national unity, for without unity China could not resist Japan. Mao, however, believed that unity was to be obtained only through struggle, as unity could not be bought cheaply. If it came cheaply, the unity would not be durable enough for a mass war against Japan. The Sian incident made Chiang give up his method. Thereafter a debate was to develop in the CCP between Wang Ming's broad cooperation to achieve unity *for* struggle and Mao's limited cooperation to achieve unity *through* struggle.

With his more orthodox view on the lack of political consciousness of the peasants, Wang was anxious to take the national revolution back to the cities where the KMT dominated. His original plan for a national defence government and anti-Japanese allied armies did not imply an overhaul of the government in Nanking, only its reform to include representatives of the other parties and popular bodies. Later he went even further to advocate unity of command, discipline, supply, equipment, and planning of the anti-Japanese allied forces.[245] According to him, unity without sincere cooperation could not ensure a successful resistance to Japan.[246] For him, therefore, everything must be for the resistance war and for unity. To be sure, he still had a considerable following in his party and the backing of the authority of the CI and the USSR. China's need for Russian aid tended to enhance his status in the CCP. Furthermore, in Central and South China there were guerrilla bands soon to be grouped together to form the New Fourth Army under Hsiang Ying, a follower of Wang Ming. Wang's personal prestige in the ECCI, his eloquence, and his real power made him a considerable figure capable of challenging Mao's leadership.

Mao, on the other hand, had scarcely any trust in Chiang as an ally. The war could be localized; it could be settled peacefully and quickly be transformed into a Japanese-Chiang joint campaign against the CCP. In that eventuality, to give up the Red Army and soviet territory would be sheer folly. To prepare against such an eventuality the CCP must not only preserve its autonomy and its ability to defend itself. It must also promote what Mao called democracy and progress for the improvement of people's livelihood and mass participation in the war, turning it into a true people's war. The struggle for democracy and progress was in itself a guarantee

[245] Wang Ming, *Hsuan-chi*, 1.168–9.   [246] *Ming-pao*, 61.91.

of the solidarity of the nation. In a mass war, even if the grande bourgeoisie and big landlords turned away from fighting Japan, the CCP could still stand alone without repeating the sorrowful history of 1927.

The crux of mass mobilization for a mass war lay in an appropriate land policy and economic reform. Once again the focus of the party was on the rich peasants. Wang Ming in his 'New situation and new strategy' of 1935 came out with a land policy even more moderate than Mao's before 1931: only landlords' land was to be confiscated while rich peasants could retain their farming tools and receive an equal share of land, not just poor land.[247] To be sure, Wang at this stage was disheartened by the failure of the land revolution, regarding it as merely an armed struggle with little social and political meaning.[248] At the Wa-yao-pao Conference this more lenient land policy was accepted. The rich, middle and poor peasants were to receive an equal share of the same land while the rich peasants' investments in commerce and industry were to remain intact. Their livestock, movable property and farm tools were not to be redistributed.[249] By the summer of 1936 the CCP tempered its land policy still further to draw it closer to Wang Ming's views, in order to facilitate cooperation between the two major parties.[250]

There were pragmatic reasons for the mitigation of CCP land policy. The fundamental agrarian problems of north Shensi, for that matter of North China in general, were not high tenancy rates and a hunger for land, but a shortage of labour and how to organize labour efficiently in order to achieve high productivity. Earlier, an ultra-left land policy implemented there had proved to be detrimental to agricultural production.[251] The change in land policy in December 1935, to one of confiscating only the rich peasants' land for rent, eliminated extreme inequality in land distribution and released the middle and poor peasants' enthusiasm for mass work. Their activism was to put an end to the monopoly of local power by landlords and rich peasants. The emphasis then was not on redistribution of land, but on a fairer distribution of grain.[252]

Mao's alternative strategy was never as crude as the 'defeat both Japan and Chiang' policy described by Chang Kuo-t'ao.[253] Its essence was how to keep Chiang in the war of resistance and if Chiang made peace with Japan, how to fight on independently and win the revolution. With

---

[247] Wang Ming, Hsuan-chi, 1.97–8.   [248] Ibid. 81.
[249] Ho Kan-chih, Modern revolution, 1.191; Central Executive Committee's directive on 15 December 1935 in MTTC 5.13.   [250] MTTC 5.63–5.
[251] Mao Tse-tung, Ching-chi wen-t'i yü ts'ai-cheng wen-t'i (Economic and financial problems), 8–9 and 12.
[252] Ibid. 12–15.   [253] Ming-pao, 60.88.

inferior military strength, victory could be assured only by mass mobilization to set up, defend and enlarge base areas, and thus to hasten the arrival of a nationwide revolutionary situation. The overall strategy in the war of resistance, as in the civil war before it, had to be the encirclement of cities from the countryside, thus cutting the ground under the feet of the cities and thereby taking the revolution to the cities. Meanwhile a social revolution in the countryside was in progress that was protected by the party's army and guided by its mass line. Early in 1937, as in the summer of 1936, when Mao engaged Edgar Snow in systematic conversation, his strategy may not yet have developed in its full form. But the main points were all there. Many of Mao's comrades, particularly Wang Ming, disagreed with him and the debate within the party continued. Meanwhile fast-moving events on the national front compelled the two major parties to enter a formal alliance in April 1937, less than three months before the outbreak of the war against Japan.

CHAPTER 3

NATIONALIST CHINA DURING THE SINO-JAPANESE WAR 1937–1945

It lasted eight years. Some fifteen to twenty million Chinese died as a direct or indirect result.[1] The devastation of property was incalculable. And after it was over the Nationalist government and army were exhausted and demoralized. Thus it inflicted a terrible toll on the Chinese people and contributed directly to the Communist victory in 1949. The war with Japan was surely the most momentous event in the history of the Republican era in China.

INITIAL CAMPAIGNS AND STRATEGY 1937–1939

The fighting began in darkness, not long before midnight on 7 July 1937. Since 1901, in accordance with the Boxer Protocol, the Japanese had stationed troops in North China between Tientsin and Peiping. And on that balmy summer night, a company of Japanese troops was conducting field manoeuvres near the Lu-kou-ch'iao (Marco Polo Bridge), fifteen kilometres from Peiping and site of a strategic rail junction that governed all traffic with South China. Suddenly, the Japanese claimed, they were fired upon by Chinese soldiers.[2] A quick check revealed that one of their

---

[1] Precise and reliable figures do not exist. Two official estimates: (1) Chiang Kai-shek in 1947 stated that the number of 'sacrifices' by the military and civilians was 'ten million' (*ch'ien-wan*) – clearly a loose approximation. *Kuo-chia tsung-tung-yuan* (National general mobilization), 4. (2) The officially sanctioned *Chiang tsung-t'ung mi-lu* (Secret records of President Chiang), 13. 199, records 3,311,419 military and over 8,420,000 non-combat 'casualties'. The number who died from war-related causes – starvation, deprivation of medicine, increased incidence of infectious diseases, military conscription, conscript labour, etc. – was doubtless very large. Ho Ping-ti's estimate of 15–20 million deaths seems credible (*Studies on the population of China, 1368–1953*, 252). Ch'en Ch'i-t'ien put the total deaths at 18,546,000, but did not indicate his source (*Wo-te hui-i* (My memoirs), 235). Chiang Kai-shek's son, Wego W. K. Chiang, more recently put the number of 'casualties' at 3.2 million for the military and 'some twenty-odd millions' for civilians ('Tribute to our beloved leader', Part II, *China Post* (Taipei), 29 Oct. 1977, 4).

[2] It has been stated that the initial shooting may not have been by soldiers from the Wan-p'ing garrison, but from a third party, possibly the Communists, who hoped thereby to involve the National government in a war with Japan. The charge is not, however, supported by firm evidence. See Hata Ikuhiko, *Nitchū sensō shi* (History of the Japanese-Chinese War), 181–3; Tetsuya Kataoka, *Resistance and revolution in China: the Communists and the second united front*, 54–5; Alvin D. Coox, 'Recourse to arms: the Sino-Japanese conflict, 1937–1945', in Alvin D. Coox and Hilary Conroy, eds. *China and Japan: a search for balance since World War I*, 299.

number was missing, whereupon they demanded entry to the nearby Chinese garrison town of Wan-p'ing to search for him. After the Chinese refused, they attempted unsuccessfully to storm the town. This was the initial clash of the war.

That the Japanese must ultimately bear the onus for the war is not in question; their record of aggression against China at least since the Twenty-one Demands in 1915, and especially since they seized Manchuria in 1931, was blatant. Yet precisely what happened at Lu-kou-ch'iao and why is still debated. The Chinese have generally contended that the Japanese purposely provoked the fighting. The Japanese goal was allegedly to detach North China from the authority of the Nanking government; by seizing control of the Lu-kou-ch'iao–Wan-p'ing area, they could control access to Peiping and thereby force General Sun Che-yuan, commander of the 29th Army and chairman of the Hopei-Chahar Political Council, to become a compliant puppet. Moreover, the argument continues, the Japanese had witnessed the growing unity of the Chinese and chose to establish their domination of the Chinese mainland now before the Nationalists became strong.

Evidence supporting this contention is not lacking. In September 1936, for example, the Japanese had taken advantage of a similar incident to occupy Feng-t'ai, which sat astride the railway from Peiping to Tientsin. Later the same year they had attempted in vain to purchase some 1,000 acres of land near Wan-p'ing for a barracks and airfield. Japanese military commanders had also become concerned during the spring of 1937 that Sung Che-yuan was falling more under the influence of Nanking, thus threatening their position in North China. And, for a week prior to the incident, Peiping had been in a state of tension: rumours announced that the Japanese would soon strike; the continuation of Japanese field exercises for a week at such a sensitive spot as Lu-kou-ch'iao was unusual and disturbing; pro-Japanese hoodlums were creating disturbances in Peiping, Tientsin and Pao-ting. Significantly, too, the Japanese on 9 July informed the Chinese that the supposedly missing soldier had reappeared, apparently never having been detained or molested by the Chinese.[3]

Japanese documents of the period suggest, however, that the Japanese neither planned nor desired the incident at Lu-kou-ch'iao. In 1937, the Tokyo government was pursuing a policy emphasizing industrial development as a means of strengthening the foundations of its military

[3] Wu Hsiang-hsiang, *Ti-erh-tz'u Chung-Jih chan-cheng shih* (The second Sino-Japanese War), hereafter *CJCC* 1.359–80; Li Yun-han, *Sung Che-yuan yü ch'i-ch'i k'ang-chan* (Sung Che-yuan and the 7 July war of resistance), 179–212; Li Yun-han, 'The origins of the war: background of the Lukouchiao incident, July 7, 1937', in Paul K. T. Sih, ed. *Nationalist China during the Sino-Japanese War, 1937–1945*, 18–27; T. A. Bisson, *Japan in China*, 1–39.

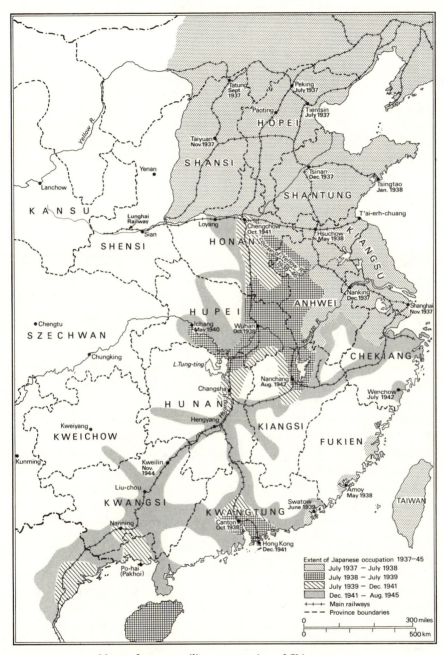

MAP 5. Japanese military occupation of China proper

forces, and the general staff as recently as June had again ordered its field commanders to avoid incidents that might provoke 'international trouble'. Officers of the Japanese army in North China were notorious, of course, for defying their superiors in Tokyo. Yet the size and deployment of the imperial forces in North China on 7 July suggests that the field commanders had made no preparations for the incident. They had only 5–7,000 men (Sung Che-yuan's 29th Army was approximately ten times that size), and most of these were engaged in manoeuvres in places where they were clearly not prepared to respond to the confrontation at Lu-kou-ch'iao. Thus only about 135 Japanese troops had been involved in the initial fighting.[4]

Whether or not the Japanese purposely provoked the Lu-kou-ch'iao fighting, the incident need not have led to a major war, for on 19 July Sung Che-yuan signed an agreement to withdraw his troops from Wan-p'ing and otherwise fully satisfied Japanese demands. But policy-makers in Nanking and Tokyo raised larger issues of principle, and these impelled the two nations into full-scale war. The National government recognized that any settlement concluded solely by regional authorities in Peiping bolstered Japanese claims that North China lay outside its sphere of authority. It consequently insisted on the preservation of full Chinese sovereignty in North China. It also advanced several (between two and four) army divisions from Central China into southern Hopei, near Pao-ting, posing a substantial threat to the Japanese forces in North China. The Japanese, on the other hand, predicated their China policy on the principle of excluding Nationalist authority from North China. And they were determined not to back down in the face of a Chinese show of strength. They therefore began reinforcing their own forces in the Peiping-Tientsin corridor.

On 25 July, the Japanese and Sung Che-yuan's forces again clashed. Three days later, the Japanese commander in North China announced 'a punitive expedition against the Chinese troops, who have been taking acts derogatory to the prestige of the Empire of Japan'.[5] Within four days, thousands of Chinese defenders lay dead, and the Japanese controlled the entire Peiping-Tientsin area. Meanwhile, the policies of the two governments were hardening. The Japanese prime minister, Prince Konoe Fumimaro, on 27 July proclaimed his determination to attain a 'fundamental solution of Sino-Japanese relations'.[6] And Chiang Kai-shek on 30 July

---

[4] Hata Ikuhiko, 162–83; Coox, 297–300; James B. Crowley, *Japan's quest for autonomy: national security and foreign policy, 1930–1938*, 310–28; Robert J. C. Butow, *Tojo and the coming of the war*, 91–5.

[5] Bisson, 28.

[6] Crowley, *Quest*, 338.

declared that 'the only course open to us now is to lead the masses of the nation, under a single national plan, to struggle to the last'.[7]

On 7 August, Chiang Kai-shek and his top advisers formally determined to wage an all-out war of resistance.[8] Chiang then made one of the greatest – and most debatable – gambles of his career. He decided to shift the major battleground of the war from North China to Shanghai. Shanghai, Nanking's strategists thought, was more suited for combat with the Japanese army than were the wide-open spaces of North China, because the constricted area of the city would nullify the Japanese superiority in tanks, artillery and logistic capabilities. An attack on the Japanese settlement in Shanghai would also divert Japanese attention from the north, enabling the Chinese there to strengthen their defences, especially of the key province of Shansi. Nanking also hoped for a political pay-off. Chinese public opinion would probably rally behind the government, as in 1932, if it took a firm stand at Shanghai. And a battle there, within a stone's throw of the large foreign community, would also draw the attention and sympathy – and possibly the intervention – of the Western powers.[9] Although pro-Nationalist writers still acclaim Chiang's gamble as a huge success, the losses probably far exceeded his worst expectations.

Chiang Kai-shek on 11 August had ordered the first three of his finest divisions – armed with German weapons and advised by General Alexander von Falkenhausen and his German staff – to take up positions inside the limits of greater Shanghai, though outside the foreign areas. The Japanese in their sector of the city (which comprised the Yangtzepoo and Hongkew sections of the International Settlement, and a salient $1\frac{1}{2}$ miles long by half a mile wide in the North Hongkew section of the Chinese city: see map 5) were caught by surprise, and they rushed in reinforcements. But when the fighting began on 13 August – there is still no agreement regarding which side started the shooting – the Chinese numbered about 80,000, the Japanese only 12,000. For a week the German-trained Chinese troops threatened to push the Japanese into the Whangpoo River. Thereafter, however, Japanese reinforcements landed on the banks of the Yangtze, on the northern edge of the city; the battle lines were now widened; and the Chinese forces had let their initial advantage slip from their grasp.

[7] Ibid. 339.
[8] Hsu Long-hsuen and Chang Ming-kai, comps. History of the Sino-Japanese War, 1937–1945, 1.357; Hsiang-hsiang Wu, 'Total strategy used by China and some major engagements in the Sino-Japanese War of 1935–1945', in Paul K. T. Sih, ed. Nationalist China, 52.
[9] Wu Hsiang-hsiang, 'Total strategy', 52–4; Ch'en Ch'eng, Pa-nien k'ang-chan ching-kuo kai-yao (Summary of experiences during the eight-year war of resistance), 9–10; Hsi-sheng Ch'i, Nationalist China at war, 41–9.

The fighting was devastating. Guns of Japanese warships, conveniently anchored in the Yangtze and Whangpoo Rivers, pounded Chinese positions at point-blank range. The Nanking government, determined not to retreat, poured in more troops. In three months of fighting, some 270,000 Chinese troops, fully 60 per cent of the Nationalist defenders and the nucleus of Chiang Kai-shek's modernized army, were killed or wounded.[10] Japanese casualties were over 40,000. Untold thousands of civilians were also slaughtered, and large portions of the city outside the Westerners' foreign concessions were destroyed.

In early November, the Japanese landed an amphibious force in Hangchow Bay, fifty miles south-west of Shanghai, and within a week this army threatened the rear of the city's defenders. The Chinese fell back toward Nanking. Their retreat was so disorganized, however, that they failed to stop at the carefully constructed concrete fortifications near Wusih on the Shanghai-Nanking railway, that had been built in imitation of the German Hindenburg Line. Nanking fell to the Japanese on 12–13 December 1937, after which the Japanese offensive slowed while their troops engaged in the most shameful episode of the war, the 'rape of Nanking'. During seven weeks of savagery, at least 42,000 Chinese were murdered in cold blood, many of them buried alive or set afire with kerosene. About 20,000 women were raped.[11] The Sino-Japanese War had begun.

Chiang Kai-shek had long attempted to avert hostilities. Since the Nationalists came to power in 1927, he had consistently favoured a conciliatory policy, despite Japan's numerous acts of interference and aggression. Convinced that China was too weak and divided to resist a strong foreign aggressor, he had acquiesced in the Japanese occupation of the four north-eastern provinces (Manchuria), concluded truces that had vitiated Nationalist influence in North China, and submitted to Japanese pressures to quash the anti-Japanese student movement. Beginning in late 1935, however, anti-Japanese sentiment had become so virulent that the National government felt constrained to harden its response to the Japanese. And, following the Sian incident of December 1936, Chiang gradually began readying for war. He had presumably purchased his release at Sian by promising verbally that he would resist future aggression. Thus, in February 1937 he removed his allegedly pro-Japanese foreign minister, Chang Ch'ün, and he began negotiating a rapprochement with his long-time enemies, the Communists. When the

[10] F. F. Liu, *A military history of Modern China, 1924–1949*, 198.
[11] F. F. Liu, 101 and 199; Lloyd E. Eastman, 'Facets of an ambivalent relationship; smuggling, puppets, and atrocities during the War, 1937–1945', in Akira Iriye, ed. *The Chinese and the Japanese: essays in political and cultural interactions*, 293–6.

fighting broke out at Lu-kou-ch'iao, therefore, Chiang had already determined to oppose further acts of Japanese aggression. All vocal parts of the nation stood behind him, more unified than in a generation.

Chiang Kai-shek's strategy was based on the principle of 'trading space for time'. Acutely sensitive to his army's inferiority to the Japanese, he had, even before the war, conceived the strategy of retreating into the remote hinterland of south-western China. 'Even if we lose fifteen ... of the eighteen provinces of China proper,' he told a gathering of political cadres in August 1935, 'with Szechwan, Kweichow and Yunnan provinces in our control we definitely will beat any enemy, and recover all the lost territory.'[12] Chiang Kai-shek's confidence was built on the realization that China's economy and society were still in a pre-modern, pre-industrial stage. He believed, therefore, that the nation's resistance could continue regardless of how many cities and factories fell to the enemy. Should the invading armies advance into China's virtually unlimited hinterland, they would be separated from their sources of supply and become exhausted. Occasionally, as at Shanghai, he did not adhere to the principle of trading space for time. In the long run, however, the strategy succeeded much as he had anticipated. The Japanese seized the urban centres of north and east China with relative ease and advanced rapidly in pronged attacks that followed the major roads and rail lines. These communications arteries did not, however, penetrate beyond the rising hills and mountains of west China, behind which the defending Chinese took cover. And the Japanese advance consequently faltered.

Unlike Chiang Kai-shek, the Japanese had no preconceived notion of the strategy or even the goals that they wished to pursue in China. During 1934–6, Foreign Minister Hirota Kōki had formulated three general desiderata for Japan in China: (1) suppression of anti-Japanese activities; (2) de facto recognition of Manchukuo and the creation of harmonious relations between that country, Japan and China; and (3) cooperation between China and Japan in the eradication of communism. But the precise meaning of Hirota's Three Principles was never clear. After the Lu-kou-ch'iao incident, Japanese policy-makers disagreed vehemently regarding their next moves. One segment of opinion, represented chiefly by the army general staff, argued against expansion in China proper. Japan's war potential was still limited, this group contended, and the opposition of the Chinese, who were now increasingly nationalistic and

---

[12] Wu Hsiang-hsiang, 'Total strategy', 48. In fact, Chiang had conceived the plan of establishing the national capital in Szechwan, in the event of war with Japan, as early as about 1932. See Chang Ch'i-yun, *Tang-shih kai-yao* (Survey history of the Kuomintang),2.914. On the Nationalists' strategic thinking generally, see Wu Hsiang-hsiang, 'Total strategy', 37–72; and Chiang Kai-shek's speeches in his *Resistance and reconstruction: messages during China's six years of war, 1937–1943.*

united, would be far more formidable than it had been in preceding years. Most Japanese leaders, civilian as well as military, however, did not comprehend the significance of the rising tide of Chinese nationalism. Remembering the ease with which they had seized Manchuria in 1931–2, they retained for the Chinese army a profound contempt. So optimistic were these proponents of war that they claimed it would be won within three months.[13]

Still, the Japanese expansionists during the early months of the war held very limited ambitions within China proper. This became evident when, on 5 November 1937, the Tokyo government proposed to settle the China 'incident' on terms similar to Hirota's Three Principles. The Chiang government did not agree to enter negotiations, however, until 2 December. By that time Shanghai had fallen, and the Nationalist armies were falling back toward Nanking in complete disarray. These easy victories whetted the Japanese appetite and the Tokyo government was no longer willing to negotiate on the basis of its November proposals. Instead, on 22 December it presented a new, harsher set of demands. These included de jure recognition of Manchukuo; demilitarization of North China and Inner Mongolia; payment of an indemnity; and – most ominous – creation of a 'special political structure' in North China which would work toward the realization of the co-prosperity of Japan, Manchukuo and China. The Chiang government did not respond to these demands, and Tokyo in January 1938 consequently announced its determination to 'annihilate' the National government.[14]

In none of the Japanese conditions for peace, now or later in the war, did they contemplate assuming direct administrative responsibilities within China proper. Japanese expansionists did, however, propose the effective subjugation of China, especially the five northern provinces, to the political will and economic needs of Japan. These were conditions that, in China's perfervid nationalistic atmosphere of 1937–8, Chiang Kai-shek could not accept, even if he wished. Chinese resistance did not collapse after the fall of Nanking, as the Japanese expansionists had complacently anticipated. Instead, the seat of the National government was moved to Chungking while Chiang, proclaiming a 'scorched-earth' policy, directed the resistance from Wuhan.

The Japanese thus made Wuhan their next objective. First, however, they endeavoured to unite their scattered armies by seizing control of the major railways linking North and Central China. In this they were

[13] Crowley, 230; Bisson, 53, 75, 124–5; Butow, 109; John Hunter Boyle, *China and Japan at war, 1937–1945: the politics of collaboration*, 53.
[14] Boyle, 68–82; Crowley, 354–78.

ultimately successful, although, as at Shanghai, they occasionally encountered heroic and brilliantly led forces of resistance. In early April 1938, for example, as the Japanese converged on the key transportation centre of Hsu-chou in northern Kiangsu, General Li Tsung-jen's forces enticed the attackers into a trap in the walled town of T'ai-erh-chuang. Li's troops inflicted heavy casualties – Chinese claimed that 30,000 Japanese were killed – and forced the Japanese remnants to retreat. This first major Chinese victory shattered the myth of Japanese invincibility. As happened too frequently, however, the Chinese did not pursue the defeated enemy, and their victory was thus ephemeral. Hsu-chou fell on 19 May. The Japanese commanders in North China and the Nanking area could now coordinate their movement in the forthcoming campaign against Wuhan.[15]

The Japanese received another notable setback in early June 1938, near Kaifeng. As they advanced westward along the Lunghai railway, the Chinese suddenly broke open the Yellow River dikes. Bursting out of its course, the river swept across the path of the approaching Japanese and continued across the plains of Honan, into Anhwei province and thence entered the sea south, rather than north, of the Shantung peninsula. The stratagem worked brilliantly. The invaders were temporarily halted, and the campaign against Wuhan was prolonged by perhaps three months. The decision to change the course of the Yellow River has, however, been bitterly criticized, and indeed the Nationalists for many years denied that they had purposely broken the dikes. For the flood had wrought even more devastation upon the Chinese populace than upon the Japanese. Some four to five thousand villages and eleven large towns had been caught in the flood waters and over two million persons were reportedly left homeless and destitute. Even seven years later, all that could be seen of some villages was the curving roof of a temple and top branches of leafless trees that poked through many feet of river silt.[16]

The determination evident at Shanghai, at T'ai-erh-chuang, and on the

---

[15] F. F. Liu, 200; Frank Dorn, *The Sino-Japanese War, 1937–41: From Marco Polo Bridge to Pearl Harbor*, 146–68; *China handbook*, henceforth *CHB*, *1937–1943: a comprehensive survey of major developments in China in six years of war*, 354–6.

[16] Dorn, 177–8; O. Edmund Clubb, *Twentieth century China*, 225; Laurance Tipton, *Chinese escapade*, 104. Estimates of the number of persons drowned by the waters released when the dikes broke ranged as high as 325,000 and even 440,000. (See Shih Ching-han, 'Huang-fan-ch'ü ti tsai-ch'ing ho hsin-sheng' (The disaster and rebirth of the Yellow River flood area), *Kuan-ch'a* (The observer), 3.3 (13 Sept. 1947), 22; and *China Weekly Review*, 105.12 (17 May 1947), 319.) Other sources state, however, that the loss of life on both the Chinese and Japanese sides was relatively light, because the Chinese residents had foreknowledge of the plan and because the flood waters advanced slowly. (See Frank Oliver, *Special undeclared war*, 209–10; and Archives of the United Nations Relief and Rehabilitation Administration, Monograph China 119, Box 2781, 'Honan regional office: history, as of 31 March 1947', 4.)

Yellow River were, however, atypical of the Nationalists' resistance during this initial phase of the war. Many Chinese commanders were hesitant and cowardly.[17] Most of them had enjoyed regional autonomy too long to risk their lives and power merely at Chiang Kai-shek's command. Governor Han Fu-chü, for example, ignominiously abandoned Shantung province to the Japanese, although he, in contrast to most, paid for his disregard of Chiang's orders with his life. He was executed in January 1938.

Although the Japanese suffered heavy losses in their long campaign to take Wuhan, their superiority in artillery, tanks and planes finally enabled them to seize the city on 25 October 1938. Only four days earlier, having met virtually no resistance, they had also taken Canton. Surely, Japanese strategists thought, the Chinese would now capitulate.

Some members of the Nationalist government had indeed felt revulsion against the horrible destruction of the war, evidenced for example in Chiang Kai-shek's scorched-earth policy which led, among other disasters, to the burning of Changsha in November 1938. Moreover, hopes for foreign intervention against Japan were bruised in September 1938, after England and France at Munich offered up Czechoslovakia to secure peace with Hitler. Only Soviet Russia provided aid to China, and it did so – some thought – merely to prolong the war and thus weaken the National government. The true beneficiaries of the war, it was therefore contended, were the Chinese Communists, who were using their respite from Nationalist annihilation campaigns to expand territorially.

The prime spokesman for those in the government who had misgivings about the policy of resistance was Wang Ching-wei. As vice director-general of the Kuomintang, he was nominally the second-ranking leader of the Nationalist movement. Although a charismatic politician with a sizeable following within the KMT, Wang wielded little influence within the Chiang Kai-shek-dominated government. Motivated perhaps equally, therefore, by overweening political ambition and despair of altering the strategy of resistance imposed upon the Chinese people, he defected from Chungking on 18 December 1938. Subsequently, in March 1940, he established a Reformed National government in Nanking, under the virtual dominance of the Japanese, as a rival to the government at Chungking.[18]

Chiang Kai-shek, on his part, appeared not to be dispirited. The

[17] Dorn, 167, 201; 205; Boyle, 139.

[18] Standard accounts of Wang Ching-wei's defection to the Japanese are: Boyle, cited above; Chu Tzu-chia (Chin Hsiung-pai), *Wang cheng-ch'üan ti k'ai-ch'ang yü shou-ch'ang* (The beginning and ending of the drama of the Wang regime); and Gerald Bunker, *The peace conspiracy: Wang Ching-wei and the China War, 1937–1941*.

abandonment of Wuhan, he optimistically proclaimed, 'marks a turning point in our struggle from the defensive to the offensive'.[19] Despite this seeming bravado, even the Japanese recognized that, by failing to knock out the Nationalist army at Wuhan, they had lost the chance of a rapid victory. Now the Nationalist forces had retreated into the rugged mountainous areas of the country, beyond the arteries of modern communication which had hitherto facilitated the Japanese advance. The Japanese high command envisioned victory not in three months but perhaps in three years.[20]

CHINA'S MOBILIZATION FOR WAR

For several years, despite repeated Japanese provocations, Chiang Kai-shek had postponed the inevitable, believing that he must first suppress the Communists and improve the quality of the army. Yet, in July 1937, Nationalist China remained woefully unprepared for war. During the next two years, therefore, there was a flurry of measures to put the nation on a war footing.

During the Nanking decade, Chiang had particularly stressed moderniza-tin of the armed forces. A corps of German advisers, most noted of whom were Generals Hans von Seeckt and Alexander von Falkenhausen, began training a modern officer corps. Substantial quantities of weapons and materiel, mostly of German manufacture, were imported for select units of the central army. The nucleus of an air force was established, and plans were conceived to equip the navy with German-built submarines, cruisers and torpedo boats.[21]

General von Seeckt had particularly emphasized to Chiang that a highly developed defence industry was essential for the maintenance of a modern army. Considering the manifest importance of such an industrial base, however, remarkably little had been accomplished. Not until 1935 was the National Resources Commission created for the purpose of developing heavy industry. The commission in 1936 inaugurated a three-year plan of industrial development, but it was very inadequately funded until after the war began.[22] In 1937, consequently, the nation's defence industry remained in its formative stages, and the army continued to rely heavily upon foreign sources for weapons and equipment. China's arsenals did produce substantial quantities of rifles and machine-guns, but

---

[19] Hollington K. Tong, *China and the world press*, 72.   [20] Butow, 135–6.

[21] F. F. Liu, 97; William C. Kirby, *Germany and Republican China*, 217–23; Jürgen Domes, *Vertagte Revolution*, 580–5.

[22] On the National Resources Commission, see above, ch. 3. This commission had been preceded by the National Defense Planning Committee, founded in 1932, which had been charged with surveying the military, industrial, cultural, etc. requirements of national defence. See *CJCC* 2.292.

virtually all heavy weapons, as well as trucks, petrol and radio equipment still had to be imported. About 300,000 troops had received German-type training, but only 80,000 of these were fully equipped with German weapons. The remainder of the approximately 1.7 million men in the Nationalist army were, by European and Japanese standards, badly trained, poorly equipped, and divided into numerous virtually independent and mutually jealous commands.[23]

Politically, too, China had begun mobilizing for the anticipated struggle with Japan, but progress had likewise been painfully slow. Following the Sian incident in December 1936 (see above, pp. 47–8), the Nationalists and Communists began negotiating a second united front. Chiang Kai-shek and Chou En-lai met five times during the first six months of the year, but the alliance had still not been consummated when the fighting erupted in July.[24]

In the spring of 1937, Chiang Kai-shek had also taken the unusual step of inviting more than 400 of the nation's leaders to a conference at the resort area of Lu-shan to exchange views on the nation's problems. Invited to the meeting were not only prominent Kuomintang members, but leaders of the minor political parties (such as the China Youth Party, the National Socialist Party, and the Third Party) and outstanding non-partisans from scholarly and professional organizations (such as Hu Shih, Fu Ssu-nien, and Chang Po-ling). The conference was actually not convened until 16 July, by which time fighting had begun. Though the government thus tried even prior to the war to align itself with the rising anti-Japanese sentiment, it still continued to incarcerate political prisoners such as Ch'en Tu-hsiu, and it prosecuted the so-called 'Seven Gentlemen', popular leaders of the anti-Japanese National Salvation Movement.

Once fighting began, however, the pace of war preparations quickened. The united front with the Communists was finally concluded. The leadership structure of the government was totally revamped. And, by no means least important, the vast migration of the government, people and materiel to the hinterland provinces of western China began. Both the structure and environment of Nationalist rule were consequently altered, although its essential character – a dictatorial regime dependent upon military force – remained unchanged.

To mobilize the country politically, the government attempted simultaneously to strengthen the centralized, authoritarian powers of Chiang Kai-shek and to broaden its base of popular support. As early as August

---

[23] *Ibid.* 1.324–6; F. F. Liu, 112, 153–5; Dorn, 6–10; Ch'en Ch'eng, table 9.
[24] See ch. 12 below (Van Slyke). On the meetings between Chiang and Chou, see US State Dept. 893.00/14154, 23 July 1937, encl., T. A. Bisson letter to Raymond Leslie Buell.

1937, Chiang was granted new and far-reaching powers. The unwieldy Central Political Council, which had been the party organ responsible for the general supervision and direction of the government, was replaced by a Supreme National Defence Conference (Kuo-fang tsui-kao hui-i) (in January 1939, it was reorganized as the Supreme National Defence Council – Kuo-fang tsui-kao wei-yuan hui). Chiang chaired this body, which was nominally the top organ of government. At the same time, and ultimately of greater significance, the Military Affairs Commission (Chün-shih wei-yuan hui), also chaired by Chiang, assumed control not only of the military, but of all administrative functions of government. Now, according to the commission's newly revised organization law, 'the chairman [of the Military Affairs Commission], in shouldering his full responsibility of national defence, shall have supreme command of the land, naval and air forces, *and shall direct the people of the entire nation*'.[25] With this mandate, Chiang Kai-shek established within the commission eight departments that were charged with the direction of political policies, heavy industries, light industries and commerce, international relations, and civilian defence, as well as military operations. The Executive Yuan and the various ministries of the National government remained in existence, but their duties were largely taken over by the Military Affairs Commission.[26]

Within five months, however, administration of the wartime state was in utter chaos. The jurisdiction of the Military Affairs Commission was so broad, its administration so complex and unwieldy, and its relations with other governmental bodies so unclear, that the government became engulfed in confusion. As a consequence, civilian administrative responsibilities were restored, at least formally, to the appropriate organs of the government and party. And the Military Affairs Commission was again charged solely with direction of military aspects of the war effort. Despite this reorganization, the commission throughout the war continued to be the effective centre of government. Chiang Kai-shek at various times held other high-ranking posts. He was, for example, chairman of the Supreme National Defence Council, president of the Executive Yuan (that is, premier of the government), chairman of the People's Political Council, and director-general of the Kuomintang. He preferred, however, to exercise his authority through the office of chairman of the Military Affairs Commission.

Within the commission, therefore, he created an Office of Councillors (Ts'an-shih-shih; directed by Wang Shih-chieh) which concerned itself

---

[25] *CHB, 1937–1943*, 321. Emphasis added.
[26] F. F. Liu, 116–18, 121–2; Chang Ch'i-yun, 3.1152; Ch'ien Tuan-sheng, *The government and politics of China*, 185–7.

with problems of economics, finance and governmental administration generally. Even in foreign policy, the Office of Councillors frequently spoke with greater authority than did the Ministry of Foreign Affairs. There was also the Office of Aides (Shih-ts'ung-shih) – better known as the generalissimo's personal secretariat. This office, staffed with such influential personages as Ch'en Kuo-fu and Ch'en Pu-lei, determined who met Chiang and what information reached his ears, as well as advising him on all appointments to official posts. The Military Affairs Commission also included a Bureau of Censorship and a Bureau of Investigation and Statistics (Chün-shih tiao-ch'a t'ung-chi chü), the latter being the much-feared secret police directed by General Tai Li. The commission was, consequently, the seat of an informal government that, throughout the war, held virtually unlimited authority over the formal offices of the National government.[27]

Within the Kuomintang, too, Chiang Kai-shek's personal leadership was acknowledged. For several years he had aspired to the position of *tsung-li* (director-general) of the party, the office through which Sun Yat-sen had wielded dictatorial control over the Nationalist movement after the party reorganization in 1924. After Sun's death, however, that title had been forever reserved for him, and the Kuomintang had thereafter been administered, formally at least, through a committee system. Chiang Kai-shek wished to resurrect the leadership principle, believing that he was due the honour and that the lack of a single leader had caused much of the party's divisiveness and instability since Sun's death. During the Nanking decade, powerful factions within the party, such as that centring around Hu Han-min in Kwangtung and Kwangsi, had been jealous of Chiang's growing powers. But in 1938 his popularity was at a peak. At the Extraordinary Congress of the KMT in Wuhan in March 1938, therefore, he was finally accorded the title of director-general. (In Chinese, the term was *tsung-ts'ai*, not *tsung-li*, a distinction without a difference.) His dominance of the party had already been virtually complete. Yet he was elated. 'I have struggled thirty years for the party and the nation,' he exulted, 'and only today have I received recognition from the entire party. Our party has been unstable for fifteen years, and only today is it stabilized.'[28] Following President Lin Sen's death in August 1943, Chiang also assumed the office of president. During the war, therefore, all supreme positions in the party, government and military became his.

Even as Chiang consolidated his dictatorship, he endeavoured to

[27] On organization of the government, see F. F. Liu, 116–17; Ch'ien Tuan-sheng, 185–7; *CHB, 1937–1943*, 86, 322–3.
[28] Chang Ch'i-yun, 3.1214.

broaden its political base. In Wuhan in early 1938 the spirit of national unity pulsated with unprecedented and never again recaptured fervour. The Extraordinary Congress of the KMT called for the creation of both the People's Political Council (Kuo-min ts'an-cheng-hui), or PPC, and the Three-People's-Principles Youth Corps (San-min-chu-i ch'ing-nien t'uan). The PPC was a parliament-like body designed to provide a platform for popular participation in the affairs of the National government. It was initially made up of 200 members, selected in various ways designed to assure the participation of prominent persons not members of the KMT. As a result, the minor political parties and the Communists received about fifty seats; independents were granted seventy seats; Kuomintang members held no more than eighty seats. The new council was thus a remarkably representative and capable body that reflected the mood of national unity during the first year of the war.[29]

The PPC was not a fully-fledged parliament, however, for its powers were sharply limited. It could propose policies and criticize, but it could not enforce its decisions. Its powers were merely advisory. But as long as the spirit of cooperation pervaded the council, until about 1939, it was an influential organ of the government.

The Three-People's-Principles Youth Corps was a very different organization, designed to enlist the support of the nation's youth. All non-Kuomintang youth groups were now abolished – through the simple expedient of refusing them the required governmental registration – and young men and women were encouraged to flock to the leadership of Chiang Kai-shek. A second purpose of the Youth Corps, however, was to revitalize the Kuomintang. Chiang Kai-shek in 1938 continued to be bitterly disappointed with the KMT, which he felt was corrupt and ineffectual. 'Most party members,' he declared,

appear to be dejected, their living is lax, they lack enthusiasm and their work is lackadaisical. Moreover, like ordinary commoners, they indulge in ease and pleasure. They even struggle for power and for their own selfish concerns... Party members have therefore almost become a special class...and the masses...are not only cool toward the party but even become antagonistic toward it.[30]

Chiang hoped that the Youth Corps would imbue the Nationalist movement with a fresh idealism. 'The Kuomintang,' he stated, 'is the nation's arteries, but [members of] the Three-People's-Principles Youth Corps are new corpuscles within the arteries.'[31]

---

[29] On the People's Political Council, see Lawrence Nae-lih Shyu, 'The People's Political Council and China's wartime problems, 1937–1945'.

[30] Chang Ch'i-yun, 3.1226–7. On the political role of the Youth Corps, see Lloyd E. Eastman, *Seeds of destruction: Nationalist China in war and revolution 1937–1949*, 89–107.

[31] Chang Ch'i-yun, 4.1731.

Most dramatic of Nationalist China's several acts of wartime mobilization was the removal of population, government, schools and factories from the coastal areas to the interior. Prior to the war, the political, cultural and industrial centres of Chinese national life had been the cities in North China and in the coastal and riverine areas of Central and South China – in precisely the areas most easily overrun by the Japanese. Beyond those areas lay the vast provinces of the interior: Szechwan, Yunnan, Kweichow, Kwangsi, Hunan, Shensi, Sikang and Kansu.[32] Life in these provinces had changed little since the Ch'ing dynasty, but here the Nationalists made their wartime base.

Anticipating that the struggle with Japan would be a war of attrition, the National government immediately after the Lu-kou-ch'iao incident began removing key industrial enterprises to the interior. Military industries, such as aeroplane assembly plants and especially the arsenals in Nanking, Wuhan, Kwangtung and Shansi, constituted the bulk of the considerable industrial migration that began in August 1937. Private industrialists, too, were urged to move their factories out of the path of the Japanese. On 10 August, three days before fighting erupted at Shanghai, the government allocated money to the National Resources Commission to assist in transferring private factories from that city. War quickly overtook these preparations. The equipment of 146 factories, weighing 15,000 tons and accompanied by over 2,500 workers, was removed from Shanghai even as bullets were flying. The destination of most of these factories during this early stage of the war was Wuhan. Before much of the machinery could be uncrated and the factories resume production, however, Wuhan itself was endangered, and the flight to the interior resumed. Some factories were shipped by boat across Tung-t'ing Lake to Kwangsi or western Hunan; others went by rail to Sian and Pao-ch'i in Shensi. Many were put on junks and towed up the Yangtze. West of I-ch'ang, the river swirled through its narrow and steep-faced gorges, where boats often progressed upstream only when pulled by hundreds of straining, sweating trackers. Altogether, 639 private factories were removed to the unoccupied areas (of these, about three-fourths ultimately resumed production). Equipment from the two large but antiquated iron-and-steel plants at Wuhan, including the Hanyang Steel Works, represented a major part of this transshipment (37,000 tons). In addition, there was the machinery of 115 textile factories weighing 32,000 tons, and of 230 machine-making plants weighing nearly 19,000 tons. Joining these

[32] Because the Japanese armies generally succeeded in occupying only the cities, railway lines and coastal areas, sizeable parts of other provinces, such as Kwangtung, Fukien, Chekiang, Kiangsi, Hupei and Honan remained more or less under the jurisdiction of the National government.

factories in flight were 42,000 skilled workmen, 12,000 of whom came with the financial assistance of the government.[33]

The Nationalists have depicted this industrial migration as evidence of the heroic dedication of the Chinese people. Notable though the achievement was, its effect has been vastly exaggerated. The amount of machinery removed, totalling some 120,000 tons, was actually insignificant relative to both the existing industrial plant and Nationalist China's wartime needs. More important, if the government had planned this industrial migration in advance – as it might easily have done, because it had long anticipated the war – the operation might have been carried out far more safely and extensively. Actually, instead of standing as a monument to Chinese patriotism, the industrial migration betrayed a distressing degree of self-serving. When the arsenals were removed, for example, not only machinery, raw materials, and workers and their families were shipped, but everything owned by the workers, including house-doors and windows, was moved. And workers in the arsenals competed vigorously with each other for the limited means of transportation, sometimes even shooting at each other.[34] Private industrialists received lucrative inducements from the government. They were guaranteed profits of 5–10 per cent for a period of five to seven years, and were promised low-interest loans and free factory sites.[35] The large majority of industrialists, who were not given such attractive promises, preferred the amenities of Hong Kong or of the International Settlement in Shanghai to the rigours and uncertainties of the interior. Chinese financiers likewise ignored the government's appeals to transfer their investments to the interior. Billions of Chinese dollars lay idle in Hong Kong and Shanghai, or took flight to the United States. Thus, some Chinese evinced an exemplary spirit of national dedication and unity, but most industrialists and financiers felt little or no personal involvement in the cause of Chinese resistance, and showed little confidence in the government's war bonds. They did not allow patriotism to dull their business instincts.[36]

---

[33] 'Chan-shih hou-fang kung-yeh shih ju-ho chien-li-ti' (How the wartime industry in the rear was established), *Hsin-shih-chieh yueh-k'an* (New world monthly), 15 March 1944, 10–15; Li Tzu-hsiang, 'K'ang-chan i-lai Ssu-ch'uan chih kung-yeh' (Szechwan's industry during the war), *Ssu-ch'uan ching-chi chi-k'an* (Szechwan economics quarterly), hereafter *SCCC*, 1.1 (15 Dec. 1943), 27–33; Hsu Ti-hsin, 'K'ang-chan i-lai liang-ko chieh-tuan ti Chung-kuo ching-chi' (China's economy during the two stages of the war), *Li-lun yü hsien-shih* (Theory and reality), 1.4 (15 Feb. 1940), 34–44; *CHB, 1937–1943*, 436–9; Chang Kia-ngau, *The inflationary spiral: the experience in China, 1939–1950*, 211–18; Hubert Freyn, *Free China's New Deal*, 41–2.

[34] 'Chan-shih hou-fang kung-yeh shih ju-ho chien-li-ti', 12.

[35] *CHB, 1937–1943*, 438.

[36] Shih Hsi-min, 'K'ang-chan i-lai ti Chung-kuo kung-yeh' (Chinese industry during the war), *Li-lun yü hsien-shih*, 1.4 (15 Feb. 1940), 53–4; Lin Chi-yung, 'K'ang-chan ch'i-chung min-ying

Universities also joined the migration to the interior. Since they had been the fountainhead of opposition to Japanese imperialism, the Japanese army wreaked a special vengeance upon them. On 29 July 1937 Japanese planes bombed Nankai University in Tientsin. The next day, Japanese artillery pummelled the remains of the campus. Finally, using kerosene, they set flames to the ruins in order to complete the destruction of this anti-Japanese centre. Tsing-hua University in Peiping was first systematically stripped by Japanese looters, and then its buildings were converted into a barracks, hospital, bar, brothel and stables for the imperial army. Other universities, in Shanghai, Nanking, Wuhan and Canton, were repeatedly bombed.[37]

Students and professors became a part of the tide of refugees to the interior. By late 1939, only six of the universities, colleges and vocational schools originally in Japanese-occupied territory remained there. Of the rest, fully fifty-two educational institutions had fled into the interior, while twenty-five took refuge in the foreign concessions or Hong Kong. Those that joined the exodus to the west sometimes had to travel 2–3,000 miles before finding a wartime haven. Three of China's most noted universities (Tsing-hua, Peita and Nankai), for example, first fled to Changsha in Hunan, where they established a joint campus. By February 1938, however, the students and faculty had to move again, this time to Kunming, the capital of Yunnan. One group went by rail and ship by way of Canton and Hanoi. The second group, consisting of 257 students and eleven professors, trekked over a thousand miles, mostly on foot, to the new campus.

The war exacted a heavy toll on the educational establishment. Seventeen institutions had been forced to close; thousands of youths had their education halted. Some students, of course, stayed at home, but hundreds of others joined the Nationalist army or the Communist guerrillas, or participated in troop entertainment or nursing corps. For those who continued their studies, conditions in the refugee universities were often wretched. There were severe shortages of textbooks, library materials and scientific apparatus. Professors frequently had lost their lecture notes and other reference materials. Both students and professors, too, found living conditions harsh. Temples, ancestral halls or mud-and-wattle huts were

ch'ang-k'uang ch'ien-Ch'uan chien-shu' (Summary account of the move of privately-owned factories and mining to Szechwan during the war), *Ssu-ch'uan wen-hsien* (Records of Szechwan), 62 (1 Oct. 1967), 4–7; Freyn, *Free China's New Deal*, 12–3; Edgar Snow, *The battle for Asia*, 149; Barbara W. Tuchman, *Stilwell and the American experience in China, 1911–45*, 184.

[37] On education during the war, see Hubert Freyn, *Chinese education in the war*; William P. Fenn, *The effect of the Japanese invasion on higher education in China*; John Israel, 'Southwest Associated University: survival as an ultimate value', and Ou Tsuin-chen', 'Education in wartime China', both in Paul K. T. Sih, ed. *Nationalist China*.

converted into classrooms and dormitories. Wooden crates served as desks; lighting was inadequate.

High morale, at least for a time, partially compensated for these material deprivations. Students felt they were defying the hated aggressor simply by continuing their education. Government authorities agreed that they were the nation's future leaders and could better serve the nation by preparing for the tasks of reconstructing the nation after the war than by serving in the army. Except for occasional air raids and other inconveniences, therefore, the educational system continued to operate on a business-as-usual basis. Moreover, because virtually all students received government financial aid and were exempt from military conscription, university enrolment grew from 42,000 students in 1936 to 79,000 in 1944.

The influx of several million refugees deeply affected the provinces of west China.[38] Hitherto they had been isolated, barely touched by the modernizing influences from the coastal areas. Many of the refugees, by contrast, were middle- and upper-class sophisticates accustomed to wealth, power, and modern amenities. They were often condescending to the more rustic natives, whose customs appeared quaint and whose language was virtually incomprehensible. They also resented the discriminatory prices and rents charged by local merchants and landlords. The local provincials, on the other hand, resented the airs and arrogance of the 'down-river people' (hsia-chiang jen). The new arrivals did indeed attempt to monopolize the major functions of government and to seize control of banking, trade and the economy generally. The most desirable jobs in government offices and factories were denied the natives, whom the down-river people regarded as lazy and unskilled. As the years passed, linguistic differences ceased to obstruct communication between natives and refugees, intermarriage became increasingly common, and the double standard of prices largely disappeared. Yet the natives' resentment against discrimination in jobs and social status never wholly dissipated as long as the war lasted.[39]

[38] Ta Ch'en, *Population in modern China*, 61. The precise number of immigrants to west China is impossible to determine. Chen estimated that 3,500,000 residents of the major cities of north and east China fled from the Japanese. These probably constituted the major portion of permanent refugees in the Nationalist areas. Chen estimated that an additional 10,750,000 fled from the less urbanized areas. Many of these doubtless were farmers, who fled their homes during periods of warfare, but subsequently returned. Some estimates of the number of refugees in west China go as high as 50 million. See Chang Kia-ngau, *Inflationary spiral*, 14, 25. This, however, is surely inaccurate. Theodore H. White, *In search of history*, 79, relates how an estimate of numbers of refugees could become grossly exaggerated.

[39] Ta Chen, 62–8; Kuo-heng Shih, *China enters the machine age, a study of labor in Chinese war industry*, 9–12 and *passim*.

DETERIORATION 1939-1945: THE MILITARY

After the fall of Wuhan and Canton in late October 1938, the character of the war and conditions in the Nationalist areas changed profoundly. The fighting progressively entered a stalemate. Especially after the Japanese attack on Pearl Harbor on 7 December 1941, Nationalist leaders anticipated that the Western Allies could defeat Japan without the necessity of further Chinese sacrifices. After all, they had fought Japan alone for four and a half years already. They consequently devoted less attention to combating the Japanese than to containing the Communists, whose growing power and territorial control augured badly for national unity and stability in the postwar period. Most of all, however, the Nationalist government at Chungking found itself caught in a seemingly irreversible process of deterioration – military, economic, social, and political – that left it by 1945 weak and demoralized.

When the Nationalists did not capitulate following their defeat at Wuhan in October 1938, the Japanese leaders realized that they had misjudged the Chinese powers of resistance and that the imperial army would merely exhaust itself if it continued to pursue the elusive defenders into the hinterlands. They therefore adopted a new strategy, stressing political means to secure control of China. First, they would consolidate control of the areas overrun since July 1937. They now effectively controlled only some 10 per cent of the territory in North and Central China – primarily the major cities and areas bordering the major railways and highways. They needed to eliminate many pockets of resistance and to harness the productive capabilities of the occupied areas to the economy of the homeland.[40]

Second, the Japanese determined to wear down the Nationalists until they collapsed from 'internal disintegration'.[41] They thus simultaneously tightened their economic blockade of the Nationalist areas and began a destructive air war. In the spring of 1939 they seized Nanchang in Kiangsi, cutting the important Chekiang-Hunan railway. In November they landed an amphibious force at Po-hai (Pakhoi) in western Kwangtung, and advanced a hundred miles to take Nanning, the capital of Kwangsi. This was a damaging blow to the Nationalists, for it severed the new railway line from Hanoi over which the Chinese were obtaining fully a third of their critically needed imports. Then, in September 1940 the Japanese occupied the northern part of French Indo-China, closing the important

---

[40] F. F. Liu, 202–3; Hata Ikuhiko, 296–7; Evans Fordyce Carlson, *The Chinese army: its organization and military efficiency*, 75; *CJCC* 2.573–4.
[41] Tetsuya Kataoka, 152.

rail line between Hanoi and Kunming. Thereafter the Nationalists were dependent for supplies from the outside world upon the newly opened but barely passable Burma Road, air transport from Hong Kong (which the Japanese were to occupy in December 1941), and the long caravan and truck route from Russia (see map).

The Japanese air raids struck indiscriminately at military and civilian targets. Their purpose was less to destroy military installations and factories than to demoralize the population. Virtually all cities in the Nationalist area, including Kweilin, Kunming and Sian, were hit. Chungking, however, suffered most severely. Bombed 268 times during 1939–41, much of the city was gutted, and many thousands died (4,400 were killed in just the first two days of heavy raids in May 1939).[42]

Yet neither the air raids nor the blockade broke the Chinese will to resist. Indeed, the perseverance of the Chungking population remained firm as long as the bombings continued, and wilted only after they ceased in late 1941. The blockade was less than a complete success, in part because the Nationalists in July 1939 had legalized, and thereafter actively promoted, the trade in most goods from areas held by the Japanese. The Japanese were at a loss to stop this trade. They were incapable of guarding every foot, or even every mile, of the more than 2,000 miles of border between occupied and unoccupied China. Many Japanese also actively colluded in this commerce, so that a sizeable but indeterminate part of Nationalist China's imports during the war came through this so-called smuggling trade.[43]

A momentous discussion by the Japanese cabinet in July 1940 also affected their operations in China. Perceiving that success in China would continue to elude them unless they obtained access to the rich natural resources of South-East Asia, and convinced that the Western powers were preoccupied with the war in Europe, the Japanese leaders agreed to broaden the scope of imperial expansion beyond the China theatre. They hoped, although without conviction, that they could attain their goals in the south by diplomacy. This decision inevitably altered the character of the China war and also led, within little more than a year, to the attack on Pearl Harbor.[44]

On the Chinese side, strategic and political considerations had persuaded the Nationalist leadership to wage a war of attrition. Chiang Kai-shek claimed that the Japanese were spreading their resources of men and

[42] CJCC 587–8.

[43] Yu-Kwei Cheng, *Foreign trade and industrial development of China: an historical and integrated analysis through 1948*, 148–9.

[44] Butow, 133; Boyle, 300; Fujiwara Akira, 'The role of the Japanese Army', in Dorothy Borg and Shumpei Okamoto, eds. *Pearl Harbor as history: Japanese-American relations, 1931–1941*, 191.

equipment too thin by advancing across the expanse of China. 'The longer our enemy struggles, the more he involves himself in difficulties; while the longer we struggle, the stronger and more determined we become.'[45] Chiang, like the Japanese, also wished to avoid decisive battles, because he anticipated that the Western Allies would ultimately be drawn into the struggle against Japan. Initially he looked to the Allies merely for material aid and for economic sanctions against Japan. But after Pearl Harbor – news of which was greeted joyously in Chungking – he expected that Great Britain and especially the United States, with its enormous technological resources, would assume the major burden of defeating Japan. By 1943, the American ambassador to China, Clarence E. Gauss, observed that 'The Chinese have persuaded themselves that [they] are too tired and too worn and too ill-equipped to make greater effort, especially when such effort may not be necessary; and that [they] can sit back, holding what they have against the Japanese, and concentrate their planning upon China's post-war political and economic problems.'[46]

The chief political problem that distracted the Nationalists' attention from the Japanese was the growing friction with the Chinese Communists. After the New Fourth Army incident in January 1941 (see p. 233) the united front had virtually ceased to exist. Influential Nationalist leaders – most notably the minister of war, Ho Ying-ch'in, and the party apparatchik, Ch'en Li-fu – at various times stridently advocated a final extermination campaign against the Communists. Chiang Kai-shek resisted these pressures, in large part because he feared that the Allies would cease aiding the Nationalist army if it became openly involved in civil war. Yet, since mid-1939, he had committed many of his best troops – at various times between 150,000 and 500,000 – to blockading the Communists' base in the north-west.[47]

Although both Nationalists and Japanese after late 1938 were content to wage a war of attrition, fighting by no means abated completely. Occasionally the Japanese launched an offensive to attain limited objectives. In June 1940, for example, they seized the important Yangtze River port of I-ch'ang in order to staunch the flow of goods between the rice-bowl provinces of Central China and Chungking and to obtain an air base closer to the Nationalist area. In the summer of 1942, after General James H. Doolittle's bombing of Tokyo, the Japanese struck into Chekiang and Kiangsi with 100,000 troops to destroy air bases that might

[45] Chiang Kai-shek, *Resistance and reconstruction*, 108.
[46] *FRUS, 1943, China*, 142.
[47] Charles F. Romanus and Riley Sunderland, *Stilwell's command problems*, 303; F. F. Liu, 205; L. P. Van Slyke, ed. *The Chinese Communist movement: a report of the United States War Department, July 1945*, 71–2.

be used in future raids against the home islands. Periodically, too, they launched attacks against the Nationalist lines, less to occupy new territory than to ravage the countryside, seize or destroy recent harvests, prevent the Nationalists from amassing potentially dangerous concentrations of troops, or train recent recruits in actual combat.[48] The casualties sustained in these years of so-called stalemate – particularly during the early period – were considerable. The Chinese admitted to suffering 340,000 dead in 1940: 145,000 in 1941; 88,000 in 1942; and 43,000 in 1943.[49] Yet the battle lines from 1939 to early 1944 were not significantly altered, and the strategic balance between the two enemies was little changed for nearly six years.

The Nationalist army during the latter half of the war numbered more than 3,500,000 men.[50] It was not, however, a united, national army, but a coalition of armies which differed in degrees of loyalty to the central government as well as in training, equipment, and military capabilities. At the heart of this heterogeneous assemblage was the 'Central Army' (Chung-yang-chün). In 1941, it comprised some thirty divisions (about 300,000 men) out of a total of over 300 divisions in the entire Nationalist army. As the war progressed, Chiang added to this force so that, by the end of the war, the Central Army counted about 650,000 men. Officers in the Central Army in 1937 were typically graduates of the Central Military Academy. There they had received an introduction to modern military techniques, often during the 1930s from German instructors. Political indoctrination had bulked large in their training; officers were intensely loyal to Chiang Kai-shek.[51]

Most of the Nationalist forces, however, were direct descendants of warlord armies, commanded by men who had risen to prominence independently of the central government. Their loyalties were therefore conditional and attenuated, and they were jealous and fearful of Chiang Kai-shek's growing power. Lung Yun, governor of Yunnan, for example, resisted central government encroachments upon his provincial power, and provided a refuge for intellectuals critical of the Chungking government. Governor Yen Hsi-shan, commander of the Second War

[48] Smythe to State, 'Significant military, political and economic developments in and with respect to China during 1940', US State Dept. 893.00/14662, 29 Jan. 1941, p. 7; F. F. Liu, 203–4; Theodore H. White and Annalee Jacoby, *Thunder out of China*, 62; Hsi-sheng Ch'i, *Nationalist China at war: military defeats and political collapse, 1937–1945*, 40–82.

[49] The official Chinese figure for total wartime casualties is 3,211,419, including 1,319,958 dead. *CHB, 1950*, 182.

[50] Ch'en Ch'eng, table 9. Probably no one, however, knew the exact size of the Nationalist army. Chang Kia-ngau (*Inflationary spiral*, 127) states that the army increased from 2.5 million men in 1940 to nearly 4.5 million in 1941. *CHB, 1937–1943*, 324, gives a figure of 6 million.

[51] Charles F. Romanus and Riley Sunderland, *Stilwell's mission to China*, 35; F. F. Liu, 112–13.

Zone in North China and vice chairman of the Military Council, ruled his native Shansi as an autonomous satrapy. He prohibited units of the Central Army from entering his war zone, and maintained his own political party (the Democratic Revolutionary Comrades' Association) as a counter to the Kuomintang. Indeed, since 1941, Yen had even maintained close and amiable relations with the Japanese. Other generals with provincial origins, such as Li Tsung-jen (Kwangsi), Hsueh Yueh (Kwangtung), Yü Hsueh-chung (Manchuria) and Fu Tso-i (Suiyuan) had lost their specifically regional bases, but retained command of armies that were loyal to them rather than to Chiang Kai-shek.[52]

The relationship between those non-Central Army commanders and the central government had been altered by the outbreak of war. Throughout the Nanking decade, the power of provincial militarists had been waning. Crucial to Chiang's growing power had been his control of a politically loyal and relatively proficient army. But the destruction of Chiang's best troops at Shanghai, including the bulk of his elite German-trained divisions, caused the military balance within the Nationalist forces to shift back toward the non-Central Army commanders. Chiang's political authority diminished proportionately.

Throughout the war, Chiang endeavoured to right the political and military balance between himself and the regional commanders by inserting KMT cadres into the provincial armies and by rebuilding his central forces with newly trained officers and modern equipment. These efforts excited the suspicions and animosity of the regional generals. They complained that the central government discriminated against them by sending their divisions into decimating combat with the Japanese while Chiang held his own forces safely in reserve. They were angered by inequitable allocations of fresh supplies, for Chiang distributed the bulk of new weapons and ammunition, including Lend-Lease equipment from the United States, to his own forces rather than to the less trustworthy provincial armies.[53]

Domestic politics, in short, underlay Chiang's conduct of the war, and he took advantage of it to enhance his central power. No modern state, of course – as Chiang's supporters have argued – could easily tolerate subversively independent attitudes among its military commanders. Yet the means that Chiang employed to enhance central government powers may not have been the most efficacious. In any event, the antipathies of the provincial militarists grew keener as the war progressed. In 1944, a coalition of the leading provincial militarists was actually plotting to

[52] Lloyd E. Eastman, 'Regional politics and the central government: Yunnan and Chungking', in Paul K. T. Sih, ed. *Nationalist China*, 329–55; Hsi-sheng Ch'i, 83–131.
[53] Romanus and Sunderland, *Stilwell's mission*, 34.

overthrow Chiang's government.[54] Meanwhile many non-Central Army commanders simply defected to the Japanese. Twelve of these generals defected in 1941; fifteen defected in 1942; and in 1943, the peak year, forty-two defected. Over 500,000 Chinese troops accompanied these defecting generals, and the Japanese employed the puppet armies to protect the occupied areas against Communist guerrillas.[55]

One of the deepest flaws in the Nationalist army, exacerbated during the war, was the poor quality of the officer corps. General Albert C. Wedemeyer, senior American officer in China after October 1944, characterized the Nationalist officers as 'incapable, inept, untrained, petty...altogether inefficient'.[56] This was also characteristic of the non-Central Army senior commanders, most of whom had gained distinction and position as a result less of their military skills than of their shrewdness in factional manoeuvring and timely shifts of loyalty. Even the senior officers who had graduated from the Central Military Academy, however, sorely lacked the qualities needed for military leadership. Most of them were graduates of the Whampoa Academy's first four classes during the 1920s, when the training had been rudimentary and had lasted just a few months. By the time they were promoted to command of divisions and armies as their rewards for loyalty to Chiang Kai-shek, their comprehension of military science and technology was frequently narrow and outdated. During the 1930s, these senior officers might have taken advantage of the advanced, German-influenced training in the staff college. By that time, however, they were of such high rank that they deemed it beneath their dignity to become students again.[57]

Some of the senior commanders, of course, transcended the system. Ch'en Ch'eng, Pai Ch'ung-hsi and Sun Li-jen, for example, stood above their peers as a result of their intelligence, incorruptibility and martial talents. Significantly, however, neither Pai Ch'ung-hsi nor Sun Li-jen were members of Chiang Kai-shek's inner circle. Chiang used their talents but kept them on taut leash, because they were not Central Army men and displayed an untoward independence of mind. Ch'en Ch'eng, who was a trusted associate of Chiang, nevertheless spent much of the war under a political cloud as a result of losing a factional quarrel with Ho Ying-ch'in, the pompous and modestly endowed minister of war.[58]

[54] See below, pp. 607-8.
[55] At the end of the war, the puppet armies numbered close to one million, because many troops were recruited within the occupied areas. Eastman, 'Ambivalent relationship', 284-92.
[56] Charles F. Romanus and Riley Sunderland, *Time runs out in CBI*, 233. Ellipsis in source. See also Albert C. Wedemeyer, *Wedemeyer reports!*, 325.   [57] F. F. Liu, 55-8, 81-9, 145-52.
[58] Donald G. Gillin, 'Problems of centralization in Republican China: the case of Ch'en Ch'eng and the Kuomintang', *JAS* 29.4 (Aug. 1970) 844-7; Wedemeyer, 325; Snow, 184-5; Romanus and Sunderland, *Time runs out*, 167.

When the war began, lower-ranking officers were generally more competent than their superiors. Between 1929 and 1937, the Central Military Academy had annually graduated an average of 3,000 cadets, and about 2,000 staff officers had received advanced training. The war, however, cut deeply into the junior officer corps. Ten thousand of them had been killed in the fighting around Shanghai and Nanking at the very outset. These losses were never fully recouped, because officer training during the war deteriorated greatly, both from lowered entrance requirements and from shortened courses of study. Indeed, the percentage of officers who were academy graduates in a typical infantry battalion declined from 80 per cent in 1937 to 20 per cent in 1945.[59] Because no army is better than its junior officers, these figures provide a rough index of the deterioration of the Nationalist army during the war.

That deterioration was most evident, however, at the lowest levels, among the enlisted men. China's wartime army was composed largely of conscripts. All males between eighteen and forty-five – with the exceptions of students, only sons, and hardship cases – were subject to the draft. According to law, they were to be selected equitably by drawing lots. In fact, men with money or influence evaded the draft, while the poor and powerless of the nation were pressganged into the ranks. Frequently conscription officers ignored even the formalities of a lottery. Some peasants were simply seized while working in the fields; others were arrested, and those who could not buy their way out were enrolled in the army.

Induction into military service was a horrible experience. Lacking vehicles for transport, the recruits often marched hundreds of miles to their assigned units – which were purposely remote from the recruits' homes, in order to lessen the temptation to desert. Frequently the recruits were tied together with ropes around their necks. At night they might be stripped of their clothing to prevent them from sneaking way. For food, they received only small quantities of rice, since the conscripting officers customarily 'squeezed' the rations for their own profit. For water, they might have to drink from puddles by the roadside – a common cause of diarrhoea. Soon, disease coursed through the conscripts' bodies. Medical treatment was unavailable, however, because the recruits were not regarded as part of the army until they had joined their assigned units.[60]

---

[59] F. F. Liu, 149.

[60] Milton E. Miles, *A different kind of war*, 348, Romanus and Sunderland, *Time runs out*, 369–70. John S. Service, *Lost chance in China: the World War II despatches of John S. Service*, 33–7; Ringwalt to Atcheson, 'The Chinese soldier', US State Dept. 893.22/50, 14 Aug. 1943, encl. p. 2. Langdon to State, 'Conscription campaign at Kunming: malpractices connected with conscription and treatment of soldiers', US State Dept. 893.2222/7–144, 1 July 1944, 2–3; F. F. Liu, 137; Chiang Meng-lin, 'Hsin-ch'ao' (New tide), *Chuan-chi wen-hsueh* (Biographical literature), 11.2 (Aug. 1967) 90.

The total number of such recruits who perished en route during the eight years of the war was probably well in excess of one million.[61]

Conscripts who reached their units had survived what was probably the worst period of their military service. Yet their prospects often remained bleak. In the Central Army units, food and clothing were generally adequate. But those so unfortunate as to be assigned to some of the provincial armies – such as those of Shensi and Kansu – were so miserable, John S. Service reported, 'as to almost beggar description'.[62]

Shortage of food, not of weapons, was the paramount problem reducing the fighting efficiency of the Nationalist army. When General Wedemeyer first took up his duties as Chiang's chief-of-staff in October 1944, he concerned himself primarily with problems of troop movements and disposition. Within a month, however, he realized that the soldiers were too weak to march and were incapable of fighting effectively, largely because they were half-starved. According to army regulations, each soldier was to be issued 24 oz of rice a day, a ration of salt, and a total monthly salary which, if spent entirely on food, would buy one pound of pork a month. A Chinese soldier could subsist nicely on these rations. In fact, however, he actually received only a fraction of the food and money allotted him, because his officers regularly 'squeezed' a substantial portion for themselves. As a consequence, most Nationalist soldiers suffered nutritional deficiencies. An American expert, who in 1944 examined 1,200 soldiers from widely different kinds of units, found that 57 per cent of the men displayed nutritional deficiencies that significantly affected their ability to function as soldiers.[63]

Primitive sanitary and medical practices similarly contributed to the enervation of the Nationalist army, and disease was therefore the soldiers'

---

[61] The precise number of mortalities among the conscripts will never be known. One official source acknowledges that 1,867,283 conscripts during the war were lost. (Information provided me in July 1978 by the director of the Ministry of Defence's Bureau of Military History, based on *K'ang-chan shih-liao ts'ung-pien ch'u-chi* (Collectanea of historical materials regarding the war of resistance, first collection), 295). Unfortunately, an analysis of this figure in terms of deaths and desertions is not given. Chiang Meng-lin, who was a strong supporter of the National government and a confidant of Chiang Kai-shek, estimated on the basis of secret documents that at least 14 million recruits died before they had reached their units. This figure is too large to be credible, and it is probably meant to be 1.4 million (see Chiang Meng-lin, 91). That the mortalities among conscripts were of this order of magnitude is also suggested in Hsu Fu-kuan, 'Shih shei chi-k'uei-le Chung-kuo she-hui fan-kung ti li-liang?' (Who is it that destroys the anti-Communist power of Chinese society?), *Min-chu p'ing-lun* (Democratic review), 1.7 (16 Sept. 1949), 6–7. Chiang Meng-lin, 90–1; Langdon to State, 'Conscription campaign', 3.

[62] *Lost chance*, 36. See also *Hu-pei-sheng-cheng-fu pao-kao*, 1942/4–10 (Report of the Hupei provincial government, April-October 1942), 113.

[63] Romanus and Sunderland, *Time runs out*, 65, 243. See also Gauss to State, 'The conditions of health of Chinese troops', US State Dept. 893.22/47, 14 Sept. 1942, encl. p. 2; and Gauss to State, 'Observations by a Chinese newspaper correspondent on conditions in the Lake district of Western Hupeh after the Hupeh battle in May, 1943', US State Dept. 740.0011 Pacific War/3559, 5 Nov. 1943, encl. pp. 4–5.

constant companion. Malaria was the most widespread and debilitating affliction. Dysentery, the incidence of which greatly increased during the war because of the deteriorating physical condition of the troops, was often ignored until cure was impossible. Then, able no longer even to eat, they soon died. Scabies, tropical skin ulcers, eye infections, tuberculosis, and venereal disease were also common.[64]

During the fighting in the south-west in 1945, American observers found that the 13th Army was unable to hike even a short distance 'without men falling out wholesale and many dying from utter starvation'.[65] Another American officer, Colonel David D. Barrett, reported seeing Nationalist soldiers 'topple over and die after marching less than a mile'.[66] A reporter for the highly regarded *Ta-kung-pao* ('L'Impartial') observed that 'where troops have passed, dead soldiers can be found by the roadside one after another'.[67] Units of the Nationalist army that were especially favoured or were trained by the United States – such as the Youth Army and the Chinese Expeditionary Forces trained in India – continued to be well fed and equipped. But they were exceptions.

There did exist an Army Medical Corps, but the medical treatment it provided was described by Dr Robert Lim (Lin K'o-sheng), chairman of the Chinese Red Cross medical Relief Corps, as 'pre-Nightingale'.[68] The formal structure of the medical corps – comprising first-aid teams, dressing stations, field hospitals and base hospitals – was unexceptionable, but it was undermined by inadequate and incompetent personnel, insufficient equipment and medicines, corruption and callousness.

There were only some 2,000 reasonably qualified doctors serving in the entire army – a ratio at best of about one qualified doctor for every 1,700 men, compared to about one doctor for every 150 men in the United States Army. An additional 28,000 medical officers served in the corps, but most of these had received no formal training, and had simply been promoted from stretcher-bearers, to dressers, to 'doctors'. The few really competent doctors tended to congregate in rear-area hospitals, out of reach of seriously wounded soldiers in the front lines. Because the stretcher units were often understaffed, and medical transport scarce, a wound in

[64] White and Jacoby, 136–8; Gauss to State, 'The conditions of health of Chinese troops', encl. p. 2; Ringwalt to Atcheson, 'The Chinese soldier', encl. p. 3; Rice to Gauss, 'The health of Chinese troops observed at Lanchow', US State Dept. 893.22/52, 4 Dec. 1943, pp. 1–2.

[65] Romanus and Sunderland, *Time runs out*, 245.

[66] David D. Barrett, *Dixie Mission: the United States Army Observer Group in Yenan, 1944*, 60.

[67] Gauss to State, 'Observations by a Chinese newspaper correspondent', encl. p. 5.

[68] Gauss to State, 'The conditions of health of Chinese troops', encl. p. 2. On medical conditions in the army, see Lyle Stephenson Powell, *A surgeon in wartime China*; Robert Gillen Smith, 'History of the attempt of the United States Medical Department to improve the effectiveness of the Chinese Army Medical Service, 1941–1945'; F. F. Liu, 139–40; Szeming Sze, *China's health problems*, 44.

combat – even a minor wound – was often fatal. It could be a day before a wounded soldier received even preliminary first aid. Then he had to be hauled to dressing stations and hospitals in the rear. Rhodes Farmer, who saw wounded being transported to the rear in 1938, observed that 'gangrene was everywhere: maggots writhed in the wounds'.[69] With this kind of treatment, even minor wounds quickly became infected, and major injuries, such as a wound in the stomach or loss of a limb, were usually fatal. Few cripples were seen in wartime China.[70]

The Chinese soldier, ill fed, abused and scorned, inevitably lacked morale. This was indicated graphically by wholesale desertions. Most recruits, if they survived the march to their assigned units, had few thoughts other than to escape. Many succeeded. The 18th Division of the 18th Army, for example, was regarded as one of the better units, yet during 1942, stationed in the rear and not engaged in combat, 6,000 of its 11,000 men disappeared due to death or desertion. Ambassador Gauss commented that these statistics were not exceptional, and that similar attrition rates prevailed in all the military districts. Even the elite forces of Hu Tsung-nan – which, because they were used to contain the Communist forces in the north, were among the best trained, fed, and equipped soldiers in the army – reportedly required replacements in 1943 at the rate of 600 men per division of 10,000 men every month.[71] Official statistics lead to the conclusion that over eight million men, about one of every two soldiers, were unaccounted for and presumably either deserted or died from other than battle-related causes.[72]

[69] Rhodes Farmer, *Shanghai harvest: a diary of three years in the China war*, 136.

[70] Farmer, 137. Dorn, 65, writes that 'the Chinese usually shot their own seriously wounded as an act of mercy, since "they would only die anyway"'.

[71] Gauss to State, 'Observations by a Chinese newspaper correspondent', p. 3 and encl. p. 5.

[72] This conclusion is based on the fact that insignificant numbers of soldiers were released from the army during the war, and that, in addition to the nearly 1.8 million in the army in July 1937, 14,053,988 men were conscripted between 1937 and 1945, Yet the Nationalist army in August 1945 numbered (by Chinese count) only about 3.5 million or (by United States count) 2.7 million. Total casualties (including 1,761,335 wounded, some of whom doubtless returned to duty) were 3,211,419. An additional 500,000 or so defected to the Japanese. I have seen no figures on the number of prisoners taken by the Japanese, but the figure surely did not exceed another 500,000. Simple arithmetic suggests that at least 8 million, and perhaps as many as 9 million, men were unaccounted for. (This figure includes the 1,867,283 recruits that the government acknowledges were unaccounted for. See note 61 above.)

Sources: *CHB, 1950*, 182, 185. Figures on the size of the army are in Ch'en Ch'eng, Table 1; and Romanus and Sunderland, *Time runs out*, 382.

The above conclusion is drawn from the Nationalists' own data, but it is incompatible with their published figures for wartime desertions (598,107) and deaths due to illness (422,479). See Ch'en Ch'eng, table 10. This contradiction in the official data demonstrates the unreliability of Nationalist figures pertaining to the military. In fact, a former Nationalist general in Taiwan responded to my inquiries by asserting that the Chinese army had placed no value on mathematical exactness regarding casualties.

FOREIGN MILITARY AID

The Chinese army did not fight wholly alone, and the assistance – or lack of assistance – of its friends significantly affected the character of the Nationalists' struggle against the Japanese. From the beginning of the war, Chiang Kai-shek had placed large hopes upon foreign aid and intercession. The Western democracies did indeed sympathize with the Chinese struggle against arrant aggression, but their sympathy was only slowly translated into material assistance. Paradoxically, it was Soviet Russia that became the Nationalists' first and remarkably generous friend. Despite a decade of strained relations between Moscow and Nanking, the two governments shared a common interest in blocking Japanese expansion on the Asian mainland. Even before the Lu-kou-ch'iao incident, therefore, the Russians' policy toward the Nationalists had softened. They had encouraged the second united front. During the Sian incident, they had counselled Chiang Kai-shek's safe release. And, as early as September 1937 – without waiting for the conclusion of a formal aid agreement – they began sending materiel to the Nationalists. During 1937–9, the USSR supplied a total of about 1,000 planes, 2,000 'volunteer' pilots, 500 military advisers, and substantial stores of artillery, munitions and petrol. These were provided on the basis of three medium-term, low-interest (3 per cent) credits, totalling US $250 million. This flow of aid lessened after the war began in Europe in September 1939. Yet Soviet aid continued until Hitler's forces marched into Russia in 1941. Significantly, virtually none of the Russian aid was channelled to the Chinese Communists. According to T. F. Tsiang, China's ambassador to Russia, 'Moscow was more interested...in stirring up opposition to Japan in China than it was in spreading communism.'[73]

The Western democracies responded more slowly and uncertainly to China's pleas for aid. The French during the first year of the war loaned a meagre US $5 million for the construction of a railway from the Indo-China border to Nanning in Kwangsi. The United States bolstered China's dollar reserves, and hence purchasing-power on the international market, by buying up Chinese silver valued at US $157 million. Not until December 1938, however, nearly 1½ years after the outbreak of hostilities, did the United States and Britain grant rather modest credits to China in the amounts of US $25 million and £500,000 (US $2 million) respectively. Fearful of alienating the Japanese, moreover, the Americans and British specifically prohibited the Chinese from using these loans to buy weapons or other war materiel. Beginning in 1940, Western aid

[73] Arthur N. Young, *China and the helping hand, 1937–1945*, 18–21, 26, 54, 125–30.

gradually increased. The United States promised credits of $45 million in 1940 and $100 million in early 1941. In late 1941, too, the United States began sending armaments and other materiel to China under the terms of the recent Lend-Lease Act. The American Volunteer Group, an air contingent that became famous as the 'Flying Tigers', under the command of Claire L. Chennault, became operational in Burma in the latter part of 1941. After $4\frac{1}{2}$ years of war, the total aid of the Western democracies approximately equalled that provided by Russia.[74]

After Pearl Harbor, America's interest in the war in China increased markedly. But relations between the two countries, now allies, were fraught with vexation. A basic cause of the strain was that the United States never provided the enormous infusions of military support and material aid that the Chinese thought was due them. After the Japanese severed the Burma Road in early 1942, the principal supply route to China was the treacherous flight from India, across the rugged foothills of the Himalayas, to Kunming in Yunnan. Partly because of America's shortage of planes, the supply of materiel over the 'Hump', as this route was known, was but a trifle compared with Chungking's expressed needs. Despite these transportation difficulties, China might have received significantly more aid, if it had not been for the Western Allies' policy of defeating Germany and Italy before concentrating against Japan. During 1941 and 1942, for example, the United States assigned to China only about 1.5 per cent of its total Lend-Lease aid and only 0.5 per cent in 1943 and 1944 – though the figure went up to 4 per cent in 1945.[75] The Nationalists were deeply aggrieved by the 'Europe first' policy.

Many of the complaints and misunderstandings that vexed Chinese-American relations after 1942 swirled around the figure of General Joseph W. Stilwell. Regarded at the time of Pearl Harbor as the most brilliant corps commander in the American army, Stilwell had initially been selected for the top combat assignment in North Africa. Because of his outstanding knowledge of China and the esteem which Chief-of-Staff

---

[74] *Ibid.* 207 and *passim.*
[75] Some figures indicating the amounts of supplies brought to China over the Hump route are (in number of tons):

1942			1943			1944			1945	
May	June	Sept.	Feb.	Apr.	June	Jan.	June	Dec.	Jan.	July
80	106	2,000	3,200	2,500	3,000	14,500	18,200	34,800	46,500	73,700

Sources: F. F. Liu, 157; Herbert Feis, *The China tangle: the American effort in China from Pearl Harbor to the Marshall mission*, 42, 67, 205. On Lend-Lease, see Young, *Helping hand*, 350, 399–402.

George C. Marshall held for him, however, he was named instead to what the secretary of war, Henry L. Stimson, subsequently termed 'the most difficult task assigned to any American in the entire war'.[76] Designated chief of Chiang Kai-shek's allied staff, as well as commander of the China-Burma-India theatre, Stilwell was specifically instructed to 'increase the effectiveness of United States assistance to the Chinese Government for the prosecution of the war and to assist in improving the combat efficiency of the Chinese Army'.[77] As the American theatre commander in China, Stilwell inevitably bore the brunt of Chinese dissatisfaction with Washington's priorities. He and Chiang initially fell out over the allied defeat in Burma. They represented different worlds and did not like each other. Stilwell was, among his other qualities, forthright to a fault, innocent of diplomacy, intolerant of posturing and bureaucratic rigmarole, and given to caustic sarcasm. Chiang Kai-shek, by contrast, tended to be vain, indirect, reserved, and acutely sensitive to differences of status. Soon Stilwell dismissed Chiang as 'an ignorant, arbitrary, stubborn man', and likened the National government to the dictatorship and gangsterism of Nazi Germany. Among friends, Stilwell disparagingly referred to Chiang as 'the peanut', and in mid-1944 he privately ruminated that 'The cure for China's trouble is the elimination of Chiang Kai-shek.' 'Why,' he asked, 'can't sudden death for once strike in the proper place.'[78] Chiang Kai-shek knew of Stilwell's attitude and slighting references to him, and in turn loathed the American. At least as early as October 1943 he tried to have Stilwell transferred from China. But Stilwell had the confidence of General Marshall and retained his post until October 1944.

Compounding their personal enmity was the fact that Chiang Kai-shek and Stilwell held fundamentally different objectives. Stilwell was concerned solely with the task of increasing China's military contribution to the war against Japan. To attain this goal, he began training Chinese troops flown over the Hump to India and proposed that the Nationalist army be fundamentally reorganized. The essential problem, he asserted, was not lack of equipment, but that the available equipment was not being used effectively. The army, he contended, 'is generally in desperate condition, underfed, unpaid, untrained, neglected, and rotten with corruption'.[79] As a remedy, he proposed that the size of the army be cut by half, inefficient commanders be purged, and an elite corps of first thirty, and ultimately one hundred, divisions be trained and equipped by the United States. He

[76] Tuchman, 232.
[77] Romanus and Sunderland, *Stilwell's mission*, 74.
[78] Joseph W. Stilwell, *The Stilwell papers*, ed. Theodore H. White, 115, 124, 215, 320, 321 and 322.
[79] Romanus and Sunderiand, *Stilwell's mission*, 282.

also proposed that the American-trained Chinese divisions launch an offensive operation to retake Burma, because, as long as the Japanese controlled that country, China was dependent for foreign supplies upon the limited flow of goods over the Hump. Only by opening a land route through Burma, Stilwell thought, could sufficient materiel be imported to equip the Chinese army for a full-scale offensive against the Japanese in China.

Chiang Kai-shek placed a lower priority upon fighting the Japanese. In his view, the ultimate defeat of Japan, after the Allies had entered the war, was certain. The outcome of his struggle with the Communists was still undecided, however, and his primary concern was therefore to preserve and enhance his power and that of the National government. Stilwell's proposals to reorganize the army and to take the offensive against the Japanese were anathema to Chiang, because they threatened to upset the delicate balance of political forces that he had created. His best-equipped troops, for example, were commanded by men loyal to him, even though they were often militarily incompetent. If officers were to be assigned to posts solely on the basis of merit, as Stilwell was urging, military power would be placed in the hands of his potential political rivals. As a case in point, Stilwell held General Pai Ch'ung-hsi in high regard and would have liked to assign him a position of real authority in the Nationalist army. What Stilwell ignored, and what loomed foremost in Chiang's thinking, was that Pai Ch'ung-hsi was a former warlord in Kwangsi province with a long history of rebellion against the central government. In like manner, Stilwell in 1943 recommended that the Communist and Nationalist armies jointly launch a campaign against the Japanese in North China. To induce the Communists to participate in such an offensive, however, weapons and other materials would have to be supplied to them. Chiang, of course, could accept no scheme that would rearm or otherwise strengthen his bête noire.

More congenial to Chiang Kai-shek's purposes was Stilwell's nominal subordinate, General Claire L. Chennault. After Pearl Harbor Chennault had been reinducted into the United States army, and his 'Flying Tigers' were reorganized as the China Air Task Force (subsequently the 14th Air Force). Retaining his nearly religious faith in the efficacy of air power, Chennault in October 1942 asserted that with 105 fighter planes, 30 medium and 12 heavy bombers, he would 'accomplish the downfall of Japan...probably within six months, within one year at the outside'.[80] This fantastic plan was irresistible to Chiang Kai-shek, for it would make China a major theatre of the war — thus qualifying the National government

<hr />

[80] Claire Lee Chennault, *Way of a fighter*, 214.

for larger quotas of material aid – without requiring large expenditures of her own resources. And the army reforms and active participation in the ground war, which Stilwell was demanding, would be unnecessary.

Stilwell, backed by General Marshall and secretary of War Henry L. Stimson in Washington, vehemently opposed the Chennault plan. Its crucial flaw, he argued, was that the Japanese would attack and destroy the American air bases as soon as the air strikes became effective. With the Chinese army in its current ineffectual condition, those air bases would be completely vulnerable. But Roosevelt sided with Chennault and Chiang Kai-shek, and Chennault's air offensive began. By November 1943, Japanese bases within China and their shipping along the China coast were sustaining significant losses. Japanese authorities, moreover, feared the Americans would use the air bases at Kweilin and Liu-chou to launch raids on the home islands, damaging their war industries. Stilwell's worst fears were then soon realized. For in April 1944, the Japanese launched the Ichigo (Operation Number One) offensive, their largest and most destructive campaign in China since 1938. It sliced through the Nationalists' defensive lines, posing a threat even to Kunming, a strategic key to all unoccupied China. This military threat coincided with an economic slump and mounting political discontent.

The success of the Ichigo campaign made China's military situation desperate. Seeking a solution to the crisis, Roosevelt on 19 September 1944 demanded that Chiang Kai-shek place Stilwell 'in unrestricted command of all your forces'.[81] Stilwell, after personally delivering the message, recorded in his diary: 'I handed this bundle of paprika to the Peanut and then sat back with a sigh. The harpoon hit the little bugger right in the solar plexus, and went right through him. It was a clean hit, but beyond turning green and losing the power of speech, he did not bat an eye.'[82] But Stilwell's exultation was brief. Chiang knew that, with Stilwell in command of the war effort, political power in China would slowly perhaps, but surely, slip from his grasp. This he could not accept and with indomitable insistence he persuaded Roosevelt to recall Stilwell. On 19 October 1944, General Albert C. Wedemeyer was named Chiang's chief-of-staff and commander of United States forces in China.

JAPAN'S ICHIGO OFFENSIVE 1944

Japan's Ichigo offensive inflicted a devastating defeat upon the Nationalists. It revealed to all Chinese and to the world how terribly the Nationalist

---

[81] Romanus and Sunderland, *Stilwell's command problems*, 443–6; Tuchman, 492–3.
[82] *Stilwell papers*, 333.

army and government had deteriorated during the preceding seven years
of war. Japan's objective in this offensive was to seize or destroy the air
bases in south-central China from which Chennault's 14th Air Force was
launching its highly effective air attacks. To accomplish this, the Japanese
in April 1944 first struck into Honan to gain full control of the
Peiping-Hankow railway and so protect their rear. By late May they were
ready. Moving southward from Hankow along the Hsiang River, the
Japanese first invested Changsha, capital of Hunan province. Three times
previously it had successfully resisted Japanese attacks, but this time the
Chinese offered no firm defence, and the city fell on 18 June.

Ten days later the attack on Hengyang began. Here Hsueh Yueh's
Cantonese forces, supported by Chennault's fighter planes and bombers,
fought fiercely for six weeks. This was the single instance during the entire
Ichigo offensive where Chinese forces staged a large-scale sustained
resistance. Thereafter, however, Chinese defences collapsed. The Japanese
pushed southward to the major air bases at Kweilin and Liuchow in
Kwangsi. By November 1944 they had smashed Chennault's air bases,
formed a pathway through Central China that connected Mukden with
Hanoi, and then moved westward. They seemed unstoppable. Chinese
armies were rushed into the breach, but – according to Wedemeyer – even
well-equipped divisions 'melted away'. They 'appeared to lack spirit and
simply would not hold ground'.[83] With the road to Chungking seemingly
open to the invaders, Chiang Kai-shek bravely announced his determination
to remain in Chungking and 'die if necessary' in its defence – a
declaration that instilled slight confidence, for he had made similar vows
at Nanking and Hankow before abandoning them.[84]

In early December, however, the Japanese army suddenly halted its
advance. Why? At the time, the Japanese offensive had appeared irresistible
and rumour-mongers charged that Chiang and the Japanese had struck
an agreement that would spare Chungking. In fact, the Japanese had
stopped moving westward because the objective of Ichigo, to destroy the
American bomber bases, had been accomplished. Survival, and not
destruction of the Chungking government, had by 1944 become the
Japanese goal.

The Ichigo offensive had, however, inflicted terrible losses upon
Nationalist China. Nearly 500,000 soldiers were dead or wounded; its
territory was cut in half by the Japanese north-south corridor; fully a
fourth of its factories were lost; sources of government revenue were

---

[83] Wedemeyer, 290 and 328.
[84] Wedemeyer, 293; Romanus and Sunderland, *Time runs out*, 166.

sharply reduced; and civilian casualties and property damage were enormous.[85]

Despite the manifest deterioration of the Nationalist army by 1944, assessments of its achievements during the war have varied widely. Ho Ying-ch'in, long-time minister of war, for example, has claimed that his forces fought 22 campaigns, 1,117 important engagements, and 38,931 small engagements against the Japanese. The Communists, he claimed, by contrast 'did not move a soldier against the enemy'. General Wedemeyer similarly insisted that 'the Nationalist Government of China, far from being reluctant to fight as pictured by Stilwell and some of his friends among the American correspondents, had shown amazing tenacity and endurance in resisting Japan', whereas 'no communist Chinese forces fought in any of the major engagements of the Sino-Japanese war'.[86]

It is assuredly true that, on a number of occasions, the Nationalist forces fought heroically against the Japanese. Three times at Changsha (once in 1939 and twice in 1941) the forces of General Hsueh Yueh resisted large-scale Japanese assaults. At Ch'ang-te, Hunan, in November–December 1943, the 57th Division of the Central Army fought with extreme determination, suffering casualties of fully 90 per cent. And in western Hupei in 1943, against one of Japan's so-called rice-bowl campaigns, the Chinese lost some 70–80,000 men as against 3–4,000 casualties for the Japanese.[87]

Critics of the Nationalists have tended to minimize these instances of heroism and combativeness. They claim, for example, that the brilliant defence of Hengyang in June–August 1944 was undertaken by a non-Central Army commander, Hsueh Yueh, despite obstructions of the Chungking government; and that, in the rare instances when the Nationalists took the offensive, it was because Chiang Kai-shek needed propaganda to convince Allied leaders that the China theatre warranted more material aid. The Communists, moreover, have ridiculed the Nationalist claims to belligerence against the Japanese, asserting that, until the Ichigo campaign, fully 84 per cent of the Japanese troops were concentrated against Communist forces and only 16 per cent against the Nationalists.[88] Stilwell,

---

[85] In Kwangsi, for example, losses in the war (most of which were sustained during the Ichigo campaign) were reportedly 110,000 persons killed, 160,000 wounded, 300,000 houses destroyed, 80,000 head of ploughing oxen killed. *Hsin-min-pao* (New people's press), 20 Mar. 1946, in *Chinese Press Review* (Chungking), hereafter *CPR*, 8 (21 Mar. 1946), 6.

[86] Ho Ying-ch'in, 'Chi-nien ch'i-ch'i k'ang-chan tsai po Chung-kung ti hsu-wei hsuan-ch'uan' (Commemorating the Sino-Japanese War and again refuting the Communists' false propaganda), *Tzu-yu chung* (Freedom's bell), 3.3 (20 Sept. 1972), 26; Wedemeyer, 279 and 284.

[87] Israel Epstein, *The unfinished revolution in China*, 311; Gauss to State, 'Observations by a Chinese newspaper correspondent', p. 1.

[88] Warren I. Cohen, 'Who fought the Japanese in Hunan? Some views of China's war effort', *JAS* 27.1 (Nov. 1967), 111–15; Dorn, 321–2; Epstein, *Unfinished revolution*, 312; Li I-yeh, *Chung-kuo*

before his dismissal in late 1944, also charged the top Nationalist commanders with 'colossal ignorance and indifference', and asserted that the Nationalist army under the existing leadership was totally incapable of making positive contributions against the Japanese.[89]

Whatever may be the final judgment on the issue, it remains a fact that the Nationalist forces persevered for eight long years against an enemy who possessed a vast technological superiority. The political, economic and human costs of this war of resistance were enormous. Yet they did not abandon the Allied war effort, and their forcing the Japanese to maintain an army of about one million men in China contributed significantly to the eventual victory. In the final analysis, however, the most important historical fact is that by the latter stage of the war, from about 1942, the greater part of the Nationalist army had so lost the will to fight that it had practically ceased to be capable of effective military operations. To this generalization there were exceptions. Stilwell's and Wedemeyer's programme to create a few high-quality Chinese divisions – trained, advised and equipped by Americans – had by 1945 finally begun to bear fruit. During April–June 1945, for instance, several of these divisions fought courageously and effectively in turning back a Japanese offensive in south-west Hunan. When the war ended, eight of these divisions had completed, and twenty-two more had begun, the thirteen-week schedule of training. The remainder of the 300-odd Chinese divisions, however, remained untouched.

The general deterioration of the Nationalist army during the war against Japan had momentous consequences. For the army was the foundation of Nationalist political power. When it began to crumble, it presaged the overthrow of Chiang Kai-shek and the National government. Chiang was seemingly powerless to reverse the process of disintegration. All attempts to reform the army – as General Stilwell learned to his dismay – quickly ran aground on the shoals of domestic politics. The army, for example, was too large, relative to available material resources, to be effective; yet proposals to reduce its size were impracticable because of the opposition of the regional commanders, who would lose their power if they lost their armies. Chiang's control of the governmental administration was also too tenuous to allow needed reforms. He had repeatedly ordered, for instance, that the conscription system be made more humane. But, because the system was dominated by local elites and corrupt officials who could not be controlled or disciplined, the terrors of the system remained.

jen-min tsen-yang ta-pai Jih-pen ti-kuo-chu-i (How the Chinese people defeated Japanese imperialism), 66.   [89] *Stilwell papers*, 157, 177, 316–19.

THE INFLATION DISASTER

The debility of the Nationalist government and army that was disclosed by the Ichigo offensive was the culmination of a long and complex process of deterioration. Of the many causes of that process, inflation was the most potent. Like leukaemic blood, the depreciated currency of the National government flowed through the body politic, enfeebling the entire organism – the army, government, economy, and society generally. Initially the rate of inflation had been rather moderate. Prices rose about 40 per cent during the first year of the war. By the latter half of 1941 and through 1944, prices more than doubled each year. Thereafter the rate of increase again spurted sharply upward.[90]

The fundamental cause of this inflation was monetary. That is, the volume of currency was vastly expanded, usually through the device of government borrowing from the four government banks, which met the demand by the wholesale printing of new money. Government expenditures increased immediately after the fighting began. During the first two years of the war, the government expended large sums in relocating and developing industries in the interior. Huge sums were devoted to new roads and railways in west China, to Indo-China, and through Burma. During this two-year period, the government's annual expenditures rose 33 per cent while its annual revenues declined 63 per cent. Prior to the war, the bulk of its revenue had been derived from the commercial and urban sectors of the economy – customs duties, salt taxes and commodity taxes contributed about 80 per cent. When the Japanese overran Shanghai and the other coastal cities, these sources of revenue were largely lost. About 75 per cent of the government's wartime expenditures were met by the creation of new paper currency (see table 1).

Although the growing volume of *fa-pi* had been, and perhaps always remained, the primary force fuelling the inflationary process, non-monetary factors accelerated the price increases. Chief among these were commodity shortages and declining confidence in the currency. The exigent demand for producer goods such as machinery, metals, electrical equipment, chemicals and fuels, and their short supply, placed them in the vanguard of the price increases. Prices of metals and metal products, for instance, increased 6.8 times during the first two war years, whereas the general price index merely doubled. Most producer goods had to be imported,

---

[90] The annual increase of retail prices was 49 per cent in 1938; 83 per cent in 1939; 124 per cent in 1940; 173 per cent in 1941; 235 per cent in 1942; 245 per cent in 1943; 231 per cent in 1944; and 251 per cent in January–August 1945. The major secondary sources on the inflation are Arthur N. Young, *China's wartime finance and inflation, 1937–1945*; Chang Kia-ngau, *Inflationary spiral*; and Shun-hsin Chou, *The Chinese inflation, 1937–1949*.

TABLE I

Value of note issue in terms of prewar prices, 1937–45 (amount and value in millions of yuan)

End of the period	Amount of note issue of government banks	Average price index[a]	Value of issue in terms of prewar notes
1937, July	1,455	1.04	1,390
1938	2,305	1.76	1,310
1939	4,287	3.23	1,325
1940	7,867	7.24	1,085
1941	15,133	19.77	765
1942	34,360	66.2	520
1943	75,379	228	330
1944	189,461	755	250
1945, August	556,907	2,647	210
1945, December	1,031,932	2,491	415

[a] For December of each year, except for the months specified for 1937 and 1945.
Source: Arthur N. Young, *China's wartime finance and inflation, 1937–1945*, 304.

and Japan aggravated the shortages by clamping an economic blockade on the Nationalist areas.

The Japanese blockade, imposed in September 1937, was initially not effective, but progressively the noose tightened. After the loss of Canton and Hankow in October 1938, import prices jumped 72 per cent; they doubled again in the latter half of 1939 after the loss of the key supply link of Nanning in Kwangsi. Japan's war on Great Britain and the United States from December 1941 quickly eliminated Shanghai, Hong Kong and the Burma Road as sources of supply. A trickle of imports continued to flow over the long and expensive land route from the Soviet Union by way of Kansu and Sinkiang, and the air supply route over the Hump gradually grew in importance. Still, China's imports by 1944 had fallen to a mere 6 per cent of the prewar level.

During the first stage of inflation, 1937–9, ordinary Chinese were shielded from the worst effects because prices of consumer goods rose more slowly than those of producer goods. Most important, food prices rose only moderately – a modest 8.5 per cent in Chungking during the first two years of the war. The reason was that the Nationalist areas were favoured by excellent harvests in both 1938 and 1939 – 8 per cent above the prewar average in the fifteen provinces that now constituted unoccupied China. The prices of other daily necessities, like clothes and housing, rose more rapidly than food – the prices of clothing, for example, had approximately doubled by mid-1939. But most Chinese could defer purchases of new clothing. And the cost of housing, except in the cities where refugees congregated, did not rise sharply. As a consequence, most people during the first two years were able to absorb the effects of the inflation without extreme hardship.

During 1940, however, food prices began shooting upward, sharply affecting the people's livelihood and stimulating the entire inflationary process. Poor harvests were the initial cause of this change. In 1940 agricultural production fell 10 per cent below that of 1939, and declined an additional 13 per cent the next year. In July 1941, too, the government began collecting the land tax in grains rather than in money. This meant that less grain reached the free market, thus further upsetting the balance between supply and demand.

There were other non-monetary causes of the inflation. Domestic industrial production was generally unable to satisfy consumer demand. Such goods as cloth, medicines, paper and electric bulbs had been produced largely in the coastal cities that were now lost to the Japanese. Many small consumer-oriented factories were established in the interior during the war, but they were never able to meet more than a small fraction of the demand. Imports from the Japanese-occupied areas became an important source of consumer goods. Initially, both the Nationalists and the Japanese banned this trade. But in July 1939, with consumer demands inexorably mounting, the Chungking government legalized the trade in all but a few critical materials. Indeed, in 1943 it even created an official agency, directed by the powerful head of the military secret police, General Tai Li, to engage in and increase the trade in goods with the enemy-held areas. Still, neither this trade nor domestic production could satisfy the market. The Japanese, for their part, outlawed this trade throughout the war, but they too conspired in it.[91]

From 1940 onward, the most important non-monetary cause of the inflation was probably not commodity shortages, but lack of public confidence in the currency. In 1937–9 there was a strong tendency, especially among the rural population, to save *fa-pi*. This hoarding – a reaction against the customary shortage of money-income in the villages – had cushioned the impact of the inflation, for it reduced the volume of currency in circulation and thereby eased the demand for hard-to-obtain consumer goods. Following the poor rice harvest in the summer of 1940, however, farmers began hoarding grain rather than money. Speculators also bought up and stored large amounts of grain in anticipation of future

[91] Eastman, 'Ambivalent relationship', 275–84.

price increases. Food prices in Chungking during 1940 and 1941 consequently shot up nearly 1,400 per cent. Industrial, transport, and other workers, as a result, demanded and received substantial wage boosts. This led to a spurt in consumer spending, which led, in turn, to further hoarding of goods. An inflationary spiral thus began, which was not effectively checked until after 1949.

Initially the Nationalist authorities had avoided creating large amounts of new currency by selling bonds and foreign-exchange reserves. Soon those alternatives were exhausted. Printing new money was irresistibly easier than controlling the budgetary deficit by creating new sources of tax revenue or holding down spending. Moreover, the authorities dismissed economists' warnings about the dangers of inflation, contending that it could not become a serious danger in an agrarian society like China. Only after prices started shooting upward in 1940 and 1941 did they gradually perceive that they must raise revenues and reduce expenditures if they would prevent the entire war effort from being undercut by the process of monetary depreciation.

In 1941–2 the government began seriously searching for new sources of revenue. The income tax was extended; a so-called consumption tax, in essence a revival of the old and much detested likin, was imposed on goods in transit; and the salt tax was increased, making it the most fruitful of the government's taxes. Another revenue-raising scheme was the creation in 1942 of state monopolies for the distribution of salt, sugar, tobacco and matches. These several measures were only marginally beneficial. The income and excess-profits taxes proved to be almost totally unenforceable, partly because of purposeful evasion. The consumption tax, although lucrative, created so many obstacles to trade that it was revoked in 1945. The inadequacy of all these revenue-raising schemes is revealed in the stark fact that less than 11 per cent of the government's wartime cash expenditures were covered by tax revenues.

The most far-reaching fiscal innovation was the land tax in kind. Since 1928, the agricultural land tax had been collected in money by the provincial governments. The central government therefore had to purchase rice for its mammoth army on the open market. But with rice prices shooting upward – the average price in June 1941 was over twenty times higher than on the eve of the war – the cost of maintaining the army had become insupportable. Beginning in July 1941, therefore, the central government took over the collection of the land tax from the provinces. It also assessed the tax not in money but in rice (or, in non-rice-producing areas, other foodstuffs such as wheat and barley; in rare cases, cotton was collected). The grain thus collected was, however, still insufficient to meet the needs of the army and civil servants. The government in July 1942 therefore instituted the practice of 'compulsory purchase' (in July 1943, this was changed to 'compulsory borrowing') of foodstuffs. That is, the taxpayer was now compelled to convey to the central government not only the land tax but an additional, and approximately equivalent, amount of grain for which he was subsequently to be reimbursed.

Through these measures, the central government obtained a sure source of foodgrains. It no longer had to expend *fa-pi* to buy expensive rice on the open market. This reduced one of the several pressures to print new money. The grain tax was, however, peculiarly susceptible to peculation, which deeply disgruntled the farmers and contributed to the moral deterioration of government. Chang Kia-ngau, an unusually objective high government official, was undoubtedly correct when he concluded that 'the long term political and social effects [of the tax in kind] to a large degree outweighed the immediate advantage of securing low cost food for the army'.[92]

Though the government was not notably successful in generating new sources of revenue, it did work manfully to limit spending. Realizing in 1940 that its open-handed encouragement of economic growth was generating a potentially dangerous inflationary trend, the government tightened its credit policies and cut back on the development of industry and communications. The most substantial savings, however, were made by clamping a lid on the wages of soldiers and government officials. Recognizing that the wages of government employees could keep pace with rising prices only if enormous sums of additional money were printed, the government did not substantially increase wages until 1944. The nominal purchasing power of officials' salaries decreased between 1937 and 1944 by about 85 per cent and of soldiers by about 94 per cent. In fact, of course, officials were supported partly through subsidized food and housing; and they also supported themselves in many cases by taking on more than one job and thus securing more than one salary. It must also be recognized that the area and population governed by the Nationalist regime during the war were both considerably smaller than pre-war. At any rate, annual government expenditures, measured in constant prices, in fact declined substantially over the course of the war. Although precision is impossible, government cash expenditures in 1944 *in real terms* had fallen to less than one-fourth of its prewar expenditures. The government was starving.

[92] Chang Kia-ngau, *Inflationary spiral*, 144. See also Young, *China's wartime finance*, 25–6. On the land tax generally, see Eastman, *Seeds of destruction*, 45–70.

Whether the government was wise to economize by holding down the wages of its employees is debatable. The low wages forced many, perhaps most, government officials and military officers to engage in peculation, to enrich themselves through unauthorized forms of trade with the occupied areas, or to obtain concurrent employment to the detriment of their efficiency in their government jobs. If, on the other hand, the government had pegged soldiers' and officials' pay to the rising cost-of-living, the government deficit would have grown enormously, thus adding to the inflationary pressures. The only economically acceptable means of holding down these government expenditures would have been to reduce the size of the army and bureaucracy. This would have reduced spending and probably would have increased efficiency. For political reasons, however, this measure was not adopted.

In 1942–4, the annual increase of prices had been about 237 per cent; from just January to August 1945, prices increased 251 per cent. On the monetary side, the government issued unprecedented amounts of new currency to meet a series of soaring new expenditures – the total number of fa-pi in circulation tripled between January and August 1945. One important cause of these rising expenditures was the growing presence of the United States in China. Its troop strength in China increased from 1,255 at the end of 1942, to 32,956 in January 1945, and to 60,369 in August 1945. These forces had to be supplied largely from the local economy, and at levels of consumption utterly beyond the ken of most Chinese. In mid-1944, H. H. Kung complained that 'in China your boys need six eggs a day, and now it is cut down to four eggs. But you eat a pound of beef a day...In order to supply the meat, we are feeding [you] our oxen, used for farm purposes... Soon there won't be any animals left to help the farmers farm their land.'[93] Indeed, one American soldier in China cost as much as 500 Chinese soldiers. In addition, the decision to build and operate four large air bases for the long-range B-29 bombers, and three fighter strips, all completed in June 1944, led to further huge expenditures. From November 1944 to May 1945, the monthly cost of the American presence increased from ¥1 billion to ¥20 billion. In retrospect, it is clear that the military benefits derived from the increased American role in China – and particularly of the B-29 operations, which staged a mere twenty raids during the war – were far outweighed by the fiscal damage inflicted upon China's weakened economy.[94]

The inflationary effect of Chinese expenditures for the American

93 Young, *Helping hand* 291, 254–5. On United States troop strength in China, see Romanus and Sunderland, *Stilwell's mission*, 267; *Time runs out*, 258.
94 Young, *China's wartime finance*, 272–3; Young, *Helping hand*, 290; Romanus and Sunderland, *Stilwell's command problems*, 115; FRUS, *1944*, 6.906–7.

military is suggested by the fact that they equalled fully 53 per cent of the new currency issues during the last 1½ years of the war. Still, the expenditures of the National government itself were also rising sharply, in large part as a result of reforms initiated upon the advice of the Americans. Thirty-nine divisions of the Chinese army, for example, were singled out for modernization, training, medical treatment and improved food. Salaries of government officials and teachers were boosted in late 1944 – although this only slightly eased their difficulties. At the same time, the expenditures and loans of the newly created War Production Board, even though only about 7 per cent of the government's total expenditures, also helped push prices ever upward during the first half of 1945. By the end of the war, the average retail price index was 2,600 times higher than in July 1937.

Not all segments of society were affected equally by the inflation. A narrow stratum of hoarders, speculators and corrupt officials acquired enormous wealth. Some groups, such as landlords and industrial workers, fared well in varying degrees and at different times. The majority of the population, however, was progressively reduced to, and even below, the bare subsistence level. Table 2 indicates changes in the purchasing power of several income groups in Nationalist China, although it does not precisely reflect their relative standards of living. The majority of farmers, for instance, fared much more poorly than the table suggests, because of poor harvests, increasing taxation and rents, and the burdens of military and labour conscription.[95] Government employees like soldiers, officials and professors, on the other hand, did not fare quite as badly as the table would indicate, because they received subsidies in such forms as cheap food and housing.

The ravages of inflation upon the standard of living of officials and soldiers affected the government's viability. As early as 1940, the purchasing power of officials' wages had declined to about one-fifth of prewar levels. By 1943, real wages were down to a tenth of what they had been in 1937. Although their plight was alleviated by monthly subsidies of rice, cooking oil and so on, officials were frequently living – in the words of Chang Kia-ngau – in 'abject poverty'.[96] Single men could scarcely survive on their salaries; officials with families became desperate, preoccupied with their personal situation. Some took second jobs; many became corrupt.

Corruption was very evident. High officials with gorgeously gowned ladies drove in chauffeured automobiles through the streets of fuel-short Chungking; they purchased perfumes, cigarettes, oranges, butter, and

---

[95] Eastman, *Seeds of destruction*, 66–70.
[96] Chang Kia-ngau, *Inflationary spiral*, 64.

TABLE 2

Indices of the purchasing power of monetary income of several income groups,
1937–45

	Professors[a]	Soldiers[b]	Civil servants[c] (Chungking)	Industrial[d] workers	Farmers[e]	Rural[e] workers (Szechwan)
1937	100	100	100	100	100	100
1938	95	95	77	124	87	111
1939	64	64	49	95	85	122
1940	25	29	21	76	96	63
1941	15	22	16	78	115	82
1942	12	10	11	75	101	75
1943	14	6	10	69	100	58
1944	11	—	—	41 (April)	81	—
1945	12	—	—	—	87	—

Sources: a. Indices for 1937–42 are from Wang Yin-yuan, 'Ssu-ch'uan chan-shih wu-chia yü ko-chi jen-min chih kou-mai-li' (Prices and purchasing power in wartime Szechwan), *Ssu-ch'uan ching-chi chi-k'an* (Szechwan economics quarterly), 1.3 (15 June 1944), 263; and those for 1943–5 are the June ratios (salaries/cost-of-living) in *Economic facts*, 22.177 (July 1943), 34.479 (July 1944), 46.701 (July 1945).
b. Wang Yin-yuan, 263.
c. Chang Kia-ngau, *The inflationary spiral*, 63.
d. Chang Kia-ngau, 63–4.
e. Chou Shun-hsin, *The Chinese inflation*, 243.

other luxuries smuggled from abroad; they dined at extravagant, multi-course banquets. Not all officials, of course, were corrupt. Some bravely suffered from malnutrition and saw the health of their families decline. Many, however, succumbed to temptation because it was easy to rationalize malfeasance when their superiors engaged in gross conspicuous consumption.

Inflation similarly ravaged the well-being of students and intellectuals. Books were few, scientific equipment sparse. Students lived in poorly lit, unheated dormitories, their beds crammed together like bunks in a ship. Faculty members frequently crowded in with the families of their colleagues. Meat and fat disappeared from their diets; some ate hardly two meals a day. Malnutrition in the academic community became almost universal. During the latter stage of the war, according to the *Ta-kung-pao*, both teachers and students were living 'on the verge of starvation', 'under the most miserable conditions imaginable'.[97] Health declined; malaria and tuberculosis were common. To supplement their meagre incomes, many faculty members taught at two or more universities, sold treasured books and art objects, or carved seals and wrote calligraphy for sale. The quality

[97] *Ta-kung-pao* (Chungking), 19 Mar. 1945, p. 2 (editorial); *ibid.* 13 Apr. 1945, p. 2 (editorial).

of their teaching suffered, and their disillusionment with the government rose.[98]

The government did endeavour to ease the economic plight of officials and professors who taught at government-run universities by providing special allowances, inexpensive housing, and various daily necessities at artificially low prices. Rice at one time was sold to government employees for Yo.10 a catty, while the price on the open market was Y5.00. But the government delayed granting meaningful salary increases, because these would have increased the budget. In 1943, government expenditures would have risen by 300 per cent if officials' real salaries had been raised to prewar levels. By 1944, discontent within the bureaucracy and army had swollen so greatly that wages were sharply increased – too little and too late, for by that time prices were rising uncontrollably. The demoralization of the bureaucracy and army continued until 1949.

THE INDUSTRIAL SECTOR

Free China's wartime industry developed upon minuscule foundations. When the war broke out, the area that was to become unoccupied China – comprising about three-fourths of the nation's territory – could boast of only about 6 per cent of the nation's factories, 7 per cent of the industrial workers, 4 per cent of the total capital invested in industry, and 4 per cent of the electrical capacity.[99] During the early years of the war, however, industry in the Nationalist area boomed. Consumer demand, especially from the government and army but also from the increased civilian population in the interior, created a nearly insatiable market for industrial products. Until 1940, food prices lagged far behind the prices of manufactured goods, so that wages remained low and profit margins were high. Until the Burma Road was shut down in March 1942, the purchase of critically needed machinery, spare parts, and imported raw materials, albeit difficult and exorbitantly expensive, was still possible.[100]

---

[98] Hollington K. Tong, ed. *China after seven years of war*, 112–13; Young, *China's wartime finance*, 323. Regarding the incidence of tuberculosis, a Communist source reported that X-ray examinations in 1945 revealed that fully 43 per cent of the faculty members at National Central University in Chungking – one of the most favoured universities – suffered from the disease, as did 15 per cent of the male students and 5.6 per cent of the female students. *Hsin-hua jih-pao*, 20 Feb. 1945, in *CPR* 47 (21 Feb. 1945) 3. This report doubtless needs corroboration.

[99] Li Tzu-hsiang, 'K'ang-chan i-lai', 23; *CJCC* 2.659. See also Chang Sheng-hsuan, 'San-shih-erh-nien Ssu-ch'uan kung-yeh chih hui-ku yü ch'ien-chan' (Perspectives on the past and future of Szechwan's economy in 1943), *SCCC* 1.2 (15 Mar. 1944), 258; and *CYB, 1937–1943*, 437.

[100] Chang Sheng-hsuan, 266. New textile-spinning equipment, for instance, was imported, increasing the number of spindles in the interior from just a few thousand before the war to about 230,000. Rockwood Q. P. Chin, 'The Chinese cotton industry under wartime inflation', *Pacific Affairs*, 16.1 (March 1943), 34, 37, 39.

TABLE 3
Factories* in unoccupied China

	1936 and before	1937	1938	1939	1940	1941	1942	1943	1944	Uncertain date of origin	Total
Number of plants established[a]	300	63	209	419	571	866	1,138	1,049	549	102	5,266
Capitalization of new plants in 1937 currency[a] (thousands of *yuan*)	117,950	22,166	86,583	120,914	59,031	45,719	9,896	14,486	3,419	7,317	487,481
Factories actually in operation	—	—	—	—	1,354[b]	—	2,123[c]	—	928[d]	—	—

* By official definition, a factory used power machinery and employed at least thirty workers.

Sources: a. Li Tzu-hsiang, 'Ssu-ch'uan chan-shih kung-yeh t'ung-chi', *Ssu-ch'uan ching-chi chi-k'an* 3, 1 (1 Jan. 1946) 206.

b. Frank W. Price, *Wartime China as seen by Westerners*, 47. This figure *presumably* includes both government-owned and private factories.

c. China Handbook, 1937–1943, 433 and 441. This figure is approximate, being the sum of private factories in existence in May 1942, the factories created since 1936 by the National Resources Council (98), and the factories established by provincial governments by August 1942 (110).

d. China Handbook, 1937–1945, 363. This figure includes both government-owned and private factories.

These favourable factors led new factories to open in increasing numbers until 1943 (see table 3), and industrial output almost quadrupled between 1938 and 1943.

Despite this growth, industrial production did not remotely satisfy consumer demands. Although the population of wartime Nationalist China was approximately one-half that of the prewar period, the output of principal industrial products never exceeded 12 per cent of prewar levels. Cotton yarn, cotton cloth and wheat flour in 1944 were only 5.3 per cent, 8.8 per cent and 5.3 per cent, respectively, of their prewar figures.[101] In 1943–4, moreover, the industrial sector entered a profound crisis, and production fell off sharply during 1944. Table 4 shows the weak condition of industry during the latter half of the war. Capitalization of new factories had peaked in 1939. Thereafter, despite the increasing number of new plants, the total value of investment fell precipitously. The industrial boom had in fact ended by about 1940, but marginal operators, with limited experience and minimal financial resources, continued to open new plants in the vain expectation that the boom would resume.[102] Most of these small, marginal operations quickly folded. In 1944, only 928 factories were actually in operation in Nationalist China. They had suffered a mortality rate of 82 per cent.

Although output increased until 1943, the industrial sector in 1940 had begun to encounter obstacles that first caused the *rate* of growth to decline, and then produced the industrial crisis after September 1943.[103] The consequences of inflation were not all negative. During the eight years of war, for example, real wages of workers rose only during 1938; thereafter, to the benefit of employers, they declined.[104] But the inflation made investments in commerce and especially in speculative enterprises vastly more lucrative than investments in industry (see table 5). Hoarding of rice and other agricultural products became widespread. 'Smuggled' goods, both from occupied China and from abroad, brought huge returns that diverted capital from productive investments. It was sometimes more profitable just to hold commodities than to pay to have them processed. The price of raw cotton during 1940 and 1941, for example, rose at an average of 13 per cent a month, and investors made substantially larger profits simply by storing the cotton than by chancing long-term investment in mills that processed cotton. Thus most liquid capital – on

---

[101] Yu-Kwei Cheng, 109; Shun-hsin Chou, 94.
[102] Rockwood Q. P. Chin, 39.
[103] Liu Chi-ping, 'San-shih-san-nien Ssu-ch'uan chih shang-yeh' (The commercial economy of Szechwan in 1944), *SCCC* 2.2 (1 April 1945), 79; Li Tzu-hsiang, 'Wo-kuo chan-shih kung-yeh sheng-ch'an ti hui-ku yü ch'ien-chan' (The past and future of China's wartime industrial production), *SCCC* 2.3 (1 July 1945), 32.
[104] Shun-hsin Chou, 239–40.

TABLE 4

Indices of industrial production in Nationalist China, 1938–1945

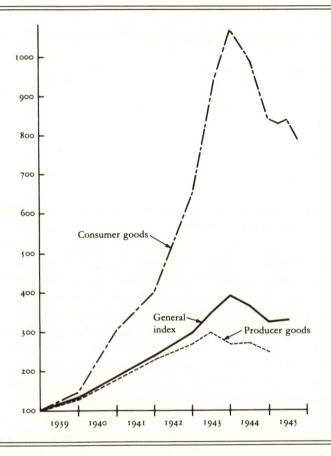

Source: a. Li Tzu-hsiang, 'Wo-kuo chan-shih kung-yeh sheng-ch'an te hui-ku yü ch'ien-chan', *Ssu-ch'uan ching-chi chi-k'an*, 2.3 (1 July 1945) 30.

b. Yu-Kwei Cheng, *Foreign trade and industrial development of China*, 110.

c. Chi-ming Hou, 'Economic development and public finance in China, 1937–1945', in Paul K. T. Sih, ed., *Nationalist China during the Sino-Japanese War, 1937–1945*, 214.

Note: There are discrepancies among these sources, although all are based upon data of the Chinese Ministry of Economics. Most significant, source *c* portrays no absolute decline in producer-goods production, but both sources *a* and *b* do indicate such a decline. The reason for the disparity may be that different commodities were included in computing the producer-goods index.

the order of 86 per cent in 1944 – had been channelled into commerce and speculation rather than production. Private modern and old-style banks increasingly withdrew from industrial investment, preferring to issue short-term commercial loans or to participate directly in hoarding and other forms of speculation. The government continued to provide

TABLE 5

Variations in real returns per individual from various types of activity,
Chungking

(1938 = 100)

Year	Agriculture	Manufactures	Retail	Speculation	US securities
1937	—	59	105	29	NA
1938	100	100	100	100	100
1939	61	106	111	297	180
1940	92	85	112	808	512
1941	109	71	119	550	1,373
1942	132	76	120	720	3,951
1943	124	69	124	263	10,260

Source: Chang Kia-ngau, *The inflationary spiral*, 60.

low-interest loans to private industry, but the value of these in constant currency was but a fraction of those provided in 1938–9. Industry consequently starved for want of working capital, an important cause of the industrial decline. Industrialists complained bitterly about the paucity of loans and the cumbrous procedures required. But those who did obtain government loans commonly used the money for speculation.[105]

Factors other than inflation aggravated the industrialists' difficulties. The tightening noose of the Japanese blockade, for example, cut off the infusions of machinery, parts, raw materials and fuels upon which China's industrial plant was heavily dependent. Much of the industrial equipment in the interior was already antiquated – machinery in the textile industry, for example, dated from the 1920s – and so its deterioration, without replacements and spare parts, was rapid. Many materials – such as high-alloy steels – were unavailable within China, and yet were crucial if production in several branches of industry was to continue.

Lack of skilled workers also hampered China's wartime industry. Locally recruited workers, recently off the farms, frequently lacked even a rudimentary acquaintance with machinery or labour discipline. Skilled

---

[105] Liu Min, 'San-shih-san-nien Ssu-ch'uan chih kung-yeh' (Szechwan's industry in 1944), *SCCC* 2.2 (1 April 1945), 35; Yung Lung-kuei, 'Chiu-chi chan-shih kung-yeh ti chi-pen t'u-ching' (Fundamental means of rescuing the wartime industry), *Chung-kuo kung-yeh* (Chinese industry), 25.8 (March 1944); Li Tzu-hsiang, 'Wo-kuo chan-shih', 36; Kuan Meng-chueh, 'Shan-hsi-sheng fang-chih-yeh chih wei-chi chi ch'i ch'u-lu' (The crisis of Shansi's textile industry and its solution), *Chung-kuo kung-yeh*, 19 (1 September 1943) 12; Juan Yu-ch'iu, 'Chin-jih hou-fang min-ying kung-yeh ti wei-chi' (The current crisis of private industry in the rear area), *Chung-kuo nung-min* (Chinese farmer), 3.1/2 (June 1943), 33; Fang Chih-p'ing *et al. Lun kuan-liao tzu-pen* (On bureaucratic capital), 36; P'an Tsu-yung, 'Hou-fang pan-ch'ang ti k'un-nan ho ch'i-wang' (Difficulties and hopes of factory management in the rear area), *Hsin-ching-chi* (New economy), 6.11 (1 March 1942), 237–9; Ch'en Po-ta, *Chung-kuo ssu-ta-chia-tsu* (China's four great families), 52.

industrial labourers, therefore, had to be recruited from cities on the coast. By 1940, however, only some 42,000 of these had followed the Nationalist government into the interior. Factory managers began poaching upon other factories in their quest for skilled employees. This competition drove up wages. It also contributed to a destructively high rate of labour turnover – in 1940, about 10 per cent a month for skilled workers and 18 per cent for unskilled. In May 1943, the monthly turnover for all workers was 23 per cent. This prodigious instability, together with the general shortage of skills and the deterioration of equipment, led to a rapid decline in worker efficiency. In textile mills, for example, it was judged to be about 60–85 per cent of prewar levels. An electrical worker estimated that the efficiency of his factory was only one-third what it had been in Shanghai.[106]

Paradoxically, some industries ran into a lack of consumer demand. The steady impoverishment of people limited their spending to only the most critical necessities. The market for textile goods became sluggish, despite the people's desperate need for new clothing, because their purchasing power had collapsed. Weakened demand also struck the manufacturers of producer goods. The iron industry, for example, had flourished prior to 1942 due to the construction of railways and air-raid shelters. When the government gave up such projects, the iron industry lapsed into the doldrums, injuring related sectors such as coal and coke. Demand for industrial machinery and military equipment remained high. But China's iron-and-steel manufacturers usually could not satisfy it, because they lacked the equipment, raw materials, and skilled labour required.[107]

To combat the inflation, the government had first tried as early as December 1938 to fix the prices of daily necessities. This quickly proved ineffective. Subsequently the government promulgated a rash of new regulations to eliminate speculation in commodities and to hold down the prices of food, industrial materials and rents. By October 1941, however, the Bank of China pronounced all these measures a 'complete failure'.[108]

The Nationalists' interest in price controls revived after the United

[106] Freyn, *Free China's New Deal*, 41; Kuo-heng Shih, 60–1, 134; *CHB*, *1937–1945*, 385; Ta Chen, 55–6 and 122, table 58; Ch'en Ta, 'Chung-Kuo lao-kung chieh-chi yü tang-ch'ien ching-chi wei-chi' (China's working class and the current economic crisis), *She-hui chien-she* (Social reconstruction), 1.4 (1 Aug. 1948), 17; Li Tzu-hsiang, 'K'ang-chan i-lai', 43; Israel Epstein, *Notes on labor problems in Nationalist China*, 20–8.

[107] Liu Chi-ping, 79; Yung Lung-kuei, 8; T'ao Ta-yung, 'Lun tang-ch'ien ti kung-yeh chiu-chi' (Current means of rescuing industry), *Chung-kuo kung-yeh* (Chinese industry), 25.11 (Mar. 1944); Liu Min, 36–7.

[108] Chang Kia-ngau, *Inflationary spiral*, 344; Young, *China's wartime finance*, 144; *Ts'ai-cheng p'ing-lun* (Financial review), 5.1 (Jan. 1941), 25–37.

States adopted an anti-inflation law in October 1942, because they inferred that price controls were the mark of a modern nation at war. Financial and economic experts, such as Franklin Ho and Arthur Young, advised the Chungking leaders against price controls, on the grounds that they left the basic causes of inflation untouched and that the government lacked the administrative means to enforce them. They warned that the controls would be ignored and public confidence impaired. Disregarding these warnings, the government instituted on 15 January 1943 a new system of price controls. Black markets were banned and violators threatened with dire punishments, up to the death sentence. Also to control prices – and increase revenues – the state created monopolies of selected commodities. Beginning in 1942, it undertook to purchase such goods in bulk and sell them at low, fixed prices. These measures governed daily necessities (rice, salt, edible oil, sugar, fuel, etc.), industrial goods (iron, steel, cotton yarn, etc.), export items (tungsten, tin, tea, pig bristles, tung oil, etc.), and miscellaneous goods such as cotton, tobacco and matches.[109]

The government's several attempts to combat inflation with price controls were ineffective. China lacked the prerequisites: that is, firm territorial and political control, an efficient and honest bureaucracy, and a functioning system of transportation and communication. Outside a few major cities, the controls were largely inoperative. Controlled commodities fled those cities to other areas. Chungking several times faced severe rice shortages, because the price of rice was higher elsewhere. Even in major cities, actual market prices exceeded the official prices by an average of 14 per cent in 1943 and 67 per cent in 1945.[110]

The price controls sometimes had ruinous consequences for industry. In 1943, for instance, the official price of raw cotton was set so low that many farmers in Shensi – which provided most of unoccupied China's raw cotton – planted wheat instead and the mills in the Nationalist area reportedly had only enough cotton to operate for half a year. Not infrequently the cost of manufacturing a product exceeded its legal fixed price. In 1943, producing a ton of iron cost Y35,000; the government price of iron was Y30,000 a ton. In 1944 the cost of mining a ton of coal ranged from Y1,870 to Y5,000; the fixed market price of coal was Y1,200 a ton. A bale of cotton cost Y15,000 to produce; yet it could be sold for only Y12,000.[111]

Finally the Ichigo campaign in 1944–5 in Honan, Hupei, Hunan, Kweichow, Kwangsi and Kwangtung hit fully one-fourth of Nationalist

[109] Chang Kia-ngau, *ibid.* 135–7, 345–9; Young, *China's wartime finance*, 35–6, 146–9.
[110] Chang Kia-ngau, *ibid.* 345–6; Young, *ibid.* 149.
[111] Kuan Meng-chueh, 7–9; Chang Kia-ngau, *Inflationary spiral*, 217; Liu Min, 37; Kan K'o-ch'ao, 'Chan-shih Ssu-ch'uan kung-yeh kai-kuan' (Survey of Szechwan's wartime economy), *SCCC* 1.2 (15 Mar. 1944), 72.

China's factories, accounting for 15 per cent or more of the total industrial capital. It also severed the remaining industrial plant of Nationalist China from its sources of supply (such as the raw cotton produced in Honan, Hunan and Hupei) and from market outlets, and destroyed investor confidence.

All these factors – inflation, lack of imports, shortage of skilled workers, withering consumer demand, obstructive price-control policies and military disaster – plunged Nationalist China's industry into a deep crisis. As one indication, arsenals in the autumn of 1944 were operating at only 55 per cent of capacity. Between 80 and 90 per cent of the iron-and-steel plants in Chungking closed between the spring of 1943 and early 1945; 50 of the 320 machine shops closed during 1944; about 185 of the 250 coal-mining units in the major coal-producing Chia-ling River area closed between 1943 and 1945.[112]

Unemployment had become a serious problem by March 1945. Mining production in 1944 was but a fraction of the 1942 levels (coal, 72 per cent; lead, 49 per cent; tungsten, 27 per cent; tin, 27 per cent; copper, 24 per cent; antimony, 6 per cent). Even cotton-handicraft production was in deep trouble by the end of 1944, largely from shortages of raw materials, transportation difficulties, and troublesome transit taxes. The industrial crisis was assuredly greater than the official production figures suggest (see table 4).[113]

The creation in November 1944 of the Chinese War Production Board, resulting in large government orders and infusions of new money, markedly stimulated some industries. Between November 1944 and May 1945, steel production increased by 52 per cent; pig iron, 46 per cent; coal, 35 per cent; and electric power, 8 per cent. Despite these increases, the general index of industrial production during the first three months of 1945 remained unchanged. Manifestly, the decline elsewhere in the industrial sector had not been impeded. The evidence is overwhelming that, on the eve of peace, Nationalist China's industry in particular, and the economy generally, were on the verge of collapse.[114]

War made the government the leading economic entrepreneur. Previously it had gained control of the banking sector, but it held only some 11 per cent of the capital in Chinese-owned industrial enterprises. By 1942, however, the Ministry of Economics reported that state-controlled

[112] Young, *Helping hand*, 335; Li Tzu-hsiang, 'Wo-kuo chan-shih', 28–9; Liu Min, 28–9.

[113] *Ta-kung-pao* (Chungking), (1 June 1945), p. 3; *CHB, 1937–1945*, 369; *Shang-wu jih-pao*, 9 Sept. 1945, in *CPR* 246 (12 Sept. 1945) 9; Chang Ta-ch'en, 'San-shih-san nien ti Ch'ung-ch'ing t'u-pu-yeh' (Chungking's handicraft textile industry in 1944), *SCCC* 2.2 (1 April 1945), 202.

[114] Chang Kia-ngau, *Inflationary spiral*, 67. See also Young, *China's wartime finance*, 141 and 316; *Shang-wu jih-pao*, 18 July 1945, in *CPR* 196 (22 July 1945) 1; *Shang-wu jih-pao*, 7 Aug. 1945, in *CPR* 217 (12 Aug. 1945) 1–4.

enterprises accounted for 17.5 per cent of the factories, 70 per cent of the capital, 32 per cent of the workers and 42 per cent of the horse-power in the Nationalist area.[115]

Three government agencies developed industry in the interior: the National Resources Commission (Tzu-yuan wei-yuan-hui), the Industrial and Mining Adjustment Administration (Kung-k'uang t'iao-cheng wei-yuan-hui) and the four government banks. The mandate of the National Resources Commission, created in 1935, was to 'develop, operate and control basic industries'. By December 1944 it operated 92 industrial units – 33 factories, 38 mines, and 21 electrical power plants. It also ran 11 industrial units conjointly with other agencies. The commission dominated the heavy and highly technical industries, in contrast to the private factories, which tended to be less mechanized and to produce light industrial goods.[116]

The initial responsibility of the Industrial and Mining Adjustment Administration, created just after the outbreak of the war, was to facilitate the removal of privately owned factories to the interior. From 1938 it also invested directly in industrial enterprises, frequently producing consumer goods in competition with private entrepreneurs – alcohol, textiles, paper and cement. In 1943 and 1944, its direct investments exceeded its loans to private industry by over 30 per cent. Sun Yat-sen had held that the government should limit its economic role to basic industries, but now it became a major participant in light industry as well.[117]

The four government banks were not 'government' banks in the usual sense, for private investors held substantial shares in three of them: the Bank of China, the Bank of Communications, and the Farmers' Bank. Like private commercial banks, all three, especially after 1940, increased their direct participation and ownership in industry and business. They did this to get tangible assets to protect the real value of their capital. This became, as Chang Kia-ngau observed, 'indistinguishable from speculation'.[118] Whatever their motives, the government banks, like the Industrial and Mining Adjustment Administration, became deeply enmeshed in the private industrial and commercial sectors.

Some critics, politically inspired, characterized the government's role in the economy as 'bureaucratic capitalism', through which officials were amassing private fortunes, squeezing out private entrepreneurs and impoverishing the common people. However, the growing economic role

[115] Parks Coble, Jr. *The Shanghai capitalists and the Nationalist government, 1927–1937*, 315–17; Ch'en Chen, ed. *Chung-kuo chin-tai kung-yeh tzu-liao* (Materials on the industry of modern China), 2.1422.
[116] *CHB, 1937–1943*, 431, 365; Ch'en Chen, 2.836–9, 853.   [117] *CHB, 1937–1943*, 438, 376.
[118] Chang Kia-ngau, *Inflationary spiral*, 189–90. See also *Ta-kung-pao* editorial, 13 Dec. 1941, cited in Ch'en Po-ta, 52.

of the National government might better be viewed as state capitalism, a rational response to the requirements of a modernizing agrarian society and to the unique economic demands of wartime. Few entrepreneurs, without government aid, could have relocated their factories or created large-scale new ones in the western provinces. Wartime China faced an especial need to rationalize the distribution of scarce resources, such as machinery, raw materials and power. It is not, therefore, the policy of state capitalism per se that can be criticized, but rather the implementation of that policy. Government enterprises were frequently inefficient, bureaucratic and corrupt, as was the government's administration elsewhere. Government-related factories, moreover, enjoyed numerous advantages – such as bank credit, raw materials, or trucks for transport – that were denied to private firms. Some companies, like the Chung-yuan Paper Mill, sought an official connection by voluntarily offering stock to the government. Failing this, private firms in large numbers foundered late in the war for want of working capital, raw materials or guaranteed markets,[119] while corrupt government officials became enormously wealthy. By the latter phase of the war, the government's economic entrepreneurship had become a political liability. In 1948 Mao Tse-tung elevated 'bureaucratic capitalism' to the level of feudalism and imperialism as a target of his New Democratic Revolution.[120]

POLITICAL DEBILITATION

An editorial in a Chengtu paper (the Hua-hsi jih-pao: West China daily) – never published, because it was quashed by the censor – trenchantly expressed the popular mood late in the war: 'Government officials are corrupt and laws are abused by them; the people's livelihood becomes daily more grievous and desperate. With the nation in hardship and the people in poverty, a small corrupt element is growing increasingly richer and living even more luxuriously. This rotten phenomenon, together with many other reactionary political factors, has lowered both the people's and the soldiers' morale nearly to the vanishing point.'[121]

Demoralization was a variable phenomenon, proceeding unevenly from

---

[119] Ch'en Chen, 2.1448–9; Chang Kia-ngau, *Inflationary spiral*, 188–90; An-min Chung, 'The development of modern manufacturing industry in China, 1928–1949', 227; Kan K'o-ch'ao, 72; Li Tzu-hsiang, 'Wo-kuo chan-shih', 34–7; Yen Hsi-ta, 'Ching-chi wei-chi yü kuan-liao tzu-pen' (The economic crisis and bureaucratic capital), *Ching-chi chou-pao* (Economics weekly), 4.6 (6 Feb. 1947) 9–11.
[120] 'On the question of the national bourgeoisie and the enlightened gentry', *Selected works of Mao Tse-tung*, 4.207–10.
[121] Penfield to Gauss, 'Censored editorial on PPC meeting', US State Dept. 893.00/9–1444, 14 Sept. 1944, encl. 1, p. 1.

place to place. In February 1939 it was reported that the martial spirit of the Hunanese was low, but morale in Kwangtung and Kwangsi was very high. In mid-1941, the people of Sikang appeared utterly indifferent while Chungking by contrast, despite – or, more probably, because of – three years of bombing, 'throbbed [to use the words of Theodore White] with the strength of a nation at war'.[122]

The demoralization of Nationalist China was largely due to the corrosive effects of inflation and the changing political and military aims of the government. After the United States and England joined the war and the Communist movement became a potent military and political force, Chiang Kai-shek and the Nationalist leaders became concerned less about surviving the Japanese onslaught than about the future of their own power. The government became conservative and repressive.

The People's Political Council, for example, had been a highly promising instrument for generating popular support. With its large number of non-KMT members, it epitomized the spirit of national unity. After 1940, however, many council members criticized the breakdown of the united front and the increase of censorship and repression. To maximize their political effectiveness, the minority party representatives in the council in March 1941 organized the Federation of Democratic Parties, a coalition of six minority parties and groups that had emerged during the 1920s and 1930s. These were typically formed of intellectuals, often foreign-educated, who resented the KMT dictatorship. There was, however, a broad ideological spread among them. The China Youth Party and the National Socialist Party were basically conservative, while the Third Party and members of the National Salvation Association were more radical. Because these minority parties hoped to dismantle the Kuomintang's one-party control of the government, however, they all spoke in the idiom of Western democracy. With the possible exception of the China Youth Party, which claimed about 30,000 members, none of them had a mass following. They were essentially congeries of intellectuals, highly elitist in outlook.[123]

Proclaiming itself a 'third force' – neither KMT nor CCP – the federation called for democratization, government by law, and freedom of speech, publication and assembly. It published the *Kuang-ming-pao*

---

[122] Peck to State, telegram, US State Dept. 893.00/14339, 28 Feb. 1939, pp. 1–3; Gauss to State, 'Transmitting copies of a report concerning some observations of a trip to Western Szechuan and Eastern Sikang', US State Dept. 893.00/14800, 18 Sept. 1941, encl. p. 8; White and Jacoby, 11, 19; Graham Peck, *Two kinds of time*, 56.

[123] *Chung-kuo ko hsiao-tang-p'ai hsien-k'uang* (Present state of the minority parties in China); 'Democracy vs. one-party-rule: the little parties organize', *Amerasia*, 7.3 (25 April 1943) 97–117; Melville T. Kennedy, Jr. 'The Chinese Democratic League', *Harvard papers on China*, 7 (1953) 136–75; Ch'ien Tuan-sheng, 351–62.

(Light) in Hong Kong and the *Min-hsien* (People's constitution) in Chungking and opened offices in major cities like Kunming, Chengtu and Kweilin. The federation spoke for intellectuals and professional people who identified with neither of the two major parties.[124]

Chungking had encouraged the PPC as long as it unreservedly supported government policies. When council members became captious and even formed a political party, however, it responded with customary ill grace. Publication of the federation's programme was suppressed by the censors, and its activities were constantly harassed by the secret police. In a government reorganization of the PPC in 1942, outspoken members of the federation lost their membership, and a reapportionment of the members assured the KMT of a dominant majority. In frustration, the Communists ceased attending meetings. Deprived of its popular and independent character, the PPC's deliberations thereafter had little impact upon government policy.[125]

The government's political style was illustrated in the National Spiritual Mobilization movement, inaugurated on 12 March 1939, the anniversary of Sun Yat-sen's death. Its objectives were to generate mass support for the government and mobilize the people for the war effort. The movement's methods, however, revealed the Nationalists' characteristic distrust of the masses. It encouraged people to swear to a 'Citizens Pact', all twelve articles of which were negatives – 'Not to act contrary to the Three People's Principles', 'Not to disobey laws and orders of the government', 'Not to participate in traitorous organizations', etc. Spiritual Mobilization – like the New Life movement of the 1930s – quickly foundered on bureaucratic inertia.[126]

Failing to mobilize the people and unwilling to permit them a meaningful role in politics, the National government remained an elitist regime, whose base of popular support eroded as the war dragged on. More and more it relied on force or the threat of force to maintain its political supremacy. Especially from 1939, as the United Front with the Communists broke down and popular discontent sharpened, the Nationalists unsheathed their weapons of repression. Wuhan in 1937–8 had seen considerable freedom of the press, but tight censorship was now reimposed. The Central News Agency invariably exaggerated victories and disguised defeats. Stories of corruption were expunged lest they

---

[124] Lyman P. Van Slyke, *Enemies and friends: the United Front in Chinese Communist history*, 169, 174–5.
[125] Lawrence Nae-lih Shyu, 'People's Political Council', 38–55.
[126] *China's spiritual mobilization: outline of the plan*; US State Dept. comment on telegram, Vincent to State, US State Dept. 893.00/14963, 13 Mar. 1943; *Kuo-min ching-shen tsung-tung-yuan yun-tung* (National spiritual mobilization movement), comp. San-min-chu-i ch'ing-nien-t'uan chung-yang t'uan-pu.

damage the war effort. Publishers were cowed by the heavy-handed pre-publication censorship, and China's wartime press was generally insipid. The Communists' *Hsin-hua jih-pao* (New China daily), published in Chungking as part of the United Front agreement, was the only newspaper that dared indicate, with symbols such as XXX, that the censors' blue pencils had reduced the original copy. Only in areas where Nationalist authority was attenuated, notably in Kweilin controlled by the Kwangsi clique (Li Chi-shen, Huang Hsu-ch'u *et al.*), and in Kunming where Lung Yun reigned, was the press able openly to express criticisms of the central government.[127]

After the New Fourth Army incident in January 1941, Communist activities were completely banned in Nationalist areas (except to a limited extent in Chungking), and known Communists were arrested. Communists, however, could take refuge in Yenan. It was individual liberals and members of the minority parties who most felt the sting of the Nationalists' political control. Ma Yin-ch'u, for example, a Kuomintang member and China's most noted economist, had criticized the large-scale war profiteering of government leaders. He was arrested in December 1940. Though freed in 1942, he was forbidden to publish on non-economic subjects and even to speak in public. Sa K'ung-liao, a well-known liberal journalist, was imprisoned in Kweilin in 1943. After the summer of 1940, many associated with the Chinese Industrial Cooperative Movement – nominally headed by H. H. Kung but tainted by radicalism because it related intimately with the common people – were arrested and some allegedly shot.[128]

Chungking's political controls fell particularly heavily upon the universities. The minister of education during most of the war (1938-44) was Ch'en Li-fu, leader of the CC clique and a fervent anti-Communist. On the pretext of eliminating invidious foreign influences (such as individualism, liberalism, and contempt for things Chinese) from the universities and raising their academic standards, Ch'en imposed rigid controls. His ministry published textbooks emphasizing China's traditions and KMT orthodoxy; it required courses in, inter alia, military training and the Three People's Principles; it provided syllabi for instructors; and it reduced student opportunities to take electives.[129] Ch'en Li-fu imposed a pervasive

[127] Lee-hsia Hsu Ting, *Government control of the press in modern China, 1900–1949*, 132–51.

[128] Hugh Deane, 'Political reaction in Kuomintang China', *Amerasia*, 5·5 (July 1941), 210–13; Lee-hsia Hsu Ting, 139–41; Gauss to State, US State Dept. 893.00/15319 (14 Mar. 1944), encl. (Memorandum by Graham Peck on unification of anti-Central Government elements), p. 6; Sa K'ung-liao, *Liang-nien ti cheng-chih-fan sheng-huo* (Two years in the life of a political prisoner), *passim*; Douglas Robertson Reynolds, 'The Chinese industrial cooperative movement and the political polarization of wartime China, 1938–1945', 306–8 and *passim*.

[129] Ou Tsuin-chen, 106–11; Jessie Gregory Lutz, *China and the Christian colleges, 1850–1950*, 386.

uniformity upon Chinese education, designed to assure Nationalist control over the nation's intellectuals and youth.

South-west Associated University (comprising Peita, Nankai and Tsinghua Universities) in Kunming was favoured by the unusually high quality of its faculty members and by the political protection of Lung Yun. Most universities, however, succumbed to Ch'en Li-fu's pressures. The KMT secret police, which Ch'en controlled, devoted much of its attention to the academic community and cowed most professors. The Three-People's-Principles Youth Corps had cells on all campuses. Ardent members served as informers.[130]

The Nationalists' main instrument of political control, besides the KMT secret police and the Youth Corps, was the Military Commission's Bureau of Investigation and Statistics. Headed by one of Chiang Kai-shek's staunchest supporters, General Tai Li, this secret service expanded from 1,700 operatives in 1935 to 40–50,000 by the end of the war. Tai Li's responsibilities included military intelligence, under-cover operations in the Japanese-occupied areas, and political control of the army.[131] But his operatives also maintained surveillance of civilians, and ran most of Nationalist China's political prisons, at least ten in number, from which spread fearsome rumours of torture, doubtless not wholly unfounded. A primary purpose of the prisons was to 're-educate' persons with 'dangerous thoughts'. Inmates who responded positively to indoctrination were usually released after a year, but some were executed. Tai Li admitted to 130 executions between 1935 and 1945, although critics hinted at far larger numbers.[132] Tai Li's organization was the most feared in Nationalist China.

By 1944, political discontent was discernible at all levels of society. The depth of unrest in the rural areas may be exemplified by conditions in Honan. In 1940 and 1941, harvests there had been poor, and in 1942 the crop of spring wheat withered from drought. Although the farmers were in desperate need of food, officials relentlessly demanded full payment of the land taxes. Sometimes the farmers' entire harvests were seized, not even leaving seedgrain for the following year. Some farmers had to sell

130 Lloyd E. Eastman, 'Regional politics', 340–1; Vincent to State, 'Meeting of Szechuan delegates of San Min Chu I Youth Corps', US State Dept. 893.408/1 (17 Mar. 1943); Langdon to Gauss, 'Activity among Chinese university students at Kunming', US State Dept. 893.42/8–3144 (31 Aug. 1944), p. 2.

131 *Tai Yü-nung hsien-sheng nien-p'u* (Chronological biography of Tai Li), comp. Intelligence Section, Defence Ministry, 25; Ch'en Shao-hsiao, *Hei-wang-lu* (Record of the black net), 102–6; H. K. Tong, *World press*, 180–1.

132 Li I-yeh, 51; Gauss to State, '"Labor camps" in China', US State Dept. 740.0011 Pacific War/3678 (24 Dec. 1943); Sa K'ung-liao, 41, and *passim; Shang-jao chi-chung-ying* (The Shang-jao concentration camp), 3, 23.

their work animals, furniture, and even their farms to satisfy the tax collectors. The result was wholesale famine in the winter of 1942–3, with many eating bark, roots and animal fodder. Cannibalism was reported. Some two or three million persons died in this tragedy; another three million took refuge outside the province. Subsequently hundreds of thousands of Honanese farmers were rounded up to transport grain in carts and wheelbarrows to collection centres, to find forage for the army's animals, to build roads, and to dig a huge 300-mile-long anti-tank trench which ultimately proved to be completely useless. Nearly a million persons were conscripted to erect dikes along the Yellow River. No pay for this labour was given to the farmers, who frequently had to provide even their own food. The depth of resentment became apparent in the spring of 1944. As Chinese soldiers retreated before Japan's Ichigo offensive, farmers ferociously attacked them. Armed with farm tools, knives and ancient guns, they disarmed 50,000 of their own soldiers, killing some – at times even burying them alive.[133]

In Hupei in 1943, a Chinese commander complained that 'the country folks...stealthily send pigs, beef, rice and wine across the line to the enemy. The country folks are willing to be ruled by the enemy, but do not wish to be free citizens under their own government.'[134] In almost every province in the Nationalist area, from Fukien and Kwangtung to Szechwan and Kansu, there were peasant uprisings, usually in protest against conscription and tax exactions. In the spring of 1943, for example, a peasant rebel force, numbering about 50,000 men, seized control of most of southern Kansu. In the autumn a band of 4,000 rose against the government in Fukien where, a United States official reported, 'the people are seething with unrest'.[135]

Active political disenchantment reverberated even inside the government. Sun Fo, son of Sun Yat-sen and the relatively liberal-minded president of the Legislative Yuan, in the spring of 1944 bitterly criticized

---

[133] White and Jacoby, 166–78; Service, *Lost chance*, 9–19; Chiang Shang-ch'ing, *Cheng-hai mi-wen* (Secrets of the political world), 157; US State Dept. 893.00/15251, encl. 1 ('Excerpts from informal report of December 26, 1943 from Secretary on detail at Sian'), pp. 1–2; Hal to Donovan, 'Recent events and trends in China', Office of Strategic Services XL2032 (4 Sept. 1944), 1–2; Rice to Atcheson, 'The conscription, treatment, training, and behaviour of Chinese Central Government troops in the Shantung-Kiangsu-Honan-Anhwei Border Area', Office of Strategic Services 116311, p. 2.

[134] Gauss to State, 'Observations by a Chinese newspaper correspondent', encl. p. 3.

[135] *Hu-pei-sheng cheng-fu pao-kao, 1943/10–1944/9* (Report of the Hupei provincial government, October 1943 to September 1944), 132; *Hu shang-chiang Tsung-nan nien-p'u* (Chronological biography of General Hu Tsung-nan), 118–21; Wu Ting-ch'ang, *Hua-hsi hsien-pi cheng-hsu-chi* (Random notes at Hua-hsi), 2.194 and 199; Service, *Lost chance*, 21; Vincent to State 'Settlement of disturbances at Penghsien, Szechuan', US State Dept. 893.00/15022 (26 Apr. 1943); Atcheson to State, 'Conditions in Kweichow province: unrest in Free China', US State Dept. 893.00/15095 (27 July 1943); US State Dept. 893.00/15300, encl. ('General report on Fukien Province' by John C. Caldwell), p. 2.

the government for its dictatorial, inefficient and repressive tendencies. The Kuomintang, he charged, had adopted 'the attitude and habit of a ruling caste', out of touch with the people. Criticisms of the government were so thoroughly suppressed that 'the people dare not and cannot speak'. Nationalist China, he warned, was emulating its enemy, Nazi Germany.[136]

The Sixth Party Congress in May 1945 – the first KMT congress since early 1938 – became a sounding board for accumulated resentments. Broadly based elements in the party denounced the pervasive corruption, opportunism, inefficiency, disregard for the public welfare, and decline of morale in party, government and army.[137] No Communist propagandist could have uttered more mordant indictments.

A coalition of provincial militarists, in concert with radical leaders of the Federation of Democratic Parties, likewise mounted a challenge to the central government. The militarists – like Lung Yun in Yunnan, Yen Hsi-shan in Shansi, and P'an Wen-hua and Liu Wen-hui in Szechwan – were vestiges of the warlord era. Their local positions had been legitimized but they were convinced that Chiang Kai-shek was using the war to gain military supremacy over their own armies. An American official reported, in April 1943, 'a bitterness and antagonism that seethes beneath the surface' between National government and these provincial militarists.[138]

A common interest brought together these military commanders and the Federation of Democratic Parties. Yunnan had become a haven for minor-party members. There Governor Lung Yun employed several Federation leaders, including P'an Kuang-tan, P'an Ta-k'uei and Lo Lung-chi, as 'advisers'; he assisted federation members financially; and he sheltered them by restricting the activities of Chiang's secret police. Members of the federation, utterly disillusioned with the central government, were convinced that the Chungking regime was 'hopeless and ... doomed'. They deplored its increasingly dictatorial and repressive tendencies.[139] By 1943–4, moreover, they had become convinced that

---

[136] Gauss to State, 'Dr Sun Fo's views on democracy and planned economy', US State Dept. 893.00/15340 (14 Apr. 1944), encl. 1, p. 3; Gauss to State, 'Dr Sun Fo's speech criticizing the present objectives and methods of the San Min Chu I Youth Corps', US State Dept. 893.00/15366 (25 Apr. 1944), encl. pp. 2–4; Gauss to State, 'Dr Sun Fo's speech to the San Min Chu I Youth Corps' (7 June 1944), in The Amerasia papers: a clue to the catastrophe of China, 1.542.

[137] Fu-hsing Chung-kuo Kuo-min-tang chien-i; Office of Strategic Services doc. L57067, 25 May 1945, 1–4; Hsin-kuan-ch'ang hsien-hsing chi (The new 'Current state of the official arena'); Eastman, Seeds of destruction, 101–2, 109–24.

[138] Drumright to Vincent, 'Threatened clash Between Chengtu police and troops of Ching Pei Ssu Ling Pu', 26 Apr. 1943, US State Dept. 893.105/93, p. 2.

[139] Chang Wen-shih, Yun-nan nei-mu (The inside story in Yunnan), 16, 42; Langdon to State 'Future political developments in China: activities of the Federation of Chinese Democratic Parties at Kunming', US State Dept. 893.00/7-1444 (14 July 1944), p. 2.

Chiang himself was the source of the government's debilities. Clarence Gauss reported in July 1944 that even liberals who a year earlier had staunchly supported him 'see no hope for China under Chiang's leadership'.[140]

A group of intellectuals of the federation and provincial militarists incongruously became partners in a scheme to overthrow the central government. Convinced that Chungking was on the verge of collapse, the conspirators hoped to abstain from using military force. They concentrated instead on creating a successor Government of National Defence. To ratify these plans, a people's congress – comprising representatives from the Kuomintang (40 per cent), the Chinese Communist Party (20 per cent), the Federation of Democratic Parties (20 per cent), and other groups (20 per cent) – was scheduled to be held in Chengtu on about 10 October 1944. At the same time Lung Yun, P'an Wen-hua, Yü Han-mou and other military commanders agreed that they would put up no further resistance to the Japanese and let them destroy Chiang Kai-shek's armies.[141]

In the end, all this plotting bore no fruit. As the American consul in Kunming remarked, 'It would indeed be difficult to imagine a more heterogeneous group of feudal barons and radicals, idealists and practical politicians.'[142] They had not taken into account the political adroitness of Chiang Kai-shek to divide and conquer his rivals. Lung Yun, a key to the entire conspiracy, withdrew from the anti-Chiang movement in January 1945 in exchange for American Lend-Lease supplies sufficient to equip three of his Yunnan divisions. Then in a carefully staged military coup in October 1945, shortly after the Japanese surrender, Chiang stripped Lung Yun of his provincial posts and brought him to Chungking, where he was kept a virtual prisoner.

The anti-Chiang conspiracy, ill-conceived though it was, was symptomatic of the profound crisis that beset Nationalist China during the last year of the war. Economic production had decreased sharply, the inflation was out of control, the army was hapless before the Japanese, government was corrupt, and political disaffection suffused all levels of society. When the war ended on 14 August 1945, therefore, Nationalist China was demoralized and weak.

[140] FRUS, 1944, 492.
[141] Eastman, 'Regional politics', 346–7.
[142] Ringwalt to Gauss, 'Proposed Government of National Defense', US State Dept. 893.00/15420 (8 May 1944), p. 3.

CHAPTER 4

THE CHINESE COMMUNIST MOVEMENT DURING THE SINO-JAPANESE WAR 1937–1945

Chinese Communist leaders had long seen the war as inevitable because their experience and their ideology convinced them that Japanese expansion in China was fuelled by irreversible forces. 'The main characteristic of the present situation,' the CCP reiterated as a litany, 'is that Japanese imperialism wants to turn China into a colony.' The CCP also saw the war as necessary and, after the end of 1935, called for unified resistance at the earliest possible moment. Mao and his followers knew that in a Sino-Japanese war they could claim, as patriots, a legitimate, honourable, and self-defined role. Indeed, they intended to claim a leading role in moral terms. For them the only alternative would be a Sino-Japanese peace from which they would surely be excluded and which might be purchased at their expense. Every delay in resistance bought time which the KMT might use to continue campaigns against the CCP. Every delay prolonged the period in which Tokyo and Nanking might come to some further accommodation, possibly including joint anti-Communist action, as Japanese Foreign Minister Hirota had proposed in August 1936.

One need not impugn the CCP's sincerity to note that termination of civil war, a broad united front and resistance to Japan would also serve the party's interest. Its platform matched the mood of urban China – of students, intellectuals, large sections of the bourgeoisie, and many workers – far better than the Kuomintang's repressive call for 'unification before resistance'. So persuasive did the united front policy become among these groups, and even among some influential factions in the Kuomintang, that it weighed heavily in Chiang Kai-shek's decision, after his release on 25 December 1936, from two weeks' captivity in Sian, to call off the civil war and adopt a stronger posture toward Japan.

The author wishes to thank Ch'en Yung-fa and Gregor Benton for their careful and critical suggestions.

I. THE EARLY WAR YEARS 1937–1938

The agreements hammered out between representatives of the KMT and CCP in the months following the Sian incident were publicly proclaimed in August and September 1937, after the Shanghai fighting began on 13 August. These agreements formed the basis of KMT-CCP relations during the first years of the war and remained nominally in force throughout it. The CCP agreed (a) to strive for the realization of Sun Yat-sen's Three People's Principles (San-min chu-i); (b) to terminate its policies of armed revolt, sovietization, and forcible confiscation of landlords' land; (c) to abolish the present soviet government; and (d) to abolish the term 'Red Army' and place Communist troops under central government command. In return, the KMT allowed the CCP to set up liaison offices in several important cities, to publish the *New China Daily*, and to nominate representatives to its two principal advisory bodies. Civil rights were considerably extended, political prisoners were released, and a subsidy was initiated to help defray administrative and military expenses of the newly 'reintegrated' territories and armies.[1]

The outbreak of war thus transformed the political and military environment for all Chinese parties and forced the Chinese Communists into fundamental reconsideration of all important policies, of strategy and of tactics. The principal issues confronting Party Central during the first year and a half of the war – from the Marco Polo Bridge incident through the sixth plenum of the Central Committee in November 1938 – were the following:

1. The united front, and particularly the question of the CCP's relationship to the Kuomintang and the National government.
2. Military strategy and tactics, including coordination of operations with Nationalist and other units.
3. Leaders and leadership, especially Mao's efforts to strengthen his position vis-à-vis Chang Kuo-t'ao (who defected to the Nationalists in April 1938) and Wang Ming (pseudonym of Ch'en Shao-yü).

During these eighteen months, policy decisions and the disputes surrounding them rose to visibility in several important party meetings (see table 6). By early 1939 these issues had been clarified, if not fully resolved, and later developments in each of these areas can be traced from this

---

[1] The monthly subsidy, which lasted until 1940, was reported to be Ch. $100,000 for administrative expenses and Ch. $500,000 for the support of three authorized divisions in the newly renamed Eighth Route Army. See James P. Harrison, *The long march to power: a history of the Chinese Communist Party, 1921–72*, 279, and cited sources.

TABLE 6
Principal CCP meetings, July 1937–December 1938

Lo-ch'uan conference. Lo-ch'uan, Shensi, *c.* 20–25 August 1937. Major issues had to do with political and military reorganization as part of the national system; attitude toward the KMT; and united front policy.

Conference of party activists. Yenan, *c.* 12 November 1937. First meeting attended by Wang Ming, just returned from Moscow. Assessment of the military and political situation after the fall of Shanghai and Taiyuan.

Politburo meeting. Yenan, 9–13 December 1937. Most complete meeting of the Politburo since the fifth plenum (January 1934). Further debate over the KMT, united front, and military policies.

Politburo meeting. Yenan, 27 February–1 March 1938. Although relatively little is known of this meeting, views contradicting Mao's preferences seem to have prevailed: the positional defence of Wuhan, mobile warfare, and continued preparations for the Seventh Congress.

Sixth plenum (enlarged) of the Sixth CCP Central Committee. Yenan, 29 September–6 November 1938. The most comprehensive meeting of party leadership between the Sixth Congress in 1928 and the Seventh Congress in 1945. All outstanding issues were considered during this very protracted series of meetings, and a very large number of important documents were produced.

foundation. The frequency of such high-level policy meetings thereafter dropped sharply; even the rectification (*cheng-feng*) sessions in 1942 and the Seventh CCP Congress (April–June 1945) announced policy rather than debating it. This phenomenon undoubtedly reflected the consolidation of Maoist leadership, though by no means unanimity and full harmony within the party.

ATTITUDE TOWARD THE KUOMINTANG: THE UNITED FRONT

From the moment of its true adoption by the CCP in December 1935, the united front was conceived as a broad appeal to all those who would heed it and respond. To all those who did, the party was willing to make substantial concessions in both substance and spirit, so long as these did not compromise fundamental principles nor ultimate Communist control of the movement. In succeeding years, the scope of the united front steadily widened and its use became more sophisticated. As early as October 1939, Mao Tse-tung was identifying the united front, armed struggle and party-building as the three fundamental problems of the Chinese revolution, whose proper understanding was tantamount to correct leadership of the revolution as a whole. Even as it announced alliance with the KMT, the CCP asked,

Should the Anti-Japanese National United Front be confined to the Kuomintang and the Communist Party? No, it should be a united front of the whole nation, with the two parties only a small part of this united front...[It] is one of all parties and groups, of people in all walks of life and of all armed forces, a united front of all patriots – workers, peasants, businessmen, intellectuals, and soldiers.[2]

Disputes centred, rather, around the spirit of the relationship, whether the CCP would observe the limits set for it by the KMT and how fully it would obey the orders of its nominal superior. During the first years of the war, these disputes were coloured by factional struggle and by personality clashes, so that fact is difficult to separate from allegation. Publicly, CCP statements praised the leadership of Chiang Kai-shek and the KMT and pledged unstinting – but vague and unspecified – unity and cooperation. Suggestions, not criticisms, were offered, most of them having to do with further political democratization, popular mobilization and the like.

Mao Tse-tung's early position on the united front with the KMT appears fairly hard and aggressive, moderated by his absolute conviction that the Kuomintang had to be kept in the war. For Mao, the united front meant an absence of peace between China and Japan. Mao's quite consistent position, in both political and military affairs, was to remain independent and autonomous. He was willing to consider, for a time, Communist participation in a thoroughly reconstituted government ('the democratic republic') primarily to gain nationwide legality and enhanced influence. But, for the most part, he sought to keep the CCP separate, physically separate if possible, from the KMT. Other party leaders, including both Chang Kuo-t'ao and the recently returned Wang Ming, apparently questioned this line.

Some sources claim that in the November and December 1937 meetings Mao's line failed to carry the day. If so, Mao was probably laying out his general position rather than calling for an immediate hardening. In late 1937 the Nationalists' position was desperate, and it was no time to push them further: Shanghai was lost on 12 November, the awful carnage in Nanking took place the following month, and, most serious of all, Chiang was seriously considering a Japanese peace offer.

But as the new year turned and wore on, the peace crisis passed. The rape of Nanking strengthened Chinese will, and in January 1938 the Konoe cabinet issued its declaration of 'no dealing' (*aite ni sezu*) with Chiang Kai-shek. Whatever his preferences might have been, Chiang now had no choice but to fight on, and most of the nation, the CCP included, pronounced itself behind him. By summer, too, at the latest, it was clear that no last-ditch defence of the temporary Nationalist capital at Wuhan

---

[2] 'Kuo-kung liang-tang t'ung-i chan-hsien ch'eng-li hou Chung-kuo ke-ming ti p'o-ch'ieh jen-wu' (Urgent tasks of the Chinese revolution following the establishment of the KMT-CCP united front), *Mao Tse-tung chi* (Collected works of Mao Tse-tung), comp. Takeuchi Minoru *et al.*, hereafter *MTTC*, 5.266–7.

was anticipated. Government organs had begun functioning in Chungking as early as the previous December, and more were moving there all the time. While morale was high and a spirit of unity prevailed, Chiang vowed to continue his strategy of drawing the Japanese deeper into China, of scorched earth, of trading space for time.

These developments strengthened Mao's position. By the time of the sixth plenum, in the autumn of 1938, the official CCP position was fully to support Chiang Kai-shek and the two-party alliance. But in private Mao also approvingly quoted Liu Shao-ch'i as saying that if Wang Ming's slogan, 'everything through the united front', meant through Chiang Kai-shek and Yen Hsi-shan, then this was submission rather than unity. Mao proposed instead that the CCP observe agreements to which the KMT had already consented; that in some cases they should 'act first, report afterward'; in still other cases, 'act and don't report'. Finally, he said, 'There are still other things which, for the time being, we shall neither do nor report, for they are likely to jeopardize the whole situation. In short, we must not split the united front, but neither should we bind ourselves hand and foot.'[3]

MILITARY STRATEGY AND TACTICS

The Chinese Communist Party entered the war in command of approximately 30,000 men, a mix of the survivors of the various Long Marches, local forces already in being, and new recruits. In the reorganization of August and September 1937, they were designated collectively the Eighth Route Army (8RA) and were subdivided into three divisions: the 115th, 120th, and 129th commanded by Lin Piao, Ho Lung and Liu Po-ch'eng, respectively. (See below, pp. 190–2 for more on these units.)

Shortly after the war began, the National government also authorized the formation of a second Communist force, the New Fourth Army (N4A), to operate in Central China. The N4A was formed around a nucleus of those who had been left behind in Kiangsi and Fukien when the Long March began in 1934. Since that time, in ever dwindling numbers, they had survived precariously in separated groups against incessant Nationalist efforts to destroy them. Their initial authorized strength was 12,000 men, but it took several months to reach that level. The nominal commanding officer of the N4A was Yeh T'ing, an early Communist military leader who later left the party, but who somehow managed to remain on good terms with both Communists and Nationalists. Actual military and political control was vested in Hsiang Ying and Ch'en I.

---

[3] 'The question of independence and initiative with the united front', Mao Tse-tung, *Selected Works*, hereafter, Mao, *SW*, 2.215–16. Dated 5 Nov. 1938.

The first major issue posed by reorganization was whether or not to accept two Nationalist proposals: first, that they assign staff officers to the Eighth Route Army; and second, that Communist and non-Communist forces operate together in combat zones designated by the Nationalists. According to Chang Kuo-t'ao, a number of ranking party members (including Wang Ming, Chu Te and P'eng Te-huai) favoured these proposals. Although this is not well documented, they may have argued that acceptance would further consolidate the united front and would justify a claim that Nationalist forces share their weapons and other equipment. Some military leaders, probably represented by P'eng Te-huai, wanted to lessen Communist reliance on guerrilla warfare in favour of larger unit operations and more conventional tactics. Mao Tse-tung and others resisted these proposals, on the grounds that they would leave the 8RA too open to Nationalist surveillance, that coordinated operations would subordinate CCP units to non-Communist forces, and that the initiatives of time and place would be lost.

Mao foresaw a protracted war divided into three stages: (1) strategic offensive by Japan, (2) prolonged stalemate (this was the 'new stage' which Mao identified at the sixth plenum), and (3) strategic counter-attack, leading to ultimate victory. He was quite vague about the third stage, except that he anticipated it would be coordinated 'with an international situation favourable to us and unfavourable to the enemy'.[4] Meanwhile, Mao was acutely aware of the CCP's strategic weakness. Such a situation, he believed, called for guerrilla warfare and for the preservation and expansion of one's own forces.

But if, in Mao's words, the CCP was not only to 'hold the ground already won' but also to 'extend the ground already won', the only alternatives were either to expand in unoccupied China, at the expense of their supposed allies, or in occupied China, behind Japanese lines and at the expense of the enemy. And when Mao said 'ground', he meant it: territorial bases under stable Communist leadership.[5] The choice was an easy one. The former alternative led to shared influence, vulnerability, and possible conflict – all of which actually took place in CCP relations with Yen Hsi-shan in Shansi. But the latter alternative clearly served the interests of resistance, and, to the extent that KMT forces had been driven out of these occupied areas, the CCP could avoid conflict with its allies.

These principles are succinctly summed up, then explained more fully, in Mao's 'Problems of strategy in guerilla war against Japan'.[6] Complexities in the real world, of course, prevented such neat and clean distinctions as Mao was able to make in his writings. The CCP could not avoid contact

---

[4] *MTCC* 6.182, 'On the new stage', Oct. 1938.
[5] The term Mao chose for 'ground' was *chen-ti*, defined as 'a staging area for military operations or combat'.   [6] Mao, *SW* 2.82.

with other Chinese forces on the exterior line and in the rear: around the perimeter of Shen-Kan-Ning, in Shansi, and in the Lower Yangtze region. Nor were the occupied areas entirely devoid of Nationalist units; early in the war, especially, significant Nationalist forces remained behind Japanese lines. But there is no mistaking Mao Tse-tung's strategic import.

LEADERS AND LEADERSHIP

At the outbreak of the war, Mao Tse-tung's position in the Chinese Communist movement was that of *primus inter pares*. Veteran comrades were prepared to argue with him over basic policy, and at least two rivals directly challenged him. These were Chang Kuo-t'ao and Wang Ming. By the end of the sixth plenum, in late 1938, Mao was well on his way toward building that coalition which would carry him to undisputed leadership by 1942 or 1943.

Chang Kuo-t'ao had suffered mortal blows to his power during and just after the Long March. In August 1935, when his temporarily stronger forces linked up with those of Mao Tse-tung in north-western Szechwan, the two clashed over a wide range of issues, including questions of leadership, of army command, and of the destination of the Long March (see above, ch. 2, note 187). Chang contested the leading position Mao had assumed at the technically irregular Tsun-yi Conference (January 1935), which he and some other Politburo members had been unable to attend. Consequently, Chang led his reconstituted army westward into the high mountains of Sikang and Chinghai, while Mao struck north-west toward Shensi and the Pao-an/Yenan region, arriving there in October 1935. But Chang was unable to hold out in this inhospitable area and, in a series of marches and counter-marches, lost much of his army to fierce, pro-KMT Muslim forces in the Kansu corridor. Finally, in October 1936 – a full year later than his rival – he and his surviving followers reached Pao-an, where Mao had already done much to consolidate his position. Chang was given nominally high posts, specifically, the vice-chairmanship of the Shen-Kan-Ning Border Region government and a place on the preparatory committee for the Seventh CCP Congress, which was later postponed and not convened until 1945. But Chang knew his star had set, and he took advantage of a ceremonial visit to Sian in the spring of 1938 to flee to Wuhan, where he denounced Mao's united front line as seeking 'defeat for all' (i.e. of both the KMT and the Japanese) during the war. A few fruitless conversations took place in Wuhan between Chang and the CCP Liaison Group stationed there, but by the time of the sixth plenum, in autumn 1938, he had been read out of the party as a renegade.

Wang Ming was a more potent rival. Having returned to China in October 1937 with Stalin's blessings and probably the authority of the Comintern, he might have expected support from those who had been closely associated with him during his period of ascendancy (see above, chapter 2) in the CCP, the somewhat derisively labelled 'returned-students'. Highly educated and articulate, Wang had spent most of his adult life in the Soviet Union. He had an easy cosmopolitanism that contrasted with Mao's parochialism and quick temper, and he was far more at home than Mao in the realm of formal Marxist theory, where he condescended to his older Hunanese comrade. Indeed, in late 1937, he 'conveyed the instruction that Mao should be strengthened 'ideologically' because of his narrow empiricism and 'ignorance of Marxism-Leninism'.[7] The two men probably felt an almost instinctive antipathy for each other, so different were their temperaments and their styles.

Whatever the orientations of Wang's former colleagues, he did not now have a clear faction behind him. Chang Wen-t'ien (Lo Fu), secretary-general of the party, mediated a number of intra-party disputes early in the war in such a way as to allow Mao's policies to prevail in most of their essentials. Ch'in Pang-hsien (Po Ku) appears to have been guided by Chou En-lai, himself a one-time associate of Wang Ming who had thrown in his lot with Mao and his group. Nor did Wang have any appreciable base in either the party's armed forces or its territorial government. Returning to a China much changed during his absence, Wang retained mainly his international prestige, his Politburo membership, and his powers of persuasion. But these considerable assets proved inadequate to an open challenge – and, indeed, Wang apparently never attempted such a showdown with Mao.

Some portray Wang Ming as the exponent of a strategy that clashed with Mao's on two fundamental issues, raising in their wake many other related points of conflict.[8] The first issue had to do with the CCP's relationship to the KMT and the central government. The second issue involved an urban revolutionary strategy based on workers, intellectuals, students, and some sections of the bourgeoisie versus a rural revolution based on the peasantry. Of course, in-fighting for leadership and personal dislike added heat to these two issues. Except in the Soviet Union, the Maoist version has held sway: Wang Ming was ready to sacrifice CCP independence in virtual surrender to the KMT, and he was unsympathetic to rural revolution.

[7] Gregor Benton, 'The "Second Wang Ming line" (1935–1938)', CQ 61 (March 1975) 77.
[8] Ibid. Also Tetsuya Kataoka, Resistance and revolution in China: the Communists and the second united front, 72ff.

This simplistic account raises puzzling questions. If his views were as Mao described them, how could Wang Ming have sought to justify them within the CCP? It is unthinkable that he would describe *himself* as a capitulationist who cared little for the peasantry. In trying to reconstruct his position we can assume that Wang Ming invoked the authority of Stalin and the Comintern after his return to China. Stalin had long wanted a Chinese resistance centring around Chiang and the KMT, a policy that Mao and the CCP adopted only reluctantly and incompletely in mid-1936, six months after Stalin's position was clear. Although the CCP moved toward such a united front in the second half of 1936 (culminating in the Sian incident, 12–25 December) more for reasons of its own than because of outside promptings, Stalin's name and the authority of the Comintern remained formidable. Not even Mao wished openly to defy Moscow's will. Wang thus had a two-edged weapon: a delegated authority from Stalin and protection against purge, for any such move would have incurred Stalin's wrath. Wang could further argue that it was the united front with the KMT that had brought an end to civil war, and, in the face of Japanese invasion, had led the CCP to an honourable and legitimate role in national affairs. Now was the time to expand and legalize that role throughout the country, rather than to remain simply a regional guerrilla movement in backward provinces. This might be accomplished, Wang apparently thought, through a reorganized central government and military structure, in which Communists would be integrally and importantly included, in response to the needs of unity and national resistance. This would, of course, require the cooperation and consent of Chiang Kai-shek. The negotiations would be difficult, but Wang's statements were sufficiently general – or vague – to allow much room for manoeuvre. Wang also implied that a 'unified national defence government' might bring the CCP a share of the financial and military resources – perhaps even some of the Soviet aid – now virtually monopolized by the Nationalists. These possibilities were tempting to many senior party members and commanders who had long suffered great poverty of means.[9] Evidently Wang Ming felt that Japanese aggression, aroused patriotism within China, and international support (especially from the Soviet Union), would eventually move Chiang to further concessions, just as they had moved him toward the united front after Sian. If so, Wang's slogan, 'everything through the united front', did not imply capitulation to Chiang, but continued pressure upon him.

[9] At the December Politburo meeting, Chang Kuo-t'ao recalls Mao sighing ruefully, 'If so much [Russian aid] can be given to Chiang Kai-shek, why can't we get a small share.' *The rise of the Chinese Communist Party, 1928-1938: volume two of the autobiography of Chang Kuo-t'ao,* 566.

Wang was soon posted to Wuhan, which during the first six months of 1938 brimmed with dedication to the war effort. The spirit of the united front pervaded all social classes and political circles, and the apparent cordiality between Nationalists and Communists surprised many. Wang may have felt that this strengthened his hand. In any case, he continued to call for a 'democratic republic' well into the spring.[10] Thereafter, realizing that Chiang Kai-shek would not consent to such sweeping changes in the government and party he controlled, Wang Ming backed off: 'The National Government is the all-China government which needs to be strengthened, not reorganized.'[11] He also called for 'national defence divisions (*kuo-fang-shih*)', a similar scaling down of his former proposals for a unified national military structure. In Wuhan, Wang was apparently able to win Chou En-lai's partial support for his programme.

The fatal flaw in Wang Ming's united front efforts lay in their dependence on the consent of the suspicious Kuomintang government. But the only leverage he had was public opinion in the Kuomintang's own constituencies.[12] Wang Ming was no capitulationist but had painted himself into a corner, whereas Mao retained much greater freedom of action.

As to the second issue, whether the revolution should be based on the countryside or the cities, Wang Ming had never lived or worked among the peasantry. Though he grew up in a well-to-do rural Anhwei family, both his instincts and his theoretical bent were quite thoroughly urban. After his return to China in late 1937, Wang rarely referred to the peasantry, and none of his known writings addressed this subject so close to Mao Tse-tung's heart. Wang nowhere called for giving up the peasant movement, but he clearly felt that without a strong foothold in the cities and among the workers and other nationalistic elements (such as students, the national bourgeoisie), the movement would eventually lose its Marxist-Leninist thrust, and pursue backward, parochial, and essentially petty-bourgeois peasant concerns. Holding the cities was thus much more important to Wang Ming than to Mao Tse-tung, who preferred to trade space for time and who – like Chiang Kai-shek after the fall of Nanking – was unwilling to see Nationalist resistance crushed in fruitless positional warfare. Wang, on the other hand, called for a Madrid-like defence of Wuhan which would mobilize the populace. Here, of course, Wang's united front conceptions and his urban bias came together, for only with KMT cooperation or tolerance could such mobilization take place.

---

[10] *Chieh-fang pao* (Liberation), 36 (29 Apr. 1938), 1. The statement was written on 11 March 1938.
[11] 'The current situation and tasks in the War of Resistance', in Kuo Hua-lun (Warren Kuo), *Analytic history of the Chinese Communist Party*, 3.363.
[12] Kataoka Tetsuya, 75.

Wang Ming meanwhile had party work to do in Wuhan. He was head of the newly-formed United Front Work Department and of the regional Yangtze River Bureau, both directly responsible to the Central Committee. In addition, he was at least the nominal leader of the Communist delegations appointed to the People's Political Council and the Supreme National Defence Council, the advisory bodies organized as sounding boards by the National government in early 1938 to symbolize multi-party unity. From these various platforms, Wang Ming proclaimed, over the head of the government, the patriotic message that was so influential in keeping urban public opinion behind resistance to Japan. Patriotism and wholehearted devotion to the war effort were his keynotes, not Mao's exhortation to 'hold and extend the ground we have already won'.

Wang also undertook organizational activities independent of the Kuomintang, particularly with youth groups, and he sought to knit a wide variety of patriotic organizations into the 'Wuhan Defence Committee'. But in August 1938 the Wuhan Defence Committee was disbanded, along with the mass organizations associated with it, and *Hsin-hua jih-pao*, the CCP paper in Wuhan, was shut down for three days as a result of its protests. With Chiang Kai-shek's decisions not to attempt an all-out defence of Wuhan nor to allow independent popular mobilization, Wang's efforts to maintain a quasi-legal organized CCP base in urban China flickered out.

Compromised by these losses and separated from party centre, Wang's influence gradually declined during 1938. In September, the CI expressed its support for Mao's leadership. The sixth plenum (October–November) thus marked Wang's substantial eclipse, and a significant strengthening of Mao's leadership. Yet the convening of a Central Committee (enlarged) plenum, rather than the anticipated full Seventh Congress, which would have required the election of a new Central Committee and Politburo, suggests that Mao was not yet ready, or perhaps able, fully to assert his primacy throughout the party. Wang continued for a time to direct the United Front Work Department, and the Chinese Women's University, and to publish frequently in party organs. But he and his views were no longer a serious threat to Mao's 'proletarian leadership', and the final discrediting of 'returned-student' influence in the 1942 rectification (*cheng-feng*) campaign was anti-climactic. After 1940, little was heard from Wang Ming.

ORGANIZATIONAL STRUCTURE AND ACTIVITIES

Both the Chinese Communist Party and its principal armies – the Eighth Route and the New Fourth – expanded greatly during the Sino-Japanese

TABLE 7

Wartime expansion of the Chinese Communist Party

1937	40,000
1940	800,000
1941	763,447
1942	736,151
1944	853,420
1945 (Seventh Congress)	1,211,128

Source: John W. Lewis, *Leadership in Communist China*, 110.

War. The first three years of the war, until 1940, saw very rapid growth. The army grew five times larger, the party twenty (see tables 7 and 8). Nor do these figures tell the whole story, for they omit the auxiliaries of the regular armies (the militia and the self-defence forces), and also tens of thousands of activists, the political infrastructure, and the mass organizations under party influence. Needless to say, such pell-mell growth brought many serious problems, since quality, experience and training were often neglected in the rush to expand.

As the tables show, both the party and the armies shrank during the early 1940s, primarily as a result of Japanese and Nationalist efforts to restrict or destroy Communist influence. By imposing cruel necessities, these efforts forced the CCP to consolidate its forces, to emphasize quality over quantity, and to organize and mobilize more effectively. This period of constriction and consolidation continued until the last year of the war. Not until the twelve months from mid-1944 to mid-1945 was there a second period of growth. These three periods, 1937–8, 1939–43, and 1944–5 were the principal phases of the Communist movement during the Sino-Japanese War.

The movement acted through the interlocking structures of party, army and government. Each of these systems had its own organization and, in addition, interacted closely with the other two. Furthermore, each reached outward and downward into society at large, seeking to create the infrastructures and mass base upon which the movement ultimately depended. Finally, administration was further complicated by enormous regional variations and the dispersal of the movement over mountains and plains, across North and Central China, behind Japanese lines and in areas contested with the KMT. One major problem of the CCP during the war was how to maintain the coherence and thrust of the movement, steering a precarious course between the Scylla of rigid centralization – unattainable, in any case – and the Charybdis of degeneration into sheer

TABLE 8

Wartime expansion of Eighth Route and New Fourth Armies

	Eighth Route Army	New Fourth Army	Total
1937	80,000	12,000	92,000
1938	156,700	25,000	181,000
1939	270,000	50,000	320,000
1940	400,000	100,000	500,000
1941	305,000	135,000*	440,000
1942	340,000	110,960	450,960
1943	339,000	125,892	464,892
1944	320,800	153,676	474,476
1945 (Apr.)	614,000	296,000	910,000

* Prior to the 4 January 1941 New Fourth Army incident. See also table 16.

localism, what the party terms 'mountain-topism' (*shan-t'ou chu-i*). Higher levels of party and army, more than regional governments, were the sinews holding the movement together from the centre in Yenan.

Party. In outline, Chinese Communist Party organization remained as it had always been, a hierarchical pyramid with the Politburo, the Standing Committee, and the Central Committee at its apex (see table 9). Policy decisions reached at this level, particularly by the Politburo or by its chairman, Mao Tse-tung, were channelled through the Secretariat, which set goals in general terms and also determined which agencies or departments should be responsible for pursuing the required tasks.

Two types of sub-structures handled the work of the party. The first were functional, task-oriented departments, responsible at the highest level directly to the Secretariat and the Politburo. The most important of these are listed, along with their directors, in table 9.

The second type of sub-structure was regional, corresponding to the areas in which the party was operating. These regional bureaus, like the Central Committee departments, were responsible to Party Central in Yenan. Downward in the chain of command, they supervised the work of branch bureaus (located mainly in the North China base areas), and lower-level committees and branches. At bureau level and below, task-oriented departments, like those at the central level, were replicated in simplified form.

Finally, the party maintained branches in government and army at all

---

[13] Harrison, *Long march*, 294. The figures for party and army should not be added together, since many army men were simultaneously party members. Perhaps one-third of the armed forces had some sort of party affiliation (full, probationary or prospective).

TABLE 9

Party organization during the Sino-Japanese War

Central Committee	
Political bureau	Mao Tse-tung, Chang Wen-t'ien, Ch'in Pang-hsien, Chou En-lai, Ch'en Yun and others
Secretariat	The above, plus Jen Pi-shih, Chu Te and K'ang Sheng (later, Liu Shao-ch'i and others)
Key Central Committee Departments	
Military Affairs	Mao Tse-tung
Organization	Ch'en Yün (later, P'eng Chen, about 1943–4)
Propaganda	K'ai Feng
United Front Work	Chou En-lai (Li Wei-han after about 1944)
Enemy Occupied Areas Work	Chou En-lai (concurrent, also K'ang Sheng, Liu Shao-ch'i and others)
Cadre Education	Liu Shao-ch'i (later, Li Wei-han)
Social Affairs	K'ang Sheng (later, Chou Hsing and Li K'o-nung)
Popular Movement	Ch'en Yun
Labour	Ch'en Yun (concurrent)
Women	Ts'ai Ch'ang
Youth	Feng Wen-pin
Press	Chang Wen-t'ien
Regional bureaus	North China, North-west China Yangtze (until 1938), South China, Central Plains (these two est. 1939), South-east China (the latter two merged in 1941 to form the Central China Bureau), and, after 1945, North-east China
Sub-bureaus (or branch bureaus)	Chin-Ch'a-Chi, Shangtung, Chin-Sui and South-eastern Shansi (part of Chin-Chi-Lu-Yü), South China
Lower-level committees	Province where applicable, county, town, district, and subdistrict

Source: Harrison, *Long march*, 293, and cited sources.

levels and in the mass organizations as well. The party thus served as a nerve system, connecting the various parts of the movement, transmitting and processing information, and issuing commands.

Military. The formal structure of the Eighth Route Army and the New Fourth Army, in North and Central China respectively, is shown in table 10. The 8RA and N4A, as the regular, full-time field forces, were the top layer of what came to be a three-layer military structure. These two armies were the best the Communists could put into the field, in training, leadership and equipment – though their equipment, at least, left much

TABLE 10

Organization of Eighth Route and New Fourth Armies

Eighth Route Army headquarters (Yenan)	
Commander	Chu Te
Deputy commander	P'eng Te-huai
Chief of staff	Yeh Chien-ying
Dir. Political Dept.	Wang Chia-hsiang (1937–8, Jen Pi-shih)
115th Division (former First Front Army; Chin-Ch'a-Chi base area)	
Commander	Lin Piao (wounded, late 1937)
Deputy commander	Nieh Jung-chen (acting CO from 1938 on)
Political officer	Lo Jung-huan
120th Division (former Second Front Army; Chin-Sui base area)	
Commander	Ho Lung
Deputy commander	Hsiao K'o
Political officer	Kuan Hsiang-ying
129th Division (former Fourth Front Army; Chin-Chi-Lu-Yü base area)	
Commander	Liu Po-ch'eng
Deputy commander	Hsü Hsiang-ch'ien
Political officer	Teng Hsiao-p'ing
New Fourth Army	
Commander	Yeh T'ing (after 1941, Ch'en I)
Deputy commander	Hsiang Ying (after 1941 Chang Yun-i)
Dir. Political Dept.	Yuan Kuo-p'ing (after 1941, Teng Tzu-hui)
Political officer	Hsiang Ying (after 1941, Liu Shao-ch'i)
Deputy political officer	Jao Shu-shih

Source: Harrison, *Long march*, 296.

to be desired.[14] Units of these two armies were available for assignment wherever needed, but each base had its own detachment. To avoid adverse Nationalist propaganda, the Communists never enlarged the top commands of the 8RA and N4A, but regiments, battalions and companies proliferated at lower levels. Actual operations were carried out by these smaller units; divisions never fought as intact units, and regiments did so only infrequently.

In the CCP base areas, two other types of forces came into being: local forces (*ti-fang chün*) and the militia (*min-ping*). Local forces, for the most part, also had full-time military responsibilities, but unlike 8RA and N4A, each remained permanently within its own territorial jurisdiction. The militia theoretically included the entire able-bodied population between the ages of 16 and 45 but, unlike the field or local forces, they were not 'divorced from production' (*t'o-li sheng-ch'an*), and were available for

---

[14] As late as 1944, the better units of the 8RA had about one-half as many rifles and carbines as total combat personnel, and even greater deficiencies in machine-guns and mortars. Artillery was almost completely missing. See Lyman P. Van Slyke, ed. *The Chinese Communist movement: a report of the United States War Department, July 1945*, 185.

part-time duty when needed. Meanwhile they carried on their regular occupations. Of course, deficiencies in training and equipment became increasingly pronounced as one descended through this military structure. The militia was armed mostly with broadswords and farm tools, their old-fashioned bird guns and rifles (*t'u-ch'iang*) having been appropriated for use by the field or local forces.

Although the creation of this military structure was a complex and difficult task, with wide variation in time and place, the Communists nevertheless gradually built up a linked hierarchy of military power reaching downward into local society. When an element of the 8RA or N4A entered an unfamiliar area, it could expect to work with auxiliaries who knew the terrain and the enemy's dispositions, and with a local population who provided logistic support, intelligence, guides and shelter. Each level was a recruiting ground for the level above, a source of training and replenishment of manpower. Indeed, most of the increases in the size of the 8RA and the N4A during the last year of the war (see above, table 8) came from wholesale redesignation of local forces.

Everywhere it went, the CCP sought to reduce traditional peasant resentment and mistrust of military service, which in folklore and bitter experience usually meant that a beloved son or husband and his badly needed labour were lost forever. But everyone was familiar with the idea of a young man working in the fields and coming to the defence of family and village when necessary. If some of these young men then moved on to full-time military service in the local forces or in the regular armies, the shock was not so great – particularly if their families were given certain tax breaks, help with their crops, and the prestige of having contributed to the Tzu-ti Chün ('the army of sons and brothers'). Indeed, enlisting a son was one way that wealthier rural families sought favour and immunity.

In public, the CCP spoke of their military forces as aroused Chinese citizens fighting against the Japanese invaders and their traitorous puppets. But in addition to this role, Communist-led forces at all levels performed many other tasks, among which were contesting for territorial control with various local rivals, enforcement of social and economic policies, security and police functions. The Communists also had to calculate how large a force 'divorced from production' each locality could support, since many party and government cadres also needed to be fed and housed through others' labour. Where ordinarily slender surpluses were further reduced by the impact of the war, economically non-productive personnel could easily become a crushing burden.

Coordination. One cannot, of course, gauge the effectiveness of an organization simply by its formal structure. Unlike the Ch'ing bureaucracy, where decision-making, implementation, and the up and down flow of communications have been substantially traced out, only certain aspects of the CCP system's functioning can be described. One frequently-used technique was rotation of key personnel from one post to another, or from one area to another, so that experience gained in the former could be brought to the latter. The outstanding example of this kind of trouble-shooting was provided by Liu Shao-ch'i, who spent the first six years of the war shuttling back and forth between Yenan and the base areas behind Japanese lines, first in North China, then in Central China, where his and Mao's theories of base-area construction were being successfully put into practice. Yet many other lower-ranking cadres were also moved about, as in 1939, when several thousand Eighth Route Army political workers arrived in Central China to beef up mass mobilization work in the New Fourth Army bases. But such rotation of personnel was always selective, never wholesale, thus ensuring continuity of leadership, familiarity with local conditions, and the maintenance of morale and discipline that come with loyalty to known leaders.

Party and army schools at various levels, based on the experience of the Kiangsi period, were another source of cadre training and indoctrination.[15] Some of these, such as Resist Japan University (K'ang-Jih ta-hsüeh) in Yenan, assigned its graduates wherever they were needed but, in addition, each major base area had its own branch of K'ang-ta and its network of cadre schools, short-term training classes, and so on. Meetings of all kinds – open and closed, large and small – became one of the hallmarks of the Communist movement. Attendance and partici-pation were virtually mandatory for party members, soldiers and activists, particularly to explain policy to the many illiterate cadres.

Printed materials were another important medium of communication and guidance. The CCP published two major newspapers for general readership, *Liberation Daily* (*Chieh-fang jih-pao*) in Yenan and the frequently censored *New China Daily* (*Hsin-hua jih-pao*) in the Nationalist capitals.[16] These and other open publications carried sanitized news reports from all over China, major international events, general statements by Communist leaders, certain documents, and propaganda. Again, each major base area published its own local newspapers and periodicals. More sensitive materials were circulated by courier in a variety of forms: secret periodicals, classified collections and reports, individual directives. Local

---

[15] Jane L. Price, *Cadres, commanders, and commissars: the training of Chinese Communist leadership, 1920–1945*, chs. 8–9.
[16] Until the summer of 1941, *Liberation* appeared at approximately ten-day intervals, in periodical form. It then shifted to daily newspaper publication.

levels often used such primitive methods as handwritten hectograph copy printed on very crude paper. Some information could be transmitted by wireless, but equipment was makeshift and scarce, with few personnel capable of operating and maintaining it. Transmitting Chinese characters by number code led to frequent errors, and of course could be intercepted.[17] Despite great difficulties and not infrequent failures, this communication system worked well enough to coordinate party, army and government efforts at various levels and in many locales.

JAPANESE INVASION AND CHINESE INITIAL RESPONSES

In July 1937 the Japanese military in China was represented most strongly by the Kwantung Army. Headquartered in the Manchurian city of Ch'ang-ch'un (Hsin-ching), its principal responsibility was to watch over Japanese interests in the puppet state of Manchukuo, but it also sought to create a pliable buffer zone in North China from which Nationalist influence could be excluded. Largely successful for a time, the Kwantung Army failed embarrassingly in late 1935, when it manoeuvred to detach five northern provinces (Hopei, Shantung, Shansi, Chahar and Suiyuan) from their connections with Nanking. This clumsy effort touched off the patriotic fire of student-led demonstrations in Peiping on 9 December 1935, a fire that soon spread to most major cities of China. In North China itself, a much smaller Garrison Army was headquartered at Tientsin under the terms of the Boxer Protocol. Its leading officers competed with the Kwantung Army for influence in northern Hopei, and their ambitions far outran the forces then at their command. It was a detachment of this Garrison Army, which totalled only about 6,000 men, that clashed at the Marco Polo Bridge on July 7 with Chinese patrols of Sung Che-yuan's much larger 29th Army.

Japanese motives in North China were economic as well as political and military. In order to link the North China economy with that of Manchukuo and the home islands, endless negotiations were taking place between Manchukuoan authorities (the Kwantung Army and the South Manchurian Railway Company), North China interests (the Tientsin Garrison Army and its economic creature, the Hsing-cheng kung-shu), and financial interests in Japan.[18] Each military command lobbied for itself

---

[17] Michael Lindsay, *The unknown war: north China, 1937–1945*, not paged. Lindsay recalls Mao's 'from masses win respect' being received, through code errors, as 'from fog win treasure'. For about a year, in 1941–2, the Japanese broke the CCP code and were able to read their transmissions.

[18] Takafusa Nakamura, 'Japan's economic thrust into North China, 1933–1938: formation of the North China Development Corporaton', in Akira Iriye, ed. *The Chinese and the Japanese: essays in political and cultural interactions*, 220–53.

with policy-makers in Tokyo, but frequently disregarded directives with which they were not in sympathy. The policy-makers in Tokyo, hardly more unified, were acutely aware of their limited control over commanders in the field. Indeed, the Japanese never found a way truly to unify their effort in China.

Shortly after 7 July, the Garrison Army was reinforced from the Kwantung Army and the home islands. Reorganized as the North China Area Army (NCAA), it soon reached a strength of about 200,000. Meanwhile, in Central China, the scene of the heaviest fighting during the first sixteen months of the war, Japanese forces totalling 250,000 were directed by what eventually became the Central China Expeditionary Army (CCEA).

In North China, the Garrison Army quickly occupied Peiping and Tientsin, then the beefed-up NCAA moved out along the spokes of the region's railway system, as shown in map 6. For the most part, the Japanese advance met light resistance. Sung Che-yuan's 29th Army, after an initial show of firmness, soon withdrew to the south. The governor of Shantung, General Han Fu-ch'ü, collapsed without a fight, opening the way across his province toward the crucial rail junction and gateway to Central China at Hsu-chou, in northern Kiangsu. (Shortly thereafter, Han was arrested and executed by Chiang Kai-shek.)

To the north-west and west, fighting was heavier. Elements of the Shansi army, under the overall command of the crafty warlord-governor Yen Hsi-shan, defended Niangtzukuan (Ladies' Pass) bravely for a time. North of Tatung, combined elements of the Shansi army and the CCP's 115th Division, commanded by Lin Piao, won a heartening but not strategically significant victory at Pinghsingkuan (Flat Pass) in late September 1937 (see below, pp. 207–8). Nevertheless, Shansi's capital, Taiyuan, fell on 9 November 1937, and the Japanese advance continued south-west along the T'ung-P'u railway line toward the great bend of the Yellow River. A year after the skirmish at the Marco Polo Bridge, the Japanese occupation of North China was approximately as shown in map 6.

This was, of course, no true occupation at all, but a network of points and lines. During its advance, the NCAA occasionally left the main communications corridors and fanned out across the countryside. Villages in their path were sometimes attacked but the NCAA made no effort to garrison the countryside, which was beyond their capacity. In North China alone, the major railway lines stretched for about 3,000 miles; simply protecting these lines and garrisoning the towns and cities along them spread thin their army of 200,000 or so. As a result, control over the deeper

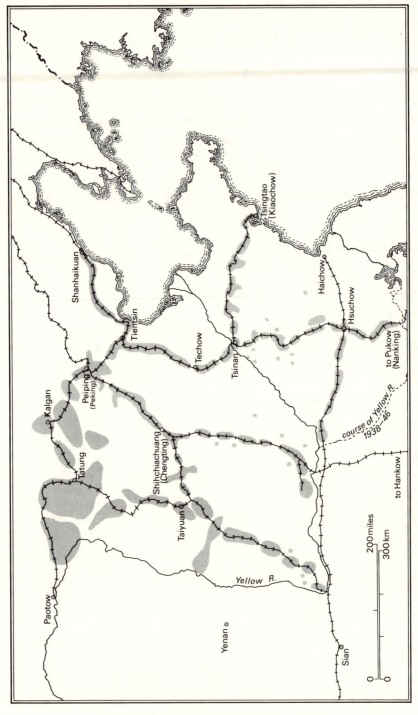

MAP 6. Japanese occupation of North China, to c. mid-1940s. *Source:* Lincoln Li; *The Japanese army in north China, 1937–1941: problems of political and economic control,* 8

TABLE 11

Major railway lines: North and Central China (c. 1942)
(distances include branches)

	miles
Peiping-Mukden, to Great Wall at Shanhai Kuan	289
Tientsin-Pukow (Tsin-Pu), to n. bank of Yangtze River	694
Peiping-Hankow (Ping-Han)	803
Peiping-Suiyuan (Ping-Sui), to Pao-t'ou	547
Tatung-Fenglingtu (T'ung-P'u), to n. bank of Yellow River[a]	420
Kiaochow-Tsinan (Kiao-Tsi)	288
Shihchiachuang-Taiyuan (Cheng-Tai)[a]	151
Techow-Shihchiachuang[b]	124
Haichow-Sian (Lung-Hai)	652
Nanking-Shanghai (Kiangnan)	109

[a] When the war began, the T'ung-P'u and Cheng-Tai lines were metre gauge rather than standard. The Japanese completed conversion of these lines to standard gauge in 1939.
[b] This link in the North China rail system was constructed by the Japanese between June and December 1940.
Source: Chang Kia-ngau, China's struggle for railway development, 86–7, 203, 205, 322–5.

countryside had to be left to Chinese collaborators. In a vague directive of December 1937, the NCAA put the burden on country-level police and unspecified local militia. But police were to number no more than two hundred per county, armed with pistols, and militia were to have only those weapons already in their possession or captured from opponents.[19] In time, a variety of more formally organized puppet organizations were charged with propaganda, rural administration, economic exploitation of conquered territories, and internal security, but the NCAA never trusted their Chinese collaborators – a characteristic, in various degrees, of the Japanese everywhere in China during the war.

In ordinary times, lightly armed police and local militias might have sufficed to maintain order outside the railway corridors. But these were not ordinary times. The Japanese invasion shattered local administration, and down to the county level the majority of magistrates and other functionaries left their posts. Below this level, local elites remained largely in place rather than abandoning their homes and property. As always in times of disorder, these local elites sought protection by enlarging or organizing quasi-military bands known by various names: min-t'uan (militia), t'uan-lien (trained bands), lien-chuang-hui (joint village associations), as well as secret societies such as the Big Swords or Red Spears. Ordinary peasants often cooperated with such groups. Bandit gangs were also a

[19] Lincoln Li, 203.

feature of chaotic times, a kind of predatory complement to the protective associations designed to keep them away.[20] Now, however, predators and protectors alike fed upon defeated Chinese armies for both men and weapons. Guns were often thrown down and left behind, while dispersing soldiers, fleeing from the railway zones, were ready for almost anything in return for food and shelter.

Although such spontaneous 'mobilization' did not in itself create resistance to the Japanese, there were also resisters on the local scene: students and teachers, especially from the larger cities, some Nationalist units, and local Communists. Students and teachers as vanguards of Chinese nationalism had touched off the National Salvation movement in December 1935. Even before the war began, many had left Peiping during summer vacation to return home or to seek safer haven in Yenan, Sian or Taiyuan. In Hopei alone during the first year of the war, the number of students and teachers at middle-school level or above dropped by 70 per cent, a combined total of 50,000.[21] Some of these dropped out or followed their universities into exile in Kuomintang-controlled Free China. But many others remained in the areas later to be incorporated into the Communist bases.

An often-cited example is that of Yang Hsiu-feng, a French-trained academic, born in 1898 in eastern Hopei. As an underground party member, he had been an active supporter of the National Salvation movement while teaching at the Hopei Provincial College of Law and Commerce in Tientsin. When the war broke out, Yang, his wife, and a few students escaped to southern Hopei, and linked up with certain Nationalist units and local leaders. But, after a falling out, Yang made contact with Communist elements in south-eastern Shansi, where a number of his former students were already active. Yang's invitation to the Communists led directly to their penetration of south Hopei, and he remained prominent in CCP affairs thereafter.

Not all Nationalist forces retreated. Some small units in North China either carried on independent resistance, or eventually became puppets under the Japanese, or affiliated with the CCP. Manchurian-born Lü Cheng-ts'ao chose the last course. A regimental commander separated from his Nationalist 53rd Army during its retreat south, he led his men east of the Peiping-Hankow railway line, into the plains of north-central Hopei. In late 1937, after his detachment had suffered considerable losses at the hands of the Japanese, Lü made contact with both local and recently-arrived Communists. With their help he organized a resistance

[20] Elizabeth J. Perry, *Rebels and revolutionaries in North China, 1845–1945*, 1–9 and ch. 6.
[21] Lincoln Li, 108.

base and, like Yang Hsiu-feng, rose in the Communist hierarchy to hold important posts after 1949.

More Communists were active in North China than has usually been realized. By 1935, anti-Communist suppression had put the party almost out of action, and many Communists and other activists were in jail in Peiping, Tsinan and Taiyuan. But in the spring of 1936, Liu Shao-ch'i took over the North China Bureau (NCB) of the CCP. Japanese pressure, the rising tide of nationalism, and united front policies brought increased tolerance, and by summer political prisoners were being quietly released. Recruitment was stepped up. Even before the war began, more than 5,000 party members were under the NCB's jurisdiction.[22]

When the war broke out a few months later, most of them were in their home towns, ready to try to organize local resistance and to welcome comrades from the Eighth Route Army. Their actions, the maraudings of bandit gangs and soldiers on the loose, and the efforts of local communities to ward off these predators – these constituted most of the 'spontaneous mobilization' created by the first shocks of the Japanese invasion. 'What evidence there is points overwhelmingly to the conclusion that the local resistance forces were not formed spontaneously and that the spontaneously organized forces were not formed for the purposes of resistance.'[23] In support of this conclusion, one finds very few examples of organized anti-Japanese activity of any kind in those zones – the cities and the railway corridors connecting them – where the Japanese invasion was most directly felt. The vast majority of the North China peasantry did not experience the Japanese presence until 1939, when the NCAA enlarged its pacification efforts beyond the railway zones. By this time, the principal North China base areas were already well established.

FORMATION OF BASE AREAS

Despite the importance of leadership struggles, high policy and ideology, it is nevertheless true that without the base areas the CCP would have been a structure without a foundation. In Mao's vivid phrase, these bases were 'the buttocks (*p'i-ku*) of the revolution', supporting its entire body. They provided haven for the party and the army, and from them came the resources of manpower, material, and popular support upon which the CCP's power ultimately depended.

---

[22] Po I-po, 'Liu Shao-ch'i t'ung-chih ti i-ko li-shih kung-chi' (An historic achievement of Comrade Liu Shao-ch'i), *Jen-min jih-pao* (People's daily) (5 May 1980) p. 2.

[23] Kathleen Hartford, 'Step-by-step: reform, resistance and revolution in the Chin-Ch'a-Chi border region, 1937–1945' (Stanford University, Ph.D. dissertation, 1980), 118–19.

1. *Shen-Kan-Ning* (an abbreviation for Shensi-Kansu-Ninghsia, i.e., the headquarters or 'Yenan area'). This was the nerve centre of the CCP, from the time of Mao's arrival at the end of the Long March in October 1935 until its capital, Yenan, was abandoned to the Nationalists in March 1947. As the only base in existence prior to the Sino-Japanese War, it produced the most voluminous and easily accessible materials on the CCP and was the CCP area most frequently visited by foreign observers, from Edgar Snow's trip in 1936 – out of which came *Red star over China* – to the journalists, foreign service officers, and military personnel of the US Military Observer Group ('Dixie Mission'; see below pp. 280–2) in late 1944 and 1945.

Shen-Kan-Ning (shown in map 7) was one of the most barren, chronically depressed, and sparsely populated regions in China. Despite its broad area (roughly the size of Ohio), it had only about 1.4 million inhabitants. Most were desperately poor, yet one estimate claimed that landlords and rich peasants comprised 12 per cent of the population and owned 46 per cent of the land. Agriculture was precarious, with a short growing season and scanty, unpredictable rainfall, which might nevertheless come in sudden cloudbursts to wash away crops and cut ravines in the defrosted loess slopes. Between 1928 and 1933, famine had stalked north-west China, including Shen-Kan-Ning (SKN); millions died and much land fell into disuse. Severe earthquakes might periodically collapse the dwellings tunnelled into loess cliffs. Along with the harshness of nature, the region had long been plagued by unrest, disorder and violence. It had never fully recovered from the terrible Muslim rebellions of the 1870s. Banditry and warlordism were endemic.

Several circumstances made Shen-Kan-Ning a special case, not representative of other base areas. (1) As the headquarters area of the CCP, most of it had passed through the agrarian revolution (confiscation of landlords' land) prior to the adoption of the milder united front land policy, so that local elite opposition was less than in other bases. (2) SKN was the only base beyond the furthest advance of Japanese armies. Although Yenan was bombed a few times, SKN was spared the problems of security and survival with which other base areas had to cope. (3) The military situation was simpler in SKN because central government and puppet forces were absent. (4) Where the bases behind Japanese lines were a mix of often scattered areas, variously consolidated, semi-consolidated, or guerrilla zones, SKN was almost entirely consolidated. (5) Because SKN was sparsely populated and backward, measures for improved livelihood could be more effective and more obvious than in other bases. Garrison units of the 8RA were freer too, to assist in these efforts.

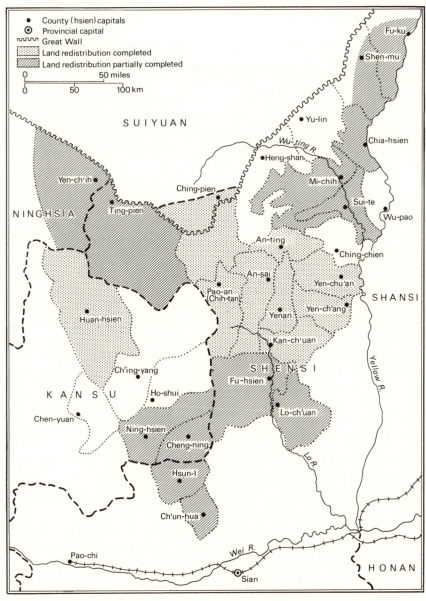

MAP 7. Shen-Kan-Ning: basic data

Territory and administration:
5 sub-regions
15 counties (*hsien*) in 1937, expanding to 29 by 1941
266 districts (*ch'ü*), 1,549 townships (*hsiang*) by 1941

Population and personnel:
Total population: *c.* 1.4 million
Armed forces in 1941: 8RA, 18,000; public security, 15,000; militia self-defence, 224,000
Party/government, 8,000

Sources: Mark Selden, *The Yenan way in revolutionary China*, 102. Basic data is taken from Selden and from Andrew Watson, *Mao Zedong and the political economy of the border region: a translation of Mao's 'Economic and financial problems'*, 12–15.

(6) The presence in SKN of Mao Tse-tung and the central party-government-military apparatus meant that policies could be carried out with close and continuous supervision from the highest levels.

Although the formal inauguration of the Shen-Kan-Ning Border Region government was announced on 6 September 1937, it had been in operation long before this time. Until the spring of 1937, it resembled the earlier Kiangsi soviet, with much responsibility vested in local military-administrative committees overseen by the party hierarchy. On the adoption of united front policies in 1937, confiscation of landlords' property was terminated, and a more participatory, 'new democratic' system was instituted – without, however, any relinquishing of ultimate party control. Assemblies were to be elected at each level, with administrative councils drawn from the assemblies to carry on the actual work of government. Although universal suffrage was proclaimed, the party could debar certain people from voting or being elected: traitors, criminals, enemy agents, defectives, and so on. KMT members could vote and run for the assemblies, but only as individuals, not as representatives of an organized political party. Furthermore, each administrative council had to be approved by and was responsible to the council at the next higher level. Party members were heavily represented in the assemblies; in councils, they usually constituted a majority. Significantly, the election process was soon terminated, and the Border Region assembly did not convene until January 1939, which meant that in name as in fact the entire structure was directed by the Border Region government, appointed by Party Central.

Chairman of the Border Region government from 1937 until well after the end of the war was one of the CCP's most respected 'elder statesmen', Lin Po-ch'ü (also known as Lin Tsu-han). Born in 1886, seven years before Mao Tse-tung, he had been an early member of Sun Yat-sen's T'ung-meng hui and of the Kuomintang. During the first united front in the 1920s, he worked for both the KMT and CCP. After 1927, he went to Moscow before returning to the Kiangsi soviet and participating in the Long March. By 1938, he was a member of the Party Central Committee.

In addition to this administrative apparatus, mass organizations – workers, women, youth – were called for and gradually began to appear at various levels, but they do not seem to have been very active during this period. Except for the militia, the military was virtually independent of these united front structures, being controlled directly by the Central Military Affairs Committee. Within two years or so, a very considerable bureaucracy was visible in Yenan and throughout Shen-Kan-Ning. Meanwhile, between 1937 and 1940 an estimated 100,000 people immigrated, mostly with the approval of the Border Region authorities.[24] Some were peasants displaced from other provinces, taking up land that had gone out of cultivation; some were veterans, disabled soldiers, and dependents. But perhaps one half came from the fallen cities of east and central China – students, teachers, journalists, writers, intellectuals of all types. In late 1938, 20,000 students were said to be awaiting permission to enter SKN.[25] Yet despite their idealism, the harshness of Yenan and the SKN base came as a shock to many. Some had difficulty adjusting not only to such spartan physical conditions, but also to a political environment in which individualism and critical independence of mind were not so valued as they had been in Peiping or Shanghai.

Although SKN remained very poor by any standard, the Border Region economy was quite stable during the first years of the war. It was a mixed economy, with some public ownership or monopoly, but with a large private sector operating under overall government supervision and price control. Except for land confiscated earlier, private ownership and cultivation were encouraged. Tenancy and hired labour were permitted, with rent ceilings and minimum wages stipulated but not always enforced. Economic burdens on the peasantry were quite light during this period. Most miscellaneous taxes had been abolished, and even the land tax had been so widely remitted that it bore on only a small proportion of the rural population. This was possible in part because of resources available from contributions and confiscation, in part because of the important Nationalist subsidy, and in part because of extensive trade with areas outside SKN.[26] These conditions were to change dramatically by 1940.

For Mao Tse-tung, the period from mid-1936 to mid-1939 was one of unusual security and release from day-to-day pressures, and he had more time now for study and reflection than at any time in the past. With the assistance of his idea man, Ch'en Po-ta, Mao wrote during these years many of his most penetrating and significant essays.[27] It is from this period that one begins to hear, with increasing frequency, of 'the thought of Mao Tse-tung' and 'the sinification of Marxism'.

2. *Shansi*. Shansi lay just across the Yellow River on the east of SKN;

---

[24] Peter Schran, *Guerrilla economy: the development of the Shensi-Kansu-Ninghsia Border Region, 1937–1945*, 99. Another 86,000 immigrants arrived between 1941 and 1945.

[25] John Israel and Donald W. Klein, *Rebels and bureaucrats: China's December 9ers*, 179.

[26] The importance of this subsidy has usually been overlooked. The total subsidy of Ch. $600,000 per month was equivalent in mid-1937 to US $180,000 (at an approximate exchange rate of 3.35 : 1) or US $2,150,000 per year. 'This sum sufficed in 1938 to meet more than the entire public expenditures of 1936. It thus appears that the alliance relieved the SKN border region government of all previous financial difficulties for a period of nearly two years.' Schran, 183.

[27] Raymond F. Wylie, *The emergence of Maoism: Mao Tse-tung, Ch'en Po-ta, and the search for Chinese theory, 1935–1945*, chs. 2–4.

its south-west corner extended to T'ung-kuan, gateway to Sian and Shensi province at the great eastward bend of the Yellow River. CCP forces going behind Japanese lines had to cross Shansi, through which communications also had to pass back and forth between Yenan and all the North China bases. Except for Shantung, all these bases were headquartered in the mountains of eastern Shansi.

Nowhere was the CCP's united front more effective than in Shansi, and this effort was well under way before the outbreak of the war. Above all, this meant dealing with the warlord-governor of the province, Yen Hsi-shan, and the CCP made him a united front target second only to Chiang Kai-shek. By instinct and temperament, Yen was clearly anti-Communist. But his instinct for survival was even stronger, and this had served him well in maintaining his hold over Shansi for more than two decades. Yen feared any penetration of his bailiwick, quite apart from its political colouration; by early 1937 he feared Chiang Kai-shek and the Japanese more than the Communists.[28] When Yen called for reinforcements to help counter a Communist invasion of south-west Shansi in the spring of 1936, Chiang and the central government began to move in on Shansi, and this continued during the manoeuvring touched off by the Sian incident of December 1936. The Japanese threat had been evident from the time of the North China autonomy movement in late 1935, if not earlier, and the fighting in Suiyuan just to the north, during November 1936, clearly indicated the Kwantung Army's intention to outflank Shansi and bring it into its political and economic sphere. Japanese agents were also intriguing within the province. Shansi's resources, especially the Ching-hsing coal mines, powerfully appealed to the Japanese expansionists.

Yen Hsi-shan was acutely aware that his Shansi house was not in order. His armies were not very effective, and his rule was tolerated rather than actively supported. In late 1935, he called for the creation of the 'Force for the Promotion of Justice', a mass organization designed to gain popular support by moderating the worst abuses of local elites and also to squeeze more money out of them for himself. By late summer 1936, Yen was ready to collaborate more actively with leftists, even with Communists. Yen's reassessment dovetailed with the CCP's united front line, which sought friends and allies – or at least acquiescent patrons – on the twin bases of anti-Japanese nationalism and some tolerance of the party's activities. In return the CCP was prepared, up to a point, to keep these activities from going beyond the bounds which would alienate the potential ally or patron. In this atmosphere, activist members of the Justice Force persuaded Yen to form the 'League for National Salvation through

[28] Donald G. Gillin, *Warlord: Yen Hsi-shan in Shansi province, 1911-1949*, esp. chs. 9-12.

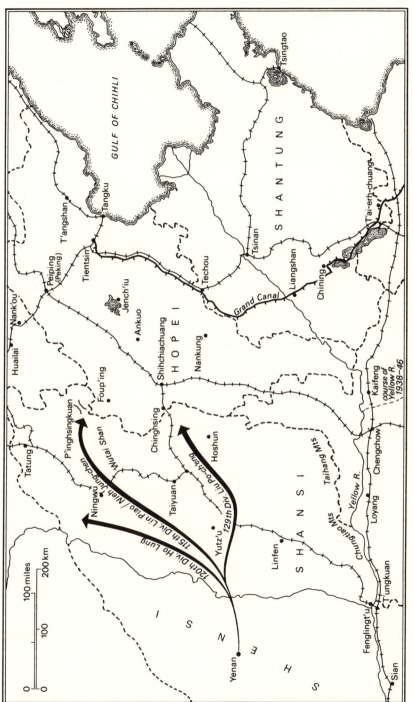

MAP 8. Eighth Route Army deployment, July–December 1937. *Source*: Johnson, *Peasant nationalism*

Sacrifice'. The Sacrifice League accordingly came into existence on 18 September 1936, the fifth anniversary of the Mukden incident, pledged to support the anti-Japanese national united front. Yen Hsi-shan is quoted as saying, at about this time, 'There *is* some risk in a united front, but if we don't collaborate with the CCP, what else can we do? For now, using the Communists is the only way, for otherwise we cannot hold off the Japanese and Chiang Kai-shek. I will use the Communists as a way of weakening the Communists.' [29]

Many individual Communists were active in the Sacrifice League from the start, along with patriotic teachers and students, liberals, and various others. Party members, such as Po I-po, recently released from prisons in Peiping or Taiyuan, set to work with a will, as a classified KMT intelligence report later acknowledged in hyperbolic terms:

Their 'loyalty' and 'hard work' far surpassed the ordinary. Furthermore, they often relinquished or would not assume positions of authority, but were quite willing to work without sparing themselves (seizing particularly on low-level work, for this is the heart of their policy). Their loyalty was like that of a dog; their docility like that of a sheep. Any lord who had such slaves would be delighted.[30]

The Sacrifice League spun off a large number of training and propaganda programmes in the military, in schools, among government officials, and in the countryside – spreading the united front message and recruiting for the party as it went.

Thus when the war broke out, there was no bar to the passage of the three main divisional commands of the 8RA across Shansi. Almost at once, the headquarters of the CCP North China Bureau moved from Peiping to Taiyuan, capital of Shansi, and Liu Shao-ch'i arrived to oversee CCP activities in the province. Prior to the fall of Taiyuan, as Japanese pressure mounted, Yen had allowed the Sacrifice League to step up the organization of military units and had turned over to them a quantity of light infantry equipment. This so-called 'New Army' – to distinguish it from what was left of the regular provincial forces, the 'Old Army' – was organized into four 'Dare-to-die columns' (*chueh-ssu tsung-tui*), each commanded by a party member who served simultaneously as political officer. Before long, about 70 of Shansi's 105 counties were headed by magistrates belonging to the Sacrifice League, and five of the seven larger administrative districts in the province were said by Communists to be in 'our hands'. All this was a promising beginning, but not much more than that. As Po I-po later told Jack Belden, the New Army's strong

[29] Po I-po, 3.
[30] Lyman P. Van Slyke, *Enemies and friends: the united front in Chinese Communist history*, 142.

point was its close relations with the people; its weak point, its lack of unity, central leadership, and military experience. Such a force, composed of students who hardly knew how to fire rifles, professors who knew nothing of tactics, and farmers who knew neither tactics nor politics, was in danger of disintegrating for lack of a directing head and of being wiped out for the lack of technique.[31]

But help was on the way in the form of the 115th, 120th, and 129th Divisions of the English Route Army, commanded by Lin Piao, Ho Lung and Liu Po-ch'eng, respectively. The North China base areas were thus born in the mountains of Shansi through the link-up of 8RA units with scattered pockets of anti-Japanese resistance behind enemy lines. As soon as possible, the Communists reached out into neighbouring provinces: Hopei, Honan, Suiyuan. Small detachments of the 115th and 129th Divisions were sent even further afield, into Shantung.

3. *Setting up the bases.* The movement of these three divisions was authorized by both Chiang Kai-shek and Yen Hsi-shan, who had been named commander of the Second War Zone. In the face of the Japanese offensive in Shansi, these units – and especially the 115th – collaborated with regular Shansi army detachments, but remained organizationally separate. From this collaboration came the first Chinese victory of the war, at Pinghsingkuan in north-eastern Shansi, on 25 September 1937. In the heavy but confused fighting in this region – most of it by elements of the Shansi army – Lin Piao set a careful ambush for the supply train at the rear of Itagaki's crack 5th Division. Caught by surprise in a narrow ravine, the Japanese were cut to pieces. Yet the Communists acquired only about 100 rifles and no prisoners; in a last-ditch measure, surviving Japanese soldiers destroyed their equipment and committed suicide.[32]

The experience of Pinghsingkuan may have helped persuade Mao and those who agreed with him of the unwisdom of conventional warfare against a superior enemy, in coordination with 'friendly armies'. In his battle report, Lin Piao – who probably sided with Mao in this debate – implicitly confirmed such a conclusion:

(1) Coordination by the friendly forces is in reality extremely bad. They decide on a plan for attack but are unable to follow through with it themselves... (7) The enemy soldiers have enormous fighting ability. We never encountered such a strong foe in the Northern Expedition or Soviet period. Their infantrymen are able to deploy themselves with individual initiative in combat situations. Although wounded, they refuse to give up arms ... (12) Our army's military skill

---

[31] Jack Belden, *China shakes the world*, 52.

[32] P'eng Te-huai, 'Kuan-yü hua-pei ken-chü-ti kung-tso ti pao-kao' (Report on work in the base areas of North China), in *Kung-fei huo-kuo shih-liao hui-pien* (Collected historical materials on the national disaster caused by the Communist bandits), 3.351.

and training still leave a great deal to be desired. In the past half year, our troops have had a chance to rest and regroup, and their discipline, morale, and regularization have progressed greatly; but in combat training we still have a long way to go.[33]

While the Japanese invasion of Shansi was still in progress, some elements of the 115th Division (about 2,000 men) under the command of Nieh Jung-chen took up positions in the north-eastern part of Shansi and in the adjacent mountainous regions of western Hopei. (Lin Piao was seriously wounded in January 1938 and returned to Yenan, then went to the USSR to recuperate.) The activities of Nieh Jung-chen in the Wu-t'ai/Fou-p'ing area marked the beginning of what was to become the Shansi-Chahar-Hopei Border Region – better known as Chin-Ch'a-Chi (CCC) after the ancient names of these provinces.

As early as November 1937, the hazy outlines of the CCC base area were beginning to take shape. Local 'mobilization committees' and other preliminary organizations were active in about thirty counties of north-east Shansi and west Hopei, twenty counties in central Hopei (east of the P'ing-Han line), and four counties in southern Chahar. Resistance groups did not yet fully control these counties, nor in many cases were they adjacent to each other. Little coordination yet existed among them.

Between 10 and 15 January 1938, the base area was formally established in a conference held at Fou-p'ing, a county town in the mountains of western Hopei. A total of 148 delegates from thirty-nine counties attended, representing some 28 'organizations' ranging from Mobilization Committees and the Salvation League through various military units to the Yellow Temple Lama Monks. It was very definitely a united front assembly, and it was fully guided by the CCP. The assembly adopted a series of resolutions endorsing anti-Japanese resistance, military mobilization, political organization and moderate economic reforms. It also endorsed the organizational structure of the CCC base, which was to guide the base for the next five years, since a full congress of the CCC base was not to meet again until January 1943. The Fou-p'ing delegates approved a nine-member administrative committee, headed by Sung Shao-wen, a Salvation League activist, concurrently magistrate of Wu-t'ai county.[34] Nieh Jung-chen was overall commander of the military district, which was separate from the civil-political hierarchy though interacting with it at all levels. This apparatus had overall jurisdiction over eleven Special Districts, the areas in which resistance organizers were most active. On

---

[33] Quoted in Kataoka Tetsuya, 64–5.
[34] Sung was a graduate of Peking University and had been imprisoned, 1933–4, for anti-Japanese agitation. See Hartford, 'Step-by-step', 84–9.

22 January 1938, Chiang Kai-shek and Yen Hsi-shan reluctantly approved the establishment of the Chin-Ch'a-Chi Border Region. Of all the bases established by the CCP behind Japanese lines, it was the only one to achieve formal central government recognition. Simultaneous with the development of CCC, Ho Lung's 120th Division was active in north-west Shansi – an area almost as poor and backward as SKN – in what was to become the Shansi-Suiyuan (Chin-Sui) base. Chin-Sui was important primarily as a strategic corridor linking the Yenan area with bases farther east, and as a shield partially protecting the north-east quadrant of SKN.

Liu Po-ch'eng moved his 129th Division into the T'ai-hang mountains of south-east Shansi, near its boundaries with Hopei and Honan. This region, together with a part of western Shantung, became the Chin-Chi-Lu-Yü base (CCLY). For most of the war, this was really two loosely integrated bases, one west of the Ping-Han railway line, the other to the east. Later to develop was the peninsular Shantung base, further from the main strength of the 8RA, where struggles between Communists, Japanese, puppets, local forces, and units affiliated with the central governments were very complex.

In Central China, certain differences from North China slowed the development of CCP influence. In the areas attacked most forcefully by Japan, especially the Yangtze delta and the Shanghai-Nanking axis, local administration often broke down, order disintegrated, and armed bands of all types quickly appeared, just as in the north. Here too, the Japanese paid scant attention at first to occupying the regions through which they passed. But elsewhere, Central China was somewhat less disrupted by the Japanese invasion. Local and provincial administrations continued to function, often in contact with Nationalist-controlled Free China. In those parts of Anhwei and Kiangsu north of the Yangtze River which had not been directly subject to Japanese attack, Nationalist armies remained, without retreating. South of the Yangtze in the Chiang-nan area, though most Nationalist forces retreated at first, some units were soon reintroduced and more followed. Many of these forces were either elements of the Central Armies or closely associated with Chiang Kai-shek, unlike the regional 'inferior brands' of military (*tsa-p'ai chün*) in the 8RA's areas. This region had been, after all, the core area of KMT power, the Nationalists were very sensitive about intrusions, and they were in a better position to thwart such efforts.

Although the New Fourth Army was smaller and for several years less effective than the Eighth Route Army, Mao Tse-tung and Liu Shao-ch'i were soon to call for aggressive base-building throughout this area, especially north of the Yangtze. Officially, the Nationalists assigned to the N4A the zone of operations shown on map 9. A monthly subsidy of about Ch. $130,000 was to be paid by the central government to help meet operating costs. North of the Yangtze, their theatre was part of the Nationalist Fifth War Zone, commanded by the formidable leader of the Kwangsi faction, Li Tsung-jen; south of the river was the Third War Zone, under General Ku Chu-t'ung, a close and trusted associate of Chiang Kai-shek. Until the sixth plenum, late in 1938, the N4A operated with rather little direct control from Yenan. Although some of the senior cadres in Hsiang Ying's headquarters – Yeh T'ing did not have much power – had been sent from Yenan, the N4A's political chain of command ran through the Yangtze River Bureau, then headed by Wang Ming. Initial military operations, almost entirely south of the river, involved getting the small N4A detachments in place, enlarging them by recruiting or absorbing miscellaneous armed bands, and carrying on such anti-Japanese activities as were within their limited power. Sometimes their ragtag appearance led local peasants to confuse them with the many bandit gangs ravaging the region; once or twice they were mistakenly welcomed as Japanese troops come to restore order. Their reception by local people – ordinary peasants and landlords alike – often depended more on their ability to disarm bandits than on their opposition to Japan.[35] Nowhere during the first year or so of the war did the Communists in Central China seek to seize administrative authority and establish the kind of bases that were beginning to take shape further north.

This situation began to change after the sixth plenum of late 1938. During 1939 the N4A expanded greatly, with the forces north of the Yangtze River becoming increasingly important, to some extent at the expense of those to the south. This military expansion was part of the increasing tension between Hsiang Ying on the one hand and Party Central on the other – Mao Tse-tung, Chou En-lai, and above all Liu Shao-ch'i. This expansion and emphasis on base-building of course brought the Central China Communists into increasingly bitter conflict with Nationalist authorities on central, provincial, and local levels.

At the sixth plenum, Liu Shao-ch'i became the highest party authority in Central China. This reflected both the decline of Wang Ming's influence and Mao's determination to achieve closer control and pursue the North China base-building policies in Central China.[36] Table 12 and map 9 show

35 Ch'en Yung-fa, 'The making of a revolution: the Communist movement in eastern and central China 1937–1945' (Stanford University, Ph.D. dissertation, 1980), 38–48.
36 The headquarters of the Central Plains Bureau was first located at Ch'ueh-shan on the P'ing-Han railway line, about half way between Chengchow and Wuhan. This was shortly after the fall of Wuhan, and the CCP may have reckoned that the Japanese would make a major push along the railway line through Hunan and Hopei, in which case the bureau would be well situated to direct operations. After it became clear that the Japanese were ignoring this section of the P'ing-Han line, the Central Plains Bureau moved eastward.

TABLE 12
New Fourth Army (late 1939)

Headquarters CO: Yeh T'ing. Vice CO/Political Officer: Hsiang Ying. Chief of Staff: Chang Yun-i. Head, Political Dept.: Yuan Kuo-p'ing. Vice-head: Teng Tzu-hui.

South Yangtze Command (formed July 1939)
  1st Detachment. CO: Ch'en I. Efforts to expand east and south of Lake T'ai during 1939 were not very successful. Most of these forces were transferred north of the Yangtze River, March–June 1940.
  2nd Detachment. CO: Chang Ting-ch'eng. In early 1939, Lo Ping-hui led part of these forces across the Yangtze to help form the 5th Detachment, placed under his command.
  3rd Detachment. CO: T'an Chen-lin.

North Yangtze Command (formed July 1939). CO: Chang Yun-i.
  4th Detachment. CO: Tai Chi-ying. Originally formed from Communist remnants surviving north of Wuhan in the Ta-pieh mountains of Hupei (near Huang-an), the old O-Yü-Wan soviet. Led by Kao Ching-t'ing, a former poor peasant butcher. Kao resisted N4A orders, discipline; refused collaboration with KMT forces. He reluctantly moved east to Lake Chao (Anhwei), was denounced as a 'tyrannical warlord', and was executed in April 1939 by order of Yeh T'ing after a public trial. Some elements of the 4th Det. were sent to help form the 5th Det. The 4th Det. served mainly as a training unit.
  5th Detachment. CO: Lo Ping-hui. Formed in spring 1939 at Lu-chiang, SW of Lake Chao; moved to Lai-an/Liu-ho area on the Kiangsu-Anhwei border, opposite Nanking, in July 1939. In late 1939, moved further east to the Lake Kao-yu/Grand Canal area in Kiangsu. 5th Det. saw much combat with both Nationalists and Japanese.
  6th Detachment. CO: P'eng Hsueh-feng. Formed in the summer of 1939 from elements sent south into Honan from the 8RA. Absorbed many local armed groups and stragglers from Nationalist armies. In early 1940, moved from eastern Honan (T'ai-k'ang/Huai-yang) eastward into northern Anhwei. 6th Det. was the main military and base-building force in northern Anhwei and northern Kiangsu.

Note: in recent years Kao Ching-t'ing has been posthumously rehabilitated; it is said he was traduced and wrongly executed in 1939.
Sources: from material in Ch'en Yung-fa, ch. 2, and Johnson, *Peasant nationalism*, 124–32.

the N4A's deployments during the first two years of the war – a general movement toward the east and north, further behind Japanese lines and away from the Nationalist rear areas. The most important of the other military forces affiliated with the N4A was the Honan-Hupei assault column led by Long March veteran Li Hsien-nien, which took up positions near those originally occupied by the 4th Detachment, north of Wuhan astride the P'ing-Han railway line. Li Hsien-nien's column was not made a formal part of the N4A until 1941, in the reorganization that followed the New Fourth Army incident. Much further east, and south of the Yangtze River, were two local semi-guerrilla groups, the Chiang-nan Anti-Japanese Patriotic Army and the Chiang-nan Assault Column led by Kuan Wen-wei. Kuan, a local CCP leader (from Tan-yang) who until 1937 had lost touch with the party, helped open up a corridor through which N4A elements could pass north of the river, across Yang-chung Island. Both these units and the 1st Detachment contested with the Chungking-affiliated Loyal National Salvation Army.

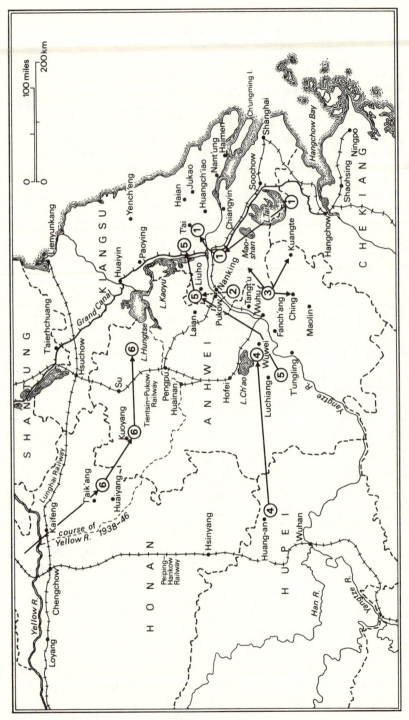

MAP 9. Disposition and movements of the New Fourth Army, to late 1940. *Source*: Johnson, *Peasant nationalism*

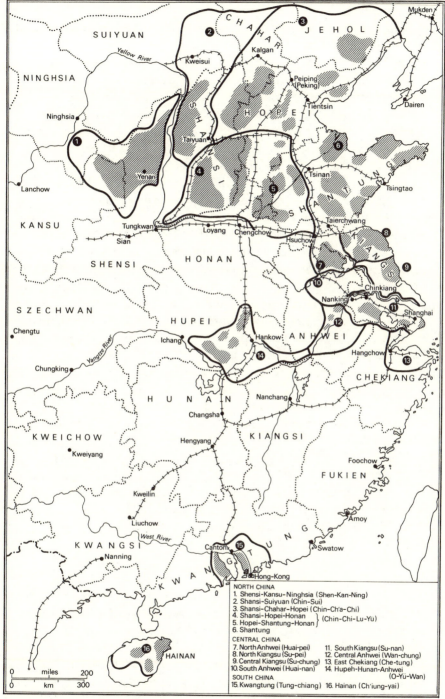

MAP 10. Communist bases as claimed overall (late 1944). *Source*: Van Slyke, *Chinese Communist movement*, xii–xiii. This map has been prepared from CCP sources dated August and October 1944.

Map 10 shows the approximate location of the Communist bases, but like most simplified CCP maps prepared late in the war for public consumption, this map shows large, contiguous areas under Communist control. This is quite misleading. The bases were in widely different stages of development and consolidation, from SKN and CCC in the north to the two shadowy and insubstantial guerrilla zones not far from Canton. A more realistic but still simplified picture would show three kinds of territories, all quite fluid. (1) Zones in which the CCP had created a fairly stable administration, able to function openly and institute reforms that were quite frankly less than revolutionary but nevertheless more far-reaching and deeply rooted in local society than any Chinese government had previously achieved. These core areas were islands within the larger expanse of bases shown on unclassified CCP maps. (2) More ambivalent regions, often referred to in Communist sources as 'guerrilla areas' and in Japanese sources as 'neutral zones'. These might contain several types of forces: Communists, KMT elements, local militia, bandits, puppet forces. In these guerrilla areas, the CCP sought allies on the basis of immediate sharing of common interests. They did only preliminary organizational work, and attempted only modest reform. (3) Areas subject in varying degrees to Japanese control. Cities, larger towns, and main communications corridors were the Japanese counterparts of the CCP's core areas, alongside which lay a fluctuating penumbra of territory where the Japanese and puppet forces held the upper hand.

In North China, especially, the railway lines both defined and divided the major base areas. Chin-Ch'a-Chi lay to the east of the Tatung-Taiyuan line, and north of the Cheng-Tai. The core areas of the base were separated from each other by the P'ing-Han, the P'ing-Sui, and the Peiping-Mukden lines. With variations, this pattern was repeated in the other base areas. The very confusion of map 11, showing a part of North China in October 1938, vividly conveys the actual complexity of the early war years.

Processes of Base Construction

The widespread disruption of government from county (*hsien*) level upward and the quasi-legal recognition granted to the CCP under the united front combined to open many opportunities to party elements. Eighth Route Army members and civilian CCP cadres represented themselves as a legitimate authority and as leaders of anti-Japanese resistance. Military and political control went hand in hand, but military affairs at first took priority. When units of the 8RA first arrived, their initial task was to link up with local Communists or 'progressives', then

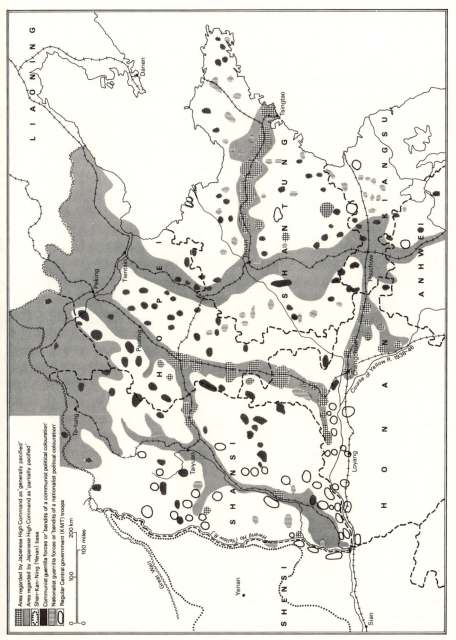

Area regarded by Japanese High Command as 'generally pacified'

Area regarded by Japanese High Command as 'partially pacified'

Shen-Kan-Ning (Yenan) base

Communist guerrilla forces or 'bandits of a communist political colouration'

Nationalist guerrilla forces or 'bandits of a nationalist political colouration'

Regular Central government (KMT) troops

MAP 11. Military situation, North China, October 1938. *Source*: Bōeichō bōei kenshūjo senshi shitsu, *Hokushi no chiansen*, map folio

to make contact with the kaleidoscope of local forces and local communities in whose midst they found themselves. Contact with native activists provided manpower, information and access to the populace. As Po I-po noted, locals lacked leadership, organization, discipline, and experience that could all be provided by outsiders, but without the locals, outsiders were likely to be distrusted, tolerated perhaps but not really supported, and could not sink roots into local society. Nationalist forces never fully mastered this linkage.

In the mountainous Shansi-Hopei borderlands, the Salvation League, headed by Sung Shao-wen, was one of the first groups with which Nieh's units made contact. Across the P'ing-Han railway, on the plains of north-central Hopei, approaches were made to Lü Cheng-ts'ao. Liu Shao-ch'i estimated that after the war began in 1937 as many as 200 armed bands, with perhaps 30,000 participants, quickly sprang up.[37] According to Liu, they were fairly easy to win over – provided the 8RA treated them well, assisted in maintaining order, did not demand too much from them in manpower and ignored a certain amount of semi-bandit behaviour. Well-entrenched bandit groups and local protective associations posed more difficult problems. Dealing successfully with them was a long process, which might have to be repeated as the base areas expanded or were forced to move. Bandits and vagrants (*yu-min*) were both a threat to local order and a source of recruits to militia forces organized by the 8RA. Despite their unpopularity with local peasants, upon whom they frequently preyed 'as upon meat and fish', many vagrants were enlisted. P'eng Chen recalled that 'the overwhelming majority actively participated in the anti-Japanese movement. At this time, the masses were, in general, still waiting to see what would happen. Most of the vagrants, with no family obligations and scant attachment to the status quo, rose up first and together with a minority of revolutionary activists, formed a path-breaking vanguard.'[38] But P'eng and other party cadres also knew that they wanted mainly to keep their bellies filled, and that they would take whatever side delivered more. 'If it gives milk,' vagrants often said, 'then call it mother.' Liu Shao-ch'i directed local cadres to handle organized bandit groups in whatever manner seemed best: to ally with them and win them over, to recruit their men and leave their leaders isolated, or to attack and break them up. In core areas, bandit groups were to be brought to heel or offered the opportunity to leave. But, according

---

[37] Liu Shao-ch'i, 'Chien-ch'ih Hua-pei k'ang-chan chung ti wu-chuang pu-tui' (Firmly support armed groups taking part in the north China war of resistance), in Chieh-fang she, *K'ang-Jih min-tsu t'ung-i chan-hsien chih-nan* (Guide to the anti-Japanese national united front), 5.42.

[38] P'eng Chen, *Chung-kung 'Chin-Ch'a-Chi pien-ch'ü' chih ko-chung cheng-ts'e* (Various policies in the CCP's 'Chin-Ch'a-Chi Border Region'), 6b.

to Liu, 'if local bandits active in the enemy-occupied area are strong enough to wreck the enemy's order, and if the anti-Japanese forces are relatively weak there, then we should persuade and unite with the bandits'.[39] This kind of united front with lumpen elements added manpower and weapons, and gradually reduced disorder in the base areas.

Local associations were a more difficult problem than bandits, according to Liu Shao-ch'i, who noted their long history in China and the impetus added by wartime conditions. The Red Spears, the Heaven's Gate Society, and joint village associations (*lien-chuang-hui*) were all 'pure self-defence organizations sharing the goals of resisting exorbitant taxes and levies and harassment by army units or bandits'. Generally controlled by local elites and 'politically neutral', they could summon mass support because they appealed to the 'backward and narrow self-interests' of the peasantry while the secret societies added superstitious beliefs to other forms of influence. They were ready to fight all intruders, including anti-Japanese guerrilla forces. Moreover, if a small force settled in their vicinity, they often attacked it for its weapons, even if it posed no threat. The associations had no permanent military organization but could respond to a summons with 'a very large military force', so long as the action took place in their local area.

Liu Shao-ch'i summarized the approaches that had proved most effective. (1) Take no rash action. (2) Strictly observe discipline; make no demands and do not provoke them, but be very watchful. (3) Scrupulously avoid insulting their religious beliefs or their leaders; show respect. (4) When they are harassed by the Japanese or by puppets, help in driving them away. (5) Win their confidence and respect by exemplary behaviour and assist them in various ways. (6) Most important, carry on patient education, propaganda and persuasion in order to raise their national consciousness, to lead them into the anti-Japanese struggle, and to provide supplies voluntarily to guerrilla forces. (7) Seek to break up associations that serve the Japanese. (8) Do not help the associations to grow, especially in the base areas or in guerrilla zones. (9) In enemy-occupied territories, help push the associations' self-defence struggles in the direction of the anti-Japanese movement. Finally, Liu noted that sometimes superstition could be turned to advantage. Some secret societies believed that Chu Te, commander of the Eighth Route Army, must be descended from their patron deity and founder of the Ming dynasty, Chu Yuan-chang. Relations between these secret societies and local 8RA units were particularly good. In short, said Liu, 'in many regions of North China, the anti-Japanese united front in rural villages

[39] Liu Shao-ch'i, 'Chien-ch'ih', 45–6.

depends mainly on how our relations and work with the associations is handled'.[40]

Thus the intrusion of Communist influence behind Japanese lines did not in the first instance depend upon nationalism, socio-economic programmes or ideology. In fact, it was quite feasible for possessors of military power to live off the Chinese countryside with a different ideology, or with no ideology at all, as the following description of Sun Tien-ying makes clear:

One of his [Sun's] lieutenants said to me, 'The reason we have an army is so that everyone gets to eat,' the implication being that whether or not they fought was unimportant. From the beginning of the war to the end of the war, he manoeuvred between the Communists and the central government, even going over to the Japanese for a time... When the war broke out, he rounded up his former associates to fight Japan. The central government designated his force the New Fifth Army, with headquarters in Lin-hsien, Honan ... Because of connections with the secret societies (pang-hui), he had contacts everywhere, so of course it was easy to do business and manage things. Although Lin-hsien is a small, out-of-the-way place, even goods from Shanghai could be bought and enjoyed.[41]

Everywhere, the CCP viewed military and political control as the essential prior condition for all other work. The distinction between consolidated, semi-consolidated and guerrilla zones measured the different degrees of such control. At an early stage, the situation might be described as 'open', in the sense that individuals and groups in society had a variety of options which the CCP was unable to prevent them from exercising. In these circumstances, the united front recognized the party's relative weakness, and it relied mainly on persuasion, accommodation, infiltration and education.

At the other extreme was a 'closed' situation, in which the CCP was powerful enough to define the options and to shape both the incentives and the costs of choice in such a way as to produce the desired behaviour. If necessary the party could impose coercive sanctions, even violence, upon those who opposed it. As this control was achieved and deepened, a kind of political revolution took place, even without any change as yet in social and economic structure. The party and its followers were wresting power from the traditional rural power holders, but establishment of control was a gradual and uneven process, influenced by terrain, by local society, and by the presence of competing or hostile forces. Even in the most successful of the base areas, Chin-Ch'a-Chi, progress was difficult. The masses did not spontaneously rally to the Communist side.

---

[40] Ibid. 48.
[41] Ch'ü Chih-sheng, K'ang-chan chi-li (A personal account of the war of resistance), 37.

Of the middle peasants, poor peasants, and other 'impoverished masses', P'eng Chen wrote, 'While the base area was being created, their capacity for political and organizational independence did not really show up ... but after these same peasants actually engaged in a certain amount of struggle (when the initiative came from the top down), they gradually awakened and found the courage to resist.' Finally, in late 1941, he could say, 'With regard to the class relationships within this region, we hold a dominant position in military and political affairs; the basic masses have already turned over and achieved dominance. But economically, the landlord-bourgeois class is still definitely predominant.'[42]

One question that runs through much of the history of the Chinese Communist movement is whether or not conditions existed in certain areas that made them more susceptible than other areas to Communist penetration, organization and control. In particular, did conditions of poverty, exploitation and social dislocation create a riper situation for Communist activity than existed in more prosperous and socially integrated areas? The answer appears to be that 'there was no single pattern of Communist success or influence in China ... The expansion of Communist forces in any area during any period was likely to be better correlated with [prolonged] Communist presence in the vicinity than with any other social phenomenon.'[43] Indeed, Mao, Liu and other leaders never accepted the position that specific social and economic conditions made some areas suitable and others unsuitable for base area construction. On the contrary, Mao believed that in principle bases could be built anywhere that the party had an opportunity for sustained operation. For example in May 1938 he insisted that bases could be established on the plains, as well as in more difficult terrain.[44] When these leaders cite local conditions (tenancy, usury, etc.), they do so to provide concrete examples to be applied flexibly in other areas, not to suggest that it was *only* under such conditions that base construction was possible. Although tenancy rates in much of North China were rather low – and rent reduction policies therefore had limited appeal – Communist leaders argued that there were other problems, other forms of exploitation, that could serve in its stead. It was up to cadres at the local level to analyse social and economic conditions in their region and set to work in the spirit of general directives. The question of whether conditions in a particular area were bringing the peasants more exploitation and misery or remaining about the same, or even improving slightly, did

[42] P'eng Chen, 1a.
[43] Roy Hofheinz, Jr. 'The ecology of Chinese communist success: rural influence patterns, 1923–1945', in A. Doak Barnett, ed. *Chinese Communist politics in action*, 72, 77.
[44] Mao Tse-tung, 'Problems of strategy in guerrilla war against Japan', Mao, *SW*, 2.95.

not interest Communist leaders or local cadres. They were convinced there was enough misery and injustice everywhere in the countryside to fuel revolutionary change.

Still, the Communists did not succeed in creating base areas everywhere, nor were they always able to maintain bases once established. The most successful bases *were* located in poorer regions: in mountainous areas, in marshlands, and in other remote areas – in short, in traditional bandit lairs such as those used by Sung Chiang and his fellows in the picaresque novel *Shui-hu chuan*. And for the same reasons. Distant from centres of population and state control, often straddling provincial boundaries, these peripheral areas offered greater security and better opportunities for uninterrupted work than did densely populated plains nearer to large cities and major communication routes.[45] In short, geography (one might even say military geography) might be more important to the success of a particular base than its social and economic structure.

What enabled the Communists to survive and grow was the combination of military-political control and popular support, both expressed in interlocking organizational structures reaching down (at least in consolidated bases) to the village level. Control came first, but what the Communists did with that control marked the difference between them and their rivals. Political, economic and social changes accompanied the extension and deepening of control in a phased and mutually interactive way. Ideally, no reform should be undertaken until the party was confident of its ability to carry it out successfully. Conversely, every change should further enhance the control of the party and the 'basic masses'. If properly handled, therefore, each change strengthened both control and support and prepared the way for the next change.

When a particular reform (an election, a production compaign, a struggle meeting) was called for, it was usually understood that this referred to the consolidated and perhaps to the semi-consolidated regions, but not to guerrilla areas which were too 'open'. Furthermore, many policies were not carried out all at once, even in consolidated bases. Instead, they were first instituted in carefully prepared 'model districts' where intensive preliminary work and concentration of personnel made success likely. The spectacle of a particularly notorious landlord humiliated in public and deprived of some or all of his property then served as a powerful example elsewhere. Other landlords, not yet so painfully singled

---

[45] G. William Skinner describes China as being made up of nine macro-regions, each of which contains a core area usually associated with rorer basins and plains. The peripheries are much poorer than the cores – indeed, they are 'exploited' by the cores for cheap labour, timber, natural resources, etc. Provincial boundaries often – but not always – follow peripheries and enclose cores. See G. William Skinner, ed. *The city in late imperial China*, 211–20.

out, were 'persuaded' to cooperate, especially when assured that their property would not be confiscated and that they would continue to receive their rents and interest, albeit on a reduced scale. More important, peasants were emboldened to define themselves in class terms, to overcome ingrained attitudes of fatalism, of passive resignation, and of community harmony – in short, to *act*. Each action made the next one easier, and burnt the bridges back to old ways. A tenant might for a time secretly pay his landlord the original, unreduced rent out of fear of retaliation or in the interest of community harmony. But once he had spoken out against him in a struggle meeting, he had probably passed the point of no return.

For the first time some peasants were beginning to think of themselves – often hesitantly or reluctantly – as political and social actors in their own right, rather than as the passive objects of action by others. The party's goal was a guided but also voluntary participation that it called 'democracy'. Alexis de Tocqueville was enunciating a general principle when he wrote, 'Patiently endured so long as it seemed beyond redress, a grievance comes to appear intolerable once the possibility of removing it crosses men's minds.'[46] P'eng Chen thus describes how the same tenants who once conspired to pay their full rent now came 'to settle scores' (*ch'ing-suan*) with landlords, refusing to pay any rent at all or demanding compensation. Poor peasants often roughed up landlords encountered on the roads or at market. 'In sum, everything was turned upside-down ... Corrections have now begun [mid-1940], and the struggle between the two sides is being held within a certain compass.'[47]

As control was being established, three sets of relationships provided the issues over which organization and mobilization might begin: (1) between landlord and tenant, focusing on rent; (2) between creditor and debtor, focusing on interest; and (3) between government and governed, focusing on taxes.[48] These issues were used to sharpen class struggle against 'feudal elements'. Step-by-step measures opened local society for deeper Communist penetration and broader organization, but at each step those being organized had to perceive actual benefit to themselves without

---

[46] Quoted in Arthur L. Stinchcombe, *Theoretical methods in social history*, 34. Note also Leon Trotsky: 'In reality the mere existence of privations is not enough to cause an insurrection; if it were, the masses would be always in revolt. It is necessary that the bankruptcy of the social regime, being conclusively revealed, should make these privations intolerable, and that new conditions and new ideas should open the prospect of a revolutionary way out. Then in the cause of the great aims conceived by them, those same masses will prove capable of enduring doubled and tripled privations.' In *ibid*. 33–4. Trotsky viewed spontaneous insurrection as an unlikely 'herd mutiny'.

[47] P'eng Chen, 4b.

[48] Ch'en Yung-fa, 175. The issues posed by these relationships were not limited to rent, interest and taxes. There were other elements as well (e.g. water rights, labour service, customary 'favours', *droit de siegneur*, etc.).

excessive risk, or else they might not respond. Concrete measures had to be found with immediate or near-term payoff, described in the vivid, earthy language to which peasants were accustomed – reserving the rhetoric of class struggle for a later date.

The first benefits brought to the local populace would depend on circumstance and had to be coordinated with the logistic needs of the CCP military and administrative personnel moving into the area. As P'eng Te-huai described it,

We provided for ourselves according to the principle of 'those with money contribute money, those with strength contribute strength'. Having set up a base area, we could collect national salvation grain levies where we had political power. Where we had not yet established base area political power, we relied on contributions, loans, requisitions, and confiscation of traitors' assets; we did not depend on the Kuomintang to issue rations or supplies.[49]

Although rent and interest reduction were stated policy, neither could be systematically carried out until control had been established to the consolidated areas of the more advanced bases. Rent reduction was described as fulfilling Sun Yat-sen's pledge to lower rents by 25 per cent (from an average rent-to-harvest ratio of 50 per cent down to 37·5 per cent) as part of the 'land to the tiller' programme which was an official but ignored element of Kuomintang ideology. This made it difficult for KMT supporters, including landlords, to criticize what the CCP was doing. From the outside, CCP rent policy looked quite moderate. Yet the complexity and variety of land relationships enabled the party to act with restraint or severity as the local situation and the mood of the cadres seemed to call for. Landlord obstructionism courted charges of damaging the cause of resistance and in effect collaborating with the enemy.[50] This could lead to severe sanctions, even confiscation of property. In any case, landlords' options were limited: 'Their land is in the rural areas and cannot be carried off into the cities.' P'eng Chen went on to write,

Generally, the enlightenment of landlords in the Chin-Ch'a-Chi Border Region took place after the basic masses had stood up, democratic rule had been firmly established, and their feudal dictatorship had been broken down. This proves that if peasants and landlords do not pass through the necessary struggles, the enlightenment of the landlords is not possible, nor is adjustment of landlord-peasant relationships.[51]

[49] P'eng Te-huai, *Tzu-shu*, 227.
[50] Landlords resisted both actively and passively. If they did not have armed manpower at their command, they might call in nearby militia (see above, ch. 6). They sometimes passed intelligence to Nationalists, puppets or Japanese agents. They used a combination of threats, cajolery and bribery to try to keep local peasants in line. More passively, they might appear to cooperate with the new regime. A common tactic was to enlist a son in the 8RA, or to become a local activist.
[51] P'eng Chen, 3a.

Interest reduction was difficult to carry out, and might also be more radical than it looked if it involved cancellation of principal or accrued interest on past loans. These losses, combined with lowered rates on new loans, often persuaded potential lenders to hold their money in reserve. Shrinkage of rural credit caused hardship, since many poor peasants required loans to survive, particularly during the spring famine in north and north-central China, when the previous year's grain stores were running low and the harvest of winter crops in May and June was still some weeks off. Furthermore, not all lenders were rich merchants or landlords. Poor and middle peasants might have a little cash, too little to invest in land or commerce, which they loaned out for additional income. Families lacking labour power – widows or childless couples – might sell land they could not cultivate in order to have money to loan. Consequently interest reduction succeeded only when the base area government itself had sufficient resources to make credit available at the prescribed interest rate.

Taxes also could be changed only slowly. Unlike Shen-Kan-Ning, bases behind Japanese lines received no outside subsidies and, as P'eng Te-huai indicated, had to rely on their own efforts. During the first two years of the war, even Chin-Ch'a-Chi was able to make only modest structural changes in the tax system, by abolishing many but not all of the miscellaneous and surtaxes that had proliferated above and beyond the basic land tax in most parts of China during the first decades of the twentieth century, and by imposing a customs duty on trade with Japanese-occupied areas. Other reforms aimed at more effective collection of the land tax by registering 'black land' (*hei-t'ien*: land formerly untaxed because it was kept off the tax rolls), and by reducing corruption so that taxes collected actually wound up in official coffers. Remaining deficits were made up by internal loans and by other ad hoc measures.

In 1939, administrative control had advanced sufficiently to permit a more regularized tax system, the 'rational burden' (*ho-li fu-tan*) plan, to be instituted in the core areas of the CCC base. Under this plan, each county was assigned a tax quota which was in turn subdivided by township and village, according to estimated total assets and capacity to pay. The village quota was then divided among the resident families, according to a calculation intended to be steeply progressive. In addition, very wealthy families were separately assessed.[52] Rent and interest reductions were designed to make the tax system more effective by preventing landlords

[52] Michael Lindsay, 'The taxation system of the Shansi-Chahar-Hopei Border Region, 1938–1945', *CQ* (Apr.–June 1970) 2–3; Kataoka Tetsuya, 124–32. Regardless of class, desirable commercial, industrial or handicraft activities were not taxed, and taxes were remitted on lands newly opened or returned to cultivation.

and rich peasants from recouping their tax payments by passing them on to tenants and debtors. Clearly, this system could not work unless its authors had confidence in those who would have to carry it out at county and village levels. P'eng Chen's report notes that it was not until well into 1939 that CCC was able to certify or replace village heads, set up village representative councils, and create a unified administrative system – and even then only in consolidated areas.[53]

The rational burden tax system was used, somewhat later, in similar form in other bases, as was the second major change, a shift from money to grain as the main unit of fiscal calculation. In CCC, the government kept its main accounts in units of millet, or their equivalent. Salaries and tax quotas were thus separated from currency fluctuations. Cadres and other functionaries were on a supply system, and received only the most meagre pocket-money income. Troops or others travelling on official business were issued grain coupons (*liang-p'iao*), which they could exchange for grain anywhere within base area jurisdiction. When a village paid its tax quota, it could deliver either grain or coupons, or a mixture of the two. Since villages were responsible for transporting their tax grain to the collection depot, they preferred the convenience of the coupons.[54]

When Communist cadres and village leaders chose, they could impose confiscations, levies, contributions, and rational-burden taxes in such a way that particular individuals or categories of local residents experienced pronounced changes in their economic condition. This worked to the advantage of tenants, poor peasants, and middle peasants, and to the disadvantage of rich peasants and landlords, especially the latter. One scholar claimed that the 'tax and rent reduction program of the CCP was revolutionary. It amounted to confiscation by instalment.'[55]

Although this assessment may be correct for certain villages in the core areas of Chin-Ch'a-Chi, it overstates what happened elsewhere in CCC and in other bases. By its own admission, the CCP lacked the capacity to carry out these policies throughout the base areas. Even where such radical transformation was within their power, the Communists usually settled for somewhat less, so long as it deepened their control and helped mobilize peasant support. For one thing, landlords and rich peasants were the most productive and economically effective operators on the rural scene, if not through their own direct labour then because of their access to capital, draft animals, tools, know-how, and understanding of market conditions. Moreover the class demarcations the CCP used as shorthand represented only very crudely the more complex reality in which peasants

[53] P'eng Chen, 9b.   [54] Lindsay, 'Taxation system', 3.   [55] Kataoka Tetsuya, 129–32.

perceived themselves.[56] Despite Communist concepts of class struggle and the reality of resentment of the rural poor toward those who took advantage of them, strong traditions of community solidarity, habits of social harmony, and fatalistic acceptance of things as they were discouraged radical action. Indiscriminate measures against those whom the Communists designated 'landlords', 'rich peasants', or more simply 'feudal elements' could well intimidate ordinary peasants, who might fear they would be next despite promises to the contrary. The literate and educated were also clustered in these petty rural elites, and if the party was to recruit local cadres capable of handling day-to-day administrative tasks, many would have to come from these groups. Finally, the Communists realized that news of harsh treatment would spread to other areas, making their penetration and united front with local elites more difficult.

By the second anniversary of the Marco Polo Bridge incident, the Chinese Communists were in an unprecedented position. Twice before the movement had grown rapidly and twice it had come face to face with extinction. Both times, in 1927 with the bloody breakup of the first united front and in 1934–5 with the hardships of the Long March, survivors had nursed the sparks of revolution and coaxed them back to life. Now, as a result of the war, the Communists were stronger and more widely spread, with armies, territories and followers scattered across North and Central China. Leadership was more unified than before, yet no longer was there a single dominant centre, such as Shanghai or the Kiangsi soviet, where the Communists might possibly be dealt a mortal blow.

Viewed from the perspectives of 1927 and 1935, the growth in CCP power was impressive. But in comparison with the strength of the Nationalists and their affiliates, or with the Japanese and puppet forces, and in comparison also with the vastness and social complexity of these new territories, this growth in CCP power appears much more limited. Would it be able to survive a third great challenge?

[56] The standard shorthand classification was as follows: *Landlord*: lived entirely on rents and other income; did not personally engage in labour. *Rich peasant*: engaged in agricultural or other labour, but had excess land to rent out. *Middle peasant*: self-sufficient owner-operator. Did not rent land either in or out. *Poor peasant*: owned some land, but not enough to support his family; rented land to make up the difference. *Tenant*: owned no land, but had recognized rights of cultivation (annual, long-term, or permanent) to land owned by others. Paid rent on all land cultivated. *Farm labourer*: hired labour, either as a regular hired hand or for a stipulated period of days, weeks, etc.

   This scheme belied the enormous variety of land tenure arrangements, as the Communists well knew (see above, ch. 5). Some very poor peasants rented out all their land because age or ill-health prevented them from cultivating it. Tenants were occasionally landlords as well, owning no land in their own name, but living off sub-let rents. Consequently, in classifying peasants, local cadres also stressed income/consumption levels, life styles, and degree of cooperation with the party's policies.

II. THE MIDDLE YEARS 1939-1943

Transition to the second phase of the war began in early 1939, as the result of the stalemate foreseen by Mao at the sixth plenum in late 1938. Mao had predicted that during this protracted 'new stage' the forces of resistance (meaning principally, of course, Communist-led forces) would grow stronger. In reality the balance sheet was mixed. In Shantung and in Central China, new bases came into being, but in much of North China territory, manpower and population were lost to Japanese consolidation. Base area economies faced severe problems and the peasantry suffered more intensely than at any other time.

Stalemate had two dimensions. The first was growing Nationalist resentment over Communist expansion, which contrasted so strikingly with their own losses. While the Nationalists were being driven out of the regions of their greatest wealth and power in the central and lower Yangtze basin, losing the cream of their armies in the process, the CCP was seeping into the broad countryside behind Japanese lines, extending its influence over territory and gaining popular support.

The second dimension was the Japanese desire – and need – to consolidate the territories they had nominally conquered, and to derive economic benefit from them. After all, the rationale for the China incident was to use China's labour and resources to augment Japanese strength, not to drain its treasure away in China's vast territories.

'Why, oh why,' lamented a Japanese colonel, 'didn't we cut the China Incident short, after we had attained our initial objectives? It was senseless of us to get lured into the hinterland...All we ever ended up with was real estate, not popular support from those we "liberated"...We bogged down, deeper and ever deeper, in that endless morass of attrition.'[57] The Japanese authorities – still divided and competing among themselves – sought to improve their situation in several ways. A new peace offensive was aimed at Chiang Kai-shek simultaneously with efforts to set up a 'reformed' Nationalist government under Wang Ching-wei, who had fled Chungking in December 1938. More collaborators and puppets were recruited. Finally, the Japanese undertook forceful military, political and economic measures to establish territorial control and eliminate opposition.

[57] Quoted in Alvin D. Coox and Hilary Conroy, eds. *China and Japan: a search for balance since World War I*, 303.

'FRICTION' WITH THE NATIONALISTS

The Communists used the euphemism 'friction' (*mo-ts'a*) to describe their conflicts with the Nationalists during the middle years of the war. By 1939, what had appeared to many observers – perhaps erroneously – as an unexpectedly cordial entente began to fade. In early 1939, the KMT Central Committee adopted a series of measures to restrict the CCP.[58] Military clashes began in the summer and continued into the autumn and winter with growing frequency and intensity, most of them taking place in and around the North China bases. The Communists called the period between December 1939 and March 1940 'the first anti-Communist upsurge'. Of course, each side called the other the aggressor, and claimed self-defence against unwarranted attack. But strategically this north China 'upsurge' was a Nationalist effort to check the unauthorized expansion of the CCP beyond the areas assigned to them and to regain influence in areas already lost to the Communists or the Japanese. Chiang Kai-shek spoke as a traditionalist insisting on his legal rights, while the Communists insisted on their evolutionary right to question the moral value of the government's legal rights.

During 1939, the Nationalists began to blockade Shen-Kan-Ning all around its southern and western perimeter. Within a year, this blockade numbered nearly 400,000 troops, including some of the best remaining Central Armies under the overall command of Hu Tsung-nan. The blockade halted further Communist expansion, particularly in Kansu and Suiyuan, and it ended direct contact between SKN and Communists active in Sinkiang (Chinese Turkestan), adjacent to Soviet Central Asia. The Sinkiang Communists, including Mao Tse-tung's brother, were liquidated in 1942. Sharp fighting broke out on the Kansu-Shensi border and in the north-east corner of SKN along the Great Wall near Suite, as the blockading forces probed for soft spots. Elements of Ho Lung's 120th Division had to be called back from the Chin-sui base across the Yellow River to beef up SKN's regular garrison.

Economically, the blockade was even more serious. The central government's subsidy to the Border Region budget was cut off during 1939. Trade between the Border Region and other parts of China was brought to a near standstill, a serious blow to a region unable to supply itself with many basic commodities.

Nationalist and regional forces also sought to intrude their military and

---

[58] These were (a) 'Measures to restrict the activities of other parties', (b) 'Measures to deal with the Communist problem', and (c) 'Measures for guarding against Communist activities in Japanese-occupied areas'. See Van Slyke, *Enemies and friends*, 97.

administrative authority into Hopei, Shansi, Honan, and Shantung – regions now viewed by the CCP as their base areas. In opposing these efforts, the CCP predictably accused their rivals of harming the resistance and damaging the people's interests. The 'experts in dissension' were said to be working with the Japanese and their puppets. Noting the increasing collaboration of regional units with the Japanese, the CCP implied that this was a deliberate and cynical tactic called 'crooked-line patriotism' (*ch'ü-hsien chiu-kuo*) to preserve these units for future anti-Communist operations. Even so, the CCP sought to avoid an open rupture with the Nationalist government in Chungking. In public, the CCP consistently described these military clashes as initiated by local commanders exceeding orders from higher authority, even though they knew this was not the case. Chiang Kai-shek, of course, could not deny this fiction, and it appeared to justify a vigorous Communist response.

Mao Tse-tung enunciated the general policy for resisting these efforts: 'justification, expedience and restraint' (*yu-li, yu-li, yu chieh*).[59] The CCP should fight, in other words, when they could claim justification for doing so, and when they could gain an advantage. But they should not press the attack beyond the limits of Nationalist tolerance or to the detriment of their public image as selfless patriots. CCP forces should keep the initiative as fully as possible in their own hands, deciding when and whether to engage and when to break off.

The most spectacular episode of the 'first anti-Communist upsurge' was the rupture with Yen Hsi-shan in December 1939. All through the summer and autumn, tension in Shansi had been growing, as Yen and his conservative followers associated with the Old Army saw the Sacrifice League and the Dare-to-die Corps of the New Army amalgamate with Communist forces. When the base areas and the Japanese occupation took over most of his province, Yen was forced into exile at Ch'iu-lin, across the Yellow River in Shensi. In November, Yen ordered his Old Army to disarm the Dare-to-die forces with the help of central units sent by Hu Tsung-nan. Out of the bloody fighting that ensued, these elements one by one broke free of even nominal provincial control, and completed their linkup with Communist forces. More than 30,000 went over to the Communists. A KMT intelligence agent summed it up with rueful eloquence:

This is the way the Communists always work. At first they were full of sweet words, flattery, and obsequious distortions, in order to open things up and cover their actions ... But once they were fully fledged, and once the low-level base had been achieved, they turned at once and bit ... We guessed in our hearts that

[59] 'Current problems of tactics in the anti-Japanese united front', Mao, *SW* 2.427.

things might end like this, but we weren't aware of how fast events were moving
... nor did we believe this could happen at the very moment when the CCP's
calls for 'united front' and 'maintenance of unity for resistance' were filling the
skies.[60]

A month or so later, in February and March 1940, elements of the 8RA
beat back this so-called upsurge. Chang Yin-wu's forces were disarmed
and dispersed on the plains of north Hopei. To the south, Chu Huai-ping
and Shih Yu-san were pushed out of the base area, as was the KMT-
appointed provincial governor, Lu Chung-lin. Although a few non-
Communist forces remained in the area, the CCC and CCLY bases were
never again seriously threatened by forces affiliated with the central
government. In apparent confirmation of CCP charges, Shih Yu-san was
executed later that year by the central government for his collaboration
with the Japanese.

By late 1939, CCP central authorities asserted that 'the regions in which
we can now expand our armed forces are limited principally to Shantung
and Central China'.[61] In these two areas, the CCP was still trying to carve
out bases in which they could operate.

The situation in Shantung was confused. After the Japanese invasion,
most of the Nationalist-affiliated forces had remained in the province,
whereas Communist forces and bases were weaker and more widely
separated than further west. Not until late 1938 did significant 8RA units
from the 115th and 129th Divisions, under Hsü Hsiang-ch'ien and Lo
Jung-huan, enter the province to link up with the Shantung column and
local guerrillas, including the remnants of a large band that had recently
been decimated by the Japanese.[62] These actions led to clashes with both
the Japanese and various Nationalist-affiliated groups, both of which were
stronger than the Communists at this time. Until late 1940, CCP clashes
with these Nationalist forces were bloodier than those with the Japanese.

The CCP knew that their Chinese rivals were deeply suspicious of one
another, and that their attitudes toward the CCP varied widely. The main
Nationalist forces had not been closely affiliated with the central
government or Chiang Kai-shek, but were under independent, sometimes
disaffected regional commanders. Communist tactics were summed up in

[60] Quoted in Van Slyke, *Enemies and friends*, 142.

[61] 'Chung-yang kuan-yü tsai Shan-tung Hua-chung fa-chan wu-chuang chien-li ken-chü-ti ti chih-
shih' (Central directive concerning development of armed forces and establishment of base areas
in Shantung and Central China), 28 January 1940, *Chung-kung tang-shih ts'an-k'ao tzu-liao* (Reference
materials on the history of the CCP), 4.138.

[62] David Paulson, 'War and revolution in North China: the Shandong base area, 1937–1945'
(Stanford University, Ph.D. dissertation, 1982), 75–7. This was the column led by a subordinate
of Han Fu-ch'ü, Fan Chu-hsien, who led a growing number of resistance fighters, until he was
surrounded and defeated in November 1938. Fan was wounded and committed suicide to avoid
capture.

slogans: 'develop progressive forces, win over fence-sitters, isolate die-hards'; 'flatter top echelons, enlist the middle ranks, hit the rank and file'; and 'win over Yü Hsueh-chung, isolate Shen Hung-lieh, eliminate Ch'in Ch'i-jung.'[63] Unlike the other North China bases, however, the Communists were for several years unable to neutralize Nationalist forces in Shantung, and might not have been able to do so even then, had Japanese mop-up campaigns not weakened them.

By November 1940, Hsu Hsiang-ch'ien claimed considerable progress, but acknowledged that Shantung was not yet a consolidated base. CCP efforts were most successful along parts of the Shantung-Hopei border, around the Taishan massif in central Shantung, and near the tip of the peninsula, far to the east. Elsewhere, he said, 'progressive forces are still weak'. Regular 8RA troops numbered perhaps 70,000, far below the levels called for by party centre – 150,000 regulars and 1.5 to 2 million self-defence forces.[64] Virtually no systematic economic reforms had yet been instituted. The familiar confiscations, collections of national salvation grain, contributions and loans were used alongside the conventional tax system which was adjusted to favour the poorer peasants.

Communist expansion in Central China was even more fraught with danger of large-scale conflict with central government forces than was the case further north. Whereas in most of North China 'friction' resulted from rapid Communist expansion into a partial vacuum, in Central China the CCP's base-building efforts required that they displace an existing Nationalist military-administrative presence with close ties to Chiang Kai-shek and the Chungking government.

The burden of this expansion was carried primarily by the 6th Detachment (northern Anhwei and Kiangsu) and by the 5th Detachment, strongly reinforced by 15,000 to 20,000 8RA troops under Huang K'o-ch'eng. As Ch'en I's 1st Detachment crossed from south to north, through the corridor provided by Kuan Wen-wei's local forces, they too became actively engaged. This expansion, responding to directives from Mao and Liu which became increasingly urgent through the latter part of 1939 and into 1940, brought the N4A forces north of the river into ever more frequent and sharper conflict with Nationalist authorities in Anhwei and Kiangsu, especially with forces under the Kiangsu governor, Han Te-ch'in.

South of the river, however, Hsiang Ying did not directly challenge Chungking's commanders. Perhaps he had been influenced by Wang Ming, as Mao later charged, or perhaps he saw no alternative. His forces – the three detachments, plus the headquarters unit – were heavily outnumbered

---

[63] Paulson, *War and revolution*, 94.   [64] *Ibid.* 107.

by Ku Chu-t'ung's Nationalist units, to say nothing of the Japanese and their puppets. Despite Mao's insistence that bases could be built anywhere, the Shanghai-Hangchow-Nanking triangle was an exceptionally difficult environment. Hsiang Ying and his followers had survived with great tenacity and courage in the mountains of South China between 1934 and 1937, in the face of savage search-and-destroy missions that were not called off until the war broke out. It seems unlikely that those who could weather such experiences would suddenly become 'right-wing capitulationists'. More plausibly, Hsiang Ying's 'accommodations' and 'compromises' reflected the true balance of power in this region. By spring 1940, however, Mao was pressing Hsiang Ying even harder:

in all cases we can and should expand. The Central Committee has pointed out this policy of expansion to you time and again. To expand means to reach out into all enemy-occupied areas and not to be bound by the Kuomintang's restrictions but to go beyond the limits allowed by the Kuomintang, not to expect official appointments from them or depend on the higher-ups for financial support but instead to expand the armed forces freely and independently, set up base areas unhesitatingly, independently arouse the masses in those areas to action and build up united front organs of political powers under the leadership of the Communist Party.[65]

The contest between the Nationalists and the Communists involved more than struggles for control of territory behind Japanese lines. It also involved national-level politics, ideology and leadership. To the CCP, one worrisome development was the campaign, all during 1939, to increase Chiang Kai-shek's prestige and formal power. More titles were added to his list of top party, government and military posts. In early 1939, the Central Executive Committee named him 'director-general' of the Kuomintang, reminiscent of the title previously borne by Sun Yat-sen. Furthermore, during the summer and autumn of 1939, there was talk of constitutional rule. In November, the KMT announced plans to convene a constitutional assembly a year later. If Chiang could fulfil these long-awaited promises, he and his government might have a new legitimacy and greater popularity.

Mao Tse-tung and his colleagues could not let these moves go unchallenged. If the KMT was to have a paramount leader and authoritative spokesman, the CCP should have one also. It is no accident that his famous 'On the new democracy' was written in late 1939 and published the following January.[66] Its substance had been anticipated in earlier statements, but its timing and full development were influenced by the

---

[65] 'Freely expand the anti-Japanese forces and resist the onslaughts of the anti-communist die-hards', Mao, *SW*, 2.431.

[66] Mao, *SW*, 2.339–84. This version has undergone considerable editing. The original text, with later changes indicated, may be found in *MTTC* 7.147–206.

KMT constitutional movement. It was the CCP's entry in the competition, both a bid for support (away from the KMT) and a statement of the multiclass united front coalition the CCP desired to lead. The apparently temperate and moderate tone of 'On the new democracy' persuaded many Chinese that the CCP had either diluted its revolutionary objectives or had deferred them to a distant future. But here, as in so many other CCP statements, language was used on two levels of meaning. To those in Kuomintang-controlled areas, the text invited an interpretation according to the liberal values of Anglo-American democracy: popular participation, multi-party government, legally protected civil rights. But in the territories the CCP controlled, the same words had more authoritarian, class-based connotations. In classified inner-party documents not for public consumption the ambiguity was dropped, and one can see clearly the tough, patient and flexible commitment of the party not only to resistance but also to social control and social change.

During this same period, the Communists professed a deep concern over the danger of Nationalist capitulation to Japan, not only on the battlefields behind Japanese lines, but at the highest levels. To be sure, some of this was propaganda, but behind the propaganda was genuine worry. During late 1939 and early 1940, all politically aware Chinese knew that Japan was negotiating with the mercurial Wang Chang-wei, who had fled Chungking a year earlier. A 'reorganized national government' in Nanking was finally established in March 1940, the most formidable collaboration to date.

Less well known was that, at the same time, the Japanese were seeking an understanding with Chiang Kai-shek himself, through intermediaries in Hong Kong. 'Operation Kiri', as this effort to 'spread a feast for Chiang' was called, had elements of both high intrigue and low comedy. Chiang's reported interest in peace may have been a hoax designed to further discredit Wang Ching-wei, who was kept waiting in the wings until Operation Kiri had fallen through, but even if Chiang had no intention of coming to terms with the Japanese, the Communists could not be sure of the outcome of this multi-pronged peace offensive until after its failure.

Never had China been so isolated as she was by the middle of 1940. In Europe, the 'phony war' ended in the spring with the German blitz across the Low Countries. France was soon knocked out, and England seemed likely to fall. Japan took advantage of the situation to demand the severance of China's last tenuous links with the outside world: the Burma Road, trade with neutral Hong Kong, and the railway line from Hanoi to Kunming. Meanwhile Russia was engaged in a nasty and embarrassing war with Finland and was cutting back on its military aid to the

Nationalists. The United States was only gradually moving away from isolationism and clearly considered England more important than China. In Chungking and elsewhere in Free China, signs of war weariness, despair and demoralization were visible.

THE NEW FOURTH ARMY INCIDENT[67]

In these circumstances, Mao's call for aggressive expansion was either a bold gamble that Chiang would not capitulate to Japan or urgent preparation to be as well situated as possible, should a KMT-CCP split take place. In Central China, the scale and tempo of the fighting continued to grow, beginning in the last months of 1939, when Lo Ping-hui's 5th Detachment clashed with elements of Han Te-ch'in's Kiangsu army near Lake Kaoyu. In the months that followed, Kuan Wen-wei's forces ranged all along the left bank of the Yangtze and made frequent contact with Lo's troops farther north. Lo also began to receive some 8RA reinforcements, moving south via the territories held by the 6th Detachment. Clearly a major confrontation was shaping up in north and central Kiangsu.

Meanwhile, the South Yangtze Command was faring rather badly. Nationalist commanders Leng Hsin and Ku Chu-t'ung were so severely restricting its activities that Mao and Liu gradually abandoned the idea of trying to establish a consolidated base in this area. During the late spring and early summer, Ch'en I transferred most of his 1st and 2nd Detachments north of the Yangtze. In September, the 3rd Detachment followed, moving across the river to the vicinity of Lake Chao, where the 4th Detachment was stationed. This left only the Headquarters Detachment under Yeh T'ing and Hsiang Ying still south of the Yangtze, at Ching-hsien in southern Anhwei.

As the military situation moved toward a showdown, negotiations began in June 1940 between KMT and CCP representatives. At issue were Communist operating zones and the authorized size of the CCP-led armies. Proposals and acrimonious counter-proposals were exchanged without agreement. The KMT considered it a concession to allow the CCP free rein north of the pre-1938 course of the Yellow River, with the exception of southern Shansi, which was to remain the bailiwick of Yen Hsi-shan. In return, all 8RA and N4A units were to evacuate Central China. In essence, the KMT was offering the CCP what it already had in return for giving up what it might be about to get by force of arms. A series of deadlines was issued by Nationalist authorities, without clear indication of the consequences of their violation.

On the surface, the CCP appeared partly to comply. The movements

---

[67] This account is based largely on material contained in Ch'en Yung-fa, ch. 1, and on information supplied by Gregor Benton.

of Ch'en I and the South Yangtze Command might look like obedience, although actually they were responding to orders of their own superiors, not to those of the Nationalists. Hsiang Ying's continuing delays and evasions during the autumn and winter of 1940 remain somewhat puzzling. He may have felt, quite justifiably, that Mao had lost confidence in him and that he would lose his command as soon as he reached that north bank of the river. Moreover, Yenan's directives were sometimes ambiguous and contradictory. He may also have wanted to reach secure agreements with KMT commanders concerning evacuation routes and safe conduct out of the area.

For a time, Han Te-ch'in kept the bulk of his forces – an estimated 70,000 men, far outnumbering the N4A – in north Kiangsu, blocking the expansion of the 6th Detachment and further southward intrusions by 8RA troops. But by midsummer he realized he would have to counter the build-up of N4A forces in central Kiangsu or risk writing it off to the Communists. A confused sequence of engagements followed, culminating in a decisive battle in early October 1940, near the central Kiangsu town of Huang-ch'iao. Over four days, several main force units of Han's 89th Army were destroyed, and others dispersed. This was also the signal for the 6th Detachment to move more aggressively in the north. In the aftermath, one of Han's principal commanders entered collaboration with the CCP, another defected to Wang Ching-wei's Nanking government. Although Han Te-ch'in was able to retain a foothold in Kaingsu until 1943, his real power was broken. Not much was made of the battle of Huang-ch'iao in the Chinese press: the KMT did not want to publicize a disastrous defeat, and the Communists were content to remain silent about an episode that contradicted their professed united front policy.

Quite understandably, during the autumn, after Han Te-ch'in's defeat, KMT-CCP negotiations took a turn for the worse. In early December, Chiang Kai-shek personally ordered all N4A forces out of southern Anhwei and southern Kiangsu by 31 December; the entire 8RA was to be north of the Yellow River by the same deadline, to be joined a month later by the N4A. Discussions then ensued between Yeh T'ing and Ku Chu-t'ung's deputies concerning the route to be taken, safe conduct, and – incredibly – the money and supplies to be given to the N4A to assist it in moving.[68] On 25 December Mao Tse-tung ordered Hsiang Ying to evacuate at once, but not until 4 January 1941 did Yeh and Hsiang actually begin to move. Almost at once, Ku Chu-t'ung's forces harassed and dispersed the N4A's Headquarters Group, which included administrative personnel, wounded soldiers and dependents, as well as combat-ready

[68] Ch'en Yung-fa, 95–7.

troops. In an effort to regroup, they moved south-west to Mao-lin, where they were surrounded by Nationalists and during the next several days cut to pieces.

Losses were high on both sides. The CCP suffered an estimated 9,000 casualties. Hsiang Ying twice tried unsuccessfully to break out of the blockade on his own and was denounced as a deserter by Yeh T'ing, who took over full command of the doomed forces. Hsiang Ying finally made good his escape, only to be killed a couple of months later by one of his bodyguards, for the N4A's gold reserves which he had taken with him. To the very end Hsiang either failed or refused to seek refuge in Liu Shao-ch'i's domain north of the Yangtze. The unfortunate Yeh T'ing was arrested and spent the rest of the war in prison; finally released in 1946, he died a month later in a plane crash, along with several other ranking party members. On 17 January Chiang Kai-shek declared the New Fourth Army dissolved for insubordination. Direct contacts between Yenan and Chungking virtually ended, and CCP military liaison offices in a number of Nationalist-held cities were closed.

Such was the New Fourth Army incident, also called the South Anhwei incident. Clearly an act of retribution for the defeats inflicted on Han Te-ch'in in north and central Kiangsu, it ended any realistic chance for a consolidated Communist base south of the Yangtze. Still, in a strategic sense, these losses were more than compensated for by the gains achieved further north – and, in fact, a few months later the reorganized N4A began quietly to reintroduce some units into this region, where they carried on guerrilla activities without a secure territorial base.

In marked contrast to the silence surrounding the Huang-ch'iao fighting, the New Fourth Army incident was the subject of bitter and prolonged controversy. The CCP charged that this was a second 'anti-Communist upsurge', even more serious than the first. Presenting themselves as martyred patriots, they characterized their antagonists as those who

want to put an end to the War of Resistance by what they call Sino-Japanese cooperation in 'suppressing the Communists'. They want to substitute civil war for the war of resistance, capitulation for independence, a split for unity, and darkness for light ... People are telling each other the news and are horrified. Indeed, the situation has never been so critical as it is today.[69]

The Nationalist rejoinder, of course, was that provocations had been many and serious and that breaches of military discipline could not be tolerated, but reluctance to detail its own defeats at CCP hands forced it into vague generalities. The CCP had much the better of this propaganda battle and

[69] 'Order and statement on the southern Anhwei incident', Mao, *SW* 2.454.

the political capital that could be made of it. 'If it is politically valuable to be thought of as a national hero, it is even more valuable to be a national martyr ... No single event in the entire Sino-Japanese War did more to enhance the Communists' prestige vis-à-vis the Nationalists than the destruction of the New Fourth Army headquarters while it was "loyally following orders"'.[70]

Many concerned Chinese and other observers were indeed 'horrified' and feared the open resumption of civil war. Although civil war did not ensue, the events culminating in the New Fourth Army incident have been seen, with few exceptions, as marking the breakdown of the second united front. This view is wrong on two counts. First, the CCP saw the united front as a strategy to be flexibly applied to all political, military and social forces in China, from the top of the central government down to the smallest village. Relations with Chiang Kai-shek and the Kuomintang regime as a whole were important, but in no way constituted the whole of the united front. Even with respect to Chiang and the Nationalists, however, the customary interpretation is misguided. Throughout the war, a cardinal goal of the united front was to prevent peace between Japan and the Nationalists. Thus, when clashes between CCP forces and those of the central government on so large a scale as at Huang-ch'iao and Mao-lin could take place without leading to peace with Japan and full-scale resumption of civil war, this was not the end of the united front but its fundamental vindication.[71] If friction on such a scale could somehow be tolerated by Chiang Kai-shek, fears of his accommodation with Japan in the future were greatly eased.

Reorganization of the Communist political and military presence in Central China followed in the wake of the New Fourth Army incident. The Central Plains and South-east China Bureaus of the CCP were merged and renamed the Central China Bureau with Liu Shao-ch'i in charge, reflecting the importance of this area to Party Central. The New Fourth Army was also completely reorganized and substantially regularized. Ch'en I became its new acting commander (since Yeh T'ing was in prison), directing the seven divisions into which the force was now divided. Each of these divisions had a territorial responsibility, and in each region the CCP claimed the establishment of a base (see map 12 and table 13). Indeed, base area construction got under way in earnest only after the friction of 1940 and the New Fourth Army incident. In the years that followed, the operating zones of the First to Fourth Divisions contained expanding enclaves of consolidated territory, where military dominance was combined with open party activity, administrative control, development of mass

[70] Johnson, *Peasant nationalism*, 139–40.   [71] Kataoka Tetsuya, 226–8.

TABLE 13

The New Fourth Army after 18 February 1941

Headquarters

Acting Commander: Ch'en I
Vice Commander: Chang Yun-i
Political Commissar: Liu Shao-ch'i
Chief of Staff: Lai Ch'uan-chu
Chief, Political Department: Teng Tzu-hui

Division	Commander	Political Commissar	Previous designation	Operating area
First	Su Yü	Liu Yen	First Detachment	*Central Kiangsu military area:* the region bounded by the Yangtze on the south, the Grand Canal on the west, a line between Huaiyin and the coast on the north, and the Pacific Ocean on the east.
Second	Chang Yun-i (concurrently army vice-commander)	Lo Ping-hui	Fourth and Fifth Detachments	*South Huai military area:* the region bounded by the Yangtze and a line between Nanking and Hofei on the south, Hofei to Pengpu on the west, the Huai River on the north, and the Grand Canal on the east.
Third	Huang K'o-ch'eng	Huang K'o-ch'eng	Part of Eighth Route Army	*North Kiangsu military area:* the region north of Huaiyin and Founing, bounded on the west by the Grand Canal.
Fourth	P'eng Hsueh-feng	P'eng Hsueh-feng	Sixth Detachment	*North Huai military area:* the region bounded by the Huai River on the south, the Tientsin-Pukow railway on the west, a line between the Grand Canal and Hsuchou on the north, and the Grand Canal on the east.
Fifth	Li Hsien-nien	Li Hsien-nien	Honan-Hupeh Volunteer Column	*The Hupeh-Honan-Anhwei military area:* Li Hsien-nien's guerrilla area north of Hankow.
Sixth	T'an Chen-lin	T'an Chen-lin	Third Detachment	*South Kiangsu military area:* the region around Lake T'ai. T'an Chen-lin's unit, which had evacuated north of the river in September 1940, re-entered the mountainous Kiangsu-Chekiang border area in 1941.
Seventh	Chang Ting-ch'eng	Tseng Hsi-sheng	Second Detachment	*Central Anhwei military area:* both banks of the Yangtze westward to Susung, in Anhwei. This area contained the fewest regular forces (5,000) at the end of the war, owing undoubtedly to the presence of strong KMT forces and the area's strategic value to the Japanese.

Sources: Johnson, *Peasant nationalism*, 144–5, checked against material in Ch'en Yung-fa and Kataoka Tetsuya. Map 12 is derived from this table.

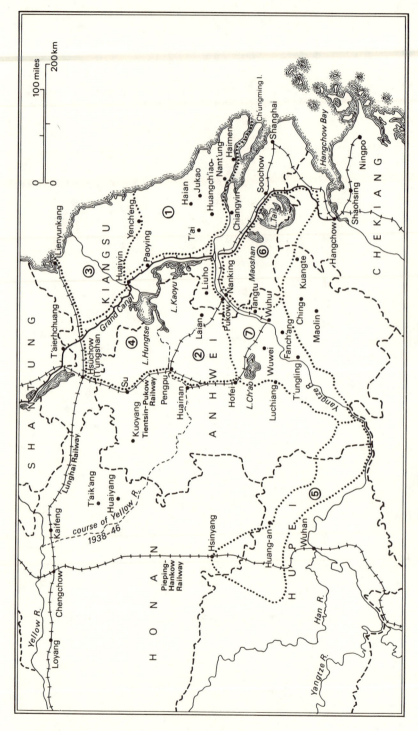

MAP 12. Disposition of New Fourth Army after the 'New Fourth Army incident'

organizations, local elections, and socio-economic reforms. The other three regions wavered between semi-consolidated and guerrilla status.

The worst of the KMT-CCP conflict was now over. When CCP documents speak of a third upsurge, in 1943, they refer to a frankly political effort. With the exception of Shantung, where a fairly strong Nationalist presence continued longer, the balance of power among Chinese forces behind Japanese lines had come by mid-1941 to favour the CCP. In succeeding years the preponderance became ever greater, until by the end of 1943 the Communists were virtually unchallenged by Chinese rivals. This thought may have been in Chiang Kai-shek's mind in September 1943 when he spoke to the KMT's Central Executive Committee: 'I am of the opinion that first of all we should clearly recognize that the Chinese Communist problem is a purely political problem and should be solved by political means...'[72] In most areas behind Japanese lines, the Nationalists no longer had the capacity to attempt any other sort of solution.

JAPANESE CONSOLIDATION

Simultaneously with the 'friction' between the KMT and the CCP, the Japanese were trying to control and exploit the territories they had nominally conquered. Treating friction and consolidation separately does some violence to the real complexity and difficulty of the problems the CCP faced in dealing with both at the same time. At times, the CCP was fighting a two-front war. But if the worst of KMT-CCP friction was over by 1941, the most serious and painful challenges of Japanese consolidation were still to come. The two chronologies must be superimposed if something approaching reality is to be recovered.

The Japanese knew that consolidation was an urgent task because most of the territory behind their army's furthest advances was largely out of their control. Some areas could be put in order by fairly straightforward means: restoring local administration and policy authority, repairing transportation and communication lines, enrolling Chinese personnel (usually untrustworthy, it turned out) as police or militia under puppet governments, registering the local population and requiring them to carry identity cards. In time-honoured Chinese fashion, techniques of collective security were widely used. One was the familiar *pao-chia* system in one form or another. A variant was the 'railway-cherishing village'. A village was assigned a nearby stretch of track; if residents failed to 'cherish' it,

[72] US Department of State, *United States relations with China, with special reference to the period 1944-1949*, 530. Hereafter *China white paper*.

TABLE 14

Damage to North China railways (Jan. 1938–Oct. 1940)

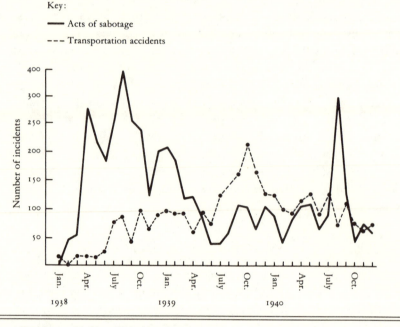

Key:

—— Acts of sabotage

--- Transportation accidents

Source: Bōeicho senshi shitan, *Hokushi no chiansen*, 1.407.

they were held collectively responsible. Yet the laxity of early Japanese control in North China was vividly illustrated by three young foreigners during the summer of 1938. On vacation from teaching in Peiping, and curious to know what was going on, they loaded their bicycles on a southbound train, got off at the Paoting station, and pedalled west until they encountered 8RA detachments.[73]

Early in the war, commanders wanted to use mobile warfare, but Mao insisted on de-escalation and dispersal of the 8RA and N4A into small units as nuclei for combat, recruitment, political work, and base area construction. With this strategy, few engagements could be very dramatic or significant. Each skirmish had to be carefully planned, utilizing local intelligence and the element of surprise so that the detachment could hit and run before its limited ammunition was gone or enemy reinforcements could arrive. Small Japanese patrols and puppet units might be ambushed in order to obtain weapons and other material as well as inflict casualties. Active collaborators or Japanese-sponsored administrative personnel

[73] Lindsay, *Unknown war*, not paged.

might be assassinated. Above all, the Communists aimed to disrupt transportation: to mine roads, to cut down telegraph poles and steal the wire, to cut rail lines and sabotage rolling stock. Sometimes they carried off steel rails to get material for their primitive arsenals, or tried to cause a derailment. Destroying a bridge or a locomotive was a major accomplishment. Table 14 shows how effectively the Communists used these opportunities in North China.

Both the Communists and the Japanese knew that these tactics had little influence on the strategic balance but were effective at other levels. To the Japanese, these actions were like numerous small cuts – painful, bleeding, and possible sources of infection. Few areas in the countryside were safe. Japanese sources document the growing exasperation of field commanders as they tried to eliminate resistance, restore administration, collect taxes, and prepare for the more effective economic exploitation of conquered territory. Guerrilla warfare against the Japanese cannot be assessed in conventional terms of battles won, casualties inflicted, terrain occupied. It must also be evaluated politically and psychologically, as Mao frequently emphasized. Since the wartime legitimacy of the CCP depended on its patriotic claims, enough military action had to be undertaken to maintain credibility. Moreover, military success was crucial to gaining the support of the 'basic masses', persuading waverers to keep an open mind, and neutralizing opposition. 'It was not that people always chose the side that was winning, but that few would ever join a side they thought was losing.' As one experienced cadre observed,

Among the guerrilla units ... there is a saying that 'victory decides everything'. That is, no matter how hard it has been to recruit troops, supply the army, raise the masses' anti-Japanese fervor or win over the masses' sympathy, after a victory in battle, the masses fall all over themselves to send us flour, steamed bread, meat, and vegetables. The masses' pessimistic and defeatist psychology is broken down, and many new guerrilla soldiers swarm in.[74]

Later, when the Japanese began to extract a heavy price for each engagement, whether victorious or not, this attitude changed.

In North and Central China, Japan's earliest pacification sweeps posed few problems for the CCP. Initially, the Japanese made few distinctions among the various Chinese forces. They simply tried to mop up or disperse them, regardless of their character. They soon realized, however, that these sweeps were only making it easier for the CCP to expand. By the second half of 1939 the Japanese were being more discriminating. Chinese non-Communist forces stood aside while the Japanese hunted for

[74] Kathleen Hartford, 'Repression and Communist success: the case of Jin-Cha-Ji, 1938–1943' (unpubl. MS.) 370–1.

the 8RA, the N4A, and their local affiliates. The Japanese also made more positive appeals to the non-Communists. According to Japanese army statistics, during the eighteen months between mid-1939 and late 1940, about 70,000 men from more or less regular Nationalist units in North China alone went over to the Japanese. The Japanese also had informal 'understandings' with several regional commanders whose units totalled perhaps 300,000 men.[75] This was, of course, the 'crooked-line patriotism' against which the CCP so strongly inveighed.

When pacification efforts began in earnest in late 1939 and 1940, some differences became apparent in the strategies employed by Japanese armies in North and Central China. In North China, the approach was heavily military in its emphasis, political tactics being limited mainly to the enlistment of collaborators. Authorities in Central China did not hesitate to use military force, either, but they sought to supplement this force with more comprehensive political and economic solutions through the formation of tightly controlled 'model peace zones'. Although both strategies ultimately failed, they brought enormous difficulties to the Chinese Communists, until the Japanese were forced to ease off in 1943 because of the burdens of the Pacific War against the United States.

When the Communists survived Japanese consolidation and repression most observers attributed it to mass mobilization and popular support, tracing that support either to anti-Japanese nationalism aroused by the invaders' brutality or to socio-economic reforms and the 'mass line'. No doubt both these factors played some part, but careful examination of detailed intra-party documents shows that repression also demobilized peasant support and terrorized populations into apathy, grudging acquiescence, or active collaboration with the Japanese. And in a locale that had been reduced from consolidated to guerrilla status, the capacity and will were frequently lacking to administer complex reforms in systematic fashion. Passive and defensive survival strategies were at least as important in weathering these storms as what lay behind the heroic public images projected by the party.

Consolidation in North China

Systematic pacification in North China in late 1939 and 1940 worked outward from the areas held more or less firmly by the Japanese and puppets, into guerrilla and contested zones. The ultimate goal was to crush resistance or render it ineffective. The approach was first to sweep an area clear of anti-Japanese elements, then set up a series of inter-connected

[75] Kataoka Tetsuya, 200–6.

strong points capable of quickly reinforcing each other. This was to be followed by extension of puppet government to take increasing charge of civil administration and 'pacification maintenance', while Japanese forces repeated the first steps farther out in contested territory. Violence was employed selectively against individuals, groups or villages charged with acts of resistance. Selective violence aimed to deter active participation in Communist-led programmes, to deprive Communist forces of a population willing to harbour them, and to persuade informers to come forward. Such, at least, was the strategy. While it fell far short of achieving Japanese objectives, it was effective enough to cause the 8RA great concern.

In practice, the framework of this strategy was the main transport lines. Railways and roads, adequately fortified and protected, would separate resistance forces from one another and deprive them of mobility, one of their most effective weapons. These 'cage' (*ch'iu-lung*) tactics made it possible to enlarge pacified areas by nibbling outwards 'as a silkworm feeds on mulberry leaves' (*ts'an-shih*). In addition, this approach aimed at the more effective economic exploitation of North China. To this end, the Japanese worked hard to improve and extend both the railway and road networks. When the war began, both the Cheng-T'ai (Shihchiachuang-Taiyuan) and the T'ung-P'u (Tat'ung-T'ungkwan) lines in Shansi province were metre-gauge, incompatible with the standard-gauge lines of the rest of China – part of Yen Hsi-shan's scheme to prevent penetration of his province (see map 6 and table 5). By the end of 1939, the Japanese had used forced labour to convert both lines to standard gauge. One benefit was the greater ease with which high-quality anthracite coal could be moved from the Ching-hsing mines (on the Cheng-T'ai line) to industrial users in North China and Manchukuo. Of the newly constructed roads and railway lines, the most important was the Te-Shih line (from Te-chow in north-eastern Shantung to Shihchiachuang); its construction began in June 1940 and was completed in November, connecting the Tientsin-Pukow, Peiping-Hankow and Cheng-T'ai lines and thus facilitating troop movements and the transport of raw cotton. With the completion of the Te-Shih link, the Japanese had direct connections between the point of their furthest advance, at the elbow of the Yellow River, and all the major cities of North China, and beyond to Manchukuo. Communist sources began to speak of the 'transportation war', and to note with concern the moats and ditches, the blockhouses, and the frequent patrols protecting the lines.

Both militarily and economically, these measures weighed heavily on Communist-led forces in North China and on the populations under their control, particularly on the plains of central and eastern Hopei. One measure of their effectiveness was the rapid decline in 'acts of sabotage' against North China railways in 1939 and the first half of 1940 (see table 14; but 'transportation accidents' almost certainly includes covert sabotage). A cadre in Chin-Ch'a-Chi reported that, in mid-1940, 'The enemy has adopted a blockhouse policy, like that of the [Kiangsi soviet]. They are spread like a constellation. In central Hopei alone, there are about 500, separated by one to three miles.'[76] Normal trading patterns were disrupted as Japanese or puppets occupied administrative-commercial centres, and peasants were caught between regulations imposed by the Communists and those enforced by the other side. Finally, landlords, moneylenders, loafers, bandits – all those who felt abused by the new order in the base areas – could take advantage of pacification programmes to try to recover lost influence or simply gain revenge. Some turned informers. After 8RA and local units had been driven away, they might kill remaining cadres or activists and settle scores with their peasant supporters. Until the 'first anti-Communist upsurge' was defeated, local elites and other disaffected elements might also find Nationalist support. It was even possible for an armed band to operate for several months in consolidated regions of the CCC base, killing cadres as they went.[77] Of this period, P'eng Te-huai later recalled,

Under the enemy's brutal pressure, the masses in a few districts even wavered or capitulated. From March to July 1940, large areas of the North China bases were reduced to guerrilla regions. Before the Cage-bursting battle [i.e. 100 Regiments], we controlled only two county seats, P'ing-hsün in the T'ai-hang mountains and P'ien-kuan in north-west Shansi. Masses who had previously had only one set of obligations now had two [toward the anti-Japanese regime and toward the puppet regime].[78]

The situation in North China had not yet reached a crisis, but it was certainly serious. Some action was necessary to regain the initiative.

The Battle of the Hundred Regiments

On 20 August 1940, the Eighth Route Army launched its largest sustained offensive of the war on Japan. Screened from observation by the 'green curtain' of tall crops, and making the most of the element of surprise, a force of 22 regiments (about 40,000 men) attacked the transportation network of North China, singling out the rather lightly defended Cheng-T'ai line for particularly heavy assault. All the major railway lines

---

[76] *Ibid.* 206. Translation paraphrased.   [77] Hartford, 'Repression', 432–4.
[78] P'eng Te-huai, *Tzu-shu*, 235. If P'eng is correct, then the CCP did not control *any* county seats in the Chin-Ch'a-Chi base at this time.

and motor roads were brought under attack and repeatedly cut. Heavy damage was inflicted on roadbeds, bridges, switching yards, and associated installations. Facilities at the important Ching-hsing coal mines were destroyed and production halted for nearly a year. This first phase of the campaign, lasting about thee weeks, gave way to a second phase during which the main targets were the blockhouses and other strongpoints the Japanese had pushed out into contested areas. This shift corresponded to shifting vulnerabilities: while the Japanese were actively using the strongpoint system, the transportation network was less securely defended; conversely, when outlying detachments were pulled back to stem the attacks on railways and roads, the blockhouses were more attractive targets. Indeed, the campaign aimed to force the Japanese to give up their cage and silkworm strategy, pull back to well-defended garrisons and leave the countryside once again to the Communists. During this second phase of the campaign many more regiments entered the fray, until a total of 104 were involved. Years later, P'eng Te-huai, the commander responsible for the Hundred Regiments, said cryptically that they joined in 'spontaneously', without orders from his 8RA headquarters.[79] By early October, the second phase was drawing to a close, and a third was developing, during which reinforced Japanese columns sought to engage and destroy 8RA units. Several fierce counter-attacks punctuated the next two months, after which the Hundred Regiments campaign was considered at an end.

The background of the Hundred Regiments offensive – who authorized and planned it and for what reasons – still remains unclear. The Japanese response to this campaign was so ferocious that it looked in retrospect to have been a mistake, and some leaders, especially Mao, may have wished to disavow it. There are indirect hints in his writings during the succeeding months and years that he viewed it critically, and he may have had misgivings all along. It was not his sort of military strategy. Over twenty years later, during the Cultural Revolution, Red Guards charged that Mao had not even known of the plan in advance, due to the deliberate duplicity of P'eng Te-huai, who was then being denounced. Though this seems unlikely, it may have some substance. Writing in his own defence against these charges, P'eng stated that after 8RA headquarters, which was located not in Yenan but in Chin-Ch'a-Chi, had planned the operation, it sent mobilization orders downward to each regional command, and also notified the Central Military Affairs Commission, headed by Mao. In the original plan, the action was to begin in early September. But, writes P'eng,

In order to prevent enemy discovery and to insure simultaneous surprise assaults, thereby inflicting an even greater blow to the enemy and the puppets, we began about ten days ahead of the original schedule, i.e. during the last week of August. So we did not wait for approval from the Military Affairs Commission (this was wrong), but went right into combat earlier than planned.[80]

There is also the question of the spontaneous action of over eighty regiments, unauthorized by 8RA headquarters, to say nothing of Yenan.

If P'eng Te-huai's account – written in 1970, shortly before his death – is accepted, then Mao and Party Central had no hand in conceiving or planning the Hundred Regiments campaign, and the 'grand strategy' motives for undertaking it disappear, except as they may have been considered by P'eng and his colleagues. One of these alleged motives was to counter any tendency toward capitulation on the part of Chiang Kai-shek and the Chungking regime: if the war heated up and the CCP threw itself into the fray, any accommodation between Chiang and the Japanese would look like cowardly surrender. Related to this explanation was the sensitivity of Communist leaders to the charge that they were simply using the war to expand their influence, avoiding the Japanese and leaving most of the real fighting to KMT armies. The Nationalists were giving much publicity to their claim that deliberate and cynical CCP policy was to devote 70 per cent of its efforts to expansion, 20 per cent to coping with the KMT, and only 10 per cent to opposing Japan.[81] A third suggested motive was to divert attention from the New Fourth Army's offensives against Nationalist forces in Central China, which were peaking at just about this time.

P'eng Te-huai acknowledged that the campaign was 'too protracted', but defended its importance in maintaining the CCP's anti-Japanese image in the wake of anti-friction conflicts, in demonstrating the failure of the cage and silkworm policy, in returning no fewer than twenty-six county seats to base control, and in keeping 'waverers' in line. Even if these reasons were less important than regional and tactical considerations in undertaking this campaign, there was no bar to using them for propaganda after the fact. Whatever misgivings Mao and Party Central may have had, they kept them to themselves. Mao radioed congratulations to P'eng on his smashing victory, and in public statements the Hundred Regiments were made the stuff of legends.

[80] *Ibid.* 236-7. P'eng also asserted that the military actions of the first anti-Communist upsurge were planned and executed on his orders alone without any prior knowledge or approval from Yenan. If so, Mao and his colleagues in Yenan must have felt great frustration at being unable to control senior commanders in both North China and Central China.

[81] This has become an article of faith in Nationalist histories. I have examined this issue in some detail and believe that no such policy was ever enunciated; in this sense the charge is a fabrication. But in some times and places, actual CCP behaviour approximated this division of effort. See Van Slyke, *Enemies and friends*, 159.

Mopping-up campaigns after the Hundred Regiments (1941–1943)

If the Hundred Regiments campaign aimed to defeat Japanese pacification efforts, it hardly succeeded. Shocked and stung by the 8RA's action, the North China Area Army redoubled its efforts to bring North China under control. Under General Tada and his successor, General Okamura Yasuji (July 1941–November 1944), the Japanese inflicted brutal and sustained violence on all the North China bases. Between 1941 and 1944, about 150,000 Japanese troops were assigned full-time to pacification duty, assisted by about 100,000 Chinese in units of widely varying description and effectiveness. The balance of the NCAA (150,000 to 200,000 men) was assigned to other tasks such as garrisoning major cities, and containing Nationalist forces. Communist regulars were estimated at about 250,000 in the base areas and 40,000 in SKN.

The Japanese and their Chinese auxiliaries invested even more than before in the construction of moats, ditches, palisades and blockhouses. Japanese sources claimed that by 1942 their forces had built 11,860 km of blockade line and 7,700 fortified posts, mostly in the Hopei plains and foothills of the Taihang mountains. A huge trench ran for 500 km along the west side of the P'ing-Han railway line, with a depopulated and constantly patrolled zone on either side. The 250 Japanese outposts established in southern Hopei by December 1940 were more than quadrupled by mid-1942. These were the principal measures for control over the plains areas, and by the end of 1941 all of the Communist bases in such terrain had been reduced to guerrilla status. Many main force units (such as those of Lü Cheng-ts'ao and Yang Hsiu-feng) were forced to move west into the mountains in order to survive.

What distinguished the new Tada-Okamura approach from earlier tactics were the much larger and more protracted search-and-destroy missions sent into the core areas of the mountain bases, and the substitution of indiscriminate, generalized violence for the selective repression employed prior to the Hundred Regiments' offensive. These were the infamous 'Three-all' mop-up campaigns: kill all, burn all, loot all. Frustrated by their continuing inability to distinguish ordinary peasants from Communists, the Japanese made war on all. After trying to seal off important consolidated regions of the base areas, the Japanese sent in very large detachments, seeking out Communist forces, civilian cadres and activists. But, in addition, they sought to destroy base facilities and stockpiles of war material, to disrupt agriculture by burning crops or interfering with planting and harvesting, and to carry off stores of grain. Entire villages were razed, and all living things found in them killed. Unlike the earlier mop-ups, which swept an area and then departed, these

TABLE 15

Japanese campaigns and blockade system in Chin-Ch'a-Chi

Campaign began	Duration (months)	Troop strength	Targeted area
August 1941	2+	100,000	Pei-yueh
Early 1942	3+	40,000	East Hopei
May 1942	3+	50,000	Central Hopei
September 1943	3	40,000	Pei-yueh

Status of blockade system in Chin-Ch'a-Chi, December 1942

	Pei-yueh	Central Hopei	East Hopei	P'ing-pei	Total
Base points and forts	1,219	1,635	329	175	3,358
Highways (in *li*)	9,238	11,987	3,062	2,618	26,905
Blockade ditches (in *li*)	1,779	5,000	924	282	7,985
Blockade walls (in *li*)	395	502	N/A	N/A	897

Source: Hartford, 'Repression', 345, 347.

campaigns left troops in the targeted areas for considerable periods of time to 'comb' back and forth, and to establish at least temporary strongpoints in the more accessible areas of mountainous bases. The data in Table 15 show how extensive these operations were in Chin-Ch'a-Chi; similar campaigns were mounted against all the North China bases.

These mopping-up campaigns took a heavy and painful toll of the rural population through which they passed. Undoubtedly, those harsh tactics and the atrocities that so frequently accompanied them did indeed cause many peasants, rich and poor alike, to harbour deep hatred of the Japanese and commit themselves more fully to the Communist side. But inner-party sources also depict many instances in which this repression served even more effectively than earlier efforts to drive a wedge between the party and peasantry:

If we only stress concealment...we are bound to be divorced from the masses. The morale of the masses cannot be sustained for long either. On the other hand, if we only seek fleeting gratification in careless fighting, we may also invite still more cruel enemy suppression. That will also alienate the masses.[82]

Communist spokesmen acknowledged that, in the North China bases, population under party control fell from 44 million to 25 million, and the 8RA declined from 400,000 to 300,000.[83] Local sources paint an even

[82] Yang Ch'eng-wu, quoted in Kataoka Tetsuya, 280.
[83] Many of the 25 million were living in semi-consolidated or guerrilla areas; the population in consolidated areas declined even more sharply than these general figures would indicate. Only

grimmer picture. By 1942, 90 per cent of the plains bases were reduced to guerrilla status or outright enemy control. In the mountainous T'ai-yueh district of the Chin-Chi-Lu-Yü base, a cadre admitted that 'not a single county was kept intact and the government offices of all its twelve counties were exiled in Chin-yuan'.[84] All twenty-six county seats occupied in the wake of the Hundred Regiments fighting were lost.

Although Japanese pacification was aimed mainly at the 8RA, this was not always the case. Nationalist forces with whom the Japanese had been unable to reach 'understandings' were attacked also, partly to free more forces for anti-Communist action, partly to keep pressure on Chiang Kai-shek, and partly to have more successes to report. The most significant of these actions took place during the spring of 1941 in southern Shansi, when over twenty divisions under General Wei Li-huang were pushed south of the Yellow River (the Battle of the Chung-t'iao Mountains, or the Chūgen campaign). Almost as important were later actions in Shantung against Yü Hsueh-chung and Shen Hung-lieh. These cleared additional areas for Communist penetration once Japanese and puppet forces withdrew; the consequences became fully evident when Japanese pressure on the Communists moderated during the last phase of the war.

Japanese consolidation in Central China

The China Expeditionary Army followed a different pattern from that pursued by the North China Area Army. Although the total forces available to the CEA were larger than those of the NCAA (c. 300,000 in Central China, and another 165,000 in the south), a smaller proportion was devoted to pacification, perhaps 50,000 to 75,000. Most of the remainder of the CEA was deployed opposite Nationalist units in Hupei, Hunan and Kiangsi. On the other hand, larger and presumably more effective puppet forces could be employed in the Lower Yangtze region because of its proximity to the Nanking regime of Wang Ching-wei.

Japanese and puppet forces concentrated on the area of greatest strategic importance to them: the Nanking-Shanghai-Hangchow triangle,

---

a part of 8RA losses was due to direct combat casualties. Other factors included reassignment of some regulars to service as guerrilla forces (to strengthen the latter, to merge more closely with the local population, to reduce burdens of troop support); elimination of inferior or disabled soldiers; and desertion. One CCP document from late 1939 (presumably Chin-Ch'a-Chi) gave two examples of desertion rates: 16·4% in 'one main force unit', and 20·8% in 'one newly established guerrilla unit'. Desertion was particularly serious when a unit was moved out of its home area; peasant-soldiers in the local forces often refused to leave. This was yet another motive for reducing some full-time soldiers to militia status.

[84] Warren Kuo, *History*, 4.75.

together with the region just north of the Yangtze River and east of the Grand Canal. The Wuhan region, farther west, was also heavily pacified. These efforts and a strong Nationalist presence in Hupei prevented Li Hsien-nien and the N4A's 5th Division from setting up a fully consolidated base in the Ta-pieh Mountains until late in the war. But other areas in Kiangsu, Anhwei and Honan were deemed less significant from either a military or economic viewpoint. Japanese forces maintained control over major transportation routes in east-central China and over the major cities. Occasional sweeps were sent through remoter areas. These were rather easily evaded by N4A elements but inflicted serious damage on Chungking-affiliated forces.[85]

Not until the second half of 1941 did the Japanese begin serious pacification in the Yangtze delta, with the adoption by General Hata Shunroku of a plan to establish 'model peace zones'. This was a phased programme in which carefully defined areas were to be brought under ever tighter military, political and economic security. When one zone had reached a certain level of development, an adjacent area would be added. The first step was to carry out intense clearing operations in order to drive out all resistors and begin with a clean slate. Tight boundary controls were then enforced, using dense bamboo palisades or other defensive works. Within the zone, local police undertook careful population registration, and administrative personnel were assigned a comprehensive programme of 'self-government, self-defence, and economic self-improvement'. In the most developed of the model peace zones, Japanese troop density reached 1·3 per sq. km., three and a half times larger than in North China. Harsh coercion was applied as necessary. As a result, security within the model peace zones in the northern Yangtze delta became quite good. Tax revenues collected by agents of the Nanking regime went up sharply, as did compulsory labour service. Japanese soldiers and well-known local collaborators claimed, with relief, that they could come and go without fear of ambush.

Yet even at their most successful, these efforts were not a general solution to the problem of Chinese resistance, either Nationalist or Communist. The model peace zones required so much manpower and other resources that they were very limited in extent. By 1943, when such efforts no longer had high priority, only a few such zones were classified as having passed through all the planned phases, the remainder being stalled in one or another preliminary stage. The only such effort well to the north of the Yangtze was the late (February 1944) and almost completely futile creation of a new province, Huai-Hai, with its capital

85 Ch'en Yung-fa, 110–11.

at Lienyunkang. And even within the securest of the model peace zones, both the Communists and the Nationalists were able to maintain a continuing low-level presence.

Further reasons for the limited success and ultimate failure of the model peace zones were that many tasks had sooner or later to be turned over to the Chinese themselves, either Wang Ching-wei appointees or recruits from the local populace. Both were the constant despair of the Japanese: the former because of their incompetence, corruption and factional disputes; the latter because they would do only what they felt compelled to do or what was in their self-interest. In the end, the model peace zones bore witness to the short-term and territorially limited effectiveness of superior power. They also demonstrated that such a solution was no solution at all across the vast breadth and population of 'occupied China'.

CCP RESPONSES: SURVIVAL AND NEW POLICIES

The combined effects of friction and pacification confronted the Chinese Communist Party with its most serious and prolonged crises of the Sino-Japanese War. Ironically, these challenges were exacerbated because Communist military and political expansion early in the war had often stressed rapid growth at the expense of consolidation and deep penetration of the villages. At the same time, after three good years, adverse weather led to poor harvests in 1940 and 1941, adding to already serious economic problems. The CCP's responses to these challenges, begun in piecemeal fashion, were as many-sided as the problems themselves. Some existing policies were overhauled and adapted to new circumstances. Some new policies were continued long after the immediate difficulties had been overcome, while others were ad hoc, common sense measures to minimize losses or gain new support. In retrospect the new pattern can be seen as early as 1940. By 1942 it was in full swing. The Maoist leadership now saw it as an integral whole.

Inseparable from the urgent practical tasks of this arduous period was the definitive elevation of Mao Tse-tung as the supreme leader and ideological guiding centre of the CCP. Between 1942 and 1944, the last major elements were added to complete 'the thought of Mao Tse-tung', and the last remnants of opposition to his primacy were removed or silenced. From this time, at the latest, the movement bore the indelible stamp of his policies and personality. The experience of these years shaped the CCP. Like the Long March a decade earlier, the Yenan era took on an independent existence – part history, part myth – capable of influencing future events.

New policies in Shen-Kan-Ning

Economic problems. The principal economic changes in Shen-Kan-Ning during the middle years of the war have already been mentioned: the end of the Nationalist subsidy, the blockade, and poorer harvests than in the years immediately preceding. These changes had profound, widespread and enduring effects. They very nearly caused the economy of SKN to collapse. Looking back on this period, Mao wrote in 1945: 'When [the war] began we had food and clothing. But things got steadily worse until we were in great difficulty, running short of grain, short of cooking oil and salt, short of bedding and clothing, short of funds.'[86]

The Nationalists' eonomic warfare deprived SKN of its principal source of 'hard currency' and either cut off or greatly changed the terms of its trade with other regions of unoccupied China. The party, government and army bureaucracies together with large numbers of immigrants, made the Border Region's resources, insufficient even in normal times, all the more inadequate. The goal of the party, therefore, was to bring the region as close as possible to economic self-sufficiency. Although full autarky was impossible, considerable progress was eventually made. Meanwhile economic conditions deteriorated rapidly.

All sources agree on the severity of the problems. Deprived of its main source of Nationalist *yuan* currency, yet continuing to depend on external trade for cotton cloth and nearly all manufactured goods, SKN once again adopted its own Border Region currency so that *yuan* reserves could continue, so far as possible, to finance essential imports. After 1939, these circumstances fuelled an inflation even more rapid than that experienced in Chungking (see table 16). In all areas of the economy, 1941 was the year of deepest crisis.

Loss of revenue, rapidly worsening terms of external trade, and inflation forced the Communists to find new income. Confiscations and 'voluntary' contributions were no longer fruitful, because most landlords and other holders of wealth had already passed through the agrarian revolution, before the more moderate united front land policies came into effect. They now had nothing more to give. Reluctantly but inevitably, the party was forced to impose taxes on virtually the entire population of Shen-Kan-Ning. Taxes were of three general types: (1) grain levies, based on actual production rather than landholdings; (2) other taxes in kind, particularly of straw and wool; and (3) taxes in cash. These levies were most sharply felt by the middle and lower-middle peasants, who up

---

[86] Mao, *SW*, 3.328–9.

TABLE 16

Price indices, 1937–1945: 'Free China' and Yenan

	'Free China'	Yenan
1937	100	100
1938	145	143
1939	323	237
1940	724	500
1941	1,980	2,200
1942	6,620	9,900
1943	22,800	119,900
1944	75,500	564,700
1945	179,000	N/A

Sources: for 'Free China', Arthur N. Young, *China's Wartime finance and inflation, 1937–1945*, 152; for Yenan, see Schran, *Guerrilla economy*, 184.

until this time had paid few if any taxes. The poorest one-fifth or so of the peasantry (those with an annual per capita income of up to about one hundred pounds of grain) remained exempt from grain levies and other taxes in kind, but by 1941 grain tax levies had increased twenty times over those collected in 1938 – a burden that created considerable popular resentment. Thereafter, tax levels dropped off a bit until the substantial decline in 1945, which was probably caused by a poor harvest and reduction of public sector expenditures following the Japanese surrender (see table 17).

In 1941, this burden was very close to estimates of taxes collected by provincial authorities in the early 1930s, but it was much fairer, being imposed on a sharply progressive basis. To ease the tax load on poorer elements of the peasantry and to mitigate as much as possible their resentment, Party Central began in mid-1940 to issue more urgent calls for rent and interest reduction, hoping thereby partially to substitute one exaction for another.

Taxes in kind on straw and wool, earlier abolished by the Border Region government, were reimposed in 1941. The straw was badly needed as fodder for transport animals in both the civilian and military sectors, and wool deliveries helped meet the need for textiles.

Several types of cash taxes were either imposed for the first time, or raised to higher levels. Sales taxes on a wide range of commodities and services resembled the often condemned 'miscellaneous taxes and surcharges' of previous regimes, but they were calculated in such a way as to discourage unnecessary consumption of imported products and luxuries such as tobacco, liquor, and religious items. Various commercial taxes were also collected from the many small-scale private enterprises

TABLE 17
TABLE 17
SKN grain tax levies, 1937–45
(in piculs: 1 picul = c. 330 lbs.)

	Grain produced	Grain collected	%
1937	1,260,000	10,000	0.8
1938	1,270,000	10,000	0.8
1939	1,370,000	50,000	3.6
1940	1,430,000	90,000	6.3
1941	1,470,000	200,000	13.6
1942	1,500,000	160,000	10.7
1943	1,600,000	180,000	11.3
1944	1,750,000	160,000	9.1
1945	1,600,000	125,000	7.8

Source: Schran, Guerrilla economy, 128,188.

still existing in SKN; in 1941 these brought in about 8 million SKN *yuan* (equivalent to 30,000 piculs of millet).

Since income from these taxes was insufficient, such expedients as deficit financing and increased corvée labour were also employed. But Mao warned that juggling finances and increasing demands on SKN's populace were no long-term solution:

All empty words are useless; we must give the people visible material wealth ... The primary aspect of our work is not to ask things of the people but to give things to the people. What can we give the people? Under present conditions in the Shen-Kan-Ning Border Region, we can organize, lead, and help the people to develop production and increase their material wealth. And on this basis we can step-by-step raise their political awareness and cultural level.[87]

It was above all in the production campaigns that the party and the region finally stemmed economic deterioration and achieved stability – albeit at a lowered level – once again. No campaign of the period received more attention; in December 1942, Mao published his own extensive yet unfinished essay on 'Economic and financial problems'. Although ideology lurks in the background, nearly all his proposals stand on their own. Many were commonsense, pragmatic measures that rural reformers had advocated for years, but had been unable to carry out. Space permits mention of only the most important areas in which production was significantly raised. Table 17 shows that between 1937 and 1944, grain production increased almost 40 per cent. Cotton production was nil at the beginning of the war and still negligible in 1939; by 1944, it had reached 3 million catties of lint and twice that in seed. Livestock also

[87] Watson, *Mao Zedong*, 232.

recorded impressive gains. Given the poor endowments of SKN and very modest new technological inputs, this was a remarkable achievement obtained by better and more varied organization, widened market incentives, and dramatic increases in cultivated land. Between 1937 and 1945, sown area almost doubled (from 8·6 to 15·2 million *mou*).[88]

The output of the weaving industry paralleled the production of raw cotton. A mere 7,370 bolts (*c.* 25 m² per bolt) in 1938, it doubled over each of the next two years, reached 45,000 bolts in 1942, then shot up to 105,000 bolts in 1943.[89] Natural resource extraction (salt, coal, a few primitive oil and gas wells), irrigation, expanded pasturage, and afforestation were all actively developed. By 1944, many problems still faced leaders and local cadres alike in Shen-Kan-Ning, but by that time the economic perils of the middle years of the war had been sufficiently overcome to permit relative security, renewed and deepened popular support or acceptance, and a tempered self-confidence.

Rectification. In the ideological and political realms, the most visible effort was the 'rectification campaign'.[90] It formally began on 1 February 1942, when more than one thousand party cadres assembled in Yenan to hear Mao Tse-tung address the opening of the CCP's Party School. Cadre education and concern for the party's ideological soundness had always been an important concern, as can be seen in the earlier writings of Mao, Liu Shao-ch'i and others. But the decision to launch this particular campaign was probably made at an 'enlarged session' of the Political Bureau, held in September 1941, which called for 'development of a party-wide ideological revolution' and elimination of 'factions which formerly existed and played an unwholesome role in the history of our party.'[91] Unfortunately, none of the documents of this very significant meeting are presently available and little is known about it.

The campaign was never formally declared to be over, but by the second half of 1944 its principal goals were apparently thought accomplished and it no longer made a major claim upon the time and attention of party members. Throughout, the rectification campaign was an intra-party exercise, limited to party members, none of whom could ignore the compelling force of Mao's addresses and statements delivered during the spring and summer of 1942. In Shen-Kan-Ning, no party member could

---

[88] Schran, 120.

[89] Schran, 146. Textile production data are broken down into various sectors (percentages for 1943): home industry (44%), state-owned enterprises (31%), capitalist enterprises (19%), Chinese Industrial Cooperatives (6%).

[90] 'Rectification' is the customary translation of *cheng-tun tso-feng*. *Cheng-tun* means to set things aright by a very thorough shaking up; *tso-feng* refers to all aspects of the way one does things, to one's 'work style'.

[91] Wylie, 166.

avoid the incessant small-group sessions in which rectification documents were struggled through to proper understanding and internalization. For the party as a whole, this was an arduous exercise in discipline and consensus-building.

The rapid expansion of the party during the first few years of the war had made for an extremely heterogeneous membership, the majority of which was organizationally inexperienced and new to Marxism-Leninism, to say nothing of the evolving body of Mao's thought. Intellectuals, students, illiterate peasants, hard-bitten Long March veterans, even some sons of landlords all joined the expanding party. Young men and women from middle-class families in Shanghai and Peking were thrown together with villagers who had never been further from home than the nearest market town and who instinctively distrusted all outsiders. It was no secret that numerous incompetents, opportunists, and spies had made it into the party. Mao's most recent rivals – Chang Kuo-t'ao and Wang Ming – still had sympathizers among mid-echelon cadres. If, from Mao's standpoint, the party was successfully to meet the challenges facing it and be prepared for the uncertainties of the future, these elements had to be purified, fused, and honed.

His own doctrines would lead the way, justified and undergirded by the principles of Marxism-Leninism. This was the 'sinification of Marxism', 'the creative application of Marxism-Leninism to the concrete realities of China'.[92] Coached by ideologues such as Ch'en Po-ta and assisted by such experienced and able colleagues as Liu Shao-ch'i, Chou En-lai and Ch'en Yun – among others – Mao Tse-tung now felt ready to claim both ideological and personal dominance over the Communist movement in China.

In his address to the Party School on 1 February 1942, Mao sounded the keynotes. After routine praise for the basically sound condition of the party, he defined its three principal defects as 'subjectivism, sectarianism, and party formalism'. He enlarged on all three in later pronouncements.[93] Mao gave these vague-sounding terms vivid, earthy meanings which are by no means easy to summarize. Subjectivism referred mainly to those who regarded abstract book-knowledge of Marxism-Leninism as a

[92] See Stuart Schram, ch. 14 below. A functional analysis of Mao's ideology, drawing a distinction between 'thought' (*ssu-hsiang*) and 'theory' (*li-lun*), may be found in Franz Schurmann, *Ideology and organization in Communist China*, 2nd ed., 21ff. Schurmann argues that Chinese Communists distinguished between pure theory – the general and abstract principles of Marxism-Leninism, valid everywhere – and the creative application of these principles to concrete situations ('thought'). For the historical evolution of Mao's ideological/political primacy, see Wylie, *The emergence of Maoism*. Wylie disputes Schurmann's analysis.

[93] *MTTC* 4.63. Many of the *cheng-feng* documents may be found in Boyd Compton, *Mao's China: party reform documents, 1942–44.*

talisman or panacea, but made no effort to apply its principles to actual problems. These half-baked intellectuals were like chefs who studied recipes but never cooked a dish, or those who 'merely take the arrow in hand, twist it back and forth, and say again and again in praise, "excellent arrow, excellent arrow" but are never willing to shoot it'. Instead,

Our comrades must understand that we do not study Marxism-Leninism because it is pleasing to the eye, or because it has some mystical value.... It is only extremely useful.... We must tell them honestly, 'Your dogma is useless', or, to use an impolite phrase, it is less useful than shit. Now, dogshit can fertilize a field, and man's can feed a dog, but dogma? It can't fertilize a field or feed a dog. What use is it?[94]

But if Mao's most scathing remarks were directed at dogmatic intellectuals who acted like the mandarins of old, subjectivism also had an opposite side: empiricism. This was the tendency to view each situation exclusively in its own terms and to rely only upon one's own experience, with no ideological guidance. Empiricism was more likely to be encountered in poorly educated peasant cadres whose horizons were narrow. In both cases, Mao called for the wedding of theory with practice.

Sectarianism was nearly as serious. Here Mao spoke of democratic-centralism, charging the sectarians (naming only Chang Kuo-t'ao, already read out of the party, but again implying Wang Ming) with forgetting centralism – the ultimate authority of the Central Committee, now clearly controlled by Mao and his followers. Sectarianism had seemingly prosaic dimensions as well, affecting the relations between local cadres and outsiders, between army and civilian cadres, between old and new cadres, and between party members and those outside the party. Sometimes individual units or localities put their interests ahead of the general good by 'not sending cadres on request, sending inferior men as cadres, exploiting one's neighbors and completely disregarding other organs, localities, and men. This reveals a complete loss of the spirit of communism.'[95] Although these problems sounded ordinary, they were both serious and quite intractable. Their effects might be ameliorated, but were never fully removed.

Mao then turned to the subject of 'party formalism', or *tang pa-ku*, devoting an entire address to this subject.[96] *Pa-ku* summoned up for Mao's listeners memories of the rigidly structured 'eight-legged' essays which had been the centrepiece of the old imperial civil service examination

---

[94] *MTTC* 8.75; Compton, 21–2. Such crudities have been expunged from Mao's *Selected works*.

[95] Compton, 27.

[96] 'Oppose party formalism' (8 Feb. 1942). Contained in Compton, 33–53. The short extracts below are drawn from this source (sometimes retranslated).

system. Although he spoke of *pa-ku* most directly in terms of the way in which many party members attempted to communicate with the masses (in literature, propaganda, directives, etc.), he clearly meant this rubric to cover all manifestations of dogmatic subjectivism and sectarianism: 'if we oppose subjectivism and sectarianism but do not at the same time eradicate party formalism, they still have a place to hide'. Once again using the language of the *lao-pai-hsing*, the ordinary peasant, Mao described – perhaps with deliberate irony – eight ways in which *pa-ku* formalism showed itself. It was wordy, windy and disgusting, 'like the lazy old woman's long, foul-smelling footbindings which should be thrown into the privy at once'. It was pretentious, abstract, insipid, cliché-ridden; worse, it made a false show of authority and aimed to intimidate the reader or hearer. It contained many foreign terms and constructions which had little meaning for the average person, but seemed very learned. It often lapsed into irresponsibility and pessimism, to the detriment of the people, the resistance, and the revolution. No one, Mao asserted, would understand or listen to a party that spoke in *pa-ku* style, much less want to follow it or join it.

Writers, intellectuals, former students and educated cadres generally were obviously the principal object of Mao's attack. They were, of course, more numerous in the Shen-Kan-Ning base than anywhere else, and many of them were becoming restive and dissatisfied. Just a few weeks after Mao's speeches before the Party School and the issuance of a central directive on cadre education, a number of prominent intellectuals loosed a barrage in the pages of *Liberation Daily*.[97] Ting Ling, the famous woman author, criticized the party's compromises in the area of sexual equality and the gap between noble ideals and shabby performance more generally. Others such as Ai Ch'ing and Hsiao Chün added their voices. Perhaps the most biting critique was contained in an essay entitled 'Wild lilies', by an obscure writer, Wang Shih-wei, who employed the satiric *tsa-wen* (informal essay) style made famous by Lu Hsun. Although none of these critics questioned the legitimacy of the party or the necessity for revolution, they felt that art had an existence apart from politics and they graphically portrayed the dark side of life in Yenan. By implication, they were asserting the autonomy of the individual and the role of the intellectual as social critic, just as they had – with party blessing – before the war in Kuomintang-controlled areas of China.

[97] Merle Goldman, *Literary dissent in Communist China*, 21ff. At this time the chief editor of *Liberation Daily* was Ch'in Pang-hsien (Po Ku), and one of his associates was Chang Wen-t'ien. Both had belonged to Wang Ming's faction in the early 1930s, though they had later moved much closer than he to the Maoist camp. Yet without their approval, the dissidents could not possibly have had their writings published in *Liberation Daily*. Ting Ling was the paper's cultural affairs editor.

What had been praiseworthy in Shanghai during the early 1930s, however, was unacceptable in Yenan a decade later. These intellectuals must have felt they were taking a risk, but they could hardly have anticipated the severity of the party's response. All of them were severely criticized and made to recant, though most were eventually rehabilitated. Wang Shih-wei, less prominent and more corrosive than most, was repeatedly attacked in mass meetings, discredited, jailed, and secretly executed in 1947.

If his February addresses and other party directives had failed properly to educate the intellectuals, Mao was ready to go further. He took these steps in May 1942, in the lengthy 'Talks at the Yenan Forum on art and literature'. Here he laid down, in explicit detail, the role of intellectuals under the leadership of the Chinese Communist Party. This statement remained authoritative throughout Mao's lifetime, and continues after his death to exert its influence. In brief, 'Talks' denies the independence and autonomy of the mind, apart from social class. One can only speak or write from a class standpoint; intellectuals are quite wrong to think that there is some objectively neutral ground upon which they can stand. Since this is so, art is one form of politics and the question then becomes *which* class it will represent. Revolutionary intellectuals must take their stand with the proletariat for otherwise they serve the bourgeoisie or other reactionary classes, even when they deny they are doing so. It follows that the ultimate arbiter and guide for literature and art is the Chinese Communist Party (led by Mao Tse-tung), since this is the vanguard, the concentrated will, of the working classes.

Mao thus turned the tables on the intellectuals: no longer independent critics, they were now the targets of criticism. So long as intellectuals were willing to play the role of handmaidens to the revolution, as defined by the CCP, they were needed and welcomed. There was no denying their creativity and their skills, but these talents were to be valued only within the limits set by the party. Socialist realism was to be the major mode of literature and art, given naturalistic Chinese forms that would be at once accessible to the masses and expressed in their own idiom, not that of Shanghai salons. This meant that intellectuals had to go among the peasants and workers, absorb their language and experience the harsh realities of their lives. Altogether, Mao was calling for the transformation of party intellectuals and of party members more generally.

By April 1942, the Central Committee had published a list of twenty-two documents to serve as the basis of cadre study and examination.[98] The

---

[98] See Compton, 6–7. The list contained six items by Mao; five Central Committee documents (probably authored in whole or in part by Mao); one each by Liu Shao-ch'i, Ch'en Yun and K'ang Sheng; a propaganda guide; an army report; three by Stalin; one by Lenin and Stalin; one by

means employed to inculcate their teachings included the now familiar small-group study and struggle sessions, usually involving 'criticism and self-criticism'. Straightforward instruction combined with peer pressure, self-examination and coercive persuasion were designed to build to ever higher levels of intensity until catharsis and commitment were achieved. Mao likened the process to the curing of a disease: 'The first step in reasoning [sic] is to give the patient a good jolt: yell at him, "You're sick!" so the patient will be frightened and break out all over in sweat; then you can treat him effectively.' Yet the object is to '"cure the disease, save the patient"...The whole purpose is to save people, not cure them to death.' 'Savage struggle' and 'merciless attack' should be unleashed on the enemy, but not on one's comrades.

Mao's apotheosis did not, of course, occur suddenly in the midst of the *cheng-feng* campaign. His own instincts for power, his success in building an influential and able coalition, and the proven effectiveness of his policies were the main causes of his gradual rise to unchallenged pre-eminence during the years after the Long March. As noted above (pages 231–2), the parallel rise in stature of Chiang Kai-shek also played a role. With the outbreak of the Pacific War in December 1941, Chiang instantly became a leader of world renown and the symbol of China's resistance to Japan. By late 1943, Chiang stood recognized at the Cairo Conference as one of the Big Four, and publication of his famous – or notorious – *China's destiny* a few months earlier was part of a bold effort to claim exclusive leadership domestically. Mao and the CCP vigorously disputed this claim.[99] Put crudely, if there was a cult of Chiang, there had also to be a cult of Mao; an anonymous 'Party Central' would not do.

Political and organizational issues. As we have already seen, political power in Communist-controlled areas was exercised at all levels through the interlocking structures of party, government, army and mass organizations. These structures were better developed in Shen-Kan-Ning than in the bases behind Japanese lines, and superimposed upon them was the apparatus of Party Central and the headquarters of the Eighth Route Army. These organizations were much more comprehensive and effective than those of imperial or Republican China. They were also democratic

---

Dimitrov (Comintern head); and the 'Conclusion' to the *History of the CPSU*. Four of the documents from the USSR were added later, as if by afterthought.

[99] Mao and his supporters (especially Ch'en Po-ta) took this challenge very seriously, probably using it to argue within the party that nothing should be done to hamstring Mao or compromise his image. As late as 1945 (at the Seventh CCP Congress), Mao acknowledged that 'it [the KMT] still has considerable influence and power.... We must lower the influence and position of the Kuomintang in the eyes of the masses and achieve the opposite with respect to ourselves.' See Wylie, 218–25.

in the specific sense that they enlisted – or required – broad participation by many elements of the populace, but not in the sense that the governed elected their ultimate leaders or determined policy. Yet the realities of political control and popular support fell well short of the standards set by the party itself and of the public image it tried to project. It was some of these shortcomings that intellectuals such as Ting Ling and Wang Shih-wei had dared to expose publicly, in a style unacceptable to the party. In its confidential materials, however, party leaders at various levels candidly acknowledged similar difficulties.

One problem was a growing bureaucracy and creeping routinization, an almost inevitable consequence of such rapid expansion not only in governing Shen-Kan-Ning itself, but also in directing an increasingly far-flung war effort in the base areas far from Yenan. Many cadres were 'withdrawn from production', a burden that bore heavily on a population facing economic distress in a backward region.[100]

A second problem lay in the fact that political structures did not fully penetrate the village (*ts'un*) level, but usually stopped at the next higher township (*hsiang*) level, with jurisdiction over a variable number of villages. Party Central was also concerned about the administrative 'distance' between county (*hsien*) and township (*hsiang*) levels.[101] Moreover, coordination of activity at each level was hampered by the emphasis on hierarchy. Despite the interlocking nature of the major organizational structures, each had its own vertical chain of command to which it primarily responded. Different units at the same level often had difficulty working with one another. This tendency was most pronounced in the party and the military, where 8RA cadres often looked down on their civilian counterparts. Low morale was a problem, if a survey published in April 1942 is typical: in the Central Finance Office (*Chung ts'ai-t'ing*), 61 per cent of party members surveyed reported themselves 'discontented' (*pu-an-hsin*) with their work assignment.[102]

100 Only crude estimates are possible. Party membership is not directly useful, since many low-ranking party members did engage in production. In late 1941, there were about 8,000 officials who received grain stipends (Selden, 152). This figure apparently does not include upper-echelon party cadres nor the garrison forces of about 40,000, most of which, up to this time, were also non-producers. The total, therefore, may have reached 50,000. In a population of 1.4 million, probably no more than one-third were males between the ages of 15 and 45. Thus, perhaps as many as 10% of the able-bodied male population of SKN was withdrawn from production.
101 Evasion at the village level is graphically portrayed in an officially celebrated short story, 'Li Yu-ts'ai's clapper-talk', by the folk-writer Chao Shu-li. The unlikely hero, an impoverished and illiterate farm labourer with a talent for satiric spoken rhymes (clapper-talk), uses pointed doggerel to expose village big-wigs who for years had hoodwinked party cadres on their tours of inspection from district headquarters.
102 *Chieh-fang jih-pao* (3 April, 1942). The survey also revealed that 87% had joined the party after the outbreak of the war; 39% were illiterate. This is the only such 'public opinion survey' known to me.

Such difficulties were attacked in two closely related new policies which bore the unmistakeable stamp of Mao Tse-tung. Both began in December 1941, a few months before the rectification campaign. The first, called 'crack troops and simple administration' (ching-ping chien-cheng), aimed to cut back the civil and military bureaucracy. The second, 'Hsia-hsiang' (to the villages), was designed to penetrate the villages more deeply, in part by transferring downward many cadres removed from higher levels. These policies combined to decentralize many political and economic tasks, thus providing a better balance between vertical command structures and lateral coordination at each level. In the process, many civil and military cadres were ordered back into production; for most, that meant to engage in farming, land reclamation, or primitive industry. Especially marked for transfer to basic levels were young intellectuals, both to be toughened by the harsh conditions of life among the peasants (a corrective to subjectivism, dogmatism and formalism), and to contribute their badly needed skills to the conduct of village affairs.

These campaigns were actively pushed during the winters of 1941, 1942 and 1943, when they could be timed to coincide with the slack agricultural season. Army units were directed to produce as much as possible of their own food and other supplies, in a modern form of the t'un-t'ien (garrison farm) system of medieval times. The model project for this was at Nan-ni-wan, about thirty miles south-east of Yenan, where the 359th Brigade of the 8RA was assigned full-time for several years to agricultural and rudimentary industrial development. By 1943, the brigade claimed it was supplying about 80 per cent of its own needs. Even Mao Tse-tung, an inveterate chain-smoker, cultivated a symbolic tobacco patch outside his cave in Yenan.

Although hard evidence is unavailable, these policies undoubtedly had some effect, particularly in organization and mobilization. 'Yet the failure to report accomplishments in the aggregate, the emphasis on exemplary achievements such as the Nanniwan project, and the [repeated] promulgation of the policy of "better troops and simpler administration"...suggest also that the progress may not have been so significant.' In early 1943, during the third round of 'simpler administration', a senior leader acknowledged that the number of full-time officials had grown from 7,900 in 1941 to 8,200.[103]

Given the general tone of these reforms in Shen-Kan-Ning and the emphasis on 'mass line' and 'from the masses, to the masses', it is

---

[103] The quotation is from Schran, 193. For personnel data, see Selden, 215–16. This leader (Lin Po-ch'ü, chairman of the SKN government) stated that 22,500 persons, exclusive of the military, were supported at public expense.

surprising that mass organizations as such seem to have played no prominent role. Our only data on such organizations in SKN come from 1938, when 30 per cent of the population (421,000 out of 1,400,000) was said to be enrolled in peasant associations; at the same time, about 25 per cent of women and 32 per cent of men were members of women's organizations and of the part-time militia, respectively. 'One suspects that these organizations for the most part lapsed into inactivity and that their functions were taken over principally by government and party.... In between...periods of intense activity [such as the 1942 rent-reduction campaign] their membership and organization existed largely on paper.'[104]

United front. Worsening relations with the Nationalists and the impact of Japanese consolidation brought more attention to united front work, not less. Beginning in mid-1940, CCP headquarters repeatedly issued confidential directives stressing the importance of such work in approaches to 'friendly armies', to all but the most pro-Japanese or anti-Communist organizations, and to all classes and strata of society. United Front Work Departments (UFWD) had been established in 1937 under the Central Committee, and at lower levels as well. The importance accorded this work is indicated by the fact that from late 1939 (when Wang Ming was transferred) until 1945 or 1946, Chou En-lai's principal responsibilities were as head of the central UFWD and the closely related Enemy Occupied Areas Work Department. He repeatedly called for the further extension and reinvigoration of UFWD at all levels, insisting upon its importance and implying that it had fallen seriously into neglect under his predecessor.[105]

The united front, thus, was not simply a tactical device but part of a general strategy of particular value in times of weakness or crisis. Each concrete problem, from local affairs to national policies, could be analysed as having three components: the party and its dedicated supporters, a large intermediate stratum (or strata), and 'die-hard' enemies. The goal was to isolate the 'die-hards' by gaining the support or neutrality of as many intermediate elements as possible. Isolated enemies might then be dealt with one by one. As early as October 1939, Mao had asserted that 'the united front, armed struggle, and party-building are the three fundamental questions for our party in the Chinese revolution. Having a correct grasp of these three questions and their interrelations is tantamount to giving correct leadership to the whole Chinese revolution.'[106] Applications of this strategy, however, were tactical and extremely flexible, aimed at

---

104 Selden, 142–3.
105 See Van Slyke, *Enemies and friends*, 116–21.
106 Mao, 'Introducing *The Communist*', Mao, *SW*, 2.288.

carefully defined groups or organizations. Precisely because the united front served long-range revolutionary goals, it avoided ideological formulae, seeking in each case to find and exploit those individuals, issues, incentives or pressures that might further the party's cause:

> In the past, the usual approach was toward making political contacts; very rarely was serious work done to make friends, even to the point of remaining aloof and uncooperative. Hereafter, we must use all possible social connections (family, fellow townsmen, classmates, colleagues, etc.) and customs (sending presents, celebrating festivals, sharing adversities, mutual aid, etc.), not only to form political friendships with people, but also to become personal friends with them so that they will be completely frank and open with us.[107]

In this spirit the CCP began in the spring of 1940 to publicize the 'three-thirds system' (*san-san chih*). According to this approach, popular organs of political power – but not the party or the army – should if possible be composed of one-third Communists, one-third non-party left-progressives, and one-third from 'the intermediate sections who are neither left nor right'. As Mao explained,

> The non-party progressives must be allocated one-third of the places because they are linked with the broad masses of the petty-bourgeoisie. This will be of great importance in winning over the latter. Our aim in allocating one-third of the places to the intermediate sections is to win over the middle bourgeoisie and the enlightened gentry.... At the present time, we must not fail to take the strength of these elements into account and we must be circumspect in our relations with them.[108]

The policy thus aimed to make base area regimes more acceptable to the upper levels of the rural population, but it represented no relinquishment of Communist leadership. In practice, representation varied widely. Mao's directive itself had noted that 'the above figures for the allocation of places are not rigid quotas to be filled mechanically; they are in the nature of a rough proportion, which each locality must apply according to its specific circumstances'.

In Shen-Kan-Ning, the proportion of party members in popular organs after 1941 conformed fairly well to the one-third guideline for CCP members. In a few cases, elected party members withdrew, with public fanfare, from their assembly seats in order to conform more closely to the desired ratio. Border Region leaders felt that the policy was quite helpful in allaying the fears and enlisting the support of the middle and upper strata of the peasantry, who had been hardest hit by the steep

---

[107] From a directive of the Central Committee United Front Work Department, 2 Nov. 1940. See Van Slyke, *Enemies and friends*, 269.

[108] 'On the question of political power in the anti-Japanese base areas', Mao, *SW*, 2.418.

increases in taxes – even though poorer peasants had misgivings about former landlords and evil gentry worming their way back into positions of influence. This partly real, partly symbolic improvement of their political fortunes, combined with their share of production increases, kept these social strata well in line – particularly since they had few alternatives.

Altogether, then, the economic, ideological and organizational/political steps taken in Shen-Kan-Ning between 1940 and 1944 may not have fully measured up to the public image the CCP sought to project, nor the assessment sometimes made by outside observers. But they were impressively effective nevertheless, particularly when contrasted with the performance of the Nationalist regime during the same period.

New policies in bases behind Japanese lines

The North and Central China base areas behind Japanese lines faced crises not only more severe but somewhat different from those in Shen-Kan-Ning during the middle years of the war. For example, SKN did not have to cope with military attacks, nor was it forced to move from one area to another. SKN's administrative apparatus was much more fully developed than those in the base areas, and prewar socio-economic change had progressed much further. Because the CCP-controlled regions behind Japanese lines were so varied and the data concerning them so fragmentary, base-by-base treatment is impossible in the space available here. We are thus constrained to describe events and policies in rather general terms, illustrating them with examples from one or more bases. This will distort complex realities by making them appear more uniform than they actually were.

In the face of Japanese military pressure, all base area organs undertook a wide range of active and passive defence measures. Villagers, grain stores, animals and other possessions were evacuated to safer areas or went into hiding. Valuables were buried. Military units dispersed after planting primitive mines and booby traps, and merged with the peasantry, though this was scant protection when the Japanese tried to kill all who fell into their hands, or when they could be identified by collaborators or resentful local elites anxious to settle scores.

Many bases, especially those on the North China plain, literally went underground into what became an astonishing network of caves and tunnels, often on two or more levels and linking up a number of villages. Multiple hidden entrances, blind alleys, and subterranean ambush points frustrated Japanese pursuers. When the Japanese countered by trying to flood the tunnels or by pumping poison-gas into them, the Chinese responded with diversion channels and simple air locks.

Survival depended on the organized leadership of the party and the army, and on the tenacity of the peasantry. But where bases had to evacuate or reduce their operations to guerrilla status, the existence of other bases where they might take haven was also essential. Those left behind, whether cadres or ordinary peasants, were encouraged to take on 'white skins and red hearts', that is, to acquiesce when there was no other choice. Despite the ingenuity and courage with which the Chinese peasantry met these challenges, departure from a particular locale of most of the party-led apparatus and main force military units sometimes imposed too heavy a burden upon local self-defence forces. On occasions when they collapsed, villages reverted to the control of local elites who often took violent revenge. Meanwhile, in more secure settings, organized activity continued, as the exiles waited to restore or reactivate the infrastructures of their home districts. The network of bases across North and Central China provided the Communist-led movement with a resilience and capacity for recovery possessed by no other Chinese forces.

That the surviving core areas were able under these conditions to pursue their political, social and economic objectives at all was remarkable. Yet they did so quite actively, with varying degrees of success. Chin-Ch'a-Chi and some parts of Chin-Chi-Lu-Yü undertook the most extensive and effective reforms. The Central China bases, most of which came into sustained operation about two years later, were less advanced. Shantung lagged even further behind.

Economically, the shift from the first to the second phases of the war was less abrupt in these bases than in SKN because they had always operated under difficult conditions and without any outside subsidy. But they too had for a time depended upon contributions – 'those with strength give strength, those with money give money' – loans, and some confiscations. The shift to 'rational burden' and ultimately to a unified progressive tax system took place as political control and administrative machinery became more effective. In Chin-Ch'a-Chi, the rational burden system was adopted in 1939, and gave way to the unified progressive tax plan in 1941. In fact, however, several systems were operating at the same time, depending on whether the region in question was a consolidated core area, a recently established base, or a guerrilla zone. None of the other bases behind Japanese lines were able to adopt the unified tax system. While the land tax was the principal source of revenue, many of the older surtaxes had to be continued as a supplement, especially in partly

TABLE 18

Land tax as a percentage of total production

	Chin-Sui	Pei-yueh
1937	Bases not yet established	
1938	N/A	6.27
1939	N/A	7.12
1940	N/A	9.71
1941	24.6	14.98
1942	17.4	13.62
1943	19.61	10.07
1944	19.35	8.9
1945	21.0	N/A

Source: Li Ch'eng-jui, 'K'ang-Jih chan-cheng shih-ch'i chi-ko jen-min ken-chü-ti ti nung-yeh shiu-shou chih-tu yü nung-min fu-tan' (Agricultural tax systems and peasant burdens in people's revolutionary base areas during the anti-Japanese war), *Ching-chi yen-chiu* (Economic research), 2 (1956) 108–9.

consolidated or guerrilla areas. In contested areas, collection was not only difficult but limited by the fact that peasants there were doubly burdened – taxed by the Japanese or puppet regimes as well as by the Communists. If Communist data are accurate, the land-tax burden was much heavier in the Chin-Sui base than in SKN, and about the same in the consolidated Pei-yueh region of Chin-Ch'a-Chi (after 1941; before that it was considerably heavier). As in Shen-Kan-Ning, taxes peaked in 1941, then slowly declined. The per household burden was twice as heavy in consolidated areas as in other regions.

Like Shen-Kan-Ning, the bases behind Japanese lines sought to achieve economic self-sufficiency by issuing their own regional currency, establishing banks, and imposing taxes on trade in and out of the base. These taxes raised some revenue, but their principal purpose was to discourage trade:

Territorial autarky was the goal, but for opposite reasons [from SKN]. The Japanese were to be isolated in the cities, deprived of the foodstuffs and raw materials which the surrounding countryside produced. To this end, trade was to be prevented rather then promoted. In the extreme the base areas had to revert to subsistence economy to the greatest possible degree, against the will and the active intervention of the enemy.[109]

Such policies, of course, were difficult or impossible to enforce in contested areas. As in Shen-Kan-Ning, cooperatives, simple industries, handicrafts, and other productive activities were encouraged, and were for the most part untaxed.

[109] Schran, 251.

TABLE 19

Class composition in 35 villages, Chin-Ch'a-Chi

	1937		1943	
	% families	% land	% families	% land
Landlord	2.42	16.43	1.91	10.17
Rich peasant	4.50	21.93	7.88	19.56
Middle peasant	35.42	41.69	44.31	49.14
Poor peasant & farm labourer	47.53	19.10	40.95	20.12

Sources: Chao Kuo-chün, *Agrarian policy*, 64. See Hartford, *Step-by-step*, 169–228 *passim*, for efforts to calculate changing income differentials in core areas of Chin-Ch'a-Chi.

The extraction of taxes was accompanied, as we have seen, by rent and interest reduction. Once again, Chin-Ch'a-Chi took the lead, but as late as October 1943, a directive noted that 'in many areas rent reduction has not been realized', and urged cadres 'to organize the peasants to carry out the provision that rent must not exceed 37·5 per cent of the principal crops'.[110] The Central China bases were considerably later. In the Huai-pei base (northern Anhwei), only 9,000 tenant families had benefited by 1941. By 1943, the movement had accelerated, with some 43,000 famil-ies affected; in the following year, the number probably doubled, as the base expanded.[111] Finally, in the Shantung base, serious rent and interest reduction had hardly begun prior to the winter of 1943–4. Many cadres doubted the importance of the policy, since tenancy rates were not high; some considered this to be thankless and difficult work, much less attractive than military service; others, concerned about shaky political control, feared that a hard line would excessively alienate still-powerful local elites.[112]

Available evidence bears out P'eng Chen's observation that property relations in base areas underwent no great structural change during the war. Probably inequalities in income were reduced more than inequality of property ownership. All the tax systems bore heavily on the rich, and actual practice often exceeded the regulations, particularly under the rational burden tax system. If this was the situation in an advanced base, it is likely that other bases would show less change, not more.

Production campaigns were stressed, just as in Shen-Kan-Ning. Quanti-

[110] Chao Kuo-chün, *Agrarian policy of the Chinese Communist Party, 1921–1959*, 51.
[111] Ch'en Yung-fa, 234.
[112] Hsueh Mu-ch'iao, *K'ang-Jih chan-cheng shih-ch'i ho chieh-fang chan-cheng shih-ch'i Shan-tung chieh-fang-ch'ü ti ching-chi kung-tso* (Economic work in the Shantung liberated areas...), 52ff.

TABLE 20
Grain production, Pei-yueh region

	piculs
1940	1,860,000
1941	1,478,000
1942	1,552,000
1943	2,191,000
1944	2,360,000

tative data are scarce, but in the Pei-yueh region of Chin-Ch'a-Chi, grain production declined rather sharply from the 1940 level until the upturn in 1943 and 1944 (table 20).[113] Production campaigns also had political motives. Benefits could not indefinitely be brought to the poorer peasantry at the expense of the wealthy without wholesale confiscation, which the united front and common sense precluded. Mobilization initially achieved on the basis of limited class struggle could, however, be continued through organization for production managed by peasant associations and labour exchange teams. Leading cadres often encouraged production campaigns in precisely these terms, as a sublimated form of class struggle and popular mobilization.[114]

While the CCP tried to increase the active participation of the populace, the other side of the coin was to weaken and isolate those who opposed the new order. In public statements these measures were almost always described as 'democratic', with emphasis on their moderation and consistency with *San-min chu-i*. In confidential reports and directives, however, this vocabulary was often replaced with that of class struggle and structural change. The two levels of discourse referred to the same phenomena. Despite the heavy admixture of propaganda in the former, the party did not see the two as contradictory, because of its definition of 'democracy' (if others read their own definitions into the term, that was their business) and because the explicit content of its policies did not at this time aim at revolutionary transformation. 'Superiority' (*yu-shih*) not 'dictatorship' (*chuan-cheng*) was the goal.

Through the innumerable details of the specific measures undertaken at various levels in different regions and bases, certain patterns can be discerned: imposition of military and political control from the top down, investigation and replacement where necessary of personnel within the

[113] Derived from data in Li Ch'eng-jui, 108-9. Some of the decline in 1941 and 1942 was probably due to fluctuations in the size of the base and to the mopping-up campaigns of those years.
[114] See Ch'en Yung-fa, 338ff.

existing administrative apparatus, further penetration of that apparatus by party cadres followed by structural and procedural changes. Alongside this takeover of the political machinery lay the military (regular units, local forces, self-defence corps or militia) and the mass organizations, especially peasant associations from which landlords and most rich peasants were excluded.

When these developments had reached a certain level of maturity, but not before, direct elections were held for a limited number of administrative posts and representative assemblies up to county level. Higher level assemblies – where they existed – were elected indirectly by those at the next lower level. Although assemblies nominally supervised administrative committees at the same level, the latter were clearly in charge, with the assemblies meeting rather infrequently as sounding boards and to approve action proposed or already taken. Despite occasional irregularities, the party carried out elections with procedural honesty. But the slate of nominees was carefully screened in advance, and few seats were contested. Instead, the election campaigns were designed to educate and involve the local population in the political process: guided participation was the hallmark of base area democracy. Election campaigns began in Chin-Ch'a-Chi in 1939, but not until 1943 was a full Border Region assembly convened – the only time it met during the course of the war. Sub-regional elections in Chin-Chi-Lu-Yü began a little later. Bases in Central China and Shantung initiated local elections considerably later, in 1942. Nowhere save in Shen-Kan-Ning and Chin-Ch'a-Chi were base-wide assemblies elected.

As in Shen-Kan-Ning, the three-thirds system was carried out in the base areas as part of renewed attention to the united front, despite the misgivings of poorer peasants. Like the united front as a whole, three-thirds was never intended to compromise party control and leadership but to make it more effective. But in the bases, three-thirds was less thoroughly implemented than in SKN. In thirteen *hsien* in the Wu-t'ai region (a part of Chin-Ch'a-Chi), a 1941 election resulted in seating between 34 and 75 per cent CCP members. As late as 1944, a Kiangsu district reported party electees as comprising 60–80 per cent, and made no mention of three-thirds. As P'eng Chen noted, three-thirds 'cannot be made a written regulation, because to fix the three-thirds system in legal terms would be in direct opposition to the principles of truly equal and universal suffrage', but he also observed that 'when we brought up and implemented the three-thirds system and strictly guaranteed the political rights of all anti-Japanese people, the landlords finally came to support and participate in the anti-Japanese regime'. A classified KMT intelligence report (April

1944) confirmed the frequent effectiveness of the CCP's united front: 'Gentry who in the past had been dissatisfied ... filled the skies with praise, feeling that the [CCP] government wasn't so bad after all, that it could recognize its own mistakes and ask for criticism....The Central Government has been away from them too long.'[115]

Although some local activists came forward spontaneously, recruitment of good village leaders from the right strata of the rural population was difficult. Some who came forward were unsuitable, or were later found to have been incompetent or corrupt. A small but significant minority were KMT agents, collaborators, or under the influence of local elites. Negative attitudes were deeply rooted: narrow conservatism, submissiveness and fatalism, lack of self-confidence, an aversion to contact with officials and government, a desire to remain inconspicuous, apprehension that one might excite envy or resentment from one's neighbours. Furthermore, poor peasants were usually illiterate and inexperienced in affairs larger than those involving their own families, and they might resent being pressed into troublesome but uncompensated service. To a degree that troubled higher levels, many of these feelings were also expressed by party members in the villages. Local cadres often reported these attitudes in the colourful and direct language of the peasants themselves. These images, therefore, must be placed alongside the more familiar portrayals of the dedicated and militant peasant, fighting to protect village and nation, working to build a new and better society. Rural China was a kaleidoscope of attitudes, interests and social groups to which no simple depiction does justice.

Organizational measures such as 'crack troops, simple administration' and 'to the villages' were applied in some bases but hardly mentioned in others. Not surprisingly, Chin-Ch'a-Chi pushed these policies in 1942 and 1943, including a substantial simplification of the Border Region government itself. But in most bases, bureaucratism in the Yenan sense seems not to have been perceived as a serious problem – indeed, lack of administrative personnel was quite often bemoaned (commandism, the practice of issuing arbitrary and inflexible orders, was widely deplored). Since the party was already and overwhelmingly in the villages, 'to the villages' had little meaning. Regular army units and local forces were so often engaged with military tasks that they had less opportunity than the SKN garrison to participate in production, though they helped out when they could.

Cadre education looked quite different in most bases than in Shen-Kan-Ning: it was simpler in ideological content and more oriented toward

115 The data and quotations in this paragraphs are taken from Van Slyke, *Enemies and friends*, 150 3.

accomplishment of specific tasks like running local elections, carrying out rent reduction, organizing production, or military recruitment and training. In these bases, few party cadres had the time or educational background to engage in the study of documents or prolonged discussions of dogmatism, subjectivism and formalism. As a result, *cheng-feng* was mentioned less frequently than in SKN, and usually with different meaning. To rank and file members rectification meant mainly invigorating party branches, overcoming negative attitudes, regularization of work, and the constant, painful task of weeding out undesirables. Basic party doctrine and major writings were presented in simplified form, sometimes as dialogues or aphorisms easily memorized. Straight indoctrination and struggle sessions were employed more than 'criticism/self-criticism'. Good and bad models of party behaviour were held up for emulation or condemnation. Meetings were held as opportunity allowed. Training and other campaigns were timed to coincide with seasonal activities: rent and interest reduction campaigns peaked at the spring and autumn harvests, elections were usually held in the early winter after the harvest, army recruitment was easiest during the nearly annual 'spring famine'.

For better educated cadres, standards were somewhat higher. Usually these were 'outside' cadres working at district or regional levels. Liu Shao-chi'i, in particular, tried to transplant Yenan-style rectification to the bases over which he had jurisdiction through the Central China Bureau. The same corpus of documents was designated for study and criticism/self-criticism meetings were called. In 1942, Liu Shao-chi'i's approach to rectification 'had an impact, however, only among high cadres of the army and other organizations under close supervision of the regional party headquarters'.[116]

The middle years of the war imposed great pressures on the Chinese Communist Party. But where in 1927 and in 1934-5 the movement had narrowly avoided annihilation, the mid-war crises did not threaten the party's very existence. By 1940, under wartime conditions, the Communist movement had sufficient territorial reach and popular support to weather the storm. Yet this outcome was not inevitable, as the experience of Nationalist guerrillas showed. The CCP's base of popular support, reinforced and enhanced by organizational control and step-by-step reforms, was both genuine and incomplete. The party's mandate had to be continually renewed and extended. It had to call upon all its resources and experience, to face difficulties realistically, to recognize its short-comings, and above all to persist.

[116] Ch'en Yung-fa, 532ff.

III. THE LAST YEARS OF THE WAR 1944–1945

On the fifth anniversary of the war (7 September 1942), Mao Tse-tung wrote in a *Liberation Daily* editorial that 'the war of resistance has in fact entered the final stage of the struggle for victory'. Although he characterized the present period as 'the darkness before dawn' and foresaw 'great difficulties' ahead, he suggested that the Japanese might be defeated within two years.[117]

Mao was too sanguine in this prediction, but there were signs that the tide was turning against the Axis powers. The heroic Russian defence of Stalingrad, the highwater mark of the German offensives in the east, was followed closely by the Allied invasion of North Africa. In the Pacific, the battles of the Coral Sea (May) and Midway (June) clearly foreshadowed American command of the seas. In August, US Marines landed on the Solomon Islands to take the offensive against Japan.

On the battlefields of China in late 1942 and particularly in the Communist-controlled base areas, harbingers of victory were still a long way off. But over the following year, as 1943 wore on, the warmer winds of change were unmistakable. Even the Japanese high command in Tokyo – though the CCP could hardly have known it – had begun to plan on avoiding defeat rather than achieving victory. What the Communists could see, however, was the decline of intensive pacification efforts and the increasing withdrawal of Japanese forces from the deep countryside. Occasional quick sweeps, like those of the early period of the war, replaced and protracted mop-up campaigns of 1941 and 1942.

OPERATION ICHIGO AND ITS CONSEQUENCES

In fact, the Japanese were preparing for their greatest military offensive in China since 1937–8, Operation Ichigo.[118] The main aim of this campaign, which in one form or another had been stalled on the drawing-boards since 1941, was to open a north-south corridor all the way from Korea to Hanoi, thus providing an overland alternative to the sea lanes which had been swept virtually clear of Japanese vessels capable of bringing essential raw materials to the home islands. A secondary goal was to destroy the American airfields in south-east China.

Ichigo began in April 1944, with campaigns against Chengchow and

---

[117] Mao, *SW*, 3.99.
[118] This summary of Operation Ichigo draws heavily on Ch'i Hsi-sheng, *Nationalist China at war: military defeats and political collapse, 1937–1945*, 73–82.

Loyang, then swept south through Honan along the P'ing-Han railway. During the summer, the heaviest fighting took place south of the Yangtze River, in Hunan, as the Japanese sought to clear the railway line between Wuhan and Canton. Changsha fell to the invaders in June, Hengyang in August. By early winter, the north-south link-up had been achieved, and the Japanese advance was swinging westward to take the airfields at Kweilin, Liuchow and Nanning. To the north-west lay Kweiyang, beyond which stretched the road to Chungking. So serious did the threat appear that in December American and British civilians were evacuated from the wartime capital, and dire predictions of defeat or capitulation were rampant. In fact, however, the Japanese advance had spent itself and could go no further.

Japanese losses were dwarfed by the damage inflicted on the Nationalists. Chungking authorities acknowledged 300,000 casualties. Japanese forces were ordered to destroy the best units of the Nationalist central armies first, knowing that regional elements would then collapse. Logistical damage was also enormous: equipment for an estimated forty divisions and the loss of resources from newly-occupied territories, especially in Hunan, 'the land of fish and rice'.

Politically, too, Ichigo was a disaster for the Nationalists, as incompetence and corruption (despite some brave fighting in Hunan) were laid bare for nearly half a year, both in Chungking and on the battlefield. Nowhere was this more striking than in the opening phase of Ichigo, which coincided with the great Honan famine in the spring of 1944. Neither the Chungking government nor the civilian-military authorities in Honan had prepared for the famine, though its coming was clearly foreseen. Far from providing relief when the famine hit, the authorities collected taxes and other levies as usual. Profiteering was common. When Chinese forces fled in the face of Ichigo, long-suffering peasants disarmed and shot them, then welcomed the Japanese. Tens of thousands starved to death in Honan during the spring of 1944.[119] Although the second half of 1944 saw the successful culmination of the Allied campaign in Burma and the reopening of an overland route into south-west China, these victories, achieved under US tactical command and with the participation of US and British forces, did not compensate for the Nationalists' losses elsewhere or redeem their damaged prestige.

The strains of Operation Ichigo and closer scrutiny of Chinese politics by the United States provided greatly expanded opportunities for Communist work in the 'big rear area' – the regions controlled to one degree or another by the Nationalist government in Chungking. Until the

[119] Theodore White and Annalee Jacoby, *Thunder out of China.*

fall of Hankow in late 1938, the CCP had enjoyed considerable latitude for open and semi-open work. Thereafter, Nationalist censorship and repression again forced it underground, except for officially sanctioned liaison groups and journalists. At all times, of course, the CCP tried to infiltrate the Nationalist government organs and military units, a secret war fought by both sides with considerable success. But the situation was still so dangerous that instructions from Yenan were to lie low, maintain or improve one's cover, and await changes in the working environment.

As the Ichigo offensive rolled on south and south-west, dissident regional elements began talking quietly about the possible removal of Chiang Kai-shek. Yunnan province, under the independent warlord Lung Yun, was a haven for liberal intellectuals and disaffected political figures clustered around South-west Associated University in Kunming – which was also the China terminus of the Burma Road and the 'over the Hump' air transport route from India. In September 1944, when the currents of Ichigo, the Stilwell crisis, and anti-Nationalist dissidence all swirled together, a number of minor political parties and splinter groups came together to form the China Democratic League.[120] As in the wake of the New Fourth Army incident in early 1941, these figures sought to play moderating and mediating roles. Most believed in liberal values and democratic practices, and called for fundamental but non-violent reforms in the Nationalist government. Although the Democratic League lacked a popular base and was by no means a unified movement, league intellectuals – many of them Western-trained – nevertheless had an influence upon educated public opinion and foreign observers out of all proportion to their own limited numbers. Both as individuals and as members of the Democratic League, they seemed to speak, many believed, for all the right things: peace, justice, freedom, broader participation in government.

For the most part, the CCP was content to let the Democratic League speak in its own voice (though it did have operatives in the league). If the KMT undertook reform or granted concessions, the CCP and not the Democratic League would be their true beneficiary. On the other hand, when the Nationalists stonewalled or counter-attacked the league, they further compromised themselves as reactionary and drove more moderates toward the CCP. Neither the Democratic League's idea of a 'third force' nor darker talk of some sort of anti-Chiang coup produced any results. But both provided new opportunities for the CCP to improve its image at the expense of Chiang Kai-shek and the KMT.

---

[120] For the dissidents, see Ch'i Hsi-sheng, 113–17; for the Democratic League and its relations with the CCP, see Van Slyke, *Enemies and friends*, 168–84.

TABLE 21

Japanese and puppet forces in China, June 1944

	North China	Central China	South China	Total
Japanese	220,000	260,000	80,000	560,000
Puppets (not classified by geographical area)				
(1) enlisted from regular or regional Nationalist units			*c.* 480,000	
(2) enlisted by force from the peasantry or by integration of bandits, vagrants, etc.			*c.* 300,000	
(3) collaborating local militia and police			*c.* 200,000	
Sub-total			*c.* 1,000,000	
Total				1,560,000

Source: 'Chung-kung k'ang-chan i-pan ch'ing-k'uang ti chieh-shao' (Briefing on the general situation of the CCP in the war of resistance), *Chung-kung tang-shih ts'an-k'ao tzu-liao* (Reference materials on the history of the Chinese Communist Party), 5.226–8, 233. This was a briefing given on 22 June 1944 to the first group of Chinese and foreign journalists to visit Yenan.

POLITICAL AND MILITARY EXPANSION

The Japanese committed nearly 150,000 troops to the Honan phase of Ichigo, and over 350,000 to the Hunan-Kwangsi phase. Although the total number of Japanese troops in North and Central China did not markedly decline, the demands of Ichigo's second phase pulled many experienced officers and men out of these theatres, replacing them with garrison troops or with new recruits from the home islands. The Japanese also increased their reliance on puppet forces, to take up some of the military slack. According to Yeh Chien-ying, chief-of-staff in Yenan, the situation in June 1944 was as shown in table 21.

On the Communist side, the party and the army resumed their growth, but during the last phase of the war the pattern of expansion in the party differed from that in its armed forces. From approximately mid-1943 to the end of the conflict in mid-1945, the party expanded once again, though at a much slower pace than in the first years of the war. As noted above (table 7), the CCP grew by about 100,000 (*c.* 15 per cent) from mid-1943 to mid-1944. At the time of the Seventh CCP Congress (April 1945), Mao claimed a party membership of 1·2 million, an increase of 40 per cent over that of just a year earlier, and more than 60 per cent above the 1942 low. Thus, by the end of the war, nearly half the party's membership had less than two years' experience.

TABLE 22

Chinese Communist forces, 1944–1945

	8RA	N4A	Total
1944 (June)	320,000	153,676	474,476
1944 (October)	385,000*	185,000*	570,000
1945 (March)	513,000*	247,000*	760,000
1945 (April)	614,000*	296,000*	910,000

* Assuming same proportions as in June 1944.
Sources: this is a composite table. The June 1944 total is from the report cited in table 30, n. 139, by Yeh Chien-ying. October 1944 and March 1945 figures were published in *Chieh-fang jih-pao* (17 March 1945). The April figures are those claimed by Mao Tse-tung at the Seventh CCP Congress.

In contrast to the continuous expansion of the party, the army remained for several years almost constant in size, recruiting only a little more than enough to replace casualties. This situation changed abruptly during the second half of 1944. In less than one year, Communist authorities claimed a virtual doubling of their full-time armed forces (field forces plus local units).

This rapid growth partly responded to the opportunities for territorial expansion in 1944 and 1945, but also anticipated Japan's defeat, and the importance which the army would then have, both as an instrument of policy (taking over Japanese-held territory or contesting with the Nationalists), and as a bargaining chip (since the terms of any negotiated settlement would reflect the realities of power in being). Most of this growth came from rapid integration of regional forces into the field forces; the large numerical increases claimed for the 8RA and the N4A, therefore, derived more from reclassification than from new recruitment. Below these full-time forces were the part-time people's militia – about 1·5 million for North China and a half million for Central China. Members of the militia were quite useful as village security and policy auxiliaries and in local intelligence, short-distance courier service, supply transport, stretcher bearing, etc. But their training was rudimentary and virtually no weapons could be assigned to them. The militia was not expected to serve as a regular combat force, and it rarely did so.

Yeh Chien-ying reported a sharp increase in the number of military engagements from mid-1943 to mid-1944 over those of previous years; at the same time, however, the scale of the engagements was smaller, a greater proportion of engagements were against puppet forces, and the casualty ratio increasingly favoured the CCP. Between mid-1943 and mid-1944, Communist casualties numbered 29,000, less than half the 64,000 suffered between mid-1941 and mid-1942.[121]

In a recurrence of some of the controversies of the first months of the war, some military leaders argued for a rapid expansion and a shift from traditional guerrilla tactics to more conventional operations. Some high-level leaders apparently wanted to attack small and intermediate cities at once. During the spring of 1944, with Ichigo under way, the Eighth Route Army carried out probing operations in Hopei around the strategic Shihchiachuang rail junction and even briefly occupied the important city of Paoting. During this period, too, the plains bases were reactivated in both north and south Hopei. In principle, Mao agreed with a forward strategy and in positioning the party to take advantage of Japan's eventual defeat. In the spring of 1944, he urged his comrades to 'pay attention to work in the big cities and along the main lines of communication and raise the work in the cities to a position of equal importance with that in the base areas'. Yet he still counselled caution, flexibility, and a realistic assessment of the party's capacities:

Our party is not yet sufficiently strong, not yet sufficiently united or consolidated, and so cannot yet take on greater responsibility than we now carry. From now on, the problem is further to expand and consolidate our party, our army, and our base areas in the continued prosecution of the war of resistance; this is the first indispensable item in our ideological and material preparation for the gigantic work of the future.[122]

Mao also worried that his field commanders might act impetuously and without coordination or understanding of the full strategic picture. On several occasions he inveighed against precisely this sort of 'mountain-top-ism'; memories of the unauthorized Hundred Regiments offensive and of his inability to control Hsiang Ying must have come to mind.

There was no reason, however, to hold back in those areas where the CCP had first established its bases, and where the Nationalist presence had already been cleaned out. In these regions, the only questions were tactical – how much could be accomplished with the resources at hand, and how much Japanese or puppet opposition could be expected. Much more sensitive was the issue of opening extensive new base areas in regions still claimed by the KMT or only recently lost as a result of Operation Ichigo. Chu Te, Yeh Chien-ying and Ch'en I all indicated that much thought had been given to such expansion; they apparently found the prospects very appealing. In the upshot, although the CCP did move into some of these areas, it did so cautiously, selectively, and with a low profile.

During the last year of the war, the CCP rang the changes on political,

---

[121] *Chung-kung k'ang-chan i-pan ch'ing-k'uang ti chieh-shao*, 238.   [122] Mao, *SW* 3.171–2.

social and economic policies previously developed, doing so both with confidence born of success and with a realistic appreciation of the limitations of its influence and power. In newly 'liberated' areas, the CCP acted very much as it had in earlier waves of expansion, doing whatever was necessary to get an initial toehold, then extend its influence. In established bases, stress was placed on both production campaigns and class struggle. Most frequently, class struggle meant further extension of rent and interest reduction.

In many bases – including some core areas – rent and interest reduction had not been thoroughly carried out, or rural elites had tried to undo the reforms already imposed. Campaigns with names like 'investigate rent – reduce rent' (ch'a-tsu chien-tsu) were seen at all levels and in all areas. Many detailed and vivid documents reported shockingly poor performance. Cadres were regularly criticized for their lack of understanding and interest in mass work. Evasion and corruption were not uncommon. Peasant involvement was too often spotty and grudging.

How should one interpret these reports? On the one hand, they seem to have come from consolidated districts, where systematic surveys were possible. Yet it is in just such areas that one would have expected the reforms to have been most thorough and effective. This may suggest that in semi-consolidated or guerrilla zones, little if any rent or interest reduction had been accomplished. But, on the other hand, these reports are designed to spur the movement, to show that much remained to be done, and to highlight errors – in short, to serve as strongly negative examples. Yet even if one accepts the didactic purpose of these documents and discounts for exaggeration, the very need for them shows that full achievement of even these limited reforms was beyond the party's capacity. Furthermore, experience had shown that the imposition of more radical economic policies not only lowered production but often frightened and alienated many middle peasants, even though such policies were not aimed at them.

Although there was no weakening of the commitment to revolutionary change in the Chinese countryside, party leaders realized that premature, poorly-planned efforts to achieve it were doomed to failure and that abstract preaching had little persuasive power. 'Nationalism' and 'class struggle' had to be given palpable, concrete meaning on a daily basis before they could be understood and accepted by a peasantry unschooled in such vague notions. Mao's caution was not so much a lack of confidence as it was a realistic appraisal of the still limited capacities of the party and its military forces. And by 1944, a new actor was playing an important role on China's already crowded stage: the United States.

THE UNITED STATES AND THE CHINESE
COMMUNISTS

When the Japanese attacked Pearl Harbor (7 December 1941), the Sino-Japanese War merged with the Second World War. Through most of 1942, the United States was in retreat or on the defensive against Japan, and could provide little direct assistance to the struggle in China. Europe had priority over Asia, and before long the strategy of island-hopping across the Pacific took precedence over efforts to defeat Japan on the Asian mainland. The China-Burma-India (CBI) theatre, under command of General Joseph W. (Vinegar Joe) Stilwell, became a backwater of the war, important primarily to keep large numbers of Japanese troops tied down and as a site for Allied air bases. Like all other nations, the United States recognized the Nationalist regime, headed and symbolized by Chiang Kai-shek, as the legitimate government of China.

In order to keep Chiang in the struggle (he sometimes hinted – or threatened – that China was exhausted and might not be able to go on) and to compensate politically for the meagre military aid being sent to China, President Roosevelt urged that China be recognized as one of the Big Four and that the century-old 'unequal treaties' be abolished. Both were accomplished, over deep British misgiving, in 1943. The long-range goal of the United States was to help a 'unified, democratic, and friendly' China become the centre of postwar stability in Asia.

Under the confusing cross-currents of events was the strategic import of US involvement – that Japan would eventually be defeated mainly by the Americans. This was soon clearly understood by both Chiang Kai-shek and Mao Tse-tung. Neither leader had much incentive to undertake anti-Japanese combat for purely military reasons, if to do so would weaken forces needed later to cope with the domestic rival. Although Mao could not acknowledge it in such terms, this was the 'international situation favourable to us and unfavourable to the enemy' that he had predicted in his 1938 treatise, 'On the new stage'.

Direct contacts between Americans and the Chinese Communists in the early and middle years of the war were very limited. Between 1937 and early 1942, US embassy staff members met occasionally with members of the CCP liaison team in Wuhan and Chungking. These meetings took place more often after the US entry into the war, and sometimes involved both American military and foreign service officers. Despite increasingly insistent requests, the Nationalists declared all base areas out-of-bounds to foreigners. Only a few refugees, like Michael Lindsay or Clare and William Band, and sympathizers, like Agnes Smedley, reported on the

Communist regions. At last, when Vice-President Henry Wallace visited China in June 1944, during Operation Ichigo, embassy officials persuaded him to press their request to visit Yenan upon Chiang Kai-shek. As a concession to this representative of an obviously impatient President Roosevelt, Chiang reluctantly authorized the creation of a US Observer Group in Yenan. A press delegation left at once; by August the official group was in place and functioning. Thus the 'Dixie Mission' was born.[123] Headed by a colourful old China hand, Colonel David D. Barrett, the group included political as well as military observers, such men as John S. Service and John P. Davies whose reports and recommendations later became so controversial during the inflamed debates in the US about the 'loss of China'. Virtually all Western journalists on the China beat wrote dispatches and books about 'Red China'. Their experience recalled that of Edgar Snow in 1936. Now, as then, the Communists seemed unusually open, forthcoming, and concerned to get their story before the world.

The timing was significant. In 1944 and 1945 the CCP was resurgent, while Nationalist shortcomings were glaringly exposed by Operation Ichigo and by the final clash between Chiang Kai-shek and General Stilwell, resulting in the latter's recall. During the more difficult middle years of the war, when the CCP was wrestling with problems of survival and carrying on the rectification campaign, Nationalist recalcitrance had prevented US observers from seeing the Communists at first hand.

For Mao and the CCP, the United States was a wild card. To all appearances, the US was committed to Chiang Kai-shek and the Nationalists. But the United States was also committed to winning the war against Japan as quickly as possible and to a unified, democratic and peaceful China after the war. If the US perceived the Communists as a dedicated and effective anti-Japanese force – in welcome contrast to Nationalist performance during Ichigo – perhaps war material and financial backing might come their way. After all, to gain victory over Germany and Japan, the US was working with the widest variety of allies, regardless of their professed ideologies. But clearly the CCP could not present itself to the United States in a favourable light if it was openly fighting the Nationalists, taking advantage of their misfortunes during 1944.

Establishment of the Dixie Mission was limited recognition by the United States, and the Chinese Communist leaders seized the opportunity to offer assistance (to downed airmen, to prepare for an Allied landing in North China) and to widen the avenues of direct communication. Full recognition and military assistance were the maximum prizes to be won,

---

[123] John S. Service, Dixie's most famous member, speculated that this name came from the song lyric, 'Is it true what they say about Dixie?' Dixie was of course the rebel side.

but any friendly association with the US, any wedge between the US and the Nationalists, was desirable so long as it did not curtail CCP initiative and autonomy. Whether or not this was a principal motive, the CCP did in fact use restraint in areas where they might have come into conflict with the Nationalists, and moved forward with prudent speed where such action could demonstrate their effectiveness in the war against Japan.

The recall of Stilwell in October 1944 was a keen disappointment to the CCP, for it showed the continuing strength of Chiang Kai-shek's influence over American China policy. Meanwhile, changes in personnel – Wedemeyer for Stilwell as theatre commander and Patrick J. Hurley as Roosevelt's special representative (later ambassador) – seemed unpromising.[124] The Communists soon made their assessment of Hurley, who, as Roosevelt's personal envoy, seemed to have a special authority to speak for the United States. Hurley believed that the CCP was not really revolutionary; he had been told by Molotov himself that the Russians considered them synthetic communists and would agree not to meddle in Chinese domestic politics. Hurley was convinced that when the CCP realized they could expect no assistance from the USSR, they would be willing to make their peace with the Kuomintang. Conversely, the CCP would be more intransigent if it believed it might obtain recognition or support from either the Soviet Union or the United States. Hurley also felt confident that he could persuade Chiang Kai-shek to accept CCP participation in a multi-party government. More than once he likened the CCP to the Republican Party in the United States – both were opposition parties, each seeking a larger role in the country's political life.

Hurley's surprise visit to Yenan in early November led to the joint drafting of a five-point proposal more sweeping in its language – partly inspired by his fondness for the Gettysburg Address – than anything the CCP had previously entertained. But when Hurley returned to Chungking with this document, which he himself had signed, Chiang Kai-shek refused to consider it. Hurley, in essence, reversed his field and disavowed the proposals he had helped to draft. CCP disappointment over Stilwell's recall deepened into disillusion with Hurley and the United States.

The political positions of the two Chinese parties had, however, been considerably clarified. In brief, the Nationalists insisted that the CCP place itself under the civil and military authority of the Chinese government as

---

[124] Hurley apparently received only verbal instructions from FDR, and from the start operated independently of the Department of State, which he held in considerable contempt. He later claimed his mission was to prevent a Nationalist collapse, to sustain Chiang Kai-shek, to harmonize relations between the generalissimo and the American commander, to prevent economic collapse, to unify all military forces in China for the purpose of defeating Japan, and to promote internal unity in China. See below, ch. 13.

a precondition to discussing reform and reorganization. Since the Kuomintang was the government of China, it could not negotiate with the CCP as an equal any more than Lincoln could have negotiated a division of the United States with Jefferson Davis. The Communist position was the Nationalist's mirror image: satisfactory political and military reforms must come first as a precondition to participation in a restructured government. The CCP considered itself the political equal – and the moral superior – of the Kuomintang, and it had no intention of submitting its territories or its armed forces to outside control. The call for formation of a 'coalition government' (*lien-ho cheng-fu*) was first enunciated by the CCP in mid-September 1944. Thereafter, until well after the end of the war with Japan, coalition government remained the centrepiece of both the CCP's negotiating position and its propaganda campaigns, just as improvements in its political and military situation in the base areas were made with civil war in mind.

With the evidence of Stilwell's recall and Hurley's inconsistency, CCP leadership apparently gave up on the possibility of being recognized by the US as coequal with the Kuomintang in the Chinese political arena. By late 1944, Chou En-lai was refusing to return to Chungking – a clear statement that the CCP believed that negotiations with the KMT would be fruitless. His brief visit to Chungking in January 1945 confirmed that the impasse had grown more bitter than ever.

Yet, even then, the party did not entirely abandon hope of receiving military assistance from the United States. There had been recurrent discussion of landing US forces in North China as a step toward the invasion of Kyushu (tentatively scheduled for October 1945). The Communists apprised Wedemeyer of the location of coastal base areas both north and south of the Shantung peninsula. From October to December 1944, sporadic discussions ensued concerning the possibility of joint US-CCP military operations on a fairly large scale – apparently without Hurley's knowledge. Extravagant language was exchanged. American colonels suggested that full equipment for up to 25,000 guerrillas was not out of the question; at one point, Mao indicated a desire to visit Washington and a willingness to have his forces serve under American commanders: 'We will accept your help with gratitude any time, now or in the future. We would serve with all our hearts under an American General, with no strings or conditions attached.... If you land on the shores of China, we will be there to meet you, and to place ourselves under your command.'[125]

When Hurley heard of these conversations, he quickly put an end to

[125] Quoted in James B. Reardon-Anderson, *Yenan and the great powers*, 56.

them and demanded a full investigation, feeling that his own efforts at a political settlement had been undermined by persons on Wedemeyer's staff and in his own embassy. By February 1945, when Hurley and Wedemeyer returned to Washington for consultations related to the Yalta Conference, the CCP had apparently all but written off hopes of recognition and support from the United States. KMT–CCP negotiations were also, for the moment at least, dead.

THE SEVENTH CONGRESS

In organizational terms, the culminating event of the last phase of the war was the convening of the long-heralded, long-deferred Seventh National Congress of the Communist Party of China, the first such gathering since the dark days of the Sixth Congress, held in Moscow in 1928. As we have noted, plans for the Seventh Congress had been well under way by early 1938, until 'wartime pressures' led to its indefinite postponement, with the sixth plenum of late 1938 taking its place. Nor did a seventh plenum meet until immediately before the Seventh Congress, nearly six years later. In the interim Mao had built his coalition, weakened or removed his rivals, and developed his ideology as the guiding centre of the Chinese Communist movement. By 1944, at the latest, Mao Tse-tung had risen far above his former peers, and was now overwhelmingly the dominant leader of the CCP. If any of his comrades had misgivings about this apotheosis, they kept silent in public.[126]

The timing of the Seventh Congress was influenced by both international and domestic considerations. Internationally, the rapid march toward victory in both Europe and Asia required that the CCP set forth its strategic line in the clearest and most forceful terms. Domestically, the CCP's Seventh Congress was timed to meet simultaneously with the Kuomintang's Sixth National Congress, to pose an alternative to the KMT at every point, and to upstage Chungking. Once again, a thrust by one contender led to parry and counter-thrust by the other. This 'congress of solidarity and victory' – hailed as 'one of the most important events in the history of modern China' – met from 23 April to 11 June, 1945, a full fifty days. The major business before the congress was the following:

(1) Acknowledgment of Mao Tse-tung as the unquestioned leader of the Chinese Communist Party and the Chinese revolution, and parallel acknowledgment of 'the thought of Mao Tse-tung' as the guide to all analysis and action. This spirit, indeed, pervaded the entire congress. It

---

[126] It appears that the doughty P'eng Te-huai expressed some such misgivings at the seventh plenum. See Wylie, 262.

was clearly expressed in the 'Resolutions on certain questions in the history of our party', which had been formally adopted by the seventh plenum a few days earlier, although, judging from its placement in volume 3 of the *Selected works*, it may have been drafted as early as mid-1944. This was nothing less than 'the new Maoist version of party history that was to become the official orthodoxy...one momentous process – the emergence and struggles of Mao's correct line prior to 1935, and its initial triumph and gradual, victorious development since Tsunyi.'[127] This view of history was also incorporated into the new party constitution, which further stated: 'The Chinese Communist Party takes the thought of Mao Tse-tung – the unified thought of Marxist-Leninist theory and Chinese revolutionary practice – as the guide to all its work.' If these affirmations were not enough, the congress also heard self-criticisms from a number of returned-students, including Po Ku (Ch'in Pang-hsien), Lo Fu (Chang Wen-t'ien) and Wang Ming.

(2) Political and military reports, delivered by Mao and Chu Te respectively, in order to define in authoritative terms the party's line, present and future. Mao's political report was the lengthy and comprehensive 'On coalition government' (later substantially edited for inclusion in the *Selected works*). This treatise can be viewed as a continuation of 'On new democracy', since it sets forth the CCP's view of China's present situation and future prospects as explicit alternatives to those of the KMT. The coalition government for which Mao called was essentially the new democratic government described five years earlier, 'under the leadership of the working class'. Although unity was the keynote, it was hardly a unity the KMT could accept. Indeed, models for a nationwide coalition government already existed: 'In every one of the Liberated Areas... popularly elected governments, that is, local coalition governments, have been or are being set up.' Mao also claimed that the pledge to implement Sun Yat-sen's Three Principles of the People had been 'completely carried into effect in China's Liberated Areas'.[128]

Yet 'On coalition government' drew a careful line between minimum and maximum programmes, and sought to keep open as many options as possible. In this regard, Mao was providing justification for the policies he had already been following for about a year: to recognize that competition with the Kuomintang might be either political or military, or some mixture of the two. The overall tone of this report, however, was quite aggressive and challenging. Mao did not rule out negotiation and compromise, but this was not the prevailing tone.

(3) The adoption of a new party constitution, following a lengthy report

[127] Wylie, 261.   [128] Mao, *SW* 3.269-70.

by Liu Shao-ch'i during which he praised Mao in such fulsome terms – 'Our Comrade Mao Tse-tung is not only the greatest revolutionary and statesman in Chinese history, but also the greatest theoretician in Chinese history' – that some have guessed he may not have been entirely sincere. This constitution replaced the one adopted at the Sixth Congress in 1928 (and would remain in force until the Eighth Congress in 1956, when – significantly – all references to the 'thought of Mao Tse-tung' were deleted). The constitution of 1945, reflecting of course the preferences of Mao Tse-tung, differed from its predecessor in several ways.[129] Chief among these was the greater centralization of power both in the party as a whole, and at its apex, where for the first time there was created the post of chairman of the Central Committee, who was concurrently chairman of the Central Political Bureau and the Central Secretariat. The new constitution also gave greater representation to the rural areas, put more stress on intra-party democracy, and dropped all references to the Soviet Union and to the international revolutionary movement. The 1945 Constitution had a strongly home-grown flavour, much different from that of the Sixth Congress, seventeen years earlier.

(4) Election of the new Central Committee (44 regular and 33 alternate members) and the staffing of the higher echelons of the party. Precisely because there were so few surprises, those few stood out: Li Li-san ranked 15th, well above Chou En-lai (23rd); Ch'en Po-ta, Mao's ideological expert, was no higher than 3rd on the alternate list. Perhaps because of his collisions with Mao, P'eng Te-huai ranked low (33rd), much lower than his military responsibilities might have suggested; the same was true of Yeh Chien-ying (31st). Wang Ming and Po Ku were the last two names on the list.[130]

THE CHINESE COMMUNISTS AND THE SOVIET UNION

During the last phase of the war in China, the role played by the USSR was, for the most part, that of a brooding presence rather than an active participant. It was only with her declaration of war on 8 August 1945 – just six days before Japan's surrender – that the USSR suddenly and forcefully emerged from the shadows to centre stage in East Asia. This did not mean, however, that other actors in China could ignore her. On the contrary, the United States and the Chinese Nationalists as well as the Chinese

---

[129] This summary follows that presented in Conrad Brandt, et al. A documentary history of Chinese communism, 419–21.

[130] Ibid. 292. See also Donald W. Klein and Anne B. Clark, Biographic dictionary of Chinese communism, 1921–1965, App. 50, 1081–9.

Communists had to include the USSR in all their calculations. Until Japan's abrupt surrender, following the two thermonuclear attacks, official US policy was to get the Soviet Union into the war against Japan as soon as possible. This attitude underlay Roosevelt's approach to Stalin at the Yalta Conference (February 1945) and continued to affect Truman as late as the meetings at Potsdam in July. But rivalry and mutual suspicion were already gnawing away at the alliance.

Chiang Kai-shek's goal was to forestall recognition and support of the CCP by either the US or the USSR. Chiang's principal means for achieving this was to offer to Stalin concessions that only he could deliver, in return for the USSR's exclusive recognition of him and his government. Needless to say, this goal had to be pursued in Stalin's direction with the greatest discretion, and this was much on Chiang Kai-shek's mind during the visit of Vice-President Henry Wallace to China in June 1944. In conversations over three days, Chiang time and again complained of the CCP's duplicity and disobedience, and alleged that the Chinese Communists were subject to control from Moscow. He urged that 'Roosevelt act as an arbiter or "middleman" between China and the USSR'. In response to Wallace's urging that points of possible conflict between China and the USSR be resolved, Chiang promised to do 'anything that was not detrimental to the sovereignty of the Chinese government'. Roosevelt almost certainly believed he had wide latitude to explore Sino-Russian relations with Stalin. In a letter to Chiang, he wrote: 'I welcome the indication given me by Mr Wallace of your desire for improved relations between the USSR and China, and your suggestion that I use my good offices to arrange for a conference between Chinese and Russian representatives is being given serious thought.'[131] These thoughts were an important element in Roosevelt's secret conversations with Stalin at Yalta. In essence, Roosevelt was using concessions by China to induce Russia to enter the war against Japan, feeling justified that in doing so he was also contributing to the improvement of Sino-Russian relations which Chiang had indicated he wanted and would pay for. In return, Stalin and Molotov indicated to Hurley that they did not consider the Chinese Communists to be communists at all, that they were not supporting the CCP, and that they were ready to recognize and deal with Chiang Kai-shek on the basis of their understanding of the Yalta discussions.

Hurley informed Chiang Kai-shek of the Yalta Conference in mid-June, negotiations between China and the USSR began the following month, and the Sino-Soviet Treaty of Friendship and Alliance was signed on 14 August 1945, the very day of Japan's capitulation. Chiang got what he

131 *China white paper*, 549–60.

wanted: a pledge of recognition and non-interference, and a promise to give moral support and military aid entirely to the 'National Government as the central government of China'. The price was high – an inflated understanding of the Yalta terms, plus several other loose ends – and led subsequently to bitter Nationalist denunciation of the US role in these events. Russia thus returned to a position more advanced than any she had held under the tsars prior to the Russo-Japanese War. Meanwhile, Russian forces quickly overran all of Manchuria and North Korea, most of the conquest being completed in the days following the Japanese surrender. On 19 August, Russian and Chinese Communist military units linked up for the first time in history.

Throughout the war, the CCP had either praised and defended the USSR or it had kept silent. But clearly Mao was playing an independent hand and had reason for deep displeasure with much that the Russians had done: exclusive aid to the Kuomintang early in the war, the Nazi-Soviet pact of 1939, the treaty of neutrality with Japan in 1941, continued and only occasionally critical recognition of Chiang Kai-shek. He probably suspected that Stalin did indeed harbour doubts about him as the first Chinese Communist leader to come to power without help or blessing from the Kremlin, about his policies, and above all about the CCP's prospects of success. In what was undoubtedly a deliberate decision by Mao, the CCP's Seventh Congress almost totally ignored the Soviet Union and Stalin.[132]

The CCP press in Yenan and Chungking had barely finished celebrating the Soviet entry into the conflict on 8 August when Japan surrendered and the Sino-Soviet treaty was announced. The joy of victory must have been tempered by the disappointment of the treaty. Although in public the CCP tried to put the best possible face on it, party leaders were hurt, angry and bewildered. One mid-level cadre must have spoken for many:

In order to maintain and stabilize the peace in the Far East, the Soviet Union has signed the Sino-Soviet Friendship Treaty. This is beneficial to the people of China and the world, but not to Japan and all other warmongers. At the same time, however, in order to carry out its duty under this treaty, the Soviet Union cannot directly aid us, and this imposes certain limitations upon us.... We do not understand actual Russian policy.[133]

Mao later recalled with bitterness, 'They did not permit China to make revolution: that was in 1945. Stalin wanted to prevent China from making revolution, saying that we should not have a civil war and should

---

[132] In the rather brief sections of 'On coalition government' devoted to the international situation, Mao referred to the USSR only as one of the three (or five) great nations jointly defeating the fascist powers. The USSR is accorded no leading role, and Stalin's name is not mentioned.

[133] Quoted in Reardon-Anderson, 103 (but retranslated).

cooperate with Chiang Kai-shek. Otherwise, the Chinese nation would perish.'[134]

PROSPECTS

The surrender of Japan was, of course, an event of great and joyful significance across China's war-torn land. It symbolized the end of the foreign aggression, and the hope of all Chinese that genuine peace might at last be achieved after seemingly endless pain and death. But Japanese surrender did not mean that the war was over in China, since the Japanese invasion was only one part of a complex, many-sided political and military conflict, all other aspects of which continued much as before. Even with the Japanese, shooting continued as Japanese troops responded to orders from the Nationalists to hold their positions and refuse surrender to Communist forces.

Thus Mao and his colleagues hardly had time to pause and congratulate themselves on the progress they had made since 1937. In 'The situation and our policy after the victory in the war of resistance against Japan' (13 August 1945), however, Mao took time to look both backward and forward. The past was portrayed in black and white; no shades of grey entered the description of the Kuomintang and its leaders, either prior to or during the Sino-Japanese War. According to Mao, the risk of civil war was very great, because Chiang Kai-shek and his foreign backers would try to seize a victory that rightly belonged to the people. Mao was hard-headed enough to see that the balance of power in China did not yet favour the CCP: 'That the fruits of victory should go to the people is one thing, but who will eventually get them...is another. Don't be too sure that the fruits of victory will fall into the hands of the people.' Some of these fruits – all the major cities and the eastern seaboard – would surely go to the KMT, others would be contested, and still others – the base areas and some Japanese-occupied countryside – would go to 'the people'. The only question was on what scale the struggle would be fought: 'Will an open and total civil war break out?... Given the general trend of the international and internal situation and the feelings of the people, is it possible, through our own struggles to localize the civil war or delay the outbreak of a country-wide civil war? There is this possibility.' It was in this spirit that Mao Tse-tung, Chou En-lai, and General Patrick Hurley flew from Yenan to Chungking on 28 August to discuss with Chiang Kai-shek the problems of peace, democracy and unity.

Finally, Mao Tse-tung stressed self-reliance. He identified the United States as a hostile imperialist power and insisted that no direct help from

[134] Stuart Schram, *Chairman Mao talks to the people*, 191.

the Soviet Union was needed: 'We are not alone...[in the world, but] we stress regeneration through our own efforts. Relying on the forces we ourselves organize, we can defeat all Chinese and foreign reactionaries.' Yet at the same time, 'Bells don't ring till you strike them...Only where the broom reaches can political influence produce its full effect. ...China has a vast territory, and it is up to us to sweep it clean inch by inch... We Marxists are revolutionary realists and never indulge in idle dreams.'

CHAPTER 5

THE KMT-CCP CONFLICT 1945–1949

By 1944 the American government had become increasingly anxious to quell the dissension that was undermining the anti-Japanese war effort in China, and forestall a possible civil war that might involve the Soviet Union on the side of the CCP once the Japanese surrendered. The negotiations between the KMT and CCP, broken off after the New Fourth Army incident in 1941, had been resumed by 1943. The Americans became actively involved with the arrival in China of Major General Patrick J. Hurley, President Roosevelt's personal representative to Chiang Kai-shek, in September 1944. Appointed US Ambassador a few months later, Hurley's mission was, among other things, 'to unify all the military forces in China for the purpose of defeating Japan'.

The Hurley mission: 1944–1945

Optimistic interludes to the contrary notwithstanding, the first year of Hurley's efforts to promote reconciliation between the leaders of China's 'two great military establishments' bore little fruit. The Communist position announced by Mao at the Seventh Party Congress in April 1945 called for an end to KMT one-party rule and the inauguration of a coalition government in which the CCP would share power. This proposal gained the enthusiastic support of the nascent peace movement in the KMT areas, where fears of renewed civil conflict were mounting as the fortunes of the Japanese aggressor declined. But it was not the sort of proposal that the KMT government was inclined to favour. Then on the day Japan surrendered, 14 August, Chiang Kai-shek invited Mao to journey to Chungking to discuss the outstanding issues between them. Mao eventually accepted, and Ambassador Hurley personally escorted him to the government's wartime capital from his own at Yenan. The ambassador continued to play his mediator's role in the subsequent negotiations.

Mao returned to Yenan on 11 October. General principles had been agreed upon, but the details of implementation had yet to be devised. Chou En-lai remained in Chungking to work toward that end. The general principles announced in their 10 October agreement, at the close of the talks between Chiang and Mao, included democratization, unification of military forces, and the recognition that the CCP and all political parties were equal before the law. The government agreed further to guarantee the freedoms of person, religion, speech, publication and assembly; agreed to release political prisoners; and agreed that only the police and law courts should be permitted to make arrests, conduct trials, and impose punishments.

According to the agreement, a political consultative conference representing all parties was to be convened to consider the reorganization of the government and approve a new constitution. The Communists agreed to a gradual reduction of their troop strength by divisions to match a proportional reduction of the government's armed forces. The Communists also agreed to withdraw from eight of their southernmost and weakest base areas.[1] The government had bowed to the Communist demand for an end to one-party KMT rule; the Communists had abandoned their demand for the immediate formation of a coalition government. In so doing, both sides were acknowledging the widespread desire for peace on the part of a war-weary public, and the political advantages to be gained from apparent deference to it.

A key issue on which not even superficial agreement could be reached, however, was that of the legality of the remaining ten Communist base areas and their governments. Chiang Kai-shek demanded that they be unified under the administrative authority of the central government; the Communists not surprisingly demurred. Even more crucial: while their leaders were thus engaged in talking peace, the Communist and government armies were engaged in a competitive race to take over Japanese-occupied territory north of the Yangtze. That territory included the strategic North-east provinces (Manchuria, as they were then known), where the Communists were rushing to create a new base area.

General Douglas MacArthur, Supreme Commander of the Allied Powers (SCAP), in his General Order Number One, authorized the Chinese government to accept the Japanese surrender in China proper, the island of Taiwan, and northern Indo-China. The forces of the Soviet Union were to do the same in Manchuria. But the government, from its wartime retreat in the south-west, was at a clear disadvantage in taking

---

[1] *China white paper.* 2.577-81; Mao Tse-tung, 'On the Chungking negotiations', *Selected works,* hereafter Mao, *SW*, 4.53-63.

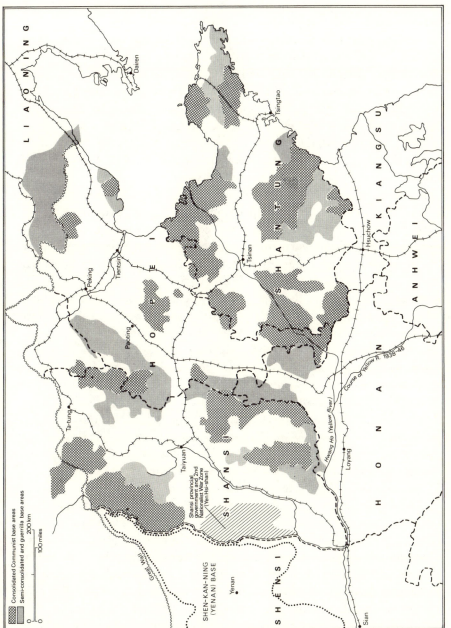

MAP 13. Zones under substantial Communist control in August 1945

Consolidated Communist base areas

Semi-consolidated and guerrilla base areas

over from the Japanese north of the Yangtze, since the Communists already controlled much of the North China countryside.

Anticipating Japan's surrender, Chiang Kai-shek had ordered Communist forces on 11 August 1945 to maintain their positions. But in accordance with conflicting orders from Yenan, Communist troops launched an offensive on all fronts against Japanese-held keypoints and communications lines to compel their surrender. Mao and the commander of the Communist armies, Chu Teh, cabled a rejection of Chiang's 11 August order five days later.

On 23 August, therefore, the commander-in-chief of government forces, General Ho Ying-ch'in, ordered General Okamura Yasuji, commander of Japanese forces in China, to defend Japanese positions against Communist troops if necessary, pending the arrival of government troops. The Japanese were also ordered to recover territory recently lost or surrendered to Communist forces, and offensive operations were undertaken following this order. From late August to the end of September, more than 100 clashes were reported between Communist forces on the one hand, and those of the Japanese and their collaborators on the other, acting as surrogate for the KMT government. As a result of these operations, the Communists lost some twenty cities and towns in Anhwei, Honan, Hopei, Kiangsu, Shansi, Shantung and Suiyuan.[2] Among their gains was Kalgan (Changchiak'ou), then a medium-sized city with a population of 150,000-200,000, and capital of Chahar province. Taken from the Japanese during the final week of August 1945, Kalgan was a key trade and communications centre for goods and traffic moving north and south of the Great Wall. Because of its size and strategic location not far from Peiping, Kalgan became something of a model in urban administration for the Communists and a second capital for them until it was captured by government forces one year later.

The United States also intervened on the government's behalf, transporting approximately half a million of its troops into North China, Taiwan and Manchuria. A force of 53,000 US marines occupied Peiping, Tientsin and other points in the north pending the arrival of government troops. The US War Department order authorizing such assistance had instructed that the principle of non-involvement in the KMT-CCP conflict not be infringed. Yet the order contained an implicit contradiction, since the two parties to the conflict viewed their race to take over from the Japanese as part of their mutual rivalry. The US thus compromised the principle of 'non-involvement' from the start in a manner that would

---

[2] *Hsin-hua jih-pao* (*New China daily news*), Chungking, 17 and 20 Sept., 5, 6 and 22 Oct. 1945 (translated in *Chinese Press Review*, hereafter *CPR*, same dates except Oct. 23 for the last cited). Also *Foreign relations of the United States*, hereafter *FRUS*, *1945*, 7.567-68.

characterize the American role in China throughout the period. The Chinese Communists began at once to protest the American garrison duties and troop movements as US interference in China's domestic affairs.[3]

The presence of the Russians further complicated the clash of interests in China at the end of the Second World War. The Soviet Union entered the war against Japan on 9 August 1945, in accordance with the Yalta Agreements of 11 February 1945. Soviet troops had just begun entering Manchuria when the Japanese surrendered on 14 August, the same day that the Soviet and Chinese governments announced the conclusion of a treaty of friendship and alliance between their two countries. During the negotiations, Stalin had conveyed assurances to the Chinese representative, T. V. Soong, that Soviet forces would complete their withdrawal from the North-east within three months after a Japanese surrender.[4] The deadline for Soviet withdrawal was thus set for 15 November 1945.

The Chinese Communists were in a position to take maximum advantage of those three months during which the Russians occupied the cities and major lines of communications in the North-east, and no one controlled the countryside. During this time, while government forces were leap-frogging over and around them in American transport planes and ships, elements of the Communist Eighth Route and New Fourth Armies were entering Manchuria by junk from Shantung and overland on foot from several northern provinces. They were joined by a small force of North-eastern troops led by Chang Hsueh-szu, a son of the Manchurian warlord Chang Tso-lin, which had been cooperating with the Communists' guerrilla activities against the Japanese in North China. Another son, the popular Young Marshal, Chang Hsueh-liang, remained a hostage to the KMT-CCP united front under house arrest in KMT territory for his role in the 1936 Sian incident.

There is little evidence of direct Soviet military assistance to the Chinese Communists at this time. But large quantities of arms and equipment from the 700,000 surrendering Japanese troops in the North-east did find their way either directly or indirectly into Chinese Communist hands.[5] The soviets also adopted delaying tactics at a number of points to prevent the Americans from landing Government troops at North-east ports. Finally, Chou Pao-chung and remnants of his old Communist North-east anti-Japanese allied army, which had fled across the border into the Soviet Union, returned with Soviet forces in 1945. Other remnants of this army, which the Japanese had effectively destroyed by 1940, emerged

[3] *FRUS, 1945*, 7.576, 577.   [4] *Ibid.* 612.
[5] *China white paper*, 1.381. Most of the arms and equipment of the 1.2 million Japanese troops that surrendered elsewhere in China went to the government armies.

from prison and from underground at this time and began reorganizing at once in cooperation with the Communist forces arriving from North China.

By early November, the KMT government was aware that Soviet withdrawal on schedule would mean immediate occupation of much of the North-east by the Chinese Communists. Despite American assistance, the government had already lost the race to organize a military and civilian takeover operation for Manchuria. The Chinese government therefore negotiated with the Soviets who formally agreed both to extend their stay and to allow government troops to enter the region by the conventional routes. New dates were set for Soviet withdrawal, first early December and then early January. The date was extended twice more, by which time the Soviets had more than overstayed their welcome. They did not actually complete their evacuation from Manchuria until early May 1946.

Meanwhile, on 15 November, with some of his best troops transported from the south and deployed along the Great Wall, Chiang Kai-shek attacked Shanhaikuan, the gateway to Manchuria at the point where the Wall meets the sea. He then proceeded to fight his way into the North-east to take by force a region which had been controlled for fourteen years by the Japanese and before that by the family of the Old Marshal, Chang Tso-lin, but never by the KMT government. The still feeble Chinese Communist forces in the region were as yet no match for Chiang's American-equipped units. His strategy to take over the North-east, aided by the Americans and no longer obstructed by the Soviets, thereafter proceeded apace.

The Soviets took advantage of their delayed departure to augment their war booty, dismantling and removing with their departing forces tons of Manchuria's most modern Japanese industrial equipment.[6] With the action shifting increasingly to the battlefield, the continuing negotiations between the antagonists appeared pointless and Chou En-lai returned to Yenan in late November. Yet these economic and political costs paled beside the strategic military error, later admitted by Chiang himself, of transporting his best American-equipped troops directly to the North-east from their deployment area in Yunnan and Burma without first consolidating control of the territory in between. Whether these troops would have been more successful in the battle for North China than they were in the North-east must remain for ever an unanswered question. But some of Chiang Kai-shek's best divisions entered the North-east never to re-emerge. His decision to commit them to the takeover of that region was a blunder that would come to haunt the generalissimo, for it was in

[6] *Ibid.* 2.596–604.

the North-east, with the failure of these troops to defeat the Communist forces there, that his cause was finally lost.[7]

Meanwhile, several more acts had yet to be played out on the diplomatic stage. Also in late November 1945 Hurley resigned as ambassador to China, damning certain American foreign service officers as he went for allegedly undermining his mediation effort by siding with the CCP. These charges would fester for years before culminating in the anti-Communist allegations of the McCarthy era.[8] But in December 1945, President Truman immediately appointed General George Marshall as his special envoy to take up the mediator's task cast aside by Hurley. The president instructed Marshall to work for a ceasefire between Communist and government forces, and for the peaceful unification of China through the convocation of a national representative conference as agreed upon by Mao and Chiang during their Chungking negotiations.

The Marshall mission: 1946

Marshall arrived in China on 23 December 1945. The US was just then completing delivery of equipment for 39 divisions of the government's armed forces and eight and a third wings for its air force, fulfilling agreements made before the Japanese surrender. Despite the obvious implications of the American supply operation completed within the context of the developing civil war in China, Marshall's peace mission produced immediate results.

Agreement was quickly reached on the convocation of a Political Consultative Conference (PCC) and a committee was formed to discuss a ceasefire. This was the 'Committee of Three', comprising General Marshall as chairman, General Chang Chün representing the government and Chou En-lai representing the CCP. A ceasefire agreement was announced on 10 January 1946, the day prior to the opening of the PCC. The agreement called for a general truce to go into effect from 13 January, and a halt to all troop movements in North China. The right of government forces to take over Manchuria and the former Japanese-occupied areas south of the Yangtze River was acknowledged by the

[7] Chiang Kai-shek, *Soviet Russia in China: a summing-up at seventy*, 232–3. Li Tsung-jen later claimed that his advice against this troop deployment went unheeded (*The memoirs of Li Tsung-jen*, 435).

[8] Hurley's first charges against the Foreign Service officers were made in his letter of resignation, reprinted in *China white paper*, 2.581–4; also, *FRUS, 1945*, 7.722–44. Among the many accounts now available of this inglorious episode are: O. Edmund Clubb, *The witness and I*; John Paton Davies, Jr. *Dragon by the tail*; Joseph W. Esherick, ed. *Lost chance in China*; E. J. Kahn, Jr. *The China hands*; Gary May, *China scapegoat*; John S. Service, *The Amerasia papers*; Ross Y. Koen, *The China lobby in American politics*; and Stanley D. Bachrack, *The Committee of One Million: 'China Lobby' politics, 1953–1971*. See also Kenneth W. Rea and John C. Brewer, eds. *The forgotten ambassador: the reports of John Leighton Stuart, 1946–1949*.

ceasefire agreement. An executive headquarters was set up in Peiping to supervise the ceasefire and began functioning at once. It was led by three commissioners representing the government, the CCP and the United States. Its truce teams were to be made up of equal numbers of government and CCP personnel, with the American role confined to that of assistance only.

The PCC met from 11 to 31 January 1946 for the declared purpose of seeking a peaceful solution to the KMT-CCP conflict. Great hopes were placed in this conference, if not by the two main antagonists, then at least by all other concerned parties. For a time it was the chief focus of popular attention and even after the hopes were shown to be illusory, the authority of the PCC agreements was invoked by the government to legitimize a number of its subsequent political actions.

The PCC participants, although not democratically elected, were acknowledged by all to be representative of the major and minor political groupings within the Chinese political arena. The participants comprised 38 delegates: eight from the KMT, seven from the CCP, five from the Youth Party, two from the Democratic League, two from the Democratic-Socialist Party, two from the National Salvation Association, one from the Vocational Education Association, one from the Rural Reconstruction Association, one from the Third Party, and nine non-partisans.

Agreement was reached on virtually all political and military issues outstanding between the KMT and the CCP. The agreements concerned: the reorganization of the national government; a political programme to end the period of KMT tutelage and establish constitutional government; revision of the 1936 Draft Constitution; membership of the proposed National Constitutional Assembly which would adopt the revised constitution; and reorganization of government and CCP armies under a unified command.

The PCC provided that a three-man military committee be formed to devise plans for implementing conference resolutions calling for general troop reductions and the integration of CCP forces into a unified national army. This group, the Military Sub-committee, was made up of General Chang Chih-chung for the government and Chou En-lai for the CCP, with Marshall serving as adviser. They announced agreement on 25 February, with plans for a massive troop reduction on both sides. This was to be accomplished within 18 months, at the end of which there would be roughly 840,000 government troops in 50 divisions, and 140,000 troops in 10 divisions on the Communist side, which would be integrated into the national army. Agreement was also reached on the disposition of these forces with the majority of the Communist divisions to be deployed in

North China, reflecting the area of their greatest strength and concentration.

Unfortunately, there was no superior authority capable of enforcing either the ceasefire or the military and political accords. Dependent only on the mutual trust and good faith of the adversaries themselves for implementation, the agreements came apart very quickly once the initial momentum, generated by the arrival in China of General Marshall and the convocation of the PCC, had passed. Perhaps the two main parties to the agreements were sincere in concluding them. From the hindsight of history, they appear rather to have been a cynical manoeuvre entered into by both rivals in order to pacify Chinese public opinion and the American ally, while buying time for the most advantageous possible deployment of their mutual armed forces. In fact, the truth may lie somewhere in between, since both Chiang Kai-shek and Chou En-lai subsequently indicated that genuine disagreement had existed within their respective parties at this time on the merits of working out a compromise accommodation between them.[9] The implication is that the two parties were perhaps still undecided in early 1946, and that the resolve to settle their differences through full-scale war emerged only with the progressive breakdown of the agreements reached at that time.

Right-wing elements within the KMT, opposed to the PCC resolution, were able to revise the party's position on a number of points at a meeting of KMT's Central Executive Committee in March 1946. The two most significant revisions placed curbs on provincial autonomy and provided for the continuation of presidential government, as opposed to the cabinet system approved by the PCC. Subsequently, the KMT also refused to grant the CCP and its political ally, the Democratic League, joint veto power in the 40-member State Council which was to be the highest organ of state power prior to the establishment of constitutional government.

The two parties therefore claimed that the KMT had violated both the letter and the spirit of the original PCC agreements, and refused to participate further in their implementation. The government, undeterred, proceeded unilaterally in accordance with the PCC agreements. The National Constitutional Assembly was convoked in November 1946 for the purpose of adopting the revised draft of the 1936 Constitution. The new constitution was promulgated on 1 January 1947; elections were held later in the year for delegates to the First National Assembly, which met during April 1948, to choose the nation's president and vice president.[10]

---

[9] Lyman P. Van Slyke, *Marshall's mission to China, December 1944–January 1947*, 1.353–4; and *FRUS, 1949*, 8.358.

[10] On the negotiations over the ceasefire agreements of 10 January see *FRUS, 1946*, 9.1–130. On the PCC and the breakdown of the agreements it produced: *ibid.* 131–77, 177–341; Van Slyke,

Meanwhile, troop reductions and the unification of the armies made even less headway than political reorganization. In this area, the Communists appeared the more intransigent, refusing even to provide the lists of their military units as required by the 25 February military reorganization accord. Blame for the disintegration of the ceasefire, however, seemed to fall about evenly on both sides. For example, General Marshall sought permission in late January to send an Executive Headquarters truce team to the Manchurian port of Yingkou, where clashes were reportedly taking place. The CCP approved but the government initially declined and then dithered over their authority. Truce teams did not actually enter Manchuria until early April, by which time hostilities were already well advanced. In Marshall's view, the government was not only responsible for refusing to honour the ceasefire in Manchuria and to allow truce teams to operate there, but also for numerous other violations of the ceasefire agreement both in South and North China.[11]

The Communists, for their part, had built up their strength so rapidly in the North-east that they were able to challenge the advancing government forces and did so repeatedly. Communist troop movements in Manchuria were technically not a violation of the agreements since the troop movement prohibition applied only to North China and not the North-east. But hostilities then occurred at many points. When the Russians finally began their withdrawal in mid-March, they apparently acted in coordination with Chinese Communist forces which were ready to move in behind them as they evacuated most of Manchuria's major cities, including Mukden (Shenyang), Changchun, Kirin, Harbin and Tsitsihar.

At Mukden, government troops were able to evict Chinese Communist forces within 24 hours. But at Changchun, units led by Chou Pao-chung engaged advance government forces and local militia for three days before entering the city on 18 April. Government forces succeeded in capturing Szupingkai on 19 May, but only after more than a month of fighting. After this defeat, the Communists then withdrew from Changchun and government units occupied that city on 23 May. In North China, the Communists also openly violated the terms of the truce with offensive troop movements in Shantung, along the Tientsin-Pukow railway, and in northern Kiangsu.[12]

Marshall's mission, 1.8-68; Carsun Chang, *The third force in China*, 142-222; and Ch'ien Tuan-sheng, *The government and politics of China*, 317-45, 375-81. The constitution adopted by the National Constitutional Assembly is translated in Appendix D of the latter volume. Conference resolutions and news releases concerning the March 1946 meeting of the KMT Central Executive Committee are in *China white paper*, 2. 610-21, 634-9.   [11] Van Slyke, *Marshall's mission*, 1.49-63.
[12] O. Edmund Clubb, *Twentieth-century China*, 267-71; Lionel Max Chassin, *The Communist conquest of China: a history of the civil war, 1945-1949*, 77-82.

With the ceasefire in disarray, Marshall temporarily withdrew as formal mediator but continued to act as an intermediary between the two sides. In this capacity, he succeeded in arranging a two-week truce for Manchuria commencing 7 June 1946. During that time negotiations were to be conducted, so as to bring about: (1) an end to the fighting in the North-east; (2) the resumption of rail communications in North China, where Communist forces were blocking the vital north-south railway links as well as the Tsinan-Tsingtao line, thus disrupting the northward movement of the government's military transport and southward-bound coal shipments for its industrial base in the Lower Yangtze valley; and (3) the implementation of the 25 February military reorganization agreement. Chiang Kai-shek declared that this would be the last time he would attempt to resolve his differences with the CCP at the conference table, and similar statements appeared in the KMT press.

Marshall resumed formal mediation and the truce was extended to the end of June, but agreement was not reached. The major stumbling block as the truce expired was the Communists' unwillingness to permit government administration of northern Kiangsu following the agreed withdrawal of CCP forces from that region. The Communist side insisted on the continuation of all existing local governments in areas of North China to be evacuated by their troops. By this time, however, the government's plans for a full-scale offensive against the Communist areas were already complete and the CCP was aware of them, making further negotiations a futile exercise.

The failure of the Marshall mission and its implications for US China policy

The Marshall mission was not formally terminated until 6 January 1947. But with the expiration of the truce period on 30 June, and in the absence of the agreements necessary to extend it, the failure of the American peace mission appeared inevitable. A new US ambassador, Dr J. Leighton Stuart, was named to fill the post which had remained vacant since Hurley's resignation. After his arrival in July, Stuart shared with Marshall the increasingly thankless task of mediation until the latter's recall to the US in early 1947. But the fate of their continuing effort had been sealed by the government's coordinated general offensive against the Communist-held areas, which began within days after the expiration of the June truce.

Shortly after the offensive began and apparently not yet aware of its import, the Americans tried one last time to salvage the negotiations. They proposed on 1 August the formation of a five-man negotiating committee with two government representatives, two for the CCP, and Ambassador

Stuart as chairman. Chiang Kai-shek demanded as a precondition wide-ranging Communist troop withdrawals – from virtually all of the areas that were the targets of his offensive. The Communists refused to agree until the status of the local governments in the areas from which they were to withdraw had been solved to their satisfaction. Military operations continued meanwhile and on 19 August, shortly after government forces bombed Yenan, the Communists declared a general mobilization for war throughout the areas under their authority.

With the government attack against the Communist-held city of Kalgan in progress, Marshall recommended to Washington in early October that he be recalled, arguing that the peace negotiations were now clearly being used as a cover for government military operations against the Communist areas. To forestall Marshall's resignation on these grounds, Chiang Kai-shek declared a short truce at Kalgan, which the CCP rejected as unsatisfactory. Chou En-lai, the Communists' chief negotiator throughout 1946, demanded instead a withdrawal of government forces to their positions at the time of the original 13 January truce in China proper, and of the 7 June truce in the North-east. The government declined and its forces captured Kalgan on 10 October.

The government then unilaterally convened the National Assembly. The CCP and the Democratic League refused to participate on the grounds that the KMT had not honoured the terms of the PCC resolutions on government reorganization. Chou En-lai returned to Yenan on 19 November, a gesture marking the formal withdrawal of the CCP from the mediation exercise. In early December, the Communists indicated their unwillingness to accept further American mediation and forwarded to Nanking their preconditions for resuming negotiations, namely, dissolution of the National Assembly and withdrawal of government forces to their January positions. These conditions were naturally unacceptable. Both sides had by now determined that they had more to gain on the battlefield than at the conference table.

As the year 1946 progressed, Marshall's role as mediator had grown increasingly difficult. Although it could not be foreseen at the time, his problems contained all the elements of the trauma that would overtake US China policy in the years to come. The hardening postures of the KMT and CCP toward each other in 1946 were paralleled by a growing resentment on both sides over the role being played by the US. The war party within the KMT – led by the CC clique of the brothers Ch'en Kuo-fu and Ch'en Li-fu – saw the American mediation effort as frustrating their plans to exterminate the Communists, the only solution to the problem in their eyes. This view would later be pursued with great vengeance by sympathizers in the United States.

Perhaps more significant was the general resentment within the KMT government generated by American demands for its reform. Prime Minister T. V. Soong noted, with reference to this gratuitous advice, that in the old days 'for one government to tell another it should do these things would mean war'.[13] Yet Chinese and American leaders both knew that the latter had no means of inducing the former to implement the wide-ranging political, economic and military reforms necessary to revive the government's sinking fortunes. Moreover, KMT leaders were also well aware that however dissatisfied the Americans might be with them, capitalist America would still support them in any showdown with the Communists.[14]

The Communist side was also aware of this basic fact of international political life. But their protestations highlighted the more immediate contradiction inherent in Marshall's position although, to be sure, the Communists did not choose to escalate the pressure on this point until even the pretence of possible success for the mediation effort could no longer be maintained. Nevertheless, Marshall had been placed in the awkward position of attempting to mediate a peace settlement while simultaneously representing a country that was the chief source of aid and support for one of the two parties to the dispute.

Only about half the arms and equipment promised to the KMT government under the 39 army divisions and air force supply programme had been delivered when Japan surrendered. The remainder was delivered later, when the enemy it would be used against was already clearly visible. The US had also aided the government in its race with the CCP to take over the former Japanese-occupied territories by transporting government troops into those areas. In some cases, US marines were even used to hold them in trust pending the government's arrival. On 25 February 1946, the same day the military reorganization agreement was announced, the US authorized the formation of a military advisory group in China to aid and assist the government in developing its armed forces. The group was set up in March. The Americans also contributed US $500 million to the China aid programme of the United Nations Relief and Rehabilitation Administration, the great bulk of which was delivered to the KMT areas. On 14 June 1946, the Lend-Lease 'Pipeline' Credit Agreement was concluded, whereby the US extended additional credit to the Chinese government for the purchase of civilian-type equipment and supplies contracted for during the Second World War but not yet delivered under

---

[13] John Robinson Beal, *Marshall in China*, 330.

[14] For a recent re-statement of this earlier belief, see Nancy Bernkopf Tucker, 'Nationalist China's decline and its impact on Sino-American relations, 1949–1950', in Dorothy Borg and Waldo Heinrichs, eds. *Uncertain years*, 153; and the same author's *Patterns in the dust*.

the wartime lend-lease programme. And in August, after the KMT offensive against the Communist areas had already begun, the Americans concluded yet another agreement authorizing the sale on credit of US $900 million worth of war surplus property to the KMT government for a net sum of $175 million. This 'civilian-type' property included small ships, vehicles, construction materials, air force supplies and materiel, and communications equipment. At the same time, negotiations were under way for a treaty of friendship, commerce and navigation between the US and Chinese governments.[15]

Such assistance may have been entirely legitimate for the recognized government of a major American ally. But within the context of Chinese domestic politics, Marshall's position as an impartial mediator between the rival parties was compromised from the start by his country's continuing strategic support for the KMT government. The Communists escalated their propaganda attacks against this relationship during the summer of 1946, accusing the US of strengthening the government's military power and thereby encouraging the KMT to seek a military solution to the conflict. Implicitly acknowledging the validity of this charge, the US placed an embargo on the shipment of arms and ammunition to China beginning in late July 1946. This was part of Marshall's declared 'efforts to influence China's governmental course of action and the determined stand and plans of political reactionaries, civil and military.'[16]

Nevertheless, the embargo, partially lifted in October and rescinded entirely in May 1947, exemplified the constraints built into Marshall's mission by his country's China policy. The ban came too late to have any restraining influence on the government's war plans or the course of the negotiations. It therefore did little to mollify the Communists. Indeed, any utility it might have had in this respect was almost immediately undermined by the August decision to sell $900 million worth of war surplus property to the government. Yet anti-Communist critics in the US would soon seize upon the embargo as an important issue in their attack on US China policy, claiming that the consequent shortage of munitions was a crucial factor in the defeat of the government's armies.

Hence the American mediation effort pleased virtually no one and accomplished little except to provide Marshall, soon to be named US secretary of state, with first-hand experience as to the futility of attempting to intervene in the Chinese civil war. Lacking the means to induce KMT

---

[15] China white paper, 1.225–9, 311–12; also FRUS, 1945, 7.527–721 passim; Tsou Tang, America's failure in China, 1941–50, 429–30.
[16] FRUS, 1946, 10.753.

compliance with any of its demands, the US still could not for reasons of its own domestic and international political concerns withdraw support completely from the KMT government in its struggle with the CCP. Thus neither could the gesture of the 1946 arms embargo induce the government to alter significantly its war plans or win any goodwill from the Communist side. Instead, the embargo's only lasting result was to heighten the resentment of the Chinese government ally and its supporters in the United States. Meanwhile, other forms of material aid and diplomatic support for that government continued as it embarked upon the course of all-out war. Perhaps the greatest failure of the Marshall mission was not that it had so little influence on the course of the civil war in China, but that the Americans should ever have assumed their mediation effort might actually do so. That erroneous assumption was part of a more deep-seated belief on the part of many in the United States, growing out of its Second World War role as the chief arbiter of Asia's fortunes, that in one way or another American policy-makers had the power and responsibility to determine the political fate of China.

THE DECLINE OF KMT RULE

The KMT government in August 1945 could claim authority over all the country's major cities, its entire industrial base, and more than three-quarters of a total population estimated at about 450 million. That government had not only won acclaim as the leader of Free China against the Japanese, but had also led China into the arena of world politics where it had come to be recognized as one of the great powers. Hence it was not surprising that Chiang Kai-shek and the government he led gambled on an all-or-nothing solution for their 'Communist problem' at the end of the Japanese war.

The government's armies numbered over 2.5 million men in 1945, more than double the Communist forces, and also enjoyed a clear superiority of arms, equipment and transport capability. Communist forces – with little fighting experience other than guerrilla warfare, with no air force, navy, nor anything comparable to the government's American-trained and equipped divisions – appeared to most observers to be no match for the Nationalists. Chiang and his generals, like the Americans who were supplying and training their armies, were impressed with modern fire-power and expected it to win in China as it had just done against Japan. That this did not happen was a surprise to almost everyone except perhaps the Communists. Before pursuing the course of the civil war of 1946–9, let us look at the contemporary process of decay within Nationalist China.

For the eventual Communist victory was founded upon the weaknesses of the old society and the political establishment which governed it.

Contemporary participants and observers did not need to subscribe to the CCP's theoretical explanations concerning feudalism, imperialism, landlord domination of the countryside, and the leading families' monopoly of the urban economy, to understand the gravity of the KMT's problems. These were clearly visible during the 1940s and were described repeatedly by diplomats and foreign correspondents, as well as an only partially-controlled Chinese press. 'Incompetent and corrupt' was the catchphrase used to describe the government's performance in virtually every sphere from the conduct of war to school administration. In March 1947 Professor Ch'u An-p'ing, founder and editor of *Kuan-ch'a* (The observer), the most popular journal of political commentary in KMT China during the late 1940s, summed up a widely held view:

The basis of the present regime's support has been the urban population: government employees and teachers, intellectuals, and business and industrial circles. At present, no one among these people has any positive feelings toward the Nanking regime. The KMT's tyrannical style of behaviour is causing deep hatred among liberal elements; as for civil servants and teachers, the skimpiness of their salaries since the end of the Anti-Japanese War has caused them to lose hope in the present political regime; the government officials by indulging in corrupt practices and creating every kind of obstruction have caused extreme dissatisfaction in business and industrial circles; and the violent rise in prices due to erroneous financial and monetary policies and the continuation of the civil war is causing sounds of resentment to be heard everywhere among the urban population.[17]

Takeover from the Japanese

After 1927, urban China was KMT territory and its heartland was the main coastal cities together with those along the Yangtze River valley. Most of that area came under Japanese occupation during the Second World War, while the KMT government retreated into the south-west. The beginning of popular urban disillusionment with the government came during the reassertion of its authority over the occupied territories after the Japanese surrender. By the end of 1945, virtually every sector of the population in the nation's major urban centres had acquired specific grievances for which the government's policies and the behaviour of its officials could be held directly responsible.

The hallmark of the period was the takeover process itself, referred to

---

[17] Ch'u An-p'ing, 'Chung-kuo ti cheng-chü' (China's political situation), *Kuan-ch'a*, 8 March 1947, p. 3.

in Chinese as *chieh-shou*. Civilian and military officials representing the government took control of all offices of the Japanese-sponsored administration and all properties, both public and private, owned by the Japanese and their collaborators. All assets were supposed to be either returned to their original owners if taken illegally, or handed over to new owners in accordance with officially established procedures. In the interim, factories were supposed to cease production; the movement of goods in or out of sealed warehouses was prohibited; and occupants of buildings were supposed to vacate them.

As the officials returned and the process unfolded, however, it became common to substitute one or more homophonous characters in writing the term *chieh-shou*, thus transforming its meaning into robbery or plunder. The takeover policies themselves were either ill-conceived or improperly implemented, and there were few institutional safeguards to inhibit abuse. As a result, the takeover process everywhere devolved into an unseemly scramble as the arriving officials raced each other to lay claim to enemy property. Everything was fair game: industrial machinery, public buildings, houses, vehicles, even furnishings and office equipment – all requisitioned for the use or profit of whoever was able to lay the first or at least the strongest claim to them. The carpet-bagging official from Chungking became the symbol of the period. According to popular saying he had but five concerns: gold bars, automobiles, houses, Japanese women, and face.[18]

Meanwhile, hundreds and thousands of workers suddenly found themselves unemployed due to the suspension of industrial production. Its cause was twofold, namely, the takeover process in the coastal areas, and the closure of wartime industries in the hinterland. Factory-owners and businessmen in Free China had expected to be compensated with enterprises taken over from the Japanese and their collaborators, since some had suffered considerable losses in following the government to the south-west during the war. Instead, the government ignored these political obligations, while letting its officials and others take over the industrial wealth of occupied China. But the economy in the recovered areas soon deteriorated to the point where it was often more profitable to dismantle and sell factory machinery, which many did, than to operate it. More than a year after the surrender, the Ministry of Economic Affairs admitted that only 852 of the estimated 2,411 factory units taken over from the Japanese and their collaborators had actually resumed operation.[19]

[18] Wang Chien-min, *Chung-kuo kung-ch'an-tang shih-kao* (A draft history of the Chinese Communist Party), 3.544.
[19] *Ho-p'ing jih-pao*, Shanghai, 13 Nov. 1946 (*CPR*, 27 Dec.).

By late 1946, there were many other reasons for the industrial depression; but it had begun with the disruption created by the bizarre behaviour of government officials racing to take over the wealth left by the Japanese.

These transgressions were compounded by the government's official attitude towards and treatment of the population in the former occupied areas. Initially the government was compromised after VJ Day by its need to rely on Japanese and Chinese puppet troops to maintain 'law and order', that is, it had to rely on the armed forces of the defeated enemy to prevent a Communist takeover of North China cities, and towns. The Japanese and their collaborators were permitted to function for an uncertain period as the Chinese government's political representatives. In the midst of the public outcry over the issue, regulations governing the punishment of collaborators were issued in late September 1946, but they contained a number of loopholes and were only selectively applied. Despite the arrest of several prominent collaborators, there was no systematic effort to settle all the claims and accusations before some impartial court or official body. Many who had served the Japanese in official capacities were entrusted with equally influential posts by the returning government.

While the government was compromising itself over the collaborator issue, however, its officials were returning clothed in self-righteousness inherited from the hardships they had suffered to sustain Free China's struggle in the hinterland. The official posture of condescension was particularly evident in the takeover of Taiwan and Manchuria. Both regions had long been under Japanese rule, Taiwan for half a century. The mutual hostility that developed between the Taiwanese and the takeover personnel from the mainland culminated in the bloodily suppressed rebellion of February 1947.[20] In the North-east, it was commonly said afterwards that a rebellion would have broken out there as well, except that everyone who wanted to rebel simply crossed over to the Communist side.

The issue was perhaps most explicitly stated in the government's policy of educational reconversion which formally stigmatized teachers and students. Special courses in KMT ideology were made mandatory for students by order of the Ministry of Education. Those who had graduated from colleges, universities and middle schools during the occupation were required to pass a written examination in order to retain their status as graduates. Teachers were also supposed to pass examinations designed to test their knowledge of and loyalty to the KMT. The resentment arose not so much over the courses themselves, since the underlying aim was generally supported and the examinations were not particularly rigorous.

[20] George H. Kerr, *Formosa betrayed, passim.*

Rather the issue was the stigma officially attached to the re-education process. In announcing it, the Ministry of Education asserted that all students who had attended schools in areas controlled by the collaborator government were assumed to have been corrupted, and until they were re-educated and their thoughts purged, they would be unfit for further education. As 'puppet students' they should be helped to 'wash off their ideological stains'.[21] But with the public scandal created by the venality of the newly-arrived officials from the south-west, local people initially on the defensive soon rose to question why such individuals should presume to sit in judgment on anyone.

Yet, despite its transgressions during this period, the KMT government suffered little more than a loss of prestige and public confidence. There were few calls for anything more drastic than the restoration of that confidence through the correction of the errors committed. Unfortunately for the government, most of the issues that aroused such disillusionment after the Japanese surrender were never satisfactorily resolved, becoming instead a prelude for what was to follow. Hence, what might have been forgotten as a temporary postwar lapse came to be recognized afterwards as the beginning of the end of popular urban support for the KMT government.

Economic incompetence: the policy of inflationary finance

Monetary inflation probably contributed more than any other single issue during the civil war years to the loss of urban public confidence in the KMT's ability to govern. The policy of inflationary finance began during the Anti-Japanese War when the government was cut off from the coastal and Yangtze River cities which had been its main base of financial support. By 1945, government income, not including bank credits, equalled only one-third of expenditures and the deficit was made up almost entirely by printing-press money. In the resulting inflation average prices rose over two thousand times between 1937 and August 1945. The gap between government income and expenditure continued throughout the civil war years, as did the principal means of bridging it, while the effects of the ensuing hyper-inflation played themselves out to their inevitable conclusion. Perhaps the most dangerous consequence of the decision to rely on printing press money was that it allowed those who made it to believe there was an easy solution to the nation's financial difficulties.

---

[21] *Chung-mei jih-pao*, Shanghai, 20 Nov. 1945 (*CPR*, 20 Nov.); also, *Shih-shih hsin-pao*, Chungking, 12 Sept. 1945 (*CPR*, 12 Sept.); *Chung-yang jih-pao*, Chungking, 12 Sept. 1945 and *Ta-kung-pao*, Chungking, 11 Sept. 1945 (both in *CPR*, 13 Sept.).

Government leaders not surprisingly opted to finance their war against the CCP in the same manner as that against the Japanese. The result was a government with neither the will nor the ability to do anything but watch over the deterioration of the nation's urban economy.

The inflation provided ready-made issues for a labour force suddenly freed, in August 1945, from the constraints of eight years of Japanese rule and ten years of KMT domination before that. After Japan's surrender the KMT was unable to re-create the network of organizational control with which it had contained the labour movement from 1927 to 1937. Now labour flouted the officially established procedures for the resolution of labour-management disputes. With its old strike-breaking tactics no longer effective, the government had no choice but to accept labour's demand for automatic wage adjustments corresponding to the rise in the cost of living. But this decision, announced in April 1946, not only accelerated the upward wage-price spiral; it also compromised the government's long-standing alliance with business and industry and roused the resentment of entrepreneurs, who felt the concession to labour was contributing to their own rising production costs. Meanwhile, official statistics demonstrated the KMT's inability to pacify labour. In 1936, just prior to the Japanese invasion, there had been 278 strikes and labour disputes recorded for the whole country. By comparison, in 1946 there was a total of 1,716 strikes and labour disputes recorded in Shanghai alone. In 1947 the number for that city reached 2,538.[22]

The government often charged that labour's aggressiveness was the work of professional Communist agitators. The labour movement, at least in Shanghai, did indeed appear to be well infiltrated.[23] But the issues were ready-made and available for exploitation by anyone. As the economy became disrupted by rampant inflation and the consequent contraction of business and industry, urban labour had no form of protection or unemployment benefits, and so refused, as did other sectors of the public on many occasions and in a variety of ways, to comply with the government's pleas for cooperation.

High wage payments were but one of many problems responsible for stifling industrial production. These included continuing increases in energy and transport costs: increasing trade and production taxes; high interest rates; and declining demand due to the reduction in real

[22] *China Weekly Review: monthly report*, 31 Jan. 1947, p. 13; *Ta-kung-pao*, Shanghai, 26 Feb. 1947 (*CPR*, 5 March); and *Lih pao*, Shanghai, 7 Jan. 1948 (*CPR*, 12 Jan.).

[23] See for example, Liu Ch'ang-sheng, *et al. Chung-kuo kung-ch'an-tang yü Shang-hai kung-jen: Shang-hai kung-jen yun-tung li-shih yen-chiu tzu-liao chih erh* (The Chinese Communist Party and the Shanghai workers: Shanghai labour movement historical research materials number two), *passim.*

purchasing power. By late 1947 these conditions had resulted in a general contraction of industrial output.

But in order to increase its income, the government allowed the continued existence of an irrational tax system which placed numerous and often exorbitant levies on legitimate business operations, while it left untouched the personal incomes of speculators and profiteers. The government's foreign trade policy also resulted in an unfavourable balance which harmed local producers. These conditions were only partially corrected by reforms in November 1946, aimed at encouraging exports and restricting imports.

The KMT government was vulnerable to the charge that instead of promoting economic development it encouraged bureaucratic capitalism, meaning the use of public office for personal enterprise and profit. Government officials and their associates used their connections to obtain foreign exchange, import commodities, and gain other advantages not readily available to the ordinary entrepreneur. One example was a scandalous government loan in 1946 to Shanghai rice merchants, who used it, apparently with official connivance, for speculative purposes, causing a further rise in the price of rice.[24] Meanwhile, when the government offered bonds for sale during the first half of 1947, capitalists were reluctant to buy. Similarly, some businessmen were said to have large sums of money which they refused to invest in their own enterprises because the profits would have been more uncertain than those which could be gained through speculation. The opportunities for speculation included buying, selling and hoarding commodities; speculating on the securities market; investing in gold and foreign currencies; and lending at black-market interest rates. The result was further cutbacks in production, collapsing enterprises and rising unemployment.

Emergency reforms of 1947 and 1948

The government launched two ambitious campaign-style reform programmes aimed, it was said, at the overall stabilization of the economy. The first was proclaimed on 16 February 1947, when all wages were frozen at their January levels, and ceilings placed on the prices of certain essential commodities, foremost among them rice, cotton and fuel. Trading in and hoarding of gold and foreign currencies by private persons was prohibited. Measures were also introduced to curb the flight of capital to Hong Kong. Yet the failure of the system of price controls was inevitable, first because

---

[24] *Hsin-wen pao*, 12 June 1946; *Shih-shih hsin-pao*, 14 June 1946; *Ta-kung-pao* 19 June 1946; and *Wen hui pao*, 9 July 1946, all Shanghai (all *CPR* for the same dates).

it was limited in scope, and second because it was not uniformly implemented, being rigorously enforced only in the cities of the Shanghai-Nanking area. Production costs therefore continued to rise, as did prices generally, while only the market prices of the essential commodities remained frozen. The price of rice in areas where it was grown soon reached levels higher than in the cities where it was to be sold. The continuous rise in the price of raw cotton made textile production unprofitable. Coal and edible oil were similarly affected. A rice shortage developed. A black market in US dollars was in existence by early April, and most of the essential commodities on the price control list emerged on the black market soon thereafter. The government was unable to provide the guaranteed allocation of these commodities to workers under the proposed factory ration scheme, and decided instead to pay subsidies corresponding to the value of the goods that would have been allocated to each worker. But the subsidies covered only the costs of essential commodities which were increasingly unavailable at the fixed prices, while those of everything else continued to rise. During the month of May, the wholesale price index for Shanghai rose 54 per cent, in comparison with a 19 per cent increase during the month prior to the start of the reform programme. Finally, under the combined pressures created by labour's demand that wages be unfrozen, the collapse of the rice market, and rice riots which spread to more than a dozen cities during late April and May, all of the emergency reform measures were formally abandoned.[25]

With this experience so recently concluded, the 19 August 1948 emergency reform programme was only a last gesture by desperate men foundering in the economic chaos they had themselves created. It was evident from the start that this new reform effort could not succeed because it contained the same flaws responsible for the failure of the 1947 programme. Yet government leaders declared, in August 1948, that this was their last chance; the reform programme had to succeed because they had no other means at their disposal with which to try to stabilize the economy and revive public confidence. When the programme was abandoned at the end of October, the only achievement anyone could think of was that it had allowed the government to confiscate US $170 million worth of gold, silver and foreign currencies from the public, in accordance with the regulation that all such holdings had to be exchanged for the new currency, the Gold Yuan. The most overtly indignant group in Shanghai, where the new programme had been most stringently enforced, was not the long-suffering middle class but business and

[25] Chang Kia-ngau, *The inflationary spiral: the experience in China, 1939-1950*, 72-3, 350-2.

industry – previously a major pillar of KMT support. Some three thousand businessmen, including some of Shanghai's most prominent, had been imprisoned at the start of the campaign. Later they denounced the 'quack doctors' who had used the four million people of Shanghai as 'specimens for an experiment' and demanded punishment for the officials who had devised it. Foremost among them was Chiang Kai-shek's son, Chiang Ching-kuo, who had been responsible for enforcing the reform measures in Shanghai.[26]

The assertion has nevertheless been made that the inflation also cost the government the support of the urban salaried middle class. The main groups making up this middle-income minority were the intellectuals, that is, college professors, school teachers, writers and journalists; and government employees. While this is too simple an explanation for their growing dissatisfaction with the KMT and the government it led, the soaring prices and depreciating currency did create a major burden for this sector of the population. Its impoverishment began during the Anti-Japanese War when inflation reduced their real incomes to between 6 and 12 per cent of their pre-1937 salaries. By 1946, according to one estimate made in Kunming, the real income of college teachers there had been reduced by 98 per cent.[27] And while it could at least decree that the wages of labour be pegged to the cost-of-living index, the government was not able to do the same for its own employees. These included the majority of college teachers whose pay scales as employees in state-financed institutions were comparable to those of other civil servants. The salaries of all public employees were revised upwards on the average of once quarterly. But these adjustments were never proportional to the rise in the cost of living. It was regularly claimed in the late 1940s that the real incomes of teachers and civil servants were not sufficient to maintain their basic livelihood in terms of food, clothing and shelter.

The new impoverishment of the intellectual community did, moreover, help to inspire the students' anti-war movement. Indeed, the professors themselves apparently precipitated the widespread Anti-Hunger Anti-Civil War demonstrations during the spring of 1947, which demanded among other things a reduction in military expenditures and an increase in the budget for education. Clearly, the hardships created by the use of printing-press money to finance the war effort provided one major issue for those opposed to that effort and helped to undermine support for it.

[26] *Ta-kung-pao*, Shanghai, and *Chung-hua shih-pao*, Shanghai, 2 Nov. 1948 (both in *CPR* of same date); Chang Kia-ngau, *Inflationary spiral*, 357–60; Lloyd E. Eastman, *Seeds of destruction*, 172–202.

[27] *Ta-kung-pao*, Shanghai, 30 Aug. 1946 (*CPR*, 31 Aug.); also Chang Kia-ngau, *Inflationary spiral*, 63–5; and Chou Shun-hsin, *The Chinese inflation, 1937–1949*, 244.

But, even so, the intellectuals as a group, like the civil servants, did not actually abandon the government until it was defeated militarily.

Political incompetence: the mismanagement of the peace movement

If their impoverishment was the main fact of economic life for China's intellectuals during the 1940s, their dominant political preoccupation was opposition to the civil war. The government refused to acknowledge the legitimacy of this protest, treating it instead as a contrivance of the Communist underground. Because of this misconception and the repression that followed therefrom, it was the government and not the CCP which ultimately had to bear the heavier burden of public censure for the military conflict.

Thus the student protest movement did not simply spring up full-blown but developed in the course of the students' demonstrations and the government's reaction to them. There were four major demonstrations which aroused nationwide attention. The December First movement (1945) was the smallest of these. The principal action was in Kunming where four young people were killed and several others seriously injured on 1 December 1945 by unknown assailants attempting to intimidate the anti-war protesters. As a result of this violent act, what had begun as a campus anti-war meeting at South-west Associated University came to be known as the first major protest of the period. In late December 1946 and January 1947, a series of anti-American demonstrations protested the alleged rape of a Peking University student by a US marine. The behaviour of the marines was only the immediate provocation. Beyond that the students queried why American military personnel were in China at all and whether they were not in fact participants in the civil war on the side of the government. The momentum generated over this issue grew into the Anti-Hunger Anti-Civil War movement which swept through universities and secondary schools in most major cities throughout the country during May and June 1947. This last big 'student tide', as they were called, merged with the Movement to Protest American Support of Japan between April and June 1948.

Despite local concerns and personalities that were often involved, the basic motivations of the national student protest were the same everywhere. The students' primary demands were an immediate end to the civil war; an end to US backing for the KMT in that war; and a shift in public expenditure from military to civilian priorities. The government responded initially by trying to divert the movement into other channels. Besides the informers and secret agents planted by the authorities in schools where students were most active, students sympathetic to the government, such as members of the KMT San-min-chu-i Youth Corps, were supposed to organize and lead student activities as loyal Nationalist supporters. Yet it was common knowledge that the brightest and most energetic student leaders in the country's best schools were all critical of the government and its war policy.

Nevertheless, government decision-makers remained constricted by their belief that if only the very few 'real' Communist agitators among the students could be eliminated, their movement could be controlled.[28] The consequent harsh tactics in turn further alienated the students. Their leaders, particularly officials of the university self-governing associations, were the chief targets of beatings, arrests and abduction by an assortment of law enforcement personnel. On the basis of tip-offs by informers, the arrest of student activists became a common occurrence. Blacklists of activists and suspected underground Communists were drawn up. These students, if not caught off campus, might be apprehended in night raids on school dormitories. Students arrested or abducted often simply 'disappeared'. Execution was the anticipated punishment for genuine Communist agents if their identity could be ascertained. Torture was also a common means of extracting information.

In this manner, what had begun as a manoeuvre to publicize the students' demands for a peaceful solution to the KMT–CCP conflict soon developed into a movement that challenged the authority of the KMT government. Of greatest significance in this respect were not the students who physically fled to the Communist side, for these seem to have been relatively few in number. More important was the wider resentment engendered by the government's attempts to subdue the protest movement. This probably did not transform the students into Communists or sympathizers. But it did intensify the students' opposition to the government and their refusal to support its war against the CCP.

The reasoning behind the students' demands was spelled out by the older generation of intellectuals in a steady stream of commentary criticizing the war and the disaster it was wreaking upon the nation. They assumed, as did most foreign observers, that the war was likely to continue indefinitely because neither side could defeat the other – the general view until about mid-1948. The costs of the war included the inflation that had completely disrupted the urban economy and the further impoverishment of the rural areas. Besides the printing press, the government's finance was also dependent upon a land tax, compulsory

---

[28] Ch'en Li-fu, head of the powerful CC clique within the KMT, expressed this view in an interview with Doak Barnett (Barnett, *China on the eve of Communist takeover*, 50).

purchase of grain at lower than market prices, and collection of grain on loan. These levies together with additional requisitions to support local needs, the abuses associated with conscription, and the disruptions caused by a poorly disciplined and underpaid army in the field, created in many areas an insupportable burden for the peasantry. The many wartime requisitions meant increased opportunities for graft on the part of local officials, while inflation increased the incentives. In describing conditions in the countryside, the term 'blood-sucking devil' was a favourite epithet of urban-based writers, and was used with reference to the local *hsiang, chen, pao* and *chia* officials. These constituted the basic levels of administration where, the critics argued, the war was actually creating the very conditions most favourable to the continued growth of the CCP.

The government's failure to win popular backing for its war against the CCP was also evident in the general inclination to blame it more than the CCP for the war. This was acknowledged at the time and a number of reasons were offered in explanation. First, the government, as the legitimate ruler of China, alone had the power to reform itself and end the war. Hence the anti-war petitioners in the KMT areas directed their effort against the government in the hope of compelling it so to act. Second, the Communists had won the balance of popular opinion during the peace negotiations of 1945-6. There was a general belief that they had been sincere, for example, at the Political Consultative Conference in January 1946, when they agreed to several compromises aimed at avoiding all-out war. The government lost credibility in this contest when the KMT Central Executive Committee unilaterally broke a number of conference agreements a few weeks later. Reinforcing this impression was the disruption of a meeting at Chiao-ch'ang-k'ou in Chungking on 10 February 1946, held to celebrate the successful conclusion of the Political Consultative Conference. This was followed by an attack on the offices of the CCP newspaper in Chungking a few days later. Both incidents were commonly thought to have been the work of thugs hired by elements within the KMT opposed to the conference agreements.[29]

Finally, the most important reason for directing anti-war sentiment primarily against the government was the general assumption that the strength of the CCP was being built upon the shortcomings of the KMT. The government was held responsible for not having remedied its defects during twenty years in power. Professor Ch'ien Tuan-sheng presented the

---

[29] For the commonly accepted view of who was responsible for the violent incident on 10 February, see John F. Melby, *The mandate of Heaven*, 88–9. For the KMT right-wing's version of the same incident, see Chung-kuo lao-kung yun-tung shih pien-tsuan wei-yuan-hui, ed. *Chung-kuo lao-kung yun-tung shih* (A history of the Chinese labour movement), 4.1585–7.

political version of this argument in an analysis of the relationship between KMT militarism and the CCP's armed opposition. He traced the military influence within the KMT back to Sun Yat-sen's alliances with warlords. What was then a marriage of convenience soon grew into a force within the KMT that could not easily be eliminated. When reorganized in 1924, the KMT tried to cut itself off from the warlords, but then proceeded to develop a military establishment of its own at the Whampoa Military Academy. In the late 1920s, after the Northern Expedition, the military period of KMT development should have ended; but in fact the period of political tutelage prescribed by Sun Yat-sen had no way to begin. Chiang Kai-shek the military leader had taken over political leadership as well. Chiang then began to fight the Communists, which made military control a continuing necessity. A mutually reinforcing relationship developed thereafter between the growing strength of the CCP and the expansion of Chiang's power within the KMT government. His Whampoa Academy men constituted the core of the military clique within the KMT. Because of their access to Chiang and their control of the army, they became the most important element within the KMT and the government. And once a military faction gained political power, concluded Ch'ien, opposition political parties also had no recourse except to arms. Hence the dominance of the military within the KMT and a government that was ultimately responsible for the civil war. He expressed a common sentiment in his demand that the military be removed from politics and brought under the control of a unified civilian government.[30]

Government responsibility for the war was asserted even more strongly by the economist, Professor Wu Ch'i-yuan. Unlike most of his colleagues, who tended to see the inflation as a consequence of the war, Professor Wu saw the war as a consequence of the government's economic policies. These had resulted in progressive economic deterioration and division of wealth. Middle-income groups, 'except for cliques of corrupt officials', had all seen their incomes eroded by the inflation. At the same time, the peasants were suffering all kinds of oppression, including 'depredations caused by soldiers, bandits, grain requisitions, conscription, and natural disasters'. 'With society in such a state,' queried Professor Wu, 'would there not be a civil war whether or not there was a CCP?'[31] But it was usually Ch'u An-p'ing, the editor of *Kuan-ch'a* (The observer), who

---

[30] Ch'ien Tuan-sheng, 'Chün-jen pa-hu ti Chung-kuo cheng-fu' (China's government usurped by military men), *Shih-tai p'i-p'ing*, Hong Kong, 16 June 1947, pp. 2–3. For a later scholarly treatment based on the same hypothesis, see, Ch'i Hsi-sheng, *Nationalist China at war: military defeats and political collapse, 1937–1945*.

[31] Wu Ch'i-yuan, 'Ts'ung ching-chi kuan-tien lun nei-chan wen-t'i' (Talking about civil war problems from an economic viewpoint), *Kuan-ch'a*, Shanghai, 7 Sept. 1946, pp. 3–4.

articulated popular sentiments most dramatically, as in his response to the American ex-diplomat William Bullitt's recommendation, in 1947, that more US aid be given to the KMT government:

Mr Bullitt advocates aid for this government because it is anti-Soviet and anti-Communist.... Is it possible that Mr Bullitt has not considered under what circumstances the CCP has risen to the position it occupies today? In this writer's view, the corrupt control of the KMT is the major factor which has created the rising power of the CCP.... If, in the past twenty years, politics had not been so corrupt and incompetent, how could people have been made to feel that the future is so empty that they have turned and entrusted their hopes to the CCP?[32]

Like the students, however, the older generation did not appear to welcome a CCP-dominated government. Ch'u An-p'ing, for example, looked to the British Labour Party's victory in 1946 to prove that it was possible to realize socialism and democracy without going the way of Moscow. As for the CCP, what he feared was the kind of political life it seemed to espouse. He queried whether the CCP was not really anti-democratic and whether there was much difference between Communists and fascists in this respect. He and his colleagues expressed reservations about the CCP's attitudes toward the individual, toward censorship, toward intellectual and political freedom, and toward literature and art. These liberal intellectuals suggested that if the KMT's performance left much to be desired on all these counts, the CCP would undoubtedly be worse.[33] Nor was anyone willing to argue that the CCP's ultimate aim was anything but the realization of communism. However, they did not think the CCP would ever be able to achieve it by force of arms.

The perceived military stalemate was therefore thought to provide a basis for compromises on both sides, and for a coalition government wherein the two parties could each serve as a check upon the other. General Marshall had given up this cause as hopeless in 1946 but non-Communist non-KMT intellectuals in China continued for almost two more years to hope that it might somehow succeed. The end result for the KMT government was that even key groups within its own constituency refused to support its struggle with the CCP. In the absence of reforms that might have made the war seem worth while, KMT leaders had no means of reversing the popular conclusion that they were sacrificing the interests of the nation as a whole in order to perpetuate

---

[32] Ch'u An-p'ing, 'P'ing P'u-li-t'e ti p'ien-ssu ti pu-chien-k'ang ti fang Hua pao-kao' (A critique of Bullitt's biased unhealthy report on his visit to China), *Kuan-ch'a*, 25 Oct. 1947, p. 5.

[33] Ch'u An-p'ing, 'Chung-kuo ti cheng-chü', 6. Chang Tung-sun, 'Chui-shu wo-men nu-li chien-li "lien-ho cheng-fu" ti yung-i' (Reflections on our intention to strive to establish a 'coalition government'), *Kuan-ch'a*, 5 April 1947, p. 7; Chou Chung-ch'i, 'Lun ko-ming' (On revolution), *Kuan-ch'a*, 25 Jan. 1947, p. 10; Yü Ts'ai-yu 'T'an chin-t'ien ti hsueh-sheng' (Discussing today's students), *Kuan-ch'a*, 24 April 1948, p. 18.

themselves in power. Even so the great majority of students and intellectuals who had raised their voices so persistently in favour of peace and political reform did not actually abandon the government until its fate was sealed on the battlefield.

THE GROWTH OF COMMUNIST POWER

The political mandate extended to the CCP from urban China was thus ambivalent, coming not directly but as a vote of non-confidence for the KMT. The informed urban public was generally aware, however, that the true source of the CCP's growing power lay in its rural social and economic policies. And it was specifically land reform that was most often cited as the basis of the CCP's strength in the countryside, allowing it to 'put down roots' there while the government was doing nothing to meet that challenge.

Yet, contrary to popular assumptions created in large measure by the Communists' own propaganda, their appeal to the peasantry was not based solely on the issue of tenancy. During the Anti-Japanese War they had abandoned land reform in favour of the overtly more moderate rent and interest-rate reduction policy designed to facilitate a united front of all classes against the Japanese invader. In areas immediately threatened by the enemy, even rent reduction was temporarily deferred in deference to that objective. But the policy was evolving in more secure areas, albeit without formal public acknowledgement, until by 1945 it included an attack against a long list of other grievances. These included local tyrants, low wages, corruption, unpaid taxes, spies, bandits, thieves, and even loose women. The party had explicitly redefined the double reduction policy to mean the elimination of 'all the most flagrant exploitations', both political and economic, in the countryside. This was an important development in North China, the Communists' main area of expansion after 1937, because peasants there often owned the land they tilled and tenancy was not always a key issue.

Equally significant were the methods being used to implement the policy. The liquidation struggle, or the struggle to settle accounts of past exploitation, became an important instrument of the party's land policy after 1943, and remained so thereafter. On the basis of the peasants' claims, the amount of past exploitation for whatever reason was fixed and calculated in terms of cash, grain, or other property. The proceeds were collected from the exploiters and redistributed in different ways which became more direct and egalitarian over time. This method not only allowed the peasants to be schooled in all the many forms of exploitation by encouraging them to recall every past injustice; it also drew them directly into the struggle by forcing them to state their claims openly and directly against the power holders in the village. The positive economic appeal to the poor thus contained a complementary destructive force. Together they represented the full political significance of the CCP's land policy. It aimed to destroy not merely the economic superiority of the main 'struggle objects', that is, landlords and rich peasants, but also the political power structure which supported them and which they supported. This then made it possible for the Communists to replace that structure with one loyal to them and sustained by the active interest of the peasants mobilized in the struggle.

Closely associated with the struggle technique and equally significant both in terms of destructive potential and precedents set for the future was the mass movement method of implementing the party's land policy. The guiding principle was Mao's oft-quoted 1927 'Report on an investigation of the peasant movement in Hunan', and especially the concept that, 'in correcting wrongs, it is necessary to go to extremes or else the wrongs cannot be righted'. Applying this principle, Mao wrote in November 1945 that rent reduction had to come as a result of mass struggle, not as a favour from the government, and that in the struggle 'excesses' could not be avoided. But 'as long as it is really a conscious struggle of the broad masses, any excesses that have occurred can be corrected afterwards'.[34] Indeed, such excesses were not only not harmful but were positively beneficial in weakening the 'forces of feudalism'. Li Yü, chairman of the CCP-sponsored Shantung provincial government, placed the concept of excesses or leftism in its operational context in terms of the 'law of the mass movement'. In the initial phase of a movement, excesses could be dangerous since the masses were not yet sufficiently aroused to resist the enemy. Only after organizations had been basically established, cadres trained, activists discovered, and the peasants propagandized was the stage set for the second or struggle phase of the movement. During this phase, leftism and excesses could not be avoided. The cadres were to 'help the masses attack the landlords, smash the reactionary control of the landlord class in the countryside, and establish the superior power of the masses'. Landlord counter-attacks had to be resisted repeatedly until the landlords understood that they had no alternative but to acquiesce. This led to the third stage, when unity became the guiding principle. For leadership cadres, Li explained, the most serious error lay neither in being excessively right nor excessively left, but in misjudging

---

[34] Mao Tse-tung, 'Rent reduction and production are two important matters for the defence of the liberated areas', Mao, *SW* 4.72.

the point at which the limits of one phase had been reached and the next should begin within the context of the developing mass movement.[35] The party had discovered not only the issues that aroused the peasantry but also how to harness the destructive energies of the spontaneous peasant violence that regularly rose and fell in response to local grievances but with little lasting result.

The land policy and the class friction it generated could become the 'mother of all other work' in a village, however, only after certain military and political preconditions had been met in the area as a whole. The basic prerequisite, established during the Japanese war, for the successful implementation of rent reduction was the capacity to protect it against its enemies both military and political. The anti-Japanese resistance mobilized the manpower and the CCP provided the leadership necessary to establish those preconditions all across North China as the strength of the Japanese began to recede in 1943. Such military and political security on so large a scale was a condition the Chinese Communist movement had never enjoyed prior to the 1940s, and it grew directly out of the Communists' successful effort to build a resistance movement against the Japanese.

After 1945, the party's land policy could then become the key to the CCP's relationship with the 'basic masses' of North China and that policy was founded on a direct appeal to the poor and landless. In addition to the material incentives provided by the distribution of the 'struggle fruits', the Communists could also offer a solution for what the peasantry as a whole apparently perceived as its most immediate grievance: the corrupt and arbitrary use of political power and social position within the village community. In exploiting these issues – together with all the others associated with the ownership and use of land, unpaid labour and indebtedness – the CCP had found the formula for transforming the military-political movement it had mobilized to resist the Japanese into one that could build a new indigenous power structure, sustained by popular participation and support once the Japanese were defeated.[36]

The May Fourth Directive of 1946, which formally marked the shift from the reduction of rents and interest rates back to land reform, did not therefore represent that sharp a distinction between the two policies. The directive in fact only acknowledged a development that had been in process within the Communists' liberated areas for several years. In accordance with that development, the directive authorized several

---

[35] Li Yü, *Lun ch'ün-chung lu-hsien yü Shan-tung ch'ün-chung yun-tung* (On the mass line and the mass movement in Shantung).

[36] Suzanne Pepper, *Civil War in China: the political struggle, 1945–1949*, 229–77.

different methods of transferring wealth from those who had it to those who did not, including land sales and a land contribution scheme. But these were soon abandoned because they were carried out in the absence of any retribution against the exploiters and power holders. The more typical sequence being followed in 1946-7 was the settling accounts struggles followed by increasingly egalitarian efforts to redistribute the struggle fruits. This process culminated in the complete expropriation of the landlords, including their land, houses and all moveable property; and the more or less equal redivision of all village lands and other means of production – as formalized in the 1947 Agrarian Law.

Towards the end of 1946, not long after the start of the government's military offensives against the Communists' liberated areas, Mao summarized the role of land reform in the Communists' defence strategy. He asserted that the peasants had only stood firmly with the Communists against the attacking KMT forces where the May Fourth Directive had been carried out and the land problem solved 'radically and thoroughly'. The peasants, he claimed, took a 'wait-and-see attitude' wherever this had not been done or where land reform was neglected on the excuse of preoccupation with the war. He therefore directed that all areas, regardless of the military situation therein, should lead the peasants in implementing the May Fourth Directive.[37]

Other party documents also indicated clearly that the party regarded land reform as the basic condition for winning a genuine mass response to the army recruiting drives. In early 1947, in twelve counties along the Shantung-Honan border, 50,000 young men were reported to have rallied to the Communist colours in the immediate wake of land reform. It was claimed that a similar recruiting drive in the same area in 1946 prior to land reform had failed to develop into a 'large-scale mass movement'.[38]

Army recruiting was, of course, only the most direct and immediately essential of the military support tasks which the Communists' style of warfare made necessary. The reliance of the regular army on an extensive civilian support network in a 'peoples' war' style of fighting had developed during the Anti-Japanese War and continued after 1945, even though guerrilla warfare now played a less important role. This civilian support network included militia units, local defence corps, women's associations and village peasant associations.

[37] Mao Tse-tung, 'A three months' summary', Mao, *SW*, 4.116. The May Fourth Directive was not published, nor Liu Shao-ch'i's authorship acknowledged, until the early 1980s.
[38] Hsu Yün-pei, 'Ts'an chün yun-tung chien-pao' (A brief report on the army recruiting movement), in *I-chiu-ssu-ch'i-nien shang-pan-nien lai ch'ü tang wei kuan-yü t'u kai yun-tung ti chung-yao wen-chien* (Important documents on the land reform movement during the first half of 1947 from the (Hopei-Shantung-Honan) regional party committee), 69-74.

Militia units were organized, ideally several thousand men per county, to support the regular army by being responsible for sentry duty, garrisoning newly-occupied areas, diversionary activities and the like. The militia also protected local party and government organizations, guarded prisoners, suppressed local anti-Communist activities, exposed enemy agents, and kept communication lines open.

Local self-defence corps were organized at the village and district levels. Their main tasks were to transport supplies to the front, and transfer captured war materiel and the wounded to the rear. They organized military transport and stretcher teams in the villages to carry out this work. All able-bodied civilian men between the ages of 16 and 55 were obliged to participate in it as required by the army.

The women's associations maintained village sentry systems to keep watch on inter-village travellers; and also assisted with hospital work and handicraft production to support the war effort.

The village peasant associations were responsible for the army recruiting drives and, similarly, youth associations mobilized their members to join the army and perform rear-service work.

Finally, all civilians in the war zones were expected to obey the orders of military units and of the local political authorities in support of the war effort by repairing defence installations, digging trenches, aiding the wounded, and voluntarily reporting on the activities of enemy agents.[39]

While this was the ideal pattern, its realization depended on first carrying through the land reform process. And this was not as easy as the contemporary accounts issued by the New China News Agency were wont to imply. These portrayed the relationship between land reform and peasant participation on the side of the CCP in terms of material incentives and fear of landlord revenge.[40] Yet intra-party documents from the same period indicated that the causal relationship was not so direct nor the results so easily achieved. Instead, the peasants were often afraid to participate in the struggle because they feared the KMT might return and allow the struggle objects to take their revenge, which indeed many did. These fears were reinforced by the reality of the heavy losses suffered

[39] This outline of wartime support tasks is based on three proclamations issued for the liberated areas of Shantung immediately after the Japanese surrender: 'Shan-tung sheng jen-min tzu-wei tui chan-shih ch'in-wu tung-yuan pan-fa' (Wartime logistics mobilization methods of the Shantung people's self-defence corps), 17 Aug. 1945; 'Chan-shih jen-min chin-chi tung-yuan kao-yao' (Wartime emergency mobilization outline), 18 Aug. 1945; and 'Min-ping hsien ta-tui kung-tso kao-yao' (Work outline of the county militia brigades), all in *Shan-tung sheng cheng-fu chi Shan-tung chün-ch'ü kung-pu chih ko-chung t'iao-li kang-yao pan-fa hui-pien* (A compilation of various regulations, programmes and methods issued by the Shantung provincial government and the Shantung military region), 18–26, 40–2.

[40] For example, Hsinhua News Agency, Yenan, 9 Nov. 1946 (translated in *For your information*, 10 Nov. 1946); and Hsinhua News Agency, dispatched by Sidney Rittenberg for Agence France Presse, 5 Dec. 1946 (trans. in *FYI*, 6 Dec. 1946).

during the government's 1946–7 advances into the base areas. In addition, peasants were often reluctant to leave their families and newly-won plots of land to participate in the war. The reluctance of the peasants was, moreover, mirrored in a lack of resolve on the part of local cadres. For example, some military cadres entertained no genuine class hatred. They had entered the army primarily to resist the Japanese and protect their families. Many were themselves of landlord or rich peasant origin and had never thought of destroying feudalism, much less turning over their family property to the peasants. Since landlords had participated in the anti-Japanese resistance, some cadres even pitied them and sought to protect them. Many local civilian cadres also disliked army recruiting work. They had to try to overcome the peasants' initial reluctance to struggle against the landlords, born of the fear that the KMT would return; and then immediately ask the peasants to defend their new lands against the threat of the advancing KMT armies.[41]

As an antidote for these failings the party prescribed the mass line method of recruiting and outlined the procedure. At village mass meetings, activists should explain the importance of the recruiting campaign and encourage the peasants to express their reservations. All the mass organizations in the village were expected to participate in overcoming the peasants' doubts and the traditional notion that good men did not become soldiers. The peasants' associations would discuss and decide who should and should not volunteer; and the women's groups were called upon to mobilize their members to encourage the menfolk to do so. After the understanding of the villagers was thus developed, emulation campaigns could be launched using the example of progressive villages to influence the more backward. Individual villages should name model families and model peasant volunteers as an inspiration for others. If necessary at this stage, CCP members themselves should come forward and take the lead in joining the army.

In villages where land reform had not yet been thoroughly carried out, the recruiting campaign could develop simultaneously with the division of land and property. Not only would landlord property be distributed to the peasants but in addition, allegedly evil landlords might be imprisoned or even killed. Declared one report: 'It is necessary to destroy their feudal control.... Experience proves that only if the landlord's land

[41] *Sung Jen-ch'iung t'ung-chih liu-yueh shih-wu-jih tsai chung-yang-chü tang hsiao kuan-yü cheng-chih kung-tso ti pao-kao* (Comrade Sung Jen-ch'iung's report on political work at the central Party School on 15 June), 1–2; and several reports compiled in *I-chiu-szu-ch'i-nien shang-pan-nien*, 69–70, 55, 63–4. The peasants' desire to remain on their newly-won plot of land is also highlighted in Chou Li-po's novel about land reform in the North-east: *Pao-feng tsou-yü* (The hurricane).

and grain are all distributed and he falls to the level of a middle peasant
... will it be impossible for him to resume his old attitude in the village.'[42]
Clearly, the provision of material benefits to the peasantry was not land
reform's only objective. Equally important was the destructive force, both
economic and political, that the movement generated. Hence one
criticism, raised against the land contribution movement that was promoted
for a time in some border regions in 1946, was that it accomplished the
task of economic redistribution without struggle. As a result, it could not
achieve the overthrow of the landlords, nor the political and psychological
liberation of the peasants.[43] Mao declared, in October 1948, that during
the preceding two years the party had 'mobilized some 1,600,000 of the
peasants who obtained land to join the People's Liberation Army'.[44] The
link between the benefits proffered and the support received, however,
was the struggle movement. For it enabled the Communists to transform
the nascent class consciousness, inspired by property redistribution, into
the specific kinds of support necessary to fight the war. The key
consideration was that the struggle movement with its many targets
destroyed the political and economic domination of the rural ruling class.

The subsequent construction of a new village power structure was the
final step in making land reform the 'mother of all other work'. Peasants
who participated most actively in the multi-featured accusation movement
provided new recruits for the CCP and new local leadership. Those who
had received land and property became the backbone of the peasant
associations and other village organizations. And this was the institutional
structure, administered by the peasants themselves, that the Communists
could then rely on to assume responsibility for collecting the grain tax,
raising a local militia, organizing military transport teams, and exerting
social pressure on reluctant volunteer recruits. These were the roots the
party put down in the countryside, which could indeed guarantee the
supplies of grain and manpower necessary to sustain the military struggle
with the KMT government.[45] In this manner, the party was able to harness
the destructive energies roused by both the Japanese invasion and the
unequal distribution of wealth and power in the Chinese countryside. This
achievement highlighted the KMT government's failure to respond

---

[42] Li Chen-yang, 'Chia-chi pien yu-chi ch'ü t'u kai ti chi-tien t'i-hui' (Understanding a few points
about land reform in the Chiahsiang-Tsining guerrilla area), in *Kung-tso t'ung-hsün, 32: yu-chi
chan-cheng chuan-hao*, supplement, 15.

[43] 'Kuan-ch'e kuan-hsing keng-che yu ch'i t'ien chi-ko chü-t'i wen-t'i ti chih-shih' (Directive on
some concrete problems in the thorough implementation of land-to-the-tiller), in *I-chiu-szu-ch'i
nien shang-pan-nien*, 14.

[44] Mao Tse-tung, 'On the September meeting', Mao, *SW*, 4.271.

[45] The classic eyewitness account of land reform during the civil war years is William Hinton,
Fanshen: a documentary of revolution in a Chinese village.

similarly to the challenges provided by the Japanese and by the inertia of the country's underlying agrarian foundations.

THE CIVIL WAR 1946-1949

In early November 1946 Chiang Kai-shek confided to Marshall that, whereas previously the KMT government had been divided on the question, agreement had recently been reached: force was the only means of settling the conflict with the CCP.[46] That decision was based on a persisting miscalculation not only of the Communists' weakness but also of his own strength. During his year in China, Marshall had tried repeatedly to warn Chiang about some of the dangers he faced. At one point, Marshall had even admonished that the government's actions 'would probably lead to Communist control in China' since the 'chaotic condition now developing would not only weaken the Kuomintang but would also afford the Communists an excellent opportunity to undermine the government'.[47]

In October 1946 Marshall appraised the Communists' military strategy, pointing out to Chiang that although in retreat they were not surrendering. While they were giving up their cities, the Communists were not losing their armies and clearly had no intention of doing so since they refused to stand and fight. With their main strength preserved, they were in a position to create endless trouble for him militarily.[48] Finally, as he was preparing to leave China, Marshall again advised Chiang that the Communists were now so strong a military and political force that the KMT government could probably not destroy them by military means. To this Chiang replied that there would be no difficulty in solving the Communist problem once their military forces were destroyed, which he was confident could be accomplished within eight to ten months.[49]

His strategy was first to recapture cities and towns on all fronts and to gain control of the major communications arteries north of the Yangtze. From these strongpoints and railway corridors, government forces would then move out into the Communists' liberated areas to re-establish control over minor points and ultimately the countryside itself. In accordance with this strategy, government forces launched their July 1946 general offensive, which Communist historiography marks as the start of the Third Revolutionary Civil War.

[46] Van Slyke, *Marshall's mission*, 1.353-4.
[47] *Ibid.* 196.
[48] *China white paper*, 1.202.
[49] Van Slyke, *Marshall's mission*, 1.407.

The first year, 1946–1947: retreat

During the first year of the war from July 1946 to June 1947, government forces captured virtually all the cities and towns in the North-east with the exception of Harbin; recaptured the county towns of northern Kiangsu; occupied Kalgan and Yenan; gained control of large portions of Hopei and Jehol provinces; and cleared much of the Lunghai and Tsinan-Tsingtao railway lines. Thereafter, the fighting moved back and forth across all China's major railway systems north of the Yangtze. In addition to the east-west Lunghai line running from the sea in northern Kiangsu to Paochi near the Kansu-Shensi border, and the Tsinan-Tsingtao line transversing Shantung, these railways included the north-south Tientsin-Pukow (Tsin-Pu) and Peiping-Hankow (P'ing-Han) lines. In Manchuria, the railways that provided the main focal points for the fighting were the Peiping-Mukden line, the only one running from North China to the North-east provinces, and the railways linking the four major cities of Mukden, Szupingkai, Changchun and Kirin. As the fighting developed, the two main theatres of the war were Manchuria and east China, that is, northern Kiangsu and Shantung.

Communist forces were renamed the People's Liberation Army (PLA) in July 1946. They remained largely on the defensive before the government advance, following a policy of strategic withdrawal from the towns back to the countryside. In September, Mao Tse-tung outlined the strategy and tactics the PLA would follow. During the Anti-Japanese War, explained Mao, the dispersal of Communist forces into small units for guerrilla warfare had been primary and the concentration of forces for mobile war supplementary. With the changing conditions of the civil war, the position of the two would be reversed. However, the government's forces were on the offensive, stronger and better armed than those of the Communists. Hence the latter's time-honoured operational principle of 'concentrating a superior force to wipe out the enemy forces one by one' had to remain unchanged until the power balance could be reversed.

Complete annihilation and quick decision were the hallmarks of this kind of fighting. Annihilation of enemy units had become the PLA's main source of weapons and an important source of its manpower as well, since captured enemy soldiers were regularly integrated into the Communist armies. The objective of wiping out the enemy's forces was to destroy his ability to fight, not to win territory. The purpose of seeking a quick solution was to permit a swift escape with a minimum of casualties in the event that the enemy could not be destroyed. 'Using this method we shall

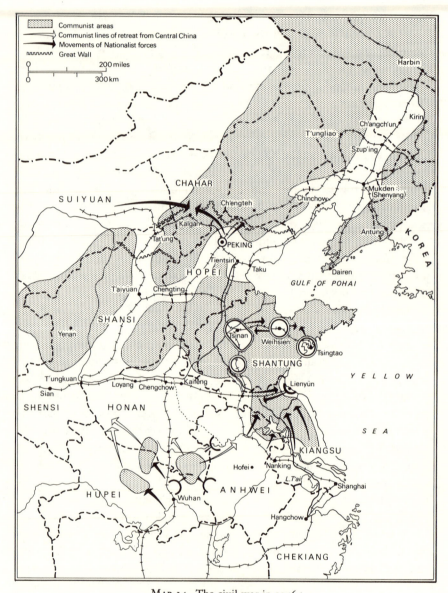

MAP 14. The civil war in 1946

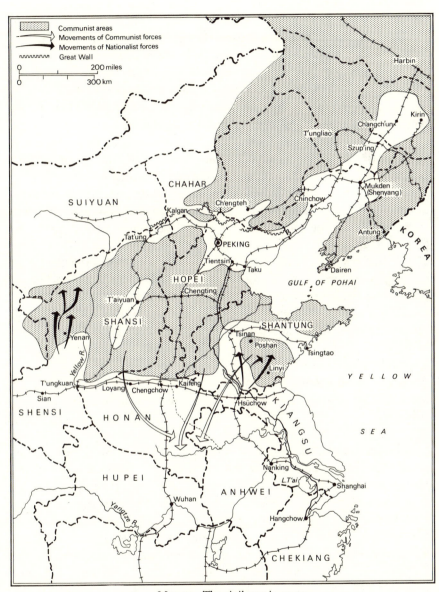

MAP 15. The civil war in 1947

win,' asserted Mao. 'Acting counter to it we shall lose.'[50] Here in summary form were the operational principles which would soon become famous.

The government offensive during the first week of July 1946 moved to surround Communist units led by Li Hsien-nien and Wang Chen on the Honan-Hupei border north of Hankow. They broke out of the encirclement and made their way back to the Communist base area in Shensi. The government had eliminated the threat they posed in the area, but the forces themselves survived to fight another day. In Shantung, the government declared the Tsinan-Tsingtao line to have been cleared of Communist forces on 17 July. But due to their continuing harassment, railway traffic still had not resumed by the end of September. Also in July, government units crossed the Yellow River and moved into southern Shansi. In the eastern part of the province, however, Communist forces were able to cut the railway line running from the capital, Taiyuan, to Shihchiachuang.[51]

The July offensive in northern Kiangsu began with government forces moving north from the Yangtze and east from the Tientsin-Pukow railway. At the time, the Communists controlled twenty-nine counties in the region. By the following spring, government forces had retaken all the county seats there and county governments were being re-established under KMT control. Everywhere, the Communists followed the principle of withdrawing before the advance of a superior force. The army regulars retreated together with most of the militia, the party cadres and their families. This strategy of survival preserved their main forces but at heavy cost.

Shansi-Hopei-Shantung-Honan. Documents captured by government armies when they had entered one of the Communists' major base areas, the Shansi-Hopei-Shantung-Honan Border Region (Chin-Chi-Lu-Yü), revealed the extent of the losses suffered there. The government's gains were both extensive and unanticipated in that region. Of the 64 counties in the Hopei-Shantung-Honan sub-region, for example, 49 were occupied by government forces. Of the 35 county seats controlled by the Communists there in mid-1946, 24 had also fallen by January 1947. The CCP had not expected this. They had to revise their plans and began preparing for a long-term guerrilla war. Party documents spelled out the strategy: the Communists' regular army units and militia would remain intact while the enemy's units were gradually being destroyed. With 80–90

[50] Mao Tse-tung, 'Concentrate a superior force to destroy the enemy forces one by one', Mao, *SW*, 4.103–7.   [51] *FRUS, 1946*, 10.231–3.

per cent of his forces on the attack, Chiang Kai-shek had no source of replacements. 'So long as we keep up our spirits and continue to destroy Chiang's forces coming into our territory,' noted one of the documents, 'then we will not only stop the enemy's offensive, but must also change from the defensive to the offensive and restore all of our lost area.'[52] The strategy was sound, but exhortations were not enough to keep spirits up during the bleak winter of 1946–7.

The principle of withdrawal as a tactic of guerrilla warfare should have included the evacuation of the local population as well as the military and political units, the objective being to save human life, village organization, and the grain stores. In 1946, however, the villages were not prepared for the reversion to guerrilla warfare conditions. As a result, cadres and defence forces fled and unarmed peasants paid with their lives and property while the village organizations were destroyed. As in northern Kiangsu, local KMT-sponsored governments were quickly set up to replace them. Following soon after came the return-to-the-village corps (*hui hsiang t'uan*). These were armed units led by landlords and others bent on re-establishing their position. They began settling accounts of their own, seizing back the land and grain that had been distributed by the Communists to the peasants. Reports of revenge and retaliation abounded.[53] The documents acknowledge that thousands of peasants were killed in this region. Destroyed with them during only a few months was an old Communist base area that had taken nearly a decade to build. In districts subsequently recaptured, returning Communist forces were cursed by the peasants for having failed to protect them. The peasants were unwilling to restore peasant associations, form new militia units, or even attend an open meeting, so little faith did they have in the staying power of the Communists in such areas.[54]

The plans for another long-term guerrilla war like that waged against the Japanese did not fully materialize, however, because by May 1947 the government's offensive had already begun to weaken. Its forces were now spread too thinly across a vast area, unable to occupy minor keypoints as the Japanese had been able to do at the height of their penetration of

[52] Ch'ü tang wei, 'Kuan-yü k'ai-chan ti-hou yu-chi chan yü chun-pei yu-chi chan te chih-shih' (Directive on developing and preparing guerilla warfare in the enemy's rear), 20 Nov. 1946, *Kung-tso t'ung-hsun, 32: yu-chi chan-cheng chuan-hao* (Work correspondence, no. 32: special issue on guerrilla warfare), 49–50; also, Ch'ü tang wei, 'Chi-lu-yü wu-ko yueh lai yu-chi chan-cheng te tsung-chieh yü mu-ch'ien jen-wu' (A summary of the past five months of guerrilla war in Hopei-Shantung-Honan and present tasks), 2 Feb. 1947, *Kung-tso t'ung-hsun, 32*, p. 37.

[53] For an eyewitness account of these incidents, see Jack Belden, *China shakes the world*, 213–74.

[54] 'Chi-lu-yü wu-ko yueh...', 42; Kuan-yü k'ai-chan ti-hou...', 48–52; and 'P'an Fu-sheng t'ung-chih tsai ti wei tsu-chih-pu chang lien-hsi hui shang te tsung-chieh fa-yen' (Statement by Comrade P'an Fu-sheng at a joint conference of organization department heads of the sub-district party committees), 8 March 1947, in *I-chiu-szu-ch'i-nien shang-pan-nien*, 38.

this same region. Meanwhile, the main forces of the Communists' regular army, still largely intact, had stopped retreating and had been able to launch a number of small counter-attacks. In Shantung, Communist forces were beginning to seize the initiative, and in Manchuria they were already engaging in limited offensives. The party was claiming that a total of ninety enemy brigades had been destroyed nationwide and that when the figure reached one hundred the military balance would favour the Communist side.[55]

In fact, the military balance did shift rapidly in 1947. US military analysts had predicted in September 1946 that the government offensive would bog down within a few months due to overly extended communications lines which would require ever more troops to defend. These same analysts, however, foresaw a protracted stalemate due to the superior training and equipment of the government forces: foreign observers 'generally agreed that the Communists cannot win either in attack or defence in a toe-to-toe slugging match with National Government forces'.[56]

No one anticipated the speed and skill with which Communist commanders would be able to transform their anti-Japanese guerrilla experience into campaigns of mobile warfare. The Communists were soon deploying larger units than they had used against the Japanese to harass and destroy their enemy's forces piecemeal while preserving and building their own strength. Losses were replaced by integrating militia units and captured enemy soldiers into the regular armies, and by large-scale military recruiting campaigns that accompanied land reform in the Communist areas in 1946–7. The development of Communist political power in the countryside that was an integral part of land reform also made possible the civilian support work necessary to sustain these military operations in areas that had not borne the brunt of the 1946 government offensive.

The North-east. The earliest successful application of this strategy occurred in Manchuria under the direction of Lin Piao, overall commander in the North-east. His forces had been pushed north of the Sungari River by the end of 1946, and government troops were poised for a spring offensive against their final objective, Harbin. But Lin then began a series of hit-and-run raids into government territory, which would allow him to seize the initiative in Manchuria by midsummer and culminate in decisive

---

[55] Chang Erh, 'Chiu-ko yueh yu-chi chan-cheng tsung-chieh yü chin-hou jen-wu' (A nine-month summary of the guerrilla war and future tasks), May 1947, *Kung-tso t'ung-hsun*, 32, 19.
[56] *FRUS, 1946*, 10.235–6.

victory two years later. His timing was appropriate for a strategy of surprise and feint, since the onset of the bitterly cold North-eastern winter was an unlikely season to initiate military manoeuvres. In November 1946, when Lin Piao's forces first launched a small diversionary attack across the frozen Sungari, the significance of their action was not apparent. After this brief foray southwards they quickly withdrew. An estimated force of 60,000 men crossed the river again on 6 January 1947. This time government troops suffered heavy casualties during at least one engagement and were able to take few prisoners before the intruders withdrew. Government commanders were therefore apprehensive as they anticipated a third drive, which occurred in mid-February. But it was over by the end of the month. Lin Piao's units withdrew quickly rather than meet a concentration of government forces, which this time refused to be trapped as they had been during the January operations.

The fourth Communist drive across the Sungari lasted from 7 to 18 March 1947. It inflicted heavy damage on one government division and captured large quantities of arms and ammunition before again retreating. The significance of these limited military excursions was now apparent: government forces had been weakened and, more important, their strategic plans for the North-east disrupted. The threat to Harbin was delayed and the Communists' position strengthened. Lin Piao then launched his fifth drive across the Sungari in May 1947, embarking on a well-coordinated campaign which marked the beginning of the end of the battle for Manchuria. A force of 400,000 men participated in the May–June operations with advances in central, southern and south-western Manchuria. The target of the main force was Szupingkai, midway between Manchuria's two main cities, Changchun and Mukden. During the five-week seige of Szupingkai, the attacking Communist troops suffered some 40,000 casualties and could not prevent the arrival of government reinforcements sent to relieve the Szupingkai garrison. After lifting the seige of the city on 30 June and withdrawing across the Sungari, Lin Piao personally accepted responsibility for the tactical errors that led to the government's defensive victory at Szupingkai.

Despite Lin's defeat, however, his North-east Field Army had gained the initiative and would retain it until final victory the following year. Government troops had been forced to abandon their outposts on the north bank of the Sungari and between the river and the Changchun-Kirin sector, advancing the front line some 150 miles south of its position six months previously. The government-held cities of Changchun, Kirin and Mukden were isolated by the destruction of their connecting railway lines, some of which were not restored until after the war. Government forces suffered losses in arms, supplies, manpower, and morale from which they also never recovered.[57]

As the Communists moved on to the offensive in the North-east and elsewhere, government armies lapsed into a strategy of static defence. Typically they would either withdraw too late from over-extended strongpoints which had ceased to have any strategic value; or they would remain inside them behind walls and trenches leaving the initiative to their adversary to lay seige or not as he chose. The cause of the government's developing Manchurian debacle, according to US military analysts at the time, was the initial over-extension of its forces and the ineptitude of their leadership, most notably that of their commander, General Tu Yü-ming. Yet the transfer of command in the North-east to General Ch'en Ch'eng in mid-1947, after the Communists' fifth offensive, and his removal in early 1948 after the sixth offensive, did little to retrieve the government's declining fortunes in the region. Its forces were still superior in equipment and training. But it was increasingly apparent that the Communists excelled in strategy and tactical application, as well as morale or fighting spirit and sense of common purpose.

The morale factor naturally had many roots. Besides the negative effects of corruption, incompetence, and losing strategies on the KMT side was, especially in the North-east, the issue of regionalism. A key goal of the government's takeover in the North-east after the Second World War was to prevent the re-emergence there of the semi-autonomous power base dominated by the family of the Old Marshal, Chang Tso-lin. Consequently the overwhelming majority of the troops sent to the area were units from elsewhere in China. The government partitioned the three North-east provinces into nine administrative divisions and filled virtually all the top posts therein with outsiders. The government's local allies tended to be landlords and others who had collaborated with the Japanese, since these were the only elements loyal neither to the Communists nor to the Young Marshal, Chang Hsueh-liang, son and heir apparent to Chang Tso-lin. Perhaps because of his continuing popularity, the Young Marshal was kept under house arrest for his role in kidnapping Chiang Kai-shek during the Sian incident and was removed to a more secure exile on Taiwan, although his release had been widely expected.

---

[57] This account of the early Sungari River offensives is based on the following accounts: *Civil war in China, 1945-50*, tr. Office of the Chief of Military History, US Dept. of the Army, 81-3; *Military campaigns in China, 1924-1950*, tr. W. W. Whitson, Patrick Yang and Paul Lai, 125-9; William W. Whitson and Huang Chen-hsia, *The Chinese high command: a history of Communist military politics, 1927-71*, 306-9; and *FRUS, 1947*, 7.26-7, 36-7, 49-50, 88-9, 130-1, 134-7, 157-9, 166-8, 171-3, 178-81, 192-3, 195-6, 198-9, 203, 208-12, 214-17, 240-1.

After the Japanese surrender, initial support for the KMT in the North-east appeared genuine according to contemporary accounts. But the 'southerners' soon wore out their welcome. Resentment created by their discriminatory takeover policies and the venality of their officials quickly produced a resurgence of regionalism. Regional loyalties might not have weighed so heavily had the government's record in the North-east been less open to criticism. People in the North-east, as in Taiwan, a region with an even longer history of Japanese rule, were often heard to comment that Japan had given them better government than the KMT. In particular, the government's effort against the Communists in the region could hardly have succeeded without the participation of local leaders. Yet so great was the KMT suspicion of them and the power they represented that it spurned even such aid as they were willing to offer. Li Tsung-jen in his *Memoirs* traces this error to Chiang Kai-shek himself, who remained 'prejudiced against native Manchurians'. Thus a locally formed North-east Mobilization Commission volunteered to organize a defence force to fight the Communists. But the offer was refused, although government commanders were never able to organize an effective local guerrilla force themselves. General Ma Chan-shen, a cavalry officer who had served under both the Old and Young Marshals, agreed to work with the government and was made a deputy commander of the North-east Command, but he was never given anything to do nor any troops to lead. Meanwhile, government commanders in the North-east were obliged to rely on 'outsiders' as their major source of troop replacements. Due to the failure of their recruiting drives in the North-east, government forces had to bring replacements for their lost and damaged divisions from areas inside China which could ill afford to lose them.[58]

The Communists took full advantage of the popular resentment these measures aroused. They avoided the central government's arrogant attitude toward the people of the North-east and used local talent wherever possible. Most of the surviving units from the old North-east army of Chang Tso-lin and Chang Hsueh-liang went over to the Communists, as did one of the latter's younger brothers, General Chang Hsueh-szu. The Communists welcomed them as allies and allowed them to retain their identity as a non-Communist force under the overall command of Lin Piao. As the Communist administered areas expanded, the North-east Field Army was able to replenish its regular units by recruiting locally; it organized an effective second-line force of local irregulars and mobilized more than a million civilian support workers to serve under its logistics command.

[58] Li Tsung-jen, 434; *FRUS, 1947,* 7.141–2, 144–5, 211–12, 232–5.

A contemporary writer summarized the Communists' successes:

It should be known that when the Chinese Communists pull up the railway tracks, or bury land mines, or explode bombs, it is not the Communists that are doing it; the common people are doing it for them. The Chinese Communists had no soldiers in the North-east; now they have the soldiers not wanted by the central government. The Chinese Communists had no guns; now they have the guns the central government managed so poorly and sent over to them, and sometimes even secretly sold to them. The Chinese Communists had no men of ability; now they have the talents the central government has abandoned.[59]

There could be few better examples of how poorly the KMT government was served by its habit of disregarding popular demands and sensibilities.

Shantung. The Communists' retreat in the important Kiangsu-Anhwei-Shantung sector was more difficult to reverse than that in Manchuria. Government forces were not as over-extended in this region, and the Communists lacked the safe sanctuary for retreat that Lin Piao enjoyed north of the Sungari. Nevertheless, the commander of Communist forces in east China, Ch'en Yi, used the same strategy and tactics to equal advantage. In Shantung, Communist troops under Hsu Shih-yu were defeated at Kao-mi in early October 1946, in a relatively large-scale action fought for control of the Tsinan-Tsingtao railway. This was reopened under government control and the Communists were reported to have suffered some 30,000 casualties before retreating northward. Then in early January 1947, Communist units retreating from northern Kiangsu joined with others from central Shantung to counter-attack their pursuers at Tsao-chuang in southern Shantung. Government forces were defeated with the loss of some 40,000 men and twenty-six tanks, with which the Communists began building an armoured column of their own. Ch'en Yi could not hold his newly-won positions, but evacuated his headquarters in Lin-yi county town in time to successfully ambush part of the force sent to surround him. The ensuing defeat of government forces in the vicinity of Lai-wu in February cost them another 30,000 men and control of the Tsinan-Tsingtao railway, which was again closed to through traffic.

The government's answer was a major campaign against Ch'en Yi's base in the I-meng Mountains during April and May 1947, using some twenty divisions, about 400,000 men, against an estimated 250,000 Communists. But government losses were again heavy, including 15,000 men claimed

59 Ch'ien Pang-k'ai, 'Tung-pei yen-chung-hsing tsen-yang ts'u-ch'eng-ti?' (What has precipitated the grave situation in the North-east?), *Ch'ing-tao shih-pao* (Tsingtao times), 19 Feb. 1948, reprinted in *Kuan-ch'a* (The observer), Shanghai, 27 March 1948, p. 16.

to have been killed or wounded during the epic battle of Meng-liang-ku in south-central Shantung, from 14 to 16 May. The government's 74th Reorganized Division, veteran of many encounters with Communist forces in the region during the preceding year, was completely annihilated. With the majority of his troops dead on the battlefield, the division commander, Chang Ling-fu, and his staff committed suicide. Still outnumbered, however, Ch'en Yi was finally forced to withdraw from the field in July, leaving government forces to claim victory at the battle of Nan-ma in central Shantung. But the bulk of Ch'en's army was left to re-group and fight again.

KMT military historians subsequently provided a candid assessment of Communist strengths and government errors during the 1947 Shantung campaigns: government commanders failed to judge Ch'en Yi's intentions and so failed also to contain his forces as they retreated out of northern Kiangsu. Later, in the vicinity of Tsao-chuang, government forces crowded the road and moved too slowly, stopping to rest along the way. Ultimately they were trapped by their strategy of defending points and lines, while the Communists' main force remained essentially intact. With their front line too widely extended and without sufficient mobility, government forces were unable to prevent individual units from being isolated, surrounded, and crushed individually. They lacked experience in night fighting. Coordination was poor between ground, air, and artillery units. And the tank battalion was immobilized by rain and mud.

The adversary, by contrast, was lightly equipped and able to move rapidly into and about the battle area. The Communists' use of 'shifting forces' at Tsao-chuang was typical. They outmanoeuvred their opponents through swift troop movements from one point to another, sabotaging the government's communications and attacking its troop reinforcements in the process. When Ch'en Yi's main force withdrew form Lin-yi, it moved secretly at night along paths in the hills beside the main road. Air reconnaissance failed to detect this and government forces were consequently ambushed from trenches dug along the road. The defeat at Meng-liang-ku was also blamed on faulty intelligence and the failure of air reconnaissance. Thinking Ch'en Yi's main force had moved much further north, the 74th Division was thus surprised and encircled in a locality where sustained defence was impossible. Moreover, central Shantung had long been Communist territory and its manpower and materiel were thoroughly mobilized. The result was fast accurate intelligence and a well-organized supply system. By contrast, government communications were never secure, its troop replacements always arrived late, and supplies were insufficient. 'Compared with the Communists,' noted the military historian's account, 'all our intelligence, propaganda, counter-intelligence and security were inferior.'[60]

The second year, 1947-1948: counter-attack

At the end of summer, 1947, Mao evaluated the results of the first year of the war and spelled out plans for the second. Chiang Kai-shek had committed 218 of his total 248 regular brigades and had lost over 97 of them, or approximately 780,000 men by Mao's reckoning. Mao reported CCP losses as 300,000 men and large amounts of territory occupied by the advancing government forces. The main task for the second year would be to abandon the strategy of withdrawal and carry the fight directly into government territory. The secondary task was to begin taking back the areas lost during the preceding year and destroy the occupying forces.[61]

Central and North China. In the summer of 1947, the Communists launched the second phase of the war with a developing nationwide counter-offensive. Liu Po-cheng, the 'one-eyed general', commander of the Shansi-Hopei-Shantung-Honan Field Army, on 30 June dramatically led 50,000 men across the Yellow River in south-western Shantung, diverting government forces from their campaign against Ch'en Yi farther east. While Ch'en retreated into Shantung, Liu's forces marched across the Lunghai railway into Honan ending in a thrust 300 miles to the south, where he set up a new base area in the Ta-pieh Mountains on the Hupei-Honan-Anhwei border, the site of the old O-Yü-Wan soviet established in the 1920s.

In a related action in late August, a smaller force of 20,000 men from Liu's army led by Ch'en Keng crossed the Yellow River in southern Shansi, moving south into the Honan-Shensi-Hupei border area and then linking up with Liu's columns. A month later, Ch'en Yi led part of his East China Field Army back through south-western Shantung and into the Honan-Anhwei-Kiangsu Border Region where they could compensate for the movement of Liu's army out of the area. The Communists had thus pushed the war southward into government territory in Central China and opened up a new theatre of operations between the Yellow and Yangtze Rivers. These initiatives brought together the forces of Ch'en

---

[60] *Civil war in China*, 86-99; also, *Military campaigns*, 139-45; Whitson and Huang, 230-9; and *FRUS, 1947*, 7.27, 58-9, 68-9, 72-3, 171-2, 244.
[61] Mao Tse-tung, 'Strategy for the second year of the war of liberation', Mao, *SW*, 4.141-2.

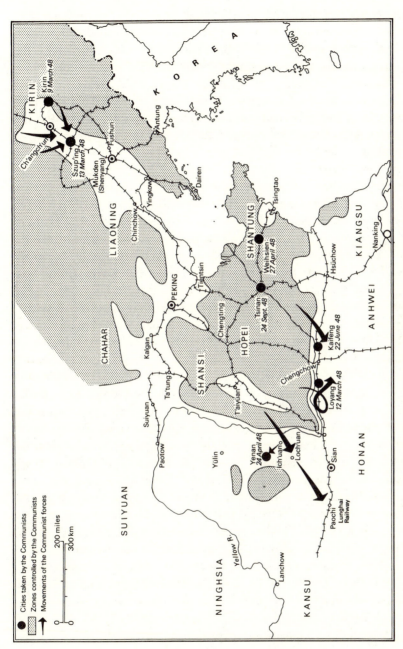

MAP 16. The CCP offensive, spring and summer 1948

Yi, Liu Po-ch'eng and Ch'en Keng, positioning them to coordinate some of the most strategically important operations of the war. In the interim they could attack all the major communications arteries in Central China and interrupt rail traffic between the Yangtze valley and the north.[62]

Meanwhile, other units of the East China Field Army in eastern Shantung and northern Kiangsu were fighting a succession of minor battles, and by mid-1948 had gained all Shantung province except a few isolated government strongpoints including the capital, Tsinan, and the port of Tsingtao.[63]

In November 1947, units from the Chin-Ch'a-Chi (Shansi-Chahar-Hopei) Field Army led by Nieh Jung-chen won an important victory with their capture of Shihchiachuang. With this key rail junction the Communists gained large quantities of materiel; control of the Peiping-Hankow railway; and the site for a new capital which they had lacked since the fall of Yenan in March 1947. The Shihchiachuang campaign also made it possible to merge the Communists' two main North China base areas – Chin-Ch'a-Chi and Chin-Chi-Lu-Yü (Shansi-Hopei-Shantung-Honan) – into one continuous territory. In addition, by the end of 1947 they had gained possession of most of the Inner Mongolian provinces of Jehol and Chahar, and all of Shansi and Hopei except for a few major cities and towns.

Capture of Yenan had provided a psychological boost for the Nationalist war effort, although it proved to be a military liability tying down troops that could have been more useful elsewhere. As one commentator put it, Hu Tsung-nan's removal from southern Shansi to attack Yenan in early 1947 had merely traded thirty reasonably prosperous Shansi counties for forty-five impoverished ones in Shensi.[64] In early spring 1948, P'eng Te-huai went on the offensive. Although the government transferred some 20,000 men from the Kaifeng-Loyang sector in Honan to reinforce Hu Tsung-nan in Shensi, they could not hold Yenan and the two changed hands in April 1948. Hu had to abandon Yenan in order to pursue P'eng Te-huai, who suddenly moved out toward Szechwan. P'eng was stopped in May by a decisive defeat near Paochi, the western terminus of the Lunghai railway, and forced back into northern Shensi. Yet despite this setback, the Communists remained in possession of most of the province including Yenan.

The Communists immediately exploited the weakness in the govern-

---

[62] Mao Tse-tung, 'On the great victory in the North-west', Mao, *SW* 4.215-16n; Whitson and Huang, 174-6; *FRUS, 1947,* 7.269-70.

[63] Mao, *SW* 4.217n.

[64] Li Tzu-ching, 'Chin-nan chieh-fang ch'ü ti tou-cheng ch'ing-hsing' (The struggle situation in the liberated districts of south Shansi), *Kuan-ch'a,* 6 March 1948, p. 15.

ment's Honan defences, created by the transfer of forces into Shensi, by moving against Loyang on the Lunghai railway. The city changed hands three times, ending in victory for Ch'en Keng's forces in early April 1948. CCP units were then in a position to capture Linfen, the last government stronghold in southern Shansi, in mid-May, linking up the Communist areas of Shansi with those of Liu Po-ch'eng's base in Central China. By the end of the month the armies of Ch'en Yi, Ch'en Keng and Liu Po-ch'eng, under the overall command of Ch'en Yi, had converged on Kaifeng in a coordinated operation that lasted for several weeks. They occupied the city, capital of Honan, in mid-June. Although Ch'en Yi's forces could not hold Kaifeng and were actually defeated in a subsequent battle nearby, the Loyang-Kaifeng campaigns were major turning points in the war. The Communist armies had demonstrated their ability to sustain the offensive on several fronts simultaneously, and to engage in large-scale positional battles in open country, the final step in moving from guerrilla operations to mobile warfare. And whereas previously the main fighting had been in Shantung and Manchuria, now the Loyang-Kaifeng operations, following close upon those at Shihchiachuang and Yenan, had created a major new battle zone in North China. These victories also made possible the expansion and unification of hitherto separate Communist border regions. The Shansi-Chahar-Hopei and the Shansi-Hopei-Shantung-Honan Border Regions were merged into the North China Liberated Area in May 1948. A unified North China People's government was established in August with its capital at Shihchiachuang.[65]

The North-east. One final turning point by mid-1948 was the reversal of the power balance in Manchuria. September 1947 brought the start of Lin Piao's sixth offensive across the Sungari, aimed this time to isolate completely the major cities of central and south Manchuria and cut land communications with North China by severing the Peiping-Mukden railway line. These goals were essentially achieved by the end of November.[66] Preliminary attacks heralding the onset of the seventh offensive began in mid-December. Command of Nationalist forces in the North-east passed from Ch'en Ch'eng to General Wei Li-huang. But Lin Piao was now strong enough to attack on three fronts simultaneously. At the start of his seventh offensive, Communist forces converged on Mukden from the north, west and south. When reinforcements were flown into the city from Changchun and Kirin, however, Lin immediately

65 *Civil war in China*, 144–53; *Military campaigns*, 145–52; Chassin, *Communist conquest*, 168–77; Mao Tse-tung, 'A circular on the situation', Mao, *SW* 4.226n.
66 *FRUS, 1947*, 7.257–8, 270–1, 287–8, 290, 298, 302, 306–8, 315–20, 356–8, 362–3, 373–80.

shifted his main operations northward in the direction of those two cities, besieging neighbouring Szupingkai for the third time in two years. The city surrendered on 13 March; the Nationalists had already abandoned Kirin a few days earlier. During the three months of fighting from mid-December to mid-March 1948, Lin Piao's forces captured a total of nineteen cities and towns.[67]

At this time, Chiang Kai-shek rejected the suggestion put forward by the head of the US Army Advisory Group, Major General David Barr, to take advantage of the reduced Communist pressure around Mukden and withdraw from the North-east while it was still possible.[68] Chiang thus lost his last chance to save what was left of the armies he had committed to the takeover of Manchuria. By mid-1948, the power balance there had shifted irreversibly against him. The Communists now claimed to have 700,000 regular troops in the region, plus 330,000 local or second-line forces, and 1.6 million civilian support workers. The government's increasingly demoralized troops numbered only about 450,000 with no effective second-line replacements.[69]

Nationwide, according to the government's estimates, the strength of its regular armies had been reduced by one-third by June 1948, in comparison with mid-1945. Government forces now numbered 2,180,000 men, only 980,000 of whom were armed. The Communist side had 1,560,000 regular troops and 700,000 irregulars, of whom an estimated 970,000 were armed. Heavy weapons numbered 21,000 on the government side as opposed to 22,800 with the Communists.[70] And as Mao had pointed out earlier, Communist gains were being made at the expense of the government's losses, since captured enemy materiel comprised the main source of arms and ammunition for the PLA, and surrendered government soldiers an important source of new recruits.

The third year, 1948-1949: victory

In March 1948, Mao was able to report that the government's armies retained the initiative in only two sectors, both in Central China, and were on the defensive everywhere else. He predicted that the CCP would probably establish a central people's government in 1949, by which time they would have captured one or two of China's largest cities and merged into one continuous area all of North-eastern China, North China,

[67] Mao Tse-tung, 'On the great victory in the North-west', Mao, SW, 4.216n; Whitson and Huang, 310-11; Civil war in China, 121-4; FRUS, 1947, 7.403-4, 411-15; FRUS, 1948, 7.1-4, 8-9, 22-4, 26-7, 36-7, 58-9, 65-6, 86, 93-5, 97-9, 103-6, 115, 121-2, 127-8, 143-5, 152-3.
[68] China white paper, 1.325.   [69] Whitson and Huang, 312; FRUS, 1948, 7.340-3.
[70] Chassin, Communist conquest, 177.

Shantung, north Kiangsu, Honan, Hupei, and Anhwei. He estimated the defeat of the KMT within three years.[71]

The Communists now had the men, weapons, organization and experience necessary to sustain large-scale positional engagements. These began with the successful siege of Tsinan, capital of Shantung, in September 1948. The Communists' spring operations had completely isolated the city and Ch'en Yi's troops campaigning in Honan had returned to Shantung by September. As in Manchuria earlier, Chiang Kai-shek's American advisers warned him that the situation of his troops at Tsinan was hopeless. But again Chiang refused to evacuate them. The attack on the city began on 16 September, and was over within ten days. The majority of the demoralized garrison had essentially refused to fight and some actually defected to the Communists, a sure sign that the tide was turning.[72]

The transformation from passive defence into defection and surrender that occurred at Tsinan was repeated several times over during the final year of the war, as the psychological effect of the government's accumulating defeats took hold. This undoubtedly helped speed up the timetable for destruction of the government's forces, which occurred in the course of three decisive campaigns fought between mid-September 1948 and the end of January 1949. These campaigns, planned as a coordinated general offensive against three major concentrations of government armies, were: the Liaohsi-Shenyang (Mukden) campaign, 12 September – 2 November, which ended in the complete defeat of the Nationalist armies in Manchuria; the Peiping-Tientsin campaign, 21 November – 31 January, which ended government resistance in North China; and the Huai-hai campaign, 6 November – 10 January, which removed the last major obstacle to the Communists' march southward to the Yangtze and beyond.

The Liaohsi-Shenyang campaign. This was Lin Piao's eighth and final offensive campaign in Manchuria, confirming his reputation among military historians and the Chinese public alike as one of China's great military leaders.[73] Considering the scale of operations, the end for the

---

[71] Mao Tse-tung, 'A circular on the situation', Mao, *SW* 4.219–26.

[72] *China white paper*, 1.319–20, 331–2; Mao Tse-tung, 'The concept of operations for the Huai-Hai Campaign', Mao, *SW*, 4.282n; *Civil war in China*, 156–7; *Military campaigns*, 158–60; *FRUS, 1948*, 7.464, 467–71, 478, 480–6.

[73] The reappraisal of Lin Piao's pre-1949 military career occurred in 1974–5, as part of the national campaign to criticize him following his death allegedly in a plane crash while trying to flee to the Soviet Union. If private conversations with ordinary Chinese are any indication, the military critique was the least convincing part of the propaganda campaign against him. For examples of that critique, see *Hsueh-hsi yü p'i-an* (Study and criticism), 9 (1974) 19–26, and 8 (1975) 18–22; *Hung-ch'i* (The red flag), 1 (1975) 39–44; *Li-shih yen-chiu* (Historical research), 1 (1975) 24–30.

government came almost as rapidly in the North-east as at Tsinan, albeit not quite so ingloriously. Lin Piao's troops numbered approximately 700,000 for this final Manchurian offensive against something under 500,000 on the government side. The three main targets were government troop concentrations at Chinchow, a key supply centre on the Peiping-Mukden railway, at Mukden itself, and at Changchun. The largest concentration was the Mukden garrison numbering 230,000 men.

The attack on Chinchow began on 12 September, although the objective was not immediately apparent due to diversionary operations against Changchun. Government troops in the vicinity of Chinchow were surrounded and isolated within two weeks. By the end of September the airfield was under attack and ammunition was already running low, making it necessary to supply the garrison by air drop. Despite heavy preliminary fighting at nearby points, most notably at Yi hsien, the Chinchow garrison was unable to withstand a sustained attack by Communist forces, two government divisions defected, and the city surrendered on 15 October.

A relief force of some 100,000 men sent out from Mukden in early October failed to break through in time to save Chinchow. Lin Piao's second major objective then became the annihilation of this force before it could return to Mukden. Feigning a march to the south-west, he instead moved his main force north-east from Chinchow. Again despite heavy fighting the relief column could not break out of the trap Lin had so swiftly laid, and surrendered on 28 October. With the Mukden garrison reduced by half its strength, the city capitulated on 2 November, after only minimal resistance. Meanwhile, at Changchun, both civilians and military had been reduced to near-starvation by Communist encirclement. The 60th Army, composed of troops from Yunnan known to be unreliable, defected to the Communists on 17 October. Other units soon surrendered there as well, ending all resistance.

Despite his earlier proven incompetence, General Tu Yü-ming rejoined the North-east command during the battle, while Chiang Kai-shek personally took over the direction of military operations from his command post in Peiping. It may never be possible to untangle the effects of the Communists' strengths as opposed to the government's weaknesses. But as the US consul-general at Mukden cabled on 27 October: 'Government military tactics North-east past week resemble comedy errors if consequences government were not so tragic'. By mid-November, exactly two years after Lin Piao had launched his first offensive across the Sungari, the last government garrisons in the North-east had either surrendered or were fleeing southward. The government had lost at least

400,000 troops including some of its best, together with all their arms and equipment during this final phase of the battle for the North-east.[74]

The Peiping-Tientsin campaign. Lin Piao's armies began their march southward immediately following their victory in Manchuria. The subsequent Peiping-Tientsin campaign brought a combined force of 890,000 regular Communist troops from the North China and North-east Field Armies under the overall command of Lin Piao, against some 600,000 troops led by one of the government's more capable commanders, Fu Tso-i. Lin Piao's main force moved rapidly south of the Great Wall and into the Peiping-Tientsin region, supported to the west by Nieh Jung-chen's North China Field Army already threatening Kalgan. Nieh's objective around Kalgan had been to discourage Fu from weakening his defence of Peiping by sending aid to the North-east. With that area now secure, the new objective was to prevent Fu from moving south to reinforce government troop concentrations in northern Kiangsu, target of the Communists' crucial Huai-Hai campaign, which began in early November. Communist strategy for the Peiping-Tientsin region therefore aimed at surrounding Fu Tso-i's forces at five points, dealing with each in turn so as to cut off their escape and prevent reinforcements from reaching them as well.

Within two weeks after the main troop movements out of Manchuria began on 21 November, Lin's forces had reached the outskirts of Tientsin and a major deployment area to the north-west of Tangshan. Within two more weeks they had consolidated their positions. The first major attack was at Fu's weakest point, Hsin-pao-an, north-west of Peiping, where the garrison was defeated by Nieh Jung-chen's forces on 22 December. Two days later Kalgan also surrendered. Meanwhile, the Communist encirclement of Peiping and Tientsin was being steadily strengthened. The Nationalist commander at Tientsin, determined to resist, flooded a large area outside the city to block the Communist advance. He then refused to surrender without a fight, but Communist forces prevailed after the 14–15 January battle of Tientsin. The nearby port of Tang-ku fell two days later, its 50,000-man garrison fleeing by sea. In this crisis, with escape routes blocked, all nearby troop concentrations defeated, and his 200,000 troops at Peiping now overwhelmingly outnumbered, Fu Tso-i negotiated a settlement. He agreed on 22 January to withdraw his forces from the city without fighting and to reorganize them into the PLA. Communist

[74] *Civil war in China*, 124–9; *Military campaigns*, 155–7; Mao Tse-tung, 'The concept of operations for the Liaohsi-Shenyang campaign', Mao, *SW* 4.261–6; Whitson and Huang, 312–19; *FRUS, 1948*, 7.457–8, 463, 469–70, 474, 477–8, 486–7, 495, 501–4, 508–9, 520, 522–5, 527–32, 537–8, 548–9.

troops entered Peiping on 31 January. In the Peiping-Tientsin campaign the government had lost close to another half million troops, together with two of China's most important cities.[75]

The Huai-Hai campaign. The third decisive campaign of the civil war occurred concurrently with the Peiping-Tientsin operations. The famous 65-day battle of the Huai-Hai was fought between 6 November 1948 and 10 January 1949. The main battle zone was bounded on the north by the Lunghai line and on the south by the Huai River, hence the name Huai-Hai. Fighting centred around the city of Hsuchou, seat of the government's Bandit Suppression Headquarters, strategically positioned at the junction of the Lunghai and Tientsin-Pukow railways. The battle climaxed the collaboration of Ch'en Yi, Liu Po-ch'eng and Ch'en Keng, commanders of the PLA's East China and Central Plains Field Armies, who had been campaigning together in the region for more than a year.

The two sides were about evenly matched in terms of regular troop strength: each committed upwards of half a million men. But the Communists with their already well-developed civilian support network were able to mobilize an additional two million peasants for the massive logistical effort necessary to sustain their battlefield operations. The military and civilian support work actually extended into four provinces: Kiangsu, Shantung, Anhwei and Honan, and was coordinated by an ad hoc General Huai-Hai Front Committee headed by Teng Hsiao-p'ing. The main government commanders were Liu Chih, Tu Yü-ming and Huang Wei, with Liu Chih in overall command and Chiang Kai-shek personally overseeing operations as he had done during the final Manchurian campaign.

The Huai-Hai battle unfolded roughly although not precisely in accordance with a three-phase 'concept of operations' drafted by Mao Tse-tung and issued on 11 October 1948. The entire campaign was completed within two months as the plan directed. During the first phase, the objective was the annihilation of the army led by Huang Po-t'ao. This was accomplished by Ch'en Yi's forces in the vicinity of Nien-chuang on the Lunghai railway between Hsuchou and the Grand Canal in a battle which lasted two weeks as planned, between 6 and 22 November.

The second phase, 23 November – 15 December, entailed the destruction of government forces in the vicinity of Shuang-tui-chi, south of Hsuchou

---

[75] *Civil War in China*, 142–4; *Military campaigns*, 165–7; Mao Tse-tung, 'The concept of operations for the Peiping-Tientsin campaign', Mao, *SW*, 4.289–93; *FRUS, 1948*, 7.532–5, 557, 592, 638–40, 643–50, 663–73, 680–1, 691–3, 700–5, 723–5; *FRUS, 1949*, 8.19, 30–1, 36, 44, 46–59, 71–2, 75–7, 87–8, 98.

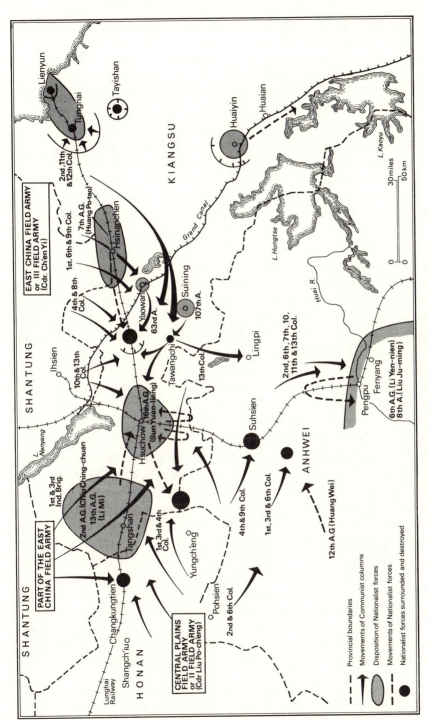

MAP 17. The battle of Huai-Hai, November 1948–January 1949

Within the map:

SHANTUNG

KIANGSU

HONAN

ANHWEI

Lunghai Railway

Shangch'iuo

Changkungtien

Tangshan

Yungchêng

Pohsien

Suhsien

Suining

Yaowan

Tawangchi

Lingpi

Pengpu

Fenyang

Huai R.

L. Hungtse

L. Kaoyu

Huaiin

Huaian

Lienyun

Tunghai

Tayishan

Hsinanchen

Ihsien

L. Nanyang

Grand Canal

Hsuchow 16th A.G.
(Sun Yuan-liang)

EAST CHINA FIELD ARMY
or III FIELD ARMY
(Cdr. Ch'en Yi)

7th A.G.
(Huang Po-tao)

1st, 6th & 9th Col.

2nd, 11th
& 12th Col.

4th & 8th
Col.

10th & 13th
Col.

63rd A.

107th A.

13th Col.

2nd, 6th, 7th, 10,
11th & 13th Col.

6th A.G. (Li Yen-nien)
8th A.(Liu Ju-ming)

4th & 9th Col.

1st, 3rd & 6th Col.

12th A.G (Huang Wei)

2nd & 6th Col.

CENTRAL PLAINS
FIELD ARMY
or II FIELD ARMY
(Cdr Liu Po-ch'eng)

PART OF THE EAST
CHINA FIELD ARMY

2nd A.G. (Chou Ching-chuan)
13th A.G.
(Li Mi)

1st & 3rd
Ind. Brig.

1st, 3rd & 4th
Col.

30 miles
50 km

Provincial boundaries
Movements of Communist columns
Disposition of Nationalist forces
Movements of Nationalist forces
Nationalist forces surrounded and destroyed

not far from the Tientsin-Pukow railway. The Communists anticipated that government reinforcements would come from the eastern terminus of the Lunghai line, brought in by sea from Tsingtao. Chiang Kai-shek instead ordered reinforcements under Huang Wei to come from Central China. Despite this change Huang Wei's army was quickly surrounded. Relief columns sent north from the Huai River area around Pengpu, Anhwei, were turned back by Communist guerrillas. Nor did the main reinforcements moving south from Hsuchou ever reach him, being themselves surrounded and destroyed in phase three of the campaign.

Phase three also was not fought in the locality anticipated by the Communists' original plan, but unfolded instead in an area just to the south-west of Hsuchou in the vicinity of Ch'en-kuan-chuang on the Anhwei-Kiangsu border. Communist forces trapped and destroyed three government armies here – the main force in the Hsuchou region totalling almost 300,000 men – as they moved out of the city in accordance with Chiang Kai-shek's order to reinforce Huang Wei. The advance army led by Sun Yuan-liang was encircled and virtually wiped out in early December. Tu Yü-ming commanded the remainder of the Hsuchou garrison together with Ch'iu Ch'ing-ch'üan and Li Mi. Ultimately surrounded and besieged by the combined armies of Ch'en Yi and Liu Po-ch'eng, Tu's forces were inadequately supplied by air and reduced to near starvation. They finally surrendered during an assault between 6 and 10 January.

The government lost another half million troops during the Huai-Hai campaign, with some 300,000 taken prisoner and the remainder dead or injured. Commanders Huang Po-t'ao and Ch'iu Ch'ing-ch'üan were killed in battle, while Huang Wei and Tu Yü-ming were both taken prisoner. Generals Sun Yuan-liang and Li Mi escaped the battlefield disguised as beggar and merchant respectively. The defeat removed the last main government defence line north of the Yangtze.[76]

Chiang Kai-shek and his commanders had no one but themselves to blame for their defeat at Huai-Hai. The battle marked not just the end of effective government resistance in mainland China, but the culmination of years of military errors and mismanagement, defects that had become characteristic of Nationalist military operations. Chiang himself is credited with having made the decision to fight on the Hsuchou plain instead of withdrawing as advised to the natural barrier of the Huai River. He furthermore placed overall command of the battle in the hands of Liu

[76] Whitson and Huang, 178-86, 240-3; Seymour Topping, *Journey between two Chinas*, 24-48; Mao Tse-tung, 'The concept of operations for the Huai-Hai campaign', Mao, *SW*, 4.279-82; *Civil war in China*, 157-60; *Military campaigns*, 161-4.

Chih and Tu Yü-ming, hardly his most capable generals. Finally, Chiang Kai-shek personally interfered with battle plans and issued operational orders while the fighting was in progress, as was his custom. With so much power concentrated in the hands of one man, responsibility for the failures could not but be concentrated there as well.

Despite the valour that many government units displayed on the battlefield, they found themselves once again outmanoeuvred by superior PLA strategy and tactics. The Communists as usual attacked weaker points, first at Nien-chuang and then Shuang-tui-chi, while the government's main forces remained unengaged at Hsuchou. When these finally moved out, they were as usual too late and too slow, their vehicles clogging the roads out of town. They were then pursued, surrounded and destroyed piecemeal at Ch'en-kuan-chuang in the time-honoured tradition of guerrilla warfare – except that this time the venue was an open battlefield containing a total of one million men.

Government commanders had never learned the lessons of speed and decisiveness that had been mastered by their adversaries. But government commanders also lacked an adequate understanding of mechanized warfare and the use of air power. Hence they were never able to gain the advantages they should have enjoyed from their absolute monopoly in both areas. Their defence was marred not only by disunity and indecision but by inadequate tactical planning, intelligence and logistical support as well. As a result they found themselves repeatedly surprised, hemmed in, and immobilized. During this and other battles, their performance seemed to confirm the judgment of one of the KMT's staunchest American supporters, William C. Bullitt, that 'There is not a single Government general who has the military training and technical skill to handle the over-all problems of logistics involved in meeting the attack of a Communist army of more than 2,000,000 men.'[77]

PLA commanders, by contrast, seemed able to adapt at will to changing battlefield situations. They were united, most immediately, by years of cooperation in applying a strategy that elevated flexibility in the field to the highest art of defensive warfare. They were then successful in applying these principles to increasingly large-scale offensive operations. In particular, their civilian support network was an indispensable feature of their success. Horse carts, wheelbarrows and carrying poles provided the chief means of conveyance on the Communists' supply lines, underscoring the old maxim that primitive things which work are better than modern

[77] 'Report by consultant William C. Bullitt to the Joint Committee on Foreign Economic Cooperation Concerning China', 80th Congress, 2nd session (24 December 1948), 12, quoted in Tsou Tang, 491.

things that don't. The Communists had crafted their war machine on the basis of the human and material resources most readily at hand. As a result, their civilian manpower network provided the logistical and intelligence support necessary to sustain their military operations, ultimately negating the initial advantages enjoyed by the government armies in numbers, training and materiel.

More generally, as the Communists moved onto the offensive in 1947, government commanders had lapsed into a strategy of passive defence from which they never freed themselves. They remained as if stunned once the enemy they had forced into retreat on all fronts in 1946 suddenly turned and began the counter-attack. The antiquated custom of withdrawing behind city walls continued to dominate government military thinking long after the Communists' battlefield performance had rendered such operational concepts obsolete. But when government forces did move out, they were regularly overwhelmed by their opponents' tactical superiority, further reinforcing their own defensive mentality.

The Communists' experience with fighting a stronger adversary during the Anti-Japanese War thus paid off handsomely after 1945. Government armies, for their part, had used the opportunity provided by the Japanese invasion neither to develop an effective guerrilla movement nor to master the art of modern warfare that Joseph Stilwell and others had tried to teach them. When the Japanese were removed from the scene and the two Chinese armies were left to face each other, government commanders could not match the performance of their enemy. By the latter half of 1948 this had developed into an effective integration of guerrilla tactics with mobile and positional warfare, allowing the Communists to orchestrate simultaneous coordinated offensives by a force of well over one million fighters.

Shortly after the fall of Tsinan in September 1948, Chiang Kai-shek had indicated that a thorough overhaul of military strategy, tactics, training and field organization was in order. In particular, the practice of holding strongpoints regardless of the cost would have to be abandoned.[78] Chiang had apparently at last grasped the nature of his military problems, but that understanding had come too late.

THE DEMISE OF THE KMT GOVERNMENT AND FAILURE OF AMERICAN POLICY

After the conclusion of the 1948-9 winter campaigns, all that followed was anti-climax. With its main forces destroyed, the demise of Chiang Kai-shek's government was a foregone conclusion. On 14 January 1949,

[78] *China white paper*, 1.332.

the Communists issued their conditions for peace, a harsh eight-point proposal very different from their negotiating posture in 1945–6. Now they were demanding, among other things, Chiang Kai-shek's punishment as a war criminal, the integration of his remaining armed forces into the PLA, and the abolition of the KMT government. Chiang declined to accept the conditions but on 21 January resigned the presidency. Vice-President General Li Tsung-jen succeeded him as acting president and opened formal peace negotiations. A government delegation led by Chang Chih-chung arrived in Peiping on 1 April, but was able to gain little beyond the eight-point conditions of 14 January, and a 20 April deadline for their acceptance. The KMT government rejected the conditions and the PLA began its advance across the Yangtze immediately the deadline had passed.

The PLA had used the intervening months to rest, regroup and reorganize. In early 1949, its field armies were renamed in preparation for their movement out of the regions where they had fought their major battles, P'eng Te-huai's North-west Field Army was redesignated the First Field Army; Liu Po-ch'eng's Central Plains Field Army was reorganized as the Second Field Army; Ch'en Yi's East China Field Army became the Third Field Army; and Lin Piao's North-east Field Army became the Fourth Field Army. Nieh Jung-chen's North China Field Army was formally deactivated later in the year.

On 21 April, the armies of Ch'en Yi and Liu Po-ch'eng moved together once more, crossing the Yangtze along a 300-mile front. Against minimal resistance they took the KMT capital, Nanking, on 24 April; Hangchow, capital of Chekiang, on 3 May; Nanchang, capital of Kiangsi, on 22 May; and Shanghai on 27 May. In mid-May, Lin Piao's army crossed the Yangtze in the vicinity of Wuhan, taking that city on 16–17 May. His progress was temporarily checked in southern Hunan, where a large force led by Pai Ch'ung-hsi blocked Lin's march southward from July to October. Both sides reported heavy casualties before Pai was finally forced to withdraw from the field in early October. Lin then proceeded more or less unobstructed, occupying Canton on 14 October and Kweilin on 22 November. It was late April 1950, however, before Lin's forces had finally eliminated all resistance in Kwangsi and Hainan Island.

In the north and north-west, the Shansi warlord, Yen Hsi-shan, held out in his capital, Taiyuan, until 24 April 1949, when the city surrendered to Nieh Jung-chen. Sian surrendered a month later to P'eng Te-huai, and Lanchou did the same at the end of August after the three main government commanders in the north-west refused to cooperate in the defence of Kansu.

The KMT government disintegrated as it retreated one step ahead of the advancing Communist armies. On 23 April, Acting President Li Tsung-jen fled Nanking for Canton, the new capital, where the government ministries had been relocating since the start of the year. Yet even the trauma of having lost the northern half of the country was not sufficient to galvanize a unified anti-Communist opposition among the KMT's cliques and factions. Chiang Kai-shek continued to manipulate military and political affairs first from his retirement home at Fenghua, Chekiang, and then from Taiwan, where he established a personal headquarters in July 1949. He resumed active control of KMT affairs about the same time. Earlier in the year he had successfully removed to Taiwan the Nationalist air force and navy, together with some of the best of the remaining army divisions loyal to him, and the government's US $300 million worth of gold, silver, and foreign exchange reserves.

Chiang's plan, which only gradually became apparent in 1949, was to abandon all the Chinese mainland and retreat to a fortress in Taiwan from which he could rebuild his own power. There he would await the inevitable onset of the Third World War between the United States and the Soviet Union which would, he thought, allow him to fight his way back under American aegis to the realm he had lost. During the half year of his retirement from public office, he worked with some determination to implement this plan. For example, he acted to undermine Li Tsung-jen's attempt to organize – together with his fellow Kwangsi clique member, General Pai Ch'ung-hsi – a credible defence south of the Yangtze. Fearing the challenge of his own plans and power should they succeed, Chiang refused to allocate the arms, ammunition and money needed by Pai Ch'ung-hsi in midsummer when his forces were blocking Lin Piao's advance in southern Hunan. Similar requests for assistance in the north-west were also denied, adding to the hopelessness of the disunited defence command in that region.[79]

By October, when Lin Piao's army occupied Canton, the KMT government had removed to its Second World War capital, Chungking. Chiang Kai-shek rejoined it there in mid-November. As the PLA's First and Second Field Armies moved through the south-west in the autumn of 1949, Chiang moved what remained of his government from Chungking to Chengtu, and then on to Taiwan on 9 December. Li Tsung-jen's plan to establish a separate resistance movement in South China never materialized. He was away from Chungking when Chiang arrived there and refused to return. Li proceeded to Hong Kong and then departed in early December for medical treatment and exile in the United States. Taiwan became the refuge for some two million KMT supporters, including half a million survivors of Chiang's armed forces.

[79] FRUS, 1949, 8.280–8, 290, 293–4, 327–8, 476–7, 489, 493, 552–3; Li Tsung-jen, Memoirs, 517–28.

While Chiang and the remnants of his government were flying from city to city in search of a final resting place, a new Political Consultative Conference was organized in Peiping. It met from 21 to 28 September, and was attended by 662 representatives from the CCP, the Democratic League, other democratic groups, labour, peasants, business and industry. Among other things, the conference adopted the Common Programme of the People's Republic of China and designated Peiping the official capital, formally changing its name back to Peking (Beijing) on 27 September. Four days later, on 1 October, Mao Tse-tung officially proclaimed the founding of the People's Republic.

For the United States, the dilemmas apparent in its China policy since 1944–5 had now overwhelmed it. America's KMT ally was defeated and the basis for any relationship with the new Communist government had been all but destroyed. The closest the United States ever officially came to an accommodation with the Chinese Communists was during 1946, when the mediation efforts of the Marshall Mission sought to bring the CCP into a coalition government. The distance between the CCP and the Americans grew with the failure of that effort and the escalation of military hostilities. The Americans continued their diplomatic and material support for the KMT and abandoned the idea of a coalition government that would include the CCP.

In reality, the United States had few options open to it in post-Second World War China. The global context of America's China policy grew increasingly important during these years when the Chinese civil war developed simultaneously with the expansion of Communist power in Europe. The first and most basic assumption of United States foreign policy was that Europe was its primary sphere of interest. Hence the dominant portion of United States aid and concern was channelled in that direction with the Truman Doctrine, aid to Greece and Turkey, and the Marshall Plan for Western Europe. The Cold War and consequent political pressures in the United States precluded any substantive tilt toward the Chinese Communists. The growing furore over the Hurley charges showed the constraints preventing that option. KMT leaders were correct in their estimate that, however unpalatable they might be to the United States, the latter had little choice but to support them. The same forces that precluded a tilt toward the CCP precluded also a complete withdrawal of support from the KMT.

But the weakness of the KMT government showed what a great effort would have been required to prop it up. General Marshall warned, after he became secretary of state, that the Chinese government was evidently incapable of eliminating the CCP as a political threat in China. Hence for any such effort to succeed, he advised the US Congress in 1948, 'it would be necessary for the US to underwrite the Chinese Government's military effort, on a wide and probably constantly increasing scale, as well as the Chinese economy. The US would have to be prepared virtually to take over the Chinese Government and administer its economic, military and governmental affairs.' That was so grandiose an undertaking that he felt compelled to advise against it. He recommended the only realistic alternative in his view, namely, a programme of limited economic aid.[80]

One final consideration was the estimate prevailing from about 1946, that while the KMT government could not eliminate the Communists as a political force in China, neither did the Communists have the strength to defeat the government militarily. Hence the American policy-makers' decision to let China simmer on the back burner, while the main thrust of the anti-Communist effort was directed toward Europe. In May 1947, therefore, the ten-month arms embargo imposed during the Marshall Mission was lifted. But the Nationalist requests in May and June for large-scale economic aid were rejected. Instead, President Truman sent General Wedemeyer, commander of United States forces in China at the end of the Second World War, back to China on a fact-finding mission. After one month in China during July and August 1947, Wedemeyer addressed an assembly of KMT dignitaries including Chiang Kai-shek himself. The general presented an uncompromising critique of the government they led, warning that their survival depended on drastic political and economic reforms. On returning to Washington, he nevertheless proposed an expansive economic and military aid programme for the KMT government, together with an international trusteeship for Manchuria to contain Communist influence there.[81] The KMT spurned Wedemeyer's demands for its reform while the Truman administration, fearing active involvement in the Chinese civil war, rejected the idea of sending to China the 10,000 officers required for his military aid proposals. The policy of limited assistance to the KMT government seemed the only realistic solution, albeit complicated by the demands of the China lobby on the one hand and economy-minded members of Congress on the other. But given the existing constraints, the basic decisions against wider intervention and for limited assistance were rationally made.

In the end, of course, the policy of limited assistance pleased no one and gained nothing. It was unable to delay disaster for the KMT government on the Chinese mainland. Yet it also earned the condemnation of the non-Communist anti-war movement there, as an American attempt

---

[80] *China white paper*, 1.382-3. The US policy of limited assistance to China is analysed in Tsou Tang, 349-493.

[81] *China white paper*, 2.758-814.

to promote its own interests by disregarding those of China through continuing support for the unregenerate Chiang Kai-shek. But it was not the policy itself that was at fault, so much as the erroneous estimates on which it was based with respect to the Chinese Communists and the underlying assumptions which led to those estimates. For the policy was founded on the mistaken calculation of the Communists' chances of victory. The prevailing view was, as Marshall advised Congress in 1948, only that the government could not defeat the Communists, not that they might actually defeat the government. The American public was never prepared for the latter contingency. Nor did American policy-makers ever appear to contemplate that China could be governed by any party other than the KMT, or the KMT led by anyone other than Chiang Kai-shek. After the military campaigns of late 1948, when even Chiang Kai-shek had accepted the inevitable, American diplomats turned to the idea of north-south partition as a possible solution. The anticipated scenario for the civil war in China was thus protracted stalemate of one form or another.

The weaknesses of the KMT government were readily apparent to all observers; only the strength of the Communists was not. The voices of the American foreign service officers, who tried to explain this towards the end of the Second World War, were silenced after the Hurley affair, and there were no United States diplomatic observers in the Communist areas during the subsequent civil war years. Meanwhile, the antipathy towards the presumed threat seemed to preclude even the serious contemplation of it, relegating that exercise to the forbidden zone of subversive activity. The most basic failure of the Americans, therefore, was to deny themselves the ability to consider on any terms other than their own the nature of the Communist-led Chinese revolution. Hence they could not estimate that the Communists might prevail, much less grasp the reasons why. Consequently, they also had no real understanding of the changes in the KMT government that would have been required before it could defeat its enemy; or of the time that would have been required to realize such reforms even had there been the will to do so; and no understanding as to how the United States could inspire such a will when it was otherwise clearly lacking. The tones of desperation that crept into American diplomatic despatches in late 1948 and early 1949, as they assessed stop-gap remedies for the ever more 'rapidly deteriorating situation', attest to the lack of understanding on all those counts. This failure led in turn to years of painful and inconclusive recriminations over the 'loss of China' and the responsibility of individual Americans for it, as though China was theirs to lose.

In later years, however, it eventually became acceptable to contemplate the event more dispassionately. Much speculation then arose about 'what might have been', as various attempts of Chinese Communist leaders during the 1940s to establish official contacts with the United States became more widely known. These included Mao's statements to the Dixie Mission in 1944; the invitation to American Ambassador J. Leighton Stuart to visit Peiping in the summer of 1949; and Chou En-lai's extraordinary approach to the Americans at this same time, using the Australian journalist, Michael Keon, as intermediary.[82] The United States failed to respond positively to any of these overtures from the Chinese Communists. Yet whether there could have been anything more than a communications channel between them seems doubtful, however rational the larger possibilities might have been in hypothetical terms. Preoccupied as they were with the expanding power of the Soviet Union and their irreducible fear of communism, American makers of policy and public opinion were in no mood to experiment with more flexible and selective approaches toward the new Chinese government during the McCarthy era of the early 1950s. Nor did the Chinese Communists expend undue effort to hold themselves apart from the mounting Cold War tensions of the period. The strident anti-American themes of the official CCP pronouncements that pursued Stuart out of China in August 1949 were matched by the uncompromising anti-Communist tones which dominated contemporary American diplomatic reports and public opinion in general. Together these Chinese and American postures indicated differences so great that they would require more than two decades to surmount.

[82] On the Dixie Mission, see Esherick, ed. *Lost chance*; on the Peiping invitation: Topping, 81-90; Shaw Yu-ming, 'John Leighton Stuart and US-Chinese Communist rapprochement in 1949', *CQ* 89 (March 1982) 74-96; *FRUS, 1949*, 8.766-70, 779, 784-5, 791; on Chou En-lai's approach to the Americans and a similar one to the British: *ibid.* 357-60, 372-3, 388, 389, 397-9, 496-8, 779-80; and Edwin W. Martin, 'The Chou demarche', *Foreign Service Journal* (November 1981), 13-16, 32.

BIBLIOGRAPHY

Abend, Hallett et al. *Can China survive?* New York: Ives Washburn, 1936

Amerasia: a monthly analysis of America and Asia. New York: Amerasia, Inc. 11 vols. March 1937–July 1947. Superseded *China Today* (subtitle varies). Ed. by P. Jaffe and others.

The Amerasia papers: a clue to the catastrophe of China. 2 vols. Prepared by the Subcommittee to Investigate the Administration of the Internal Security Act and Other Internal Security Laws of the Committee on the Judiciary, United States Senate. Washington, DC: US Government Printing Office, 1970

Bachrack, Stanley D. *The Committee of One Million: 'China Lobby' politics, 1953–1971.* New York: Columbia University Press, 1976

Barnett, A. Doak. *China on the eve of Communist takeover.* New York: Praeger, 1963

Barnett, A. Doak, ed. *Chinese Communist politics in action.* Seattle: University of Washington Press, 1969

Barrett, David D. *Dixie Mission: the United States Army Observer Group in Yenan, 1944.* Berkeley: Center for Chinese Studies, University of California, 1970

Beal, John Robinson. *Marshall in China.* Garden City, NY: Doubleday, 1970

Belden, Jack. *China shakes the world.* New York: Harper, 1949

Benton, Gregor. 'The "second Wang Ming line" (1935–38)'. *CQ* 61 (March 1975) 61–94

Benton, Gregor. 'The origins and early growth of the New Fourth Army'. Unpublished manuscript

Bergson, Abram. *The economics of Soviet planning.* New Haven: Yale University Press, 1961

Bertram, James M. *First act in China: the story of the Sian mutiny.* New York: Viking, 1938. Also published as *Crisis in China: the story of the Sian mutiny.* London: Macmillan, 1937

Bisson, Thomas Arthur. *Japan in China.* New York: Macmillan, 1938

Bōeicho bōei kensujo senshi shitsu. *Hokushi no chiansen* (Pacification war in North China). 2 vols., map folios. Tokyo: Asagumo shimbunsha, 1968

Borg, Dorothy and Heinrichs, Waldo, eds. *Uncertain years: Chinese-American relations, 1947–1950.* New York: Columbia University Press, 1980

Boyle, John Hunter. *China and Japan at war, 1937–1945: the politics of collaboration.* Stanford: Stanford University Press, 1972

Brandt, Conrad, Schwartz, Benjamin and Fairbank, John K. *A documentary history of*

Chinese communism. Cambridge, Mass.: Harvard University Press; London: Allen & Unwin, 1952

Braun, Otto. *A Comintern agent in China 1932–1939,* trans. by Jeanne Moore. Intro. by Dick Wilson. Stanford: Stanford University Press, 1982. First published in German in 1975 as *Chinesische Aufzeichnungen* (1932–1939). Berlin: Deitz Verlag (GDR)

Buck, John Lossing. *Land utilization in China: a study of 16,786 farms in 168 localities, and 38,256 farm families in twenty-two provinces in China, 1929–1933.* 3 vols. Nanking: University of Nanking; Chicago: University of Chicago Press, 1937; 2nd printing, New York: Paragon Book Reprint Corp., 1964

Bunker, Gerald E. *The peace conspiracy: Wang Ching-wei and the China War, 1937–1941.* Cambridge, Mass.: Harvard University Press, 1972

Bush, Richard Clarence, III. 'Industry and politics in Kuomintang China: the Nationalist regime and Lower Yangtze Chinese cotton mill owners, 1927–1937'. Columbia University, Ph.D. dissertation, 1978

Butow, Robert J. C. *Tojo and the coming of the war.* Princeton: Princeton University Press, 1961

Cambridge history of China. Cambridge: Cambridge University Press. Vol. 3, *Sui and T'ang China 589–906, part 1,* ed. by Denis Twitchett, 1979; vol. 10, *Late Ch'ing 1800–1911, part 1,* ed. by John K. Fairbank, 1978; vol. 11, *Late Ch'ing 1800–1911, part 2,* ed. by John K. Fairbank and Kwang-Ching Liu, 1980; vol. 12, *Republican China 1912–1949, part 1,* ed. by John K. Fairbank, 1983

Carlson, Evans Fordyce. *The Chinese army: its organization and military efficiency.* New York: Institute of Pacific Relations, 1940

Cavendish, Patrick. 'The "New China" of the Kuomintang', in Jack Gray, ed. *Modern China's search for a political form,* 138–86

'Chan-shih hou-fang kung-yeh shih ju-ho chien-li-ti' (How the wartime industry in the rear was established). *Hsin-shih-chieh yueh-k'an,* 15 March 1944, 10–15

Chang, Carsun (Chang Chün-mai). *The third force in China.* New York: Bookman, 1952

Chang Ch'i-yun. *Tang-shih kai-yao* (Survey of party history). 5 vols. Taipei: Chung-yang wen-wu, 1951

Chang Ch'ih-chang. *Chi-luan wen-ts'un* (Collected essays of Chi-luan [Chang Ch'ih-chang]). Taipei: Wen-hsing shu-tien, 1962

Chang, John K. 'Industrial development of Mainland China, 1912–1949'. *Journal of Economic History,* 27.1 (March 1967) 56–81

Chang, John K. *Industrial development in pre-Communist China: a quantitative analysis.* Chicago: Aldine, 1969

Chang Kia-ngau. *China's struggle for railway development.* New York: John Day, 1943

Chang Kia-ngau. *The inflationary spiral: the experience in China, 1939–1950.* Cambridge, Mass.: MIT Press, 1958

Chang Kuo-p'ing. *Pai Ch'ung-hsi chiang-chün chuan* (A biography of General Pai Ch'ung-hsi). Canton, 1938

Chang Kuo-t'ao. *Wo-ti hui-i* (My recollections). *Ming-pao yueh-k'an* (Ming-pao monthly), Hong Kong, 1.3–6.2 (March 1966–Feb. 1971). Reissued in three volumes, Hong Kong, 1973. Trans. under the title *The rise of the Chinese Communist Party* by R. A. Berton

Chang Kuo-t'ao, Liu Ning et al. *I-ko kung-jen ti kung-chuang chi ch'i-t'a* (A working man's confession and other essays), n.p., n.d.

Chang P'ei-kang. 'Min-kuo erh-shih-san nien ti Chung-kuo nung-yeh ching-chi' (China's agricultural economy in 1934). *Tung-fang tsa-chih* 32.13 (1 July 1935) 133–45

Chang Sheng-hsuan. 'San-shih-erh-nien Ssu-ch'uan kung-yeh chih hui-ku yü ch'ien-chan' (Perspectives on the past and future of Szechwan's economy in 1943). *Ssu-ch'uan ching-chi chi-k'an*, 1.2 (15 March 1944) 258–70

Chang Ta-ch'en. 'San-shih-san-nien ti Ch'ung-ch'ing t'u-pu-yeh' (Chungking's handicraft textile industry in 1944). *Ssu-ch'uan ching-chi chi-k'an*, 2.2 (1 April 1945) 202–4

Chang Tung-sun. 'Chui-shu wo-men nu-li chien-li "lien-ho cheng-fu" ti yung-i' (Reflections on our intention to strive to establish a 'coalition government'). *Kuan-ch'a*, 5 April 1947, pp. 5–7

Chang Wen-shih. *Yun-nan nei-mu* (The inside story in Yunnan). Kunming: K'un-ming kuan-ch'a, 1949

Chao Kuo-chün. *Agrarian policy of the Chinese Communist Party, 1921–1959*. New Delhi: Asia Publishing House, 1960

Chao Shu-li. *Li-chia-chuang ti pien-ch'ien* (Changes in the Li village). Shansi: Hua-pei hsin-hua shu-tien, 1946

Chapman, H. Owen. *The Chinese revolution, 1926–1927*. London: Constable, 1928

Chassin, Lionel M. *The Communist conquest of China: a history of the civil war, 1945–1949*. Cambridge, Mass.: Harvard University Press, 1965

CHB. See *China handbook*

Ch'en Chen and Yao Lo. *Chung-kuo chin-tai kung-yeh shih tzu-liao* (Source materials on the history of modern industry in China). 4 collections totaling 6 vols. Peking: San-lien, 1957–61

Ch'en Chen-han. 'Cheng-fu yin-hang hsueh-shu chi-kuan yü fu-hsing nung-ts'un' (Government, banks, academic institutions, and revival of the villages). *Kuo-wen chou-pao*, 10.46 (20 Nov. 1933), articles pp. 1–8

Ch'en Ch'eng. *Pa-nien k'ang-chan ching-kuo kai-yao* (Summary of experiences during the eight-year war of resistance). n.p.: Kuo-fang-pu shih-liao-chü, n.d.

Ch'en Ch'i-t'ien. *Wo-ti hui-i* (My memoirs)

Ch'en Hsueh-chao. *Man-tsou chieh-fang-ch'ü* (Wanderings in the liberated areas). Shanghai: Shang-hai ch'u-pan kung-ssu, 1950

Ch'en, Jerome. *Mao and the Chinese revolution*. London: Oxford University Press, 1965

Ch'en, Jerome. 'Resolutions of the Tsunyi conference'. *CQ* 40 (Oct.–Dec. 1969) 1–38

Ch'en, Jerome. 'Ideology and history'. Report on the visit of the North American delegation on socialism and revolution to the People's Republic of China, June–July 1980, xeroxed for circulation, 1980

Ch'en, Jerome. 'The Chinese communist movement to 1927'. *CHOC* 12.505–26

Ch'en Kung-po. *The Communist movement in China: an essay written in 1924*. Ed. with an introduction by C. Martin Wilbur. New York: Columbia University Press, 1960

Ch'en-pao (The morning post). Peking. 15 Aug. 1916–

Ch'en Po-ta. *Chung-kuo ssu-ta-chia-tsu* (China's four great families). Hong Kong: Chung-kuo, 1947

Ch'en Shao-hsiao. *Hei-wang-lu* (Record of the black net). Hong Kong: Chih-ch'eng, 1966

Ch'en, Ta. *Population in modern China*. Chicago: University of Chicago Press, 1946

Ch'en Ta. 'Chung-kuo lao-kung chieh-chi yü tang-ch'ien ching-chi wei-chi' (China's working class and the current economic crisis). *She-hui chien-she*, 1.4 (1 Aug. 1948) 17–19

Ch'en Tu-hsiu. 'Kao ch'üan-tang t'ung-chih-shu' (Letter to all the comrades of the party). 10.12.1929. Mimeographed

Ch'en Tun-cheng. *Tung-luan ti hui-i* (Memoirs of upheaval). Taipei: Yuan-hsia, 1979

Ch'en Yung-fa. 'The making of a revolution: the Communist movement in eastern and central China, 1937–1945'. 2 vols. Stanford University, Ph.D. dissertation, 1980

Chen, Yu-Kwei. *Foreign trade and industrial development of China: an historical and integrated analysis through 1948*. Washington, DC: University Press of Washington, 1956

Ch'eng Chi-hua et al. *Chung-kuo tien-ying fa-chan-shih* (A history of the development of Chinese cinema). 2 vols. Peking: Chung-kuo tien-ying, 1963

Ch'eng Yuan-chen. 'Ko-hsin yun-tung chih-hsu ch'eng-kung pu-hsu shih-pai' (The renovation movement can only succeed and must not fail). (Renovation weekly), 1.5 (24 Aug. 1946) 3–5

Chennault, Claire Lee. *Way of a fighter*. New York: G. P. Putnam Sons, 1949

Chesneaux, Jean. *The Chinese labor movement, 1919–1927*, trans. by H. M. Wright. Stanford: Stanford University Press, 1968

Ch'i Hsi-sheng. *Nationalist China at war: military defeats and political collapse, 1937–1945*. Ann Arbor: University of Michigan Press, 1982

Chiang Kai-shek. *Resistance and reconstruction: messages during China's six years of war, 1937–1943*. New York: Harper, 1943

Chiang Kai-shek. *Chiang tsung-t'ung yen-lun hui-pien* (President Chiang's collected speeches). 24 vols. Taipei: Cheng-chung, 1956

Chiang Kai-shek. 'Tzu-shu yen-chiu ko-ming che-hsueh ching-kuo ti chieh-tuan' (Stages traversed in studying revolutionary philosophy), in Chiang Kai-shek, *Chiang-tsung-t'ung yen-lun hui-pien*, 10.48–60

Chiang Kai-shek. *Chiang-tsung-t'ung ssu-hsiang yen-lun chi* (Collection of President Chiang's thoughts and speeches). 30 vols. Taipei: Chung-yang wen-wu, 1966

(Chiang Kai-shek). *Chiang tsung-t'ung mi-lu* (Secret records of President Chiang). 15 vols. Taipei: Chung-yang jih-pao, 1974–78

Chiang Shang-ch'ing. *Cheng-hai mi-wen* (Secrets of the political world). Hong Kong: Chih-ch'eng, 1966

Chiao-fei chan-shih (History of the war to suppress the bandits), ed. by History Bureau, Ministry of Defence, Republic of China, Taipei. 6 vols. 1962

Cheih-fang jih-pao (Liberation Daily news), Yenan, 1941–; Shanghai, 1949–

Chieh-fang pao (Liberation). Published at approximately weekly intervals in Yenan by the CCP Central Committee, from May 1937 to July 1941; thereafter became *Liberation Daily*.

Chieh-fang she, comp. *K'ang-Jih min-tsu t'ung-i chan-hsien chih-nan* (Guide to the anti-Japanese national united front). Yenan: 1938–40

Ch'ien Pang-k'ai. 'Tung-pei yen-chung-hsing tsen-yang ts'u-ch'eng-ti?' (What has precipitated the grave situation in the Northeast?). *Ch'ing-tao shih-pao* (Tsingtao times), 19 Feb. 1948, reprinted in *Kuan-ch'a,* 27 March 1948, pp. 16, 14

Ch'ien T'ang. *Ko-ming ti nü-hsing* (Revolutionary women). Shanghai: Kuang-wen she, 1949

Ch'ien Tuan-sheng. 'Chün-jen pa-hu ti Chung-kuo cheng-fu' (China's government usurped by military men). *Shih-tai p'i-p'ing* (Modern critic). Hong Kong, 16 June 1947, 2–3

Ch'ien Tuan-sheng. *The government and politics of China.* Cambridge, Mass.: Harvard University Press, 1950, reprinted 1961

Chin Fan. *Tsai Hung-chün ch'ang-cheng ti tao-lu shang* (On the route of the Red Army's Long March). Peking: Chung-kuo ch'ing-nien ch'u-pan-she, 1957

Chin, Rockwood O. P. 'The Chinese cotton industry under wartime inflation'. *Pacific Affairs,* 16.1 (March 1943) 33–46

China handbook 1937–1943: a comprehensive survey of major developments in China in six years of war, comp. Chinese Ministry of Information. New York: Macmillan, 1943. *China handbook, 1937–1944: . . . in seven years . . .* Chungking: Chinese Ministry of Information, 1944. *China handbook, 1937–1945 (Chan-shih Chung-hua chih),* new edition with 1946 supplement. New York: Macmillan, 1947. *China handbook, 1950,* comp. China Handbook Editorial Board. New York: Rockport Press, Inc., 1950

China Quarterly. Quarterly. London, 1960–. 1960 to Dec. 1976 published by Congress for Cultural Freedom; from Dec. 1976 by the Contemporary China Institute of the School of Oriental and African Studies, University of London

China Weekly Review. Shanghai, 1917–

China white paper. See United States Department of State, *United States relations with China*

The China year book, ed. by H. G. W. Woodhead. London: George Routledge & Sons, Ltd., 1912–21; Tientsin: The Tientsin Press, 1921–30; Shanghai: The North China Daily News & Herald, Ltd., 1931–9

Chinese Press Review, comp. by United States Consulates. Chungking, 1942–5; Shanghai, 1946–9

Chinese Recorder. Shanghai, 1867–1941

Chinese Republican Studies Newsletter. Semi-annual 1975–83. From 9.2 (Feb. 1984) became *Republican China*

Ching-chi chou-pao (Economics weekly). Shanghai, Nov. 1945–

Ching-chi yen-chiu (Economic research). Peking, April 1955–

CHOC. See *The Cambridge history of China*

Chou Chung-ch'i. 'Lun ko-ming' (On revolution). *Kuan-ch'a*, 25 Jan. 1947, pp. 6–10

Chou Shun-hsin. *The Chinese inflation, 1937–1949*. New York: Columbia University Press, 1963, reprinted 1969

Chu Tzu-chia (Chin Hsiung-pai). *Wang cheng-ch'üan ti k'ai-ch'ang yü shou-ch'ang* (The beginning and ending of the drama of the Wang regime). 6 vols. Hong Kong: Wu Hsing-chi shu-pao-she, 1974

Ch'u An-p'ing. 'Chung-kuo ti cheng-chü' (China's political situation). *Kuan-ch'a*, 8 March 1947, pp. 3–8

Ch'u An-p'ing. 'P'ing P'u-li-t'e ti p'ien-ssu ti pu-chien-k'ang ti fang Hua pao-kao' (A critique of Bullitt's biased unhealthy report on his visit to China). *Kuan-ch'a*, 25 Oct. 1947, pp. 3–5

Ch'ü Chih-sheng. *K'ang-chan chi-li* (A personal account of the war of resistance). Taipei, Chung-hua, 1965

Ch'ü Ch'iu-pai. 'Chung-kuo hsien-chuang yü Kung-ch'an-tang ti jen-wu' (The present situation in China and the tasks of the CCP), report at the November conference, in Hu Hua, *Chung-kuo hsin-min-chu chu-i . . . tzu-liao*, 220–2

Chung, An-min. 'The development of modern manufacturing industry in China, 1928–1949'. University of Pennsylvania, Ph.D. dissertation, 1953

Chung-kung k'ang-chan i-pan ch'ing-k'uang ti chieh-shao (A briefing on the Chinese Communist war activities). Photocopy with English title. Chieh-fang-she, comp. n.p., 1944

Chung-kung tang-shih ts'an-k'ao tzu-liao (Reference materials on the history of the CCP). Chung-kung chung-yang tang-hsiao tang-shih chiao-yen-shih (Party history research office of the CCP central party school), ed. Nei-pu fa-hsing (internal use only). 10 vols. Peking: Jen-min, 1979

Chung-kung ti cheng-chih kung-tso (The political work of the Chinese Communist Party), Kiangsu Provincial Committee, n.d.

Chung-kuo ko hsiao-tang-p'ai hsien-k'uang (Present state of the minority parties in China). n.p., 1946

Chung-kuo Kung-ch'an-tang tsai Chiang-hsi ti-ch'ü ling-tao ko-ming tou-cheng ti li-shih tzu-liao (Historical materials concerning the revolutionary struggles led by the CCP in Kiangsi). ed. by Kiangsi Jen-min ch'u-pan-she, Kiangsi, 1958. See Liu P'ei-shan

Chung-kuo kung-yeh (Chinese industry). Nanking, Nov. 1932–; Kweilin, Jan. 1942–

Chung-kuo lao-kung yun-tung shih pien-tsuan wei-yuan-hui, ed. *Chung-kuo lao-kung yun-tung shih* (A history of the Chinese labour movement). 5 vols. Taipei: Chung-kuo lao-kung fu-li ch'u-pan-she, 1959

Chung-kuo nung-min (The Chinese farmer). Canton: Farmers' Bureau of the Central Executive Committee of the Kuomintang of China, Jan. 1926–; also Chung-king, Feb. 1942–. Photolithographic reprint edn. of Canton pub., Tokyo: Daian, 1964

Chung-yang jih-pao (Central daily news). Nanking, 1928–

'Chung-yang kuan-yü tsai Shan-tung Hua-chung fa-chan wu-chuang chien-li ken-chü-ti ti chih-shih' (Central directive concerning development of armed forces and establishment of base areas in Shantung and Central China), 28 January 1940

Chung-yang t'ung-hsin (Central newsletter). Organ of the Central Committee of the Chinese Communist Party, Aug. 1927–

Civil war in China, 1945–50. Taiwan: translated and prepared at the field level under the auspices of the Office of the Chief of Military History, (US) Dept. of the Army; Library of Congress microfilm 51461

CJCC. See Wu Hsiang-hsiang, *Ti-erh-tz'u Chung-Jih chan-cheng shih*

Clopton, Robert W. and Ou Tsuin-chen, trans. and ed. *John Dewey, lectures in China, 1919–1920.* Honolulu: East-West Center, 1973

Clubb, O. Edmund. *Twentieth century China.* New York: Columbia University Press, 1964; 3rd edn. 1978

Clubb, O. Edmund. *The witness and I.* New York: Columbia University Press, 1974

Coble, Parks M. *The Shanghai capitalists and the Nationalist government, 1927–1937.* Cambridge, Mass.: Council on East Asian Studies, Harvard University, 1980

Cochran, Sherman. *Big business in China: Sino-foreign rivalry in the cigarette industry, 1890–1930.* Cambridge, Mass.: Harvard University Press, 1980

Compton, Boyd. *Mao's China: party reform documents, 1942–44.* Seattle: University of Washington Press, 1952

Coox, Alvin D. 'Recourse to arms: the Sino-Japanese conflict, 1937–1945', in Alvin D. Coox and Hilary Conroy, eds. *China and Japan*

Coox, Alvin D. and Conroy, Hilary, eds. *China and Japan: a search for balance since World War I.* Santa Barbara: Clio Press, 1978

CPR. See *Chinese Press Review*

CQ. See *The China Quarterly*

Crowley, James B. *Japan's quest for autonomy: national security and foreign policy, 1930–1938.* Princeton: Princeton University Press, 1966

CWR. See *China Weekly Review*

CYB. See *The China year book*

Davies, John Paton, Jr. *Dragon by the tail: American, British, Japanese, and Russian encounters with China and one another.* London: Robson, 1974

Deane, Hugh. 'Political reaction in Kuomintang China'. *Amerasia*, 5.5 (July 1941) 209–14

Degras, Jane. *The Communist International 1919–1943: documents.* 3 vols. London: Oxford University Press for Royal Institute of International Affairs, 1956, 1960, 1965

Deliusin, L. P. See Grigoriev, A. M.

Dirlik, Arif. 'Mass movements and the left Kuomintang'. *Modern China*, 1.1 (Jan. 1975) 46–74

Dirlik, Arif. 'The ideological foundations of the New Life Movement: a study in counterrevolution'. *JAS* 34.4 (Aug. 1975) 945–80

Domes, Jürgen. *Vertagte Revolution: die Politik der Kuomintang in China, 1923–1937.* Berlin: Walter de Gruyter & Co., 1969

Dorn, Frank. *The Sino-Japanese War, 1937–41: from Marco Polo Bridge to Pearl Harbor.* New York: Macmillan, 1974

Eastman, Lloyd E. 'Fascism in Kuomintang China: the Blue Shirts'. *CQ* 49 (Jan.–March 1972) 1–31

Eastman, Lloyd E. *The abortive revolution: China under Nationalist rule, 1927–1937.* Cambridge, Mass.: Harvard University Press, 1974

Eastman, Lloyd E. 'Regional politics and the central government: Yunnan and Chungking', in Paul K. T. Sih, ed. *Nationalist China during the Sino-Japanese War, 1937–1945*, 329–62

Eastman, Lloyd E. 'Facets of an ambivalent relationship: smuggling, puppets and atrocities during the war, 1937–1945', in Akira Iriye, ed. *The Chinese and the Japanese*, 275–303

Eastman, Lloyd E. *Seeds of destruction: Nationalist China in war and revolution 1937–1949.* Stanford: Stanford University Press, 1984

Epstein, Israel. *Notes on labor problems in Nationalist China.* New York: Institute of Pacific Relations, 1949

Esherick, Joseph W., ed. *Lost chance in China: the World War II despatches of John S. Service.* New York: Random House, 1974

Fan-Chiang yun-tung shih (History of the anti-Chiang movement), ed. by Chung-kuo ch'ing-nien chün-jen she. Canton: 1934

Fang Chih. 'Min-tsu wen-hua yü min-tsu ssu-hsiang' (National culture and national thought). *Wen-hua chien-she* (Cultural reconstruction), 1.2 (10 Nov. 1934) 15–20

Fang Chih-p'ing et al. *Lun kuan-liao tzu-pen* (On bureaucratic capital). Canton: Tsung-ho, 1946

Farmer, Rhodes. *Shanghai harvest: a diary of three years in the China War.* London: Museum Press, 1945

Feis, Herbert. *The China tangle: the American effort in China from Pearl Harbor to the Marshall mission.* Princeton: Princeton University Press, 1953

Feng Yü-hsiang. *Wo so-jen-shih-ti Chiang Chieh-shih* (The Chiang Kai-shek I know). Hong Kong: Wen-hua kung-ying-she, 1949

Fenn, William P. *The effect of the Japanese invasion on higher education in China.* Kowloon: China Institute of Pacific Relations, 1940

Feuerwerker, Albert. 'The foreign presence in China'. *CHOC* 12.128–207

Freyn, Hubert. *Chinese education in the war.* Shanghai: Kelly & Walsh, 1940

Freyn, Hubert. *Free China's New Deal.* New York: Macmillan, 1943

FRUS. See United States Department of State, *Foreign Relations of the United States.*

Fu-hsing Chung-kuo Kuo-min-tang chien-i: Hsin-sheng tsa-chih-she chih liu-tz'u ch'üan-kuo tai-piao ta-hui tai-piao i-chien shu (A proposal to revive the Kuomintang: a recommendation from the New Life Magazine to representatives in the Sixth Party Congress). n.p.: [1945]

Geisert, Bradley Kent. 'Power and society: the Kuomintang and local elites in Kiangsu province, China, 1924–1937'. University of Virginia, Ph.D. dissertation, 1979

Gillin, Donald G. *Warlord: Yen Hsi-shan in Shansi province, 1911–1949*. Princeton: Princeton University Press, 1967

Gillin, Donald G. 'Problems of centralization in Republican China: the case of Ch'en Ch'eng and the Kuomintang'. *JAS* 29.4 (Aug. 1970) 835–50

Goldman, Merle. *Literary dissent in Communist China*. Cambridge, Mass.: Harvard University Press, 1967

Gray, Jack, ed. *Modern China's search for a political form*. London: Oxford University Press, 1969

Grigoriev, A. M. 'The Comintern and the revolutionary movement in China under the slogan of the soviets (1927–1931)', in R. A. Ulyanovsky, ed. *The Comintern and the East,* 345–88. Evidently a translation of L. P. Deliusin, ed. *Komintern i vostok*

Guillermaz, Jacques. *A history of the Chinese Communist Party, 1921–1949*. London: Methuen; New York: Random House, 1972. Trans. by Anne Destenay of *Histoire du parti communiste chinois 1921–49*. Paris: Payot, 1968

Harrison, James Pinckney. *The long march to power: a history of the Chinese Communist Party, 1921–72*. New York: Praeger, 1972

Hartford, Kathleen. 'Repression and Communist success: the case of Jin-Cha-Ji, 1938–1943'. Unpublished manuscript

Hartford, Kathleen. 'Step-by-step: reform, resistance and revolution in the Chin-Ch'a-Chi border region, 1937–1945'. Stanford University, Ph.D. dissertation, 1980

Hata Ikuhiko. *Nitchū sensō shi* (History of the Japanese-Chinese war). Rev. edn, Tokyo: Kawade shobō shinsha, 1971

Hatano Ken'ichi, comp. *Gendai Shina no kiroku* (Records of contemporary China). Monthly. Peking: 1924–1932. 23 reels

HC. See Mao Tse-tung, *Hsuan-chi*

HCPP. See *Hung-ch'i p'iao-p'iao*

Heinlein, Joseph H., Jr. 'Political warfare: the Chinese Nationalist model'. American University, Ph.D. dissertation, 1974

Heinzig, D. 'The Otto Braun memoirs and Mao's rise to power'. *CQ* 46 (April–June, 1971) 274–88

HHLY. See *Hsing-huo liao-yuan*, also Liu Po-ch'eng for *HHLY* Hong Kong

Hinton, William. *Fanshen: a documentary of revolution in a Chinese village*. New York: Random House, 1968

Ho, Franklin L. 'The reminiscences of Ho Lien (Franklin L. Ho)', as told to Crystal Lorch, postscript dated July 1966. Unpublished manuscript in Special Collections Library, Butler Library, Columbia University

Ho, Franklin L. 'First attempts to transform Chinese agriculture, 1927–1937: comments', in Paul K. T. Sih, ed. *The strenuous decade: China's nation-building efforts, 1927–1937,* 233–36

Ho Kan-chih. *Chung-kuo hsien-tai ko-ming shih* (A history of the modern Chinese revolution). Peking: Pei-ching kao-teng chiao-yü ch'u-pan-she, 1958, 2 vols; Hong Kong: San-lien, 1958. English edn, Peking: Foreign Languages Press, 1960

Ho Ping-ti. *Studies on the population of China, 1368–1953*. Cambridge, Mass.: Harvard University Press, 1959

Ho Ying-ch'in. 'Chin-hou chih Chung-kuo Kuo-min-tang' (The Chinese Kuomintang from now on). *Chung-yang pan-yueh-k'an*, 2 (Oct. 1927) 99–103

Hofheinz, Roy, Jr. 'The Autumn Harvest uprising'. *CQ* 32 (Oct.–Dec. 1967) 37–87

Hofheinz, Roy, Jr. 'The ecology of Chinese communist success: rural influence patterns, 1923–1945', in A. Doak Barnett, ed. *Chinese Communist politics in action*, 3–77

Holland, W. L. and Mitchell, Kate L., eds., assisted by Harriet Moore and Richard Pyke. *Problems of the Pacific, 1936. Aims and results of social and economic policies in Pacific countries: proceedings of the sixth conference of the Institute of Pacific relations, Yosemite National Park, California 15–29 August 1936*. Chicago: University of Chicago Press, 1937

Hsia, Tsi-an. *The gate of darkness: studies on the leftist literary movement in China*. Seattle: University of Washington Press, 1968

Hsiao Cheng. *T'u-ti kai-ko wu-shih-nien: Hsiao Cheng hui-i-lu* (Fifty years of land reform: the memoirs of Hsiao Cheng). Taipei: Chung-kuo t'u-ti kai-ko yen-chiu-so, 1980

Hisao Tso-liang. *Power relations within the Chinese communist movement, 1930–1934*. Seattle: University of Washington Press, 1961

Hsiao Tso-liang. *The land revolution in China, 1930–1934: a study of documents*. Seattle: University of Washington Press, 1969

Hsiao Tso-liang. *Chinese communism in 1927: city vs. countryside*. Hong Kong: The Chinese University of Hong Kong, 1970

Hsin-ching-chi (New economics). Chungking, 1938–

Hsin hua jih-pao (New China daily news). Hankow, 1938–; Chungking, 1942–

Hsin kuan-ch'ang hsien-hsing chi (A new 'current situation in officialdom'). n.p.: 1946

Hsin-shih-chieh yueh-k'an (New world monthly). Chungking, July 1932–

Hsing-huo liao-yuan (A single spark can start a prairie fire). ed. by The People's Liberation Army. 10 vols. Peking: Jen-min wen-hsueh ch'u-pan-she,, 1958–63

Hsu Fu-kuan. 'Shih shui chi k'uei-le Chung-kuo she-hui fan-kung ti li-liang?' (Who is it that destroys the anti-Communist power of Chinese society?) *Min-chu p'ing-lun*, 1.7 (16 Sept. 1949) 5–7

Hsu Long-hsueh and Chang Ming-kai, comps. *History of the Sino-Japanese War, 1937–1945*, trans. by Wen Ha-hsiung. Taipei: Chung Wu Publishing Co., 1971.

Hsu Ti-hsin. 'K'ang-chan i-lai liang-ko chieh-tuan ti Chung-kuo ching-chi' (China's economy during the two stages of the war). *Li-lun yü hsien-shih*, 1.4 (15 Feb. 1940) 33–46

Hsu Yun-pei. 'Ts'an chün yun-tung chien-pao' (A brief report on the army recruiting movement), in *I-chiu-ssu-ch'i nien shang-pan-nien lai ch'ü-tang-wei kuan-yü t'u-kai yun-tung ti chung-yao wen-chien* (Regional party commission's important documents concerning land reform movement since the first half of 1947), 69–77. Chi-Lu-Yü ch'ü-tang-wei, June 1947

Hsueh-hsi yü p'i-p'an (Study and criticism). Shanghai, Sept. 1973–

Hsueh Mu-ch'iao. *K'ang-Jih chan-cheng shih-ch'i ho chieh-fang chan-cheng shih-ch'i Shan-tung chieh-fang-ch'ü ti ching-chi kung-tso* (Economic work in the Shantung liberated areas during the anti-Japanese and civil wars). Peking: Jen-min jih-pao she, 1979

Hsueh Yueh. *Chiao-fei chi-shih* (A factual account of the campaigns against the bandits). Taipei, 1962

Hu Hua. *Chung-kuo hsin-min-chu chu-i ko-ming-shih ts'an-k'ao tzu-liao* (Historical materials on the Chinese new democratic revolution). Peking: Shanghai: CP, 1951

Hu Hua. *Chung-kuo ko-ming-shih chiang-i* (Lectures on the history of the Chinese Revolution). Revised edn. 2 vols. Peking: Chinese People's University, 1979

Hu-pei-sheng-cheng-fu pao-kao, 1942/4–10, 1942/4–10 (Report of the Hupei provincial government, April–October, 1942). n.p: n.d.

Hu-pei-sheng-cheng-fu pao-kao, 1943/10–1944/9, 1943/10–1944/9 (Report of the Hupei provincial government, October 1943 to September 1944). n.p.: n.d.

Hu shang-chiang Tsung-nan nien-p'u (Chronological biography of General Hu Tsung-nan). Taipei: Wen-hai, n.d.

Hua-tzu jih-pao (The Chinese mail). Hong Kong, 1864–

Hung-ch'i (The red flag). Official organ of the centre of the Chinese Communist Party, Nov. 1928–1933

Hung-ch'i (The red flag). Peking, 1967–

Hung-ch'i p'iao p'iao (Red flag flying). 16 vols. Peking: Chung-kuo ch'ing-nien ch'u-pan-she, 1957–61

Hung-hsing (The red star), ed. by the General Political Department of the Red Army, 1932–4

Hung-se Chung-hua (Red China). Official organ of the Soviet Republic of China, 11 Dec. 1931–12 Dec. 1936

Hung-se wen-hsien (Red documents) Yenan, 1938

Huntington, Samuel P. *Political order in changing societies*. New Haven: Yale University Press, 1968

I-chiu-ssu-ch'i nien shang-pan-nien lai ch'ü-tang-wei kuan-yü t'u-k'ai yun-tung ti chung-yao wen-chien (Important documents on the land reform movement during the first half of 1947 from the regional party committee). n.p.: Chi-Lu-Yü ch'ü tang wei, June 1947

International Press Correspondence. Organ of the Executive Committee of the Communist International. English edn, 1925–35

Iriye, Akira, ed. *The Chinese and the Japanese: essays in political and cultural interactions*. Princeton: Princeton University Press, 1980

Israel, John. *Student nationalism in China, 1927–1937*. Stanford: Published for the Hoover Institution, Stanford University Press, 1966

Israel, John. 'Southwest Associated University: survival as an ultimate value', in Paul K. T. Sih, ed. *Nationalist China during the Sino-Japanese War, 1937–1945*, 131–54

Israel, John and Klein, Donald. *Rebels and bureaucrats: China's December 9ers*. Berkeley: University of California, 1976

JAS. See Journal of Asian Studies
Jen-min jih-pao (People's daily). Peking, 1949–

JMJP. See Jen-min jih-pao

Johnson, Chalmers A. *Peasant nationalism and communist power: the emergence of revolutionary China, 1937–1945*. Stanford: Stanford University Press, 1962; 2nd rev. edn 1966

Journal of Asian Studies, 1956–. Quarterly. (*Far Eastern Quarterly* 1941–56)

Juan Yu-ch'iu. 'Chin-jih hou-fang min-ying kung-yeh ti wei-chi' (The current crisis of private industry in the rear area). *Chung-kuo nung-min*, 3.1/2 (June 1943) 33–5

Kahn, E. J., Jr. *The China hands: America's Foreign Service Officers and what befell them*. New York: Viking Press, 1975

Kan K'o-ch'ao. 'Chan-shih Ssu-ch'uan kung-yeh kai-kuan' (Survey of Szechwan's wartime economy). *Ssu-ch'uan ching-chi chi-k'an*, 1.2 (15 March 1944) 64–72

K'ang-Jih chan-cheng shih-ch'i chieh-fang-ch'ü kai-k'uang (The liberated areas during the anti-Japanese war). Peking: Jen-min, 1953

K'ang-Jih min-tsu t'ung-i chan-hsien chih-nan (Guide to the anti-Japanese national united front). 10 vols. Yenan, 1937–40

Kao T'ing-tzu. *Chung-kuo ching-chi chien-she* (Chinese economic reconstruction). Shanghai: CP, 1937

Kapp, Robert A. *Szechwan and the Chinese Republic: provincial militarism and central power 1911–1938*. New Haven: Yale University Press, 1973

Kataoka Tetsuya. *Resistance and revolution in China: the Communists and the second united front*. Berkeley: University of California Press, 1974

Kennedy, Melville T., Jr. 'The Chinese Democratic League'. *Harvard papers on China*, 7 (1953) 136–75

Kerr, George H. *Formosa betrayed*. London: Eyre & Spottiswoode, 1966

Kim, Ilpyong J. *The politics of Chinese Communism: Kiangsi under Soviet rule*. Berkeley: University of California Press, 1974

Kirby, William Corbon. *Germany and Republican China*. Stanford: Stanford University Press, 1984

Klein, Donald W. and Clark, Anne B. *Biographic dictionary of Chinese communism, 1921–1965*. 2 vols. Cambridge, Mass.: Harvard University Press, 1971

Ko-ming wen-hsien (Documents of the revolution), comp. by Lo Chia-lun et al. Taipei: Central Executive Committee of the Chung-kuo Kuomintang, many volumes, 1953–

Ko-ming yü chan-cheng (Revolution and war) n.p., Aug. 1932–

Koen, Ross Y. *The China lobby in American politics*. New York: Harper & Row, 1974

Kuan-ch'a (The observer). Shanghai, 1947–

Kuan-ch'a chi-che. (The observer's correspondent). 'Ts'ung chan-chü k'an cheng-chü' (Looking at political conditions from the military situation). *Kuan-ch'a*. Shanghai, 28 Feb. 1948, pp. 14–16

Kuan-ch'a chi-che. (The observer's correspondent). 'T'u-ti kai-ko, ti-tao chan' (Land reform, tunnel warfare). *Kuan-ch'a*, 3 April 1948, p. 14

Kuan Meng-chueh. 'Shan-hsi-sheng fang-chih-yeh chih wei-chi chi ch'i ch'u-lu' (The crisis of Shensi's textile industry and its solution). *Chung-kuo kung-yeh*, 19 (1 Sept. 1943) 6–13

Kuhn, Philip A. 'Local self-government under the Republic: problems of control, autonomy, and mobilization', in Frederic Wakeman, Jr. and Carolyn Grant, eds. *Conflict and control in late imperial China*, 257–98

Kung-ch'an tang-jen (The Communist). No data

Kung Ch'u. *Wo yü Hung-chün* (The Red Army and I). Hong Kong: Nan-feng ch'u-pan-she, 1954

Kung-fei huo-kuo shih-liao hui-pien (Collected historical materials on the national disaster caused by the communist bandits). Chi-chi-mi (top secret). 3 vols. Taipei: Chung-hua min-kuo k'ai-kuo wu-shih-nien wen-hsien pien-tsuan wei-yuan-hui, 1964

Kung-tso t'ung-hsun, 32: yu-chi chan-cheng chuan-hao (Work correspondence, number 32: special issue on guerrilla warfare). n.p.: Chi-Lu-Yü ch'ü tang wei min-yun pu, June 1947

Kuo-chia tsung-tung-yuan (National mobilization). n.p.: Hsing-cheng-yuan hsin-wen-chü, 1947

Kuo Hua-lun (Warren Kuo). *Chung-kung shih-lun* (An analytical history of the CCP). 4 vols. Taipei: Kuo-chi kuan-hsi yen-chiu-so, 1969

Kuo-min ching-shen tsung-tung-yuan yun-tung (National spiritual mobilization movement), comp. by San-min-chu-i ch'ing-nien-t'uan chung-yang t'uan-pu. n.p. 1944

Kuo, Thomas C. *Ch'en Tu-hsiu (1879–1942) and the Chinese communist movement.* South Orange, NJ: Seton Hall University Press, 1975

Kuo, Warren (Kuo Hua-lun). *Analytical history of the Chinese Communist Party.* 4 vols. Taipei: Institute of International Relations, 1966–71

Kuo-wen chou-pao. (Kuowen weekly, illustrated). Tientsin Kuowen Weekly Association, 1924–37

Lary, Diana. *Region and nation: the Kwangsi clique in Chinese politics, 1925–1937.* London: Cambridge University Press, 1974

League of Nations, Council Committee on Technical Cooperation between the League of Nations and China. *Report of the technical agent of the council on his mission in China from the date of his appointment until April 1st, 1934*

Lei Hsiao-ts'en. *San-shih-nien tung-luan Chung-kuo* (Thirty years of China in turmoil). Hong Kong: Ya-chou, 1955

Leyda, Jay. *Dianying: an account of films and the film audience in China.* Cambridge, Mass.: MIT Press, 1972

Li Ang (Chu P'ei-wo, Chu Hsin-fan). *Hung-se wu-t'ai* (The red stage). Chungking, 1942; Peking, 1946

Li Ch'ang. 'Hui-i min-hsien tui' (Reminiscences of the National Salvation Vanguard), in Li Ch'ang et al. *I-erh-chiu hui-i-lu* (Memoirs of December 9), 3–34. Peking: Chung-kuo ch'ing-nien ch'u-pan-she, 1961

Li Ch'eng-jui. 'K'ang-Jih chan-cheng shih-ch'i chi-ko jen-min ken-chü-ti ti nung-yeh shui-shou chih-tu yü nung-min fu-tan' (Agricultural tax systems and peasant burdens in people's revolutionary base areas during the anti-Japanese war). *Ching-chi yen-chiu* (Economic research), 2 (1956) 100–15

Li Li-san. *Fan-t'o* (Anti-Trotsky). n.p., n.d. Mimeographed

Li, Lincoln. *The Japanese army in north China, 1937–1941: problems of political and economic control*. Tokyo: Oxford University Press, 1975

Li-lun yü hsien-shih (Theory and reality) Shanghai, 1939–

Li-shih yen-chiu (Historical research). Monthly. Peking, 1954–66, 1975–

Li Ta. 'Ko-hsin yun-tung ti ta ching-shen' (The great spirit of the renovation movement). *Ko-hsin chou-k'an*, 1.6 (31 Aug. 1946) 5

Li Tsung-jen and Tong Te-kong. *The memoirs of Li Tsung-jen*. Boulder, Colo.: Westview Press, 1979

Li Tzu-ching. 'Chin-nan chieh-fang ch'ü ti tou-cheng ch'ing-hsing' (The struggle situation in the liberated districts of south Shansi). *Kuan-ch'a*, 6 March 1948, p. 15

Li Tzu-hsiang. 'K'ang-chan i-lai Ssu-ch'uan chih kung-yeh' (Szechwan's industry during the war). *Ssu-ch'uan ching-chi chi-k'an*, 1.1 (15 Dec. 1943) 17–43

Li Tzu-hsiang. 'Wo-kuo chan-shih kung-yeh sheng-ch'an ti hui-ku yü ch'ien-chan' (The past and future of China's wartime industrial production). *SCCC* 2.3 (1 July 1945) 26–41

Li Yü. *Lun ch'ün-chung lu-hsien yü Shan-tung ch'ün-chung yun-tung* (On the mass line and the mass movement in Shantung). n.p.: Chung-kung Chiao-tung-ch'ü tang wei, February 1946

Li Yun-han. *Sung Che-yuan yü ch'i-ch'i k'ang-chan* (Sung Che-yuan and the 7 July war of resistance). Taipei: Chuan-chi wen-hsueh, 1973

Li Yun-han. 'The origins of the war: background of the Lukouchiao Incident, July 7, 1937', in Paul K. T. Sih, ed. *Nationalist China during the Sino-Japanese War, 1937–1945*, 3–32

Lilley, Charles Ronald. 'Tsiang T'ing-fu: between two worlds, 1895–1935'. University of Maryland, Ph.D. dissertation, 1979. (Ann Arbor: University Microfilms International, 1980)

Lin Chi-yung. 'K'ang-chan ch'i-chung min-ying ch'ang-k'uang ch'ien-Ch'uan chien-shu' (Summary account of the move of privately-owned factories and mines to Szechwan during the war). *Ssu-ch'uan wen-hsien*, 62 (1 Oct. 1967) 3–9

Lindsay, Michael. 'The taxation system of the Shansi-Chahar-Hopei Border Region, 1938–1945'. *CQ* 42 (April–June 1970) 1–15

Lindsay, Michael. *The unknown war: north China, 1937–1945*. London: Bergstrom & Boyle, 1975

Liu Ch'ang-sheng et al. *Chung-kuo kung-ch'an-tang yü Shang-hai kung-jen: Shang-hai kung-jen yun-tung li-shih yen-chiu tzu-liao chih erh* (The Chinese Communist Party and the Shanghai workers: Shanghai labour movement historical research materials number two). Shanghai: Lao-tung ch'u-pan-she, August 1951

Liu Chen-tung. 'Chung-kuo ch'u-lu wen-t'i' (The question of China's way out). *Kuo-wen chou-pao*, 10.24 (19 June 1933) 1–6 (sep. pag.)

Liu Chi-ping. 'San-shih-san-nien Ssu-ch'uan chih shang-yeh' (The commercial economy of Szechwan in 1944). *Ssu-ch'uan ching-chi chi-k'an*, 2.2 (1 April 1945) 75–81

Liu, F. F. *A military history of modern China, 1924–1949*. Princeton: Princeton University Press, 1956

Liu Min. 'San-shih-san-nien Ssu-ch'uan chih kung-yeh' (Szechwan's industry in 1944). *SCCC* 2.2 (1 April 1945) 27–43

Liu Ning. See Chang Kuo-t'ao

Liu P'ei-shan. 'Hui-i Hsiang-Kan pien-ch'ü ti san-nien yu-chi chan-cheng' (Recollections of three years' guerrilla warfare in the Hunan-Kiangsi border region), in *Chung-kuo Kung-ch'an-tang tsai Chiang-hsi ti-ch'ü ling-tao ko-ming tou-cheng ti li-shih tzu-liao* (Historical materials concerning the revolutionary struggles led by the CCP in Kiangsi). Chiang-hsi jen-min, 1958

Liu Po-ch'eng et al. *Hsing-huo liao-yuan* (A single spark can start a prairie fire). Hong Kong: San-lien, 1960. See also *Hsing-huo liao-yuan*

Liu Shao-ch'i. 'Lun kung-k'ai kung-tso yü mi-mi kung-tso' (On open work and secret work). *Kung-ch'an tang-jen* (The Communist). Yenan, 1939. Manuscript. Copy in the Hoover Institution

Liu Shao-ch'i. 'Chien-ch'ih Hua-pei k'ang-chan chung ti wu-chuang pu-tui' (Firmly support armed groups taking part in the north China war of resistance), in *K'ang-Jih min-tsu t'ung-i chan-hsien chih-nan* (Guide to the anti-Japanese national united front). 5. 39–54

Liu Shou-sung. *Chung-kuo hsin wen-hsueh shih ch'u-kao* (A preliminary draft history of modern Chinese literature). 2 vols. Peking: Tso-chia ch'u-pan-she, 1956

Liu Ta-chung. *China's national income, 1931–1936: an exploratory study*. Washington, DC: Brookings Institution, 1946

Liu Ta-chung and Yeh Kung-chia. *The economy of the Chinese mainland: national income and economic development, 1933–1959*. Princeton: Princeton University Press, 1965

Lo Chia-lun. See *Ko-ming wen-hsien*

Lötveit, Trygve. *Chinese communism, 1931–1934: experience in civil government*. Lund, Sweden: Studentlitteratur, 1973; Copenhagen: Scandinavian Institute of Asian Studies Monograph Series, no. 16, 1973

Lutz, Jessie Gregory. *China and the Christian colleges, 1850–1950*. Ithaca: Cornell University Press, 1971

Malraux, A. *Anti-memoirs*, trans. by T. Kilmartin. New York: Holt, Rinehart & Winston, 1968

Mao Tse-tung. *Hsuan-chi* (Selected works). Chinese ed. Peking, 1966

Mao Tse-tung. *Mao Tse-tung chi* (Collected writings of Mao Tse-tung), ed. by Takeuchi Minoru. 10 vols. Tokyo: Hokubōsha, 1970–2

Mao Tse-tung. *Ching-chi wen-t'i yü ts'ai-cheng wen-t'i* (Economic and financial problems). Hong Kong: Hsin-min-chu ch'u-pan-she, 1949

Martin, Edwin W. 'The Chou demarche'. *Foreign Service Journal*, Nov. 1981, 13–16, 32

May, Gary, with intro. by John K. Fairbank. *China scapegoat: the diplomatic ordeal of John Carter Vincent*. Washington, DC: New Republic Books, 1979

McLane, Charles B. *Soviet policy and the Chinese communists, 1931–1946*. New York: Columbia University Press, 1958

Melby, John F. *The mandate of Heaven.* Toronto: University of Toronto Press, 1968

Miao Ch'u-huang. 'Chung-kuo kung-nung hung-chün ch'ang-cheng kai-shu' (A brief account of the Long March of the Workers' and Peasants' Red Army of China). *Li-shih yen-chiu* (Historical research), 2 (1954) 85–96

Miao Ch'u-huang. *Chung-kuo Kung-ch'an-tang chien-yao li-shih* (A brief history of the Chinese Communist Party). Peking: Hsueh-hsi tsa-chih-she, 1957

Miles, Milton E. *A different kind of war: the little-known story of the combined guerrilla forces created in China by the US Navy and the Chinese during World War II.* Garden City, NY: Doubleday, 1967

Military campaigns in China, 1924–1950. See Ministry of National Defence

Min-chu p'ing-lun (Democratic review) Hong Kong, July 1949–

Miner, Noel Ray. 'Chekiang: the Nationalists' effort in agrarian reform and construction, 1927–1937'. Stanford University, Ph.D. dissertation, 1973

Ming-pao yueh-k'an (Ming-pao monthly). Hong Kong, 1966–

Ministry of National Defence, War History Bureau. *Military campaigns in China, 1924–1950,* trans. by W. W. Whitson, Patrick Yang and Paul Lai. Taipei, 1966

Moore, Barrington, Jr. *Social origins of dictatorship and democracy: land and peasant in the making of the modern world.* Boston: Beacon Press, 1966

MTTC. See Mao Tse-tung, *Mao Tse-tung chi*

Nakamura Takafusa. 'Japan's economic thrust into North China, 1933–1938: formation of the North China Development Corporation', in Akira Iriye, ed. *The Chinese and the Japanese,* 220–53

'Nan-ch'ang ta-shih chi' (Important events at Nanchang). *Chin-tai-shih tzu-liao,* 4 (1957) 130

Nathan, Andrew J. 'A factionalism model for CCP politics'. *CQ* 53 (Jan.–March 1973) 34–66

North China Herald. Weekly. Shanghai, 1850–

North, Robert C. *Kuomintang and Chinese Communist elites.* Stanford: Stanford University Press, 1952

Oliver, Frank. *Special undeclared war.* London: Jonathan Cape, 1939

Ou Tsuin-chen. 'Education in wartime China', in Paul K. T. Sih, ed. *Nationalist China during the Sino-Japanese War, 1937–1945,* 89–123

Ou Tsuin-chen. See Clopton, Robert W.

Paauw, Douglas S. 'The Kuomintang and economic stagnation, 1928–1937'. *JAS* 16.2 (Feb. 1957) 213–220

P'an Tsu-yung. 'Hou-fang pan-ch'ang ti k'un-nan ho ch'i-wang' (Difficulties and hopes of factory management in the rear area). *Hsin-ching-chi,* 6.11 (1 Mar. 1942)

Paulson, David. 'Leadership and spontaneity: recent approaches to communist base area studies'. *Chinese Republican Studies Newsletter,* 7.1 (Oct. 1981) 13–18

Peck, Graham. *Two kinds of time: a personal story of China's crash into revolution.* Boston: Houghton Mifflin, 1950; first half reprinted 1968

Pei-p'ing she-hui tiao-ch'a so. See *Ti-erh-tz'u Chung-kuo . . .*

P'eng Chen. *Chung-kung 'Chin-ch'a-Chi pien-ch'ü' chih ko-chung cheng-ts'e* (Various policies in the CCP's 'Chin-Ch'a-Chi Border Region'). n.p.: T'ung-i ch'u-pan-she, 28 Jan. 1938. Manuscript in Hoover Institution, Stanford University

P'eng Shu-chih. 'Jang li-shih ti wen-chien tso-cheng' (Let historical documents be my witness). *Ming-pao yueh-k'an*, 30 (June 1968) 13–22

P'eng Te-huai. *P'eng Te-huai tzu-shu* (The autobiography of P'eng Te-huai). Shan-tung: Jen-min, 1981

Pepper, Suzanne. *Civil war in China: the political struggle 1945–1949*. Berkeley: University of California Press, 1978

Perkins, Dwight H., with the assistance of Yeh-chien Wang, Kuo-ying Wang Hsiao [and] Yung-ming Su. *Agricultural development in China, 1368–1968*. Chicago: Aldine, 1969

Perry, Elizabeth J. *Rebels and revolutionaries in North China, 1845–1945*. Stanford: Stanford University Press, 1980

Po I-po. 'Liu Shao-ch'i t'ung-chih ti i-ko li-shih kung-chi' (An historic achievement of Comrade Liu Shao-ch'i). *JMJP* 5 May 1980

Polachek, James. 'Gentry hegemony: Soochow in the T'ung-chih Restoration', in Frederic Wakeman, Jr. and Carolyn Grant, eds. *Conflict and control in late imperial China*, 211–56

Powell, Lyle Stephenson. *A surgeon in wartime China*. Lawrence, Kansas: University of Kansas Press, 1946

Price, Frank W. Preface to *Wartime China as seen by Westerners*. Chungking: The China Publishing Co. Preface dated 1942

Price, Jane L. *Cadres, commanders, and commissars: the training of the Chinese communist leadership, 1920–1945*. Boulder, Colo.: Westview Press, 1976

'Ranisha no soshiki to hanman kōnichi katsudō no jitsurei' (The organization of the Blue Shirts and examples of anti-Manchukuo, anti-Japanese activities), in *Ranisha ni kansuru shirō* (Materials on the Blue Shirts). n.p.: [1935?]

Rea, Kenneth W. and Brewer, John C., eds. *The forgotten ambassador: the reports of John Leighton Stuart, 1946–1949*. Boulder, Colo.: Westview Press, 1977

Reardon-Anderson, James B. *Yenan and the Great Powers: the origins of Chinese Communist foreign policy, 1944–1946*. New York: Columbia University Press, 1980

Red China. See *Hung-se Chung-hua*

Red Flag. See *Hung-ch'i*

Red Star. See *Hung-hsing*

Reynolds, Douglas Robertson. 'The Chinese industrial cooperative movement and the political polarization of wartime China, 1938–1945'. Columbia University, Ph.D. dissertation, 1975

Romanus, Charles and Sunderland, Riley. Vol. 1. *Stilwell's mission to China*. Washington, DC: Office of the Chief of Military History, Dept. of the Army, 1953; vol. 2. *Stilwell's command problems*, same pub., 1956; vol. 3. *Time runs out in CBI*, same pub., 1959

Sa K'ung-liao. *Liang-nien ti cheng-chih-fan sheng-huo* (Two years in the life of a political prisoner). Hong Kong: Ch'un-feng, 1947

SCCC. See *Ssu-ch'uan ching-chi chi-k'an*

Schram, Stuart R., ed. *Mao Tse-tung unrehearsed: talks and letters, 1956–71*, trans. John Chinnery and Tieyun. Harmondsworth: Penguin, 1974; American edn, *Chairman Mao talks to the people: talks and letters: 1956–1971*. New York: Pantheon Books, 1974

Schran, Peter. *Guerrilla economy: the development of the Shensi-Kansu-Ninghsia Border Region, 1937–1945*. Albany: State University of New York Press, 1976

Schwartz, Benjamin I. *Chinese communism and the rise of Mao*. Cambridge, Mass.: Harvard University Press, 1951

Schwartz, Benjamin I. 'Themes in intellectual history: May Fourth and after'. *CHOC* 12.406–51

Selden, Mark. *The Yenan way in revolutionary China*. Cambridge, Mass.: Harvard University Press, 1971

Service, John S. *The Amerasia papers: some problems in the history of US–China relations*. Berkeley: University of California Press, 1971

Service, John S. *Lost chance in China: the World War II despatches of John S. Service*, ed. by Joseph W. Esherick. New York: Random House, 1974

Shan-tung sheng cheng-fu chi Shan-tung chün-ch'ü kung-pu chih ko-chung t'iao-li kang-yao pan-fa hui-pien (A compilation of various regulations, programmes, and methods issued by the Shantung provincial government and the Shantung military region). n.p.: Chiao-tung ch'ü hsing-cheng kung-shu, 1945

Shang-jao chi-chung-ying (The Shang-jao concentration camp). Rev. edn. Shanghai: Hua-tung jen-min, 1952

Shaw Yu-ming. 'John Leighton Stuart and US–Chinese Communist rapproche-ment in 1949: was there another "lost chance in China"?' *CQ* 89 (March 1982) 74–96

She-hui chien-she (Social reconstruction). Nanking, 1948–

She-hui hsin-wen (The social mercury). Shanghai, Oct. 1932–July 1937

Sheng Li-yü. *Chung-kuo jen-min chieh-fang-chün san-shih-nien shih-hua* (An informal history of the 30 years of the People's Liberation Army of China). Tientsin: Jen-min, 1959

Shigemitsu, Mamoru. *Japan and her destiny*, trans. by O. White. London: Hutchinson, 1958

Shih Ching-han. 'Huang-fan-ch'ü ti tsai-ch'ing ho hsin-sheng' (The disaster and rebirth of the Yellow River flood area). *Kuan-ch'a*, 3.3 (13 Sept. 1947), pp. 22–3

Shih Hsi-min. 'K'ang-chan i'lai ti Chung-kuo kung-yeh' (Chinese industry during the war). *Li-lun yü hsien-shih*, 1.4 (15 Feb. 1940) 48–55

Shih-hua (Honest words). Official organ of the central bureau of the Central Soviet, 30 Oct. 1930–7 Feb. 1931

Shih Kuo-heng. *China enters the machine age: a study of labor in Chinese war industry*, ed. and trans. by Hsiao-tung Fei and Francis L. K. Hsu. Cambridge, Mass.: Harvard University Press, 1944

Shih-pao (The eastern times). Shanghai, 1904–

Shih-shih hsin-pao (The China times). Shanghai, 1924–

Shih-tai p'i-p'ing (Modern critic). Hong Kong, Jan. 1939–

Shu-wen. 'Ch'en Li-fu t'an CC' (Ch'en Li-fu chats about the CC). *Hsin-wen t'ien-ti*, 20 (1 Feb. 1937) 13

Shyu, Lawrence Nae-lih. 'The People's Political Council and China's wartime problems, 1937–1945', Columbia University, Ph.D. dissertation, 1972

Sih, Paul K. T., ed. *The strenuous decade: China's nation-building efforts 1927–1937*. Jamaica, NY: St John's University Press, 1970

Sih, Paul K. T., ed. *Nationalist China during the Sino-Japanese War, 1937–1945*. Hicksville, NY: Exposition Press, 1977

Skinner, G. William, ed. *The city in late imperial China*. Stanford: Stanford University Press, 1977

Smedley, Agnes. *The great road: the life and times of Chu Teh*. New York: Monthly Review Press, 1956; London, 1958

Smith, Robert Gillen. 'History of the attempt of the United States Medical Department to improve the effectiveness of the Chinese Army Medical Service, 1941–1945'. Columbia University, Ph.D. dissertation, 1950

Snow, Edgar. *The battle for Asia*. New York: Random House, 1941

Snow, Edgar, *Random notes on Red China, 1936–1945*. Cambridge, Mass.: East Asian Research Center, Harvard University, 1957

Spence, Jonathan. *The Gate of Heavenly Peace: the Chinese and their revolution 1895–1980*. New York: Viking Press, 1981

Ssu-ch'uan ching-chi chi-k'an (Szechwan economic quarterly). Chungking, 1943–

Ssu-ma Hsien-tao. *Pei-fa hou chih ko-p'ai ssu-ch'ao* (The doctrines of the various cliques after the Northern Expedition). Peiping: Ying-shan-she, 1930

Stilwell, Joseph. See Romanus, Charles; Tuchman, Barbara W.

The Stilwell papers. Arr. and ed. by Theodore H. White. New York: Schocken Books, 1948

Stinchcombe, Arthur L. *Theoretical methods in social history*. New York: Academic Press, 1978

Sun Fo (Sun K'o) et al. *T'ao Chiang yen-lun-chi* (Anti-Chiang messages). Canton, 1931

Sung Jen-ch'iung t'ung-chih liu-yueh shih-wu-jih tsai chung-yang-chü tang-hsiao kuan-yü cheng-chih kung-tso ti pao-kao (Comrade Sung Jen-ch'iung's report on political work at the Central Party School on 15 June). n.p.: Chin-Chi-Lu-Yü chün-ch'ü cheng-chih pu, December 1947

SW. See Mao Tse-tung, *Selected works*

Sze, Szeming. *China's health problems*. Washington, DC: Chinese Medical Association, 1944

Ta-kung-pao ('L'Impartial'). Tientsin, 1929–; Hankow, 1938–; Chungking, 1938–; Hong Kong, 1938–

Tai Yü-nung hsien-sheng nien-p'u (Chronological biography of Tai Li), comp. by Intelligence Section, Defence Ministry. Taipei, 1966

Tamagna, Frank M. *Banking and finance in China*. New York: Institute of Pacific Relations, 1942

Tang ti kai-tsao (Reconstruction of the party). n.d.

T'ang Leang-Li. *The inner history of the Chinese Revolution.* London: Routledge, 1930

Tang Leang-li. *Suppressing communist bandits in China.* Shanghai, 1934

T'ao Ta-yung. 'Lun tang-ch'ien ti kung-yeh chiu-chi' (Current means of rescuing industry). *Chung-kuo kung-yeh,* 25 (Mar. 1944) 10–12

Thornton, Richard C. *The Comintern and the Chinese Communists, 1928–1931.* Seattle: University of Washington Press, 1969

Ti-erh-tz'u Chung-kuo lao-tung nien-chien (Second year book of Chinese labour), ed. by Pei-p'ing she-hui tiao-ch'a so (Peiping Social Survey Institute), 1930

Ti-erh-tz'u kuo-nei ko-ming chan-cheng shih-ch'i shih-shih lun-ts'ung (Discourses on the history of the second revolutionary war period), ed. by Shih-hsueh shuang-chou-k'an she, Peking: San-lien, 1956

Tien Hung-mao. *Government and politics in Kuomintang China, 1927–1937.* Stanford: Stanford University Press, 1972

Ting, Lee-hsia Hsu. *Government control of the press in modern China, 1900–1949.* Cambridge, Mass.: East Asian Research Center, Harvard University, 1974

Tipton, Laurence. *Chinese escapade.* London: Macmillan, 1949

Tong, Hollington K. (Tung Hsien-kuang), ed. *China after seven years of war.* New York: Macmillan, 1945

Tong, Hollington K. *China and the world press.* Nanking, Feb. 1948

Tong, Hollington K. *Chiang Tsung-t'ung chuan* (A biography of President Chiang). 3 vols. Taipei: Chung-hua wen-hua, 1954

Topping, Seymour. *Journey between two Chinas.* New York: Harper & Row, 1972

Tou-cheng (The struggle). Official organ of the Central Committee of the Chinese Communist Party, c. 1928?–1934?

Ts'ai-cheng p'ing-lun (Financial review) Hong Kong, 1939–

Ts'ai T'ing-k'ai. *Ts'ai T'ing-k'ai tzu-chuan* (Ts'ai T'ing-k'ai's autobiography). 2 vols. Hong Kong: Tzu-yu hsun-k'an-she, 1946

Ts'ao Po-i. *Chiang-hsi su-wei-ai chih chien-li chi ch'i peng-k'uei* (The establishment and collapse of the Kiangsi soviet). Taipei: Cheng-chih ta-hsueh, 1969

Tsou Tang. *America's failure in China, 1941–50.* Chicago University Press, 1963

Tuchman, Barbara W. *Stilwell and the American experience in China, 1911–45.* New York: Macmillan, 1970

Tucker, Nancy Bernkopf. 'Nationalist China's decline and its impact on Sino-American relations, 1949–1950', in Dorothy Borg and Waldo Heinrichs, eds. *Uncertain years: Chinese-American relations, 1947–1950,* 131–71

Tucker, Nancy Bernkopf. *Patterns in the dust: Chinese-American relations and the recognition controversy, 1949–1950.* New York: Columbia University Press, 1983

Tung-fang tsa-chih (Eastern miscellany). Shanghai, 1904–48

Ulyanovsky, R. A., ed. *The Comintern and the East.* Moscow: Progress Publishers, 1979

United States Department of State. *United States relations with China, with special reference to the period 1944–1949.* Washington, DC, 1949. Reissued with intro. and index by Lyman Van Slyke as *China white paper.* 2 vols. Stanford: Stanford University Press, 1967

United States Department of State. *Postwar foreign policy preparation, 1939–1945*

United States Department of State. *Foreign relations of the United States*. Various subtitles: *1945, the Far East, China*, vol. 7, pub. 8442 (1969); *1946, the Far East, China*, vol. 9, pub. 8561 (1972); *1946, the Far East, China*, vol. 10, pub. 8562 (1972); *1947, the Far East, China*, vol. 7. pub. 8613 (1972); *1948, the Far East, China*, vol. 7, pub 8678 (1973); *1948, the Far East, China*, vol. 8, pub. 8583 (1973); *1949, the Far East, China*, vol. 8, pub. 8886 (1978); *1949, the Far East, China*, vol. 9, pub. 8774 (1974). All published Washington, DC: US Government Printing Office

United States War Department. See Van Slyke, Lyman P.

United States War Department, Military Intelligence Division. 'The Chinese Communist movement', 1945, in *Institute of Pacific Relations, hearings before the subcommittee to investigate the administration of the Internal Security Act and other internal security laws of the Committee on the Judiciary*. United States Senate, 82nd Congress, 1951–2

Van Slyke, Lyman P. *Enemies and friends: the united front in Chinese Communist history*. Stanford: Stanford University Press, 1967

Van Slyke, Lyman P., ed. *The Chinese Communist movement: a report of the United States War Department, July 1945*. Report prepared by the Military Intelligence Division. 'Originally published in 1952 . . . as an appendix to official transcript of the 1951 Senate hearings on the Institute of Pacific Relations.' Stanford: Stanford University Press, 1968

Van Slyke, Lyman P., ed. *Marshall's mission to China, December 1945–January 1947: the report and appended documents*. 2 vols. Arlington, Va.: University Publications of America, 1976

Vogel, Ezra. 'From friendship to comradeship'. *CQ* 21 (Jan.–Mar. 1965) 46–60

Wakeman, Frederic, Jr. and Grant, Carolyn, eds. *Conflict and control in late imperial China*. Berkeley and Los Angeles: University of California Press, 1975

Wales, Nym (Snow, Helen Foster). *Red dust*. Stanford: Stanford University Press, 1952

Wang Cheng. 'The Kuomintang: a sociological study of demoralization'. Stanford University, Ph.D. dissertation, 1953

Wang Chien-min. *Chung-kuo kung-ch'an-tang shih-kao* (A draft history of the Chinese Communist Party). 3 vols. Taipei: Wang Chein-min, 1965

Wang Fan-hsi. *Chinese revolutionary: memoirs, 1919–1949*, trans. and with an intro. by Gregor Benton. Oxford, NY: Oxford University Press, 1980

Wang Ming (Ch'en Shao-yü). 'Chung-kuo hsien-chuang yü Chung-kung jen-wu' (The present situation of China and the tasks of the CCP). Speeches at the 13th plenum of the ECCI, Moscow, 1934

Wang Ming (Ch'en Shao-yü). *Wang Ming hsuan-chi* (Selected works). 4 vols. Tokyo: Kyūko shoin 1973

Watson, Andrew, ed. *Mao Zedong and the political economy of the Border Region: a translation of Mao's 'Economic and financial problems'*. Cambridge: Cambridge University Press, 1980

Wedemeyer, Albert C. *Wedemeyer reports!* New York: Henry Holt, 1958

Wen hui pao. Shanghai, 1946–

White, Theodore H. *In search of history.* New York: Harper and Row, 1979

White, Theodore H. See *The Stilwell papers*

White, Theodore H. and Jacoby, Annalee. *Thunder out of China.* New York: William Sloane Associates, 1946

Whitson, William W. with Hung Chen-hsia. *The Chinese high command: a history of Communist military politics, 1927–1971.* New York: Macmillan, 1973

Wilbur, C. Martin. 'The Nationalist Revolution: from Canton to Nanking, 1923–28'. *CHOC* 12.527–720

Wilson, Dick. *The Long March, 1935: the epic of Chinese communism's survival.* New York: Viking Press; London: Hamilton, 1971

Woodhead, H. G. W. See *China year book*

Wu Ch'i-yuan. 'Ts'ung ching-chi kuan-tien lun nei-chan wen-t'i' (Talking about civil war problems from an economic viewpoint). *Kuan-ch'a,* 7 Sept. 1946, pp. 3–4

Wu Hsiang-hsiang. *Ti-erh-tz'u Chung-Jih chan-cheng shih* (The second Sino-Japanese War). 2 vols. Taipei: Tsung-ho yueh-k'an, 1973

Wu Hsiang-hsiang. 'Total strategy used by China and some major engagements in the Sino-Japanese War of 1935–1945', in Paul K. T. Sih, ed. *Nationalist China during the Sino-Japanese War, 1937–1945,* 37–80

Wu, Tien-wei. *The Sian Incident: a pivotal point in modern Chinese history.* Ann Arbor: Center for Chinese Studies, University of Michigan, 1976

Wu Ting-ch'ang. *Hua-hsi hsien-pi cheng-hsu-chi* (Random notes at Hua-hsi). 2 vols. Taipei: Wen-hai, n.d.

Wylie, Raymond F. *The emergence of Maoism: Mao Tse-tung, Ch'en Po-ta, and the search for Chinese theory, 1935–1945.* Stanford: Stanford University Press, 1980

Yang, Martin M. C. *Chinese social structure: a historical study.* Taipei: The National Book Co., 1969

Yen Hsi-ta. 'Ching-chi wei-chi yü kuan-liao tzu-pen' (The economic crisis and bureaucratic capital). *Ching-chi chou-pao* 4.6 (6 Feb. 1947) 9–11

Young, Arthur N. *China and the helping hand, 1937–1945.* Cambridge, Mass.: Harvard University Press, 1963

Young, Arthur N. *China's wartime finance and inflation, 1937–1945.* Cambridge, Mass.: Harvard University Press, 1965

Young, Arthur N. *China's nation-building effort, 1927–1937: the financial and economic record.* Stanford: Hoover Institution Press, 1971

Yü Ts'ai-yu. 'T'an chin-t'ien ti hsueh-sheng' (Discussing today's students). *Kuan-ch'a,* 24 April 1948, pp. 17–18

Yung Lung-kuei. 'Chiu-chi chan-shih kung-yeh ti chi-pen t'u-ching' (Fundamental means of rescuing the wartime industry). *Chung-kuo kung-yeh,* 25 (Mar. 1944) 8–9

INDEX

Abend, Hallet 75
administration, *see* bureaucracy
Agrarian Law (1947) 322
agriculture: as fraction of gross domestic product 38–9; dominance of 36; problem of tenancy and rents 36–7; effect of weather on 38–9; good years for 40, 46–7; real return from in wartime 164; Japanese disruption of 247–8; *see also* land; landlords; peasants
Ai Ch'ing 258
aid to China, military: from Germany 125–6; from Russia 144; from US 144–8
air lines 41
air raids: Japanese 134–5; of Chennault 147–8, 149
American Volunteer Group 145
Anhwei 33
annihilation campaigns against Communists 33
anti-American demonstrations 314
anti-Communist campaign 34, 47; at universities 172; 'first upsurge' 227–35; 'second upsurge' 235; 'third upsurge' 239
anti-fiscal agitation *see* taxes
anti-foreign demonstrations 6
Anti-Hunger Anti-Civil War demonstrations 1974, 314
anti-imperialism, theme of CCP 88
Anti-Oppression Anti-Hunger movement 314

anti-war demonstrations 314; directed against KMT 316
arms: from Germany 125–6; removal of to interior 130
army, CCP: doubling of 277; casualties of 277–8; recruitment for 322–5, 332; civilian support network for 322–3, 332, 349–50; 1948 strength of 342; skills of 349–51; *see also* Eighth Route Army (8RA); New Fourth Army (N4A); People's Liberation Army (PLA)
army, Nationalist: peasant resistance to exactions of 192; mobilization of 125, 137; Chiang Kai-shek's relations with 137–8; officers of 138–40; casualties of 140, 150; enlisted men in 140–1; lack of food for 141; medical care in 142–3; desertions from 143; conflicting assessments of 150–1; retraining programmes 151; in Central China 209; in Operation Ichigo 273–4
August First Declaration 107
authoritarianism, of the Nanking regime 21–2
Autumn Harvest uprisings 55, 68, 69, 71

Band, Clare 280
Band, William 280
banditry: and peasant unrest 198; and the CCP armies 216
Bank of China 25, 43, 168
Bank of Communications 25, 168